American
Jewish
Year Book

American

Jewish

Year Book 1992

VOLUME 92

Prepared by THE AMERICAN JEWISH COMMITTEE

Editor

DAVID SINGER

Executive Editor

RUTH R. SELDIN

THE AMERICAN JEWISH COMMITTEE

NEW YORK

THE JEWISH PUBLICATION SOCIETY

PHILADELPHIA

ISBN 0-8276-0429-7

Library of Congress Catalogue Number: 99-4040

PRINTED IN THE UNITED STATES OF AMERICA
BY THE HADDON CRAFTSMEN, INC., SCRANTON, PA.

Preface

Two subjects of urgent concern to American Jews are explored in feature articles in this year's volume. In "Jewish Identity in Conversionary and Mixed Marriages," Peter Y. Medding, Gary A. Tobin, Sylvia Barack Fishman, and Mordechai Rimor propose a typology of intermarried families, based on levels of Jewish behavior and identification. They also examine the relationship between contemporary Jewish identity and the propensity to intermarry. Noted demographer Sidney Goldstein offers "Profile of American Jewry: Insights from the 1990 National Jewish Population Survey," a wide-ranging analysis of the most significant research in two decades on the status of American Jews.

Regular articles on Jewish life in the United States are "Intergroup Relations," by Jerome A. Chanes; "The United States, Israel, and the Middle East," by Kenneth Jacobson; and "Jewish Communal Affairs," by Lawrence Grossman.

The tumultuous events of 1990—in the Persian Gulf, Soviet Union, Eastern Europe, Germany, South Africa, and elsewhere—are reported in articles on Jewish communities around the world. Developments in Israel are covered by Menachem Shalev.

Updated estimates are provided for Jewish population in the United States (by Barry Kosmin and Jeffrey Scheckner, of the North American Jewish Data Bank) and in the world (by U.O. Schmelz and Sergio DellaPergola of the Hebrew University's Institute of Contemporary Jewry).

Carefully compiled directories of national Jewish organizations, periodicals, and federations and welfare funds, as well as religious calendars and obituaries, round out the 1992 AMERICAN JEWISH YEAR BOOK.

We gratefully acknowledge the assistance of Terry Smith and many colleagues at the American Jewish Committee, especially Michele Anish and Cyma M. Horowitz of the Blaustein Library and Deloris Kitt.

THE EDITORS

Contributors

HENRIETTE BOAS: Dutch correspondent, Jewish Telegraphic Agency and Israeli newspapers; Amsterdam, Holland.

Y. MICHAL BODEMANN: associate professor, sociology, University of Toronto, Canada; visiting professor, Humboldt University, Berlin, Germany.

JEROME A. CHANES: co-director for domestic concerns, National Jewish Community Relations Advisory Council.

M.M. CONSONNI: research fellow, Diaspora Research Institute, Tel Aviv University, Israel.

SERGIO DELLAPERGOLA: chairman, Institute of Contemporary Jewry, and director, Division of Jewish Demography and Statistics, Hebrew University of Jerusalem, Israel.

ALLIE A. DUBB: professor, Jewish civilization, and director, Kaplan Center for Jewish Studies and Research, University of Cape Town, South Africa.

SYLVIA BARACK FISHMAN: senior research associate and assistant director, Cohen Center for Modern Jewish Studies, Brandeis University; teaching associate, Brown University program in Judaic studies.

ZVI GITELMAN: professor, political science, and Preston R. Tisch Professor of Judaic Studies, University of Michigan.

SIDNEY GOLDSTEIN: G.H. Crooker University Professor and professor of sociology, Brown University; chairman, CJF National Technical Advisory Committee on Jewish Population Studies.

LAWRENCE GROSSMAN: director of publications, American Jewish Committee.

NELLY HANSSON: researcher, political science and sociology; secretary- general, Association for the Preservation of the French Jewish Cultural Heritage; Paris, France.

KENNETH JACOBSON: director, international affairs, Anti-Defamation League of B'nai B'rith.

LIONEL E. KOCHAN: visiting lecturer, Oxford Center for Post-Graduate Hebrew Studies, England.

MIRIAM L. KOCHAN: writer, translator, Oxford, England.

BARRY A. KOSMIN: director, North American Jewish Data Bank, City University of New York Graduate Center.

PETER Y. MEDDING: associate professor, political science and contemporary Jewry, Hebrew University of Jerusalem, Israel; adjunct professor, Cohen Center for Modern Jewish Studies, Brandeis University.

ROBIN OSTOW: Canada Research Fellow in sociology, McMaster University, Hamilton, Ontario, Canada.

MORDECHAI RIMOR: research associate, Cohen Center for Modern Jewish Studies, Brandeis University.

HILARY RUBINSTEIN: research fellow, history, University of Melbourne, Australia.

JEFFREY SCHECKNER: administrator, North American Jewish Data Bank, City University of New York Graduate Center.

U.O. SCHMELZ: professor emeritus, Jewish demography, Institute of Contemporary Jewry, Hebrew University of Jerusalem, Israel.

MILTON SHAIN: lecturer, modern Jewish history, University of Cape Town, South Africa.

MENACHEM SHALEV: diplomatic correspondent, *Davar*, Tel Aviv; Israel correspondent, *Forward*, New York.

GARY A. TOBIN: director, Cohen Center for Modern Jewish Studies, and associate professor, Jewish community research and planning, Brandeis University.

HAROLD M. WALLER: associate dean (academic), Faculty of Arts, McGill University, Montreal, Canada; director, Canadian Center for Jewish Community Studies.

Contents

Special
Articles

Jewish Identity in Conversionary and Mixed Marriages

by PETER Y. MEDDING, GARY A. TOBIN, SYLVIA
BARACK FISHMAN, and MORDECHAI RIMOR

INTERMARRIAGE BETWEEN JEWS AND NON-JEWS in the United
States is now commonplace. The propensity of Jews to marry non-Jews was
extremely low until the mid-1960s, but rose sharply thereafter and continued to climb in the 1980s. As a result, in many Jewish communities,
among those marrying in recent years, there are more outmarriages than
inmarriages.

This change in the underlying social and religious structure of the American Jewish community has important implications for the present and
future state of that community. On the one hand, marriage to non-Jews may
indicate the successful integration of Jews into American society and their
achievement of a high level of social acceptance. On the other, intermarriage may betoken and contribute to the decline of Judaism in America.

The subject of intermarriage evokes considerable passion among Jews
because it arouses fears about elemental issues of group survival. One aspect
of the matter is quantitative: the offspring of intermarriage may not remain
Jewish; within one or two generations there may be fewer Jews and a greatly
weakened Jewish community. Another aspect is qualitative: even if intermarriage does not lead to a decrease in the physical number of persons
living in households with a Jewish parent, questions remain as to their
Jewishness, i.e., the intensity of their communal affiliation, ethnic identification, and religious practice.

This article[1] focuses on the qualitative aspects of Jewish intermarriage in
the United States. It presents a theory of Jewish identity which provides a

[1]This article provides a more extensive and intensive analysis and theoretical treatment of
data originally discussed in Sylvia Barack Fishman, Mordechai Rimor, Gary A. Tobin, and
Peter Medding, *Intermarriage and American Jews Today: New Findings and Policy Implications. A Summary Report* (Maurice and Marilyn Cohen Center for Modern Jewish Studies,
Brandeis University, 1990).

In addition, Cohen Center researchers have explored aspects of intermarriage in *Research
Notes* (Maurice and Marilyn Cohen Center for Modern Jewish Studies): Larry Sternberg,
"Intermarriage: A First Look" (1988); Mordechai Rimor, "Intermarriage and Conversion:
The Case from the Boston Data" (1988); Mordechai Rimor, "Intermarriage and Jewish
Identity" (1989); Mordechai Rimor, "Feelings and Reactions to Intermarriage" (1989).

3

framework for the systematic empirical analysis of Jewish identification and behavior in households representing three basic marriage types: inmarriage—between two born Jews; conversionary marriage—between a born Jew and a born non-Jew who converts to Judaism; and mixed marriage—between a born Jew and a born non-Jew who does not convert to Judaism. Although, as we will show, they differ greatly, the latter two categories are often referred to collectively as intermarriage or outmarriage.

It has been notably difficult for researchers to assess the quality of Jewish life in intermarried families or to make the kinds of meaningful comparisons between conversionary and mixed-married families that could help to gauge the potential for future Jewish commitment. Among the specific issues calling for clarification are the following: What are the characteristics and extent of Jewish behavior and identification in conversionary and mixed-married households? To what degree do the offspring of conversionary and mixed marriages receive formal Jewish education? To what extent are non-Jewish identities maintained in conversionary and mixed-married households?

In an effort to better understand the relationship between marriage type and level of Jewish identification, this study employs a typology for categorizing patterns of Jewish identification and behavior. The typology makes it possible to clarify whether and under what conditions Jewish identity is maintained in such marriages and to evaluate the character and content of that Jewish identity.

The article begins with a review of the recent literature on intermarriage, indicating how the present analysis goes beyond previous work in the field. It then provides a detailed description of the data set and methodology used in the analysis. Following a discussion of background variables, the article presents a new theory of Jewish identity and a typology of conversionary and mixed marriages. Empirical analysis of the Jewish identification and behavior of the various marriage types follows. This establishes the basis for the construction of an overall index of Jewish identification that makes it possible to quantify the various categories in the typology. The typology is then expanded to include a category we call "dual-identity" households. These households incorporate Jewish and Christian identities simultaneously. The concluding section takes note of the major findings and their implications.

Review of the Literature

Numerous books and articles in the last decade have discussed the effects of the escalating rate of Jewish intermarriage on the character and vitality of individual Jewish identity and the continuity and survival of the American Jewish community as a whole. Observers differ widely in their perceptions of the consequences of the intermarriage phenomenon.[2] At one end of the spectrum are scholars who are comparatively pessimistic, some of whom predict the eventual disappearance of a distinctive Jewish community, seeing only the survival of the Orthodox. At the other end of the spectrum are scholars who are relatively optimistic, who discern the transformation and even revitalization of the American Jewish community. Rising rates of intermarriage, the latter argue, provide an opportunity to strengthen the ranks of American Jewry through an infusion of new blood or "imports"—the born non-Jewish spouses and their children.

During the past ten years, it is the optimists who have dominated the discussion of Jewish intermarriage in the United States. Thus, Egon Mayer, who has written extensively on the subject, derives encouragement from the fact that contemporary intermarried couples tend to feel closer to Judaism than to Christianity. What is more, he argues, the generally higher educational and occupational status of the Jewish spouse enhances this leaning toward Judaism.[3]

Another scholar who leans toward the optimistic view is Steven M. Cohen. He argues that the "concentration of intermarriage among the Jewishly peripheral means it is less threatening to Jewish continuity." He also takes a positive view of conversionary marriages, which "in all likelihood . . . are both quantitative and qualitative assets to the Jewish population." However, Cohen is somewhat less sanguine about the impact of mixed marriages. On the plus side, he observes that "most mixed-married Jews report not one, but several sorts of attachment to Jewish people and Jewish ritual and, less frequently, to organized Jewry." On the negative side, he asserts that "the marriages of Jews to born non-Jews vastly increase the chances that the partners will be less involved in various aspects of Jewish life," even if the Jewish spouse was peripherally involved to begin with. On the whole, Cohen maintains, intermarriage does not present a "grave threat to the Jewish continuity of large numbers of American Jewry."[4]

A significant scholarly exchange on the subject of intermarriage appeared in *Studies in Contemporary Jewry*, volume 5. Israeli demographers Sergio DellaPergola and U.O. Schmelz interpret not only rising rates of intermar-

---

[2]Interpersonal relationships in intermarried households are explored in Paul and Rachel Cowan, *Mixed Blessings: Marriage Between Jews and Christians* (New York, 1987) and in Susan Weidman Schneider, *Intermarriage: The Challenge of Living with Differences Between Christians and Jews* (New York, 1989).

[3]Egon Mayer, "Processes and Outcomes in Marriages Betweeen Jews and Non-Jews," *American Behavioral Scientist* 23, no. 4, Mar./Apr. 1980, pp. 487–518.

[4]Steven M. Cohen, "Reason for Optimism," in Steven M. Cohen and Charles S. Liebman, *The Quality of Jewish Life—Two Views* (New York, American Jewish Committee, 1987), pp. 13–17; 26–27.

riage, but also trends toward postponement of marriage and nonmarriage, low fertility rates, increasing divorce, etc., as pointing to the "decline of the conventional Jewish family." Reviewing the available survey data, they argue that "as a result of more frequent out-marriage, particularly mixed marriage, Jewish identity is generally weakened, often amalgamated with the ethnocultural heritage of an originally non-Jewish spouse or parent and frequently lost in the longer run."[5]

Aiming to refute this position, Calvin Goldscheider asserts that "there is currently about a 20 percent gain of Jewish adults through conversion relative to total in-marriages."[6] Goldscheider argues that the "growing acceptance of intermarriage and the intermarried into Jewish life" and the "increasing similarity between the intermarried and the nonintermarried in measures of Jewishness" make for a situation in which a relationship between intermarriage and Jewish discontinuity is "weak and growing weaker." Goldscheider concludes: "Concerns over the demographic implications of Jewish intermarriage for survival of the group seem exaggerated."[7]

In this debate about its quantitative implications, the impact of intermarriage on the nature and intensity of Jewish identification and behavior has been relatively neglected. Thus, while Mayer, Goldscheider, and Cohen[8] all have data showing that persons living in intermarried households are generally less Jewishly involved than those in inmarried households (except for conversionary marrieds in matters of religious performance), these qualitative aspects of intermarriage have not been subjected to systematic and detailed analysis.

This study focuses directly on the nature and intensity of Jewish identification and behavior in conversionary and mixed marriages. The analysis highlights two significant factors that elsewhere have gone unnoticed: the Jewish denominational identification of the various types of households and the simultaneous presence within them of Christian symbols and practices. Moreover, the large size of the sample used in this study[9] permits a more

---

[5]Sergio DellaPergola and Usiel O. Schmelz, "Demographic Transformations of American Jewry: Marriage and Mixed Marriage in the 1980s," and "American Jewish Marriages: Transformation and Erosion—A Rejoinder to Calvin Goldscheider," in *Studies in Contemporary Jewry*, 5, ed. Peter Y. Medding (New York and Oxford, 1989), pp. 169–200; 209–214; at 193.

[6]Calvin Goldscheider, "American Jewish Marriages: Erosion or Transformation?" *Studies in Contemporary Jewry*, 5, pp. 201–208; at 204.

[7]Calvin Goldscheider, *Jewish Continuity and Change: Emerging Patterns in America* (Bloomington, 1986), p. 28.

[8]Egon Mayer and Carl Sheingold, *Intermarriage and the Jewish Future: A National Study in Summary* (New York, American Jewish Committee, 1979); Egon Mayer, *Love and Tradition* (New York, 1985); Goldscheider, *Jewish Continuity and Change*; Steven M. Cohen, *American Assimilation or Jewish Revival?* (Bloomington, 1988).

[9]Thus, Goldscheider's sample of the Boston community contained 934 cases; Cohen's study

in-depth statistical analysis of qualitative data than ever previously undertaken.

Methodology

This article is based on data collected in eight different Jewish communities in the United States: Baltimore, Boston, Essex and Morris counties (New Jersey), Providence (Rhode Island), and Worcester, all in the eastern United States; Cleveland in the Midwest; Dallas in the Southwest; and the San Francisco Bay area in the West.[10]

These eight communities were selected from the many Jewish population surveys on file at the Cohen Center for Modern Jewish Studies at Brandeis University on the basis of four criteria. They reflect the current regional spread of American Jewry; the samples were fully representative; the data were collected between 1985 and 1988; and the questions relating to key variables were mostly identical, which permitted the files to be merged.

The analysis focuses on married couples, who are also referred to as households. In constructing a merged data set, therefore, the first step was to remove all unmarried respondents—i.e., the widowed, the divorced, the separated, singles—from the data files of each of the eight communities. Following this, a consecutive merged file was constructed via the SPSSX Data Analysis System. Consecutive merging of the variables was facilitated by the identical or almost identical wording of the questions, relating to the items (variables) that were included in the merged file.

In each of the individual community surveys a weighting factor had been applied to enable projections to be made corresponding to the estimated numbers of individuals and households in a particular community. The

of New York was based on 1,566 cases, and Mayer and Sheingold's sample totaled 446 cases. As will be explained below, the present study includes 6,673 households.

[10]*Jewish Population Study of Greater Baltimore*. Prepared for Associated Jewish Charities and Welfare Fund. Data collected during 1985. Principal investigator: Gary A. Tobin. *Jewish Population Study of Greater Boston*. Prepared for the Combined Jewish Philanthropies. Data gathered during 1985. Principal investigator: Sherry Israel. *Jewish Population Study of MetroWest, New Jersey*. Prepared for the United Jewish Federation of MetroWest. Data gathered during 1985 and 1986. Principal investigator: Gary A. Tobin. *Jewish Population Study of Greater Worcester*. Prepared for the Worcester Jewish Federation. Data gathered during 1986. Principal investigator: Gary A. Tobin. *Jewish Population Study of Greater Cleveland*. Prepared for the Jewish Community Federation. Data gathered during 1987. Principal investigator: Ann Schorr. *Jewish Population Study of Rhode Island*. Prepared for the Jewish Federation of Rhode Island. Data gathered during 1987. Principal investigators: Calvin Goldscheider and Sidney Goldstein. *Jewish Population Study of the Bay Area*. Prepared for the Jewish Federations of San Francisco, Oakland, and San Jose. Data gathered during 1986. Principal investigator: Gary A. Tobin. *Jewish Population Study of Greater Dallas*. Prepared for the Jewish Federation of Greater Dallas. Data gathered during 1988. Principal investigator: Gary A. Tobin.

merged file is based on these projected totals. Consequently, the weight applied to each community in the merged file is determined by its projected Jewish population, and not by the actual numbers in the original sample used in each community survey. As such, the merged file is fully representative of the eight communities.

No attempt has been made to weight or correct the merged file further in order to seek to make it representative of the actual proportions of these communities within American Jewry as a whole. However, the same basic trends, relationships, and patterns relating to marriage types are found in each of the individual communities. As a result, merging the file does not erase, or average out, contradictory trends and patterns in the different communities.

The total projected number of households in the merged file is 197,078, representing a total Jewish population in the eight communities of over 433,104 individuals in inmarried households, 35,266 in conversionary households, and 106,163 individuals in mixed-married households—in all, 574,533 individuals, or about 9.75 percent of American Jewry. All percentage calculations have been made on the basis of these projected numbers. However, the numbers of cases (Ns) given in the tables are the actual or unweighted Ns in the merged file for each particular question, based on a total of 6,673 households. The Ns for each variable differ somewhat, because sometimes respondents did not answer a specific question, and in some cities certain questions were not asked. Moreover, placing the actual Ns in the tables is necessary to ensure that the number of cases in any cell is large enough for statistical analysis. As cells with an actual N lower than 10 must be treated with extreme caution on statistical grounds, they have been excluded from analysis and discussion. A note to this effect appears in the tables each time this occurs.

Levels of statistical significance have been computed using the gamma value. The data in the tables presented are statistically significant at the .001 level. ("Gamma" is a measure of association used for ordinal scales and in cross-tabulations that have more than 2x2 cells. It expresses the intensity of this association, and thus provides a more rigorous measure of significance than the yes/no character of the chi-square.)

The present analysis focuses on differences between marriage types, as reflected in the pattern of identification or behavior of the household as a unit. Occasionally, however, the analysis focuses on the attributes or achievements of the individual Jewish spouse or spouses, as, for example, is the case with most of the background variables (except for income, which is a household attribute). Thus, the incidence of the various types of marriage within the different age groups, for example, is arrived at by counting each individual Jewish spouse as a single unit.

The sum of the individual Jewish spouses in all marriage types will always be greater than the sum of couples or households. Put simply, one marriage of each type (inmarriage, conversionary, mixed) adds up to three marriages. However, the sum of born Jewish partners in these three marriages is four (two in the inmarriage, and one in each of the other types). Specifically, each N in tables 3–8, 10–11, and 13–14 represents the sum of the individual Jewish spouses who answered the relevant question and may be as high as 11,120. (The N in table 5 is slightly smaller because the question was not asked in every city.) In tables 1–2, 9, 12, and 15–35, the Ns are for households.

Household intermarriage rates—the percentage of intermarried couples as a proportion of all couples, households, or marriages—are always higher than individual rates—the percentage of born Jews in intermarriages as a proportion of the total of married Jewish individuals. Thus, in the example above, the individual intermarriage rate is 50 percent (two out of four Jews are in intermarriages), while the household intermarriage rate is 66 percent (two out of three marriages are intermarriages). Or, to take actual figures from table 3: for the decade 1980–1989, the individual rates shown—62 percent inmarriage, 5 percent conversionary marriage, and 33 percent mixed marriage—have computed equivalent household rates of 45 percent inmarriage, 7 percent conversionary marriage, and 48 percent mixed marriage.

BACKGROUND CHARACTERISTICS AND MARRIAGE TYPES

Rates of Inmarriage and Intermarriage

As seen in table 1, the distribution of marriage types varies by community. For example, approximately 80 percent or more of marriages in Baltimore, Boston, Cleveland, Essex/Morris counties, and Providence are inmarriages, whereas in San Francisco and Dallas the proportions are 60 percent and 66 percent, respectively. In the merged sample, as reported in table 2, 73 percent of all marriages are inmarriages, 5 percent are conversionary, and 21 percent are mixed marriages.

Decade of Marriage

The overall distribution of marriages in the merged sample shows a consistent increase in the incidence of intermarriage since 1960 (table 3). Almost 94 percent of Jewish individuals who married prior to 1960 are inmarried; only 2 percent are in conversionary marriages and 5 percent in mixed marriages. The proportion inmarrying declines by about 10 percent in the 1960s, and by another 10 percent in the 1970s. This process becomes accelerated in the 1980s, when the rate of inmarriage declines by a further 13 percent. Conversely, the proportion entering into mixed marriages rises dramatically over time. By the 1980s, 33 percent of Jewish individuals are entering into mixed marriages.

Significantly, since the 1960s, the proportion of individuals entering into conversionary marriages has remained fairly steady, at about 5 percent. Despite what some have claimed, converts do not constitute an increasing proportion of the intermarried. To the contrary, the figures in table 3 show that they constitute a rapidly declining proportion of the intermarried, from 28–29 percent before 1970 to 13 percent in the 1980s.

Age and Generation

The basic pattern with regard to intermarriage is confirmed by examining marriages within age and generation, as presented in tables 4 and 5. The incidence of inmarriage declines steadily with age, from well over 90 percent among Jews aged 55 and older, to 70 percent among those aged 18–34. There has been a fivefold increase in the incidence of mixed marriage among younger age groups; 5 percent of those in the two oldest age groups are mixed-married, as compared with 25 percent of those aged 18–34. At the same time, the incidence of conversionary marriage more than doubles, rising from about 2 percent for those aged 55 and older, to 5 percent for those under age 44.

Tabulation of marriages by generation as presented in table 5 produces a similar but even more pronounced pattern than that seen in tables 3 and 4. While 93 percent of first-generation Jews are inmarried, only 56 percent of the fourth generation are. At the same time, the proportion of Jews entering into conversionary marriages increases threefold, from 2 percent in the first generation to 6 percent in the fourth. However, the proportion of those in mixed marriages increases more than sevenfold—from 5 percent in the first generation to 38 percent in the fourth.

Gender

In the past, Jewish men were much more likely than Jewish women to intermarry. Although rates of intermarriage and mixed marriage for both men and women have risen steadily over time, Jewish men are still more likely than Jewish women to intermarry. As seen in table 6, overall, 82 percent of Jewish men are inmarried, as compared with 90 percent of Jewish women. The proportion of inmarriages among Jewish men declines by 35 percent in three decades, from 90 percent for the period before 1960 to 55 percent in the decade of the 1980s. For Jewish women, the proportion of inmarriages declines by 28 percent during the same period, from 98 percent to 70 percent.

Significantly, since the 1960s, the decline in the proportion of inmarriages for the two sexes has proceeded apace, with a 23-percent decline among Jewish men and a 21-percent decline among Jewish women. Apart from the fact that both groups are subject to the same societal influences, the two rates are also integrally connected to each other: as increasing proportions of Jewish men intermarry, there will be fewer available Jewish males for Jewish women.

In all decades of marriage, Jewish men are consistently more likely than Jewish women to be involved in conversionary marriages, indicating the greater propensity of non-Jewish women to convert to Judaism, as compared with non-Jewish men married to Jewish women. Over three decades, the proportion of mixed marriages among Jewish women increases from 2 percent to 28 percent, while among Jewish men it increases from 8 percent to 38 percent.

Multiple Marriages

Intermarriages are more common in subsequent marriages than in first marriages, as seen in table 7. While 86 percent of first marriages are inmarriages, the proportion drops to 70 percent in second marriages and 54 percent in third or subsequent marriages. Conversely, rates of mixed marriage rise with the number of marriages, while conversionary marriages remain fairly static. Other data, not reported in table 7, indicate that individuals under the age of 45 are more likely to have multiple marriages than those over age 45. Nevertheless, when controls for age are introduced, mixed marriages are still more common in the case of multiple marriages. Multiple marriage, it appears, lowers the likelihood of choice of Jewish marriage partners, possibly because religiously suitable partners are less readily available. In addition, factors related to starting and raising a family may no longer be relevant, which may also influence these trends.

Age at First Marriage

Table 8 examines mean age at first marriage. For the entire sample, the mean age is 25 years. Inmarried men have a mean age of 25.9 years, while for women it is 23.2 years. The mean age jumps to 27.8 years for males and to 25.7 years for females in conversionary marriages, and to 27.9 years for males and 26 years for females in mixed marriages. The tendency of conversionary and mixed marriages to occur at a later age than inmarriages suggests that a substantial proportion of never-married individuals currently in their thirties and forties are likely to marry non-Jews.

Children at Home

The distribution of marriage types among households with children at home, as presented in table 9, more or less mirrors that of the whole sample (see table 2). If anything, there are slightly more mixed-married households with children at home than the proportion of mixed-marrieds in the total sample, reflecting the increased incidence of mixed marriage among the younger age groups. Overall, 24 percent of households with children at home are mixed marriages, and 4 percent are conversionary marriages. Thus, nearly three in ten families with children at home have one spouse who was not born Jewish, and the vast majority of these constitute mixed marriages.

Education, Occupation, Income

Marriage type is related to socioeconomic status, but in ways that defy conventional wisdom, which associates intermarriage with high socioeconomic achievement and integration. The data reported here indicate the opposite—higher socioeconomic status is associated with lower levels of mixed marriage, higher rates of conversion, and higher rates of inmarriage. Education, occupation, and income alone are weakly associated with marriage-type variation, but these associations are stronger when age group is introduced as a variable. Generally, lower socioeconomic status is associated with higher rates of intermarriage and much higher rates of mixed marriage. This is particularly noticeable in the 18–34 age group, as seen in table 10. For example, 74 percent of those with a graduate degree in that age group are inmarried, compared with 69 percent of those with a college degree, 63 percent of those with some college, and 59 percent of those with a high-school diploma or less. Conversely, 41 percent of those with a high-school education are in mixed marriages, but only 19 percent of those with graduate degrees. There are also differences in the incidence of conversionary marriages. In the 18–34 age group, 7 percent of those with graduate degrees are in conversionary marriages, as compared with under 1 percent of those with a high-school diploma or less. Overall, similar but less pronounced marriage patterns appear for the 35–44 age group but are not present among those aged over 45 years.

Again, as the data in table 11 indicate, in the 18–34 age group, between 72 percent and 75 percent of those in professional, executive, and sales positions are inmarried, as compared to 61 percent of those in clerical positions, and 54 percent of those in blue-collar and service occupations. Conversely, while the proportion of mixed-marrieds is about 20 percent in the three highest occupational categories in the 18–34 age group, it climbs to 45 percent in the lowest occupational category. As with education, these patterns are apparent, but less so, in the 35–44 age group, but for the most part are not present in the older age groups.

This general picture is further corroborated by the household income data. While table 12 shows that the proportion of mixed marriages is at its lowest where income is highest, that is, among those earning over $150,000, the opposite does not appear to be true, and there does not appear to be any association between lower income and higher rates of mixed marriage. However, when broader income categories are used, lower income does turn out to be associated with mixed marriage. Overall, 26 percent of those with incomes below $75,000 are mixed-married as compared with 18 percent of those earning over $75,000. The picture is sharpened further when we control for age, as shown in table 13.

The data demonstrate clearly that there is a strong association between lower income and higher rates of mixed marriage among those aged under 45, but that it does not exist at all among those over 45. Thus in the under 45 age group, 37 percent of those earning under $30,000 and 33 percent of those earning between $30,000 and $75,000 are mixed-married, while 21 percent among those earning over $75,000 are. Conversely, 56 and 59 percent, respectively, of the two lower income groups are inmarried, compared with 72 percent of those earning over $75,000. Turning to those over 45 years, the differences between the rates of mixed marriage of the three income groups are extremely small. The rate of mixed marriage is slightly higher in the middle income group (17 percent) than among the lower and higher income earners (12 percent and 15 percent, respectively).

In all, greater proportions of younger Jews than of older Jews are better educated, in more prestigious occupations, and earn higher incomes. Why they are more likely to inmarry than those young people who do not achieve these educational, occupational, and income levels, and why the latter are more likely to marry out, is not clear from our data. One possible explanation is that within a community in which high levels of achievement are the norm, low achievers will be less attractive marriage partners and more limited in their choices than high achievers. Conversely, low achievers in terms of Jewish norms may still be relatively high achievers by the norms of American society as a whole and may seek to maximize these assets outside the Jewish community rather than compete within it against higher achievers.

Jewish Education

The data relating to Jewish education, as reported in table 14, seem to indicate that individuals who have had some Jewish education and those who have had none at all are almost equally likely to be involved in conversionary and mixed marriages. However, closer examination of the data does reveal differences based on duration of Jewish education, particularly so in younger age groups. In general, as can be seen in table 15, going from older to younger age groups, there is a linear increase in the proportion of individuals receiving more than six years of Jewish education, strikingly so among women. Thus, 45 percent of women aged 18–34, as against 21 percent of women over 65 years of age, received six or more years of Jewish education; the comparable figures for men are 46 percent and 35 percent. Similarly, the proportion of women receiving no Jewish education at all declines markedly, from 45 percent of those aged 65 and over, to 25 percent of those in the 18–34 age group. By way of contrast, the proportion of men of all age groups with no Jewish education at all is consistently much lower—in the range of 11 percent to 20 percent—and there is no linear relationship with age.

While Jewish women are both less likely than Jewish men to have received any Jewish education at all, and to have received it for more than six years, older Jewish women are also less likely to intermarry. This suggests a complex relationship between Jewish education and the propensity to intermarry. To control for these factors, table 15 presents the figures for years of Jewish education broken down by both age and gender. A comparison of those with more than six years of Jewish education and those with less or none at all confirms that Jewish education is clearly associated with higher rates of inmarriage and lower rates of mixed marriage. While this holds true for both men and women in all age groups, the association between more than six years of Jewish education and inmarriage is strongest in younger age groups: especially among men aged 35–54, and is also weakly present in the 18–34 age group; for women it is strongest among those under age 45 (particularly in the 18–34 age group).

Among those with less than six years of Jewish education, there does not appear to be a consistent relationship between number of years of Jewish education and the propensity to inmarry. In only two out of ten cases (Jewish males aged 35–44 and Jewish males aged 45–54) is there a clear linear relationship between the two, with those having up to five years of Jewish education more likely to be inmarried than those without any Jewish education. In four other cases the opposite is true—those who have not received any Jewish education are more likely to be inmarried than those with up to five years of Jewish education. In yet another four cases there is little or no difference at all.

In general, the association between inmarriage and a lengthy period of Jewish education appears strongest at a time when the incidence of inter- marriage is relatively high, as can be seen among younger men and women, and appears weakest when the incidence of intermarriage is relatively low, as in the case of older men and women. Clearly, the relationship between these two elements is not linear but is mediated by other powerful social and psychological factors, most especially the character and salience of personal Jewish identity at the time of marriage.

These background data have been concerned with the question of which Jews have a greater or lesser propensity to intermarry. Overall, they indicate that age, generation, and gender are more highly associated with intermar- riage than are the other background factors. Intermarriage rates are highest among younger and fourth-generation American Jews, particularly males. The data also show an increased incidence of mixed marriage over time, with the rates of conversionary marriage remaining fairly stable.

By the 1980s, just under half of the marriages involving Jews were mixed, forming families in which one spouse was Jewish and the other was a non-Jew. Consistently, the incidence of mixed marriage was found to be highest in the younger age groups, among whom it was only slightly low- ered by long exposure to Jewish education. Thus, in the youngest age cohorts, even those who received more than six years of Jewish education manifest a relatively high rate of mixed marriage, peaking at 25 percent among males aged 18–34 years (see table 15).

This finding of increasing mixed marriage even among strongly identified Jews suggests a hitherto unappreciated and intriguing possibility: the in- creasing incidence of mixed marriage may be associated with underlying changes in the nature of Jewish personal and group identity. These changes, in turn, have led to expectations or hopes that Jewish identity can still be maintained and transmitted in mixed marriages.

Given the increasing incidence of intermarriage, how these hopes and expectations play themselves out—in short, what happens to Jewish iden- tity in conversionary and mixed marriages—is a particularly crucial ques- tion for investigation. We begin with a theoretical analysis of the nature of contemporary Jewish identity, the underlying changes within it, and the implications for different marriage types.

CONTEMPORARY JEWISH IDENTITY
AND INTERMARRIAGE

Jewish identity is located at the core of personal identity, which Herbert Kelman defines as "the enduring aspects of the person's definition of himself ... the individual's conception of who he is and what he is over time and across situations." Included in this is "the child's cultural and ethnic heritage—the groups into which he is born." These form "an inherent part of his identity ... by virtue of the fact that the group[s] to which he belongs are usually an inevitable part of his life experience." Thus, Kelman notes, an individual's ethnic and cultural heritage "enters into who and what he is, just as his biological heritage does." The individual, therefore, "must somehow take his cultural as well as his biological heritage into account if he is to develop a firm personal identity." The group's definition of itself, its own conception of its basic values, enters into the individual's personal identity as an ongoing cultural heritage that exists independently of the individuals that bear it, being expressed in written documents, oral traditions, institutions, and symbols.[11]

A Partial Community of Shared Feelings[12]

In the past, the common denominator of Jewish identity was a community of belief based on a system of shared prescriptive values. Over the last century, however, this has shifted in the direction of a community of shared individual feelings. The community of belief constituted a total system that controlled the individual's environment with a detailed pattern of prescribed actions and fixed roles. Group membership was thus clearly defined. In contrast, the contemporary community of shared individual feelings is a voluntary and partial community of personal choice, with unclear boundaries and undefined membership. It is characterized by emotions and attachments, which, while often deep, are not always clearly articulated.

This shift in Jewish identity is paralleled and reinforced by the trend in American society in the direction of what Richard Merelman has called "the decline of group belongingness and the rise of individualization." Merelman notes that in contemporary America, "many people continue to be members and identify with groups, [but] they believe their group identities to be matters of individual choice, which can be changed without

---

[11]Herbert C. Kelman, "The Place of Jewish Identity in the Development of Personal Identity." Working paper prepared for the American Jewish Committee's Colloquium on Jewish Education and Jewish Identity, Nov. 1974, mimeo, pp. 1–3.

[12]The next two sections further develop the theory first propounded in Peter Y. Medding, "Segmented Ethnicity and the New Jewish Politics," in *Studies in Contemporary Jewry*, 3 (New York and Oxford, 1987), ed. Ezra Mendelsohn, pp. 26–45.

stigma. Group membership thus becomes voluntary, contingent, fluid, not 'given,' fixed and rigid. " [13] The process that Merelman is describing shows itself in the fact that many American Jews give strong expression to feelings of Jewishness as a central component of their personal identity even when they fail to uphold major Jewish religious beliefs and rituals. As documented in many studies, being Jewish is very important to such individuals: they express considerable Jewish pride, are comfortable with their Jewishness, are happy that they were born Jewish, relate to other Jews as family, and want their children to remain Jewish.

Despite the shift away from the community of shared belief, the religious value system remains a distinctive defining characteristic of the Jewish group at the normative and cultural levels. Popular religious observances—i.e., those relating to *rites de passage* and the holidays—continue to provide personal identity with its group aspects, even though the practices may have been selectively detached from a coherent and consistent whole. They serve as a vehicle for expressing shared feelings in familial and communal contexts, which reinforce and heighten the positive emotional affect of group belonging at the core of personal identity.

At the same time, religion differentiates and separates Jews from other groups. This implies, first and foremost, a rejection of the dominant Christian culture.[14] In Robert Bellah's words, "It is part of Jewish identity and the maintenance of the boundaries of the Jewish community to deny that Jesus is the Christ, the Messiah. This is to claim, however tacitly, that Christianity is a false religion."[15] Paradoxically, as the religious aspects of Judaism have become relatively less central to the core of Jewish identity, and shared feelings have become more important, being *not* Christian has taken on greater salience as a defining element of Jewishness.[16]

---

[13]Richard M. Merelman, *Making Something of Ourselves: On Culture and Politics in the United States* (Berkeley, 1984), p. 30.

[14]As Ben Halpern puts it, "America is really a Christian country." See the illuminating discussion in his *Jews and Blacks: The Classic American Minorities* (New York, 1971). The citation is on p. 60.

[15]Robert N. Bellah, "Competing Visions of the Role of Religion in American Society," in *Uncivil Religion: Interreligious Hostility in America*, eds. Robert N. Bellah and Frederick E. Greenspahn (New York, 1987), p. 228.

[16]Psychologist Joel Crohn, who has worked in marital counseling and ethnotherapy groups with ethnic and religious intermarriages, reports that "Christian symbols were often perceived by the Jewish partners as unwelcome and even dangerous reminders of the dominance of the Christian world." Some "perceived irreconcilable differences between the Jewish and Christian worlds." One intermarried Jewish subject in such a group, when asked by another group member, "Do you feel like learning about Christianity is somehow betraying who you are— like it's entering the bowels of the demon?" replied, "Yeah. I feel like it's a big betrayal." See Joel Crohn, *Ethnic Identity and Marital Conflict: Jews, Italians and WASPs* (New York, Institute for American Pluralism, American Jewish Committee, 1986), pp. 33, 36.

In the partial community of shared individual feelings, Jewishness forms part of the core of self-identity. As such, it can be significant without requiring the individual to raise it constantly to the level of conscious awareness. But there are also occasions in the life of the individual which do characteristically raise the issue of Jewish identity to the level of conscious awareness, among them being when choosing a marriage partner, at the birth of a child, and when making decisions about whether and how to transmit an ethnic heritage to the children. Similarly, events that affect the larger Jewish group, such as episodes of prejudice and discrimination—rejection of the group by others—may be experienced as personal rejection. Such rejection threatens all members of the community of shared individual feelings—constituting an attack on the core of personality—whether or not the attack is directed at them personally and however tenuous their own ties with the group.

Segmented and Unambiguous Jewish Identity

The Jewishness of the community of shared feelings in contemporary American society has become segmented in a number of different ways.

First, Jewishness constitutes only one segment of personal identity, existing alongside others, such as those deriving from being an American, college-educated, a high-income earner, or a social and political liberal, for example. Needless to say, the various aspects of personal identity inform and shape each other. Thus, the trait of Jewishness plays a part in how Jews act out their various roles in American society, while their various roles in American society influence their Jewish identity.

Second, the multiple aspects of identity coexist independently rather than coalescing to form a larger, integrated whole. The result is what might be termed a pluralistic personality. The significance and salience for the individual of any particular segment of his or her personal identity will vary with particular circumstances—personal, societal, historical, and so forth.

Third, neither the extent nor the intensity of the Jewish segment of personal identity is fixed. The Jewish segment may be very broad, taking in many aspects of contemporary Jewish group identity (such as religion, Israel, philanthropy, culture, group defense, friendship) or only one or a few of these. At the same time, involvement in even a single, narrow segment of Jewishness may be very intense, whereas simultaneous involvement in a number of aspects may be attenuated.

While contemporary Jewish identity is segmented in these various ways, the core of Jewishness remains unambiguous, in the sense that it is perceived by both Jews and others to be exclusively connected with the Jewish group's cultural and ethnic heritage. Thus, in families in which both parents are

Jewish and continue to identify as such, the Jewish ethnic and cultural self-identity imparted to their children is unambiguous, even when it is weak or generates ambivalence. They are Jewish and nothing else. The Jewish self-identity of these individuals defines both who they are and who they are not, irrespective of the extent and intensity of its particular form. The process of unambiguous Jewish identity formation is reinforced by values in American society encouraging individuals to build on their own cultural roots for purposes of self-esteem, individual happiness, and positive intergroup relations. Under these conditions, an unambiguous ethnic identity provides the foundation for a secure personal identity.[17]

Segmented Jewish Identity and Mixed Marriage

The existence of a segmented and unambiguous Jewish identity encourages Jews who enter into mixed marriages to assume that this will not prevent them from continuing to affirm and maintain the Jewish element at the core of their personal identity. (By the same token, their non-Jewish spouses, if they so choose, will be able to maintain a culturally different personal identity.) They see Jewish identity as a personal issue and are convinced that participation in a mixed family is compatible with strong personal expressions of Jewishness: to feel part of the Jewish people, to be proud of one's Jewishness, to attend synagogue, to perform Jewish rituals, or to support Israel. The experience of diversity and pluralism within the family may be deemed personally enriching. The rationale of mixed marriage, therefore, is that neither partner's personal identity need impinge on the other.

The structural realities of American Jewish life predispose young American Jews to meet, date, and marry non-Jews. The segmented and unambiguous character of their Jewish identity often leads them to assume or hope that intermarriage will have little effect on their Jewish feelings and commitments. Many also believe that their children will likewise be Jewish and that mixed families are not a bar to the transmission of a Jewish personal identity. These expectations are not always realized, however, and indeed run counter to the fundamental dynamics of mixed families in America. Thus, an unambiguous Jewish identity in the parental generation may turn out to be a terminal Jewish identity in the next. In order to understand why this is so, it is necessary to examine the identity dynamics in mixed and conversionary marriages.

---

[17]See Perry London and Barry Chazan, *Psychology and Jewish Identity Education* (American Jewish Committee, 1990), p. 9, who cite the theory of Henry Tajfel and John Turner that "feeling positive toward one's group is a major factor in enhancing one's self-image and self-esteem," and that "strong group identity promotes a positive sense of self."

Identity Dynamics in Conversionary and Mixed Marriages

Conversionary and mixed marriages reflect very different hopes and goals, and set in motion opposing processes. Conversion to Judaism generally indicates a desire to create an environment for identity formation that avoids competing and conflicting identities within the family and thereby increases the chances of developing an unambiguous Jewish identity in the children. Conversion to Judaism, however, is a process, not an act, and as such it is by no means easy, quick, or inexorable. Some who convert may not proceed very far along the road, may stop, or go backward, while others do indeed reach the final destination. Conversion involves a change of personal and group identity by the non-Jew, necessitating, on the one hand, distancing, disaffiliation, and cutting off ties with the usually Christian spiritual heritage and identity of the family into which the individual was born, and the adoption of Jewish symbols, behavior, and identity, on the other.

Conversion to Judaism may trigger a number of difficulties. In the first place, a Christian core identity may prove resistant to change, and may therefore manifest or reassert itself on symbolic occasions during the cycle of the year, or at critical junctures of the life cycle, unless it is consciously rejected. Secondly, it is often not clear what becoming Jewish entails in terms of the Jewish partner's desires and expectations. If it entails conversion to Judaism as a religion, then it is clear what that means and how it can be achieved. But if Jewishness involves an ethnic dimension—a relationship in blood, membership in a people characterized by shared feelings and history—it is not so clear how this may be attained, even after formal religious conversion. It may take time and experience before the convert to Judaism "feels" Jewish.

Mixed marriage involves a very different situation. A mixed family creates an environment for identity formation that is founded on the competing heritages of the Jewish and the non-Jewish spouses, both of which enter into the child's core identity. Mixed marriage thus not only decreases the likelihood that an unambiguous Jewish identity will be formed, but also raises the possibility that no Jewish identity at all will emerge. As Nathan Glazer has explained, "Their children have alternatives before them that the children of families in which both parents were born Jewish do not—they have legitimate alternative identities."[18]

In mixed-married families, the absence of agreement about fundamental matters of identity confronts the children with a choice between four alternatives: they can incorporate the identity of the Jewish parent, that of the

---

[18]Nathan Glazer, *New Perspectives in American Jewish Sociology* (New York, American Jewish Committee, 1987), p. 13.

non-Jewish parent, that of both, or that of neither. Identifying wholly with one parent may prove traumatic to the extent that it involves the rejection of the other parent, as well as part of the self. Maintaining both identities simultaneously may create tensions and conflicts that prevent the development of an integrated personal identity. Thus, the most commonly chosen solution may turn out to be identifying with neither parent and focusing on shared, general, secular values.

The range of possible Jewish identity outcomes from both conversionary and mixed marriages can be presented in the form of a typology with six cells or subtypes.

CONVERSIONARY AND MIXED-MARRIAGE TYPOLOGY

Marriage Type	Jewish Identification Level		
	Low	Medium	High
Conversionary	LC	MC	HC
Mixed	LM	MM	HM

The cells are based on the intersection of Jewish identification and marriage type. As there are three levels of Jewish identification (low, medium, and high) and two marriage types (conversionary and mixed) this results in six subtypes, three for each marriage type.

At this point, this typology does not take account of the possible simultaneous presence within the various marriage types and subtypes of a Christian identity, assuming an inverse relationship between Jewish identity and Christian elements. The existence of marriages in which Jewish and Christian identities are both maintained will be examined at a later stage and will result in an expanded typology.

Having established a theoretical framework for the examination of Jewish identity in mixed and conversionary marriages, let us now turn to the empirical data.

MARRIAGE TYPE AND JEWISH IDENTIFICATION

Denomination

Jewish identity is formed not only within the family but also within formal religious structures, such as synagogues and schools, which are generally affiliated with organized Jewish religious movements. These denominations, as they are known, represent alternative normative patterns of Jewish belief and behavior, each having different standards and expectations on a whole range of matters, including conversion to Judaism and mixed marriage.

It was argued above that, in the community of shared feelings, the religious aspect of Jewish identity continues to be central to the core of individual and group identity. One expression of this is the overwhelming extent to which American Jews think of themselves as being Orthodox, Conservative, or Reform Jews, even when they are not formally affiliated with a synagogue or temple.[19] (In the survey files, there is an additional category of "Just Jewish." Sometimes it is a specific denominational alternative; when not, it is a residual category for all who give some other broad general term of Jewish identification.) In all, denomination is likely to be strongly associated with differences in the pattern of individual Jewish identification and behavior.

The need to control for denomination is underscored by the differential distribution of the four denominations within each marriage type, as shown in table 16. Thus, Conservative Jews constitute over one-third of the total sample, but only 12 percent of the mixed-marrieds. Conversely, those who identify as Just Jewish represent less than 14 percent of the total sample but make up over one-third of the mixed-marrieds. Finally, Reform Jews represent 45 percent of the total sample but constitute 57 percent of the conversionary marrieds.

These patterns of discrepant representation are a result of the clear relationship between denominational identification and marriage type, as shown in table 17. In the case of the inmarrieds, the rank order is Orthodox, Conservative, Reform, and Just Jewish, while in the case of the mixed-marrieds it is the reverse. About nine in ten Orthodox and Conservative Jews are inmarried, as against seven in ten Reform Jews, and five in ten of the Just Jewish. Conversely, nearly half of the persons calling themselves Just Jewish are mixed-marrieds, as are over one-fifth of those identifying as Reform Jews, but only one in 15 of those calling themselves Orthodox and Conservative Jews. The overall level of conversionary marriages is low among all denominational groups—ranging between 2 percent and 7 percent—with the rank order being Reform, Conservative, Just Jewish, and Orthodox. (The very small number of Orthodox conversionary and mixed-marrieds in our sample necessitates their exclusion from all further statisti-

---

[19]See Jack Wertheimer, "Recent Trends in American Judaism," AJYB 1989, vol. 89, pp. 63–162, for a broad-ranging analysis of denominationalism in American Jewish life. Denominational self-identification in 27 recent community studies ranged between 70 and 95 percent. In the same communities, between 26 and 84 percent were currently synagogue members.

cal analyses involving denominations, leaving only Orthodox inmarrieds). It is clear, then, that persons identifying themselves with different wings of American Judaism exhibit very different marriage profiles. While Orthodox and Conservative Jews are predominantly inmarried, among those who identify as Reform, three in ten are either conversionary marrieds or mixed-marrieds, as are half of the Just Jewish. It must be emphasized, however, that these denominational figures are based on current self-identification, and their relationship to family of origin is unknown. Thus, a person who grew up in an Orthodox home and married a convert might decide that he or she would be more comfortable affiliating with a Conservative or Reform congregation. One cannot draw any conclusions from these data about possible linkages between the denomination of the family of origin and the propensity to engage in conversionary or mixed marriages.

Religious Affiliation and Identification

Synagogue membership and attendance give public expression to religious affiliation and identification. On a more private, familial level, ritual practice plays the same role.

Data on Jewish religious affiliation and identification—as measured by synagogue membership, synagogue attendance, and ritual practice—appear in tables 18, 19, and 20 for marriage types within denominations, for marriage types alone, and for denominations alone. The overall data for marriage types show that the differences between inmarrieds and conversionary marrieds are very narrow and not unidirectional. Inmarrieds are slightly more likely than conversionary marrieds to belong to synagogues, but conversionary marrieds are more likely than inmarrieds to attend synagogue regularly. Thus, 60 percent of inmarrieds belong to synagogues and 28 percent attend regularly, while among the conversionary marrieds the figures are 56 percent and 34 percent, respectively. Inmarrieds and conversionary marrieds perform Jewish rituals with almost identical degrees of frequency: 87 percent of both groups attend a Passover seder, 85 percent and 84 percent light Hanukkah candles, 68 percent fast on Yom Kippur, and 38 percent and 32 percent, respectively, light Sabbath candles.

The most striking feature of the data contained in these tables is the marked difference between inmarrieds and conversionary marrieds, on the one hand, and mixed-marrieds, on the other. For all three measures, mixed-marrieds score 30 percent to 40 percent lower than the inmarrieds and the conversionary marrieds: 15 percent of mixed-marrieds belong to a synagogue; 6 percent attend synagogue regularly (53 percent never attend); 52 percent participate in a seder; 52 percent light Hanukkah candles; 34 percent fast on Yom Kippur; and 3 percent light Sabbath candles.

For all three marriage types, the same denominational rank order from highest to lowest—Orthodox, Conservative, Reform, Just Jewish—is evident. Thus, 36 percent of Conservative mixed-marrieds are synagogue members, as against 21 percent of Reform mixed-marrieds, and 5 percent of Just Jewish mixed-marrieds. The comparable figures for regular synagogue attendance are 75 percent, 63 percent, and 25 percent, respectively. The practice of all the Jewish rituals in table 20 follows a similar pattern. For example, 76 percent of Conservative mixed-marrieds fast on Yom Kippur, as against 40 percent of Reform mixed-marrieds, and 17 percent of Just Jewish mixed-marrieds. The three apparent exceptions to this pattern do not alter this basic finding.[20]

Comparison of the different marriage types within denominations shows that Conservative and Reform conversionary marrieds are less likely than their inmarried counterparts to belong to synagogues, but are more likely to attend synagogue. The differences in synagogue membership are greatest among Conservative Jews: 68 percent of Conservative inmarrieds belong to synagogues, but only 54 percent of Conservative conversionary marrieds do; 59 percent of Reform inmarrieds and 57 percent of Reform conversionary marrieds belong. With regard to synagogue attendance, in both denominations the margin in favor of conversionary marrieds is about 10 percent: 42 percent of Conservative conversionary marrieds attend synagogue regularly, as do 32 percent of Conservative inmarrieds; among Reform Jews the equivalent figures are 33 percent and 22 percent. However, no clear pattern emerges for ritual performance: in both denominations, inmarrieds and conversionary marrieds are variously higher on different rituals. Moreover, the margins between them are very narrow, usually a few percent.

In contrast, Just Jewish conversionary marrieds consistently score higher, and sometimes much higher, than Just Jewish inmarrieds on all three measures of religious affiliation and identification. Thus, 49 percent of Just Jewish conversionary marrieds belong to synagogues, as compared with 23 percent of Just Jewish inmarrieds; 66 percent of the conversionaries attend synagogue at least a few times a year, but only 43 percent of the inmarrieds do so. Again, 86 percent of Just Jewish conversionary marrieds light Hanukkah candles and 60 percent fast on Yom Kippur, as compared with 52 percent and 33 percent, respectively, of Just Jewish inmarrieds. The differences between the two groups indicate an underlying secular orienta-

---

[20]In two cases (higher figures for seder attendance and Hanukkah candle lighting by Conservative inmarrieds than Orthodox inmarrieds and higher synagogue membership among Reform conversionary marrieds than among Conservative conversionary marrieds), the percentage differences are marginal. In the third case (higher levels of ritual performance by Just Jewish conversionary marrieds than by Reform conversionary marrieds), the actual numbers of Just Jewish conversionary marrieds are so small that these results must be treated with caution.

tion among Just Jewish inmarrieds, and a more religious orientation on the part of Just Jewish conversionary marrieds, even when this is not accompanied by current denominational identification. (There may, of course, have been some denominational affiliation in the past, during the conversion process.) Given the relatively small actual numbers of Just Jewish conversionary marrieds, however, all findings relating to them must remain somewhat tentative and will therefore be excluded from further analysis.

The considerably lower levels of religious involvement of mixed-marrieds are maintained within the various denominations. On average, mixed-marrieds are 25 percent lower than the other two marriage types on all measures of religious identification and affiliation. Thus, 36 percent of Conservative mixed-marrieds, 21 percent of Reform mixed-marrieds, and 5 percent of Just Jewish mixed-marrieds belong to a synagogue, as compared to 68 percent, 59 percent, and 23 percent, respectively, of comparable inmarrieds. Similarly, 76 percent of Conservative mixed-marrieds, 68 percent of Reform mixed-marrieds, and 35 percent of Just Jewish mixed-marrieds light Hanukkah candles, while 95 percent, 86 percent, and 52 percent of equivalent inmarrieds do so.

Mixed-marrieds calling themselves Conservative are more likely to belong to synagogues (36 percent) than Reform mixed-marrieds (21 percent). This is true despite the Reform movement's recognition of patrilineal descent and greater Conservative ideological opposition to mixed marriage.

Denominational identification is closely associated with level of religious involvement. As seen in tables 18, 19, and 20, Conservative and Reform mixed-marrieds are on average about 30 percent more likely than Just Jewish mixed-marrieds to have current synagogue membership, to attend synagogue, and to participate in ritual practice. Clearly, among mixed-marrieds a denominational self-definition is associated with a higher level of religious involvement, while Just Jewish as a self-definition indicates conscious distancing from Jewish religious identification.

The strength and stability of the relationship between marriage type and religious affiliation and identification were tested by controlling for the effects of age and family type (not shown in table). For age, the sample was divided into two groups: under 45 years of age and over 45 years of age. For family type, the sample was divided into two groups: couples with no children at all and couples with unmarried children, whether living at home or not. These controls were applied to the questions relating to synagogue membership, synagogue attendance, and ritual practice, for the three marriage types, both by themselves and within denomination. The results indicate that while both age and family type are themselves influential, the impact of marriage type and denomination are still clearly evident within age groups and family types. In general, the expected age-related and life-cycle-related influences do not diminish the strength of the association between denomination and marriage type on the one hand, and Jewish religious affiliation and identification, on the other.

Two aspects of the relationship between marriage type and Jewish religious identification and affiliation are particularly noteworthy. The first is the extent to which conversionary marriages are like inmarriages, both as a whole and within denomination. Clearly, conversion often leads to the maintenance of Jewish religious practices. At the same time, a significant proportion of conversionary marriages are low in their levels of Jewish religious practice, which raises questions about the quality and meaning of such conversions. The second aspect is the low overall level of Jewish religious affiliation and practice of mixed-marrieds, although these levels are slightly higher among those who are denominationally identified. Mixed marriage clearly militates against Jewish religious affiliation and practice.

Organizational Membership and Ties to Israel

The broad pattern of organizational membership for the three marriage types, as presented in table 21, generally parallels that for synagogue membership (see table 18). Indeed, the same rank order is evident—inmarrieds, conversionary marrieds, and mixed-marrieds. At the same time, there are some significant variations.

The data for marriage types as a whole (at the base of table 21) show that inmarrieds and mixed-marrieds respond uniformly to both organizational and synagogue membership, but with one fundamental difference: inmarrieds are uniformly quite high in their membership levels, while mixed-marrieds are uniformly low. Thus, 57 percent of inmarrieds belong to Jewish organizations and 60 percent to synagogues, whereas 16 percent of mixed-marrieds belong to Jewish organizations and 15 percent to synagogues. In contrast, however, among conversionary marriages, the level of Jewish organizational membership is significantly lower than that for synagogue membership—45 percent belong to Jewish organizations and 56 percent to synagogues.

When the data for membership in synagogues and other Jewish organizations are combined, it is found that 40 percent of inmarrieds belong to both and 24 percent to neither, 31 percent of conversionary marrieds belong to both and 30 percent to neither, and 5 percent of mixed-marrieds belong to both and 75 percent to neither.

From the data it would appear that conversion to Judaism in the sense of religious integration proceeds faster than communal integration. Apparently it takes longer to acquire and develop Jewish communal ties than it does to adopt new religious beliefs and practices. At the same time, the obstacles placed by mixed marriage in the path of Jewish self-identity seem to apply equally to both the religious and communal dimensions.

Ties to Israel were probed by means of a question asking whether any member of the household had ever made a trip to Israel. The data at the base of table 22 replicate the rank order seen previously: inmarrieds, conversionary marrieds, and mixed-marrieds. Overall, 47 percent of inmarrieds have visited Israel, as compared to 39 percent of conversionary marrieds, and 21 percent of mixed-marrieds.

When the denominational factor is taken into account (see the base of tables 21 and 22), some noteworthy exceptions emerge. On the one hand, the expected rank order for both organizational membership and visits to Israel of Orthodox, Conservative, Reform, and Just Jewish is maintained. However, with regard to visiting Israel, differences between the Just Jewish and the other denominations are rather small; indeed, only 2 percent separates Reform Jews and the Just Jewish in this regard. For Orthodox, Conservative, and Reform Jews, the level of synagogue membership is higher than the level of organizational membership, which in turn is higher than the level of Israel visits. For the Just Jewish, however, the reverse is true: the level of Israel visits is highest (34 percent), followed by organizational membership (26 percent), with the level of synagogue membership (16 percent) lowest. These data further demonstrate the underlying secular orientation of the Just Jewish, in all marriage types.

When marriage types within denominations are examined, there is a striking exception to the expected pattern: Conservative conversionary marrieds are almost as likely as Conservative inmarrieds to belong to Jewish organizations (56 percent as against 59 percent) and more likely to visit Israel (55 percent as against 47 percent). Based on this finding, the earlier suggestion that conversionary marrieds generally have a lower level of ethnic and communal identification as compared to their religious identification must be revised, since it holds only for Reform, but not for Conservatives. The explanation may lie in the interaction between denomination and conversion, perhaps in the differing standards and expectations of Conservative and Reform conversions, combined with a process of self-selection among those undertaking conversion.

Within each denomination, mixed-marrieds are consistently less likely than other marriage types to belong to Jewish organizations and to visit Israel. Moreover, their levels of participation are lower than their already low levels of religious affiliation and identification. Thus, 33 percent of Conservative, 17 percent of Reform, and 7 percent of Just Jewish mixed-marrieds belong to Jewish organizations; the comparable figures for visiting Israel are 16 percent, 20 percent, and 24 percent.

When controls are introduced for age, the results (not shown in a table) clarify further the differential processes at work among Conservative and Reform conversionary marrieds. While both Conservative and Reform in-marrieds and mixed-marrieds over the age of 45 are much more likely to have visited Israel than those under the age of 45, with Conservative and Reform conversionary marrieds the situation is reversed. Among Conservative conversionary marrieds under the age of 45, 61 percent have visited Israel, as compared to 34 percent of those over the age of 45; among Reform conversionary marrieds, 27 percent of those under the age of 45 have visited Israel, as compared to 18 percent of those over the age of 45.

It would appear that the increasing centrality given to Israel in contemporary Jewish life has in recent years found direct expression in visits to Israel as part of the conversion process, whether formally or informally. This seems particularly evident in the case of young Conservative conversionary marrieds. This process is augmented within the Conservative movement by membership in Jewish organizations: 63 percent of Conservative conversionary marrieds under the age of 45 belong to Jewish organizations, as compared with 39 percent over the age of 45. In contrast, among Reform conversionary marrieds, membership in Jewish organizations is slightly lower for those under the age of 45 than for those over the age of 45.

Jewish Philanthropy

Researchers have consistently found that contributing to Jewish causes is highly correlated with other measures of Jewish identification.[21] According to Jonathan Woocher, philanthropy constitutes one of the central tenets of American Jewry's civil religion of "sacred survival." And, indeed, in the study described here, some 80 percent of respondents report that their households contribute to Jewish causes.

The pattern of giving to Jewish causes, as seen in table 23, follows the rank order of the marriage types previously encountered for other measures of Jewish identification: inmarried (86 percent), conversionary married (81 percent), and mixed-married (57 percent). Similarly, the denominational rank order replicates the standard pattern: Orthodox (87 percent), Conservative (86 percent), Reform (83 percent), and Just Jewish (65 percent). However, the differences between Orthodox, Conservative, and Reform Jews with regard to philanthropy are narrower than for any of the other measures. Moreover, the level of participation of the Just Jewish in Jewish philanthropy is higher than for all other items of religious and communal identification. When marriage type is combined with denomination, the

---

[21]See, for example, Mordechai Rimor and Gary A. Tobin, "Jewish Giving Patterns to Jewish and Non-Jewish Philanthropy," in *Faith and Philanthropy in America,* ed. Robert Wuthnow and Virginia A. Hodgkinson (San Francisco, 1990), pp. 134–64.

same pattern of relationship between marriage type and Jewish philanthropy is maintained.

By way of comparison, 72 percent of households report that they give to non-Jewish or nonsectarian causes, which is slightly lower than the overall rate of Jewish giving. Differences between marriage type and denomination and between combinations of the two are much narrower for general philanthropic giving than for donations to Jewish causes. When giving to both types of causes is compared, within all denominations inmarrieds are more likely to give to Jewish than to non-Jewish causes, while the opposite is the case with mixed-marrieds.

Friendship Patterns

Jewish religious identification and communal affiliation are reinforced by primary groups such as family and close friends. Thus it is important to examine the relationship between marriage type and the ethnic character of friendship groups.

The patterns of friendship of the three marriage types are reported in table 24, which presents them in two categories: a predominantly Jewish friendship pattern, in which two or all of one's three closest friends are Jewish; and a predominantly non-Jewish friendship pattern, in which only one or none of one's three closest friends are Jewish.

The figures at the base of table 24 indicate an extremely strong relationship between marriage type and friends, with each marriage type maintaining its own distinctive pattern of friendship. Exactly three-quarters of the inmarrieds have predominantly Jewish friends, while one-quarter have mainly non-Jewish friends. Among the conversionary marrieds, exactly half mix with predominantly Jewish friends, while the other half have mainly non-Jewish friends. The friendship pattern of the mixed-marrieds is more or less the reverse of that of the inmarrieds: about seven in ten have predominantly non-Jewish friends, while three in ten have predominantly Jewish friends.

A somewhat more complex picture of friendship patterns emerges when denomination is taken into account. Overall, the familiar denominational rank order is evident: the Orthodox have the highest proportion of predominantly Jewish friends, followed by Conservative Jews, Reform Jews, and the Just Jewish. It is worth noting that when marriage types are compared within and across denominations, the expected distance between Conservative and Reform inmarrieds is virtually erased. However, the major deviation from the expected rank order occurs among the conversionary marrieds: Conservative conversionary marrieds are less likely to have predominantly Jewish friends (41 percent) than are both Reform conversionary marrieds (54 percent) and Conservative mixed-marrieds (49 percent).

When controls for age are introduced, as reported in table 25, the expected denominational and marriage-type rank orders are reinstated for those aged 45 and older. In this age group, 84 percent of Conservative conversionary marrieds have predominantly Jewish friends, as compared with 63 percent of Reform conversionary marrieds, and 65 percent of Conservative mixed-marrieds. But among those under 45 years of age, the previously noted deviations from the expected denominational and marriage-type rank orders are even more marked. Only 34 percent of the younger Conservative conversionary marrieds have predominantly Jewish friends, as compared with 54 percent of Reform conversionary marrieds, and 43 percent of Conservative mixed-marrieds.

The low proportion of predominantly Jewish friends among younger Conservative conversionary marrieds is consistent with the general relationship between age and friendship patterns seen in table 25: except for the Orthodox inmarrieds, for every combination of denomination and marriage type, those under the age of 45 are less likely to have predominantly Jewish friends than those over age 45. However, the difference between the two Conservative conversionary married age groups—50 percent—is twice that of the age groups for other denominational marriage types. Why this is so—since younger Conservative conversionary marrieds score relatively high on all other dimensions of Jewish identification—is not clear.

Jewish Education for the Children

The relationship between marriage type and the provision of formal Jewish education to children during the key period, ages 10–13, is shown at the base of table 26. Among the inmarried, formal Jewish education for children in the pre-bar/bat mitzvah years is almost universal (95 percent), and its incidence is only slightly lower among the conversionary marrieds (84 percent). However, the proportion receiving Jewish education drops to 41 percent among the children of mixed marriages.

This rank order among marriage types remains intact when denomination is taken into account, but some striking variations are apparent. First, among all marriage types the differences between Conservative and Reform Jews in the provision of Jewish education are minimal. Second, within both denominations, the differences between the inmarried and the conversionary marrieds, on the one hand, and the mixed-marrieds, on the other, are greatly reduced, while among the Just Jewish the gap between them is increased to the maximum. Among Conservative Jews the difference between the mixed-marrieds and the other two marriage types in providing children with formal Jewish education is 19 percent, among Reform Jews it ranges from 12 to 14 percent, but among the Just Jewish it is 100 percent. While all the Just Jewish inmarrieds provide their children with formal Jewish education, no Just Jewish mixed-marrieds do so. Denominational identification is closely related to the provision of Jewish education to the children of mixed marriages. Over 80 percent of mixed-marrieds who identify with a denomination give their children Jewish educations, but mixed-marrieds without a denominational identification do not. In all likelihood, this relationship is two-directional: attendance at Jewish schools that are denominationally affiliated usually entails formal synagogue or temple affiliation, thus providing children with a clear denominational identification. Conversely, denominational self-identification facilitates formal synagogue or temple membership, which in turn encourages the provision of Jewish education for the children.

Three main conclusions may be drawn from the foregoing analysis of the relationship between marriage type and various aspects of Jewish identification. First, there is a strong, direct relationship between marriage type and all measures of Jewish identification. Second, within the marriage types themselves, there are recurring variations that point to the existence of separate subtypes. Third, these patterns continue to show themselves even when account is taken of the strong and consistent influence of denomination, which variously mutes or reinforces the impact of marriage type but never overrides it completely. This is even more the case when the weaker and less consistent influences of family type and age are considered.

Index of Jewish Identification

Taking the analysis a step further, an index of Jewish identification was constructed, making it possible to identify the different marriage subtypes, as well as to determine the relative weight of each within the broader marriage type, within the denomination, and within the total sample.

The index of Jewish identification was constructed by combining all the various elements of Jewish identity into a single numerical score on an additive (Likert) scale. Eleven items were included: synagogue membership, synagogue attendance; Sabbath candle lighting; participation in a Passover seder; fasting on Yom Kippur; lighting Hanukkah candles; membership in a Jewish organization; donating to a Jewish charity; visiting Israel; and having predominantly Jewish close friends. In each case one point was assigned for a positive response, except for synagogue attendance, where one point was given for attendance on the High Holy Days and a few times a year, and two points for attending monthly or weekly. In order to avoid problems of standardization, only respondents who answered all of the questions were scored, thus excluding those in communities in which not all of the questions were asked and those who, for whatever reason, did not answer particular questions. As a result, the total number of respondents was reduced by about one-third. The range of possible scores is 0–11, and, following the shape of the frequency distribution, it is divided into three categories: low Jewish identification: 0–4 points; medium Jewish identification: 5–8 points; and high Jewish identification: 9–11 points.

It should be noted that the index does not include items indicating higher levels of Jewish identification, such as strict Sabbath and festival observance, keeping kosher, and daily synagogue attendance. Although the original Jewish population surveys contain such data, these and similar items that reflect traditional standards of Jewish religious identification were excluded in order to reduce the range of the index, thereby lowering the threshholds for the medium and high levels. The net effect, therefore, is to include within these two categories many individuals who would not otherwise have been included.

Measured by the index of Jewish identification, 25 percent of all respondents score high, 45 percent medium, and 30 percent low. When divided according to marriage type, as reported in table 27, the data show the same relationship between marriage type and Jewish identification for the overall index as for the individual items—there is little difference between inmarrieds and conversionary marrieds on the index, but the gap between them and mixed-marrieds is quite wide.

These data also serve as the basis for identifying and locating the various marriage subtypes in the typology of conversionary and mixed marriages and assessing their relative weights. Thus, the vast majority of conversionary marrieds (83 percent) are to be found at the middle and upper levels of Jewish identification. One-third of them (33 percent) are "high-Jewish-identification conversionary marrieds," indicating the considerable value and identity change, if not total transformation, that has resulted from conversion. Half of the total (50 percent) are "medium-Jewish-identification conversionary marrieds." The smallest group, about one-sixth (17 percent), are "low-Jewish-identification conversionary marrieds," in which conversion may be described as nominal or pro forma, to the extent that it has resulted in little or no change in identification or behavior.

The pattern for mixed-marrieds is strikingly different. Indeed, judging by these figures, mixed marriage represents an almost insuperable bar to the achievement of a high level of Jewish identification. Thus, only 1 percent are "high-Jewish-identification mixed-marrieds," who have created a family environment in which a strong Jewish identity is being maintained and transmitted. The largest single group by far, just under seven in ten (69 percent), are at the opposite end of the scale, "low-Jewish-identification mixed-marrieds." In these households, Jewish identification and behavior are peripheral. Finally, three in ten mixed marriages (30 percent) are "medium-Jewish-identification mixed-marrieds," mainly households that emphasize ritual home practices rather than communal or ethnic ties.

Taking denomination into account (see table 28) sharpens the picture even further. Looking first at differences within denomination, Conservative conversionary marrieds score somewhat higher than Conservative inmarrieds, while the pattern within Reform is dichotomous—Reform conversionary marrieds are represented more at the high and low levels of Jewish identification, and less at the medium level, than are Reform inmarrieds. Mixed-marrieds among all the denominations score much lower than the other marriage types.

Turning to differences across denominations, just under half (48 percent) of Conservative conversionary marrieds, but only a little more than a quarter of Reform conversionary marrieds (27 percent), exhibit high levels of Jewish identification. Conversely, very few Conservative conversionary marrieds (3 percent) show low levels of Jewish identification as compared with nearly a quarter (23 percent) among Reform conversionary marrieds. The largest groups in both denominations are those with medium Jewish identification; they represent about half of all conversionary marrieds.

The differences between Conservative mixed-marrieds and Reform mixed-marrieds, in contrast, are narrower, and are concentrated at the lower and middle levels of the Jewish identification index. Very few Conservative mixed-marrieds or Reform mixed-marrieds exhibit high Jewish identification, but 53 percent of Conservative mixed-marrieds are at the medium level, as compared with 41 percent of Reform mixed-marrieds. At the bottom of the scale the situation is reversed: 57 percent of Reform mixed-marrieds show low Jewish identification, as compared with 42 percent of Conservative mixed-marrieds. However, the largest differences are between Conservative and Reform mixed-marrieds on the one hand, and the Just Jewish mixed-marrieds on the other. There are no Just Jewish mixed-marrieds with high Jewish identification and only 13 percent are at the medium level; the vast majority (87 percent) are at the low level.

Identification with Non-Jewish Cultural and Religious Symbols

The foregoing discussion analyzed the extent and strength of key aspects of Jewish identification in different marriage types. Our theory of Jewish identity posited that being *not* Christian was a major defining element of Jewish identity. The creation of an unambiguous Jewish identity entails, at the very least, the absence from the home of Christian symbols and practices, even if the level of Jewish identification is low. Empirically, we can then hypothesize that Jewish identification and the incorporation of Christian practices and symbols in the home will vary inversely. Thus, in homes with medium and high levels of Jewish identification we would not expect to find Christian symbols and practices, while such symbols would be present only when Jewish identification had disappeared completely or was at a low level.

This hypothesis is explored by means of a question about having a Christmas tree at home. While this single question serves clearly to identify those who have introduced a central Christian symbol into the home, it does not indicate whether it is an isolated practice or the tip of the iceberg—part of a more extensive incorporation of Christian symbols and values into the home. However, the surveys contain no further questions that might resolve this issue. The results are reported in table 29.

It is clear that inmarrieds shun the practice: 98 percent do not have a Christmas tree. Such an unequivocal response strongly supports our theory that among inmarrieds, at least, there exists an unambiguous Jewish identity, in which being *not* Christian is a defining element. Among conversionary marrieds, 78 percent do not have a Christmas tree while 22 percent do. In contrast, among mixed-marrieds, 62 percent have a Christmas tree while 38 percent do not. Quite remarkably, more mixed-marrieds have Christmas trees than perform any single Jewish ritual. (The most widely practiced rituals are attending a Passover seder and the lighting of Hanukkah candles, which, as was previously shown in table 20, are engaged in by 52 percent of the mixed-marrieds.)

The expected denominational rank order remains firm in this area. Overall, 3 percent of Orthodox Jews have Christmas trees, as do 4 percent of Conservative Jews, 18 percent of Reform Jews, and 33 percent of the Just Jewish. The same rank order is maintained when marriage types are compared across denomination. Thus, 8 percent of Conservative conversionary marrieds as against 33 percent of Reform conversionary marrieds have Christmas trees; among mixed-marrieds, the comparable figures are 41 percent and 63 percent, and 66 percent for the Just Jewish.

Introducing controls for age, family type, and the ethnic character of friendship groups does not alter the above patterns. Indeed, family type itself is seen to have a marked impact, shown in table 30: within every denomination and marriage type (and particularly among mixed-marrieds), those who have children are consistently more likely to have a Christmas tree than those who have no children. Where marriage type, denomination, and family type are mutually reinforcing, the proportion having a Christmas tree reaches a peak. Thus, 81 percent of Just Jewish mixed-marrieds with a child at home have a Christmas tree. When controls for age are introduced, the impact of marriage type, denomination, and family is clearly apparent, both among those under 45 and those over 45. In contrast, the impact of close friends is less clear-cut (not shown in a table). While Conservative conversionary marrieds and Conservative mixed-marrieds with predominantly non-Jewish friends are more likely to have a Christmas tree than those with predominantly Jewish friends, this is not the case among Reform conversionary marrieds and Reform mixed-marrieds.

Dual-Identity Households

As we have seen, virtually all inmarried households manifest a single, unambiguous Jewish identity by virtue of the fact that Christian symbols are barred, irrespective of the level of Jewish identification. Thus, inmarried Jews, including those with a low level of Jewish identification and those without denominational identification, overwhelmingly reject the practice of having a Christmas tree in the house.

Among intermarrieds, however, the situation is more complex. Conversionary and mixed marriages constitute arenas within which various theoretically possible identity resolutions or outcomes that come to characterize the household work themselves out. Unambiguous Jewish single-identity households are one possible identity outcome, as are Christian single-identity households, secular-identity (religiously and ethnically neutral) households, and dual-identity households. A *dual-identity* household is one in which both Jewish and Christian symbols and identification are maintained side by side, even when Jewish identification is at a medium level, or higher. Indeed, under certain circumstances, Christian symbols and practices are more likely to be found in such households when Jewish practices are present than when the latter are absent.

The existence of single-identity and dual-identity households among conversionary and mixed marriages makes it necessary to expand the typology presented above. Each of the previously specified subtypes can now be divided into those that have a Christmas tree and those that do not. The expanded typology in table 31 has 12 cells instead of the previous 6, although only 11 are actually filled.

Among conversionary marrieds, "dual low-Jewish-identification conversionary-marriage households" represent a partial or incomplete conversionary process, one that has not resulted in an unambiguous Jewish identification, even at a low level, due to the simultaneous retention of a Christian identification. "Dual medium-Jewish-identification conversionary-marriage households" represent a conversionary process that involves a moderate, if not modal, acceptance of Jewish identification and values, yet is bivalent to the extent that it also incorporates certain Christian elements in the home.

In "dual high-Jewish-identification conversionary-marriage households" the value and identity transformation is still not fully achieved, since Christian symbols show themselves. The existence of a dual identity where Jewish identification is high will in all likelihood create considerable dissonance within the family.

Among mixed-marrieds, the combination of low Jewish identification and a Christmas tree in the house—"dual low-Jewish-identification mixed-marriage households"—points to people on the margins of two heritages, and perhaps even marginal in the classic sociological sense of not quite belonging to either. As against this, "dual medium-Jewish-identification mixed-marriage households" exhibit a marked degree of religious syncretism. The "dual high-Jewish-identification mixed-marriage household" cell is empty, as a result of the absence of a dual-identity subtype that both maintains and transmits a high level of Jewish identification and simultaneously incorporates Christian symbols.

The data in table 31 show 62 percent of all mixed-marrieds to be in dual-identity households, as compared with 20 percent of conversionary marrieds. Most of the conversionary marrieds in the dual-identity category exhibit medium and high levels of Jewish identification, while most of the mixed-marrieds are at the low level. Taken together, among all conversionary and mixed marriages, dual-identity households outnumber single-identity households 54 percent to 46 percent.

When denomination is examined (see table 32), it becomes clear that the formation of dual-identity households is closely related to the standard denominational rank order. Thus, among conversionary marrieds, 7 percent of Conservative Jews and 30 percent of Reform Jews are in dual-identity households, while among mixed-marrieds, 33 percent of Conservative Jews, 65 percent of Reform Jews, and 69 percent of the Just Jewish are in that category. Overall, 20 percent of all Conservative conversionary and mixed-marrieds are in dual-identity households, as compared with 56 percent in the Reform denomination. The small proportion of "dual high-Jewish-identification conversionary-marriage households" are all found among Reform Jews; there are none in the Conservative denomination.

Higher levels of Jewish identification are generally associated with single-identity households. Over two-thirds of all conversionary marrieds with medium or high Jewish identification, and 90 percent of the Conservative Jews among them, are not in dual-identity households. At the opposite end of the scale, 35 percent of the Reform, and 63 percent of the Just Jewish, low-Jewish-identification mixed-marrieds are in dual-identity households.

At the same time, a not insubstantial number of households at reasonably high levels of Jewish practice maintain Christian practices simultaneously. Thus, in the medium- and high-Jewish-identification categories, 14 percent of Conservative mixed-marrieds, 23 percent of Reform conversionary marrieds, and 29 percent of Reform mixed-marrieds are in dual-identity households. In the case of the latter, the dual-identity outcome is by far the most popular, outnumbering the single-identity households by a ratio of more than two to one.

Introducing controls for age provides a clear indication of the direction of these trends among the mixed-marrieds. Three features stand out when those under age 45 are compared with those over age 45. First, as shown in table 33, Reform identification is far more prevalent within younger mixed-married households than older ones. Thus, while 40 percent of mixed-marrieds over age 45 call themselves Reform, 60 percent of those under age 45 do so. This increase has come at the expense of the non-denominationally identified Just Jewish mixed-marrieds, whose proportion is 49 percent in the older age group and 31 percent in the younger one.

Second, the proportion of Reform mixed-marrieds in dual-identity households has increased dramatically (see table 34). While just over half (54 percent) of those over 45 are in dual-identity households, nearly three-quarters (73 percent) of those under 45 are. (Among the Just Jewish mixed-marrieds, the equivalent proportions decline from 76 percent to 68 percent.)

Third, much higher proportions of younger than of older Reform Jews with medium and high Jewish identification are in dual-identity households. Among Reform mixed-marrieds, 34 percent of those with medium and high Jewish identification under age 45 are in dual-identity households, as compared with 19 percent of those over age 45. The equivalent figures for medium- and high-Jewish-identification Reform conversionary marrieds are 29 percent and 9 percent, respectively, indicating an even greater movement in the direction of dual-identity households.

The total extent of this change is clearly illustrated in table 35, which compares the distribution of marriage types in the two age categories. Nearly one-quarter of all households (23 percent) in the under-45 age group are dual-identity intermarried households, and about one-sixth (16 percent) are single-identity intermarried households, as against 8 percent and 7 percent, respectively, in the over-45 age group. Conversely, inmarriages, which constitute the overwhelming majority of households in the older group (85 percent), represent only six in ten (61 percent) in the younger group.

CONCLUSION

The data reported above demonstrate and quantify the dramatic changes in the marriage choices of American Jews in the last four decades. With every passing generation and the coming of age of every younger cohort, more Jews have been marrying non-Jews, and mixed marriages represent an increasingly larger proportion of married couples. While males are more likely than females to marry non-Jews, the greatly heightened propensity of Jewish women to do so has narrowed the difference between them. Rates of intermarriage are consistently higher among those with lesser socioeconomic achievement, as measured by education, occupation, and income, than among those with greater achievement.

The finding that intensive Jewish education alone has not acted as a bar to intermarriage suggests that the increase in the propensity of Jews to marry non-Jews and to establish mixed families is associated with the nature and quality of contemporary Jewish identity. It was argued that the core of Jewish personal and group identity is distinguished less by "shared beliefs" and more by "shared feelings." This has led to the development of a Jewish personal identity that is both secure and unambiguous, and at the same time segmented, individualistic, pluralistic, and varied in intensity and salience.

A Jewish identity of this nature can facilitate mixed marriage by permitting Jews to marry non-Jews in the hope or assumption that they will be able to maintain their personal Jewish identity. That is to say, they will not be called upon to surrender part or all of the religious core of their personality or to deny their ethnic heritage (neither will their non-Jewish spouses), and they will be able to transmit that Jewish identity to their offspring. How these hopes and assumptions actually turn out—how Jewish identification fares in conversionary and mixed marriages—constitutes the central focus of this study. In what follows, the key findings relating to it are briefly summarized and linked to our theoretical framework, and their implications for future trends are discussed.

Conversionary Marriages

Overall, Jewish identification fares well in conversionary marriages, or at least as well as in inmarriages, if the identical proportions of both marriage types at each level of Jewish identification are the criterion. Indeed, the Jewish identification of conversionary marrieds fares even better when they are denominationally connected: the overall level of Jewish identification among Conservative and Reform conversionary marrieds turns out to be higher than that of their respective inmarrieds.

However, conversionary marriages do not fare so consistently well in developing an unambiguous Jewish identity. Here denominational differences are decisive. While very few Conservative conversionary marriages result in dual-identity households, nearly a third of Reform conversionary marriages do so.

In sum, these findings indicate that conversion usually leads to the achievement of medium and high levels of Jewish identification, and more often than not brings about a qualitative identity transformation that results in the acquisition of an unambiguous Jewish identity by the convert and the establishment of a single-identity household. At the same time, the existence of significant proportions of conversionary marrieds who remain at low levels of Jewish identification and those who maintain dual-identity households suggests that conversion "does not always work." Clearly, there are different types and levels of conversionary marriage, and in differentiating among them, greater attention needs to be paid to the content and character of the conversion process and its denominational auspices. Similarly, the effect of the actual timing of conversion—whether it takes place before or after marriage—about which we had no data, is an issue meriting further analysis.

Mixed Marriages

Despite the hopes and assumptions, Jewish identification does not fare well in mixed marriages. The overall level of Jewish identification among the overwhelming majority of mixed-marrieds is low, and in only one case (Conservative mixed-marrieds) are less than a majority in the low-Jewish-identification category. In all, the data indicate that mixed marriage and the level of Jewish identification are strongly negatively related. So few mixed-marrieds manifest a high level of Jewish identification, and denominational connection makes so little impact in this regard, that mixed marriage must be regarded as a virtual bar to the achievement of a high level of Jewish identification.

Predominantly, Jewish identification in mixed marriages is accompanied by the presence of symbols of Christian identification, resulting in dual-identity households at all levels of Jewish identification. Contrary to what might have been expected, among Reform mixed-marrieds there was clear evidence of a positive relationship between the level of Jewish identification and the incorporation of Christian symbols. That is to say, as the level of Jewish identification rises to medium, so too does the proportion of dual-identity households. This tendency has increased over time and reaches its peak in the younger age groups.

Overall, the chances of a mixed marriage resulting in a single-identity household at any level of Jewish identification are extremely slim, and the chances of it resulting in a single-identity household at a high level of Jewish identification are infinitesimal. Under these circumstances, the likelihood of creating an unambiguous Jewish identity, should such indeed be the intention or the desire, is virtually nil.

Dual-identity households are segmented and pluralist, responding to the individual needs of both partners in an intermarriage and catering to their different if not competing religious and ethnic heritages. The longer-term viability of such marriages and the actual identity resolutions arrived at by the children in these households, the bearers of both traditions, are at present unknown. If the theory of personal identity and of the unambiguous character of Jewish identity elaborated above is correct, then the least likely resolution of all is the development of a new synthesis of Judaism and Christianity, a modern version of the ancient Judeo-Christians, or Christian-Jews. It is more likely that, over time, choices will have to be made between being either Jewish or Christian or neither. The low level of Jewish identification in these households to begin with, the pull of the majority, and the strength and attraction of common secular and general values do not augur well for the choice of an unambiguous Jewish identity. Rather than meeting the hope of being able to transmit Jewish identity, mixed marriages may prove to be terminal for Jewish identity.

However these choices turn out in the future, one thing is certain. The American Jewish community as we know it, formerly based upon a heavy predominance of inmarriage that transmitted an unambiguous Jewish identity—even if the latter was not always strong and was sometimes the source of ambivalence—is rapidly being transformed. The increased rate of mixed marriage has already produced an age cohort under 45 whose marriage profile is very different from that of the cohort over 45. As we have noted, only six in ten of all households under 45 are inmarriages, and about a quarter are dual-identity households.

If the rate of mixed marriage continues to increase and present trends continue, the already low overall level of Jewish identification is likely to fall further, and dual-identity households may eventually rival if not outnumber single-identity households. Unambiguous Jewish identity may become the mark of a minority. Whether such a Jewish community can command the will and resources to support the network of Jewish institutions, causes, and activities within the community, in American society and politics, and abroad, is an open question. But the answer to it will determine the future of American Jewry.

It can be argued that current trends and patterns are neither inexorable nor irreversible and may be influenced by changes in individual attitudes and communal policies. Both individual Jews and communal leaders may take a passive or more active response to the issues. The critical differences between conversionary and mixed-married households clearly revealed by the data suggest that a more activist approach to conversion, including conversion after marriage, could have a considerable impact on future developments. By the same token, the ambiguous character of mixed-married households provides opportunities for activist policies aimed at encouraging a degree of identity transformation that might lead to conversion rather than result from it.

Moreover, the quality of Jewish life of the core of the Jewish community—the inmarried couples—may be enhanced or diluted as time goes on. Such changes will directly affect the intermarried Jewish population as well. Thus, the strength and viability of the American Jewish community will be affected at least as much by the strength and growth of the most deeply committed Jewish groups as by its success in drawing less committed groups closer to Judaism.

The size of the Jewish population, the vitality of Jewish life, and the future of the American Jewish community all depend upon a clear understanding of these phenomena and appropriate actions by individual Jews, scholars, and communal leaders.

APPENDIX

TABLE 1. MARRIAGE-TYPE DISTRIBUTION, BY COMMUNITY

Community	Number of Cases	Inmarriage (%)	Conversionary Marriage (%)	Mixed Marriage (%)	Total (%)
Baltimore	769	80	5	15	100
Boston	787	78	3	19	100
Cleveland	582	79	4	17	100
Dallas	598	66	9	24	99*
Essex/Morris County (NJ)	1,215	83	3	14	100
Providence (RI)	676	86	6	9	101*
San Francisco	1,679	60	8	31	99*
Worcester (MA)	367	71	10	19	100
Total	6,673				

*Rounding error.

TABLE 2. MARRIAGE TYPES IN TOTAL SAMPLE

Marriage Type	Number of Cases	Projected Frequency	Percent
Inmarriage	5,225	144,711	73.4
Conversionary marriage	409	10,610	5.4
Mixed marriage	1,037	41,757	21.2
Total	6,671	197,078	100.0

TABLE 3. DECADE OF MARRIAGE OF INDIVIDUALS, BY MARRIAGE TYPE

Marriage Type	Number of Cases	Prior to 1960 (%)	1960–1969 (%)	1970–1979 (%)	1980–1989 (%)
Inmarriage	7,645	94	84	75	62
Conversionary marriage	335	2	5	6	5
Mixed marriage	874	5	12	19	33
Total	8,854	101*	101*	100	100

*Rounding error.

TABLE 4. AGE OF INDIVIDUALS, BY MARRIAGE TYPE

Marriage Type	18–34 (%)	35–44 (%)	45–54 (%)	55–64 (%)	65+ (%)
Inmarriage	70	78	86	93	94
Conversionary marriage	5	5	3	3	1
Mixed marriage	25	17	11	5	5
Total percent	100	100	100	101*	100
Number of cases	1,543	3,081	2,164	2,179	2,154

*Rounding error.

TABLE 5. GENERATION OF INDIVIDUALS, BY MARRIAGE TYPE

Marriage Type	First Generation (%)	Second Generation (%)	Third Generation (%)	Fourth Generation (%)
Inmarriage	93	87	70	56
Conversionary marriage	2	2	4	6
Mixed marriage	5	11	26	38
Total percent	100	100	100	100
Number of cases	807	4,659	2,127	399

TABLE 6. GENDER OF INDIVIDUALS, BY MARRIAGE TYPE AND DECADE OF
MARRIAGE

Decade/ Gender	Number of Cases	Inmarriage (%)	Conversionary Marriage (%)	Mixed Marriage (%)	Total (%)
Prior to 1960	3,927	94	2	5	101*
Male	2,001	90	3	8	101*
Female	1,926	98	1	2	101*
1960–1969	2,056	84	5	12	101*
Male	1,074	78	8	15	101*
Female	982	91	1	8	100
1970–1979	1,900	75	6	19	100
Male	1,008	70	9	21	100
Female	892	79	3	18	100
1980–1989	952	62	5	33	100
Male	502	55	7	38	100
Female	450	70	2	28	100
Total					
Male	6,149	82	5	13	100
Female	5,681	90	1	9	100

*Rounding error.
Note: In some tables, the "Total" may differ from the sum of the Ns. This is because sometimes respondents did not answer a specific question, and in some cities certain questions were not asked.

TABLE 7. CURRENT MARRIAGE TYPE OF INDIVIDUALS IN FIRST, SECOND, AND THIRD (+) MARRIAGES

Marriage Type	First Marriage (%)	Second Marriage (%)	Third (+) Marriage (%)
Inmarriage	86	70	54
Conversionary marriage	3	6	6
Mixed marriage	11	24	40
Total percent	100	100	100
Number of cases	9,774	1,240	103

TABLE 8. MEAN AGE OF INDIVIDUALS AT FIRST MARRIAGE, BY MARRIAGE TYPE AND GENDER

Marriage Type/Gender	Mean Age
Total population	25.0
Inmarriage	24.6
Male	25.9
Female	23.2
Conversionary marriage	27.6
Male	27.8
Female	25.7
Mixed marriage	26.9
Male	27.9
Female	26.0
Total	
Male	26.3
Female	23.6

TABLE 9. PRESENCE OF CHILDREN IN HOUSEHOLD, BY MARRIAGE TYPE

Marriage Type	Number of Cases	Children in Household (%)
Inmarriage	1,629	73
Conversionary marriage	89	4
Mixed marriage	535	24
Total	2,253	101*

*Rounding error.

TABLE 10. SECULAR EDUCATION OF INDIVIDUALS,† BY MARRIAGE TYPE
            AND AGE

Education/Age	Inmarriage (%)	Conversionary Marriage (%)	Mixed Marriage (%)	Total (%)
		Marriage Type		
High school or less	88	1	10	100
18–34	59	—	41	100
35–44	61	11	28	100
45–54	86	1	13	100
55–64	95	2	4	101*
65+	95	1	4	100
Some college	86	3	11	100
18–34	63	5	33	101*
35–44	79	6	15	100
45–54	92	3	5	100
55–64	94	2	4	100
65+	95	1	4	100
College degree	83	3	14	100
18–34	69	5	26	100
35–44	79	4	18	101*
45–54	85	3	11	99*
55–64	95	2	3	100
65+	94	2	4	100
Graduate degree	81	5	14	100
18–34	74	7	19	100
35–44	80	5	15	100
45–54	84	4	12	100
55–64	87	4	9	100
65+	88	2	10	100
Number of cases	9,522	401	1,019	10,942

*Rounding error.
†Jewish respondents and spouses only.
—Less than one-half of 1%.

TABLE 11. OCCUPATION OF INDIVIDUALS,† BY MARRIAGE TYPE AND AGE

Occupation/Age	Inmarriage (%)	Conversionary Marriage (%)	Mixed Marriage (%)	Total (%)
Professional/technical	82	4	14	100
18–34	74	6	20	100
35–44	80	4	16	100
45–54	83	3	14	100
55–64	90	3	7	100
65+	91	2	7	100
Executive/managerial	82	5	13	100
18–34	72	5	23	100
35–44	76	7	17	100
45–54	84	6	10	100
55–64	89	6	6	101*
65+	93	1	6	100
Sales	85	4	11	100
18–34	75	5	21	101*
35–44	75	8	18	101*
45–54	88	4	8	100
55–64	96	1	3	100
65+	92	2	7	101*
Clerical	89	2	9	100
18–34	61	5	34	100
35–44	87	3	11	101*
45–54	95	—	5	100
55–64	96	1	4	101*
65+	98	—	2	100

TABLE 11.—*(Continued)*

Occupation/Age	Inmarriage (%)	Conversionary Marriage (%)	Mixed Marriage (%)	Total (%)
		Marriage Type		
Service/blue collar	77	2	21	100
18–34	54	1	45	100
35–44	66	4	30	100
45–54	84	1	15	100
55–64	88	3	9	100
65+	93	1	6	100
Number of cases	8,848	390	974	10,212

*Rounding error.
†Jewish respondents and spouses only.
—Less than one-half of 1%.

TABLE 12. ANNUAL HOUSEHOLD INCOME, BY MARRIAGE TYPE

Marriage Type	$5,000–10,000 (%)	$10,001–30,000 (%)	$30,001–50,000 (%)	$50,001–75,000 (%)	$75,001–150,000 (%)	$150,000+ (%)
Inmarriage	67	73	65	68	72	85
Conversionary marriage	17	4	6	7	7	3
Mixed marriage	17	23	29	25	22	12
Total percent	101*	100	100	100	101*	100
Number of cases	87	695	1,430	1,203	964	487

*Rounding error.

TABLE 13. ANNUAL HOUSEHOLD INCOME, BY MARRIAGE TYPE AND AGE

Marriage Type	Under 45 Years			Over 45 Years		
	$5,000–30,000 (%)	$30,001–75,000 (%)	$75,001–150,000 (%)	$5,000–30,000 (%)	$30,001–75,000 (%)	$75,001–150,000 (%)
Inmarriage	56	59	72	85	79	82
Conversionary marriage	8	8	7	3	4	4
Mixed marriage	37	33	21	12	17	15
Total percent	101*	100	100	100	100	101*
Number of cases	279	1,477	792	475	1,048	613

*Rounding error.

TABLE 14. JEWISH EDUCATION OF INDIVIDUALS, BY MARRIAGE TYPE

Marriage Type	Previously Received Jewish Education (%)	Did Not Previously Receive Jewish Education (%)
Inmarriage	83	86
Conversionary marriage	4	2
Mixed marriage	13	12
Total percent	100	100
Number of cases	9,158	1,862

TABLE 15. YEARS OF JEWISH EDUCATION, BY MARRIAGE TYPE, GENDER, AND AGE

| | Age and Years of Jewish Education | | | | | | | | | | | | | | |
| Marriage Type | 18–34 | | | 35–44 | | | 45–54 | | | 55–64 | | | 65+ | | |
	None (%)	No. Yrs. <5 (%)	6+ (%)	None (%)	No. Yrs. <5 (%)	6+ (%)	None (%)	No. Yrs. <5 (%)	6+ (%)	None (%)	No. Yrs. <5 (%)	6+ (%)	None (%)	No. Yrs. <5 (%)	6+ (%)
Male															
Inmarriage	62	59	67	58	70	79	71	79	91	91	83	94	93	88	94
Conversionary marriage	7	9	9	10	8	7	2	6	3	3	4	4	1	2	1
Mixed marriage	31	33	25	32	22	14	27	15	6	6	13	2	7	10	5
Number of cases	59	230	372	127	642	696	101	442	467	125	474	426	231	466	503
Age-group percentages	14	40	46	11	49	41	15	49	37	12	50	38	20	45	35
Female															
Inmarriage	65	65	86	85	78	88	91	92	96	97	97	98	99	99	98
Conversionary marriage	1	3	2	2	2	2	1	1	1	1	1	1	0	0	1
Mixed marriage	34	32	12	13	20	10	9	7	4	2	2	2	1	1	1
Number of cases	154	236	404	295	539	568	256	416	295	325	360	292	316	279	222
Age-group percentages	25	30	45	25	39	36	30	42	27	39	36	25	45	34	21

TABLE 16. DENOMINATIONAL* DISTRIBUTION WITHIN MARRIAGE TYPES

Marriage Type	Number of Cases	Orthodox (%)	Conservative (%)	Reform (%)	Just Jewish (%)	Total (%)
Inmarriage	5,042	9	39	43	9	100
Conversionary marriage	395	3	30	57	10	100
Mixed marriage	860	2	12	52	34	100
Total	6,297					

*Use of the term "denomination" always refers to the self-identification of respondents.

TABLE 17. MARRIAGE-TYPE DISTRIBUTION WITHIN DENOMINATIONS

| Denomination | Number of Cases | Marriage Type | | | Total (%) |
		Inmarriage (%)	Conversionary Marriage (%)	Mixed Marriage (%)	
Orthodox	471	92	2	6	100
Conservative	2,274	88	5	7	100
Reform	2,857	71	7	22	100
Just Jewish	695	50	4	46	100
Total	6,297				

TABLE 18. SYNAGOGUE MEMBERSHIP, BY MARRIAGE TYPE AND
DENOMINATION

Denomination/ Marriage Type	Number of Cases	Do Belong (%)	Do Not Belong (%)	Total (%)
Orthodox				
Inmarriage	435	78	22	100
Conservative				
Inmarriage	2,011	68	32	100
Conversionary marriage	124	54	46	100
Mixed marriage	130	36	64	100
Reform				
Inmarriage	2,206	59	41	100
Conversionary marriage	224	57	43	100
Mixed marriage	416	21	79	100
Just Jewish				
Inmarriage	371	23	77	100
Conversionary marriage	34	49	51	100
Mixed marriage	279	5	95	100
Total marriage type				
Inmarriage	5,023	60	40	100
Conversionary marriage	382	56	44	100
Mixed marriage	825	15	85	100
Total denomination				
Orthodox	469	74	26	100
Conservative	2,265	65	35	100
Reform	2,846	51	49	100
Just Jewish	684	16	84	100

TABLE 19.   SYNAGOGUE ATTENDANCE, BY MARRIAGE TYPE AND
            DENOMINATION

Denomination/ Marriage Type	Number of Cases	Never, or Bar/Bat Mitzvah, Weddings, Etc. (%)	High Holidays or Few Times Per Year (%)	Monthly, Weekly, or More (%)	Total (%)
Orthodox					
Inmarriage	428	10	27	64	101*
Conservative					
Inmarriage	1,973	6	62	32	100
Conversionary marriage	120	5	53	42	100
Mixed marriage	125	25	65	10	100
Reform					
Inmarriage	2,147	16	62	22	100
Conversionary marriage	217	14	53	33	100
Mixed marriage	397	37	53	10	100
Just Jewish					
Inmarriage	361	58	35	8	101*
Conversionary marriage	32	34	52	14**	100
Mixed marriage	265	75	24	1	100
Total marriage type					
Inmarriage	4,909	16	56	28	100
Conversionary marriage	369	13	53	34	100
Mixed marriage	787	53	41	6	100

TABLE 19.—*(Continued)*

Denomination/ Marriage Type	Number of Cases	Never, or Bar/Bat Mitzvah, Weddings, Etc. (%)	High Holidays or Few Times Per Year (%)	Monthly, Weekly, or More (%)	Total (%)
Total denomination					
Orthodox	461	12	28	60	100
Conservative	2,218	7	62	31	100
Reform	2,761	20	60	20	100
Just Jewish	658	65	31	5	101*

*Rounding error.
**Cell size too small for analysis.

TABLE 20. RITUAL PRACTICE, BY MARRIAGE TYPE AND DENOMINATION

Denomination/ Marriage Type	Number of Cases	Sabbath Candles		Passover Seder		Yom Kippur		Number of Cases	Hanukkah Candles*	
		Do Prac. (%)	Do Not Prac. (%)	Do Prac. (%)	Do Not Prac. (%)	Do Prac. (%)	Do Not Prac. (%)		Do Prac. (%)	Do Not Prac. (%)
Orthodox										
Inmarriage	396	76	24	89	11	93	7	195	92	8
Conservative										
Inmarriage	1,834	50	50	94	6	82	18	1,166	95	5
Conversionary marriage	117	46	54	98	2	88	12	99	99	1
Mixed marriage	112	11	89	71	29	76	24	69	76	24
Reform										
Inmarriage	1,979	27	73	88	12	59	41	1,437	86	14
Conversionary marriage	210	22	78	84	16	61	39	160	77	23
Mixed marriage	365	4	96	67	33	40	60	274	68	32
Just Jewish										
Inmarriage	362	13	87	60	40	33	67	213	52	48
Conversionary marriage	32	39	61	83	17	60	40	23	86	14**
Mixed marriage	264	0	100	38	62	17	83	167	35	65

TABLE 20.—(Continued)

Denomination/ Marriage Type	Number of Cases	Sabbath Candles		Passover Seder		Yom Kippur		Number of Cases	Hanukkah Candles*	
		Do Prac. (%)	Do Not Prac. (%)	Do Prac. (%)	Do Not Prac. (%)	Do Prac. (%)	Do Not Prac. (%)		Do Prac. (%)	Do Not Prac. (%)
Total marriage type										
Inmarriage	4,571	38	62	87	13	68	32	3,131	85	15
Conversionary marriage	359	32	68	87	13	68	32	303	84	16
Mixed marriage	741	3	97	52	48	34	66	657	52	48
Total denomination										
Orthodox	426	71	29	86	14	92	8	217	86	14
Conservative	2,063	47	53	92	8	82	18	1,334	94	6
Reform	2,554	21	79	83	17	55	45	1,871	81	19
Just Jewish	658	8	92	51	49	27	73	403	46	54

*This question was not asked in all cities.
**Cell size too small for analysis.

TABLE 21. ORGANIZATIONAL MEMBERSHIP, BY MARRIAGE TYPE AND
DENOMINATION

Denomination/ Marriage Type	Number of Cases	Do Belong (%)	Do Not Belong (%)	Total (%)
Orthodox				
Inmarriage	427	64	36	100
Conservative				
Inmarriage	1,975	59	41	100
Conversionary marriage	122	56	44	100
Mixed marriage	129	33	67	100
Reform				
Inmarriage	2,194	57	43	100
Conversionary marriage	222	39	61	100
Mixed marriage	407	17	83	100
Just Jewish				
Inmarriage	373	43	57	100
Conversionary marriage	33	34	66	100
Mixed marriage	281	7	93	100
Total marriage type				
Inmarriage	4,969	57	43	100
Conversionary marriage	377	45	55	100
Mixed marriage	817	16	84	100
Total denomination				
Orthodox	461	62	38	100
Conservative	2,226	57	43	100
Reform	2,823	47	53	100
Just Jewish	687	26	74	100

TABLE 22. VISIT TO ISRAEL, BY MARRIAGE TYPE AND DENOMINATION

Denomination/ Marriage Type	Number of Cases	Did Visit (%)	Did Not Visit (%)	Total
Orthodox				
Inmarriage	43	61	39	100
Conservative				
Inmarriage	2,007	47	53	100
Conversionary marriage	123	55	45	100
Mixed marriage	129	16	84	100
Reform				
Inmarriage	2,208	42	58	100
Conversionary marriage	224	26	74	100
Mixed marriage	418	20	80	100
Just Jewish				
Inmarriage	373	41	59	100
Conversionary marriage	34	55	45	100
Mixed marriage	281	24	76	100
Total marriage type				
Inmarriage	5,022	47	54	101*
Conversionary marriage	381	39	61	100
Mixed marriage	828	21	79	100
Total denomination				
Orthodox	468	58	42	100
Conservative	2,259	45	55	100
Reform	2,850	36	64	100
Just Jewish	688	34	66	100

*Rounding error.

TABLE 23. CONTRIBUTION TO CHARITIES, BY MARRIAGE TYPE AND DENOMINATION

Denomination/ Marriage Type	Number of Cases	Jewish Causes		Number of Cases	Non-Jewish Causes	
		Do Give (%)	Do Not Give (%)		Do Give (%)	Do Not Give (%)
Orthodox						
Inmarriage	415	88	12	412	66	34
Conservative						
Inmarriage	1,942	88	12	1,911	72	28
Conversionary marriage	117	86	14	119	72	28
Mixed marriage	128	64	36	126	79	21
Reform						
Inmarriage	2,143	88	12	2,122	76	24
Conversionary marriage	221	81	19	219	80	20
Mixed marriage	415	67	33	407	70	30
Just Jewish						
Inmarriage	370	75	25	366	69	31
Conversionary marriage	33	65	35	33	65	35
Mixed marriage	277	55	45	276	72	28
Total marriage type						
Inmarriage	4,870	86	13	4,939	72	28
Conversionary marriage	371	81	19	395	77	23
Mixed marriage	820	57	43	1,001	72	28
Total denomination						
Orthodox	448	87	13	445	66	34
Conservative	2,187	86	14	2,156	72	28
Reform	2,779	83	17	2,748	75	25
Just Jewish	680	65	35	675	70	30

TABLE 24. RELIGION OF 3 CLOSEST FRIENDS, BY MARRIAGE TYPE AND DENOMINATION

Denomination/ Marriage Type	Number of Cases	0–1 Jewish (%)	2–3 Jewish (%)	Total (%)
Orthodox				
Inmarriage	342	8	92	100
Conservative				
Inmarriage	1,502	22	78	100
Conversionary marriage	110	59	41	100
Mixed marriage	99	51	49	100
Reform				
Inmarriage	1,699	23	77	100
Conversionary marriage	189	46	54	100
Mixed marriage	330	62	38	100
Just Jewish				
Inmarriage	274	49	51	100
Conversionary marriage	29	36	64	100
Mixed marriage	231	79	21	100
Total marriage type				
Inmarriage	3,817	25	75	100
Conversionary marriage	328	50	50	100
Mixed marriage	660	69	31	100
Total denomination				
Orthodox	372	13	88	101*
Conservative	1,711	26	74	100
Reform	2,218	34	66	100
Just Jewish	534	63	37	100

*Rounding error.

TABLE 25. RELIGION OF 3 CLOSEST FRIENDS, BY MARRIAGE TYPE, DENOMINATION, AND AGE

Denomination/ Marriage Type	Under 45 Years of Age				Over 45 Years of Age			
	Number of Cases	0-1 Jewish (%)	2-3 Jewish (%)	Total (%)	Number of Cases	0-1 Jewish (%)	2-3 Jewish (%)	Total (%)
Orthodox								
Inmarriage	131	4	96	100	201	12	88	100
Conservative								
Inmarriage	654	26	74	100	800	15	85	100
Conversionary marriage	78	66	34	100	21	16	84	100
Mixed marriage	70	57	43	100	25	35	65	100
Reform								
Inmarriage	716	27	73	100	937	19	81	100
Conversionary marriage	124	46	54	100	52	37	63	100
Mixed marriage	238	64	36	100	66	51	49	100
Just Jewish								
Inmarriage	104	55	45	100	159	41	59	100
Conversionary marriage	**				**			
Mixed marriage	148	86	14	100	72	60	40	100

TABLE 25.—(Continued)

Denomination/ Marriage Type	Under 45 Years of Age				Over 45 Years of Age			
	Number of Cases	0–1 Jewish (%)	2–3 Jewish (%)	Total (%)	Number of Cases	0–1 Jewish (%)	2–3 Jewish (%)	Total (%)
Total marriage type								
Inmarriage	1,605	29	71	100	2,097	19	81	100
Conversionary marriage	220	51	49	100	82	40	60	100
Mixed marriage	456	71	29	100	163	60	40	100
Total denomination								
Orthodox	148	10	90	100	213	15	85	100
Conservative	802	33	67	100	846	16	84	100
Reform	1,078	40	60	100	1,055	22	78	100
Just Jewish	270	72	28	100	240	48	52	100

**Cells too small for analysis.

TABLE 26. JEWISH EDUCATION OF CHILDREN AGES 10–13, BY MARRIAGE TYPE AND DENOMINATION

Denomination/ Marriage Type	Receiving Jewish Education	
	Yes (%)	No (%)
Orthodox		
Inmarriage	100	
Conservative		
Inmarriage	100	
Conversionary marriage	100	
Mixed marriage	81	19
Reform		
Inmarriage	95	5
Conversionary marriage	93	7
Mixed marriage	81	19
Just Jewish		
Inmarriage	100	
Conversionary marriage**		
Mixed marriage		100
Total marriage type		
Inmarriage	95	5
Conversionary marriage	84	16
Mixed marriage	41	59
Number of cases	1,037	105

**Cells too small for analysis.

TABLE 27. CONVERSIONARY AND MIXED-MARRIAGE TYPOLOGY

Marriage Type	Number of Cases	Jewish Identification Index Low (%)	Medium (%)	High (%)	Total (%)
Inmarriage	3,378	18	50	32	100
Conversionary marriage	343	(LC)	(MC)	(HC)	
		17	50	33	100
Mixed marriage	678	(LM)	(MM)	(HM)	
		69	30	1	100
Total	4,399	30	45	25	100

Key: LC Low-Jewish-Identification Conversionary Marriages
MC Medium-Jewish-Identification Conversionary Marriages
HC High-Jewish-Identification Conversionary Marriages
LM Low-Jewish-Identification Mixed Marriages
MM Medium-Jewish-Identification Mixed Marriages
HM High-Jewish-Identification Mixed Marriages

TABLE 28. CONVERSIONARY AND MIXED-MARRIAGE TYPOLOGY, BY
DENOMINATION

Marriage Type	Number of Cases	Jewish Identification Index			Total (%)
		Low (%)	Medium (%)	High (%)	
Orthodox					
Inmarriage	194	8	26	66	100
Conservative					
Inmarriage	1,232	8	49	43	100
Conversionary marriage	110	(LC)	(MC)	(HC)	
		3	49	48	100
Mixed marriage	76	(LM)	(MM)	(HM)	
		42	53	5	100
Reform					
Inmarriage	1,609	16	59	25	100
Conversionary marriage	187	(LC)	(MC)	(HC)	
		23	50	27	100
Mixed marriage	286	(LM)	(MM)	(HM)	
		57	41	2	100
Just Jewish					
Inmarriage	226	62	30	8	100
Conversionary marriage	**				
Mixed marriage	167	(LM)	(MM)	(HM)	
		87	13	0	100

Key: See table 27.
**Cells too small for analysis.

TABLE 29. HAVING CHRISTMAS TREE, BY MARRIAGE TYPE AND
DENOMINATION

Denomination/ Marriage Type	Number of Cases	Do Have Tree (%)	Do Not Have Tree (%)	Total (%)
Orthodox				
Inmarriage	396	1	99	100
Conservative				
Inmarriage	1,834	1	99	100
Conversionary marriage	117	8	92	100
Mixed marriage	111	41	59	100
Reform				
Inmarriage	1,985	3	97	100
Conversionary marriage	210	33	67	100
Mixed marriage	367	63	37	100
Just Jewish				
Inmarriage	361	5	95	100
Conversionary marriage	32	10**	90	100
Mixed marriage	263	66	34	100
Total marriage type				
Inmarriage	4,576	2	98	100
Conversionary marriage	359	22	78	100
Mixed marriage	741	62	38	100
Total denomination				
Orthodox	426	3	97	100
Conservative	2,062	4	96	100
Reform	2,562	18	82	100
Just Jewish	656	33	67	100

**Cell size too small for analysis.

TABLE 30. HAVING CHRISTMAS TREE, BY MARRIAGE TYPE, DENOMINATION, AND PRESENCE OF CHILDREN

Denomination/ Marriage Type	No Children			Children Present		
	Number of Cases	Do Have Tree (%)	Do Not Have Tree (%)	Number of Cases	Do Have Tree (%)	Do Not Have Tree (%)
Orthodox						
Inmarriage	168	1	99	210	—	100
Conservative						
Inmarriage	700	1	99	1,018	1	99
Conversionary marriage	27	8	92	88	8	92
Mixed marriage	39	22	78	71	52	48
Reform						
Inmarriage	853	4	96	1,036	2	98
Conversionary marriage	61	26	74	141	39	61
Mixed marriage	144	55	45	217	69	31
Just Jewish						
Inmarriage	193	6	94	150	5	95
Conversionary marriage	**			**		
Mixed marriage	108	47	53	145	81	19

**Cells too small for analysis.

TABLE 31. EXPANDED CONVERSIONARY AND MIXED-MARRIAGE TYPOLOGY, BY HAVING CHRISTMAS TREE

| Marriage Type | Number of Cases | Jewish Identification Index | | | | | | Total (%) |
| | | Low | | Medium | | High | | |
		Do Have Tree (%)	Do Not Have Tree (%)	Do Have Tree (%)	Do Not Have Tree (%)	Do Have Tree (%)	Do Not Have Tree (%)	
Conversionary marriage	343	(DLC) 4	(SLC) 13	(DMC) 14	(SMC) 36	(DHC) 2	(SHC) 31	100
Mixed marriage	678	(DLM) 45	(SLM) 24	(DMM) 17	(SMM) 13	(DHM)	(SHM) 1	100

Key: SLC Single Low-Jewish-Identification Conversionary-Marriage Households
SMC Single Medium-Jewish-Identification Conversionary-Marriage Households
SHC Single High-Jewish-Identification Conversionary-Marriage Households
SLM Single Low-Jewish-Identification Mixed-Marriage Households
SMM Single Medium-Jewish-Identification Mixed-Marriage Households
SHM Single High-Jewish-Identification Mixed-Marriage Households
DLC Dual Low-Jewish-Identification Conversionary-Marriage Households
DMC Dual Medium-Jewish-Identification Conversionary-Marriage Households
DHC Dual High-Jewish-Identification Conversionary-Marriage Households
DLM Dual Low-Jewish-Identification Mixed-Marriage Households
DMM Dual Medium-Jewish-Identification Mixed-Marriage Households
DHM Dual High-Jewish-Identification Mixed-Marriage Households

TABLE 32. EXPANDED CONVERSIONARY AND MIXED-MARRIAGE TYPOLOGY, BY HAVING CHRISTMAS TREE AND DENOMINATION

Denomination/ Marriage Type	Number of Cases	Jewish Identification Index						Total (%)
		Low		Medium		High		
		Do Have Tree (%)	Do Not Have Tree (%)	Do Have Tree (%)	Do Not Have Tree (%)	Do Have Tree (%)	Do Not Have Tree (%)	
Orthodox								
Inmarriage	190	0	8	0	26	0	66	100
Conservative								
Inmarriage	1,232	0	8	1	48	0	43	100
Conversionary marriage	110	(DLC) 0	(LC) 3	(DMC) 7	(MC) 42	(DHC) 0	(HC) 48	100
Mixed marriage	77	(DLM) 18	(LM) 24	(DMM) 14	(MM) 39	0	(HM) 5	100
Reform								
Inmarriage	1,609	1	15	2	57	0	25	100
Conversionary marriage	187	(DLC) 7	(LC) 16	(DMC) 19	(MC) 31	(DHC) 4	(HC) 23	100
Mixed marriage	286	(DLM) 35	(LM) 22	(DMM) 29	(MM) 12	0	(HM) 2	100
Just Jewish								
Inmarriage	226	4	58	1	29	0	8	100
Conversionary marriage	**							
Mixed marriage	167	(DLM) 63	(LM) 24	(DMM) 6	(MM) 7	0	(HM) 0	100

Key: See table 31.
**Cells too small for analysis.

TABLE 33.   DENOMINATIONAL IDENTIFICATION OF MIXED-MARRIEDS, BY AGE

Mixed-Marrieds/Age	Number of Cases	Conservative (%)	Reform (%)	Just Jewish (%)	Total (%)
Under age 45	307	9	60	31	100
Over age 45	109	11	40	49	100

TABLE 34. EXPANDED CONVERSIONARY AND MIXED-MARRIAGE TYPOLOGY, BY HAVING CHRISTMAS TREE, DENOMINATION, AND AGE

| Denomination/ Marriage Type | Number of Cases | Jewish Identification Index | | | | | | Total (%) |
| | | Low | | Medium | | High | | |
		Do Have Tree (%)	Do Not Have Tree (%)	Do Have Tree (%)	Do Not Have Tree (%)	Do Have Tree (%)	Do Not Have Tree (%)	
Under Age 45								
Conservative								
Conversionary marriage	58	(DLC) 0	(SLC) 4	(DMC) 10	(SMC) 41	(DHC) 0	(SHC) 45	100
Mixed marriage	43	(DLM) 16	(SLM) 24	(DMM) 16	(SMM) 37	(DHM) 1	(SHM) 6	100
Reform								
Conversionary marriage	98	(DLC) 5	(SLC) 22	(DMC) 25	(SMC) 21	(DHC) 4	(SHC) 23	100
Mixed marriage	170	(DLM) 39	(SLM) 17	(DMM) 34	(SMM) 9	(DHM) 0	(SHM) 1	101*
Just Jewish								
Conversionary marriage	**							
Mixed marriage	94	(DLM) 64	(SLM) 23	(DMM) 4	(SMM) 9	(DHM) 0	(SHM) 0	100
Total marriage type								
Inmarriage	1,199	1	14	2	52	0	31	100
Conversionary marriage	181	(DLC) 3	(SLC) 14	(DMC) 18	(SMC) 32	(DHC) 3	(SHC) 31	101*
Mixed marriage	375	(DLM) 48	(SLM) 21	(DMM) 19	(SMM) 11	(DHM) 0	(SHM) 1	100

TABLE 34—(Continued)

Denomination/ Marriage Type	Number of Cases	Jewish Identification Index						Total (%)
		Low		Medium		High		
		Do Have Tree (%)	Do Not Have Tree (%)	Do Have Tree (%)	Do Not Have Tree (%)	Do Have Tree (%)	Do Not Have Tree (%)	

Over Age 45

Denomination/ Marriage Type	Number of Cases	Do Have Tree (%)	Do Not Have Tree (%)	Do Have Tree (%)	Do Not Have Tree (%)	Do Have Tree (%)	Do Not Have Tree (%)	Total (%)
Conservative								
Conversionary marriage	18	(DLC) 0	(SLC) 0	(DMC) 0	(SMC) 48	(DHC) 0	(SHC) 52	100
Mixed marriage	17	(DLM) 36	(SLM) 23	(DMM) 12	(SMM) 29	(DHM) 0	(SHM) 0	100
Reform								
Conversionary marriage	39	(DLC) 23	(SLC) 11	(DMC) 8	(SMC) 35	(DHC) 1	(SHC) 22	100
Mixed marriage	47	(DLM) 35	(SLM) 28	(DMM) 18	(SMM) 16	(DHM) 1	(SHM) 2	100
Just Jewish								
Conversionary marriage	**							
Mixed marriage	45	(DLM) 68	(SLM) 19	(DMM) 8	(SMM) 5	(DHM) 0	(SHM) 0	100
Total marriage type								
Inmarriage	1,534	2	19	1	47	0	31	100
Conversionary marriage	69	(DLC) 14	(SLC) 19	(DMC) 5	(SMC) 35	(DHC) 1	(SHC) 26	100
Mixed marriage	144	(DLM) 53	(SLM) 25	(DMM) 10	(SMM) 12	(DHM) 0	(SHM) 0	100

*Rounding error.
**Cells too small for analysis.
Key: See table 31.

TABLE 35.   HOUSEHOLD IDENTITY OUTCOMES, BY AGE

Household Identity	Under Age 45 (%)	Over Age 45 (%)
Inmarried	61	85
Single-identity intermarried	16	7
Dual-identity intermarried	23	8
Number of cases	1,755	1,747

Profile of American Jewry: Insights from the 1990 National Jewish Population Survey

by SIDNEY GOLDSTEIN

IN THE INTRODUCTION TO *The Jews in America*, Chaim Potok points up the key challenge facing the American Jewish community in the 1990s.[1] In contrast to the situation in Europe, he emphasizes, Jews have become part of the very fabric of American life. This has created both enormous opportunities and significant risks, including the potential for the disintegration of core Jewish values and the splintering of the Jewish community into a multiplicity of factions. The issue that remains open, Potok argues, is whether Jews in the United States will succeed in fashioning an authentic American-Jewish civilization, one rich in new forms of individual and communal expression, or whether they will become fully absorbed into the larger culture and disappear as a distinct group.

Epitomizing Potok's concern in the extreme is the "silent Holocaust" described by Leslie Fiedler:[2] "Not a single one of my own eight children has, at the present moment, a Jewish mate; nor for that matter do I. . . . In any case, there is no one to say kaddish for me when I die. I am, in short, not just as I have long known, a minimal Jew—my Judaism nearly non-existent —but, as I have only recently become aware, a terminal one as well, the last of a four-thousand-year line. Yet, whatever regrets I may feel, I cannot deny that I have wanted this, worked for it."

Neither the concerns embodied in Potok's assessment nor the outcome implied in Fiedler's family account are new; they have been expressed and debated for years by leading observers of the Jewish scene.[3] Some have held that American Jewry is progressively weakening demographically as a result of low fertility, high intermarriage, significant dispersion, and assimilatory losses.[4] Others argue that the demographic issues are of marginal

---

[1]Chaim Potok, "Introduction," in *The Jews in America*, ed. David Cohen (San Francisco, 1989), pp. 10–11.

[2]Leslie Fiedler, *Fiedler on the Roof* (Boston, 1991), as quoted in the *New York Times Book Review*, Aug. 4, 1991, p. 3.

[3]Edward Norden, "Counting the Jews," *Commentary*, Oct. 1991, pp. 36–43; Gideon Shimoni, "How Central Is Israel?" *Moment*, Oct. 1991, pp. 24–27.

[4]See, e.g., U.O. Schmelz and Sergio DellaPergola, *Basic Trends in American Jewish Demography*, Jewish Demography Papers (New York, American Jewish Committee, 1988).

importance and that what counts is the quality of Jewish life.[5] In the latter view, concerns about population size, growth, fertility, and migration represent misplaced emphases; concerns should focus on Judaism, Jewish culture, Jewish education, the perpetuation of Jewish communal institutions, and the linkages between the American Jewish community and Israel. Regrettably, the evidence needed to assess the validity of the different perspectives remains limited. To the extent that quality and quantity are inexorably linked in a complex fashion, it is generally recognized that we must be concerned about both, and about the connections between them. The need to do so is made all the more important by the impressive success of American Jews in their struggle over the last century for acceptance into the larger American society. Jews have reached new heights in educational achievement and occupational choice, as well as greater freedom in selection of place of residence, memberships, friends, and spouses. Together, these changes help explain associated demographic features such as later age at marriage, low fertility, more intermarriage and divorce, and high mobility. The major question is the extent to which these changes have contributed to the weakening of American Jewry, especially in terms of the ties of individual Jews to the Jewish community.

The issues are intensified because the American Jewish community has evolved from a collection of largely self-contained local communities into a national Jewish community, judged demographically by the increasing proportion of the population that is third, fourth, and higher generation American, by the extensive dispersal of the population across the United States, and by the movement of population among communities.[6] Some of the unique features of local Jewish communities—features grounded in their historic development, particular sociodemographic composition, and institutional structure—may continue and, in some cases, may even be exacerbated. But overlying such differences, ongoing trends have led individuals, both movers and stayers, to become part of familial, social, and economic networks that span the nation, reinforcing the national character of the community.

THE SEARCH FOR DATA

Recognition of the importance of a national perspective and the multiplicity of interactions between the national and the local communities has reinforced the need for demographic, social, and economic information at

---

[5]Cf. Calvin Goldscheider, *Jewish Continuity and Change* (Bloomington, Ind., 1986).
[6]*The Emergence of a Continental Jewish Community: Implications for the Federations*, Sidney Hollander Memorial Colloquium (New York, Council of Jewish Federations, 1987).

both levels. Because separation of church and state precludes a question on religion in the U.S. Census, there is no core of information about those who identify themselves as Jewish by religion. It has thus been necessary to look for alternate sources of data needed for assessment and planning purposes.[7]

A variety of alternate sources have been tapped or developed, but most have had limitations for an analysis of American Jewry. Omnibus sample surveys directed at the general population, such as the Gallup Poll, seldom include more than a few hundred Jews and often considerably fewer, so that the number of Jews is inadequate for in-depth assessment.[8] Aggregating the results of several years of such surveys helps to overcome the small-numbers problem but raises new concerns about comparability of information from year to year and about possible changes in attitudes and behavior over the interval encompassed by the surveys.

Use of census data on country of birth, and in recent censuses on ancestry, on the assumption that those born in Russia are largely Jewish, runs the risk of error due to lack of exact comparability between birthplace or ancestry and Jewish identity.[9] Information on Jews identified by the census as Yiddish speakers at home or while growing up is also subject to serious bias because of sharp age differentials in the use of Yiddish.[10] Moreover, the value of this and other approaches based on ancestry will decrease as the country origins of American Jews change and as they become further removed from their immigrant ancestors.

The same concern applies to use of distinctive Jewish names (DJNs) as a way of identifying and estimating Jews in the population.[11] This approach also loses its usefulness as the rate of intermarriage rises, especially as more Jewish women intermarry and take the "non-Jewish" names of their husbands (even if their husbands convert to Judaism).

---

[7]Barry A. Kosmin, Paul Ritterband, and Jeffrey Scheckner, *Jewish Population in the United States 1987: Counting Jewish Populations: Methods and Problems*, Reprint No. 3 (New York, North American Jewish Data Bank and CUNY Graduate Center, 1988); Sidney Goldstein, "A National Jewish Population Study: Why and How," in *A Handle on the Future—The Potential of the 1990 National Survey for American Jewry*, Reprint No. 4 (New York, North American Jewish Data Bank and CUNY Graduate Center, 1988), pp. 1–9; Steven M. Cohen, Jonathan S. Woocher, and Bruce A. Phillips, eds., *Perspectives in Jewish Population Research* (Boulder, Colo., 1984).

[8]Alan M. Fisher, "The National Gallup Polls and American Jewish Demography," AJYB 1983, vol. 83, pp. 111–26.

[9]Stanley Lieberson and Mary C. Waters, *From Many Strands: Ethnic and Racial Groups in Contemporary America* (New York, Russell Sage Foundation, 1988).

[10]Sidney Goldstein, "A Further Assessment of the Use of Yiddish in Rhode Island Households," *Rhode Island Jewish Historical Notes* 9, Nov. 1985, pp. 209–19.

[11]Barry A. Kosmin and Stanley Waterman, "The Use and Misuse of Distinctive Jewish Names in Research on Jewish Populations," in *Papers in Jewish Demography, 1985*, ed. U.O. Schmelz and S. DellaPergola (Jerusalem, Institute of Contemporary Jewry, Hebrew University, 1989), pp. 1–10.

Local Jewish communities have increasingly recognized that effective planning must be based on comprehensive, accurate assessments of the population.[12] A large number of communities have therefore undertaken their own surveys. While these have added greatly to our knowledge, that knowledge remains incomplete. The surveys have varied considerably in scope and quality: They have relied on different questionnaires, varying sampling designs and coverage of the Jewish population, and diverse tabulation plans. The absence of standardized methods and definitions (including who was to be counted as a Jew) made it difficult and sometimes impossible to compare findings across communities, either to obtain a better understanding of a particular community or to obtain insights into the national Jewish community.

Recognizing the problems of coverage and variation in quality among local studies and the need for a national profile, the Council of Jewish Federations (CJF) in 1970/71 undertook the National Jewish Population Study (NJPS-1970/71). The national sampling design relied on a combination of local Jewish federation lists of Jewish households and standard area probability methods to ensure representation of Jewish households not included on lists.[13] Housing units of the combined list and area samples were screened for Jewish occupants. Three criteria were employed to identify Jews: whether any of the occupants had been born Jewish, had a parent who had been born Jewish, or regarded themselves as being Jewish.[14]

In all, a national sample of 7,179 units, each of which had at least one member meeting one of the three criteria, was identified. The resulting weighted estimate of the national Jewish population was 5.4 million Jews. After adjusting for housing units whose religion could not be ascertained and for biases resulting from area-sample cutoffs, Bernard Lazerwitz estimated the total population to range between 5.6 and 6.0 million.[15] Of the persons identified as Jewish by one of the three criteria, 97.3 percent were born Jewish and were still Jewish at the time of the survey; 1.2 percent were born Jewish but no longer considered themselves Jewish; and 1.5 percent were not born Jewish but were reported as Jewish at the time of the survey.[16] In addition, 6.4 percent of all the members of the sampled households

[12]Lester I. Levin, "Federation and Population Studies," in *Perspectives in Jewish Population Research*, ed. Steven M. Cohen, Jonathan Woocher, and Bruce A. Phillips (Boulder, Colo., 1984), pp. 57–64.

[13]Fred Massarik and Alvin Chenkin, "United States National Jewish Population Study: A First Report," AJYB 1973, vol. 74, pp. 264–306.

[14]Bernard Lazerwitz, "An Estimate of a Rare Population Group: The U.S. Jewish Population," *Demography* 15, Aug. 1978, pp. 389–94.

[15]Ibid.

[16]Fred Massarik, "The Boundary of Jewishness: Some Measures of Jewish Identity in the United States," in *Papers in Jewish Demography, 1973*, ed. U.O. Schmelz, P. Glickson, and S. DellaPergola (Jerusalem, Institute of Contemporary Jewry, Hebrew University, 1977), pp. 117–39.

consisted of persons neither born Jewish nor currently Jewish. These were largely the non-Jewish spouses of Jewish household members or the children of mixed marriages who were not being raised as Jews. As Fred Massarik concluded, "Interpretations of the Jewish population must therefore give careful attention to the number of persons living in Jewish households and the number of members who specifically meet clear criteria of Jewishness. Failure to do so can lead to quite discrepant estimates of the total Jewish population."[17] This caveat has even greater importance in the 1990s.

NJPS-1970/71 was a milestone in the development of American Jewish demography. Unfortunately, exploitation of its rich data was limited, so that the full value of the survey for understanding the Jewish population was not realized. Nonetheless, the experience both in implementing that survey and trying to utilize the results served the Jewish community well.

In the 1970s, because the national survey was seen as obviating the need for new local surveys, few such surveys were initiated. Since 1980, however, about 50 Jewish communities, including most larger ones, have undertaken surveys. Over the last several decades, some have already done so twice, and a few, like Boston, have done so three times. Still, questions remained about how well these local surveys represented the Jewish population as a whole and, in the case of some surveys, about the quality of coverage.

In the absence of another NJPS in the early 1980s, but with keen recognition of the need for national assessments of the Jewish population, individual groups and scholars have attempted to develop national samples. Studies undertaken for the American Jewish Committee, largely by Steven Cohen, have been in the forefront of such efforts. A number of these earlier surveys[18] employed samples based on distinctive Jewish names derived from lists of persons affiliated with a wide range of Jewish organizations or activities. Whether a sample based on such lists of affiliated or identified Jews was representative of the entire adult Jewish population and especially of those at or near the margins of the community remained questionable, as Steve Cohen himself recognized.[19]

In more recent surveys, a stronger effort has been made to achieve less biased coverage by relying on a different base for developing the sample. A consumer mail panel of 200,000 households developed by a marketing and survey research firm contained 4,700 households which had been identified as containing at least one member reported as currently Jewish. Based on

---

[17]Massarik, "Boundary of Jewishness," p. 119.

[18]Steven M. Cohen, "The 1981–82 National Survey of American Jews," AJYB 1983, vol. 83, pp. 89–110; Cohen, *Attitudes of American Jews Toward Israel and Israelis: The 1983 National Survey of American Jews and Jewish Communal Leaders* (New York, American Jewish Committee, 1983).

[19]Steven M. Cohen, *Ties and Tensions: The 1986 Survey of American Jewish Attitudes Toward Israel and Israelis* (New York, American Jewish Committee, 1987).

the total sample, a demographically balanced subsample (based on region, income, population density, age, and household size) was developed containing over 2,000 Jewish households. The data collected suggest that this sample "succeeded in reaching a slightly larger number of marginally Jewish respondents" than did the earlier samples based on distinctive Jewish names.[20] Still, doubts about the representativeness of such samples were raised both by the self-selective character of participants in the panel and the fact that the sample presumably reflected current religious identification—therefore missing individuals who did not report themselves as currently Jewish by religion.

THE NATIONAL JEWISH POPULATION SURVEY OF 1990[21]

Planning for NJPS-1990

This situation presented a major challenge to any effort to undertake a national assessment of the Jewish population. In preparing for a possible new CJF national survey, advantage was taken of the many improvements introduced in sampling and survey procedures since NJPS-1970/71, the experience gained from the large number of local Jewish community surveys completed since then, and the various limited efforts to collect national data. Moreover, the new survey benefited from the much stronger professional credentials of the recent planning and research staffs of local federations, the CJF, and other national agencies, as well as the availability and commitment of a substantial number of Jewish scholars interested and often experienced in surveying and assessing both the general and the Jewish populations. Thus, there was a greater appreciation of the need for data of high scientific quality and a far greater potential for employing the most sophisticated methods to obtain such data and for using them effectively for analytic and planning purposes.

In order to correct problems of comparability among local surveys and to design better sampling methods and a core questionnaire that could be used both locally and eventually in a national survey, in 1984 CJF created the National Technical Advisory Committee on Population Studies (NTAC). In 1986, through the cooperative efforts of CJF and the Graduate

---

[20]Ibid. See also Steven M. Cohen, *Content or Continuity? Alternative Bases for Commitment* (New York, American Jewish Committee, 1991).

[21]This section draws heavily on the paper prepared for the Sidney Hollander Colloquium on the 1990 National Jewish Population Survey, cosponsored by the Wilstein Institute of the University of Judaism and the Council of Jewish Federations, July 1991.

School and University Center of the City University of New York, the Mandell L. Berman North American Jewish Data Bank (NAJDB) was founded; its goal, to enhance comparability of the data collected locally and nationally and to facilitate analysis of the various data sets. Operating through the concerted efforts of NTAC and NAJDB, planning for a 1990 National Jewish Population Survey was initiated in the late 1980s. The decision to undertake the survey coincided with worldwide interest in launching a "world census" of Jewry parallel to the 1990 round of censuses being undertaken by national governments. The October 1987 World Conference on Jewish Population, held in Jerusalem, with over 20 countries represented, recommended a stocktaking of world Jewry as the basis for obtaining information for future study and action in the Jewish population field.

The Field Survey

In late 1988, CJF's endowment committee and its board of directors approved undertaking a 1990 national Jewish population study in the United States. Organization of the sample survey was the responsibility of NTAC. In close consultation with federation planners, it designed the core questionnaire. With assistance from a number of national sampling experts, several of whom serve on NTAC, and following consultation with a number of survey companies, it developed a sample design that was intended to ensure the widest possible coverage of the Jewish population, encompassing all types of Jews, ranging from those strongly identifying themselves as Jewish, at one extreme, to those on the margins of the community or even outside it, at the other; it sought to include born Jews who no longer considered themselves Jewish and the non-Jewish spouses/partners and children of Jewish household members, as well as other non-Jewish members of the household.

Following receipt and review of proposals from a number of survey firms, CJF commissioned the ICR Survey Research Group of Media, Pa., to collect data in a three-stage national telephone survey. Since the universe of Jewish households was not known, Stage I involved contacting a random sample of 125,813 American households using computer-assisted telephone interviewing. The sampled households represented all religious groups in continental United States, as well as secular households; the Jewish households were identified among them.

This initial screening was carried on as part of the twice-weekly nationally representative omnibus market-research surveys conducted by ICR. One thousand households were contacted in each of 125 successive rounds over the course of the period April 1989 to May 1990. Each household was selected using a random-digit-dialing (RDD) methodology; within each cooperating household, to ensure random selection, the adult chosen as respondent was the one with the most recent birthday. The overall procedure allowed for an equal probability of Jews to be selected from every state (except Alaska and Hawaii) and from locations of all sizes, so that a national profile could be obtained. Representation of Alaska and Hawaii was incorporated into the national sample in the third stage of the survey.

In addition to traditional census-type questions on sociodemographic, economic, and household characteristics, the screening survey asked "What is your religion?" Only 2.2 percent of the respondents refused to reply to this question. One by-product of this phase of the study, which was conducted in tandem with CUNY Graduate Center, was a unique profile of religious identification and of denominations in the United States. In fact, the responses provide the largest contemporary data set on American religious adherence. The results of this first stage—the National Survey of Religious Identification— were publicly announced in April 1991 and received wide dissemination in the press.[22]

To ensure the comprehensive coverage desired in NJPS for current and former Jews, additional questions were included in the Stage I screening phase for those who did not respond "Jewish" to the question on current religion. Whereas in the initial screening question respondents only had to answer for themselves, follow-up questions required that respondents provide information both on themselves and on other members of the household. Three follow-up sets of screening questions were successively directed to all respondents who did not identify themselves as Jewish by religion: 1. "Do you or anyone else in the household consider him/herself Jewish?" 2. "Were you or anyone else in the household raised Jewish?" 3. "Do or did you or anyone else in the household have a Jewish parent?" A positive answer to any of these questions qualified the household for initial classification as "Jewish."

This procedure, using multiple points of qualification, more than doubled the unweighted sample of identified "Jewish households." It now added households in which respondents reported themselves as Jewish by criteria other than religion as well as households of mixed composition, which included respondents who had either indicated they had some other religious identification on the religious screening question or had even initially refused to answer. The four screening questions identified 5,146 households containing one or more "qualified" Jews.

Over the course of a year, a panel was thus created to be used in the summer of 1990 as the basis for an intensive assessment of the sociodemo-

[22]Ari L. Goldman, "Portrait of Religion in U.S. Holds Dozens of Surprises," *New York Times*, Apr. 10, 1991.

graphic, economic, and identificational characteristics of the American Jewish population. To requalify potential respondents and to minimize loss to follow-up between the initial screening and the in-depth survey, 2,240 members of the 5,146 Jewish sample identified in the early months of the screening survey were recontacted in Stage II, the inventory stage. This took place in the months before the final interview stage. During this procedure, a number of potential respondents dropped out of the survey sample due to changes in household composition or disqualification upon further review.

Stage III, the in-depth survey, was conducted during ten weeks in May to July 1990. During this stage, the entire sample of 5,146 "Jewish" households was requalified. In order to meet the original goal of obtaining about 2,500 completed interviews, 2,441 households of those qualified were interviewed, using the extensive questionnaire prepared by NTAC for in-depth assessment of the sociodemographic and economic characteristics of the American Jewish population and of a wide array of attitudinal and behavioral variables related to Jewish identity. Completed interviews were obtained from 2,439 households, encompassing 6,507 individuals; these constitute the final sample for NJPS-1990.

Identifying the Jewish Population

The results of both the screening phase and the in-depth interviews attest to the validity and importance of the view that conceptual and measurement concerns should enter not only into the initial sample selection process but also into the analytical process. The complexity and fluidity of the contemporary American Jewish community are clearly demonstrated by the survey findings, beginning with the qualifying round.

Of the 5,146 households that qualified in Stage I as having at least one Jewish member under one of the four criteria specified earlier, just under half qualified on the basis of religion, just over one-third as containing an ethnic Jew (persons who consider themselves Jews), 5 percent on the basis of some member having been raised Jewish, and another 12 percent on the basis of at least one member reporting a Jewish parent.[23] The results of this self-ascription process demonstrate that any survey that restricts its identification of the Jewish population only to those reporting being Jewish by religion runs the risk of excluding a substantial part of the total population of Jewish religio-ethnic identity.

Moreover, among the 5,146 households that were initially screened as

---

[23]Sidney Goldstein and Barry A. Kosmin, "Religious and Ethnic Self-Identification in the United States 1989–1990: A Case Study of the Jewish Population," paper presented at the Population Association of America, Washington, D.C., March 1991.

being eligible for the in-depth survey, only 3,665 of the respondents themselves qualified as Jewish under one of the four criteria and only 57 percent of these on the basis of being Jewish by religion. The other 1,481 respondents qualified because members of the household other than the respondent met one of the criteria employed in the screening phase. This situation reflects the large number of households whose members were of mixed religious/ethnic identification or contained persons of Jewish descent who did not profess to be currently Jewish. That so many households were religiously and ethnically mixed is largely due to the sharp increase in mixed marriages in the last several decades.

One might question whether individuals should be counted as part of the Jewish population if they do not regard themselves as currently Jewish, even though born of one or two Jewish parents or raised as Jews, and particularly if they currently report identification with another religion. The answer to this depends, of course, on the religious and sociological perspectives adopted and the use for which the analysis is being undertaken. The great advantage of NJPS-1990 is that it provides the information on these persons and gives scholars and planners the option of including or excluding them, depending on the purpose of the analysis. Assessment of their behavioral characteristics with respect to Jewish practices should provide a more definitive answer as to how they should be classified sociologically and demographically as well as what factors may explain their current status with respect to Jewish identity. Unless it is known how many are in each category, including those on the margins and those who have left, the community cannot design realistic programs to maintain its strength, to retain those in it—especially those on the margins—and to attract back those who have opted out.[24]

Extension and Exploitation of NJPS-1990

Two other features of NJPS-1990 are relevant to this description of the organization of the study and the plans for exploiting the data. The first relates to the efforts NTAC undertook to develop a consortium of communities which would undertake surveys, at their own expense, approximately at the same time as NJPS-1990, and which would employ as much as possible the same basic sample design and core questionnaire. Such an

---

[24]This survey, like all sample surveys, is subject to sampling error arising from the fact that the results may differ from what would have been obtained if the whole population had been interviewed. Surveys are also subject to errors arising from nonresponse and respondents providing erroneous information; NJPS-1990 is no exception. Readers interested in sampling and nonsampling errors are referred to the Methodological Appendix in *Highlights of the CJF 1990 National Jewish Population Survey* (Kosmin et al., 1991, pp. 38–39) and to other documents on NJPS-1990 available through the North American Jewish Data Bank.

arrangement was motivated by recognition that, while the size of the national sample can adequately provide reliable insights into the characteristics of the national Jewish population and allow comparisons by region and community type, it is not large enough to permit in-depth assessment of individual communities, with the possible exception of New York. While the idea of a consortium was favorably received, financial and logistic considerations restricted the number of participating communities. That they include New York and Chicago and such smaller communities as Columbus, Seattle, and South Broward County, Florida, should greatly enhance the richness of the insights gained into American Jewry in 1990, both nationally and locally, and also the opportunities for evaluating methodological aspects of the various surveys.

The second major feature of NJPS-1990, and one which sharply distinguishes it from the NJPS-1970/71, is the extensive attention paid in the early stages of the study to the uses to which the data would be put analytically and for planning purposes. A subcommittee of NTAC developed an agenda for disseminating the findings. Beginning with a report at the 1990 CJF General Assembly, and through two major news releases in 1991, the findings were publicized in leading newspapers, on national TV, and on radio. A number of papers have already been presented at professional meetings; more are scheduled. The Sidney Hollander Colloquium in July 1991, cosponsored by the Wilstein Institute of the University of Judaism and the Council of Jewish Federations, focused on the initial findings of the survey and served to encourage utilization of the data by both planners and researchers. A second conference—"A Consultation on Conceptual and Policy Implications of the 1990 CJF National Population Survey"—was sponsored in October 1991 by the Hornstein Program in Jewish Communal Service at Brandeis University.[25] Through CJF Satellite, the findings have been reviewed with local federations. *Highlights of the CJF 1990 National Jewish Population Survey*[26] was published and is available to both professionals and the public.

Most significantly, a number of scholars and planners, many of them leaders in their fields, agreed to author individual monographs, with the State University of New York (SUNY) Press undertaking to publish the series, beginning perhaps in late 1992. The monograph topics encompass, among others, the elderly, marriage and the family, population redistribution and migration, women, socioeconomic status, fertility, Jewish identity,

---

[25]A key discussion at the consultation, initiated by Steven M. Cohen and Gabriel Berger, revolved about the allocation of the surveyed population into the Jewish identity subcategories and the impact of alternative categorizations on rates of intermarriage and assimilation.

[26]Barry A. Kosmin et al., *Highlights of the CJF 1990 National Jewish Population Survey* (New York, Council of Jewish Federations, 1991).

intermarriage, philanthropy, Jewish education, apostasy, and voluntarism. While these monographs are being prepared, the authors, as well as others who will have access to the data through a public-use tape, are being encouraged to prepare papers for conferences and articles for journals. Clearly, every effort has been made to ensure that the results of the survey will be widely exploited and disseminated, thereby enhancing their value for scholarly and planning purposes.

Over the past several decades, the *American Jewish Year Book* has occupied a key role in keeping the leadership and the public informed about the demographic situation of American Jewry. In addition to its regular inventory of the size and distribution of Jews among the various localities in the United States and overseas, it has published an impressive number of articles on various demographic features of world and especially American Jewry. Among these articles have been two overviews which attempted, within the limits of available data, to present profiles of the American-Jewish population in 1970 and in 1980.[27] Between the two reports, the results of NJPS-1970/71 had become available, adding to the insights that could be drawn from individual community studies. Now, with the initial findings of NJPS-1990 available, this decennial monitoring of American Jewry's profile and of the ways it has changed in the second half of the 20th century can be undertaken again.

In doing so, as before, the emphasis will be on the major areas of demographic concern—size, composition, distribution, and the processes of marriage (including intermarriage), fertility, and migration. As far as possible, comparisons will be made with the patterns that emerged from the analysis of NJPS-1970/71, in order to gain insights into the extent and direction of change. However, differences in coverage and in the definitions and classifications used in the two surveys sometimes preclude meaningful comparisons. Most important, the 1990 profile will take advantage of the much greater attention given by NJPS-1990 to providing coverage of the full range of American Jewry, including both persons born of one or two Jewish parents but not professing to be currently Jewish and persons not born and not currently Jewish but living with persons qualifying as Jewish under the criteria employed by the survey. By doing so, a more accurate and useful overview of American Jewry can be obtained, with deeper insights into where we have come from, where we are heading, and what implications the demographic situation has for the future of the community.

In undertaking this overview, it must be stressed that the wealth of data available in NJPS-1990 can only be tapped superficially here. Simple cross-

---

[27]Sidney Goldstein, "American Jewry, 1970: A Demographic Profile," AJYB 1971, vol. 72, pp. 3–88; Goldstein, "The Jews in the United States: Perspectives from Demography," AJYB 1981, vol. 81, pp. 3–59.

tabulations are used to profile the population, without controls for other variables affecting the relationships. Fuller analyses, using multivariate techniques, must await preparation of the individual articles and monographs and the in-depth treatment that they can give to particular aspects of the Jewish demographic situation.

THE COMPLEXITY OF JEWISH IDENTITY

The fluid character of the American Jewish community is at the heart of the findings of NJPS. How many Jews there are depends on who is counted as in and who is counted as out of the population. From a policy perspective, this raises questions about how the community can retain those still in the core, how it can bring back those at the margin and those who may have left, and how it can draw in those still in situations where they must choose between being or not being Jewish. Depending on how these questions are answered over the next several decades, the Jewish population has the potential of growing or declining.

On the basis of the weighted sample,[28] NJPS-1990 estimated that 3.2 million households in the United States contained one or more persons who were Jews or former Jews, using the four criteria specified earlier. These 3.2 million households contained 8.1 million persons. The total estimated population is raised to 8.2 million by another 70,000 Jews living in nursing homes and other long-term care institutions (mainly elderly persons), 10,000 living in prisons or homeless, and 20,000 immigrants estimated to have arrived after the survey was initiated.

Just over half (4.2 million) of the 8.1 million individuals in qualified households were born Jews who regarded themselves as Jewish by religion (table 1); this number includes the 100,000 institutionalized and unenumerated persons, for whom detailed data on type of Jewish identity were not obtained). Augmented by the estimated 185,000 who indicated they were Jews by choice, about 70 percent of whom reported having beeen converted, Jews by religion numbered 4.4 million in 1990 and constituted 54 percent of all members of qualified households and almost two-thirds of all persons

---

[28]After the survey information was collected and processed, each respondent was assigned a weight. When the weights are used in tabulations of the survey data, the results provide estimates of the U.S. population in each category shown in the tabulations. The weighting method ensures that key demographic characteristics of the adult population of the total weighted sample of 125,813 responding households in Stage I matched the most current estimates of these demographic characteristics produced by the Census Bureau. The weighting procedure adjusted for noncooperating households, for those who were not at home when the interviewer telephoned, and for households which did not have telephones or had multiple lines.

of Jewish descent and preference. An additional 1.1 million persons were classified as having been born Jewish but were secular Jews; they did not report their current religion as Jewish nor did they identify themselves with any other religious group. In combination with those claiming to be Jews by religion, these 5.5 million persons compose the "core Jewish population": all those professing to be currently Jewish by religion, ethnic or cultural identity, or birth and not reporting any other religious affiliation. This population is the one which most Jewish communal agencies recognize as their clientele.

Reflecting the broad net which the screening design for NJPS-1990 employed, an additional 1.3 million persons included in the survey are persons of Jewish descent who at the time of the survey reported a religion other than Jewish. They comprise 16 percent of all household members and 19 percent of all those of Jewish descent or religious preference.

Of these, 210,000 are persons who were born or raised Jewish but who currently follow another religion.[29] A majority are offspring of intermarriages, about half of whom were raised as Christians. Comparing this number with the enumeration of Jews by choice suggests a near balance in the exchange between Jewish and non-Jewish groups of those choosing to change religious identification.

Distinct from the converts out of Judaism are those 415,000 adults of Jewish descent who were raised from birth in a religion other than Judaism. They constitute 5 percent of the 8.2 million persons encompassed in the survey and 6 percent of those of Jewish descent or preference. Usually the children of intermarriages, they report an almost equal balance of Jewish fathers and mothers. (It needs to be stressed here that the classification of individuals was based on the information provided by the respondent, not on Jewish legal—halakhic—criteria.) Interestingly, a number of these persons consider themselves Jewish by ethnicity or background, and some follow selected Jewish religious practices. Since they profess another religion, however, they are not treated as core Jews in NJPS-1990.

Exceeding the number of adults of Jewish background but not currently identified as Jews are those 700,000 children under 18 years of age who have a "qualified Jew" as a parent (stepparent in a few cases), but who are being raised in a religion other than Judaism. They constitute almost 9 percent of the 8.2 million persons represented in the survey and 10 percent of all persons of Jewish descent and preference.

Among these children, about 40 percent have a parent who either is a Jew by religion or who is a secular Jew in an interfaith marriage; these children are usually being raised in the religion of the non-Jewish parent. The

---

[29]Some have undergone formal conversion, but others have simply switched to another religion. In the text and tables of this report, all such persons are referred to as converts out.

majority of the children in this category are children of converts out of Judaism or of a parent of Jewish descent who was raised from birth as a non-Jew. Their connection to Judaism is through one or more Jewish grandparent(s). Since they have been away from their Jewish roots for two generations, they have had little opportunity for exposure to Judaism. It remains to be determined in future years whether any of this group will come to identify positively as Jews by ethnicity or to convert to Judaism if required to do so to satisfy Jewish law.

In total, the combined population represented by the core population and those of Jewish descent, some of whom regard themselves as ethnic Jews even while professing another religion, numbers 6.8 million persons. That 19 percent of the total are outside the core population attests to the cumulative impact over one or more generations that intermarriage has had on the demographics of the Jewish population. Concurrently, it suggests the heterogeneous character of the population that now constitutes, by one or another criterion, the "Jewish" population of the United States. This heterogeneity is exacerbated further because 1.35 million adult Gentiles were living with those persons identified as "Jewish" by one of the foregoing criteria. These Gentiles were not and never had been identified as Jewish by religion or ethnic origin. Most are the spouses of a "Jewish" man or woman, but some may be persons who share the living quarters as partner or roommate.

The fact that Gentiles constitute 16 percent of the 8.2 million persons encompassed in the survey highlights further the very heterogeneous nature of the Jewish population, particularly if household composition is considered. It also suggests that, to the extent that the Gentile household members, and possibly even their relatives outside the household, are affected by their interaction with the Jewish members of the household, the potential "Jewish audience" in America is far greater than the 5.5 million core population or even the larger group represented by the core Jews and those of Jewish descent. Moreover, such heterogeneity points to the challenges that Jewish communal agencies and religious institutions face in the years ahead in delineating their client population. Who, for example, should be eligible for services rendered by a home for the aged, a community center, or a family service? Who, indeed, should be eligible for burial in a Jewish cemetery? What distinctions, if any, should be drawn between Jewish individuals and Jewish households, between core Jews and Jews by descent, between Jews by either of these criteria and non-Jews living with them? While all would agree that every effort needs to be made to retain those in the core and to strengthen their Jewish identity, what efforts, if any, should be made to attract back into the core those of Jewish descent who now profess another religion? And what missionary efforts should be exerted to make "Jewish households" more homogeneous by attempting to convert to

Judaism the Gentile spouses and partners of those already in the core? Reflecting the complexity that characterizes individual Jewish identity, the composition of "Jewish households" is also complex. Of the 3.2 million units represented in the survey, only 57 percent were composed entirely of members of the core Jewish population, that is, were entirely Jewish in their current composition. Just over one-quarter (27 percent) were mixed, consisting of at least one person belonging to the core population but including at least one other who was non-Jewish at the time of the survey. As many as 16 percent had no core Jewish household members, having qualified for inclusion in the survey only because one or more members of the household were of Jewish descent even though currently professing another religion. If the number of Jewish households is restricted to those containing at least one core Jew, the total count decreases to 2.7 million units, of which two-thirds are entirely Jewish and one-third are mixed.

NUMBERS, DISTRIBUTION, AND MOBILITY

Changing Numbers, 1970/71 to 1990

At no time in American history has there been a complete enumeration of the nation's Jewish population. Any statistics on the number of Jews in the United States must therefore remain an estimate. Given the complexity of identifying who is Jewish, the estimates vary considerably, depending on the inclusiveness or exclusiveness of the criteria used and the success achieved in identifying the various subsets of the population. As the results of NJPS-1990 indicate, depending on which criteria were used, the number of Jews in the United States varies from a low of 5.5 million to a high of 6.8 million, or even up to 8.2 million if we choose to include the Gentile members of "Jewish households." In fact, some analysts of the 1990 data may conclude that there are far fewer than 5.5 million Jews if they apply halakhic criteria. Such variation for any given year, and the use of different criteria in different years, makes any evaluation of changes over time difficult if not dangerous.

NJPS-1970/71 counted persons as Jewish if they had been born Jewish, had a parent who had been born Jewish, or regarded themselves as being Jewish. It estimated the national Jewish population to be 5.4 million, or 2.9 percent of the total American population. A later adjustment of this estimate by Bernard Lazerwitz took account of housing units whose religion could not be ascertained and of biases resulting from area-sample cutoffs in field sampling for economy reasons. The resulting estimates showed the total Jewish population to range between 5.6 and 6.0 million. However, since no adjustments were ever made for the socioeconomic subcategories of the 1970/71 population, and full evaluation of the 1990 data remains to be completed, it seems advisable to continue to use the 5.4-million original estimate yielded by NJPS-1970/71 in any comparisons undertaken here between the results of that survey and those of the 1990 survey.

Table 2 shows the comparative statistics on population and households for the 1970/71 and the 1990 surveys. It clearly indicates that the extent of change in the 20-year interval varies sharply depending on the criteria used to classify individuals as Jewish. If the broadest set of criteria is used, the Jewish population increased by 40.2 percent, from 5.85 to 8.20 milllion. This is a faster rate of growth than even the total American population, which increased by 22.4 percent in this same interval. However, much of the growth in the "Jewish" population (using the broadest definition) reflects the very large increase in the number of Gentiles living with Jews.

If the comparison is restricted to individuals who are either currently Jewish or of Jewish descent, the increase is much smaller, from 5.48 to 6.84 million or 24.8 percent. Here, too, the indicated growth may be misleading, since almost one in five of the 6.8 million are not currently Jewish. The impressive growth within this category is largely attributable, therefore, to the growing number of persons who are Jewish by descent but currently profess a different religious affiliation.

Restricting the comparison to those currently Jewish, that is, in the core population, the data point to only a slight increase in the Jewish population since 1970, from 5.42 to 5.51 million or 1.8 percent. This is a far slower rate of growth than that of the American population as a whole. Nonetheless, these statistics indicate that the sharp declines in the Jewish population that some scholars anticipated after the 1970/71 survey have not been realized; yet little more than stability has been achieved, probably due to immigration from overseas. However, if Lazerwitz's adjusted data for 1970/71 are more accurate than the lower 1970/71 estimate used here, compared to our 1990 data, the population did decline in the 20-year interval by about 4.6 percent (based on Lazerwitz's medium estimate of 5.78 million Jews).

Reflecting the high rates of intermarriage and the consequent vast increase in the number of households containing a Jew (two Jews marrying each other form one household, whereas two Jews who intermarry form two households), the number of households in 1990 (3.19 million) far exceeded the number identified in the 1970/71 survey (1.95 million). Again, it needs to be stressed that half a million of the households in the 1990 survey did not include any person who was a core Jew.

The net result of the changes in the size and Jewish identity subcategories of the "Jewish population" compared to changes in the size of the population of the nation as a whole is a variable percentage of Jews in the total.

If the broadest definition is used, including Gentiles, then the proportion has risen from 2.9 percent in 1970 to 3.3 percent in 1990, and for some purposes (e.g., political), this may be the relevant statistic. However, if the comparison is restricted to all persons of Jewish descent and preference, it remains unchanged at 2.7 percent. If, further, the comparison is limited to those identified as core Jews, it decreases from 2.7 percent in 1970 to only 2.2 percent 20 years later. The drop would be even sharper if Lazerwitz's adjusted 1970 statistics were used. Clearly, unless the currently non-Jewish members of "Jewish" households are included in the count, Jews have become a smaller percentage of the total population.

Nonetheless, according to estimates emanating from the National Survey of Religious Identification,[30] made on the basis of the first stage (screening phase) of the national survey, which obtained information on the religious composition of the total American population, Jews remain by far the third largest major religious group in the United States. Restricted to the adult population and to those professing a religion, that survey found 86.5 percent of the population to be Christian (including 26.5 percent Catholic and 55.7 percent Protestant; the balance reported "Christian") and 1.8 percent Jewish. The remainder of the adult population was distributed among a number of other groups (e.g., Muslims, Buddhists, Hindus) as well as among agnostics and those reporting no religion. No single religion of the other groups exceeded 0.5 percent of the total adult population. Thus, although constituting a small minority in comparison to the overwhelming Christian majority in America, Jews are clearly the predominant minority religious group in the country.

While total numbers are an important issue, the composition and distribution of the population probably are more relevant factors affecting the dynamics of change in Jewish life in the United States. Thus, we turn next to examination of a range of compositional variables, such as geographic distribution, age, education, and occupation, as well as such components of demographic change as migration, fertility, and intermarriage. The value of NJPS-1990 for such purposes is greatly enhanced by the opportunity to compare the characteristics and demographic behavior of Jews belonging to different identity subcategories of the core population and to compare the core Jews both with those of Jewish descent who in 1990 professed another religion and with the Gentile members of the surveyed households who were born and remain non-Jewish. Such comparisons should allow some insights into how these subcategories of the population differ from one another and suggest what implications observed differences have for the future of the community. Concurrently, they may provide some insights

---

[30]Goldman, "Portrait of Religion."

into the factors accounting for the location of individuals in particular identity categories.

For purposes of analysis, the core population will be subdivided into three groups: (a) those born Jewish and reported as Jewish by religion; (b) the secular-ethnic Jews—those born Jewish but not reporting themselves as Jewish by religion and not reporting any other religion; (c) Jews by choice—those converted to Judaism and those simply choosing to regard themselves as Jewish. Since the criteria for conversion vary among denominations, this analysis does not try to distinguish between the two subgroups. The currently non-Jewish population also consists of three sub-groups: (a) converts out of Judaism—adults who were born or raised Jewish but who were following another religion at the time of the survey; (b) persons who reported Jewish parentage or descent, but who were raised from birth in another religion (some of these and of the converts out consider themselves Jewish by ethnicity or background); (c) persons who were not and had never been identified as Jewish by religion or ethnic origin.

Regional Distribution

NJPS-1970/71 documented the high mobility levels of American Jews and their increasing dispersion across the United States.[31] Migration, which has played a key role throughout Jewish history, had by 1970 become the major dynamic responsible for the growth or decline of many local Jewish communities and for the changing distribution of the Jewish population among regions of the country and among metropolitan areas.

The high level of education of American Jews and the kinds of occupations which they have increasingly been able to enter, coupled with the growing freedom of choice which Jews have had about where they reside, often result in movement away from parental family and place of origin. This often also means movement out of centers of Jewish concentration.[32] Moreover, the shift away from self-employment to employment for others can result in more frequent movement, because repeated transfers are often associated with high white-collar positions. Such geographic mobility has the potential for weakening individual ties to a particular Jewish community by reducing the opportunites for integration locally and by increasing opportunities for greater interaction with non-Jews, especially as occupational identification and affiliation take on increased importance.

Migration may also have positive effects on the vitality of Jewish life by

---

[31]Sidney Goldstein, "Population Movement and Redistribution Among American Jews," *Jewish Journal of Sociology* 24, June 1982, pp. 5–23.

[32]Sidney Goldstein, "Jews on the Move: Implications for American Jewry and for Local Communities," *Jewish Journal of Sociology* 32, June 1990, pp. 5–30.

bringing additional population to smaller communities or to formerly declining ones, thereby providing the kind of "demographic transfusion" needed to help maintain or to develop basic institutions and facilities essential for a vital Jewish community. It may also do so by bridging the traditional age and affiliation cleavages, thereby providing the social cement needed to hold the community together.[33]

Concurrently, mobility may contribute to the development of a national Jewish society, characterized by greater population dispersion and by greater population exchange among various localities.[34] Both processes require more effective networking among locations in order to ensure continuing opportunities and stimuli for mobile individuals and families to maintain their Jewish identity and their links to the Jewish community, regardless of where they live or how often they move from place to place. Greater dispersion, especially to smaller communities and to more isolated ones, also requires development of methods to ensure that such communities are better able through their own facilities or through links to other, larger communities to service the various needs of both their migrant and nonmigrant populations.[35]

In 1900, two decades after the onset of the massive movement of East European Jews to the United States, 57 percent of American Jewry was concentrated in the Northeast region of the country, reflecting the attractiveness of the major ports of entry and their nearby areas to the new settlers. Only one in five Jews lived in the South or the West; the remaining one-quarter resided in the Midwest. The continued heavy influx of immigrants over the next few decades reinforced the concentration in the Northeast and especially in New York, New Jersey, and Pennsylvania. By 1930, 68 percent of all of America's Jews were living in the Northeast region; the proportions in each of the other three regions had declined, with only 12 percent reported in the South and West combined.

With the great reduction in immigration, internal movement became an increasingly important force in redistributing the Jewish population among regions of the country. Succeeding decades witnessed a continuous decline in the percentage living in the Northeast and particularly sharp rises in the proportion living in the West and to a lesser extent in the South. For 1971, the *American Jewish Year Book* reported 63 percent of the population in the Northeast and 25 percent in the Sunbelt states of the South and the West; the Midwest had declined to only 12 percent of the total.[36] NJPS-

---

[33]Barry D. Lebowitz, "Migration and the Structure of the Contemporary Jewish Community," *Contemporary Jewry* 2, Fall/Winter 1975, p. 8.

[34]Sidney Goldstein, "American Jews on the Move," *Moment*, Aug. 1991, pp. 24–29ff.

[35]Goldstein, "Jews on the Move."

[36]AJYB 1973. The grouping of states has been changed to ensure comparability with the census assignment of states among regions.

1970/71 found slightly more (64 percent) in the Northeast, and considerably more in the Midwest, about 17 percent, and fewer in the Sunbelt, 19 percent. The difference has never been satisfactorily resolved.[37]
The trend in redistribution documented for 1970–71 has continued (table 3). According to NJPS-1990,[38] considerably fewer Jews were living in the Northeast, only 43.6 percent. Together the South and the West accounted for 45.1 percent, almost equally divided between them. The Midwest continued to contain the smallest percentage of Jews, only 11.3 percent of the total. This overall distribution pattern shows a major realignment of the Jewish population and strengthens the assumption that Jews have participated, perhaps in accentuated form, in the movement out of the Northeast and the Midwest to the South and West that in recent decades has characterized the American population generally.[39] While Jews remain heavily concentrated in the Northeast, the changing regional distribution suggests that Jews feel increasingly accepted in America and are paralleling mainstream America in shifting to the Sunbelt regions of the country.[40] Whether all types of Jews are doing so equally can be assessed by the data on regional distribution by type of Jewish identity.

Differences in regional distribution by type of Jewish identity cannot be ascribed entirely or even mainly to the effects of selective migration. They may well stem from differences in the historical development of various Jewish communities, to variations in socioeconomic and denominational composition, to the size of the local Jewish communities, and to the norms regarding intermarriage and conversion.

The NJPS-1990 sample shows that, in a comparison of core Jews and non-Jews, more of the core Jews are concentrated in the Northeast, which includes the New York, New Jersey, and Pennsylvania areas of original heavy immigrant settlement. By contrast, relatively more of the non-Jews in "Jewish" households live in each of the other three regions. This finding suggests either that regions outside the Northeast attract a disproportional number of the marginal Jews or that conditions in these regions are more conducive to marginality and the intermarriages that result in Gentile spouses and children being in "Jewish" households.

The sharp locational differences among the subgroups of core Jews confirm these regional variations. Whereas almost half of the Jews by religion

---

[37]Fred Massarik, "Jewish Population in the United States, 1973," AJYB 1974–75, vol. 75, pp. 295–304.
[38]These findings differ from the statistics reported in the 1991 *American Jewish Year Book*, whose data are based largely on reports from local federations and on local community studies.
[39]Larry Long, *Migration and Residential Mobility in the United States* (New York, 1988), pp. 137–88.
[40]Cf. William M. Newman and Peter L. Halvorson, "American Jews: Patterns of Geographic Distribution and Change, 1952–1971," *Journal for the Scientific Study of Religion*, June 1979, pp. 183–93.

are concentrated in the Northeast, less than one-third of the secular Jews and those who are Jews by choice are located there. Clearly, the Northeast, while no longer the majority area of Jewish residence in the United States, is by far the dominant location of persons identifying themselves as Jewish by religion. Both secular Jews and Jews by choice are relatively more likely to live in each of the other three regions. The differences are particularly sharp for the West. Such variable distribution may have serious implications for the future strength of Jewish identity of those living in the respective regions.

Variations in regional distribution also characterize the non-Jewish members of the sampled households. Those who are converts out of Judaism and those of Jewish descent who grew up in and now practice another religion each have a quite low proportion living in the Northeast, just over one-quarter. This is considerably below the proportion of Jews by religion and even below that of the secular Jews and the Jews by choice. Many more live in the Midwest and the South than do any of the core identity groups. However, while somewhat more live in the West than is true of Jews by religion, the percentage of both secular Jews and Jews by choice in the West exceeds the percent of the converts out of Judaism and of those of Jewish descent but now non-Jews.

Gentile household members, unlike the other non-Jewish members, are relatively more concentrated in the Northeast and less so in the Midwest and South. In fact, their distribution pattern quite closely parallels those of the secular Jews and Jews by choice. Whether this stems from high rates of marriage to secular Jews remains to be determined in the in-depth assessment of intermarriage patterns.

The net result of the differential regional concentration of the various identity subtypes is that the Jewish identificational composition of the different regions also varies. As the data in panel "b" of table 3 show, 61 percent of the sampled population in the Northeast consists of Jews by religion, compared to just under half in the South and only four in ten in the West. The relatively greater concentration of Jews by religion in the South is undoubtedly related to the heavy in-migration of older persons. Significantly, the West contains relatively more secular Jews than do the other regions. Except for the comparatively small percentage of Jews by descent/other religion in the Northeast, the regions seem to differ minimally in the concentrations of non-Jewish household members.

Compared to all other regions, in the Northeast fewer of the sampled household members are secular, Jews by choice, converts out of Judaism, and born to Jewish parents but practicing another religion. The Northeast clearly continues to be the major "bastion" of Judaism in the United States, even as its position is diluted through the redistribution of population to other regions of the country. Given such redistribution, it is also clear that the mix of Jewish identities varies considerably from region to region and that losses to the core Jewish population through intermarriage, conversion out, and children not raised as Jews are more common among those living outside the Northeast. Such a pattern has particular implications for the future of the national community if redistribution continues to be toward the Sunbelt areas.

Metropolitan/Nonmetropolitan Residence

Historically, Jews in the United States have been overwhelmingly concentrated in urban areas. In 1957 about nine out of every ten Jews age 14 and over lived in urbanized areas of 250,000 or more persons, in contrast to only 37 percent of the total American population. Almost all of the remaining Jews resided in smaller urban places; only 4 percent of the total lived in rural areas, compared to 36 percent of Americans as a whole.[41]

Greater dispersal was already evident in an analysis of changes in geographic distribution undertaken by Newman and Halvorson covering the period 1952–1971.[42] Based on data reported in the *American Jewish Year Book*, their study found that the highest growth in Jewish population occurred in counties other than those of traditional Jewish residence, many of them in areas new to Jewish settlement. By contrast, areas of high Jewish concentration in 1952 displayed moderate or low growth. The observed changes pointed to both higher rates of dispersion and continued growth associated with the processes of urbanization and metropolitanization.

This pattern of redistribution was corroborated in an analysis completed by Kosmin, Ritterband, and Scheckner,[43] which compared the distribution of Jewish population among the 30 largest metropolitan areas of Jewish residence in 1936 and 1986. In 1936, 90 percent of the country's Jewish population was found in the 17 largest metropolitan areas; by 1986, the top 30 metropolitan areas had to be considered in order to encompass so high a proportion of American Jewry. As Kosmin, Ritterband, and Scheckner conclude, ". . . there are more Jewish population centers than in the past, but with fewer Jews in each center."[44]

In 1936, only one of the 30 largest Jewish communities was farther south than Washington, D.C., or St. Louis, and that was Houston, with its 16,000

---

[41]U.S. Bureau of the Census, "Religion Reported by the Civilian Population of the United States, March 1957," *Current Population Reports*, Series P-20, no. 79, 1958.

[42]Newman and Halvorson, "American Jews."

[43]Barry A. Kosmin, Paul Ritterband, and Jeffrey Scheckner, "Jewish Population in the United States, 1986," AJYB 1987, vol. 87, pp. 164–76.

[44]Ibid.

Jews. By 1986, the Miami/Ft. Lauderdale metropolitan area had the third largest Jewish population in the United States, with 367,000 persons, and six other southern metropolitan areas were among the leading 30, including two more in Florida with a combined population of over 100,000 Jews. Similar developments occurred in the West. Only three of the leading communities in 1936 were west of the Rockies, and none of these exceeded 100,000 Jews. By 1986, there were six, and Los Angeles, with its 604,000 persons, ranked as the second largest Jewish community in the United States. Meanwhile, metropolitan communities in the East and Midwest experienced declines. The New York metropolitan area's reported Jewish population decreased from 2.6 million to 2.2 million in the 50-year interval, and Chicago's went from 378,000 to only 254,000. Declines also characterized Philadelphia, Cleveland, Detroit, Pittsburgh, and St. Louis. While some of these changes may be an artifact of the way the basic statistics were collected and/or reported, the overall pattern suggests major basic changes in patterns of Jewish population growth and distribution among metropolitan areas. The new geography has serious implications for integration and assimilation and for other areas of social, economic, political, and even religious concern.

Of particular interest is the extent to which Jews have participated in movement to smaller locations. Such dispersion, especially when it involves movement to communities with few Jewish inhabitants, has particular relevance for the strength of individual ties to the Jewish community. It has the potential of weakening opportunities both to interact with other Jews and to have easy access to Jewish facilities, agencies, and institutions. Much more research is needed on how the "Jewish environment," as indicated by density of Jewish population and facilities, affects individual Jewish identity and the vitality of the community.

Some insights into the impact of metropolitan/nonmetropolitan residence[45] can be obtained from NJPS-1990. In 1990, Jews continued to be concentrated in metropolitan areas: three-quarters of all core Jews enumerated in NJPS-1990 were living in metropolitan areas (table 4), virtually identical with the 77 percent of the total American population in 1988. Yet, as many as one-quarter of all Jews were living in nonmetropolitan areas, that is, not only outside the central cities of the 283 metropolitan areas of the United States but also beyond their suburban areas. About two-thirds of the nonmetropolitan core population lived in areas of 150,000 persons and over, but the balance were in smaller places. In all, therefore, almost 8 percent of American Jews resided in nonmetropolitan areas of less than

---

[45]Metropolitan area residents are those who live in a county that lies within a metropolitan area. Residents of nonmetropolitan areas are persons living in counties that are not in metropolitan areas; the population size refers to the number of residents of the given counties.

150,000 total population. This finding justifies the concerted efforts made by NJPS-1990 to include representation of areas with sparse Jewish populations in the national sample. Such areas were not covered in NJPS-1970/71, which may help to explain some of the differences in the findings between the two surveys, especially as this relates to Jewish identity and behavior. The residential pattern of the core Jews varies considerably by type of Jewish identity. Jews by religion were much more concentrated in metropolitan areas than either secular Jews or Jews by choice, 79 percent compared to 65 and 59 percent, respectively. Whether nonmetropolitan location leads to greater secularism and outmarriage or whether secular and intermarried persons choose to live in nonmetropolitan areas and smaller communities needs to be studied in greater depth; that they are disproportionally located in such places is clear. Whereas only one in five of the Jews by religion lived in nonmetropolitan areas, one-third of the secular Jews and four in ten of the Jews by choice did so; moreover, a substantial proportion of the latter two groups lived in nonmetropolitan areas of less than 150,000 persons.

The relation between metropolitan/nonmetropolitan residence and Jewish identity is also suggested by the residential patterns of the non-Jewish members of the sampled households. For the total group, only 60 percent were located in metropolitan areas, compared to three-quarters of the core Jews. This percentage varied minimally for the three subcategories of non-Jews, and more closely resembled that of secular Jews and Jews by choice than it did Jews by religion. That approximately four out of every ten of the non-Jews in the sampled households lived in nonmetropolitan areas, and as many as 15–18 percent in areas of less than 150,000 population lends weight to the thesis that identity is correlated with residence, either as effect or cause. It suggests for community planners that efforts to reach those more marginal to the community must give concerted attention to smaller communities of the country.

Migration Patterns

Migration is a key factor in helping to explain the national redistribution of the Jewish population. It is also the salient factor in the changing distribution between metropolitan and nonmetropolitan areas. NJPS-1970/71 documented the extensive mobility of American Jewry.[46] At that time, 17 percent of the Jewish population aged 20 and over were living in a different city or metropolitan area than that in which they had resided in 1965. As many as 9 percent had moved to a different state in the five-year interval,

---

[46]Goldstein, "Population Movement and Redistribution."

and an additional 6 percent had moved elsewhere within their state of residence. While the system of classifying persons as residentially stable or mobile differed some in 1990 compared to 1970, the information collected in NJPS-1990 suggests that the high level of migration observed for 1965–70 also characterized the period 1985–90 (table 5). About one-fourth of the Jews in the core population moved beyond their local area in the five years 1985–90. Almost 11 percent moved between states, and another 11 percent changed areas of residence within their state. Overall, both the proportion migrating intrastate and those moving a greater distance seem to have increased some over 1965–70.

The mobility levels of American Jews very closely parallel those of the total white American population; for the latter, 20 percent migrated beyond their local area between 1980 and 1985, the most recent period for which national five-year data are available. Nine percent had moved between states, and 9 percent had made intrastate moves beyond the local area. The virtually identical levels of mobility suggest that the underlying economic and social forces that account for a very mobile American population operate among Jews as well. This is not surprising, given the educational and occupational composition of the Jewish group. Evidently, the stimulus that these provide for movement outweighs any countervailing impact that ties to family and community may have for Jews.

The cumulative effect of such extensive mobility is evidenced in the proportion of Jewish adults who had moved during their lifetime (table 6). Less than one in five were living in the same city/town in which they were born. By contrast, one-quarter of all adults had moved elsewhere in their state, and almost one-half were living in a different state in 1990 from their state of birth. Those who were foreign-born constituted the remaining 10 percent of the adult population. Using this lifetime index of mobility, Jews are considerably more mobile than the general population, among whom only 30 percent had changed state of residence, and 6 percent had moved from another country. That 57 percent of all Jews were living outside their country or state of birth attests to the key role which migration occupies as a dynamic of change for American Jewry.

That it does so for both Jews by religion and secular Jews is suggested by the comparative data on migration for these groups. The comparison will be limited here to the recent migrants, i.e., to those who had moved in the five years before the survey (table 5). Ten percent of Jews by religion had made an interstate move between 1985 and 1990, and another 10 percent moved intrastate beyond their local area. Jews by choice were more mobile, and secular Jews were the most mobile of all, probably reflecting both their somewhat younger age composition and a greater willingness to leave places of concentrated Jewish settlement.

Age affects the propensity to move, since migration is closely linked to events in the life cycle. Thus, whereas 72 percent of Jews aged 18–24 resided in the same city/town in 1990 as in 1985, this was true of only 54 percent of the 25–34 age group (table 7); graduate studies, marriage, and beginning a career all help explain the heightened mobility. That as many as 22 percent of the latter were interstate migrants attests to the dramatic role of migration in this stage of the life cycle. (Similar patterns were observed for 1970.)[47] Thereafter, increasing age is associated with greater stability: A rising proportion lived in the same house in 1985 and 1990, reaching a high of 83 percent of those 65 years and over, compared to a low of only 21 percent of those aged 25–34; a corresponding reduction was noted in the percent who reported interstate migration. Nonetheless, a majority of those aged 35–44 and over one-quarter of those 45–64 years changed residences during the five-year interval, many between states or outside their local area within state; mobility is certainly not restricted to the younger segments of the population. Moreover, a considerable part of the mobility of middle-aged and older persons seems, from data not presented here, to be repeat movement.

The NJPS-1990 data also allow comparison of the five-year mobility patterns of the core Jewish adults and the currently non-Jewish members of "Jewish" households (table 5). Such a comparison indicates that the core Jews as a whole are somewhat less mobile than the total non-Jews. More of the non-Jews had changed residence locally and through moves to other parts of their state as well as outside the state, suggesting that ties to family and community may be somewhat weaker than among Jews. Examination of the subgroups within the non-Jewish group indicates, however, that greater mobility is mainly characteristic of the Gentile members of the households and, to a lesser extent, those born of Jewish parents but not raised Jewish. The converts out of Judaism displayed greater stability. Fuller explanation of these differences must await in-depth analysis, taking account of variation among groups in socioeconomic composition, in age patterns, and in strength of social ties.

That migration is not restricted to the adult population is evident in the statistics showing the percentage of persons under age 18 who were living in a state other than the one in which they were born (not shown in table). Among all the children classified as core Jews, 21 percent were interstate migrants by the time of the survey. The level of migration is considerably higher for children classified as Jewish by religion than for those categorized as secular Jews. Almost one-quarter of the former, compared to only 16 percent of the secular children, had moved interstate. The high degree of

---

[47]Ibid.

mobility among Jewish youth points to the necessity of assessing more fully the implications that such movement has on their integration into the Jewish community, particularly into systems of Jewish education.

Among the 700,000 children in the sampled households classified as currently non-Jewish, interstate migration occurred more frequently than among the Jewish children; 29 percent had made such moves, compared to only 21 percent of the Jewish children. The higher migration level of the non-Jewish children contrasts with the pattern of the parental generation, suggesting that core Jewish families with children may be less mobile than their non-Jewish counterparts in the sampled households. Specific reasons for this need in-depth evaluation.

The Impact of Mobility on Regional Distribution

NJPS-1990 provides information on the origin and destination of the interstate migrants, thereby permitting evaluation of their regional redistribution patterns across the country (table 8).

The highest migration rates characterized those core Jews born in the Northeast and Midwest; 30 percent of the former and 42 percent of the latter were living in a different region in 1990 than that in which they were born. By contrast, only 23 percent of those born in the South and even fewer, 13 percent, of those born in the West had changed region of residence.

The direction of the shift among those who moved is clearly to the Sunbelt. About half of the 838,500 leaving the Northeast moved to the South, and another third migrated to the West. Of the 335,900 leaving the Midwest, almost one-third went to the South, and just over half headed to the West. Of the much smaller numbers leaving the South and the West, almost half shifted to the Northeast; the second largest stream was the interchange between the South and the West. The direction of the overall shift is most evident in the streams for the Northeast and Midwest: Whereas 60 percent of all interregional migrants originated in the Northeast and another 24 percent in the Midwest, by 1990 only 12 percent of the interregional migrants had moved to the Northeast and 8 percent to the Midwest. By contrast, only 10 and 7 percent of all interregional migrants were born in the South and the West, respectively, but 44 and 36 percent resided in these regions by 1990. On balance, this redistribution resulted in a net loss of almost 677,000 Jews to the Northeast and 219,000 to the Midwest. By contrast, the South gained 485,000, and the West netted 411,000. Clearly, migration has produced a massive redistribution of Jews among the major regions of the United States.

The movement of the non-Jewish members of the surveyed households closely parallels that of the Jews, with a net shift from the Northeast and the Midwest to the South and the West. The former two regions experienced a lifetime loss of 115,000 and 113,000 persons, respectively, while the South gained 84,000 and the West 143,000. With the small exception of the interchange between the Northeast and the Midwest (Jews shifted from the Northeast to the Midwest, whereas for non-Jewish household members the exchange was reversed), the overall direction of interregional migration patterns of Jewish and non-Jewish household members was similar. However, the shift of the Jewish members to the South and West was more marked, reflecting the fact that relatively fewer of the non-Jews originated in the Northeast and comparatively more moved there and to the Midwest from other regions of the country.

SOCIODEMOGRAPHIC CHARACTERISTICS

Age Composition

Jews in the United States have long been characterized by a relatively older population. Reflecting the combined effects of lower fertility and the growing concentration of the large numbers of immigrants from the early 1900s among the aged, the core Jewish population continues to be older than the white population of the United States (the difference is even greater if nonwhites are included). In 1990, the median age of the Jewish core was 37.3 years, almost four years higher than the 33.6 median of the total whites (table 9). Since 1970, both the Jewish and the total population have aged, with both groups adding about four years to their median ages.

The 1990 differences in age composition suggested by the medians are reflected in the proportions in different age segments. For example, 19 percent of the Jewish group is under age 15, compared to 21 percent of all whites. These proportions are well below the 23 and 28 percent, respectively, recorded in 1970 and reflect both lower Jewish fertility and the reduction in general fertility. By contrast, relatively more Jews are aged; even excluding the 80,000 Jews living in institutions, most of whom are above age 65, 17.2 percent of the core Jewish population was age 65 and over, compared to only 13.3 percent of the white population. This difference extends even to the old aged; almost 8 percent of the Jews were age 75 and over, compared to 5.5 percent of the whites.

The differences are not as great in the middle ages, suggesting that the relative burden of supporting the dependent population, the young and the aged combined, is quite similar for Jews and for the population as a whole. However, compared to all whites, the dependency of the aged is greater for the Jews and that of the children and youth is less, although for both groups, those under age 25 still considerably outnumber the aged.

The age composition within the Jewish population also varies among the different identity subcategories. The median age of those who are born Jews and currently Jews by religion was 39.3 years, compared to a median of only 29.9 years for those classified as secular Jews. This difference is clearly reflected in the much larger proportion of secular Jews under age 25 and in the much higher percentage of aged among the Jews by religion. Even within the middle age range, 25–64 years, Jews by religion are more skewed toward the higher ages. These cross-sectional data suggest a shift toward secular identification with Judaism among younger generations, but, as these persons age, they may well shift from viewing themselves as secular to regarding themselves as Jews by religion.

Jews by choice have the highest median age, 41.1 years, for obvious reasons. Few children make a decision to change their religion or have this decision made for them. Conversion is largely an adult phenomenon, with the religion of the children being largely determined by their parents. Just over half of Jews by choice are found in the narrow age range of 25–44 years, reflecting the upsurge in recent decades in marriages of Jews to persons not born Jewish.

Finally, NJPS-1990 allows comparison of the age composition of the Jewish members of the surveyed households with those who were not Jewish at the time of the survey. Such a comparison shows that the non-Jewish members are younger than either the Jewish members or the total U.S. white population. Their median age of 31.7 is almost six years below that of the Jews and two years below all whites in the nation. This difference, like that of the Jews by choice, is probably a function of the recent high rate of intermarriage and the fact that a large proportion of the children of mixed marriages are not being raised as Jews. The particularly high proportion of children in the Jewish descent/other religion category is a case in point. The differences are even sharper if the comparison is made with those classified as Jewish by religion. In fact, the age composition of the non-Jewish members of households quite closely resembles that of the secular Jews. This suggests that the same social factors that lead more younger Jews to identify themselves as secular may also underlie the greater number of younger non-Jews, who are either descended from Jews but are not themselves Jewish or are Gentile members of the household.

The variations in the comparative age structures of the Jewish population by type of identity are important considerations for institutions and agencies in planning current programs and future directions. At the same time, these age patterns call for more research attention to whether these cross-sectional differentials are indicative of future trends; longitudinal studies are very much in order.

Gender Differentials

The gender composition of the Jewish population reflects the combined effects of a variety of demographic and social forces. In general, males outnumber females at birth, but thereafter mortality tends to be more heavily selective of males. As a result, more women than men reach the older ages. Other factors also affect sex composition, however. For Jews, sex-selective rates of intermarriage, conversion into and out of Judaism, and immigration could affect the gender composition of the different subcategories. The omission of the institutionalized population from these statistics on gender composition is also likely to significantly affect the sex ratios of the aged, since the population in nursing homes and institutions for the aged tends to be heavily female; the aged still living in households may consist disproportionally of married couples and therefore be more balanced in gender composition than the aged as a whole.

For the total core Jewish population, a near balance exists in gender composition with 98.8 males for every 100 females; this is only slightly above the 95.8 ratio for the total white population (table 10). The higher ratio for the Jews is largely attributable to the omission from the Jewish group of the institutionalized population.

Within the Jewish group, gender composition varies among the different identity categories. The sex ratio is just over 100 for both the Jews by religion and the secular Jews, but far below a balanced composition for the Jews by choice. The latter suggests that intermarriages resulting in conversion of the non-Jewish spouse more often involved a Jewish-born male whose wife chose Judaism than a Jewish-born female whose husband made such a choice. Women may also be more likely to choose Judaism for reasons unrelated to marriage.

The total non-Jews in "Jewish" households have a somewhat lower sex ratio than the Jews, and are quite similar to the total U.S. white population. While this group, too, would be affected by the omission of the institutionalized population, the effect would not be as great as for the Jews since considerably fewer of the non-Jews are in the aged group. The more important factor affecting the sex composition of the non-Jews is the sex-selective patterns of intermarriage and conversion out of Judaism. Among those who have converted out of Judaism, the sex ratio is heavily skewed toward women. Among the larger number of others of Jewish descent who were born or raised as non-Jews, the overall sex ratio is quite balanced, reflecting the large percentage of children. For those aged 25 and over, however, the sex ratio is also unusually low, possibly reflecting the greater tendency of women to acknowledge their Jewish descent. Whether this relates in any way to halakhic considerations needs further research. Such an explanation is further suggested by the high sex ratio of those reported as Gentile members of the households: 103.1 males per 100 females. But this higher ratio may also reflect a lesser tendency, especially in earlier years, of men to become Jews by choice upon marriage to a Jew.

Generation Status

The changing generation status of the American-Jewish population has great importance for the future of American Jewry.[48] In the last half century, third and higher generation Jews have had to face the American scene without massive reinforcement from immigrant flows from overseas. Although this situation has been modified by the influx of Israelis and Soviet Jews, their relatively small numbers do not seem to have significantly altered either the overall demographic composition of American Jewry or its socioreligious profile. Confronted with the growing freedom that Jews have come to experience in virtually all spheres of American life, the greater distance at which more Jews now find themselves from their immigrant origins takes on added significance.

Already in 1970, the growing Americanization of the Jewish population was evident. NJPS-1970/71 found only 23 percent of household heads in the Jewish population to be foreign-born, and one out of every five was already third generation.[49] Succeeding community surveys showed declining proportions of foreign-born and rising percentages of third generation. For example, the Boston studies of 1965, 1975, and 1985 reported the foreign-born to be 22, 12, and 8 percent, respectively, of the total population. By contrast, those with American-born parents rose from 20 to 49 to 61 percent over the three surveys.[50]

By NJPS-1990, the percentage of foreign-born in the core Jewish population had declined to 9 percent. The relation to age is clear, directly reflecting the changing volume of Jewish immigration to the United States; 17 percent of the population aged 65 and over were foreign-born, declining to only 4 percent of those under age 18. In all, 55 percent of all foreign-born persons are 45 years old and over.

Indicative of the changing generation status of the population is the number of U.S.-born grandparents (table 11, panel *a*), which can range

---

[48]Sidney Goldstein and Calvin Goldscheider, *Jewish Americans: Three Generations in a Jewish Community* (Englewood Cliffs, N.J., 1968).

[49]Massarik and Chenkin, "U.S. National Jewish Population Survey."

[50]Morris Axelrod, Floyd J. Fowler, and Arnold Gurin, *A Community Survey for Long Range Planning* (Boston, Combined Jewish Philanthropies of Greater Boston, 1967); Floyd J. Fowler, *1975 Community Survey: A Study of the Jewish Population of Greater Boston* (Boston, Combined Jewish Philanthropies of Greater Boston, 1977); and Sherry Israel, *Boston's Jewish Community: The 1985 CJP Demographic Study* (Boston, Combined Jewish Philanthropies of Greater Boston, 1987).

between none and four for any single individual. Only 2 percent of those 65 years old and over had all four grandparents U.S.-born, but four out of ten of those aged 18–24 years did so. Whereas 94 percent of the aged reported none of their grandparents born in the United States, this was true of only 23 percent of the youngest adult group. Judged by generation status, the Jewish community in the United States is clearly becoming an increasingly American-Jewish community.

To what extent is generation status associated with Jewish identity? The NJPS-1990 data point to a clear relation. Among core Jews, including children, 10 percent of the Jews by religion were foreign-born, compared to 7 percent of the secular Jews and slightly fewer of the Jews by choice (not shown in table). Much of the difference between the Jews by religion and the secular Jews stems from the larger proportion of older persons among the Jews by religion, but even in younger groups, more of the Jews by religion were foreign-born. More detailed examination shows Jews by religion had the highest proportion with no American-born grandparents (70 percent) and the lowest with all four grandparents born in the United States (9 percent). By contrast, only 38 percent of the secular Jews had no American-born grandparents, and 28 percent had all of their grandparents American-born. Not surprisingly, more Jews by choice had all their grandparents born in the United States, and fewer had no American-born grandparents. Incorporation of Jews by choice into the core Jewish population has the effect, therefore, of increasing the average generation status of the core Jewish population. That the non-Jewish members of the sampled "Jewish" households have a much higher proportion with American-born grandparents, 46 percent compared to 14 percent of the core Jews, is not unexpected.

Of special interest are the Jews who have converted out of Judaism. Overall, their generation-status profile most closely resembles that of the secular Jews; almost one-third reported all four of their grandparents as American-born, and only 30 percent had no grandparents born in the United States. Consistent with such a pattern as well as with expectations, even higher percentages of those of Jewish descent who were not born or raised Jewish reported having all four grandparents American-born, and few had no American-born grandparents.

The changing generation status of the Jewish population can best be summarized by their average number of American-born grandparents (table 11, panel b). For all Jews in the core population, this amounts to exactly 1.00. It varies, however, from a low of only 0.75 for those who are Jewish by religion to a high of 2.44 for those who are Jews by choice; secular Jews are intermediate. Moreover, within each identity group, the average number of American-born grandparents is inversely related to age. The average for young adult Jews by religion, for example, is over twice as high as for the aged. Those who converted out of Judaism most closely resembled the secular Jews, except for a considerably higher number of American-born grandparents among aged converts. Not surprisingly, the other currently non-Jewish members in the sampled households had higher averages than did the Jewish subgroups. Interestingly, however, the differences were minimal among identity groups for those aged 18–24, pointing to greater similarity among younger cohorts as the foreign-born and their children die.

While much fuller research is needed to assess the impact of generation status on Jewish identity, these data suggest that the greater distance from ethnic ties and experiences that served as integrating forces for earlier generations has altered the socioreligious profile of American Jewry. Rising Americanization, judged by generation status, seems to be associated with both higher levels of secularism and higher rates of conversion to another faith, probably largely in association with intermarriage. Generational change is inevitable and involves a complex process leading to the abandonment of traditional forms and the development of new forms of identity and expression which are seen by many as more congruent with the broader American way of life. Whether these changes have resulted by 1990 in the weakening or strengthening of American Jewry remains to be tested.

Educational Achievement

Reflecting the great emphasis placed on education, both as an intrinsic value and as a means for mobility, the Jews of America have compiled an extraordinary record of educational achievement. By midcentury, the children and grandchildren of the immigrants from Eastern Europe were averaging about 12 years of schooling, two years higher than the average of the white population.[51] Moreover, over twice as many Jews as whites in the population had completed college.[52]

NJPS-1970/71 indicated that these differentials had continued. Just over half of all Jews age 25 and older had some college education, in contrast to only 22 percent of all whites age 25 and over. Moreover, only 16 percent of the Jews, compared to 46 percent of the whites, had less than 12 years of schooling. Particularly sharp differences characterized the proportion that had some graduate education—18 percent of the Jews, compared to only 5 percent of white adults. While Jewish women, like those in the general population, had, on average, less education than men, the levels of educational achievement for both Jewish men and women were well above

---

[51]Ben Seligman and Aaron Antonovsky, "Some Aspects of Jewish Demography," in *The Jews*, ed. Marshall Sklare (Glencoe, Ill., 1958).

[52]Sidney Goldstein, "Socioeconomic Differentials Among Religious Groups in the United States," *American Journal of Sociology* 74, May 1969, pp. 612–31.

those of their counterparts in the general population.

In the 1970s it seemed likely that educational levels might remain at the very high plateau already achieved or even dip slightly, as young Jews integrated more into the larger society. Jews, it was thought, might then pattern their educational behavior more on the model of the general population. What do the data from NJPS-1990 indicate?

For the core Jewish population 25 years old and over, a college education had become increasingly common (table 12A). Almost three-quarters had at least some college, and as many as one-quarter had some graduate education. Overall, therefore, educational achievement of the adult Jewish population rose substantially between 1970/71 and 1990. The general U.S. white population also experienced an impressive improvement in its educational level, but sharp differentials persisted between them and the Jews. In 1990, almost twice as high a percentage of Jews had some college education as whites, and the percentage with graduate training was three times greater.

Some of this increase for both groups reflects the changing composition of the population aged 25 and over. As the older persons with less schooling die, and as the more educated younger population ages, the average for all ages will rise. A fairer comparison of changes between 1970/71 and 1990 and of differences between groups would be with both age and gender controlled. For such purposes, the focus here will be on the 30–39 age group (table 12B and table 13). Such a focus is useful because most of these persons are young enough to be affected by recent educational patterns, and most of them are likely to have completed their education.

In 1970/71, 83 percent of the males had some college education; 70 percent had graduated college; 45 percent had done some graduate studies. For the total white male population, the comparable levels were only 34, 20, and 11 percent. By 1990, 87 percent of the Jewish males aged 30–39 years had some college education, 69 percent had graduated college, and 37 percent had had some graduate studies. These data show no rise in levels of education among Jewish males. Sharp differences persist, however, between the Jewish males aged 30–39 and this age cohort in the white population. Only slightly more than half (52 percent) of white males aged 30–39 received some college education and less than a third (31 percent) graduated college. Only 13 percent did any graduate studies. Similar patterns characterize Jewish and white females. Clearly, educational achievement remains a very strong value in the Jewish community, even though young people in the last two decades have not achieved higher levels of education than their immediate predecessors.

Of particular interest is whether levels of education vary by type of Jewish identity. The data from NJPS-1990 strongly suggest this to be the case. It may well help to explain why the levels of education have not risen more for the younger Jewish population as a whole.

Among all adults in the three Jewish core groups, similar proportions obtained a college or graduate education. These comparisons are distorted, however, by the different age compositions of the three groups. If the comparison is restricted to those aged 30–39, a different picture emerges. Many more of the secular Jews had less than a college education, and a much higher percent of the Jews by religion had completed college than was true of the Jews by choice or of the secular Jews. Similarly, the secular Jews had the lowest percentage reporting graduate studies. These very different educational patterns suggest that the value placed on education generally associated with Jews occurs most frequently among those professing to be Jews by religion and next most frequently among those who have chosen to be Jews. Have the secular Jews assimilated the less positive attitude toward higher education that seems to characterize the American population in general? Does this help to explain why fewer younger Jews have pursued graduate studies?

Differentials extend to the non-Jewish members of "Jewish" households. Thus, among all the currently non-Jewish household members aged 30–39, almost one-third had less than a college education compared to only 14 percent of the Jewish members. Moreover, only 43 percent of the non-Jewish members had completed college and about one in five had pursued graduate studies, in contrast to 66 and 33 percent, respectively, of the Jewish members. For all three of the non-Jewish groups, the percentage who completed college was well below the levels of college completion of all three of the core Jewish groups. Moreover, the percentage of all three categories of Jews who had undertaken graduate studies was well above that of the three non-Jewish groups.

The differences among the various subcategories of core Jews and of non-Jews suggest that the intensity of Jewish identity is related to levels of education; the stronger the intensity, the higher the level of achievement. Evidently, the values and norms associated with being Jewish or becoming Jewish, especially regarding oneself as Jewish by religion, have a significant impact on the amount of education obtained. Full demonstration of this relation requires an in-depth analysis that gives attention to a number of additional variables and also uses information on the type and intensity of religious identity before and at the time that education was being pursued.

Labor-Force Status and Occupation

The labor-force participation of men and women closely reflects the life-cycle stage, being intimately tied to whether individuals are pursuing education, beginning a career, marrying and raising a family, or retiring. Consistent with patterns in the general population, the proportion of men in the core Jewish population in 1990 actively participating in the labor force rose, as education was completed, from a low of 40 percent of those aged 18–24 to a peak of 94 percent in the prime working ages 35–44. At first gradually and then precipitously, the percent in the labor force declined to 26 percent of those aged 65 and over. Compared to the levels found by the 1957 census survey,[53] the data suggest a considerably lower level of labor-force participation by Jews in recent years, especially in the younger and older ages. In 1957,[54] as many as 54 percent of men aged 18–24 were working, reflecting lower rates of college enrollment, while 46 percent of those aged 65 and over were in the labor force, reflecting a lesser tendency to retire. The latter difference even extends to the 45–64 age group, 96 percent of whom were in the labor force in 1957 compared to only 81 percent in 1990. Only in the peak ages, 35–44, is there close similarity, with well over 90 percent working in both 1957 and 1990.

The overall pattern of age differentials for women closely parallels that of men, with labor-force participation rising in 1990 from 43 percent of those 18–24 to a peak of 76 percent at ages 25–34, and then declining to only two-thirds of those aged 45–64 and 10 percent of the aged. However, the peak occurs ten years earlier, and the levels of participation are lower than those of men at all ages but the youngest. The latter reflects a somewhat lesser tendency of women to be enrolled as students (49 percent compared to 57 percent of the men).

Most significant, however, is the substantial proportion of women aged 25–44 and 45–64 in the labor force, about three-fourths of the former and two-thirds of the older group. These levels represent dramatic increases. In 1957, for example, only about 30 percent of Jewish women aged 25–44 were employed, reflecting the greater likelihood that they were engaged in home management. That labor-force participation in 1957 rose to 38 percent of those aged 45–64 resulted from the tendency of some women to enter the labor force once children were older; even this level is far below the 66 percent of women aged 45–64 in the labor force in 1990. As for men, fewer young women were labor-force participants in 1990 than in 1957, 43 percent compared to 57 percent; unlike men, however, there was minimum change

---

[53]U.S. Bureau of the Census, "Religion Reported by the Civilian Population."

[54]Since the 1970 data on labor force refer to heads of household, they are not fully comparable to the 1990 data that encompass all adult household members. To assess change, therefore, the 1957 Census survey data are used, even though the coverage of Jews differs from 1990; the 1957 data refer to persons reported as Jewish by religion. However, since Jews by religion constitute a very high proportion of the 1990 core Jewish population, and the labor-force rates of the total core and of the Jews by religion are quite similar, the differences between 1957 and 1990 in coverage are not serious.

in the proportion of employed older women, 10 percent in 1990 compared to just over 8 percent in 1957. Whether this pattern will change as women aged 25–64 (who have had more labor-force experience than earlier cohorts) age needs to be monitored in future research. It is clear that, for the age range 25–64, Jewish women's participation in the labor force has become a common pattern, with significant implications for family, fertility, income, and participation in the organized activities of the community.

The high occupational achievement of Jews, paralleling their distinctive educational record, has long been documented.[55] Community studies in every decade since the 1950s, as well as NJPS-1970/71, have shown Jews to be heavily concentrated in the upper ranks of the occupational hierarchy. Moreover, comparative data over the last four decades point to a continuing increase in the proportion of Jews engaged in white-collar work; and within the white-collar category, a shift has occurred toward more professionals and fewer managers.[56] These shifts in occupational composition likely reflect the continued operation of forces identified earlier by Simon Kuznets[57] as affecting the Jewish occupational structure: decreased self-employment as more Jews entered professional, technical, and executive positions in firms and large corporations; a decline in the share of industrial blue-collar jobs; and a lesser concentration in trade, especially small proprietorships, in contrast to many of their parents and grandparents. The non-Jewish population has also moved up the occupational hierarchy in response to changing opportunities and labor-force needs. The question then for 1990 is whether Jews persist in their occupational distinctiveness and, if so, whether the differential between Jews and non-Jews has narrowed or widened.

Differentials clearly persist (table 14). In 1990, 80.1 percent of all core Jewish employed males held white-collar positions, well above the 47.6 percent for the total white population of the United States.[58] Within the white-collar group, the differential for professionals was even sharper, with 39.0 percent of all Jewish males so employed compared to only 15.8 percent of all employed whites. The percentage employed as managers was quite similar for the two groups, but the proportion in sales and clerical work was higher for the Jewish men.

Despite these large current differences within the white-collar group, the

---

[55]Goldstein, "American Jewry, 1970"; Goldstein, "The Jews in the United States," pp. 3–59.

[56]Barry R. Chiswick, "The Economic Status of American Jews: Analysis of the 1990 National Jewish Population Survey," paper presented at Conference on Policy Implications of the 1990 National Jewish Population Survey, Los Angeles, July 1991.

[57]Simon Kuznets, *Economic Structure of U.S. Jewry: Recent Trends* (Jerusalem, Institute of Contemporary Jewry, Hebrew University, 1972).

[58]U. S. Dept. of Labor, Bureau of Labor Statistics, *Employment and Earnings*, vol. 38, Jan. 1991.

comparative data from 1970 point to continued narrowing of differences between males in the Jewish and the total white population. While the level of white-collar employment for Jewish men has declined from the 87-percent level reported in NJPS-1970/71, that of whites generally has risen. The data indicate that more Jewish males are now engaged as operatives and service workers, suggesting that for the first time in recent history, American Jews are increasingly turning to manual labor for their livelihood. This finding confirms the speculation offered in 1981 that, motivated by different values and attracted by new life-styles and income opportunities, especially during times of economic uncertainty, more Jews may turn to making a living through manual labor. Bienstock[59] may have been right when he suggested that Jews might turn in increasing numbers to opportunities in new areas where demands for services were likely to grow. As a result, the occupational structure of Jewish males in 1990 more closely resembles that of the whites than it did in 1970. The index of dissimilarity[60] declined substantially from a high of 56.9 in 1970 to 32.6 in 1990.

That some of the narrowing may be due to the changing Jewish identificational composition is suggested by the comparative data on occupational composition by identity type. Whereas 82.3 percent of the male Jews by religion are in white-collar work, only 72.4 percent of both the secular Jewish men and those males who are Jews by choice are so employed. Most of the difference is concentrated in the lower proportion of the latter two groups in sales and clerical work, although secular males also tend to have fewer managers. Furthermore, more of those not Jewish by religion are concentrated in the manual-laborer groups. If the secular Jews and the Jews by choice constitute a growing proportion of the total core population, their different pattern of occupational choice could well account for the narrowing differential between the Jewish core group and the general white population. We shall have to await the results of the more in-depth evaluation of the occupational data for fuller insights into the factors explaining this change.

Jewish women have also been characterized by much higher levels in white-collar work than all white females; and, as for men, the differentials have narrowed. In 1990, the proportion of Jewish women in white-collar work was similar to that in 1970—90 percent—but for white women generally, it had risen from 65 to 72 percent. Unlike their male counterparts, Jewish women were not characterized by a rising percent of manual workers in the two decades since NJPS-1970/71.

Within the white-collar group, the differences between Jewish women

[59]Herbert Bienstock, quoted in *New York Times*, June 25, 1972.

[60]The index shows the percent of cases that would have to be redistributed in order for the two groups to have identical distributions.

116 / AMERICAN JEWISH YEAR BOOK, 1992

and all white women held only for professionals, with over twice as many Jewish women in the group. Between 1970 and 1990, the proportion of Jewish women working as managers remained constant, but the percentage of professionals rose significantly, from 24 to 36 percent, with a corresponding drop in clerical and sales workers. These changes are consistent with the rising level of education among women.

Among the Jewish women, Jews by religion closely resembled the secular Jews and the Jews by choice in the total percentage who were in white-collar occupations; the percentage varied only between 87 and 91 percent, being highest for the Jews by religion. Although the percentage of professional women was highest for Jews by choice, much of this difference is attributable to age composition. Once age is controlled, Jews by choice have the lowest proportion of white-collar persons, including professionals, and far fewer in sales and clerical work; with age controlled, secular Jews have more in professional work than do Jews by religion. By contrast, more of the Jews by choice are in managerial positions. For all three groups, most of the small number engaged in manual work are employed as service workers. As for men, these data for women suggest that somewhat more of the secular Jews and Jews by choice than Jews by religion are in the lower ranks of the occupational hierarchy. This differential sharpens when age is controlled.

Comparisons can also be made between the Jewish members of the sampled households and the non-Jewish members. If dichotomized in terms of white-collar and blue-collar workers, the non-Jewish members tend to fall between the Jews and the total American white population. Among males, 56 percent are white-collar, in contrast to 80 percent of the core Jews and 48 percent of all whites; among females, 74 percent of the non-Jewish members are white-collar, in contrast to 90 percent of the core Jewish group and 72 percent of the white population. Age does not seem to change these patterns. Clearly, the underlying factors that account for occupational composition seem to operate in an intermediate fashion for the non-Jewish members of "Jewish" households. Multivariate assessment should indicate what these specific variables are and whether they relate to general sociodemographic conditions or to factors more closely tied to Jewish identity.

Marriage Patterns

Marriage and the family have been basic institutions for Judaism, playing a key role in providing for the future, first through reproduction and then by serving as the major agents of socialization and the transmission of values, attitudes, goals, and aspirations. Given the high value that Judaism has traditionally placed on marriage and the family and the changes occurring in these institutions in American society as a whole, a major question is whether Jews have changed their marriage patterns. If so, how, and what implications does this have for the maintenance of the demographic and social vitality of the Jewish population in the future? The 1957 census survey[61] provided one of the first opportunities to compare Jewish marital composition with that of the general population. That comparison indicated that Jews were more apt to marry at some time in their life, to marry at a somewhat later age, and to have more stable marriages.

NJPS 1970/71 found three-quarters of all men and 85 percent of all women aged 25–29 had been married; this compared to 81 and 89 percent, respectively, of men and women in this age group in the U.S. white population. Above age 35, over 95 percent of all Jewish men and 98 percent of all Jewish women had been married,[62] attesting to a strong adherence to traditional values concerning marriage.

NJPS-1990 indicates some change in the patterns suggested by these earlier surveys (table 15). By 1990, the current marital status of the Jewish population almost matched that of the general U.S. white population. Just over 26 percent of all Jewish adult males had never married, compared to 24 percent of the total adult white population; slightly more of the total whites were married and divorced than were Jews. These overall similarities are misleading, however, because of pronounced differentials among younger age groups. In the 18–24 age group, for example, only 4 percent of the Jewish men had been married, compared to 17 percent of men in the general population; by ages 25–34, just half of all Jews but two-thirds of all whites had been married. Even as late as ages 35–44, substantial differences persisted. Only by age 45 and over were the differences minimal, with approximately 92 percent or more of the men in both groups having been married.

The key question is whether these cross-sectional data indicate the likely levels of marriage of the younger cohorts. Comparison with the 1957 census statistics and the NJPS-1970/71 data shows a basic change. For example, whereas only 29 percent of Jewish men in 1957 and 17 percent of those in 1970/71 were still single at ages 25–34, this was true of half of all Jewish men in this age range in 1990. At ages 35–44, 17 percent were still single in 1990 compared to only 5 percent in 1957 and 4 percent in 1970/71. Only at age 45 and over were the levels quite similar, with 5 percent or fewer still single. The sharper differential between the younger and older groups in 1990 compared to 1957 and 1970/71 suggests that the percent married by the time they reach middle and old age may in the future be less for the currently younger segments of the Jewish population than was true earlier.

---

[61]U.S. Bureau of the Census, "Religion Reported by the Civilian Population."
[62]Schmelz and DellaPergola, *Basic Trends in American Jewish Demography*.

By 1990, like women in the general population, Jewish women were marrying at older ages than was true in 1957 and 1970/71. For example, among all Jewish women aged 25–34, in 1957, 91 percent had married and in 1970/71, 90 percent had done so, but by 1990 this was true for only half. Even at ages 35–44, a differential persisted, with 89 percent of all Jewish women having married, compared to 94 percent in 1957 and 98 percent in 1970/71. Moreover, by 1990 the decline in proportions marrying by age 45 was considerably sharper for the Jewish than for the white women. For those aged 45 and over, however, minimal change had occurred between 1957 and 1990, either for Jewish women or for white women generally; in both periods, over 90 percent were married.

As for men, the difference in patterns for the younger and older women raises questions about whether the cross-sectional patterns can point to future levels of marriage for those under age 45 in 1990. Whether changes in marriage behavior associated with higher rates of cohabitation will reduce the percentage who eventually marry, or whether other factors, such as AIDS, will lead to rising marriage rates will need monitoring over the next decade. To the extent that marriage in 1990 had been delayed for a substantial proportion of younger men and women, the impact of such delays on fertility as well as on intermarriage heightens the significance of this change in marital behavior.

Is type of Jewish identity differentially associated with marriage patterns? For men, the data point to somewhat more younger Jews by religion remaining single longer than secular Jews and especially Jews by choice. Among those aged 25–34, 51 percent were never married compared to 47 percent of the secular Jews and only 19 percent of the Jews by choice. By ages 35–44, the differences were minimal. The higher proportion of Jews by religion who pursue graduate education may explain the lower proportion who marry before age 35. For women, more of those aged 18–24 who were Jews by religion were never married than were secular Jewish women or Jews by choice. For those between ages 25 and 44 years, the percentages never married among Jews by religion and secular Jews were similar and higher than among Jews by choice. Although the differences apply to a narrower segment of young Jewish women than of men, the same explanations may hold, particularly since fewer women than men receive higher education, and women marry on the average about 2–3 years earlier than men.

AVERAGE AGE AT MARRIAGE

For those who do marry, there is no strong evidence of significant changes in age at marriage among the different age cohorts (table 16). For males in the core Jewish population, the average age at first marriage was 26.0 years and varied irregularly within a narrow range for the age groups between 25–34 and 65 and over. The 20.6-year average for those under age 25 is distorted because such a high percentage of this age cohort is still single. Since more of those single in the younger age groups may still marry later, the average age at marriage among these cohorts is likely to rise, but only time will tell how many marry and at what ages.

The average age of marriage of core Jewish women is almost three years lower than that of men. The difference tends to be narrower, however, among younger cohorts, but varies irregularly by age. The absence of a clear pattern of change in average age at marriage suggests that the percentage of persons marrying, rather than the age at which they marry, may be the more important change in marriage behavior among the Jewish population.

MARITAL STABILITY

The central role that the family has played in Jewish life has given rise to growing concern about the extent to which Jews share in the growing general tendency of broken marriages. Information on current marital status is not a good indicator since divorce can be followed by remarriage; data on current marital status do not therefore indicate the extent of divorce. Information on number of marriages and type of marital dissolution for those married more than once must also be considered.

Some insight into the extent of marital dissolution among Jews can be obtained by examining the number of marriages of the adults represented in NJPS-1990. In obtaining such an enumeration, the survey also ascertained the reason for the marital dissolution of the first marriage and of the last marriage in all cases of multiple marriage. Since few persons had married more than twice, the divorce record is complete for virtually all ever-married persons.

Among all ever-married men in the core Jewish population, 83.5 percent had been married only once at the time of the survey; 14 percent had been married twice; and 2.5 percent had been married three or more times (table 17). Marital stability was slightly higher for women, with 87.2 percent married once, only 11.2 percent married twice, and fewer than 2 percent having had three or more marriages. Overall, therefore, these data point to a relatively high rate of marital stability among Jews, particularly since some of the broken marriages were attributable to death of spouse and temporary separations rather than divorce. However, the data by age point to changing patterns and relations.

The percentage of men married more than once increases from none of those under age 25 to a high of 22 percent of those aged 45–64 years. Of those aged 65 and over, somewhat fewer had multiple marriages, but more had been married three or more times (5.4 percent) than any other group. For women the pattern was somewhat different, with the percent married more than once rising from none of those under age 25 to 18 percent of those aged 35–44 years; it then declined to only 10 percent of the oldest group. The higher level in the middle ages may reflect changing divorce patterns.

Of those married only once, NJPS-1990 found that 5.5 percent of all men and 10.4 percent of all women were divorced at the time of the survey. That the level is twice as high for women as for men points to the much higher remarriage rate of divorced men. For this subset of the ever-married population, the age data indicate a particularly high divorce rate for the small number of men who were married before age 25 (27 percent of all those who had married only once) and for women between ages 35 and 54 (about 15 percent). For the men this suggests a high risk of marital break-up of young marriages; for the women it again points to a stronger tendency to remain divorced for some time after a marriage dissolves.

Since a number of those whose first marriages ended in divorce have remarried, a more accurate basis for assessing the stability of first marriages is to examine the first-marriage divorce rate among all ever-married persons. Such assessment shows that among all ever-married men in the core population, 16.4 percent ended their first marriage in divorce. For women the comparable percentage was 18.2 percent. Of the men who remarried after their first divorce, 10.5 percent experienced a second divorce; 11.9 percent of the remarried women had also been divorced again by the time of the survey. Taking account of both first and last divorce among all ever-married persons, the evidence indicates 18 divorces for every 100 ever-married men and 19 for every 100 ever-married women. While comparative data are not available for earlier points in time, this finding suggests that divorce has become relatively common among American Jews.

Of particular interest is whether the rate of divorce varies by Jewish identity. Hypothetically, given the strong value placed on marriage and the family, divorce should occur less frequently among persons who report being Jews by religion than among those reported as secular Jews. The data (not shown in table) support such an expectation. Among the ever-married men, those classified as Jewish by religion reported 13.6 percent of their first marriages broken by divorce. The rate was almost twice as high among secular Jews (24.5 percent), and the differences generally applied across most age groups. A large difference also characterized women, among whom 16.3 percent of the Jews by religion and 27.2 percent of the secular Jews had experienced a divorce in their first marriage. Clearly, being secular is associated with greater risk of marital break-up.

The relation of marital dissolution to status as a Jew by choice differs by gender (not shown in table 15). For men, it is associated with an unusually high divorce rate. Among almost four out of every ten male Jews by choice, the first marriage ended in divorce, although the data available for this overview do not indicate if the divorced marriage involved a Jewish or non-Jewish spouse. For women the rate was only 18.4, quite similar to that of Jews by religion and well below that of secular Jews. The reasons for these gender differences among the Jews by choice need to be explored in later analyses.

If the analysis focuses on cumulative divorces in first and last marriage (for those married more than once), the same pattern of differentials by identity noted for first marriage persists. Being a Jew by religion has a positive correlation with stability as does, for women, being a Jew by choice. Secular Jews are more prone to divorce, and the greatest risks characterize male Jews by choice. These data suggest that, to the extent that changes in the identity composition of the Jewish population are associated with changing marital stability, any trend toward higher levels of secularism and intermarriage by Jewish women are likely to be associated with higher levels of marital instability.

Fertility Differentials

American Jews have been characterized by lower fertility than non-Jews, and some data sets have even pointed to below-replacement levels of Jewish reproduction.[63] This situation, coupled with the reduced immigration in the second half of the 20th century and the increasing rates of intermarriage, has given rise to concern about whether, in fact, the Jewish population in the United States will continue to grow. The debate continues and seems likely to become accentuated, in view of the evidence from NJPS-1990 showing very high rates of mixed marriage, low rates of conversion, and a high proportion of children of mixed marriages not being raised as Jews (see discussion below).

NJPS-1990 provides the opportunity to assess fertility changes in the 20 years since the 1970/71 national survey. Using that survey, DellaPergola found that since the beginning of the century, Jewish fertility was consistently lower than among total whites. He reported that "Jewish fertility levels basically followed over time the general fluctuations of the total whites, but patterns of response to period societal change were relatively earlier as appropriate to a more perfectly contracepting population."[64] Moreover, the younger cohorts of women tended toward increasingly lower

[63]Sergio DellaPergola, "Patterns of American Jewish Identity," *Demography* 17, Aug. 1980, pp. 261–73.
[64]Ibid., p. 270.

fertility, even though young ever-married women indicated an expectation of slightly more than two children. DellaPergola speculated that these expectations seemed unrealistically high, given other patterns observed. The evidence from NJPS-1990 seems to validate his doubts.

Comparison of the Jewish fertility reported in 1990 with that of all white women in childbearing years in 1988 shows Jewish fertility to be substantially below that of the general population (table 18). For example, Jewish women aged 25–29 averaged only 0.5 children, whereas white women in this age group had already had one child. By ages 40–44, Jewish women averaged 1.6 children, considerably below the 2.1 average of all white women in that age group. These differentials suggest that the motives for small families among Jews reflect a complex combination of factors involving both conditions unique to the Jews and those shared with the larger population.

The 1970/71 data showed an average completed fertility of 2.4 children for all Jewish women aged 45–49.[65] In 1990, the comparable age group had averaged only 1.9 children. This was not only 20 percent below the Jewish average for those aged 45–49 20 years earlier, but also 19 percent below the average for all white women aged 45–49 in 1988, and 10 percent below the 2.1 level needed for replacement. Clearly, Jewish fertility has declined, resulting in below-replacement fertility for those at the end of childbearing. This contrasts with the above-replacement levels achieved by Jewish women in the age groups between 50 and 65, who were in their peak childbearing years during the baby-boom period.

To date, Jewish women currently aged 35–44 have also had fewer than 2.1 children. Again, their averages are below the 2.3 levels achieved by women in this age range in 1970/71. Moreover, based on their expected completed family size, the women in the 1990 survey will remain at below-replacement levels. This suggests a marked change in fertility behavior over the past 20 years.

Even among women below age 35, except for those aged 20–24 who were just beginning childbearing, the fertility levels reported in 1990 were about half those in 1970/71 for comparable age groups. Nonetheless, as in 1970/71, in 1990 women under age 35 indicated that they expected to have more than two children. If realized, this would represent a significant reversal in fertility behavior. Like DellaPergola, however, we can question how realistic these expectations are. Ever-married women aged 20–24 in 1970/71 expected to average 2.5 children by the end of childbearing. Twenty years later, ever-married women in this same age cohort (not necessarily represented by the same women since some had died and some may have left the core Jewish group) had had only 1.7 children. For the 25–29 age group in

---

[65]DellaPergola, "Patterns."

1970/71, the 2.0 actual completed births by the end of the next 20 years also fell below the expected average of 2.2 indicated in 1970/71. Only for the women above 35, most of whom were well along in their fertility by 1970/71, did completed fertility come close to resembling expectations. While it is possible that the younger 1990 cohorts will be more realistic in their expectations than were the 1970/71 women, especially if patterns of late childbearing change, the experience of cohorts included in the 1970 study provides no sound basis for believing this will be the case.

If the age group 45–49 is used as marking the end of childbearing, comparison among the subgroups of core Jews shows considerable variation in the average number of children ever born. Whereas Jews by religion averaged 1.9 children, secular Jewish women averaged 1.7; Jews by choice constituted the only group to exceed replacement with their 2.3 average. For the next youngest group, however, most of whom had also completed childbearing, minimal difference characterized the Jews by religion and the secular Jews; each averaged about 1.6 children ever born. Again, the Jews by choice had higher fertility, averaging 1.9 children. For all three groups, fertility was below replacement levels at this late point in the reproductive cycle.

Within this overall pattern, the higher fertility of Jews by choice is notable. Their average number of children was higher than that of Jews by religion and of secular Jews at every age below 50, except the very youngest. This suggests that couples involving one spouse who converted to Judaism do not restrict the number of children below the average of all Jews. Why Jews by choice should generally have higher fertility than born Jews remains to be explored. It may be related to the differences in socioeconomic and cultural background that may also help to explain the higher fertility of the white population.

Moreover, the fertility of the Jews by choice at ages 40–44 and 45–49 is about 10 percent higher than that of converts out of Judaism, who averaged 1.8 and 2.0 children, respectively. However, for younger age groups, the number of children born by the time of the survey was higher for the converts out of Judaism. At all ages, the fertility of the converts out exceeded that of the Jews by religion and the secular Jews. How much of this higher level reflects differences in timing of childbearing rather than number of children born by the end of reproduction and how much is attributable to background factors similar to those characterizing the non-Jewish white population which the convert has presumably joined remains to be ascertained.

Except for those women within ten years of the end of the childbearing period, whose below-replacement fertility levels are consistent with expectations for completed fertility, women generally expected to have more than two children. However, in only a few age/identity categories did the expected averages exceed replacement level. These data on expectations, therefore, provide no strong evidence of a major upswing in Jewish fertility. Among all Jewish women under age 45 at the time of the survey, the average completed fertility would be only 1.9 children even if expectations were fully realized, and this would vary between the narrow range of 1.8 and 2.1 for the three categories of core Jews, with secular Jews having the lowest average and Jews by choice the highest. With an average just above 2.1, converts out of Judaism expect only slightly more children than those choosing Judaism.

The overall prospects for Jewish fertility, based on the results of NJPS-1990, therefore apppear to differ minimally from those based on NJPS-1970/71 and intervening surveys. For the immediate future and most likely for the longer run as well, birth levels among Jews seem likely to operate at below-replacement levels or at best to hover at about replacement. Coupled with the higher than average death rates that are associated with an aging population, natural increase is likely to be low or even negative. If intermarriage continues high, with low levels of conversion into Judaism and high percentages of children in mixed marriages being reared as non-Jews, there seems little prospect that the total core Jewish population of the United States will rise above the 5.5 million estimated on the basis of NJPS-1990. If anything, in the absence of strong reversals in fertility and/or intermarriage or large upsurges in immigration, the chances are more likely that the core population will decline toward 5.0 million and possibly even below it in the early decades of the 21st century. All this remains speculative, and different scenarios can be developed based on the assumptions one is willing to adopt.

Intermarriage

Interest in the levels and impact of intermarriage of Jews has a long history. Initially, it was viewed not so much as a potential threat to the demographic maintenance of American Jewry but as an index of the loss of Jewish identification and the weakening of the social and religious cohesiveness of the community. Increasingly, however, concern has focused on the effect of intermarriage on the future size of the Jewish population, especially at a time when fertility is at or even below replacement levels. This concern became particularly acute after the popularization of the concept of the "vanishing American Jew" in the 1960s, based on evidence from community studies of increasing rates of intermarriage with greater distance from immigrant origins.[66]

---

[66]Erich Rosenthal, "Studies of Jewish Intermarriage in the United States," AJYB 1963, vol. 64, pp. 3–53.

The 1957 Bureau of the Census sample survey provided the first national set of estimates of Jewish intermarriage.[67] It found that 3.8 percent of married persons reporting themselves as Jewish were married to non-Jews, and that at least 7.2 percent of all marriages in which one partner was Jewish were mixed marriages. Both these statistics are probably low since no information was collected on the earlier religion of marriage partners; couples with one converted spouse were not separately identified, so that it was not possible to ascertain the rate of conversion either into or out of Judaism.

NJPS-1970/71 provided the first nationwide set of comprehensive data on Jewish intermarriage patterns since it also ascertained the religious identity of the marriage partners before marriage.[68] Of all Jewish persons married at the time of the survey, 8.1 percent were married to a person not born Jewish. Although this level was higher than the 1957 finding, in itself it was not considered unusually high. What shocked the community was the reported rise in the level of intermarriage from less than 2 percent of those individuals who had married before 1925, to about 6 percent of those marrying between 1940 and 1960, to 12 percent of the 1960–64 marriage cohort, to a high of 29 percent of all Jews marrying in the five years preceding the survey. While such a finding was not inconsistent with earlier evidence, the magnitude of the rate, the fact that it reflected a national pattern, and projections that the rate would rise still higher aroused the community to new concerns about its demographic survival.[69]

The impact of intermarriage on demographic growth may largely be determined by the extent of conversion to Judaism of the non-Jewish partner and by the extent to which the children of interfaith marriages are raised as Jews. NJPS-1970/71 found that in 23 percent of the intermarriages in which the husband was originally Jewish, the wife converted; among those couples in which the wife was originally Jewish, only 4.0 percent of the husbands converted. Of the non-Jewish partners in intermarriages, a very substantial percentage identified themselves as Jews even though they had not undergone official conversion to Judaism, i.e., they were functioning as Jews by choice. This was true of 46 percent of the non-Jewish wives and 44 percent of the non-Jewish husbands. Moreover, the study found that 63 percent of the children of Jewish fathers and 98 percent of those of Jewish mothers were being raised as Jews.[70]

The combined findings with respect to conversion, self-identity of the non-Jewish spouse, and children being raised as Jews (even if not always

---

[67]Goldstein, "Socioeconomic Differentials Among Religious Groups."

[68]Massarik and Chenkin, "U.S. National Jewish Population Survey"; Schmelz and DellaPergola, "Demographic Consequences."

[69]Elihu Bergman, "The American Jewish Population Erosion," *Midstream*, Oct. 1977, p. 9.

[70]Massarik and Chenkin, "U.S. National Jewish Population Survey."

halakhically Jewish) meliorated the concerns raised by the high rates of intermarriage. Yet, it was also recognized that the study may have underestimated the levels of intermarriage and overestimated the gains to Judaism through conversion and identification because of inadequate representation of areas containing very low levels of Jewish concentration and of those Jews who had converted out of Judaism. The more encompassing design of NJPS-1990 was intended to correct the defects of NJPS-1970/71 in coverage of more marginal Jews and those who had converted out of Judaism. To the extent that it succeeded, the data obtained on intermarriage should be more accurate than were those for 1970/71.

NJPS-1990 estimated that 2.6 million adults were born Jewish and were married at the time of the survey.[71] Of this number, 69 percent were married to someone also born Jewish and 4 percent were married to a person not born Jewish who had chosen to be Jewish either through conversion or through self-identification. Of the Jews by choice, about 70 percent had converted. The remainder of the born Jews were married to Gentiles, including the 6 percent of born Jews who converted to another religion. Compared to the findings of NJPS-1970/71, therefore, these data point to a very substantial rise in the level of intermarriage, from 8 percent in 1970/71 to 31 percent of all born Jews.

That this higher level reflects a continuation of the trend suggested by the cohort data of the 1970/71 study is evidenced in the statistics by marriage cohort.[72] Whereas 89 percent of born Jews who married prior to 1965 married another born Jew, only 69 percent of those marrying between 1965 and 1974 did so. This percentage, in turn, declined to only 49 percent for the group marrying between 1975 and 1984, and in the five years preceding the survey, 1985–1990, it reached a low of 43 percent. Of the intermarriages, some involved conversions to Judaism or a choice on the part of the non-Jewish spouses to regard themselves as Jewish even if not formally converted. If all such Jews by choice are counted as Jewish, the percent of Jews marrying other Jews rises to 91 percent among those marrying before 1965, and to 48 percent of those marrying in the most recent period, 1985–1990. The high rate of mixed marriages in 1985–1990 means that for every new

---

[71]Intermarriage can be defined in different ways, depending on whether the Jewish identity of the marriage partners is ascertained according to religion at time of birth, at time of courtship, at time of marriage, or at time of the survey. Depending on the definition used, the rate of intermarriage will vary. Consistent with NJPS-1990's goal of encompassing current as well as former Jews, intermarriage is measured in terms of the religious identification of the current marriage partner of anyone who was born Jewish and is now married, irrespective of current Jewish identity.

[72]Egon Mayer, "Jewishness Among the Intermarried: A Record of Lost Continuity or Lost Opportunity?" Paper presented at the Sidney Hollander Colloquium on the 1990 National Jewish Population Survey, July 1991.

couple consisting of two Jewish partners there were approximately two new couples in which only one of the partners was Jewish. The magnitude of the change that has occurred in the extent of mixed marriages is indicated by the fact that among those marrying before 1965, five times as many Jewish marriages were homogamous as mixed.

The extent of change in intermarriage patterns is further illustrated by the changing levels of conversion to, or choice of Judaism by, the non-Jewish partner. Among those spouses not born Jewish in the pre-1965 marriage cohort, one out of every five chose to be Jewish. In each succeeding cohort, the NJPS-1990 data indicate that the percentage declined, reaching a low of only 9 percent in the 1985–1990 cohort. Of course, these percentages may change in future years as spouses respond to family and community pressures, as they learn more about the religion of the other spouse, and particularly as parents face decisions about the religious training and identification of their children.

One of the major concerns about the demographic implications of high rates of mixed marriages is the Jewish identity of the children of such marriages. The households identified as mixed-married in NJPS-1990, that is, households in which children live with a core Jewish and a non-Jewish parent, contained 664,000 children under 18 years of age. Of these children, only 25 percent were being raised as Jews at the time of the survey; 45 percent were being raised in another religion;[73] and 30 percent were being raised without any religion. Unless a large majority of the latter opt to be identified as Jews when they reach adulthood, most children of mixed marriages will be lost to Judaism; they will be Jews by descent only, either through the maternal or paternal line. These potential losses constitute a major challenge to the Jewish community. Seen in the context of the high rate of mixed marriage that has come to characterize the community, the failure to attract more of these children into the Jewish fold could contribute to declines in the number of Jews in the future. That virtually all of the children of Jews by choice married to born Jews were being raised as Jews points to the importance of increasing the rate at which the non-Jewish partner to a marriage chooses to become Jewish and of strengthening the opportunities that the mixed-married and their children have to develop stronger ties to the Jewish community.[74]

The changing levels of intermarriage and conversion (both formal and informal) reflect a complex set of changes in the American social structure and the position of Jews in this structure, as well as in the attitudes of Jews and non-Jews about intermarriage generally and mixed marriages in particular. The greater freedom in choosing where to be educated, in type and

---

[73]These included children reported being raised as both Jewish and something else.
[74]Cf. Mayer, "Jewishness Among the Intermarried."

place of employment, in location of residence, and in choice of friends have all contributed to greater freedom in choice of spouse. Associated with such freedom has been the greater freedom extended to both partners to decide whether, upon marriage, to make the couple religiously homogamous or to maintain individual religious identity as well as to decide in what, if any, religion to raise children.

Accompanying the structural changes that have been conducive to more mixed marriages and less conversion have been the sharp changes in attitude among the Jewish population about the acceptance of intermarriage. NJPS-1970/71 asked respondents whether "it is all right for Jews to marry non-Jews." Half maintained that it was not, and most of these disagreed strongly. The question was asked differently in 1990: "Hypothetically, if your child were considering marrying a non-Jewish person, would you: strongly support, support, accept or be neutral, oppose or strongly oppose the marriage?" Among the respondents classified as Jews by religion, only 22 percent reported that they would oppose the marriage, and far fewer of those who were secular Jews, only 4 percent, reported opposition. Indeed, one-third of the Jews by religion and 45 percent of the secular respondents said they would support such a marriage, and about half of each group said they would accept it.

Clearly, a large proportion of the Jewish population has reconciled itself to the possible or actual marriage of their children to non-Jews even though they might prefer Jewish children-in-law. Given this set of attitudes and the growing opportunities for mixed marriages to occur, there seems little likelihood that the trend revealed by both NJPS-1970/71 and NJPS-1990 will reverse itself. At best, it may reach a high level plateau. This means, as Egon Mayer has stressed, that reactive, defensive, preventive measures are not likely to achieve much in the decades ahead.[75] Rather, what he refers to as proactive, culturally, and even politically assertive measures seem more in order, measures which would lead to the strengthening of the weak ties that many intermarried still retain.

JEWISH PRACTICES AND ATTACHMENTS

Denominational Identification

Religious denomination constitutes a major dimension along which the American Jewish community subdivides itself. Denominational divisions are particularly pertinent because of the different attitudes and practices

---

[75]Ibid., p. 33.

about such issues as intermarriage and conversion, patrilineal descent, and divorce, all of which affect who is to be considered a Jew. Stimulated in part by Rabbi Irving Greenberg's provocative essay questioning whether there will be one Jewish people by the year 2000,[76] a heated debate has ensued on the demographic and religious implications these different practices have for social interaction among Jews, for their survival as one people, and even for survival demographically at a level at which Jews can remain a key segment in the larger American community.

The discussion of the complexity of defining and measuring what constitutes the Jewish population of the United States in this essay touches on these concerns only superficially. Introduction of halakhic issues would add profoundly to the complexity and would alter considerably the categories of Jewish identity used by NJPS-1990. While full discussion of the issues must await other occasions, their significance is clearly relevant to examination of the current denominational composition of the Jewish population and of changes in such identity.

For all respondents, NJPS-1990 asked: "Referring to Jewish religious denominations, do you consider yourself to be Conservative, Orthodox, Reform, Reconstructionist, or something else?" The wide range of responses, in addition to the four specific denominations, reflects the religious heterogeneity of the respondents, including those professing no religion and those reporting themselves as non-Jewish even though born to Jewish parents. A number of secular Jews and even some of the currently non-Jewish respondents indicated that they considered themselves to be identified with one of the major denominations. Whether they were responding in terms of family identity, sympathy with a particular outlook, or on some other basis cannot be ascertained. The fact that they did so testifies to the difficulty and complexity of ascertaining both who is a Jew and what types of Jews there are. The information collected from the respondents and referring to the respondents only has been weighted to reflect the denominational affiliation of all adults. The results may differ some from the actual denominational composition of the total adult population, based on giving individual members in each household the opportunity to answer for themselves.

For the entire adult core Jewish population, the largest single denomination was Reform, with 38 percent of the total (table 19). It was followed closely by Conservative, with 35 percent. Orthodox constituted 6 percent of total adults and Reconstructionist just over 1 percent. Those who indicated a nondenominational category, such as secular, just Jewish, and traditional, made up 10 percent of the total; a residue group of miscellaneous small categories accounted for almost 9 percent.

---

[76]Irving Greenberg, "Will There Be One Jewish People by the Year 2000?" *CLAL Perspectives* (New York, National Jewish Center for Learning and Leadership, 1986), pp. 1–8.

Not surprisingly, compared to the secular Jews, more of the Jews by religion were in the major denominational groups. Whereas 91 percent of the Jews by religion reported a denominational affiliation, only 25 percent of the secular Jews did so; one-fifth of the latter were in the "just Jewish"/secular category and another 52 percent said they were something else. Jews by choice, on the other hand, more closely resembled the Jews by religion in denominational composition. More of them were Reform; fewer were Conservative, and about the same proportion were Orthodox. That a total of 92 percent of Jews by choice identified denominationally, even though a considerable proportion did not go through formal conversion, suggests the significance of their having made the choice to identify as Jews.

Among those born Jewish and still Jewish by religion, denominational affiliation varies across age groups (table 20). The aged group contains the highest percent of Orthodox and the lowest percent Reform, reflecting its heavier immigrant composition. Twelve percent of all older persons, compared to only 5 percent of those between ages 25 and 64, are Orthodox. By contrast, the percent who are Reform rose from 31 percent of the aged to half of those aged 25–44, and the percentage Conservative declined with lower age to only 33 percent of those aged 25–44. A major realignment in denominational affiliation has occurred with distance from the older, more heavily immigrant or second-generation cohorts. Yet, the data for those aged 18–24 at the time of the survey suggest, as have those for some community studies,[77] that the pattern may be altering again. Among the youngest cohort, almost twice as many were Orthodox (10 percent) as among those aged 25–64, and more were Conservative than at ages 25–44. By contrast, Reform accounted for only 35 percent of the youngest cohort, a level not too far above that of the aged and well below that of the 25–44 age group. Among the 18–24 group, 10 percent identified themselves as "just Jewish"/secular. This percentage is the highest of any age group, possibly pointing to an underlying movement away from denominational identification, even among persons professing to be Jewish by religion. But this group may change once its members marry and settle in a career and a community. Whether the change in denominational identification among the young reflects a basic reversal among the Jews by religion or whether it reflects a shift of the younger Reform raised/educated Jews from the Jews by religion category into the secular category, leaving relatively more of the Jews by religion in the Conservative and Orthodox groups, needs to be researched in depth. In doing so, particular attention needs to be given to the role of Jewish education, both type and amount.

To assess changes in denominational identification, respondents were

---

[77]Calvin Goldscheider and Sidney Goldstein, *The Jewish Community of Rhode Island: A Social and Demographic Survey* (Providence, Jewish Federation of Rhode Island, 1988).

asked a parallel question about the denomination in which they were raised. Comparison of this information with that on current identification allows evaluation of changes over the course of the lifetime of the individual respondents. The data point to substantial shifts in the denominational identity of American Jewry.

For the core population, Conservative Judaism constitutes the denomination in which the largest proportion of Jews were raised, one-third (table 21). An additional 26 percent were raised as Reform Jews, and almost as many (23 percent) as Orthodox. Not even 1 percent grew up in the Reconstructionist movement. Just over four out of every five core Jews thus reported being raised in a specific denomination.

Comparison of the data on current denomination with that in which individuals were raised shows that, on balance, the proportion Conservative has hardly changed, remaining close to one-third, although specific individuals so identified may have changed denominations. On the other hand, the percentage of Orthodox declined from 23 percent to only 6 percent, and the proportion of Reform increased from 26 to 38 percent. Reconstructionists rose to 1.3 percent of all core Jews. In total, the percentage of core Jews reporting a denomination declined only slightly, from 83 percent based on denomination raised to 81 percent based on current denomination, suggesting the persistence of denominational identification among Jews despite some tendency toward greater secularism. Seven percent reported being raised as "just-Jewish"/secular and 10 percent reported such an identity at the time of the survey. For both reference periods, about 9 percent classified themselves as something else, but for most of the Jews by choice this was non-Jewish at the time they were growing up.

The dynamics of change in denominational identity can be better measured by comparing the denomination in which born Jewish and currently Jewish individuals were raised and their denomination at the time of the survey (table 22). These data point to much greater movement into the Conservative and Reform groups than into the Orthodox. Whereas 89 percent of all Orthodox respondents reported they were raised Orthodox, only 60 percent of the Conservative adults and 58 percent of the Reform reported their "origins" as being in the same denomination. Of the 11 percent of the Orthodox who were not raised as Orthodox, almost half shifted from Conservative; almost all the others had been secular/"just Jewish." Three-fourths of the 40 percent of Conservatives who were drawn from other denominations came from an Orthodox background; and most of the others were raised Reform. The situation was different for the 41 percent moving into Reform; of all adult Reform Jews, one-fourth came from the Conservative movement and about one in ten had been raised Orthodox. Clearly, most of the considerable shifting among denominations involved transitions to the denomination most nearly similar to the one in which the individual was raised. A majority of both the Reconstructionist and the "just Jewish" groups were not raised with these identities; most were drawn from the other major denominations, especially the Conservative group.

The absolute effect in numbers of the exchanges among denominations between early socialization and the time of the survey, plus the gains resulting from the addition of Jews by choice, is crudely indicated by the size of the denominations at these two points (not in table). Since adults of varied ages are included, the changes do not cover a specific number of years. On balance, over the lifetime of the respondents, the greatest numerical changes characterized the Orthodox and Reform. The former declined by about 731,000 adherents, or 73 percent, from the one million adults reported raised as Orthodox. The Reform grew by about 533,000 persons, or 46 percent, from the 1.17 million who were raised Reform. Conservative remained virtually stationary, increasing by only about 40,000, or 3 percent, from the 1.53 million who reported themselves as having been raised as Conservative Jews. The small Reconstructionist movement experienced the largest relative growth, just over 200 percent, but this increase involved only about 46,000 adults.

The number not identified with any of the four specific denominations also grew, by 112,000 persons, or 15 percent. While this finding points to some increase in secularization of the core population, the change is not particularly sharp. It is augmented, however, by those who have left Judaism entirely and by the large numbers of Jews by descent who were not raised and are not currently Jewish. On balance, therefore, these data suggest that those still classifiying themselves as Jewish have been shifting away from Orthodoxy toward Reform and secular Jewish identity.

Ritual Practices and Organizational Involvement

The heterogeneity of the population surveyed by NJPS-1990 raises questions about whether the subgroups differ in how they manifest their Jewish or former Jewish identities. Does converting out of Judaism mean cessation of all observance of Jewish ritual practices and other manifestations of Jewish identity or does some retention occur, particularly of practices that provide links to one's Jewish family? For those choosing to be Jewish, how closely do their Jewish observances resemble those of persons raised Jewish, and how much do they continue to observe the practices associated with former religious identification? Do secular Jews differ from those who reported themselves as Jewish by religion? Do secular Jews forego all ritual practice?

The data available from the large number of questions included in NJPS-1990 on ritual practice, organization memberships, philanthropy, ties to Israel, and attitudes toward a range of topics lend themselves to providing some answers to such questions. To do so thoroughly requires an in-depth assessment that is beyond the scope of this overview report. Because only a superficial evaluation, limited to a few behavioral indicators, can be undertaken here, the reader should be aware that some of the conclusions may change when fuller controls for age, denomination, family history, and other key background variables can be introduced into the analysis. The comparisons are suggestive of underlying differences and whet the appetite for fuller understanding of the reasons for the observed patterns and their implications for the future of Jewish life in the United States.

RITUAL PRACTICES

Attention turns first to selected ritual practices (table 23). Most pertain to the household as a whole, though a few questions related specifically to individual behavior are also examined. In our discussion, ritual practices are analyzed along two dimensions: in terms of the respondent's Jewish identity and other characteristics and in terms of household composition (entirely Jewish, mixed Jewish-Gentile, no core Jews). It should be noted that even though, to simplify presentation, the discussion may refer to the practices as if they were performed by the individual, the data for a given household do not necessarily reflect the behavior of the individual responding for that household.

Observance of the Sabbath is at the very heart of Judaism and lighting Sabbath candles is an important aspect of that observance. Of all respondents in the core Jewish group, 62 percent reported that candles were never lit in their households on Friday evening; only 17 percent reported lighting Sabbath candles always or usually. Not surprisingly, almost nine out of ten respondents who were either formerly Jewish or of Jewish descent never lit candles Friday evening; 11 percent did so sometimes, and 2 percent even reported regular lighting of candles. This may involve behavior by someone else in the household who is currently Jewish or may be a vestige of earlier behavior that is done without religious connotation.

Within the core Jewish group, sharp differences exist by type of identity (table 24). Whereas almost one in five of those reporting themselves as Jewish by religion reported Sabbath candles being lit in their household always or usually, and another 23 percent reported sometimes lighting candles, only 11 percent of the secular Jews fell in these two categories; almost nine in ten of the secular Jews indicated that candles were never lit in their households, virtually identical to the non-Jewish respondents. By contrast, but surprising by its magnitude, 57 percent of the Jews by religion reported never lighting candles. While adhering more closely than the secular Jews to this key element of ritual, still, a majority of Jews by religion do not practice it. The level of adherence is reported as highest among the Jews by choice. Almost one-third reported Sabbath candle lighting always or usually, and only 32 percent reported never doing so. Evidently, candle lighting has particular symbolic value in households that include a Jew by choice. The significance of this for outreach programs designed to achieve higher levels of religious homogamy in intermarried households needs to be recognized. Fuller understanding of the reasons that lead to such a differential might also prove useful in enhancing ritual practices among other segments of the Jewish population.

Consistent with the differences observed among respondents with different types of Jewish identity, sharp differences characterize household types. One in five of the entirely Jewish households lit Sabbath candles always or usually compared to just under 5 percent of the mixed households and only 1 percent of those with no core Jews as members As important, just over half of the entirely Jewish households reported never doing so. Less surprising, just over 80 percent of the mixed and almost nine out of ten of the non-core households reported no such observance.

The observance of *kashrut* (dietary laws) was also assessed. Since buying kosher meat and other kosher products has become widespread, even among non-Jews, purchase of kosher meat no longer serves as a good index of *kashrut* observance. Keeping separate dishes within the household is a more sensitive index. That it is no longer a common practice is evidenced by the fact that eight of every ten households in the core Jewish population were reported as not using separate dishes for meat and milk products. Only 13 percent did so always/usually. These statistics differed only slightly from those reported by the non-Jewish respondents, among whom 83 percent never used separate dishes, compared to 9 percent who did so always/usually.[78]

Again, the data for the subtypes within the core population point to differences. Fifteen percent of the Jews by religion reported using separate dishes, compared to only 4 percent of the secular Jews. While it is not surprising that 92 percent of the secular Jews did not practice *kashrut*, that 80 percent of the Jews by religion failed to do so points to the high degree of attenuation of this religious tradition. As with candle lighting, Jews by choice reported the highest rate of *kashrut* practice in their households. One in five such households used separate dishes always/usually, and only 59

---

[78]Some non-Jews misunderstood this question to refer to everyday dishes and those used for special occasions.

percent reported never doing so, a high percentage but well below that of the Jews by religion.

A vast majority of households, including entirely Jewish ones, reported never or only sometimes using separate sets of dishes in observance of *kashrut*. Almost four out of every five entirely Jewish units and about 90 percent of the mixed households were in these nonuse categories. Clearly, this aspect of religious behavior is now practiced by only a small minority of Jewish households, undoubtedly largely concentrated among those regarding themselves as Orthodox.[79]

Observing Passover through attendance at a seder has been one of the most common practices reported in community surveys, reflecting both its religious significance and its role in reinforcing family and community linkages. In contrast to Sabbath candle lighting and observance of *kashrut*, NJPS-1990 reveals a fairly strong continuation of seder attendance. It is, however, not nearly as universal as some community studies have reported. Almost 62 percent of the respondents in the core population reported that their households always/usually attended a seder, and another 19 percent did so sometimes. Yet, one in five indicated they never did so, suggesting that a substantial number of Jews forego this family/religious event. Most persons who are no longer Jewish but are of Jewish descent never attend a seder, but that 10 percent reported doing so always/usually and another 14 percent as sometimes suggests that family ties may lead to continued involvement in observance of Passover through seder participation on the part of these non-Jews.

Within the core group, attendance at a seder is highest for Jews by religion, almost three-fourths of whom reported always or usually participating and another 18 percent doing so sometimes. They were followed closely by Jews by choice. However, only a minority of secular Jews attended a seder at least sometimes (44 percent). Evidently, most secular Jews see little value in even observing the humanistic/cultural aspects of the Passover holiday as manifested in the seder.

Seder attendance, like Sabbath candle lighting and *kashrut*, varies by household composition. Whereas 69 percent of the entirely Jewish households were reported as having someone in the household always or usually attending a seder, only 40 percent of the mixed households and far fewer, 8 percent, of the noncore households did so. By contrast, only 14 percent of the entirely Jewish households were reported as having no one attending a seder, compared to almost four in ten of the mixed households and almost eight in ten of those having no core Jews as members.

Hanukkah, like seder attendance, has been noted as one of the mainstays

---

[79]Cf. Goldscheider and Goldstein, *Jewish Community of Rhode Island*.

of Jewish religious practice in the United States today, even though the popular importance attached to it is far out of proportion to its significance religiously, being strongly determined by its location in the secular calendar close to Christmas. Over three times as many respondents (60 percent) reported that Hanukkah candles were always/usually lit in their households as reported lighting Sabbath candles. Like attendance at a seder, observance of Hanukkah serves as an important symbol of Jewish identity. Nonetheless, a not insignificant part of the survey population does not light Hanukkah candles. Among the non-Jewish respondents, the extent of observance of Hanukkah closely resembled that of seder attendance and probably for the same reasons.

Among the core population, the observance of Hanukkah by Jews in the various identity-type categories also closely resembles the patterns already discussed for seder attendance. A large majority (70 percent) of Jews by religion always/usually lit Hanukkah candles, and only 17 percent never did so. These were followed closely by the Jews by choice. Only 16 percent of the households of secular respondents always/usually lit candles, and two-thirds never did so. Evidently, the competition of Christmas is not a major stimulus for manifesting one's Jewishness through Hanukkah candle lighting.

Like attendance at seders, lighting of Hanukkah candles is a popular practice in entirely Jewish households; just under two-thirds reported doing so always or usually. By contrast, only four in ten mixed households did so this frequently. Among households with no core Jews in them, lighting Hanukkah candles occurred regularly among only 8 percent.

Because of the increasingly religiously mixed composition of Jewish households, interest has grown in the extent to which non-Jewish practices have been introduced. Full evaluation of this requires far more in-depth analysis than is possible here. Attention to whether the surveyed households had a Christmas tree provides some initial insights.

The evidence is that this non-Jewish practice has penetrated Jewish households to a considerable degree. While 62 percent of the respondents in the core population reported never having a Christmas tree in their household, 28 percent indicated that they did so always/usually, and another 10 percent said sometimes. Whether they regarded the tree as a religious or as a seasonal symbol was not ascertained. That over one-third of the core households sometimes or always/usually had a Christmas tree is largely explained by the fact that about one-third of the households containing at least one core Jew also included at least one person who was not a core Jew, i.e., someone professing another religion. Given such a composition, the high proportion of households having a Christmas tree is more comprehensible. Not surprisingly, nine out of every ten respondents in the currently non-Jewish group reported having a Christmas tree sometimes, usually, or always.

Some households in each of the Jewish identity categories had a Christmas tree, although the frequency varies. Far fewer of the Jews by religion than of the secular Jews reported having a tree always or usually, and the Jews by choice more closely resembled the Jews by religion. The high proportion of secular Jews having a tree may reflect a high rate of mixed marriage among them. That almost half of the Jews by choice had a Christmas tree suggests that a number continue to observe Christmas in this way even while professing Judaism. This may relate to maintenance of family ties in the same way that a proportion of the Jews who have converted to another religion continue to light Hanukkah candles and to attend a seder. Whether those Jews by choice who have converted to Judaism differ from those who are Jews by choice without conversion with respect to having a tree remains to be determined.

Another perspective for viewing the practice of having a Christmas tree is in terms of household composition. As many as 10 percent of those households composed entirely of Jews reported always or usually having a Christmas tree; two-thirds of the mixed households did so as did about 80 percent of those with no core Jews as members. Given the comparatively high percentage of mixed households that regularly observe Hanukkah, this suggests that many concurrently observe both Hanukkah and Christmas. The data support such an assumption; of the four in ten mixed households that always or usually light Hanukkah candles, two-thirds also always or usually have a Christmas tree. This means that almost 30 percent of all mixed households always or usually have both a Christmas tree and light Hanukkah candles. This finding suggests that mixed religious composition quite often also involves mixed religious practices.

Next to be considered is an individual trait, fasting on Yom Kippur, the holiest day in the Jewish calendar. Of the core Jews, 48 percent reported that they personally did so, and 48 percent did not. The remainder could not for health reasons. The high percentage who did not fast reflects the comparatively low level of traditional behavior within the Jewish community. Among the currently non-Jewish population, 12 percent reported fasting, again suggesting that, like candle lighting and *kashrut*, a small number continue to observe the practices with which they became familiar while being raised in a Jewish environment. Alternatively, it may reflect deference to other members of the household who are Jewish.

Consistent with patterns already noted, fasting was far more common among Jews by religion and Jews by choice than among secular Jews. The secular Jews and the currently non-Jewish respondents were virtually identical in proportion fasting. Clearly, this is a practice very largely restricted to persons identifying themselves as Jewish by religion or choice, although it is not even observed by all the members of these identity groups.

PHILANTHROPY

Still another expression of Jewish identity is represented by charitable donations to Jewish causes. For philanthropy, as for synagogue/temple membership, behavior varied by household composition. Whereas almost two-thirds of the entirely Jewish households contributed to Jewish causes in 1989, only 28 percent of the mixed households and far fewer of the households with no core Jews did so. Interestingly, contributing to Jewish causes on the part of entirely Jewish households ranks high, along with seder attendance and Hanukkah candle lighting, suggesting that philanthropy persists as one of the key channels through which Jewish households express their Jewishness. For mixed households, Jewish philanthropy also ranks higher than such traditional ritual practices as Sabbath candle lighting, but it characterizes only a minority of such households and ranks lower than seder attendance and Hanukkah candle lighting in frequency. We can thus expect that, other things being equal, a growing proportion of mixed households will reduce the aggregate amount of giving to Jewish causes. Contributions to secular charities are much more uniform across all types of households. Two-thirds of both the entirely Jewish and the mixed composition households reported such contributions, as did just over half of the noncore units. This uniformity in secular philanthropy reenforces the significance of the differentials observed for contributions to Jewish causes.

ORGANIZATIONAL MEMBERSHIP

Identity can also express itself through participation in the organized life of the larger community, such as synagogues/temples and Jewish organizations. Respondents were asked whether they or any members of their household belonged to a synagogue or temple. Only one-third of those in the Jewish core population reported such membership. Among those respondents outside the core, only 3 percent did. Within the core group, membership was highest (56 percent) among households in which the respondent was a Jew by choice and virtually nonexistent among secular Jews. Just over one-third of the households represented by a Jew by religion belonged to a synagogue. Not surprisingly, over three times as many households composed entirely of Jews held synagogue membership as did mixed households. Data not shown here indicate that affiliated households are larger than average, suggesting a life-cycle pattern of membership wherein households with children of school age are more likely to be affiliated in order to enable their children to enroll in programs of Jewish education.[80] Such a relation evidently does not characterize a high proportion of the mixed households. How to attract their Jewish members and especially their children remains a major challenge for the community.

Membership in Jewish organizations other than a synagogue/temple is another way to express one's Jewish identity. Yet 72 percent of the respondents in the core population indicated that they were not members of any Jewish organization, and only 13 percent belonged to two or more groups. Membership in Jewish organizations was even lower among noncore respondents; only 5 percent belonged, and most of these held membership in only one group. Once again, Jews by religion and Jews by choice closely resembled each other. Although about two-thirds of both groups did not belong to any Jewish organization, somewhat more of the Jews by choice were active, reiterating earlier findings that being a Jew by choice is associated with more intense manifestation of Jewishness. In sharp contrast, secular Jews had very low affiliation rates, with only 8 percent belonging to a group.

ISRAEL VISITS

The final indicator examined here is the number of times the respondent had visited Israel. One quarter of the core respondents had been to Israel, 15 percent once and 12 percent twice. Far fewer of the noncore respondents, only 6 percent, had visited Israel. Identifying as a Jew by religion is associated with a higher rate of visiting Israel (31 percent) than is being a secular Jew or a Jew by choice (11 percent each). Aside from differences in degree of identification with Israel, the higher rate among Jews by religion may be partially explained by the popularity of organized trips to Israel for teens, in which they would have been most eligible to participate as members of synagogue/temple youth groups. This is the single index of Jewishness in which the Jews by choice more closely resemble the secular Jews than the Jews by religion and one of the few on which they have the lowest "score," although their ranking is closely shared with the secular Jews.

Overall, what do these indicators tell us about Jewish practices and affiliation in America? First, it must be stressed again that the comparisons undertaken here are superficial, not having taken account of a host of background variables that could affect the outcomes. Such analyses will have to await fuller exploitation of the rich data available in NJPS-1990. Within these limitations, the data seem to point to several conclusions. The

---

[80]Kosmin et al., *Highlights*, p. 37.

overall level of Jewish identity as manifested in ritual practice, organization membership, and ties to Israel is comparatively low for the core population and much lower still for those of Jewish descent who do not profess to be currently Jewish. It is considerably higher for entirely Jewish households than for households of mixed composition. To the extent that the latter may be a growing group because of increasing numbers of mixed marriages and the very large reservoir of children of such marriages who are not being raised as Jews, levels of nonobservance and nonmembership may rise in the future.

If observance and involvement are important mechanisms for maintaining the strength of individual identity and integration with the larger community, then, even for many core Jews, the reinforcement and the links are weak. It may well be that other mechanisms for maintaining identity and integration are replacing the traditional ones.[81] Some of these, such as social affinity through work and friendship with other Jews, can and will be measured through NJPS-1990 data. Whether they are sufficient to serve as substitutes for traditional practices and more formal involvement with the community remains to be tested.

CONCLUSION

At the heart of the findings of NJPS-1990 is the fluid character of the American Jewish community. The broad net intentionally built into the design of NJPS in its effort to identify all types of Jews in America has shown that we are constituted of different Jewish populations for different purposes, that we need to think of ourselves not so much in total numbers but in terms of who and what we are and whom the community is serving.

We consist of a central core made up of persons identifying themselves as either Jews by religion or as secular Jews, many of whom live in entirely Jewish households. Yet even within this core group wide differences exist in socioeconomic characteristics and Jewish practices. In addition, a substantial number of Jews are married to non-Jews. Still others, because of earlier family histories of intermarriage, qualify as Jewish only by descent, either having been born to a Jewish parent but not raised Jewish or having chosen to adopt another religion as a corollary of intermarriage. Forming the outer ring are Gentiles, who, though never Jewish through parentage or socialization, are members of households composed partially of current or former Jews and in this way may be affected by their exposure to Jewish values and practices and by worldwide events that have relevance for the

---

[81]Goldscheider, *Jewish Continuity and Change*.

Jewish community. In short, there is no one Jewish population in America today. From both a demographic and a planning perspective, how many we are and who we are depends on who we count as in or out, and this depends, in turn, on what our goals are—to identify the basic core, to reach out to those on the margins, to make concerted efforts to attract those still confronting choices as to who they should be.

The differences observed in both socioeconomic composition and behavioral indicators among the different categories of Jews identified by NJPS-1990 seem to justify the distinctions made by the classification system adopted for the analysis. Jews by religion are more traditional and involved in their community; Jews by choice more closely resemble those who are Jews by religion; the secularists operate closer to the margins of traditional behavior. In fact, for most indicators, Jews by choice tend to be the most observant and the most involved. In view of the high rates of intermarriage, this finding suggests that "conversion" of the non-Jewish partner should enhance the Jewish component of family life and possibly even raise the overall level of observance in the community.

Major challenges face the community as a result of the high rates of intermarriage, the persistence of low fertility, the greater dispersal of the population, comparatively high rates of marital instability, the evidence of growing secularism, the loss of the more traditional members through aging and death, and growing Americanization. Yet, there are also signals of potential for continued strength as American Jews continue their efforts to find a meaningful balance between being American and being Jewish.

The demographic base of the Jewish population seems to have reached a plateau and may well decline in future years. Only if the mixed-married and especially their children, as well as the substantial number who are secular, can be retained or brought back into the core and their ties to Judaism and the Jewish people strengthened can our numbers grow. As I have argued before,[82] the potential for continued vitality remains. Stability of numbers, or even declining numbers, need not constitute a fundamental threat to the maintenance of a strong Jewish community and to high levels of identity, although the impact of size is clearly more relevant on the local than national level because of the need for sufficient Jewish population density to allow a vital Jewish communal life. What is most important both nationally and locally is that the community be willing to develop new institutional forms designed to mitigate the negative effects of population decline and dispersal and the growing numbers of mixed households. These must provide increasing opportunities for Jewish self-identification and for greater participation of individuals in organized Jewish life, regardless of

---

[82]Goldstein, "Jews in the United States."

whether they live in large or small communities or whether they are in entirely Jewish or in mixed households. Jews will surely become increasingly American in the years ahead. The question is whether the Jewish community will enhance the opportunities and means for them to remain Jewish and possibly facilitate a more intensive identification with their Jewishness.

APPENDIX

TABLE 1. JEWISH POPULATION, BY JEWISH IDENTITY

Jewish Identity	Number	Percent of Core Jewish Population	Distribution of Total Pop. in Qualified Households
Jews by Religion[a]	4,210,000	76.3	51.4
Secular Jews	1,120,000	20.3	13.7
Jews by Choice	185,000	3.4	2.3
Core Jewish Population	5,515,000	100.0	
Converts Out	210,000		2.6
Jewish Descent/ Other Religion	415,000		5.0
Children under 18 being raised in other religion	700,000		8.5
Gentiles	1,350,000		16.5
Total population	8,190,000		100.0

[a]Includes 100,000 institutionalized and unenumerated persons.

Note: In this and all subsequent tables the following definitions are used: The Core Jewish Population consists of (1) persons born Jewish and identified as being Jewish by religion (Jews by Religion); (2) persons born Jewish reporting no current religious identity (Secular Jews); and (3) those born non-Jews but identified as Jewish by religion—whether converted or not (Jews by Choice). Non-Jewish Household Members include (1) persons born/raised Jewish reporting adherence to another religion (Converts Out); (2) persons with Jewish parent(s) brought up in and reporting other religious identity (Jewish Descent/Other Religion); (3) those born in and reporting another religion (Gentiles); and (4) children under age 18 who have a "qualified Jew" as a parent, i.e., one currently Jewish or of Jewish descent, but who are being raised in a non-Jewish religion.

TABLE 2. THE JEWISH POPULATION IN THE UNITED STATES, 1970 AND 1990

Population	1970	1990	Percent Change
Total population in Jewish households	5,850,000[a]	8,200,000[b]	+40.2
Total Jews: currently Jewish and Jewish background	5,480,000	6,840,000[c]	+24.8
Total core Jews: currently Jewish religion/identification	5,420,000	5,515,000	+1.8
Number of households with one or more Jews	1,950,000	3,186,000	+63.4
U.S. resident population	203,211,000	248,710,000	+22.4
U.S. households	63,449,000	91,947,000	+44.9
Jews as a percent of U.S. population			
Total population in Jewish HH	2.9	3.3	
Total Jews	2.7	2.7	
Total core Jews	2.7	2.2	
Average household size			
Total households with Jews	3.0	2.6	
Entirely core Jewish households	NA	2.2	
Mixed households	NA	3.2	
Households with no core Jews	NA	2.7	
Total U.S. households	3.1	2.7	

[a]Includes 50,000 institutionalized population.
[b]Includes 100,000 institutionalized and unenumerated population.
[c]Includes 700,000 children under age 18 of Jewish descent who are currently not being raised as Jews.

TABLE 3. REGION OF RESIDENCE OF POPULATION, BY JEWISH IDENTITY (PERCENT)

a. Percent Distribution by Region

Region	Core Jewish Population				Total U.S. White Population
	By Religion	Secular	By Choice	Total	
Northeast	47.8	30.4	30.4	43.6	21.1
Midwest	10.8	12.7	13.5	11.3	26.1
South	21.7	20.4	27.9	21.6	32.8
West	19.7	36.6	28.2	23.5	20.0
Total percent	100.0	100.0	100.0	100.0	100.0
Total number (in millions)	4.10	1.12	0.18	5.40	199.7

Region	Non-Jewish Household Members			
	Converts Out	Jewish Descent/ Other Rel.[a]	Gentiles	Total
Northeast	25.2	28.4	36.6	32.3
Midwest	22.6	14.7	13.8	14.9
South	31.0	29.8	23.8	26.9
West	21.2	27.1	25.8	26.0
Total percent	100.0	100.0	100.0	100.0
Total number (in millions)	0.21	1.12	1.35	2.68

TABLE 3.—(Continued)

b. Percent Distribution by Jewish Identity

	Core Jewish Population			Non-Jewish Household Members				Total Number
Region	By Religion	Secular	By Choice	Converts Out	Jewish Descent/ Other Rel.[a]	Gentiles	Total Percent	(in mill.)
Northeast	60.8	10.6	1.7	1.7	9.8	15.4	100.0	3.22
Midwest	43.9	14.1	2.5	4.8	16.3	18.5	100.0	1.01
South	47.1	12.7	2.7	3.5	17.6	17.0	100.0	1.89
West	41.1	20.8	2.6	2.3	15.5	17.7	100.0	1.96
Total	50.7	13.9	2.3	2.7	13.8	16.7	100.0	8.08

[a]Includes 700,000 children under age 18 of Jewish descent being raised in another religion.
Note: On this and subsequent tables, percentages or numbers may not always add to totals, due to rounding.

TABLE 4. METROPOLITAN/NONMETROPOLITAN RESIDENCE[a] OF POPULATION, BY JEWISH IDENTITY (PERCENT)

a. Distribution by Metro/Nonmetro Residence

| Residence | Core Jewish Population | | | |
	By Religion	Secular	By Choice	Total
Metropolitan	79.1	65.0	58.6	75.4
Nonmetropolitan 150,000+	15.2	22.2	26.2	17.0
Nonmetropolitan 40–150,000	3.5	8.8	10.1	4.9
Nonmetropolitan under 40,000	2.2	4.0	5.1	2.7
Total percent	100.0	100.0	100.0	100.0

| Residence | Non-Jewish Household Members | | | |
	Converts Out	Jewish Descent/ Other Rel.[b]	Gentiles	Total
Metropolitan	58.2	55.7	64.8	60.4
Nonmetropolitan 150,000+	26.1	26.9	21.3	24.0
Nonmetropolitan 40–150,000	5.6	9.5	8.0	8.5
Nonmetropolitan under 40,000	10.1	7.9	5.9	7.1
Total percent	100.0	100.0	100.0	100.0

TABLE 4.—*(Continued)*

b. Distribution by Jewish Identity

	Core Jewish Population				
Residence	By Religion	Secular	By Choice	Total	Number (in millions)
Metropolitan	79.1	18.3	2.6	100.0	3.76
Nonmetropolitan 150,000+	67.2	27.7	5.1	100.0	0.85
Nonmetropolitan 40–150,000	54.6	38.4	7.0	100.0	0.24
Nonmetropolitan under 40,000	62.0	31.7	6.3	100.0	0.13
Total	75.4	21.3	3.3	100.0	4.99

	All Household Members					
Residence	Current Religion Jewish	Secular Jews	Jews by Choice	Non-Jewish Members	Total	Number (in millions)
Metropolitan	56.1	13.0	1.8	29.1	100.0	5.31
Nonmetropolitan 150,000+	39.0	16.0	3.0	42.0	100.0	1.46
Nonmetropolitan 40–150,000	28.8	20.2	3.7	47.3	100.0	0.46
Nonmetropolitan under 40,000	26.4	13.5	2.7	57.4	100.0	0.31
Total	49.8	14.0	2.2	33.9	100.0	7.55

[a]Metropolitan area residents are those who live in a county that lies within a metropolitan area. Residents of nonmetropolitan areas are persons living in counties that are not in metropolitan areas; the population size refers to the number of residents of the given counties.
[b]Includes 700,000 children under age 18 of Jewish descent being raised in another religion.

TABLE 5.   FIVE-YEAR MIGRATION STATUS OF ADULTS, BY JEWISH IDENTITY (PERCENT)

Migration Status	Core Jewish Population				U.S. White Pop. Mobility 1980-85[a]
	By Religion	Secular	By Choice	Total Jews	
Same house	60.5	44.0	52.5	57.1	58.7
Diff. house/ same local area	19.2	24.0	21.2	20.1	21.4
Intrastate	9.4	18.2	13.1	11.2	9.3
Interstate	10.0	12.4	10.8	10.5	8.7
International	0.9	1.4	2.5	1.1	1.8
Total percent	100.0	100.0	100.0	100.0	100.0
Total number (in millions)	3.16	0.76	0.17	4.09	171.37

Migration Status	Non-Jewish Household Members			
	Converts Out	Jewish Descent/ Other Rel.	Gentiles	Total Non-Jews
Same house	61.1	48.3	46.2	48.3
Diff. house/ same local area	22.2	27.8	24.2	24.8
Intrastate	11.4	9.9	15.1	13.6
Interstate	4.6	13.5	13.2	12.3
International	0.7	0.5	1.3	1.1
Total percent	100.0	100.0	100.0	100.0
Total number (in millions)	0.20	0.41	1.28	1.89

[a]*Source:* U.S. Bureau of the Census, 1987.

TABLE 6. LIFETIME MIGRATION STATUS OF ADULTS, BY JEWISH IDENTITY
         (PERCENT)

Migration Status	Core Jewish Population			Total Jews
	By Religion	Secular	By Choice	
Same house	2.0	2.6	2.3	2.1
Diff. house/ same local area	18.3	14.0	10.7	17.2
Intrastate	24.8	22.2	22.7	24.2
Interstate	44.0	51.8	58.4	46.1
International	10.9	9.4	6.0	10.4
Total percent	100.0	100.0	100.0	100.0
Total number (in millions)	3.18	0.77	0.17	4.12

Migration Status	Non-Jewish Household Members			Total Non-Jews
	Converts Out	Jewish Descent/ Other Rel.	Gentiles	
Same house	0.5	3.3	2.9	2.7
Diff. house/ same local area	19.7	10.6	13.8	13.7
Intrastate	30.1	32.8	29.5	30.2
Interstate	41.7	44.9	44.3	44.2
International	8.0	8.4	9.5	9.1
Total percent	100.0	100.0	100.0	100.0
Total number (in millions)	0.20	0.41	1.29	1.90

TABLE 7. FIVE-YEAR MIGRATION STATUS OF CORE JEWISH ADULTS, BY AGE (PERCENT)

Migration Status	Age Group				
	18–24	25–34	35–44	45–64	65 & Over
Same house	54.3	21.0	48.6	73.1	82.7
Diff. house/ same local area	17.3	33.0	26.9	14.3	9.1
Intrastate	16.5	21.3	12.8	5.7	3.9
Interstate	11.5	22.1	10.4	6.2	4.1
International	0.3	2.6	1.4	0.7	0.1
Total percent	100.0	100.0	100.0	100.0	100.0
Total number (in millions)	0.42	0.84	0.92	1.02	0.90

TABLE 8. REGION OF 1990 RESIDENCE, BY REGION OF BIRTH AND INTERREGIONAL LIFETIME MIGRATION, U.S.-BORN POPULATION, CORE JEWS AND NON-JEWISH HOUSEHOLD MEMBERS

Region of Birth	Region of Residence					Distribution by Region of Birth
	Northeast	Midwest	South	West	Total	
	Core Jewish Population					
	Percent Distribution of Total Population					
Northeast	69.7	2.9	17.2	10.2	100.0	59.9
Midwest	6.9	57.6	13.3	22.2	100.0	24.0
South	11.5	4.0	76.8	7.7	100.0	9.6
West	5.9	1.8	5.4	86.9	100.0	6.5
	Percent Distribution of Outmigrants					
Northeast	—	9.7	56.7	33.6	100.0	
Midwest	16.2	—	31.4	52.4	100.0	
South	49.5	17.2	—	33.3	100.0	
West	45.3	13.6	41.1	—	100.0	
Total	11.6	8.4	44.2	35.8		100.0

TABLE 8.—*(Continued)*

Region of Birth	Region of Residence				Total	Distribution by Region of Birth
	Northeast	Midwest	South	West		
	Interregional Lifetime Migration					
Total inmigration	+161,930	+116,970	+618,330	+501,860		
Total outmigration	−838,500	−335,860	−133,570	−91,160		
Net migration	−676,570	−218,890	+484,760	+410,700		
Northeast	—	+27,040	+409,310	+240,220		
Midwest	−27,040	—	+82,440	+163,490		
South	−409,310	−82,440	—	+6,990		
West	−240,220	−163,490	−6,990	—		
	Non-Jewish Household Members					
	Percent Distribution of Total Population					
Northeast	76.1	3.7	15.2	5.0	100.0	
Midwest	7.3	57.2	15.5	19.9	100.0	
South	7.6	8.8	71.7	12.0	100.0	
West	4.1	3.0	6.8	86.1	100.0	
	Percent Distribution of Outmigrants					
Northeast	—	15.3	63.7	21.0	100.0	32.7
Midwest	17.1	—	36.4	46.5	100.0	32.2
South	26.7	31.1	—	42.2	100.0	24.7
West	29.6	21.5	48.9	—	100.0	10.4
Total	15.2	14.9	37.6	32.3		100.0

TABLE 8.—(Continued)

Region of Birth	Region of Residence				Total	Distribution by Region of Birth
	Northeast	Midwest	South	West		
	Interregional Lifetime Migration					
Total inmigration	+99,070	+97,630	+245,840	+211,010		
Total outmigration	−213,970	−210,220	−161,660	−67,700		
Net migration	−114,900	−112,590	+84,180	+143,310		
Northeast	—	−3,150	+93,160	+24,890		
Midwest	+3,150	—	+26,110	+83,330		
South	−93,160	−26,110	—	+35,090		
West	−24,890	−83,330	−35,090	—		

TABLE 9. AGE COMPOSITION, BY JEWISH IDENTITY (PERCENT)

| Current Age | Core Jewish Population | | | | Total U.S. White Population |
	By Religion	Secular	By Choice	Total	
0–14	18.3	23.9	4.5	19.0	20.7
15–24	9.5	16.3	7.3	10.9	14.2
25–34	15.0	19.9	18.0	16.1	17.6
35–44	16.8	17.0	33.1	17.4	14.9
45–64	20.0	16.2	26.9	19.5	19.3
65 & over	20.4	6.6	10.2	17.2	13.3
Total percent	100.0	100.0	100.0	100.0	100.0
Median age	39.3	29.9	41.1	37.3	33.6

| Current Age | Non-Jewish Household Members | | | |
	Converts Out	Jewish Descent/ Other Rel.[a]	Gentiles	Total
0–14	—	55.7	—	23.2
15–24	8.6	11.5	16.1	13.6
25–34	19.3	9.6	28.3	19.8
35–44	28.8	11.0	26.2	20.1
45–64	31.8	7.4	21.6	16.5
65 & over	11.7	4.7	7.8	6.8
Total percent	100.0	100.0	100.0	100.0
Median age	42.7	13.5	37.1	31.7

[a]Includes 700,000 children under age 18 of Jewish descent being raised in another religion.

TABLE 10.   SEX RATIOS[a], BY AGE AND JEWISH IDENTITY

Age Group	Core Jewish Population				Total U.S. White Population
	By Religion	Secular	By Choice	Total	
0–14	113.3	87.1	118.8	106.2	105.4
15–24	105.7	95.5	40.9	100.4	102.8
25–44	99.4	113.4	41.3	98.1	101.0
45–64	99.5	96.2	32.1	94.3	93.8
65 & over	91.0	140.0	342.6	96.5	68.9
Total	100.6	102.2	52.6	98.8	95.8

Age Group	Non-Jewish Household Members			
	Converts Out	Jewish Descent/ Other Rel.[c]	Gentiles	Total
0–14	b	112.7	—	112.7
15–24	176.8	110.4	84.6	96.4
25–44	68.6	81.4	100.6	92.7
45–64	39.3	60.4	114.6	87.3
65 & over	60.7	48.2	140.0	91.8
Total	62.2	96.6	103.1	96.5

[a]Number of males per 100 females.
[b]All females.
[c]Includes 700,000 children under age 18 of Jewish descent being raised in another religion.

TABLE 11. GENERATION STATUS: PERCENT OF GRANDPARENTS BORN IN U.S., BY AGE AND JEWISH IDENTITY, AND AVERAGE NUMBER OF U.S.-BORN GRANDPARENTS

a. Percent U.S.-Born Grandparents

Age Group	Core Jewish Population							
	By Religion		Secular		By Choice		Total	
	None	All	None	All	None	All	None	All
18–24	27.1	33.7	12.7	51.0	—	59.6	22.5	39.1
25–44	53.5	12.8	25.3	31.6	18.8	38.6	45.6	18.2
45–64	85.0	3.7	62.0	17.0	27.9	48.2	78.4	8.1
65 & over	95.8	1.1	88.7	4.2	41.7	33.4	94.3	2.0
All ages	70.0	9.3	38.3	28.4	22.6	42.3	12.5	14.1

Age Group	Non-Jewish Household Members							
	Converts Out		Jewish Descent/ Other Religion		Gentiles		Total	
	None	All	None	All	None	All	None	All
18–24	27.4	62.8	7.5	44.5	17.4	57.3	16.3	55.3
25–44	22.4	34.2	21.4	45.9	28.5	51.4	26.2	48.3
45–64	35.1	17.7	21.3	37.4	48.9	37.8	40.7	34.8
65 & over	51.7	33.4	20.3	62.0	55.4	40.0	44.2	45.6
All ages	30.0	32.4	19.6	45.8	33.0	48.7	29.5	46.2

TABLE 11.—(*Continued*)

b. Average Number of U.S.-Born Grandparents

Age Group	Core Jewish Population			
	By Religion	Secular	By Choice	Total
18–24	2.16	2.87	3.52	2.39
25–44	1.12	2.08	2.37	1.39
45–64	0.34	1.05	2.44	0.56
65 & over	0.89	0.31	2.08	0.14
All ages	0.75	1.78	2.44	1.00

Age Group	Non-Jewish Household Members			
	Converts Out	Jewish Descent/ Other Rel.	Gentiles	Total
18–24	2.71	2.93	2.83	2.84
25–44	2.09	2.49	2.46	2.43
45–64	1.66	2.28	1.80	1.89
65 & over	1.63	2.75	1.72	2.02
All ages	1.98	2.52	2.33	2.33

TABLE 12A.   EDUCATIONAL ACHIEVEMENT, BY JEWISH IDENTITY, ALL ADULTS
AGE 25 AND OVER (PERCENT)

| Education | Core Jewish Population | | | | Total U.S. White Population[a] |
	By Religion	Secular	By Choice	Total	
High school or less	28.5	25.1	21.9	27.7	62.2
Some college	18.7	21.5	20.3	19.3	17.3
College completed	26.8	25.0	29.6	26.7	11.8
Graduate studies	25.9	28.4	28.2	26.4	8.7
Total percent	100.0	100.0	100.0	100.0	100.0
Total number (in millions)	2.67	0.56	0.13	3.36	129.17

| Education | Non-Jewish Household Members | | | |
	Converts Out	Jewish Descent/ Other Rel.	Gentiles	Total
High school or less	42.7	48.8	44.5	45.2
Some college	29.6	22.2	17.6	20.0
College completed	15.3	15.1	23.8	20.9
Graduate studies	12.4	13.9	14.1	13.8
Total percent	100.0	100.0	100.0	100.0
Total number (in millions)	0.17	0.32	1.00	1.46

[a]*Source:* U.S. Bureau of the Census, Aug. 1988, table 2.

TABLE 12B. EDUCATIONAL ACHIEVEMENT, BY JEWISH IDENTITY, ALL ADULTS AGES 30–39 (PERCENT)

Education	Core Jewish Population				Total U.S. White Population[a]
	By Religion	Secular	By Choice	Total	
High school or less	12.6	19.9	10.2	14.0	50.8
Some college	16.7	29.3	29.4	20.0	21.8
College completed	34.5	26.1	32.3	32.7	16.2
Graduate studies	36.2	24.7	28.0	33.4	11.2
Total percent	100.0	100.0	100.0	100.0	100.0
Total number (in millions)	0.59	0.16	0.05	0.81	33.60

Education	Non-Jewish Household Members			
	Converts Out	Jewish Descent/ Other Rel.	Gentiles	Total
High school or less	27.6	33.7	32.3	32.1
Some college	33.6	30.3	22.3	25.3
College completed	20.3	21.8	26.7	24.9
Graduate studies	18.4	14.2	18.7	17.7
Total percent	100.0	100.0	100.0	100.0
Total number (in millions)	0.06	0.10	0.33	0.49

[a]*Source:* U.S. Bureau of the Census, Aug. 1988, table 2.

TABLE 13. EDUCATIONAL ACHIEVEMENT, BY JEWISH IDENTITY, MEN AND WOMEN AGES 30–39 (PERCENT)

Education	Core Jewish Population				Non-Jewish Household Members				Total U.S. White Pop.[a]
	By Religion	Secular	By Choice	Total	Converts Out	Jewish Descent/ Other Religion	Gentiles	Total	
					Males				
High school or less	12.4	16.6	10.6	13.2	18.4	36.9	38.2	35.9	47.9
Some college	14.5	26.2	32.2	17.8	22.6	23.1	20.5	21.2	21.5
College completed	33.2	26.5	32.0	31.7	44.8	23.0	27.3	28.3	17.5
Graduate studies	39.9	30.7	25.2	37.3	14.2	17.0	14.0	14.6	13.1
Total percent	100.0	100.0	100.0	100.0	100.0	100.0	100.0	100.0	100.0
Total number (in thousands)	296	83	18	397	24	43	161	228	16,841
					Females				
High school or less	12.8	23.3	10.0	14.7	34.5	31.5	26.9	28.9	53.8
Some college	18.9	32.4	27.7	22.2	41.7	35.5	24.0	28.7	22.0
College completed	35.8	25.8	32.6	33.6	2.3	20.9	26.1	22.0	14.9
Graduate studies	32.5	18.5	29.7	29.5	21.5	12.1	23.0	20.4	9.3
Total percent	100.0	100.0	100.0	100.0	100.0	100.0	100.0	100.0	100.0
Total number (in thousands)	297	80	31	408	32	59	173	264	16,760

a*Source:* U.S. Bureau of the Census, Aug. 1988, table 2.

TABLE 14. OCCUPATIONAL DISTRIBUTION, BY JEWISH IDENTITY AND SEX, POPULATION AGE 18 AND OLDER (PERCENT)

| Occupation | Core Jewish Population | | | | U.S. White Population[a] |
	By Religion	Secular	By Choice	Total	
			Males		
Professionals	38.8	40.1	36.7	39.0	15.8
Managers	17.8	11.8	20.2	16.7	14.3
Clerical/sales	25.7	20.5	15.5	24.4	17.5
Crafts	7.6	11.7	11.1	8.5	19.8
Operatives	5.3	9.8	11.6	6.4	19.6
Service	4.7	6.1	4.9	5.0	8.9
Agriculture	—	—	—	—	4.2
Total percent	100.0	100.0	100.0	100.0	100.0
Total number (in millions)	1.47	0.37	0.05	1.89	55.78
			Females		
Professionals	34.7	39.8	43.6	36.1	15.2
Managers	13.4	9.6	18.0	13.0	16.0
Clerical/sales	42.9	37.5	27.5	41.1	41.3
Crafts	1.7	2.0	1.3	1.8	2.2
Operatives	1.4	4.1	1.1	1.8	7.8
Service	5.8	7.1	8.5	6.2	16.5
Agriculture	—	—	—	—	0.9
Total percent	100.0	100.0	100.0	100.0	100.0
Total number (in millions)	1.51	0.36	0.11	1.98	45.73

TABLE 14.—*(Continued)*

| Occupation | Non-Jewish Household Members | | | |
	Converts Out	Jewish Descent/ Other Rel.	Gentiles	Total Non-Jews
		Males		
Professionals	20.2	31.9	27.3	27.5
Managers	9.5	10.4	13.2	12.3
Clerical/sales	12.5	20.5	15.6	16.2
Crafts	22.2	20.8	15.8	17.3
Operatives	18.1	9.7	16.4	15.3
Service	14.3	6.7	10.9	10.4
Agriculture	3.1	—	0.9	1.0
Total percent	100.0	100.0	100.0	100.0
Total number (in millions)	0.08	0.16	0.62	0.85
		Females		
Professionals	21.2	22.7	31.7	28.2
Managers	17.0	11.7	12.2	12.7
Clerical/sales	37.2	35.8	30.7	32.8
Crafts	2.8	1.3	5.1	3.9
Operatives	10.2	15.3	4.4	7.7
Service	11.6	13.3	16.0	14.8
Agriculture	—	—	—	—
Total percent	100.0	100.0	100.0	100.0
Total number (in millions)	0.12	0.23	0.59	0.93

aSource: U.S. Department of Labor, Jan. 1991, table 823.

TABLE 15.   MARITAL STATUS OF THE ADULT CORE JEWISH POPULATION BY AGE
AND SEX; AND PERCENT NEVER MARRIED BY JEWISH IDENTITY

	Marital Status					U.S. White Pop. Percent Never Married[a]
Age	Never Married	Married	Divorced/ Separated	Widowed	Total	
			Core Jewish Males			
18–24	96.2	2.8	1.0	—	100.0	83.0
25–34	49.5	46.5	4.0	—	100.0	33.7
35–44	17.4	72.5	9.2	0.9	100.0	11.7
45–64	7.4	80.8	9.4	2.4	100.0	5.3
65 & over	3.1	82.1	3.4	11.3	100.0	4.0
All ages	26.4	64.2	6.1	3.3	100.0	24.1
U.S. white	24.1	66.2	7.2	2.6	100.0	
			Core Jewish Females			
18–24	85.4	11.7	2.9	—	100.0	68.2
25–34	31.2	60.9	7.2	0.8	100.0	20.4
35–44	11.4	74.3	13.8	0.5	100.0	7.2
45–64	4.5	72.9	14.9	7.7	100.0	4.0
65 & over	1.6	56.7	4.0	37.7	100.0	4.9
All ages	19.6	63.7	9.6	7.1	100.0	16.9
U.S. White	16.9	61.9	9.0	12.2	100.0	

	Percent Never Married					
	Core Jewish Males			Core Jewish Females		
Age	By Religion	Secular	By Choice	By Religion	Secular	By Choice
18–24	97.3	93.6	100.0	89.9	74.4	42.0
25–34	51.0	47.0	19.4	31.4	32.8	22.1
35–44	17.6	16.8	17.4	11.4	11.5	11.1
45–64	7.3	8.9	—	4.5	6.6	—
65 & over	3.2	3.8	—	1.7	—	—
All ages	24.8	34.4	13.7	17.9	27.4	15.4

[a]*Source:* U.S. Bureau of the Census, May 1991, table 1.

TABLE 16. AVERAGE AGE AT FIRST MARRIAGE BY CURRENT AGE, SEX, AND
JEWISH IDENTITY, POPULATION AGE 18 AND OVER

Age	Core Jewish Population			
	By Religion	Secular	By Choice	Total
		Males		
18–24	19.7	21.4	—	20.6
25–34	25.6	24.3	24.9	25.2
35–44	26.3	25.3	24.5	26.0
45–64	25.9	25.4	26.4	25.8
65 & over	27.0	25.5	25.0	26.8
All ages	26.3	25.0	25.2	26.0
		Females		
18–24	20.5	20.3	—	20.4
25–34	23.0	23.1	23.6	23.1
35–44	24.4	23.7	23.2	24.2
45–64	21.9	21.8	24.3	22.0
65 & over	24.3	22.4	25.0	24.2
All ages	23.4	22.6	23.8	23.3

TABLE 16.—*(Continued)*

Age	Non-Jewish Household Members			
	Converts Out	Jewish Descent/ Other Rel.	Gentiles	Total
		Males		
18–24	21.0	21.1	20.9	20.9
25–34	22.5	22.5	24.2	23.8
35–44	26.7	25.0	26.9	26.4
45–64	25.4	23.7	25.4	25.1
65 & over	25.4	24.7	31.0	28.6
All ages	25.0	24.0	25.9	25.4
		Females		
18–24	17.8	19.6	18.6	18.8
25–34	20.6	21.5	23.8	22.9
35–44	21.8	22.6	24.1	23.4
45–64	19.8	20.7	23.6	21.9
65 & over	21.3	21.4	21.3	21.3
All ages	20.6	21.5	23.4	22.5

TABLE 17. NUMBER OF MARRIAGES, BY AGE, SEX, AND JEWISH IDENTITY (PERCENT)

Age	Number of Marriages			Total Percent	Number of Marriages			Total Percent
	1	2	3+		1	2	3+	
		Males				Females		
				Total Core Jewish Population				
18–24	100.0	—	—	100.0	100.0	—	—	100.0
25–34	97.6	2.4	—	100.0	92.6	6.5	0.9	100.0
35–44	81.5	16.4	2.1	100.0	82.5	14.8	2.7	100.0
45–64	78.5	20.1	1.4	100.0	84.3	13.9	1.7	100.0
65 & over	83.0	11.6	5.4	100.0	90.1	8.9	1.0	100.0
Total	83.5	14.0	2.5	100.0	87.2	11.2	1.6	100.0
				Jews by Religion				
18–24	100.0	—	—	100.0	100.0	—	—	100.0
25–34	98.0	2.0	—	100.0	92.1	6.5	1.4	100.0
35–44	85.8	13.7	0.5	100.0	85.6	12.4	2.0	100.0
45–64	83.0	15.2	1.8	100.0	84.5	13.8	1.7	100.0
65 & over	83.9	10.9	5.2	100.0	89.5	9.6	1.0	100.0
Total	86.0	11.7	2.4	100.0	87.7	10.8	1.5	100.0
				Secular Jews				
18–24	100.0	—	—	100.0	100.0	—	—	100.0
25–34	96.6	3.4	—	100.0	92.8	7.2	—	100.0
35–44	68.7	24.6	6.7	100.0	69.2	26.5	4.5	100.0
45–64	63.2	36.8	—	100.0	82.1	15.2	2.6	100.0
65 & over	84.3	6.7	9.0	100.0	100.0	—	—	100.0
Total	76.3	20.0	3.6	100.0	84.6	13.5	1.9	100.0

TABLE 17.—*(Continued)*

Age	Number of Marriages			Total Percent	Number of Marriages			Total Percent
	1	2	3+		1	2	3+	
	Males				Females			
	Jews by Choice							
18–24	—	—	—	—	—	—	—	—
25–34	100.0	—	—	100.0	96.2	3.8	—	100.0
35–44	80.5	17.3	2.2	100.0	31.3	11.9	5.7	100.0
45–64	30.9	69.1	—	100.0	87.5	12.5	—	100.0
65 & over	54.8	45.2	—	100.0	100.0	—	—	100.0
Total	61.8	37.4	0.8	100.0	88.3	9.8	1.9	100.0
	Total Non-Jewish Household Members							
18–24	100.0	—	—	100.0	100.0	—	—	100.0
25–34	89.9	10.1	—	100.0	88.6	11.0	0.3	100.0
35–44	76.4	17.2	6.4	100.0	76.4	19.2	4.5	100.0
45–64	75.5	19.4	5.1	100.0	72.4	21.3	6.3	100.0
65 & over	84.1	10.1	5.8	100.0	63.5	32.9	3.5	100.0
Total	81.6	14.4	4.1	100.0	79.1	17.5	3.5	100.0

TABLE 18. AVERAGE NUMBER OF CHILDREN EVER BORN PER WOMAN, BY AGE
AND JEWISH IDENTITY

| | Core Jewish Population | | | | |
Age	By Religion	Secular	By Choice	Total	Total U.S. White Women[a]
15–19	0.0	0.0	0.0	0.0	0.1
20–24	0.2	0.5	0.4	0.3	0.4
25–29	0.5	0.6	1.1	0.5	1.0
30–34	1.2	0.9	1.3	1.1	1.5
35–39	1.5	1.3	1.5	1.5	1.9
40–44	1.6	1.6	1.9	1.6	2.1
45–49	1.9	1.7	2.3	1.9	2.3
50–54	2.1	2.6	2.5	2.2	2.8
55–59	2.7	2.5	2.7	2.6	3.0
60–64	2.2	2.1	1.4	2.2	2.9
65 & over	2.0	1.8	2.8	2.0	2.4
Total	1.6	1.2	1.7	1.5	

| | Non-Jewish Household Members | | | |
Age	Was Jewish	Jewish Descent/ Other Religion	Gentiles	Total
15–19	0.0	0.0	0.0	0.0
20–24	1.2	0.3	0.2	0.3
25–29	1.3	0.8	0.8	0.8
30–34	1.8	1.7	1.1	1.3
35–39	1.7	1.8	1.4	1.6
40–44	1.8	2.0	1.6	1.7
45–49	2.0	2.2	2.5	2.3
50–54	2.2	3.3	2.4	2.5
55–59	3.0	5.0	2.5	2.8
60–64	2.1	2.8	3.9	3.2
65 & over	2.4	2.6	3.1	2.7
Total	2.0	1.8	1.5	1.6

[a]Source: U.S. Bureau of the Census, May 1989, table 1; U.S. Bureau of the Census, March 1984, table 270.

TABLE 19. CURRENT DENOMINATION OF CORE JEWISH ADULT RESPONDENTS, BY JEWISH IDENTITY (PERCENT)

Current Denomination	Jewish Identity			
	By Religion	Secular	By Choice	Total
Orthodox	7.0	0.8	7.9	6.1
Conservative	39.6	13.0	32.4	35.1
Reform	42.7	11.3	51.3	38.0
Reconstructionist	1.5	0.9	0.6	1.3
Just Jewish	8.0	21.7	5.7	10.1
Something else	1.1	52.4	2.1	9.4
Total percent	100.0	100.0	100.0	100.0

TABLE 20. CURRENT DENOMINATION OF ADULT RESPONDENTS WHO ARE JEWS BY RELIGION, BY AGE (PERCENT)

Current Denomination	Age			
	18–24	25–44	45–64	65 & over
Orthodox	9.7	5.2	4.8	11.8
Conservative	43.1	32.6	42.4	48.6
Reform	34.8	50.6	42.6	31.2
Reconstructionist	1.1	1.6	2.7	0.2
Just Jewish	10.3	8.0	7.2	7.8
Something else	1.0	2.0	0.3	0.5
Total percent	100.0	100.0	100.0	100.0

TABLE 21. DENOMINATION RAISED OF CORE JEWISH ADULT RESPONDENTS, BY
JEWISH IDENTITY (PERCENT)

Denomination Raised	By Religion	Secular	By Choice	Total
Orthodox	26.6	6.9	2.5	22.5
Conservative	38.0	21.7	7.8	34.3
Reform	28.4	21.5	1.4	26.3
Reconstructionist	0.4	0.1	—	0.3
Just Jewish	5.6	16.2	7.5	7.4
Something else	0.7	33.6	80.8	9.3
Total percent	100.0	100.0	100.0	100.0

TABLE 22. CURRENT DENOMINATION OF RESPONDENTS WHO WERE BORN
JEWS, BY DENOMINATION RAISED (PERCENT)

Denomination Raised	Current Denomination				
	Orthodox	Conservative	Reform	Reconstructionist	Just Jewish
Orthodox	89.1	32.4	11.7	17.1	15.5
Conservative	4.8	60.1	25.9	44.4	18.4
Reform	0.4	4.2	58.6	13.9	14.5
Reconstructionist	—	—	0.3	17.2	—
Just Jewish	5.0	1.5	2.4	5.5	46.7
Non-Jewish	0.7	1.7	1.0	1.9	5.0
Total percent	100.0	100.0	100.0	100.0	100.0

TABLE 23.   JEWISH RITUAL PRACTICES AND ATTACHMENTS OF ADULT RESPON-
DENTS, CORE JEWS AND NON-JEWS (PERCENT)

Practices	Always/ Usually	Sometimes	Never	Total Percent
		Core Jews		
Sabbath candles	16.9	20.9	62.2	100.0
Attend seder	61.7	18.5	19.8	100.0
Separate dishes	13.0	4.8	81.4	100.0a
Hanukkah candles	59.7	14.4	25.9	100.0
Christmas tree	27.6	10.1	62.3	100.0
Percent who fast on Yom Kippur				48.5
Percent belonging to one or more Jewish organizations				28.2
Percent who have been to Israel				26.2
Percent who are synagogue members				32.9
		Non-Jews		
Sabbath candles	1.6	10.7	87.7	100.0
Attend seder	10.3	13.9	75.8	100.0
Separate dishes	9.8	7.5	82.7	100.0
Hanukkah candles	9.4	10.7	79.9	100.0
Christmas tree	81.8	8.1	10.1	100.0
Percent who fast on Yom Kippur				11.6
Percent belonging to one or more Jewish organizations				5.1
Percent who have been to Israel				5.5
Percent who are synagogue members				3.2

aIncludes 0.8 percent who are vegetarians.

TABLE 24. JEWISH RITUAL PRACTICES AND ATTACHMENTS OF CORE JEWISH ADULT RESPONDENTS, BY JEWISH IDENTITY (PERCENT)

Practices	Always/ Usually	Sometimes	Never	Total Percent
	Jews by Religion			
Sabbath candles	19.4	23.3	57.3	100.0
Attend seder	71.4	17.6	11.0	100.0
Separate dishes	14.7	4.4	80.1	100.0a
Hanukkah candles	70.2	13.2	16.6	100.0
Christmas tree	20.7	7.2	72.1	100.0

Percent who fast on Yom Kippur	57.8
Percent belonging to one or more Jewish organizations	32.8
Percent who have been to Israel	30.8
Percent who are synagogue members	38.5

Practices	Always/ Usually	Sometimes	Never	Total Percent
	Secular Jews			
Sabbath candles	3.1	8.4	88.5	100.0
Attend seder	22.1	21.5	56.4	100.0
Separate dishes	4.3	3.2	91.5	100.0a
Hanukkah candles	15.9	17.9	66.1	100.0
Christmas tree	55.9	19.5	24.6	100.0

Percent who fast on Yom Kippur	10.3
Percent belonging to one or more Jewish organizations	7.8
Percent who have been to Israel	10.9
Percent who are synagogue members	5.6

Practices	Always/ Usually	Sometimes	Never	Total Percent
	Jews by Choice			
Sabbath candles	32.9	35.2	31.8	100.0
Attend seder	63.9	20.7	15.4	100.0
Separate dishes	19.4	20.1	59.4	100.0a
Hanukkah candles	64.5	21.3	14.1	100.0
Christmas tree	27.3	21.6	51.1	100.0

Percent who fast on Yom Kippur	71.5
Percent belonging to one or more Jewish organizations	38.1
Percent who have been to Israel	11.4
Percent who are synagogue members	55.5

aIncludes small percentage who are vegetarians.

Review
of
the
Year

UNITED STATES

Civic and Political

Intergroup Relations

IF ANY SINGLE EVENT IN 1990 caused American Jews some unease, it was the crisis in the Persian Gulf, which began in August and was building toward a climax at year's end. Throughout the year, Jewish groups noted increasing levels of anxiety at the grass roots about anti-Semitism; however, most indices showed that anti-Semitism had not increased and that the fundamental security of the Jewish community was not threatened. The specter of a breach in the wall of separation between church and state, and of erosion of religious liberty, troubled the American Jewish polity, particularly as the contours of the federal judiciary underwent significant changes. The 25th anniversary of Vatican II's *Nostra Aetate* symbolized the exceptional changes that had occurred in the broad realm of interreligious relationships. A simmering dispute about quotas dominated debate over the ill-fated civil-rights bill in the U.S. Congress.

Political Affairs

THE GULF CRISIS

The August 1990 invasion of Kuwait by Iraq generated an active debate on the nature of an appropriate American response. This discussion during the late summer and autumn of 1990, involving the administration and the Congress, had significant implications for the Jewish community.

Immediately following the Iraqi invasion, Jewish groups expressed support of administration efforts to forge an international consensus to force Iraq's withdrawal from Kuwait. In September and again in December, community groups also approved UN resolutions relating to the crisis, including one that authorized member nations to use "all means necessary" to curb Iraq. As the year drew to a close, Jewish groups moved toward taking stands on the use of force in the Gulf. At the end of November, the Union of American Hebrew Congregations became the first Jewish group to openly advocate the use of force in order to resolve the crisis. Other Jewish groups, however, recommended a more cautious option. The National Council of

177

Jewish Women, for example, urged President George Bush to "explore every feasible alternative to military action."

In the sharp debate that unfolded toward the end of the year over the use of force versus continuation of sanctions against Iraq, the Jewish community generally was reluctant to take a high-profile position, lest support of the resolution be perceived as a Jewish issue. This was particularly so after syndicated columnist Patrick J. Buchanan stated on an August 26 telecast of "The McLaughlin Group": "There are only two groups that are beating the drums for war in the Middle East—the Israeli Defense Ministry and its 'amen' corner in the United States." Buchanan further asserted that the Israelis wanted war "desperately" because "they want the United States to finish off the Iraqi war machine." (See "Political Anti-Semitism," below.) The desire for a low-key approach was especially evident when Rep. Stephen Solarz (D., N.Y.), an ardent advocate of the military option, called a meeting of representatives of Jewish groups to ask for their support. The Jewish representatives expressed a reluctance to be involved in that manner, but they reportedly told Solarz, "When the president makes a formal request, we are ready to be openly supportive."

Although Buchanan sought to encourage the view that American Jews were pressing for the war in Israel's interest, his suggestion of "dual loyalty" found little response among most Americans, who were in any case largely supportive of the administration's position.

At the end of November, one group, the Commission on Social Action of Reform Judaism, an arm of the Union of American Hebrew Congregations and the Central Conference of American Rabbis, affixed its signature to an interreligious statement on the Gulf condemning the Iraqi invasion and speaking of the "dangers of offensive military action by the United States." This interreligious statement was considerably less extreme in its opposition to force than the statement released by the National Council of Churches on November 16, which, in a stinging rebuke of administration policy, called for "withdrawal of U.S. troops from the Gulf." It was suggested that the church groups that signed the interreligious statement—many of whom also signed the NCC document—agreed to water down their position on pragmatic grounds. As one observer put it, "[The NCC] wanted Jewish participation and a statement they could take into a Congressman's office without being dismissed out of hand. They wanted real talking points."

The U.S. Catholic Conference, the public-affairs arm of the Catholic Church in America, took a more nuanced stance on the use of force. In a November 15 letter to President Bush, USCC president Archbishop Daniel Pilarczyk of Cincinnati suggested that there might be moral justification for the use of force to resolve the Gulf crisis, but not without a prior national assessment and discussion of the ethical dimensions of the situation.

Questions were raised during the summer and autumn with respect to the participation of Jewish personnel in Operation Desert Shield, the American military build-up in the Persian Gulf. It was reported that Jewish military personnel, particularly chaplains, were being denied entry into Saudi Arabia, and that some Jewish servicemen were being pressured to remove any Jewish identification from their dog tags. (As a matter of constitutional protection, all military personnel have the option of indicating any religion—or none at all—on their dog tags.) Jewish groups such as the Jewish War Veterans of the U.S.A. were in contact with the Defense Department regarding these allegations.

An intergroup-relations issue directly flowing from the Gulf crisis was that of harassment and scapegoating of Arab-Americans, including a number of reported physical attacks. Some Jewish groups, including the National Jewish Community Relations Advisory Council (NJCRAC), acting on behalf of national and local Jewish organizations, issued statements during the fall condemning such activity and warning that "all manifestations of bias, bigotry, and group stereotyping" were unacceptable.

THE 1990 ELECTIONS

During 1990, an election year, foreign policy—including even the Persian Gulf crisis—took a back seat to taxes and domestic economic issues. Although Israel was a factor in a few races for the House of Representatives—and anti-Semitism in at least one—neither was a significant determinative factor across the country.

While a number of Jewish incumbents in the U.S. Congress were thought to be endangered, only one was defeated in the November elections. Indeed, two new Jewish members of the House of Representatives were elected—Richard Zimmer (R., N.J.) and Bernard Sanders (I., Vt.)—increasing the number of Jews in the lower house of Congress to a record high of 33. In the Senate, the Jewish contingent remained at eight (six Democrats and two Republicans), but Sen. Rudy Boschwitz (R., Minn.) lost his seat—and his party a vote—to another Jew, Democrat Paul Wellstone. Supporters of Israel viewed the Boschwitz defeat as a blow; political analysts observed that Boschwitz, the only Jew on the Senate Foreign Relations Committee, not only was one of the leading advocates of Israel in the Senate but played a crucial role in behind-the-scenes "arm-twisting" of those senators wavering in support. One of two survivors of the Holocaust in the Congress (the other was Rep. Tom Lantos, D., Calif.), Boschwitz was active in Holocaust organizations and commemorations as well.

Boschwitz, who was seeking a third term, was defeated by political newcomer Paul Wellstone, a Jew, a 48-year-old professor of political science at Carleton College in Northfield, Minnesota. The close Wellstone–Boschwitz race was troubled—and perhaps decided—by a letter sent out by Senator Boschwitz's campaign to Jewish groups in the state saying that Wellstone had married a Christian, did not raise his children as Jews, and had no ties to the Jewish community. Jewish leaders reacted with outrage against Boschwitz. Jews account for only a tiny percentage of voters in Minnesota, but the incident resounded throughout the state. Wellstone asserted support for Israel, but indicated that he would not hesitate to criticize the policies of the Likud government on the Senate floor.

Other 1990 Senate races of note included the defeat by Jesse Helms (R., N.C.) of Harvey Gantt, after Helms resorted to the use of racial themes during the final weeks of the campaign. Although Helms, who had a mixed record on Israel, had some Jewish support, most Jews backed Gantt to become the first black senator in the South since Reconstruction. In Oregon, Sen. Mark Hatfield (R.), a longtime critic of Israel ("even before it became fashionable," in the words of Morris Amitay, past director of the American Israel Public Affairs Committee–AIPAC), defeated Harry Lonsdale. And in Iowa, Sen. Tom Harkin, supported by pro-Israel groups and by Jewish activists concerned with the domestic agenda, became the only Democratic senator from Iowa to be reelected in many decades.

In one of the more unusual races in recent memory, Bernard Sanders—a Jewish socialist running as an independent—won an overwhelming victory to become Vermont's single member of the House of Representatives.

The net loss of Republican seats in both the House and Senate pleased representatives of a number of multi-issue Jewish organizations, who had endured two very difficult legislative sessions of the 101st Congress on issues such as civil rights, church-state separation, and reproductive rights. Observers of the 1990 elections noted that both pro-Israel and multi-issue political action committees (PACs) provided money to the vast majority of congressional races in 1990, mostly to incumbents.

In another political development, efforts by pro-Arab state convention delegates to pass anti-Israel resolutions or platform planks in a number of states came to naught. In at least one state, California, the state Republican party passed a strong pro-Israel resolution at its convention in March, but only after overcoming stiff opposition on the part of pro-Arab delegates.

In gubernatorial races, California Democrats, in a primary election held in June, chose Dianne G. Feinstein as their candidate for governor. She was defeated, however, in the November general election by the Republican candidate, Sen. Pete Wilson. Bruce Sundlin of Rhode Island (D.) remained the only Jewish governor, with Democratic governors Madeline Kunin of Vermont and Neil Goldschmidt of Oregon not seeking reelection in 1990.

In Arkansas, a Ku Klux Klan supporter and former leader of the American Nazi party, Ralph Forbes, was defeated by a black candidate, Kenneth Harris, by a landslide margin in a Republican runoff election in June for lieutenant governor. The white-supremacist candidate had received a 46-percent plurality in the primary election in May, short of the majority needed to clinch the primary. According to the Anti-Defamation League, Forbes was associated with an affiliate of the anti-Semitic and racist Christian Identity Movement, and had been the campaign manager of Louisiana white-supremacist David Duke's 1988 presidential campaign. In another expression of anti-Semitism, Rep. Gus Savage of Chicago (D., Ill.), victorious in his reelection bid, assailed "Jewish money" and Jewish control of the media in a campaign speech.

In December, a group of Jewish Democratic leaders formed the National Jewish

Democratic Council, for the purposes of encouraging Jewish candidates at all levels and of promoting greater Jewish involvement in the Democratic party. They hoped to maintain the pattern of a Jewish majority voting for Democratic candidates in presidential, congressional, statewide, and local elections. (According to polling data, 74 percent of Jewish voters supported Democratic candidates in the November 1990 congressional elections.) Republican Jews had already formed such an organization, the National Jewish Coalition, organized during 1980 to support Ronald Reagan in his bid for the presidency. Both groups stressed that they were independent of their respective party's official organizations. Political observers suggested that the motivation for forming the Jewish Democratic Council was to prevent recurrence of what happened in 1988, when seven state Democratic party conventions adopted resolutions supporting Palestinian "self-determination," and the issue was debated at the 1988 Democratic national convention.

Finally, the Reverend Jesse Jackson declined to run for the Washington, D.C., mayoralty, but easily won election to one of two "shadow" Senate seats for the District of Columbia, and was expected to use his position to lobby for D.C. statehood.

Soviet Jewry

LOAN GUARANTEES

To help meet the costs of the heavy influx of Soviet Jews to Israel, early in 1990 Israel requested a $400-million guarantee from the U.S. government for commercial loans from banks for the purpose of Soviet Jewry settlement. According to Secretary of State James Baker's March 1 testimony before the foreign operations subcommittee of the House Appropriations Committee, the administration's condition for the $400-million loan guarantee was that the funds not be used in the occupied territories. President Bush's March 3 statement objecting to Israeli settlements in the West Bank (and East Jerusalem, for that matter) was based on the perception that sizable numbers of Soviet Jews were being settled in those areas; in fact, asserted the Israeli government, a tiny fraction—less than 1 percent—was being settled there. Subsequent statements by various administration officials suggested that the United States would indeed not link loan guarantees to the end of settlement activity per se, but only to the settlement of Soviet Jews in those areas. Throughout much of the year, the administration declined to say whether it would in fact support the $400-million guarantee. Finally, in October, armed with Israeli assurances that the money would not be used to settle Soviet Jews in the West Bank or the Gaza strip, the administration indicated that it would provide final approval of the guarantees.

Meanwhile, in the Congress, Senators Patrick Leahy (D., Vt.) and Robert Kasten (R., Wis.) introduced legislation in early February that provided guarantees for $400 million of housing loans. Senate passage of the FY 90 supplemental appropriations bill, which had strong bipartisan support, occurred in April. Companion legislation was approved the same month by an overwhelming margin in the House of Representatives. Rep. Gus Savage (D., Ill.), who had made assertedly anti-Semitic remarks after he won his primary reelection campaign in late March, tried unsuccessfully to strip the $400 million from the House bill.

There was little domestic fallout during 1990 over the protracted negotiations between the Israeli and American governments. American Jewish groups took the public posture that the negotiations were "mostly technical difficulties" to be resolved between the two governments without major American Jewish communal involvement.

WAIVER OF JACKSON-VANIK

President Bush's partial waiver on December 12 of the Jackson-Vanik Amendment—good until July 1991—was the culmination of yearlong discussions within both the Jewish community and the administration, and between Jewish groups and administration officials on the issue. Jackson-Vanik, passed in 1974 in reaction to a Soviet decision to put a steep tax on émigrés with higher academic degrees (most of whom were Jews), imposed restrictions on U.S. trade with the Soviet Union and linked "most-favored-nation" (MFN) status to Soviet-Jewish immigration. With significant changes in the U.S.-Soviet climate, particularly with respect to the easing of emigration restrictions and promises to introduce more liberal emigration laws, a number of Jewish organizations publicly supported easing the Jackson-Vanik restrictions. Under the law, the president could waive Jackson-Vanik for a one-year period if he were able to demonstrate to the Congress that doing so would promote freer emigration. The waiver could be extended each year unless both houses of Congress voted to disapprove such an extension.

Among Jewish groups, the two leading Soviet Jewry advocacy organizations, the National Conference on Soviet Jewry (NCSJ) and the Union of Councils for Soviet Jews (UCSJ), were split on the waiver issue. The NCSJ, in a reevaluation of its policy, announced in early December that it would support waiver. NCSJ had previously asserted that it would support a Jackson-Vanik waiver only if a number of conditions, including assurances of a continuing high level of Jewish emigration, were met. The UCSJ, for its part, maintained the position that a waiver would remove any incentive for the Soviet Union to codify free emigration into its laws. Indeed, President Bush, who met with Soviet president Mikhail Gorbachev in Washington in June, indicated before the summit that codification was an issue for the administration as well. Nonetheless, on December 12, the president decided to waive a number of Jackson-Vanik restrictions on agricultural credits for the Soviet Union. He did not, however, lift the important provision that barred the USSR from receiving MFN trade benefits.

While other Jewish groups were generally supportive of waiver, arguing that demonstration of support for Gorbachev for his role in increasing emigration was indicated, it was unclear on what precise conditions the administration based its waiver. In 1989, for example, Bush had called for "passage . . . and faithful implementation of an emigration law." What constituted implementation? queried analysts; in fact, did the administration yet require this provision in 1990? None of those analysts following the issue had any answers.

Finally, the first "Solidarity Sunday" amid *glasnost*—and the first in three years— was held in New York on May 1. The traditional cry of "Let My People Go!" was changed to "Bring My People Home!" as rally planners, who had canceled the demonstrations in 1989 and 1990 because conditions for Soviet Jews continued to improve, now looked toward public support of resettlement.

Anti-Semitism and Extremism

The standard indices for measuring anti-Semitism offered somewhat contradictory evidence this year about the state of Jewish security: an increase in incidents of vandalism and harassment related to anti-Semitism, but a continuing decline in anti-Semitic attitudes, as measured by public-opinion surveys.

The annual Anti-Defamation League (ADL) audit of anti-Semitic incidents for 1990 reported 1,685 episodes, an 18-percent increase over the 1,432 such incidents reported during 1989, and the highest total reported in the 12-year history of the audit. Of the 1,685 incidents reported, 927 were acts of vandalism directed at Jewish institutions and Jewish-owned property, and included 38 serious crimes of arson, bombing, and vandalism. This was a record number as well. Additionally, the ADL audit reported 758 acts of harassment, threats, and assaults against Jewish individuals, their property, and their institutions. Incidents in this category increased 29 percent over the previous year and were at a record number. The total ADL figure marked the fourth straight year of increasing levels of anti-Semitic acts nationwide.

The ADL report further noted a trend in the growing numbers of anti-Semitic incidents occurring on college campuses and a "resurgence" of anti-Semitic incidents seemingly motivated by the developing Persian Gulf crisis toward the end of the year. While the ADL had in 1989 underscored signs of growing neo-Nazi, violence-mongering "skinheads," in 1990 the league reported a sharp decrease in the number of skinhead-related anti-Semitic incidents. The number of hard-core skinheads in 1990 remained unchanged from the estimated 3,000 activists in 31 states reported by the ADL and other monitoring groups in 1989. It was not clear to observers whether the number had indeed peaked in 1989.

According to the May 1990 Roper Organization poll conducted annually for the American Jewish Committee, on the key question of which groups have too much power in the United States, respondents continued to rank Jews near the bottom of those groups listed. The 8-percent figure of those who responded "Jews" to this indicative question was unchanged from the previous year's poll. Other significant Roper findings included: on the "dual-loyalty" question, a large plurality—44 percent—of respondents disagreeing with the proposition "American Jews are more loyal to Israel than to the United States." The percentage agreeing—28 percent—was up slightly over the 1989 number.

Other evaluative criteria by which anti-Semitism is measured showed no evidence of an increase during 1990. Most significant, in the view of analysts, was the fact that "conflict" situations—situations that tend to polarize society and can lead to an increase in anti-Semitic expression—did not produce any increase in anti-Semitism in 1990, continuing the pattern of four decades. This, despite the perception among many Jews that there was greater expression of anti-Semitism in the general community than was reflected in the survey data or the assessments of Jewish groups.

In the view of many Jewish communal leaders and of seasoned observers, a distinction had to be made between anti-Semitism—which surely exists and must be monitored and counteracted by Jewish communal agencies—and basic Jewish security, which is rooted primarily in the strength of constitutional protections and democratic institutions, which in 1990 remained stable in the United States.

EXTREMIST GROUPS

According to organizations monitoring extremist-group activity, membership in most such groups continued to decline. Still, the ADL claimed that the decade-long decline in the strength of the Klan had come to a halt, with membership in 1990 remaining approximately the same as in 1989. According to the ADL and Klanwatch, some areas of the country showed indications of possible Klan growth. The ADL placed the membership of all hate groups in the United States during 1990 at fewer than 20,000.

A significant development in countering extremist activities was the October verdict in a civil trial against Tom Metzger, a former Klan leader who headed the racist organization White Aryan Resistance (WAR), and his son John, leader of the Aryan Youth Movement. These two national extremist organizations reportedly had sizable followings among racist skinheads. In *Engedaw Berhanu v. Tom Metzger et al.*, a jury in Portland, Oregon, returned a $12.5-million verdict against the Metzgers, White Aryan Resistance, and two skinhead followers in connection with the 1988 murder of an Ethiopian immigrant by the skinheads. The jury found that the Metzgers and WAR were vicariously liable for the immigrant's death because they had actively encouraged the skinheads to commit acts of racial violence. The ADL and the Southern Poverty Law Center cooperated in bringing the lawsuit on behalf of the plaintiff in *Berhanu* under various statutes, including the Oregon racial intimidation law that allows individual victims of hate crimes to bring a civil action for relief. Analysts suggested that lawsuits like *Berhanu* sent a clear message that illegal harassment on the basis of religion and race would be countered not only in the criminal courts, but in civil actions as well.

In another case involving criminal prosecution of extremists, in March five members of a white supremacist group were convicted in a Dallas federal district court of firearms violations and conspiracy to violate the civil rights of Jews, blacks, and Hispanics. The charges against the five stemmed from a series of anti-Semitic and racist incidents committed in 1988, including vandalism of religious institutions and beatings of individuals.

ANTI-SEMITISM ON THE CAMPUS

Reports from college and university campuses around the country seemed to indicate a growth of anti-Semitic expression along with a rise in the number of bias incidents in general on campuses, many of them with highly diverse populations. A study conducted by the National Jewish Community Relations Advisory Council (NJCRAC) at the request of the Council of Jewish Federations and released in November, found that behavioral anti-Semitism was in fact not pervasive on college campuses and concluded that "the vast majority of Jewish students feel comfortable on most American campuses." The study did find that troubling incidents of anti-Semitism occurred in connection with campus visits of extremist speakers, and were more likely to be linked to the political debate surrounding events in the Middle East, especially on those campuses having a large foreign—especially Arab—student population. To a significantly smaller degree, campus anti-Semitism was expressed in random incidents of vandalism and graffiti, according to the NJCRAC report.

While the numbers of incidents of anti-Semitic vandalism on the campus, as reported by the Anti-Defamation League, jumped from 69 incidents at 54 institutions in 1989 to 95 incidents at 57 institutions in 1990, the number of such incidents was small relative to the total campus population, and indeed represented a minuscule percentage of the total number of "bias" incidents reported on the campus. Indeed, according to the National Institute Against Prejudice and Violence, since 1986 more than 250 campuses around the country had reported a range of racist and bias-related incidents, with virtually every minority group a target. Both the NJCRAC and the National Institute Against Prejudice and Violence found that bias and racism were far more pervasive problems on the campus than anti-Semitism.

Invited speakers bearing a largely anti-Semitic message, such as Kwame Toure (black activist Stokely Carmichael) and Nation of Islam leader Louis Farrakhan, continued to travel the campus circuit during 1990, often serving as flash points for anti-Semitic acts. In response to the speakers' appearances, Jewish communal organizations, both on and off the campus, encouraged university administrators to issue statements that condemned messages of hate while supporting free speech. On a number of campuses, university administrators did demonstrate leadership in denouncing campus anti-Semitism. On the University of Wisconsin campus and in the Madison, Wisconsin, community, which experienced a series of 24 incidents, from

July to September, ranging from vandalism of Jewish fraternities, Hillel houses, and synagogues to the cutting of a brake cable on a bus parked in the synagogue parking lot, a broad intergroup coalition and the university administration strongly repudiated anti-Semitism and other forms of bigotry.

A troubling campus-related episode was the publication of a quote from Adolf Hitler's *Mein Kampf* in the October 3 issue of the *Dartmouth Review*, an alternative, politically conservative weekly newspaper published by students but unaffiliated with Dartmouth College. In the incident, which took place on Yom Kippur, a quote from Theodore Roosevelt on the newspaper's masthead was replaced with the Hitler quote. Dartmouth president James O. Freedman immediately denounced the newspaper, and the *Review* issued an apology, suggesting that it had been a victim of sabotage on the part of an unknown staff member.

ANTI-SEMITISM IN THE BLACK COMMUNITY

In August, black filmmaker Spike Lee's film *Mo' Better Blues* was attacked by Jewish groups for its stereotypical depiction of two Jewish jazz-club owners, Moe and Josh Flatbush. The ADL said that "Spike Lee's characterization of the Flatbush brothers as greedy and unscrupulous dredges up an age-old and highly-dangerous form of anti-Semitic stereotyping." In a *Los Angeles Times* survey of film critics, many agreed that the characterization was anti-Semitic, but many also defended Spike Lee's right of free artistic expression. Around the time of the film's release, in July, a speaker at the annual convention of the National Association of the Advancement of Colored People (NAACP) in Los Angeles asserted that black entertainers had been held back because of the "century-old problem of Jewish racism in Hollywood." Benjamin J. Hooks, executive director of the NAACP, did not repudiate the comment, although he said that it did not represent the organization's views.

The rap group Public Enemy, which had caused consternation among Jewish groups for the anti-Semitic comments made by one of its members, "Professor Griff," during 1989, spurred protest again this year, with the release of its new album in January. A single, "Welcome to the Terrordome," contained lyrics that revived the anti-Semitic slander of deicide. The ADL called upon Walter Yetnikoff, president of CBS Records, the album's distributor, to repudiate the racism and anti-Semitism articulated in the record. Yetnikoff responded with a statement condemning bigotry in music. In a related matter, the music industry in 1990 agreed to voluntary uniform labeling of albums with offensive lyrics, prompting legislators in 13 states to withdraw pending bills calling for mandatory labeling.

Minister Louis Farrakhan, who had been the focal point of controversy for several years in his role as head of the some-10,000-member black organization Nation of Islam, asserted in a *Washington Post* interview on March 1 that he was "not an enemy of Jews." He said he wished to end the bitter antagonism that had characterized his relationship with the Jewish community since his 1984 assertion that Judaism was "a gutter religion." Observers suggested that Farrakhan's overture was part of an effort to win a more prominent role in national politics for his organization.

A report published by the American Jewish Committee, "What Do We Know About Black Anti-Semitism?" provided a comprehensive analysis of published survey evidence on black attitudes toward Jews. Among the conclusions of the AJC report were that blacks tend to be more anti-Semitic than whites at the same levels of education (but *not* that as education levels rise in the black community, so does anti-Semitism—a commonly held belief); and that generally, a greater percentage of blacks (37 percent) than whites (20 percent) score as anti-Semitic on standard attitudinal scales. The review further showed that the percentage of blacks scoring as anti-Semitic on those scales had decreased perceptibly from 1964, but the decrease was smaller than that for whites. Analysts noted that the data on black anti-Semitism were fragmentary and limited, and that no recent comprehensive survey of black attitudes toward Jews had been conducted.

A study by sociologist Hubert Locke of three cities—St. Louis, Seattle, and Buffalo—suggested that the popular perception that black anti-Semitism is widespread may be unfounded. The study, *Black Protestantism and Anti-Semitism*, published in 1990 and based on Locke's earlier research, suggested that the souring of relationships between leadership of the two communities was a result of battles over such contentious issues as affirmative action and should not be "generalized as a characteristic of the . . . attitudes of black citizens toward Jewish people as a general proposition."

POLITICAL ANTI-SEMITISM

On the political front, the activities of two individuals raised questions about racial politics and a possible reemergence of political anti-Semitism. In Louisiana, former "grand wizard" of the Knights of the Ku Klux Klan David Duke mounted a strong bid for the U.S. Senate seat held by Democrat J. Bennett Johnston. Duke, 40, who headed the National Association for the Advancement of White People, had been elected in 1989 to the state legislature in Louisiana. Running on an anti-establishment platform as a Republican in the October election, Duke garnered 605,681 votes—43.5 percent of the total, including an estimated 55 percent of the white vote. Johnston, in gaining more than 50 percent of the total vote, avoided a runoff in November. It was a matter of concern to many that the Louisiana Republican party failed to repudiate Duke.

Observers suggested that Duke's strong showing in the Louisiana senatorial vote was a step in an effort aimed at moving white supremacy and other racial politics off the margin and back into the mainstream of American politics. At the same time, it appeared that many, if not most, white voters for Duke cast their ballots in favor of Duke's populist "anti-government" stance—including his call for an end to affirmative-action programs—rather than explicitly for racist reasons. At year's end, Duke was reportedly considering a race in 1991 for governor of Louisiana.

In general, election campaigns during 1990 were free of anti-Semitism, a key criterion in the assessment of the nature and extent of anti-Semitism. One exception was the public attack considered by Jewish groups to be anti-Semitic made by Rep. Gus Savage (D., Ill.) of Chicago against Jewish contributors to his opponent, who was also African-American. Savage was repudiated by some black leaders, but not by any in Chicago.

One issue raised for Jewish organizations by the Duke and similar campaigns was the limitation placed on partisan political activity by Section 501(c)(3) of the Internal Revenue Code, which governs most nonprofit organizations in the Jewish community. In Louisiana, a number of groups joined forces to form the Louisiana Coalition Against Racism and Nazism, a political action committee, for the purpose of countering Duke's 1990 candidacy.

In a September 14 *New York Times* column, op-ed writer A.M. Rosenthal accused conservative syndicated columnist Patrick J. Buchanan of anti-Semitism and indeed of "blood libel." The impetus for the Rosenthal denunciation was Buchanan's charge that only Israel and American Jews (he called them Israel's "amen corner") were backing the Gulf war (see above). Rosenthal wrote: "We are not dealing here with country-club anti-Semitism but with the blood libel that often grows out of it: Jews are not like us but are others, with alien loyalties for which they will sacrifice the lives of Americans." In his printed response of September 19, Buchanan denied that he was anti-Semitic, and, in a pointed reference to ADL national director Abraham H. Foxman, averred that such charges were smoke screens for "amen-corner" protectors.

In both his syndicated columns and on television, Buchanan had evidenced hostility to Israel and to many Jewish concerns for some years. He questioned the viability of the Jewish state and the validity of continued American support of Israel, proclaimed the innocence of convicted Nazi war criminal John Demjanjuk, and supported the presence of the Carmelite convent at Auschwitz. Jewish groups were reluctant during the 1990 Buchanan fray to label the columnist an out-and-out anti-Semite, or to call for removal of his column or other censoring. "The organized Jewish community does not feel that Pat Buchanan should be muzzled," said the National Jewish Community Relations Advisory Council, reflecting the view shared by many Jewish leaders. "We're very unhappy about what Pat Buchanan says, but the place for counteraction is in the marketplace of ideas," the group's spokesman noted. Nevertheless, there was serious concern among a number of analysts about Buchanan's remarks, particularly as they reflected a reaction triggered by a "conflict" situation, in this case the Gulf crisis.

HOLOCAUST REVISIONISM

Holocaust revisionism—denial of the Holocaust or of its extent by pseudo-scholarly means—was expressed in a number of campus settings during 1990. In February, Donald Hiner, a part-time instructor of history at Indiana-Purdue University, taught in his classes that the Holocaust was a "myth," and that "none of it makes sense unless you look at it from the prospect of Israel getting a lot of wealth from the story." Following fact-finding by the Indianapolis Jewish Community Relations Council and other Jewish groups, the college dean characterized Hiner's classroom remarks as "lies and slander."

DISCRIMINATORY CLUBS

Discriminatory practices by private clubs, although generally on the decline, were exposed in a number of situations that garnered national headlines in this year. The exclusion of Jews, including Henry Bloch, a prominent Jewish citizen in Kansas City, by the Kansas City Country Club prompted Tom Watson, a champion golfer, to resign from the club in protest in December. "It's something I can't personally live with," said Watson. Bloch was subsequently invited to join the club. Jewish groups welcomed the decision in August by the Shoal Creek Country Club of Birmingham to admit its first black member. Shoal Creek was the site of the 1990 Professional Golfers' Association championship tournament. And in Orlando, Florida, the women's tennis team of the Jewish Community Center faced expulsion from the Orlando-based Women's Amateur Invitational League (WAIT) for refusing to play matches on the premises of a country club with discriminatory membership policies. Finally, in August, the Senate Judiciary Committee passed a resolution characterizing it as "inappropriate" for nominees to the federal bench and Justice Department appointees to be members of discriminatory private clubs. Jewish groups welcomed the Judiciary Committee action.

LEGISLATIVE AND JUDICIAL ACTIVITY

The Hate Crimes Statistics Act was passed by the 101st Congress and signed into law by President George Bush in April. This legislation, which enjoyed wide support within the Jewish community as furthering the goals of the Religious Violence Act (passed by the 100th Congress), requires the U.S. Attorney General to acquire data on crimes that manifest prejudice based on race, religion, sexual orientation, or ethnicity. Passage of the statistics act reflected widespread concern about the reported increase in hate violence in America.

Most states had laws on their books on bias-motivated violence and intimidation, other hate crimes, or data reporting; however, the constitutionality of such statutes was challenged in a number of states. One such case, *R.A.V. v. St. Paul*, was accepted in 1990 for review by the U.S. Supreme Court. In *R.A.V.*, the Minnesota

Supreme Court—the first state supreme court to interpret hate-crimes statutes—upheld a St. Paul city ordinance making it a crime to place on public or private property a burning cross, a swastika, or any other symbol likely to arouse "anger, alarm, or resentment on the basis of race, color, creed, religion, or gender." While acknowledging that the St. Paul ordinance raised free-speech concerns, the court interpreted the law as applying only to conduct that is violence-provoking and therefore "outside First Amendment protection," and not to expression that is merely offensive. On a related issue, the U.S. Supreme Court this year struck down federal and state laws making it a crime to burn the American flag, asserting that the government could not prosecute "expressive conduct" (*U.S. v. Haggerty* and *U.S. v. Eichman*). A similar judgment had been reached in the 1989 *Texas v. Johnson*. Jewish groups applauded the Court's action in these cases and were opposed to a proposed constitutional amendment that would have given the Congress and the states the power to prohibit physical desecration of the flag. (It was defeated in the House of Representatives, 254–177.) The proposed amendment was triggered by the decisions in *Haggerty* and *Eichman*, and was opposed by the Jewish community both on the grounds of freedom of expression and of frivolously amending the Constitution. Jewish groups were divided on *R.A.V. v. St. Paul*.

In at least one state, New York, a bias-related crimes bill was stalled as a result of opposition by some members of the legislature, based on provisions of the bill that would extend protection to homosexuals and put bias crimes in a special category.

OTHER MATTERS

The U.S. Supreme Court decided in 1990 to hear a case involving alleged discrimination against Americans working abroad, *Equal Employment Opportunity Commission v. Aramco*. In this case, the U.S. Court of Appeals for the Fifth Circuit ruled that Title VII of the Civil Rights Act of 1964, prohibiting job discrimination on the basis of race, sex, religion, or national origin, did not apply to U.S. citizens working abroad. Although the individual involved in *Aramco* was not Jewish, Jewish groups expressed concern over the appeals-court decision. *Aramco* was the first such case to reach the Supreme Court, and a decision was expected during 1991. The American Jewish Congress joined in an *amicus* brief in the case, and the American Jewish Committee and the Anti-Defamation League were considering such action as well.

In a widely publicized incident in December, the head of the international team in charge of editing the Dead Sea Scrolls, Harvard professor John Strugnell, was dismissed from his editorial post after attacking Jews, Judaism, and Israel. Strugnell was quoted in the Israeli newspaper *Ha'aretz* on November 9 as saying "Judaism is originally racist"; "the correct answer of Jews to Christianity is to become Christian"; Judaism "is a horrible religion; it's a Christian heresy"; and other such assertions.

Catholic-Jewish Relations

The 25th anniversary of *Nostra Aetate*, commemorated in the autumn of 1990, provided a backdrop for Catholic-Jewish relations during the year, both internationally and in the United States. The promulgation in 1965 by the Second Vatican Council of *Nostra Aetate*, "In Our Time," the Vatican "Declaration on the Relation of the Church to Non-Christian Religions," marked a special moment in the history of the Church and its relation to Judaism. *Nostra Aetate* redefined the ways in which Catholics view Jews, and, in essence, rejected and repudiated Christian anti-Semitism. The 25th anniversary of the document symbolized these exceptional changes that had occurred in Catholic-Jewish relations since 1965 and was commemorated in numerous programs around the United States.

THE VATICAN

The Church, via Vatican statements and programmatic initiatives on the part of Catholic bodies in a number of countries, continued its call for repudiation of anti-Semitism, as consistent with Vatican II declarations. On March 16, Pope John Paul II called on all Catholic churches around the world to engage in "systematic study" of the Second Vatican Council's teaching on Jews and Judaism. The pope's call came at a meeting with a delegation of American Jewish leaders in Rome, which ended a two-year hiatus in such high-level meetings brought on, in the view of most observers, by tensions over the Auschwitz convent issue. (The last meeting between the pope and Jews had taken place in September 1987.) The delegation urged the pope to take a leading role in combating anti-Semitism that might emerge in the newly liberalized societies in Eastern Europe and the USSR. At the meeting, the pope reaffirmed the Church's adherence to *Nostra Aetate* and proposed a "systematic study of the [Second Vatican] Council's teaching" on the irrevocable nature of God's bond with the Jewish people. This was the first time that individual Catholic churches were directed by the Vatican to address issues such as anti-Semitism.

A highly significant development in Vatican-Jewish relations was the promulgation in Prague on September 6 of a statement of the Holy See's Commission on Religious Relations with the Jews, "Anti-Semitism: A Sin Against God and Humanity." The statement, issued by an international Catholic-Jewish liaison committee, asserted: "That anti-Semitism has found a place in Christian thought and practice calls for an act of *teshuvah* (repentance) and of reconciliation on our part." Among other recommendations, the Prague declaration called for the monitoring and prompt countering of all trends and developments that threaten an upsurge of anti-Semitism in Eastern and Central Europe and the inclusion of *Nostra Aetate* teachings in curricula, including those of theological seminaries, in order to eliminate the Catholic "teaching of contempt." "One cannot be authentically Christian and engage in anti-Semitism," asserted the declaration. Analysts of Christian-Jewish relations suggested that the Prague document helped to repair the rift in international Catholic-Jewish relations resulting from papal meetings with Yasir Arafat and Austrian president Kurt Waldheim, and by the prolonged controversy over relocating a Carmelite convent from the Auschwitz/Birkenau death-camp site.

A second meeting between Pope John Paul II and a delegation from the International Jewish Committee for Interreligious Consultations (IJCIC), held in December, represented a further step in the discussion of anti-Semitism. The meeting, originally scheduled for November, was postponed because of an internal dispute within the Synagogue Council of America, the umbrella body for Jewish rabbinical and synagogue organizations that serves as the American secretariat for IJCIC. The rescheduled meeting in Rome, on December 6, was held in conjunction with a 25th-anniversary commemoration of *Nostra Aetate*. At the meeting, according to IJCIC chairman Seymour D. Reich, the pope "went beyond the language of [the] Prague [declaration], which called for dissemination [of the new Church teachings], and he called for implementation." This development was consistent with a pattern of Vatican actions in recent years that included the noteworthy February 1989 document *The Church and Racism: Toward a More Fraternal Society*, which included statements on anti-Zionism, anti-Semitism, and Nazism that were viewed by Jewish groups as positive.

While these developments were welcomed by most Jewish organizations in America and worldwide, the ambiguous and indeed sometimes ambivalent nature of Vatican-Jewish relations was also in evidence. The meeting between Pope John Paul II and PLO leader Yasir Arafat on April 6, their third meeting since 1982, drew strong protests from Jewish organizations. Arafat reportedly used his meeting with the pope to carry further his campaign against Soviet Jewish *aliyah*. Jewish groups expressed disappointment that the pope did not publicly call upon Arafat to condemn terrorism, including the murder of Palestinians by other Palestinians.

As during past years, official Catholic documents considered during 1990 had ramifications for relations with Jews. A draft of a new catechism for the Roman Catholic Church, the *Catechism for the Universal Church*, issued in September, was part of an effort by the Vatican to codify Vatican II teachings—in particular, the opposition to anti-Semitism and a commitment to promoting constructive Christian-Jewish cooperation—for educational use. Nonetheless, concern was expressed that the draft's extensive use of "typology" and "prefiguration" was supersessionist in nature. According to Rabbi A. James Rudin of the American Jewish Committee, "By using typology the catechism's authors see the entire Hebrew Scriptures as a clear 'prefiguration,' an intermediate step, a prelude to the coming of Jesus"; as such, according to Rudin and other analysts, the catechism ran counter to Vatican II teachings. Additionally, the catechism's views on the Pharisees and on the Jewish messianic idea were deeply troubling to Jewish analysts of the document. Summing up the catechism's deficiencies, Rudin said: "*Nostra Aetate*, the Vatican 'Notes' [on *Nostra Aetate*], the many constructive statements that have been issued by various bishops' conferences since 1965 have given great impetus to positive Catholic-Jewish relations, but they have had little or no effect upon the Catechism's authors. The

Catechism takes almost no note of the robust quality of the encounter."

Jewish communal officials attributed significance to the catechism and other documents because the Catholic Church, more than other religious bodies, operates by means of official documents that receive global usage. With respect to the forthcoming Vatican document on the Church and the *Shoah*, some observers suggested that, in order to avoid the protests that greeted publication of the Vatican's 1985 "Notes" on *Nostra Aetate*, the draft of the document be reviewed by a group of Jewish scholars prior to its issuance.

Jewish leaders were disappointed that the Vatican did not indicate any intention during 1990 to grant full, formal, and normal recognition to the State of Israel, although it had previously asserted that there were no theological bars to recognizing Israel. (The Vatican maintains that it does recognize the State of Israel on a *de facto* basis.) It is widely believed that the reason for Vatican reluctance to normalize relations with Israel is fear over possible consequences of recognition for Catholic communities in Middle Eastern countries. Additionally, according to Rabbi Marc Tanenbaum, a longtime observer of Vatican-Jewish relations, "Israel is not interested, in this stage, in pushing for full diplomatic relations with the Vatican. Israel does not want to invite Vatican pressure for a Palestinian homeland, and so it is in Israel's interests to remain relatively silent." Support for formal Vatican recognition continued to be expressed during 1990 by individual American bishops and by officials of the National Conference of Catholic Bishops and the U.S. Catholic Conference.

OTHER CATHOLIC-JEWISH MATTERS

Jewish groups were not happy when New York's John Cardinal O'Connor, on May 10, sharply criticized the Israeli government over its handling of the St. John's Hospice issue, raising the question of a possible "conspiracy" to drive Christians out of Israel. (See "Protestant-Jewish Relations.") However, O'Connor stated in an address to the American Jewish Committee on May 17 that guaranteeing access to the holy places in Jerusalem did not necessarily mean that Israel must relinquish control of the city. Cardinal O'Connor, a member of the three-bishop National Conference of Catholic Bishops committee on Middle East affairs, said that the "juridical status of Jerusalem" and "what nation controls Jerusalem are irrelevant so long as there is free access to the holy places for members of all religious persuasions." Although Jewish groups took sharp exception to Cardinal O'Connor's May 10 characterization of the move of the Jews into the hospice as "obscene," and other comments, O'Connor was considered to be a friend of Israel, especially within Church councils.

The Passion Play performed every ten years at Oberammergau, Germany, a sometimes-serious obstacle to Christian-Jewish relations, was performed before more than 500,000 people between May and September. In May 1989 the Anti-

Defamation League, the American Jewish Committee, the Brooklyn-Queens Archdiocese, and representatives of Oberammergau undertook to deal with the concerns about and criticisms of the play that had been expressed since the last production. Despite some changes, however, the 1990 production continued to use the traditional 1634 text. In the words of Rabbi Leon Klenicki of the Anti-Defamation League, "The play, despite revisions, is not yet in accordance with the teachings of the Second Vatican Council nor of subsequent Vatican guidelines on Passion Plays." Play officials averred that a new Passion Play production, with a new text, would be mounted in 2000.

The issue of the Carmelite convent at the Auschwitz/Birkenau death-camp site, which had been a focus for Catholic-Jewish tensions during the 1980s, came closer to resolution in 1990. Following rounds of meetings and discussions, including intervention by the Vatican in the matter, Bishop Henryk Muszynski, chairman of the Polish Episcopate's Commission on Dialogue with the Jews, announced on February 6 that construction would begin in the spring of 1990 on an interfaith center, outside the death-camp site, in which the nuns from the convent would be relocated. Indeed, on February 19, ground was broken for the center. In a separate albeit related development, Tadeusz Mazowiecki, Poland's prime minister, announced in London in January that the Auschwitz museum, set up during the Stalinist period, would be redesigned "to do justice to the tragedy of the Jewish people." Bishop Muszynski confirmed that the future of the museum "will be considered in consultation with Jewish organizations." This affirmation was welcomed by Jewish leaders in Poland and elsewhere.

Concerns were expressed within the Jewish community over a proposal to the Vatican to consider Queen Isabella of Spain for sainthood in the Roman Catholic Church. Queen Isabella, who in March 1492 signed the edict of expulsion of Jews from Spain, is viewed as a despot by both Jews and Muslims, who were subject to torture, forced conversion, and expulsion during her reign from 1474 to 1504. Isabella's cause, which was being promoted by individuals in the Spanish Catholic clergy, was still in the early stages of study. She had yet to be declared "venerable," the first of three stages in the sainthood process. (The other two are beatification and sainthood itself.) Under Vatican rules, after being declared venerable, a person needs two attributed miracles in order to qualify for sainthood. The Vatican reported in 1990 that there were no miracles attributed as yet to Isabella. While the U.S. National Conference of Catholic Bishops did not articulate a position on the Isabella canonization, individual American bishops raised serious questions about the sainthood proposal.

In November, the Anti-Defamation League and the American Jewish Committee announced that they were rejoining the International Jewish Committee for Interreligious Consultations (IJCIC). The "unity" move was undertaken to enable these community-relations agencies to participate in the December papal meeting.

Protestant-Jewish Relations

The bipolar character of Protestant-Jewish relations in the United States continued during 1990: generally critical in terms of Israel and the Middle East; positive in other areas but with some divergence over priorities on their respective domestic agendas.

ST. JOHN'S HOSPICE

The news that 150 Jewish settlers had occupied a building belonging to the Greek Orthodox Church in the Christian Quarter of Jerusalem's Old City on April 11, during Christian Holy Week, caused significant consternation in the Christian community, including in the United States. Tensions were exacerbated by the revelation that Israel's Ministry of Housing had provided substantial financial aid for purchase of the building's lease from its present tenant. American Jewish organizations, joined by Jerusalem mayor Teddy Kollek and other Israeli leaders, were quick to condemn the action, asserting that the incident was idiosyncratic, an aberration of long-standing policy of sensitivity to religious and ethnic diversity in the Old City.

The Middle East Council of Churches, a consistent anti-Israel voice since its founding, called for a public campaign during the Easter season of "prayer and action for peace in the Holy Land." Elements of the campaign included a "Prayer from Jerusalem," distributed by the National Council of Churches (NCC) and intended for use in churches on Palm Sunday, April 8; and "Prayers for the Peace of Jerusalem," for the Christian Pentecost on June 3. The National Jewish Community Relations Advisory Council, in an analysis of the Holy Week prayer on behalf of a consortium of Jewish groups, concluded, "The true purpose of the prayer is to transmit anti-Israel attitudes within a liturgical setting. . . . The prayer is a theological screen for political extremism and distortion." And the National Conference of Christians and Jews (NCCJ) characterized the prayer as "triumphal, contradicting the NCC's work to overcome such attitudes," and asserted that the prayer recalls "the worst uses of Christian Holy Week as a club against Jews." The NCCJ cautioned that the prayer's use could "cause Jewish-Christian tensions in U.S. communities." However, consistent with a long-recognized pattern on matters having to do with Israel and the Middle East, the issue had very limited play in local churches and even less among those in the pews.

PROTESTANT DENOMINATIONS AND ISRAEL

Exemplifying national denominational views on Israel was the resolution adopted by the General Assembly of the Presbyterian Church (U.S.A.), the main denominational body for Presbyterians in the United States, at its General Assembly in June. The resolution, "Continuing Concern for the Israeli/Palestinian Situation," took a more hostile posture than that body's 1989 resolution on Israel, recommending that the U.S. Congress "make the continuation of U.S. aid contingent upon an end to further settlements in the occupied territories, and an end to human-rights violations as enumerated by the U.S. State Department in its Annual Report." It further recommended that the State Department "designate 10 percent of all appropriated aid for Israel to be used exclusively for the educational, medical, and economic benefit of Palestinians in the occupied territories." Jewish community-relations organizations were encouraged to meet with local presbyteries and to make positive "overtures" on Israel, with an eye to the next (1991) assembly.

The National Council of Churches underwent leadership changes during 1990, and signaled Jewish groups that it would seek to enhance Christian-Jewish relations, particularly through expansion of the activities of the reactivated Office of Jewish-Christian Relations. Although General Secretary James A. Hamilton said that the NCC would seek to moderate its previously harsh posture on issues involving the Middle East, NCC response on the national level to the Persian Gulf crisis raised questions for Jewish groups. The General Board of the NCC, meeting in November, issued a message that linked the crisis with a call for withdrawal of Israeli forces from the West Bank and for convening an international conference to resolve the Israeli-Palestinian issue.

A positive development in denominational activities was the "Message" on Jewish-Christian relations, issued in May by the United Church of Christ (UCC; formerly New England Congregational). The UCC reaffirmed its 1987 condemnation and repudiation of anti-Semitism and of supersessionism. "God has *not* abrogated the Jews' covenant," asserted the UCC statement. The UCC followed the pattern of positive declarations on Jews and Judaism that had emerged from a number of denominations in recent years.

Black-Jewish Relations

Black-Jewish relations during 1990 continued to be troubled, in the eyes of most observers. One element was the specter of black anti-Semitism that haunted large segments of the American Jewish community (see above). One analyst, Earl Raab, director of Brandeis University's Perlmutter Institute for Jewish Advocacy, suggested, "American Jews may tend to overstate the extent of black hostility towards them, and, in so doing, may tend to understate the importance to their security of more general race-connected problems in the country." In general, despite the rise in race-connected violence, race-related problems were not considered top priorities on the Jewish communal agenda. Rather, attention was paid to specific situations as they arose.

MANDELA VISIT TO U.S.

Tensions between Jewish groups and Nelson Mandela, the long-imprisoned South African National Congress leader, threatened to mar the black leader's first visit to the United States in June. Many Jews were unhappy that Mandela had, on a number of occasions, equated the nationalist struggle of black South Africans with the Palestinian struggle, and in March he reiterated his support of the Palestine Liberation Organization and of Libyan leader Muammar Qaddafi. In the hope of avoiding unpleasant confrontation, leaders of six Jewish groups arranged to meet with Mandela in Geneva on June 10, hoping to have him clarify his views on Israel before his scheduled arrival in the United States on June 20.

At the Geneva meeting, American Jewish leaders reaffirmed the Jewish community's unqualified opposition to apartheid and its strong support of the international arms embargo of South Africa. As for Mandela's views, they were summed up by ADL national director Abraham H. Foxman in a letter to the *New York Times* published on June 24: "We left with no doubt about his recognition of the legitimacy of the Zionist endeavor and the right of the Jewish people to a state in the Middle East."

Mandela, as expected, was embraced by the black community in the United States. He was warmly welcomed by most Jewish groups as well. He addressed an ecumenical service at New York's Riverside Church at which the presence of Jewish communal leadership was especially prominent. "It was an important continuation of the communication begun in Geneva," according to American Jewish Committee official Rabbi A. James Rudin. But soon into his American visit, Mandela, on national television, caused consternation when he stated that he considered Yasir Arafat a "comrade-in-arms." At the same time, rearticulating a theme from the Geneva talk, Mandela said, "We have been very much influenced by the lack of racialism amongst the Jewish communities."

Mandela's seemingly contradictory statements highlighted the potential for conflict in two of the basic missions of Jewish community-relations agencies: their role as human-relations organizations, promoting black-Jewish dialogue and opposing apartheid; their role as "defense" organizations, defending fundamental Jewish interests, particularly when the State of Israel is perceived to be under attack. The distress of most Jewish leaders over many of Mandela's comments was mostly kept under wraps, largely for fear of exacerbating black-Jewish tensions. One Jewish group, the Community Relations Council of the Greater Miami Jewish Federation, formulated a distinction that many subscribed to: "We separate Mr. Mandela's role as a symbol for the struggle for freedom and equality in South Africa from that of Mr. Mandela's statements as an individual who supports terrorists, terrorism, and oppression." Summing up the Mandela visit in terms of black-Jewish relations, it appeared that the restraint of the Jewish community with respect to Mandela's comments prevented further disruption in black-Jewish relations but also underscored the sensitive nature of those relations.

Church-State Issues

CHANGES IN FEDERAL JUDICIARY

Changes in the federal courts, especially on the U.S. Supreme Court—resulting from appointments during the Reagan and Bush administrations—had a profound effect on developments in the area of church-state separation during 1990. A shift in the Supreme Court's stance on these matters was signaled by decisions and opinions in a number of cases over 1989 and 1990, with both the "establishment" and "free exercise" clauses of the First Amendment coming under attack.

One important development was the surprise resignation in July of Associate Justice William J. Brennan, Jr., after 34 years on the Supreme Court, where he exercised leadership within the "separationist" camp. Named to replace him by President George Bush was relatively inexperienced David H. Souter, 50 years old, who had served 12 years as a state judge in New Hampshire and had just been appointed to the U.S. Court of Appeals for the First Circuit in April 1990. His record—including writings on judicial matters—was considered meager. In the view of most observers of church-state separation, Souter's replacement of Justice Brennan further diminished the core support for the High Court's position on church-state issues.

The sizable number of Bush administration nominations to the federal judiciary—72 through 1990—led, in the view of a number of analysts, to the tipping of a delicate balance between "conservative" and "liberal" jurists on the U.S. Supreme Court and on many federal courts of appeal. Jewish civil-liberties and -rights organizations expressed increasing concern during 1990 about threats to fundamental Bill of Rights protections resulting from the changing contours of the federal bench.

"ESTABLISHMENT-CLAUSE" MATTERS

On June 5, the U.S. Supreme Court decided a significant "equal-access" case, *Mergens v. Board of Education of Westside Community Schools*, testing the constitutionality of the Equal Access Act. The act, passed by Congress in 1984, required schools that established a "limited open forum" policy—namely, that permitted non-curriculum-related groups and clubs to meet—to allow religious, social, or philosophical clubs to meet on school property during noninstructional hours. The High Court upheld the act by an 8–1 margin, ruling that official recognition by the Omaha high school of a Christian Bible club did not breach the constitutionally required separation of church and state. An *amicus* brief was filed in *Mergens* by the Anti-Defamation League on behalf of the National Jewish Community Relations Advisory Council and other Jewish groups, who expressed dissappointment in the Court's decision. In the aftermath of *Mergens*, analysts suggested that civil-liberties groups, including local Jewish communal organizations, would be called upon to monitor high schools that chose to permit religious clubs to ensure that no coercion or proselytizing took place.

A reemerging battleground related to schools and religion was that of public aid to parochial schools in the form of vouchers and tuition-tax credits, and aid for remedial programs in schools. Growing dissatisfaction with the existing structure of public-school education had led some states to consider programs, including voucher and tax-credit systems, that would enhance parental choice in selecting their children's schools. In some cases, the universe of available choices included sectarian institutions. In one notable development on this issue, Ballot Measure 11, a voter referendum in Oregon that would have established a tuition tax-credit program "for education outside the public schools" in that state, was defeated by more than a 2–1 margin in the November election.

With respect to public-sector aid to remedial programs, two cases were on appeal in federal courts during 1990. In *Pulido v. Cavazos* and *Barnes v. Cavazos*, federal district courts ruled that publicly funded off-premises remedial programs for private and parochial schools were permissible. Previous Supreme Court rulings had invalidated attempts to use public funds to aid religiously related schools for auxiliary services under Title I of the Elementary and Secondary Education Act of 1965. Jewish groups were divided on this issue.

School prayer, a heatedly debated issue in recent years both in the Congress and in the courts, had a relatively low profile during 1990. In *Doe v. Human*—a case testing the legality of voluntary Bible classes during regular school hours in an elementary school—a federal district court decision halting the practice was affirmed by the U.S. Eighth Circuit Court of Appeals.

In Congress, in prior years a battleground for school prayer, a measure supporting voluntary school prayer that had passed the House of Representatives in 1989 failed passage in 1990 in the Senate. The measure, an amendment to vocational rehabilitation legislation, would have forbidden the allocation of federal vocational funds to any agency that has "a policy of denying . . . prayer in public schools by individuals on a voluntary basis." Introduction of this measure indicated an apparent shift in the tactics of school-prayer proponents, who now sought to introduce school-prayer legislation under the cover of other legislative vehicles, thereby bypassing the Senate and House Judiciary committees, which in recent years had not been supportive of school-prayer measures.

The issue of religious holiday observances in schools was addressed by a broad coalition of religious and educational groups that produced a pamphlet, *Religious Holidays in the Public Schools: Questions and Answers*, emphasizing the need for objective teaching about religious holidays rather than their celebration. The pamphlet was well received by school officials around the country, but a number of Jewish groups continued to view "teaching about religion" as possibly leading to more damaging practices.

The related issues of "values education," teaching religion, and teaching about religion reemerged, with a number of states considering the adoption of textbooks that included material on religious matters. Points of controversy on this issue were sharpened in June, with the issuance of a joint statement of the Synagogue Council of America and the National Conference of Catholic Bishops, calling for the introduction of programs and materials in schools on "civil and personal values," and encouraging congregations to press for "moral instruction" in the schools.

Other areas involving religion in the schools, such as prayers at graduation, baccalaureate ceremonies, and distribution of religious literature—situations previously considered by most observers to be "on the margin"—surfaced in federal and state courts during 1990. The case law on these situations was mixed, since issues such as distribution of religious literature raised free-speech as well as church-state questions.

The state of the law on religious symbols (including so-called menorah-crèche cases) remained unclear. In the last major case on the subject heard by the Supreme Court (*County of Allegheny v. American Civil Liberties Union of Greater Pittsburgh, et al.*, 1989), the Court ruled that a religious symbol standing alone, such as a nativity scene or a menorah, violates the establishment clause. However, following *Lynch v. Donnelly* (1984), the Court found that secular symbols accompanying the religious symbol—placement of a Christmas tree alongside a Hanukkah menorah— had the effect of making the entire display secular, and therefore constitutionally permissible. The issue of a religious symbol standing alone in a public park, arguably a public forum and therefore subject to free-speech protections, was not addressed by *Allegheny County*.

The Supreme Court in 1990 refused to review *Kaplan v. City of Burlington*, in which a federal appeals court ruled that placement of a menorah standing alone in a public park violated the establishment clause. However, a federal district court ordered the City of Pittsburgh to permit Lubavitch to erect its menorah on the steps of City Hall, a public forum. The city had refused to permit the menorah display because, under *Allegheny County*, the crèche could not be displayed at the nearby courthouse. The district court held that this was not sufficient justification for denying Lubavitch's right of religious free speech. According to Marc D. Stern, co-legal director of the American Jewish Congress, "A case-by-case approach is being taken, so that the 'public-forum' doctrine will not swallow up the Establishment Clause."

The Lubavitch/Chabad organization continued its efforts to place menorahs in as many communities around the country as possible. In most of those cases that were litigated—Beverly Hills, Cincinnati, Boca Raton, and Grand Rapids—Chabad won. (In Beverly Hills, the judge required placement of a Christmas tree together with the menorah.) In Atlanta, the federal district court ruled that a menorah could not be placed outside the state capitol, not on constitutional grounds, but on the basis of a state law prohibiting free-standing displays of any sort outside the capitol.

There was some federal-court activity in a number of communities surrounding non-holiday-related religious symbols on public property, in which the courts generally ruled that such placement was unconstitutional.

Most mainstream Jewish groups maintained the position that any public support of religious symbols—including their display on public property—violates the establishment clause. However, recognizing that changes in the country's judicial climate meant that they could no longer rely on the federal courts to enforce this view, it seemed likely that groups would increasingly seek protection from state constitutions and courts.

The question of prayer in the courtroom was ruled on this year. In *North Carolina Civil Liberties Union v. The Honorable H. William Costangy*, a federal district court in North Carolina barred a state-court judge from opening his court sessions with a self-composed prayer.

In another area of church-state separation, a case testing the constitutionality of a New Jersey fraud-protection law as applied to *kashrut* regulation was decided this year. In *Ran-Dav v. New Jersey*, a state court found that the law and accompanying regulations did not violate the establishment clause. Jewish groups had long held that the state has a legitimate interest in protecting consumers against fraud, and that this interest, even in areas involving religion (such as the dietary laws), was not compromised by the First Amendment.

The first effort to codify this principle on a federal level was mounted by Rep. Stephen Solarz (D., N.Y.). In August, Solarz introduced into the House of Representatives the Public Disclosure of Religious Dietary Certification Act, which would require manufacturers of products labeled as kosher to file certain information with the U.S. Food and Drug Administration. While the legislation, developed by Agudath Israel of America, an Orthodox group, raised some questions with respect to its constitutionality, by and large most other Jewish groups supported the bill's principle. The bill died with the adjournment of the 101st Congress.

"FREE EXERCISE"-CLAUSE MATTERS

A serious and potentially crippling blow to the free exercise of religion occurred in April 1990, when the Supreme Court, in *Employment Division of Oregon v. Smith*, rejected the "compelling state interest" standard in use since 1963 in free-exercise cases. This test held that where the free exercise of religion conflicts with an otherwise valid law of general applicability, the government must demonstrate a compelling interest in order to deprive a person of his or her religious rights. In *Smith* the Supreme Court held that two Native Americans, dismissed from their jobs as drug counselors because of their sacramental ingestion of peyote—an illegal hallucinogenic drug—were not entitled to unemployment compensation. The Court held that the use of peyote was not protected by the free-exercise clause, because the law banning the use of the drug did not single out Native Americans or their church but applied to everyone equally.

In a stunning departure from settled jurisprudence, Justice Antonin Scalia, writing for the 6–3 majority in *Smith*, asserted that the Oregon law had no free-exercise implications and, thus, that the "compelling state interest" standard need not be applied. Additionally, Justice Scalia called into question the role of the courts in safeguarding the rights of religious minorities. He noted that, while a state might legitimately grant a "religious-practice exemption," such an exemption was not "constitutionally required. . . . It may be fairly said that leaving accommodation to the political process will place at a relative disadvantage those religious practices that are not widely engaged in."

The fallout from *Smith* was felt in some situations at the state and local levels and in several cases in federal courts and the U.S. Supreme Court. Within days of the decision in *Smith*, in a 7–2 decision, in *Minnesota v. Hershberger*, the Supreme Court set aside a 1989 Minnesota Supreme Court decision that exempted members of the Old Order Amish from complying with a highway safety law. The Amish had maintained that the law placed an unconstitutional burden on their free exercise of religion, and the Minnesota court had exempted the Amish, on religious grounds, from observing the traffic law. The Supreme Court, citing *Smith*'s rejection of the "compelling state interest" test, ordered the Minnesota court to review the case under the Scalia guidelines.

Observers of church-state relations averred that the principle of religious freedom would be dangerously eroded by the decision in *Smith*. Jewish groups were concerned, for example, that kosher slaughter could be in jeopardy, or that zoning regulations could be used to exclude houses of worship. The *Smith* decision may have effectively demolished the constitutional protection that had shielded religious groups, including those with unpopular views and conduct, from the legislative will of intolerant majorities.

At least one other Supreme Court case in 1990 was decided on the basis of Scalia's *Smith* opinion. The U.S. Supreme Court reversed a landmark case, *City of Seattle v. First Covenant Church*, in which the Washington Supreme Court ruled for the church—which had resisted landmarking status—on the basis that preservation was not a "compelling state interest." The U.S. Supreme Court vacated the Washington court's ruling. And in Rhode Island, in *Yang v. Riley*, a case testing the right of Hmong Laotians to refuse to have autopsies performed, a federal district court judge revised his opinion in light of *Smith* and ruled against the Hmong religious principle. Rhode Island subsequently passed autopsy legislation protective of religious rights. Analysts of free-exercise law suggested that, in the aftermath of *Smith*, discrete legislation in many areas would have to be carefully scrutinized in terms of religious protection, or special laws passed.

Legislation was introduced on July 30 in the 101st Congress to remedy *Smith*. The Religious Freedom Restoration Act, sponsored by Rep. Stephen Solarz (D., N.Y.), was drafted by a broad coalition of religious and civil-liberties groups. Despite wide-ranging support, however, the measure failed of passage in 1990. Reintroduction of the bill in the 102nd Congress was expected by coalition members.

In a related development, legislation was introduced, but failed to pass, in the

101st Congress to reverse the 1986 Supreme Court decision in *Ansonia v. Philbrook*. In *Philbrook* the Supreme Court rejected arguments by religious employees seeking to broaden the standard in use for "reasonable accommodation" for Sabbath and holiday observance. Religious-liberty organizations vowed to press for passage of legislation to remedy *Philbrook* in the 102nd Congress.

TAXATION OF RELIGION

Taxation of religious institutions, a most sensitive area, was tested in the courts this year, with *Jimmy Swaggart Ministries v. California Board of Education* decided in January by the U.S. Supreme Court. From 1974 to 1981, the Louisiana-based Swaggart group held 23 religious "crusades" in California, during which the ministries sold religious and nonreligious merchandise and were taxed on these sales, as well as on mail-order merchandise. Swaggart's request for a refund of the sales tax, contending that churches ought not be taxed for disseminating doctrine and carrying on worship, was denied. A unanimous Supreme Court ruled that the mere fact that the imposition of a tax made religious activity marginally more expensive was not unconstitutional. Church-state observers suggested that, with the decisions in *Swaggart* and the 1989 *Texas Monthly v. Bullock*, the heretofore-assumed principle of the exemption of religious organizations from certain types of taxation could no longer be assumed or asserted.

OTHER CHURCH-STATE MATTERS

The controversy over provisions of federal child-care legislation that impinge on church-state separation continued during 1990. The legislation, the Act for Better Child Care Services (known as the "ABC" bill), was passed by the Senate (S. 5) this year, in spite of the opposition of many groups in the organized Jewish community, including the National Jewish Community Relations Advisory Council, the American Jewish Congress, the National Council of Jewish Women, the Anti-Defamation League, the American Jewish Committee, and the synagogue bodies of the Conservative and Reform movements, as well as groups such as Americans United for the Separation of Church and State. These organizations maintained that the ABC bill permitted sectarian institutions to receive public money for child care with no prohibitions on sectarian worship or instruction. ABC also permitted, in effect, the use of child-care vouchers for sectarian purposes at day-care facilities. Sen. Robert Dole (R., Kan.), a supporter of the ABC bill, had warned in 1989 that the bill, if passed, would lead to litigation because of church-state concerns.

The House version of the child-care bill, H.R. 3, passed on March 29 by a 265–145 margin. The bill included an earlier amendment by Rep. Richard Gephardt (D., Mo.) that permits the use of vouchers in church-run day-care facilities, even if sectarian education is provided. Rejected, by 297–125, was an amendment by Rep.

Don Edwards (D., Calif.) that would have barred the use of federal funds for sectarian worship or instruction, and prohibited religious discrimination in the hiring of child-care workers by sectarian institutions that receive federal funds. Jewish groups awaited the promulgation of administrative regulations governing the measure.

The debate on this issue led analysts to suggest that differences over the provision of social services in sectarian settings could lead to both a breakdown in consensus within the Jewish community and increasing strains in coalitional relationships with other groups.

A legal test of a group's right to maintain a sectarian or parochial character emerged this year. In *Welsh v. Boy Scouts of America*, an atheist sued the Boy Scouts, alleging that its policy of refusing membership to children who don't believe in God discriminated on the basis of religion in a place of public accommodation. A federal judge in Chicago ruled that the claim had merit. For Jewish groups, the case raised questions about the ability of the quasi-religious organizations that abound in the Jewish community to restrict membership to Jews.

In the area of religion and politics, New York archbishop John Cardinal O'Connor caused a furor on June 14 when he warned Catholic office-holders that "they are at the risk of excommunication" if they support abortion rights. While most Jewish groups did not publicly comment on the cardinal's remarks, which appeared in the weekly archdiocesan newspaper *Catholic New York*, Jewish community-relations organizations had long-standing positions opposing the use of ecclesiastical sanctions with respect to public-policy matters.

Civil Rights

The long-standing dispute over quotas dominated debate on civil-rights legislation in the 101st Congress. The Civil Rights Act of 1990 (S. 2104 and H.R. 4000), introduced in February, aimed at strengthening remedies for gender, racial, religious, and ethnic on-the-job discrimination in hiring, promotion, and termination. The bill also amended Title VII of the Civil Rights Act of 1964 to allow for punitive damages in cases of gender, religious, or ethnic discrimination. (Under present Title VII law such damages were available only to victims of racial discrimination.) Among other things, the legislation would make it easier for a plaintiff to prove the discriminatory effect of employment practices and to require employers to defend the legitimacy of such practices.

The Bush administration objected to S. 2104/H. R. 4000 on the grounds that the legislation would result in the imposition of minority hiring quotas. (The administration supported a substitute civil-rights bill, which used a different test for discrimination.) Jewish groups, working within a larger coalition spearheaded by the Washington-based Leadership Conference on Civil Rights (LCCR), engaged throughout the year with congressional leaders and administration officials in an effort to garner administration support. The Senate adopted the Civil Rights Act by a wide margin in July; the House passed its very similar version of the bill on October 17. President Bush vetoed the legislation, citing the quota issue. Neither body mustered the two-thirds majority needed to override a presidential veto.

The fact that Jewish groups, which were mostly on record as opposing quotas, gave strong support to the legislation, was intended to send the message that quotas were not an issue. Jewish groups, including NJCRAC, ADL, the American Jewish Congress, the National Council of Jewish Women, the American Jewish Committee, and synagogue bodies of Orthodox, Conservative, and Reform movements, and other organizations, expressed the view that legislative language that eased challenges to employment practices would not result in hiring or promotion quotas. These groups expressed disappointment over the Bush veto. One Jewish organization, Agudath Israel of America, opposed the bill because it believed that the legislation would indeed result in quotas. Reintroduction of civil-rights legislation was expected in 1991.

In one of the last decisions handed down in its 1990 term, the U.S. Supreme Court in June decided *Metro Broadcasting v. Federal Communications Commission*, a case involving FCC policies that gave minority broadcasters special preference in obtaining FCC licenses. In a 5–4 decision, the Court upheld the constitutionality of the FCC policies. Justice William Brennan ruled that the FCC policies do not violate the "equal-protection" clause of the 14th Amendment, since they are consistent with "longstanding congressional support" for achieving the important governmental objective of broadcast diversity.

Reaction of Jewish groups to the *Metro Broadcasting* decision was mixed: the Anti-Defamation League, which had filed an *amicus* brief supporting Metro Broadcasting, was disappointed in the ruling. It had argued that the FCC policies, in that they gave preferences to certain groups, were unconstitutional. The American Jewish Committee, which had filed a brief on behalf of the FCC, argued that the FCC policies considered minority status only to the degree of acting as an "enhancement" in the awarding of contracts, and not as the guarantee of such awards.

The decision in *Metro Broadcasting* was considered to have important intergroup-relations ramifications, because the High Court had been sending conflicting messages on affirmative action. Supreme Court decisions in 1989 forced state and local governments to revamp numerous affirmative-action programs; in *Metro Broadcasting*, however, a case in which federal programs to aid minority businesses were at risk, the Court ruled that such programs were constitutional. One implication of the decision in *Metro Broadcasting*, according to Jewish groups, was that the Congress might implement race-based affirmative-action programs simply to promote diversity.

Nazi War Criminals

DEMJANJUK CASE

The controversy over the trial of John Demjanjuk in Jerusalem continued, with developments both in the United States and in Israel. (Demjanjuk, the man accused of being "Ivan the Terrible" who operated the gas chambers at Treblinka, was extradited to Israel by the United States in 1986. After a lengthy and often contentious trial, he was convicted on April 18, 1988, of crimes against the Jewish people, crimes against humanity, war crimes, and crimes against persecuted people. On April 25, 1988, Demjanjuk was sentenced to death. In 1989, the Israeli High Court of Justice, which had planned to hear an appeal of Demjanjuk's conviction and death sentence, granted a six-month delay, based on reported new defense evidence that Demjanjuk was a victim of mistaken identity.) The Israeli High Court finally heard Demjanjuk's appeal on June 22. The burden of the defense case was that a different person—one identified as "Marczenko"—was "Ivan the Terrible." The prosecution claimed that Marczenko was Demjanjuk's mother's maiden name, and that "Marczenko" and Demjanjuk were one and the same person. There was no decision in 1990 on the appeal.

In the United States, Demjanjuk's family petitioned the Justice Department in February to produce transcripts of the interviews conducted by the department's Office of Special Investigations that had led to the ex-Cleveland autoworker's denaturalization in 1988. Judge Louis Oberdorfer of the U.S. district court in Washington, D.C., denied the family's request. (Judge Oberdorfer had earlier, in 1987, upheld a request under the Freedom of Information Act to produce other documents.) In December, James Traficant (D., Ohio), a supporter of Demjanjuk's claims, released what he claimed to be evidence of mistaken identity. Congressman Traficant's evidence was dismissed by a Justice Department official in December.

OSI INVESTIGATIONS

The Justice Department's Office of Special Investigations (OSI) continued its investigations of individuals who were suspected of being Nazi war criminals and were alleged to have lied when they entered the United States or applied for citizenship. Through 1990, 33 Nazi war criminals were stripped of their citizenship, and 29 of them were deported from the United States. OSI investigations were in process on more than 600 suspected war criminals.

The case of Boleslavs Maikovskis continued to garner attention. Maikovskis, 86, of Mineola, N.Y., had been the subject of a lengthy Immigration and Naturalization Service (INS) investigation. The INS began deportation proceedings against Maikovskis in 1976 on the ground that he lied about his past when he applied for a visa to enter the country in 1951. The intention of the INS at that time was to deport

Maikovskis to the Soviet Union, where he had been tried *in absentia* in 1965 and sentenced to death for war crimes, specifically, the killing of Jews and others in the area of Audrini, Latvia, in 1942. But Maikovskis slipped out of the United States in 1987 and traveled to West Germany, where he was arrested in October 1988. Maikovskis, who was charged in January with war crimes in a Muenster, West Germany, court, faced a life sentence.

Among other Nazi war criminals whose cases reached closure during 1990 was Martin Zultner, 78, who moved to Austria in 1975 and voluntarily relinquished his American citizenship in October rather than face deportation proceedings. An OSI complaint alleged that Zultner, when he arrived in the United States in 1950, concealed SS service at Mauthausen during 1943–45. The citizenship of Anton Tittjung, 66, was revoked in December by a federal district court, likewise on the grounds of concealment of wartime service in Mauthausen. Jakob Habich, 77, of Chicago, in the United States since 1955, had assertedly concealed his membership in Nazi SS Death's Head battalions and his service as a prison guard in Auschwitz, and was deprived of his citizenship in March. The OSI, citing Habich's fragile medical condition, agreed not to deport him. Bruno Karl Blach, 69, an SS guard in Dachau from 1940 to 1943, was extradited to West Germany by a Los Angeles federal district court order in January. Blach, who entered the United States in 1956 and never became an American citizen, was sent to Duisberg, West Germany, to stand trial for mass murder in Germany and Austria. Albert Ensin, 68, of Stoughton, Massachusetts, who was not a U.S. citizen, was ordered not deported by a U.S. immigration judge for health reasons.

OUTSIDE THE U.S.

The case of Arthur Rudolph, 83, who was deported from the United States to West Germany in 1983, came to public attention again this year. Rudolph was the Nazi rocket scientist who was invited to the United States in 1957 and headed the "Saturn 5" project at the Marshall Space Center at Huntsville, Alabama. He chose deportation over the alternative of remaining in the United States and facing criminal charges.

In July Rudolph arrived in Canada, intending to remain in Canada on an extended visit. An American organization based in Huntsville, "Friends of Arthur Rudolph," with support of Rep. James Traficant (D., Ohio)—who had been active in support of Demjanjuk—advocated on behalf of the former NASA scientist. In December, Rudolph was found by Canadian immigration authorities to be not admissible, on the grounds that there was sufficient evidence that he had been an accessory to war crimes. Rudolph had already voluntarily returned to West Germany on August 13.

Other Holocaust-Related Matters

During 1990 the German Democratic Republic, in a reversal of a 40-year policy, formally acknowledged for the first time its share of responsibility for Jewish victims of Nazi persecution. On April 12, a statement of apology for the Holocaust, asking forgiveness of the Jewish people, was read in the Volkskammer, East Germany's first freely elected parliament. In June, the first individual reparations claim against the new East German regime was filed by a Philadelphia attorney on behalf of a survivor. In September, the two Germanys, as part of their Unification Agreement, committed themselves to negotiate new restitution agreements with the Conference on Jewish Material Claims Against Germany for certain categories of Holocaust survivors.

A noteworthy event was a Conference on Moral Courage During the Holocaust and in a Post-Holocaust World, convened in May by the Jewish Foundation for Christian Rescuers, founded by Rabbi Harold Schulweis of Encino, California, and Eva Fogelman of New York, and now a project of the Anti-Defamation League; and by Princeton University's Woodrow Wilson School. The issue of Christian rescuers of Jews during the Nazi era—the "Righteous Among the Nations"—had received scant attention, and indeed some scorn, among some in the survivor community. The Princeton conference, together with the activities of a number of scholars and those of the Jewish Foundation, gave visibility to this relatively neglected area of Holocaust-related activity and study.

The Pollard Affair

In March, Jonathan J. Pollard filed a motion with the U.S. district court for the District of Columbia, to have his 1986 plea of guilty set aside. Pollard had pleaded guilty and was convicted in June 1986 of spying for Israel and was serving a life sentence. Pollard's attorneys contended that the government had violated a number of promises made in the plea-bargain agreement, chiefly not to seek a life sentence. Were their petition granted, Pollard would be entitled to a trial on the espionage charges. However, in September, U.S. district court judge Aubrey Robinson denied Pollard's plea-withdrawal motion. Observers noted that courts do not readily grant such motions.

Meanwhile, sporadic campaigns throughout the year on Pollard's behalf were mounted by members of Pollard's family and other activists. Jewish groups in the United States, while not adopting a formal advocacy role, explored with Justice Department officials questions regarding the circumstances surrounding Pollard's sentencing and allegations of discrimination, civil-rights abuses, and anti-Semitism.

JEROME A. CHANES

The United States, Israel, and the Middle East

RELATIONS BETWEEN THE United States and Israel in 1990 focused primarily on three areas: the Arab-Israeli peace process, with its continuing ups and downs; Israel's request for financial assistance in the absorption of Soviet Jewish immigrants; and the crisis in the Persian Gulf that began to unfold in August.

The Peace Process

In December 1989 Secretary of State James Baker had succeeded in persuading Israel and Egypt to accept "in principle" his five-point plan for negotiations between Israel and the Palestinians, which included preliminary talks among the United States, Egypt, and Israel, a list of Palestinians satisfactory to Israel, and plans for an Israeli-Palestinian dialogue in Cairo. As the year ended, Baker was seeking a date for a Washington meeting of Israeli foreign minister Moshe Arens, Egyptian foreign minister Ahmad Esmat Abdel-Meguid, and himself.

Early in January, a meeting date had still not been set. There were reports that it might not take place at all because of the wide gulf between the sides on conditions each wanted attached to the Baker plan. Israel interpreted the plan to support its refusal to deal even indirectly with the PLO, while Egypt assumed that it provided for the PLO to approve the Palestinian negotiations. Commenting on such reports on January 8, State Department spokeswoman Margaret Tutwiler denied that the United States had given up on chances for the meeting: "Secretary Baker has always said as long as there is hope, he would stay engaged. We have no reasons for him not to be engaged right now." Two days later, after the Israeli inner cabinet gave no response to the latest U.S. bid, she indicated that the secretary was increasingly impatient at the lack of movement and that he might turn to "other areas of the world clamoring for his attention." The comments were believed to be directed mostly at Israeli prime minister Yitzhak Shamir and his coalition government. Tutwiler added that Baker had not given up and had actually resumed his personal involvement—missing for the past month—with phone calls to Meguid and Arens.

Talk of uncertainty about a U.S. role led the Egyptian foreign minister to fly to Washington on January 16 to appeal for continued involvement. Reports indicated that Cairo was alarmed not only by news of U.S. distancing but also by Shamir's recent comment—regarding the influx of Soviet Jews (January 14)—that a "big Israel" was required to accommodate the newcomers. Meguid said the next day that the comment did "not serve the interests of peace in the Middle East and it would be better if Shamir stopped making such statements." After meeting with Baker, Meguid told reporters that Egypt wanted to pursue the process but added that no progress had been made on a three-way meeting. Egyptian diplomacy continued closer to home when it was announced, the next day, that Israel's finance minister, Labor leader Shimon Peres, would visit Cairo the following week at the invitation of President Hosni Mubarak to discuss the negotiations. The invitation was seen as a slap at Likud leaders Shamir and Arens.

The differing perspectives within the unity government of Israel surfaced in full force during Peres's visit to Cairo on January 24. On arrival at the airport, he told reporters that the parties "are very near an agreement" on direct talks between Israel and the Palestinians and that such talks "can be started rather soon." Shamir chief of staff Yossi Achimeir, upon hearing of Peres's words, rejected his comments—"I don't know on what basis he said this"—and denied that Shamir had dropped his opposition to deported Palestinians taking part in the proposed talks. Later in the day, following his meeting with Mubarak, Peres reiterated his optimistic assessment and indicated that he and the Egyptian leader had agreed on compromises that would allow two West Bank residents deported by Israel to join the Palestinian negotiating team and permit Arab residents of East Jerusalem to take part. Reports suggested that Peres would submit the ideas agreed upon to a vote by the 12-member Israeli cabinet, and if the proposal were defeated, Labor would pull out of the government.

At the very time that stories were coming out of Washington that Baker might meet Arens and Meguid in Europe in mid-February, the process was sidetracked when a tour bus in Egypt carrying a group of Israeli academics and their wives was attacked by assailants armed with rifle and grenades, killing 8 and wounding 17. Mubarak, who had snubbed Shamir on several recent occasions, called him to express sympathy for the families of the victims. Israel expressed satisfaction at Egypt's response, but because of the tragedy, a much-anticipated session of the Likud party's Central Committee was postponed, as was the possibility of a three-way meeting the following week in Geneva.

On February 12, the Likud meeting was finally held. Disorder and chaos characterized the event. Housing Minister Ariel Sharon announced his resignation from the government on the grounds that the party was making concessions on its principles not to deal with the PLO or to give up any territory. Shamir, after a long speech, broke from the agenda and asked the 3,000 delegates for a show of support. As hands shot up, and amid the shouts of Sharon supporters, the prime minister declared himself the victor and marched from the room.

Tension grew when, ten days later, the Labor party's Central Bureau voted unanimously to leave the government if Likud did not accept Labor's compromise formula for starting negotiations by March 7. While Labor had made earlier threats to leave, this was taken more seriously. Labor was perceived to have improved its political standing due, on one hand, to Likud squabbling and, on the other, to commitments of support from enough smaller parties to enable it to form a government without Likud.

In the United States, a note of optimism was sounded by Assistant Secretary for

Mid-East Affairs John Kelly in testimony on February 28 before the House Foreign Affairs subcommittee on Europe and the Middle East. Kelly told chairman Lee Hamilton (D.,Ind.) that he believed the three-way meeting would take place in March. Official sources, elaborating on Kelly's prediction, indicated that they expected the Israeli cabinet to accept within several days the latest U.S. proposals for a Palestinian delegation to include some members who were residents of East Jerusalem but who also had residences in the West Bank, and others who had been expelled from the territories by Israel.

Amid Israel's internal bickering over the process, Baker dropped a bombshell from Washington. On March 1, speaking before a House subcommittee, the secretary said that the United States would tie Israel's request for $400 million in loan guarantees for housing Soviet immigrants to a halt in new Israeli settlements (see below). Baker also said that the United States had "done pretty much what we can do, we think, from our end" to get the talks started and we "are awaiting a response from the Israeli government." A close aide to Shamir described him as "quite angry" over the timing of the settlements remark. Adding fuel to the fire, the day after the hearing, President George Bush said in Palm Springs, California, "We do not believe there should be new settlements in the West Bank or Jerusalem," thus appearing to challenge Israel's right to build in East Jerusalem.

On March 6, one day before the Labor deadline, Likud leaders agreed to open talks with the Palestinians, but only if East Jerusalem Arabs were excluded from the process. Likud also reserved the right to walk out of any negotiating session with Palestinians if they believed the PLO was trying to control or direct the discussions. Likud said it would not proceed until Labor accepted these conditions, its leaders pointing out that, in light of President Bush's comments on Jerusalem in such blunt terms and on the eve of a critical political decision, "we see the danger Jerusalem is in now, and we couldn't allow ourselves to put any question marks on it."

On Wednesday, March 7, the inner cabinet met to consider the critical issue, but failed to complete the discussion, postponing the vote until Sunday, March 11. That morning, the inner cabinet met in an acrimonious three-hour meeting. Likud rejected Labor's demand that the body vote on Baker's plan. Labor ministers stormed out and told reporters that they would try to bring the government down through a no-confidence vote. Peres summed up Labor's position: "We have said that the minute the peace process is terminated, this will put an end to the present Government. We shall draw the necessary conclusions from the new situation, which means that the present situation has reached an end, and we shall check all other alternatives." The next day Shamir beat Peres to the punch when he dismissed the finance minister, prompting the rest of Labor's cabinet ministers to resign.

ISRAELI GOVERNMENT FALLS

Two days later Peres got his revenge. By a 60–55 vote, with the abstention of five members of the Orthodox Shas party, the Knesset defeated Shamir in a confidence vote, thereby dissolving the government, the first time the Knesset had ever done so. Shamir, as a result, became the head of a transitional, caretaker government. All awaited the decision the following week by President Chaim Herzog to give either Shamir or Peres an opportunity to form a new government.

U.S. officials were reported to be unfazed by the developments in Israel, indicating that the fall of the government would cause a short-term pause in the peace process but could actually enhance prospects for Israeli-Palestinian negotiations in the long run. These officials noted that the government fell trying to resist the Baker plan and, citing the religious party vote, expressed relief that the president's recent comments on Jerusalem seemed to have had little effect on the Knesset vote.

On March 20, President Herzog chose Shimon Peres to try to form a new government because he believed that Labor had "the most reasonable and best chance to win the widest Knesset support." Peres said that if he succeeded in forming a government, he would immediately approve the Baker proposal. U.S. reaction was generally low-key; however, on April 19, the State Department called on Israel to choose a government "capable of saying yes" to U.S. proposals for negotiations with representatives of the Palestinians.

On April 26, after five weeks of unsuccessful effort to win support, Peres gave up his bid to form a government. The next day Herzog turned to Shamir. How the U.S. government felt about the Peres demise and the possibility of a new Shamir government soon became clear. Shamir had mocked Peres's assertion that Shamir's refusal to say "yes to Baker" had stalled the peace process: "I must say there is something perhaps ridiculous in the very slogan 'Yes to Baker' . . . If there is understanding and cooperation between us and the United States, no one can expect we will accept every proposal or idea of an American secretary of state."

The State Department was quick to respond. On April 30, in a stinging rebuke, it said that Shamir had torpedoed the U.S. initiative "on the verge" of direct negotiations between Israel and the Palestinians. It went on to say, "Saying yes to Secretary Baker's [proposal] meant saying yes to Israel's [own peace proposal], yes to Israeli-Palestinian dialogue, and yes to peace. Continuing to say no will give us very little to work with."

Shamir, like Peres, went through difficult weeks of bargaining with the small parties to form a government. With his final deadline only hours away, on June 8, the Likud leader announced that he had succeeded in bringing together a government deemed by some as the most conservative ever formed in Israel. The agreement reached with a variety of smaller parties stated as among its priorities "dealing with the massive immigration that is coming here and its absorption," as well as "strengthening, expanding and developing" Jewish settlements in the territories.

President Bush told reporters in Omaha that Israel's forming of a new government was an internal matter, but the tenor of his remarks made clear his attitude: "Israel can do what it wants with its government, and I'll work with whoever that country puts forward as their government. But they know the policy of the United States on peace talks. U.S. policy is firm. We want the peace talks to begin."

On June 11, the new government became official, with 62 of the 120 Knesset members voting approval. Tensions between Prime Minister Shamir and the U.S. administration resumed immediately. Two days after taking office, Shamir appeared to be hardening his previous position, saying that Israel would not negotiate with any Palestinian who opposed the idea of autonomy for the territories. Meanwhile, new defense minister Moshe Arens spent his first full day in office visiting the two largest Jewish settlements in the West Bank, and Police Minister Roni Milo, a close aide to Shamir, said that the Baker plan was "no longer relevant." At the same time, new foreign minister David Levy spoke in softer tones: "I will say to our American friends that this is not an extremist government. This is not a government opposed to peace."

Baker was not slow to react to Shamir. Testifying before a congressional committee, he delivered what *Newsweek* called a U.S. administration's "sharpest public rebuke to an Israeli government since the 1956 Suez crisis." First, he detailed how Shamir had scuttled his own peace plan. Then he complained that Israel's new government was posing more obstacles to talks. In the *coup de grace*, he offered the White House phone number: 1-202-456-1414 and said, "When you're serious about peace, call us."

Israeli leaders reacted with anger, Avi Pazner, Shamir's media aide, complaining that Baker had misunderstood Shamir, that there were no new conditions, and that Baker could have found this out had he contacted the prime minister. Where was the usual honeymoon? Pazner asked. "It's usual to give a new government 100 days of grace. We didn't even get a few days, not even 100 hours."

Israel's response to U.S. criticism that it was to blame for the stalled peace process was to direct attention to another issue, the absence of peace talks between the Arab states and Israel. On June 19, speaking before high-school students in Petah Tikvah, Shamir invited Syrian president Hafez al-Assad "to come, to talk, to conduct negotiations and maybe to get to peace." On June 25, Syria gave its first reaction to the Shamir invitation in the form of a commentary by the state-run Damascus radio, calling the gesture "a trick." On the same day, Syrian defense minister Gen. Mustafa Tlas said he had warned his combat troops of an attack from Israel.

Meanwhile, President Bush indicated in a news conference on June 20 that he had written the Israeli prime minister a letter to determine his "seriousness about the peace process." Officials said that the letter asked again for a positive response to Baker's request for Israeli agreement to open talks with Palestinians in Cairo based on Shamir's plan. When asked the next day by reporters for the administration's next move, Baker resorted to the George Shultz approach: "We can't make it happen, we can't impose it. The parties in the region have to want it. We can't want it any more than they do. That's what it really boils down to." Shamir's response came several days later. According to reports, the letter committed Israel to continue to work with the United States to promote a dialogue with a Palestinian delegation, but reiterated Israel's resistance to the participation of deportees and Arabs from East Jerusalem.

On June 26 and 27, Egyptian foreign minister Meguid met in Washington with Bush and Baker in what were described as sessions to discuss "prospects for reviving" the peace effort and "how we work together to do so." No new ground was broken.

The month of July was characterized by Israeli efforts to ease tensions with Washington and alter the image of the government as extremist. Defense Minister Arens steered Israeli forces away from conflict with Palestinians in the West Bank and Gaza, Foreign Minister Levy softened his former resistance to Israeli-Palestinian negotiations, and Housing Minister Sharon concentrated on housing for Soviet immigrants. As the month ended, no apparent direction was evident in the peace process.

And then the Middle East exploded.

The Gulf Crisis

On August 2, the forces of Iraq invaded Kuwait and within hours had overrun the small emirate. The invasion, which shocked the world, quickly became the focal point not only of Middle East but of world diplomacy.

For Israel, the move by Saddam Hussein was not so startling; indeed, Israel had been warning about his aggressive intentions for a decade and more. In 1981, Menachem Begin decided to deal with a growing Iraqi nuclear potential by ordering Israel's Air Force to destroy Iraq's nuclear reactor at Osirak. For that Israel was widely condemned, including by the United States.

During the 1980s Iraq was consumed with its war with Iran, which ended in 1988. As 1990 began, speculation grew about what Saddam Hussein would do next. Some analysis maintained that eight years of war were enough, that he would need a respite to rebuild. Others, however, noted that Saddam was moving toward making Iraq a Middle East superpower. The *Christian Science Monitor* reported in January that ambitious programs were under way in almost every aspect of the military— ballistic missiles, chemical and biological warfare, munitions, tank production, and nuclear weapons. Perceptions of an Iraq gone amok heightened when Iraq hung an Iranian-born British journalist, Farzad Bazoft, on March 15, on charges of espionage, despite appeals from Margaret Thatcher and others. Thatcher described it as "an act of barbarism deeply repugnant to all civilized people," and recalled Britain's ambassador in protest.

On March 30, a federal indictment was unsealed in San Diego accusing four Iraqis and the export manager of a London-based front company of conspiring to smuggle 40 nuclear-warhead detonation capacitors into Iraq from the United States. The Iraqi News Agency quoted a Foreign Ministry spokesman as denouncing the arrests as part of an anti-Iraq campaign on the part of the British government, news media, and "Zionists." The Western criticism spurred Saddam to give a belligerent speech on official Baghdad radio on April 2. Boasting that he had acquired advanced chemical weapons, he said that if the United States and Britain thought their criticism would provide political and diplomatic cover for Israel to strike at Iraq, they were mistaken: "Because, by God, we will make the fire eat up half of Israel if it tries to do anything."

In Washington, the Bush administration criticized Hussein's remarks as "deplorable and irresponsible" and called for concrete steps "to rid the region of chemical and other conventional weapons and to move toward peace." In Jerusalem, Shamir answered for his nation: "Let there be no doubt. Israel will also know how to defend itself in the future and defeat the evil designs of its enemies." Meanwhile, Jordan's King Hussein and Egypt's Hosni Mubarak rallied to Saddam's side, echoing the Iraqi leader's claims that his country was the target of a Western-inspired campaign of hostility. Early in May, Yasir Arafat ordered several thousand of his forces from Jordan and other Arab nations to be relocated in Iraq for training, a move seen as an effort to cooperate more closely with Saddam, to fight off challenges from hard-liners within his own organization, and to enhance his status among Arab leaders.

Saddam renewed his threats against Israel at the opening session of an Arab summit meeting in Baghdad on May 28, called to seek ways to stem large-scale immigration of Soviet Jews to Israel: "If Israel attacks, we will hit back strongly, and if it uses weapons of total destruction against our nation we will use against it the weapons of total destruction we have. There can be no concession on liberating Palestine." Late in June, Saddam continued his war rhetoric in an interview with the *Wall Street Journal*. He said that another Middle East war was "inevitable" unless the United States blocked Israeli policies aimed at dominating the Arab world. Saying Iraq would strike only if Israel struck first, he asserted: "We shall respond to an Israeli attack whenever it comes and wherever."

Saddam's aggressive language continued in July, but it shifted away from Israel and toward Kuwait and the Arab emirates. The issue was these states' oil production, which Iraq claimed was excessive, thereby weakening oil prices and hurting the Iraqi economy. In a nationally broadcast address on July 17, he charged that their oil production policies were the result of American influence seeking "to undermine Arab interests and security." Ominously, he threatened to use force against these countries: "Iraqis will not forget the saying that cutting necks is better than cutting means of living. O God almighty, be witness that we have warned them. If words fail to protect Iraqis, something effective must be done to return things to their natural course and to return usurped rights to their owners." The next day Iraq made public a letter to the Arab League accusing Kuwait of stealing Iraqi oil, building military installations on its territory, and reducing oil income by cooperating with an "imperialist-Zionist plan" to depress oil prices through overproduction.

On July 24, it was reported that Iraq had moved nearly 30,000 elite army troops to its border with Kuwait, and that the Bush administration had put U.S. warships in the Persian Gulf on alert. The following day, the United States called for a diplomatic solution to the crisis, saying there was "no place for coercion and intimidation in a civilized world." On July 25, Saddam summoned U.S. ambassador April Glaspie and, according to reports, conveyed a message to President Bush that Iraq sought to end the crisis peacefully and avoid a confrontation with the United States. On the same day, however, U.S. officials announced that Saddam's forces on the Kuwait border had grown to 100,000. (Later on, the meeting with Hussein became highly controversial, as questions were raised about whether Ambassador Glaspie had been sufficiently firm with Saddam, and if not, whether her conduct was her own doing or a result of instructions from Washington.)

On August 1, talks between Iraq and Kuwait that were being hosted in Jiddah, Saudi Arabia, by King Fahd broke off after only one session. Early the next morning, the Iraqi army invaded Kuwait; within hours it had seized control of Kuwait City and its rich oil fields and driven the emir of Kuwait into exile. President Bush immediately denounced the invasion as "naked aggression," and the UN Security Council issued a unanimous call for an immediate, unconditional Iraqi withdrawal.

On August 6, the Security Council passed Resolution 661, which called on the UN's 159 member states to halt all trade and other financial dealings with Iraq and occupied Kuwait. Two days later, at a news conference, Secretary of Defense Cheney and Chairman of the Joint Chiefs of Staff Colin Powell indicated that after consultation with King Fahd, the president had ordered U.S. military deployment to Saudi Arabia on August 6 and that the first American forces had taken off for the Gulf on August 7.

On the same day, the president, in a televised address, said that the "mission of our troops is wholly defensive," and they "will not initiate hostilities." Bush explained U.S. goals in the struggle: "First, we seek the immediate, unconditional and complete withdrawal of all Iraqi forces from Kuwait. Second, Kuwait's legitimate government must be restored to replace the puppet regime. And third, my administration, as has been the case with every President from President Roosevelt to President Reagan, is committed to the security and stability of the Persian Gulf. And fourth, I am determined to protect the lives of American citizens abroad."

On the same day, August 8, Iraq announced that it had annexed Kuwait, leading the Security Council, on August 9, to declare the annexation "null and void" under international law. The following day, in a historic decision, an emergency Arab League summit in Cairo voted to send troops to Saudi Arabia and other Gulf states to protect against further Iraqi attack. The Security Council, throughout the matter, continued to give the United States and others in the coalition further discretion. On August 25, it authorized the U.S.-led naval armada to use force to prevent violations of the UN economic sanctions.

ISRAEL'S RESPONSE

Israeli officials condemned the invasion, pointing to its broader significance. Avi Pazner, senior aide to Shamir, said: "I think it's time the world, especially the big powers, open their eyes and see where the real threat to peace and stability comes from in the Middle East. And it does not come from our conflict here with the Palestinians." Defense Minister Moshe Arens compared Saddam's invasion to events in the 1930s, when a "cruel and brutal dictator was gobbling up one country after another." He indicated that Israel had no intention of getting involved in any fighting with Iraq unless Iraqi troops moved into Syria or Jordan or "if Iraq takes aggressive actions against Israel."

The question of Israel's role in the affair was to become a recurring theme in the developing conflict. Early reports suggested that the crisis was bound to improve Israel's relations with the United States, strained during the past six months over the peace process. A senior Israeli government official told the *Washington Post* on August 5, "We are the big winners of the whole situation. It's like a God-given gift for us. It changes the perception of almost everything, above all the priorities of the U.S.-Israeli relationship." It was assumed that pressure on Israel in the peace process would be deferred, especially with the PLO in a new predicament as a Saddam ally that had also been cultivating the United States. On August 7, during a special Knesset discussion on the crisis, Arens read a statement that officially put forth Israel's position. "I ought to stress that the Iraqi invasion of Kuwait does not constitute a strategic change from Israel's standpoint. But the moment we see that we face a change—for instance, the entry of the Iraqi army into Jordan—we will act."

The Bush administration's decision to send military forces to Saudi Arabia and also to enlist Arab allies against Iraq was warmly praised by Shamir, who called it a "credible action, very encouraging to the free world." Meanwhile, it was widely noted that, while Israel saw itself as America's closest ally in the Middle East, the United States was not asking Jerusalem for help. As Simcha Dinitz, chairman of the Jewish Agency, told the *New York Times*, Israel needed "to keep a low profile because, in the U.S.'s efforts to draft the Arab world in a move against Iraq, Israel isn't any help." On August 8, Arens reiterated Israel's view that Iraq's invasion "does not represent a geostrategic change for Israel." He also commended the U.S. embargo policy against Saddam, saying it could be effective, noting that Hussein had made reversals at other times in the past.

On the same day, in an interview published in the weekly *Paris Match*, Shamir said that Israel had no desire to intervene in the Iraq-Kuwait conflict, but that there was a difference between Israel and Kuwait "and it is a big one, the Jewish state is not Kuwait and Iraq better not forget it."

Also on August 8, when Saddam announced the annexation of Kuwait, he pledged to fight what he called a "criminal force" assembling in the region under American leadership. At the same time he made comments about Israel and the

Palestinians which were seen as the beginning of a campaign aimed at dissuading other Arab states from participating in an economic embargo of Iraq. By invoking the Palestinian cause and implying that Kuwait was a stop on the road to the liberation of Jerusalem, Saddam was seen as going over the heads of Arab leaders who opposed him and straight to the masses.

When Iraqi military officials the same day threatened an all-out attack, after accusing Israel of disguising its aircraft in American markings, Israelis of all stripes began to prepare themselves emotionally for the possibility of war. Military officials in Israel were quoted as fearing that Saddam intended to attack Israel if the United States and other countries struck Iraq. This was seen as a way to draw other Arab states into the conflict on Iraq's side. Ze'ev Schiff, the respected military analyst for the newspaper *Ha'aretz*, wrote that the Iraqi lie "is apparently designed to pave the way for the launching of land-to-land missiles at Israel, in the event that the Americans launch air strikes against Iraq." *Yediot Aharonot*, the mass-circulation daily, ran a headline: "Apprehension in Israel: Conflict in the Gulf Could Reach Us." And the circumspect *Ha'aretz* proclaimed: "Estimation in Jerusalem: Iraq Is Likely to Launch a Missile Attack Against Israel," while Israel radio began to discuss the possibility of issuing gas masks to every citizen.

On August 12, Saddam addressed his nation on the crisis and offered the proposal that "all cases of occupation" in the region "be resolved simultaneously." Spelling out what he meant, he said that he referred to "immediate and unconditional Israeli withdrawal from occupied Arab lands in Palestine, Syria, and Lebanon; a Syrian withdrawal from Lebanon; mutual withdrawals by Iraq and Iran and arrangement for the situation in Kuwait." This linkage of the Arab-Israeli conflict to Iraq's invasion of Kuwait (though he never spoke of withdrawing from Kuwait) remained an underlying theme during the crisis.

The White House responded immediately, saying that the U.S. government "categorically regrets" the proposals. The administration statement urged enforcement of the UN Security Council resolutions calling for Iraq's "immediate, complete and unconditional" withdrawal and the restoration of Kuwait's legitimate government. It labeled Saddam's proposals as "another attempt at distracting from Iraq's isolation and at imposing a new status quo." In a news conference on August 14, Bush was asked whether the United States had an "across-the-board policy" against annexation of captured lands in the Middle East, clearly a reference to Saddam's proposal. The president refused to bite, saying, "I can only address myself to the current situation," that the invasion of Kuwait "is unacceptable."

One week later, Shamir told an Israeli television audience that the government was worried about a possible Iraqi attack on Israel but remained determined not to get involved in the crisis. He showed no displeasure with the U.S. request that Israel maintain a low profile, recognizing that any Israeli action might jeopardize U.S. relations with cooperating Arab states, that "it is in the interest of the United States that Israel not be involved now." Furthermore, he denied that Israel was failing to fulfill a role as a strategic asset to the United States, that in fact everything Israel was doing was "in agreement" with Washington. Shamir summarized Israel's posture: "It's clear that someone wants us to become involved in this conflict and that's Iraq and Saddam Hussein. He wants to make this into an Arab-Israeli conflict . . . but we have no intention of helping Saddam Hussein to involve us in this conflict."

Israel reacted more strongly to the mediation effort launched by UN Secretary-General Javier Pérez de Cuéllar, which raised Israeli concerns that a weak diplomatic compromise would allow Saddam to achieve some of his war aims and would be an invitation to aggression. On August 28, Defense Minister Arens stated on Israel television that, if Saddam "stays in power and retains the weapons, there will be grounds for concern here, in this region, and, I think, throughout the world. I hope this will not be the way the crisis ends." Zalman Shoval, newly appointed Israeli ambassador to Washington, said bluntly that the "whole Middle East and particularly Israel would be in grave danger" if Saddam survived.

With such stories circulating, Shamir felt compelled to explain to a Knesset committee, on August 28, that the Israeli government was not pressing the United States to go to war: "Israel isn't pushing the United States to do anything. Who are we that we'd push the only superpower in the world today? We aren't pushing the U.S. into any kind of war." Several days later, the *Washington Post* reported that on August 26 President Bush had sent Shamir a letter expressing thanks for Israel's willingness to be helpful in the Gulf situation. The letter was described by unnamed sources as having an "exceedingly warm tone"; the contrast was noted to the situation only a month earlier when Shamir was regarded within the administration as an untrustworthy ally whose obstructionist position on peace talks with the Palestinians had made him unwelcome in Washington.

ARMS SALES

A persistent issue in U.S.-Israeli relations during the Gulf crisis was that of arms sales. It first came to light on August 28, when the Defense Department indicated that it had agreed to sell Saudi Arabia a $6-billion emergency package of advanced weaponry, including F-15 fighter planes, M-60 tanks, and Stinger antiaircraft missiles. This sale was seen as significant because it exceeded the limits Congress had imposed on the Saudi Air Force for more than five years. That included a limit of 60 F-15s; the sales projected would increase the total number of F-15s in Saudi Arabia by early 1991 to 120.

In response, the director general of Israel's Defense Ministry, Gen. David Ivri, flew to Washington to meet with Pentagon officials to discuss Israeli needs. Reports indicated that Israel was asking for two batteries of Patriot missiles, designed primarily for use against aircraft but which also could be used against incoming missiles. It was noted that Israel had considered buying the Patriot system before the crisis but had decided against it because of the high cost.

Meanwhile, in September, the arms issue moved to a more serious level when it was revealed that the Pentagon was recommending one of the largest U.S. arms sales in history to Saudi Arabia, over $20 billion in advanced weapons. Included in the package—which was an expansion of the $6-billion deal reported in August—were F-15s, air-to-air missiles, Apache helicopters, Stinger antiaircraft missiles, and more. Shortly after the news broke of the sale recommendation, Israeli defense minister Arens visited Washington, where he told Defense Secretary Dick Cheney and National Security Advisor Brent Scowcroft that the sale and the soaring costs to Israel as a result of the crisis had severely eroded Israel's military position. After his meeting with Cheney, Arens told reporters that large-scale sales to the Saudis without adequate compensation for Israel "could upset the military balance in the area, and that would be destabilizing." It was reported that he had asked for an infusion of military aid on the order of $1 billion in 1990. Pentagon officials quoted Cheney as having reiterated the American "commitment to maintain Israel's qualitative military edge." Reportedly, Arens was also told that in view of the large-scale American military presence in the Middle East, the threat generally to Israel in the near term and the chance of any Arab attack other than from Iraq had been reduced. In the long term, it was acknowledged, Israel's needs would have to be addressed.

On his return to Israel on September 19, Arens said, "There are signs that Washington is beginning to understand Israel's needs" as a result of the Gulf crisis. Other reports indicated that the Arens visit had not met Israel's expectations; when asked about that in a briefing, State Department spokeswoman Margaret Tutwiler said only that the entire issue of arms aid to Israel remained "under discussion."

In Washington, the size of the projected Saudi sale generated a political uproar in Congress. House Appropriations subcommittee chairman David Obey (D., Wis.) called the plan "widely large" and "grossly oversized." Within days, on September 21, the White House announced a compromise on the Saudi sale, saying that after consultations with Congress, the sale would proceed "in phases." The White House went on to say that the sale "constitutes a key dimension of our overall strategy toward the Persian Gulf and could serve as well to protect American lives." It was reported that the first part of the sale, an emergency package, would be up to $8 billion, and was not expected to meet any serious opposition in Congress. The second phase, however, was seen by some members of Congress as still questionable.

LINKAGE

The issue of linkage of the Gulf crisis to the Arab-Israeli conflict surfaced again early in September. Soviet foreign minister Eduard Shevardnadze, in a speech in Vladivostok on September 4, described Iraq's seizure of Kuwait as one of "several highly complex interlocking problems" troubling the Middle East that required an international conference to seek a coordinated solution. He went on to say that Israel's agreement to such a conference "could exert a positive influence on the overall situation in the Middle East and on efforts to defuse the crisis."

The following day, Secretary Baker and Foreign Minister Levy met in Washington, the first high-level meeting between Israeli and American officials since the crisis began. After the meeting, Baker said they had agreed "that we should not link the situation between Israel and the Palestinians with the situation in the Persian Gulf, as some have suggested." He also thanked Israel publicly for maintaining its low profile in the Persian Gulf crisis. Levy responded in kind, indicating that he was returning to Israel with a "good feeling about the commitments to the needs of Israel." He said that Israel was keeping a low profile, "not because Israel is not an important factor on the scene, and not because there is no danger lurking or threatening Israel," but because Israel "stands firmly with the United States and understands what great tasks it is undertaking." Levy and Baker also indicated agreement on the importance of establishing a "credible" Arab-Israeli peace process which, according to Baker, was one of the best ways to prove that Saddam's approach was not the wave of the future in the Middle East. The next day Levy met with Bush, a meeting arranged by Baker after their session. The tenor of the meeting was reported to have been positive, once again highlighting the changed atmosphere since the Gulf crisis began.

On September 9, Bush and Soviet president Mikhail Gorbachev met in Helsinki, with the U.S. president rejecting efforts to link the Gulf crisis to the Arab-Israeli conflict but indicating that he might not oppose an international conference as long as it was not linked. Israeli leaders were low-key in their response; Avi Pazner, Shamir's press adviser, noted that the United States's "priority is to find a solution to the crisis in the Persian Gulf, and as to the future, it is much too early to tell what will happen." Clearly, the Middle East peace process remained on hold.

On September 14, Baker met with President Hafez al-Assad of Syria, in Damascus, the first high-level U.S.-Syrian meeting in more than two years. The session was seen as an effort to draw attention in the Arab world to hard-line Syria's participation in the struggle against Saddam Hussein, as a way to legitimize the coalition in Arab eyes in a way that no other country could. Syria had already dispatched 3,000 troops to Saudi Arabia. At a news conference, Syria's intent to cooperate with the U.S.-led effort against its old enemy, Saddam, was highlighted by Foreign Minister Farouk al-Sharaa's rejection of linkage: "Let me make it clear to you that I don't believe there is a linkage between the two questions. We are not linking the Gulf crisis with the Arab-Israeli crisis at all."

On September 23, Saddam Hussein stepped up his rhetoric, threatening to attack oil fields in Saudi Arabia and Israel if his nation was "strangled" by the economic sanctions imposed by the UN. The Iraqi statement, issued in the name of the Revolutionary Command Council, described the "prime objective" as "the liberation of Palestine from the usurpation of the Zionist usurpers." Bush administration officials described the latest Saddam outburst as part of his continuing political strategy aimed at splitting the international coalition opposing him, but also indicated that the events of July had taught them not to discount his threats as mere bravado. As one Pentagon official said: "It's a deliberate step in his plan to keep what he's got and drive our coalition apart. At the same time, we're not sloughing this off. He has the capability to do these things."

In Israel, Shamir responded to this most bellicose statement yet from Saddam: "We, of course, are taking his threats seriously and preparing for them, to anticipate, prevent, and God forbid, if he'll really attack, to repay him."

On September 26, Levy met Baker in Washington to discuss Saddam's threat. Reportedly, Levy pointed out that before Saddam's latest remarks, he had talked about "retaliating" against Israel with chemical weapons for any Israeli attack on Iraq, but now had changed his threat and begun talking about an Iraqi first strike on Israel. This new threat, Levy reportedly said, made it more difficult for Israel to maintain its low profile and made more urgent the need for U.S. assistance. Baker was said to have told Levy that the administration was "committed to Israel's security and you can count on that fact" if Israel were attacked.

One official was quoted as saying that Israel had "some legitimate concerns and we want to address them." Nothing concrete, however, emerged. In an interview after the meeting, Levy acknowledged that Washington's request for a low Israeli profile, made within hours after Iraq's invasion, had caused "a malaise about U.S.-Israeli relations" in his country. He continued: "The low profile was pursued so vigorously by Washington that it was made to seem Israel had vanished from the region. The U.S. administration knew what we were doing. But to American public opinion—to the man in the street—it was made to seem we weren't there."

On October 1, President Bush addressed the opening session of the UN General Assembly and expressed hope for a diplomatic solution to the crisis. Regarding the Arab-Israeli conflict, he made comments which were read by some as implicit linkage: "In the aftermath of Iraq's unconditional departure from Kuwait, I truly believe there may be opportunities for Iraq and Kuwait to settle their differences permanently, for the states of the Gulf themselves to build new arrangements for stability, and for all the states and peoples of the region to settle the conflict that divides the Arabs from Israel." The change was noted from the president's remarks at Helsinki in which he had said that the issue of a homeland for the Palestinians was a matter "separate and apart" from the Kuwaiti invasion. Bush later told reporters that he had not meant to imply linkage.

Early in October, Saudi leaders made comments that reflected their sense of urgency about defeating Saddam, while appearing loyal to the Arab cause against Israel. Defense Minister Sultan Ibn Abdal-Aziz warned Israel to stay out of the crisis and said that if each of the two found itself at war with Iraq, Saudi Arabia would fight in isolation and not allow Israel to come to its defense. These comments were the first in public by a senior Saudi official on the prospect of Saudi Arabia and Israel finding themselves at war with Iraq at the same time. On October 2, the Saudi foreign minister, Prince Saud al-Faisal, told the UN that Iraq should give up Kuwait to strengthen the right of Palestinians to claim a homeland in Israeli-occupied territory. The prince was seen as trying to show that Arab concern for the

Palestinians was constant, but that primacy had to go to resolving the immediate Kuwaiti issue.

The seriousness with which Israel took Saddam's threats was manifest on October 9, with the announcement that the military had begun handing out gas masks and chemical-warfare defense kits to the population. Shamir noted that Saddam had "made his threats many times and we must take his threats seriously."

The following day, events took place in Jerusalem that led to renewed strains between the United States and Israel and fueled Arab efforts to isolate Israel and keep the question of linkage alive.

TEMPLE MOUNT INCIDENT

On October 10, a struggle took place outside the Al Aksa Mosque on the Temple Mount involving Israeli policemen, hundreds of demonstrating Arabs, and thousands of Jews praying at the Western Wall during Sukkot, resulting in 19 Palestinians killed and more than 100 wounded. Mayor Teddy Kollek described the event as the most violent in Jerusalem since the 1967 war, the death toll the largest in a single day since the beginning of the *intifada*. Immediately, sharp differences were expressed as to how the violence erupted. Israeli officials claimed that Palestinians had come to the mosque not to pray but for violence, citing rocks thrown from the Temple Mount onto Jewish worshipers, creating a provocation calculated to distract the world from the Gulf crisis. Palestinians said that the events occurred when demonstrators seeking to prevent Jewish radicals from laying a cornerstone for a new Jewish temple were indiscriminately shot upon by police.

At a White House news conference the next day, the president rejected efforts to use this incident to create linkage: "Saddam Hussein is trying to, from the very beginning, justify the illegal invasion of Kuwait by trying to tie it to the Palestine question. And that is not working. The Arab world is united, almost united, against him. And I don't think if he tries now to use this unfortunate incident to link the two questions, I don't think that will be successful. And certainly I will be doing what I can to see that it is not successful."

That said, it was apparent early on that the effort to pacify the Arab coalition regarding the incident would lead the United States to come down hard on Israel. Bush rebuked Israel that day for not acting "with greater restraint." And he added that he hoped no one questioned "our interest in seeing a solution to the Palestine question, to the implementation of the Security Council resolutions."

Later that day, the United States asked the Security Council to approve a resolution condemning Israel for "excessive" use of force in the Jerusalem incident. The proposed draft never referred to the Israelis hit by stones directly but only referred to "innocent worshipers" and called on the UN to investigate and report back. It was described as by far the most critical resolution of Israel ever introduced by the United States. Israel's acting UN representative, Johanan Bein, said that Israel was being made a "sacrificial lamb" in order for the United States to maintain its coalition against Saddam.

Things then went from bad to worse between the two governments. On October 12, the Security Council passed a resolution condemning Israel and calling for a mission of the secretary-general to go to the region to investigate the matter and report back before the end of October. The next day, Israel's cabinet officially denounced the UN decision and declared it would not cooperate with the mission. David Levy focused on two points in explaining Israel's position. First, he said, accepting the delegation would mean accepting that "Jerusalem is not our legal capital and questioning our sovereignty over it." Secondly, he noted, in the resolution "no attention is paid to the savage attack of agitators against the calm Jewish worshipers praying on a holy day in a holy place."

On October 15, Bush declared that he wanted to see Israel drop its opposition to the UN mission. The United States had succeeded in watering down the resolution, and the longer Israel dragged out the issue, the more difficult it would be to pass any new anti-Iraq resolutions. According to Margaret Tutwiler, Baker had sent a message to Levy that the United States would have supported UN action on the Jerusalem incident even without the Gulf crisis. And he warned that if Israel did not cooperate, "there will be some who will compare you, even though it is not justified, to Saddam Hussein and his rejection of Security Council decisions."

In a speech before the Knesset on October 15, Shamir lashed out at the West, accusing it of hypocrisy and saying that "Israel will not pay the price of the lessons that the international community must extract from" its problems in the Arab world. Without mentioning the United States by name, Shamir complained that Israel was "expected to put up with the renewed and massive supply of arms and advanced weapons to [Arab] states, to agree to negotiations with the terrorist organizations, and to ignore the words of incitement and hatred that are constantly voiced and written in the Arab states."

Meanwhile, Jerusalem mayor Teddy Kollek said he would meet with the UN delegates, if asked: "It's haughty not to. I am confident enough of our situation and in the situation of Jerusalem that I can receive and answer anyone who comes here. This is a view of strength and not weakness."

On October 18, the government sent word that it would be willing to give the secretary-general a copy of the findings of its own inquiry into the shootings. The next day, Pérez de Cuéllar rejected the Israeli offer, saying "I can't make a report on the basis of the Israeli findings," and Security Council members from the Arab and nonaligned nations sought another resolution criticizing Israel. This one would cite article 25 of the charter requiring countries to obey council orders, would deplore Israel's refusal to cooperate with the secretary-general, urging it to reconsider, and would instruct the secretary-general to prepare a report on protecting Palestinians even if he could not send envoys to Israel.

On October 23, the council decided to put off voting on the new resolution while the Bush administration tried to persuade Israel to cooperate with UN representatives. The next day Israel rejected the U.S. appeal made in a letter from Bush to Shamir. Immediately thereafter, the United States voted with the rest of the council to deplore Israel's refusal to cooperate. As in the case of the October 12 vote, diplomats noted that the U.S. vote was largely influenced by its desire to preserve the international coalition opposing Saddam, the argument being that an American veto would embarrass the Arab states by casting the United States in the role of Israel's protector. Israel's acting representative, Johanan Bein, said at the council meeting that the PLO had deliberately sidetracked the council from the Gulf crisis by involving it in the Palestinian question: "It appears Saddam Hussein has been let off the hook."

In more moderate tones than in its reaction to the first resolution, Israel criticized the Security Council decision and rejected calls to reconsider its refusal to accept a UN investigative team. Shamir aide Avi Pazner said that Israel was "sorry that the United States supported an anti-Israel resolution because they are playing into the hands of Saddam Hussein."

Meanwhile, an Israeli commission named to investigate the incident issued its report on October 26. While the report sharply criticized senior Israeli police commanders, concluding that they had not adequately prepared for the possibility of trouble, it put the responsibility for the violence and killings on the Palestinians: "[T]he use of live ammunition in the Temple Mount under the prevailing conditions was found to be justified because the police officers were afraid for their lives." It said further that Muslim extremists incited the Palestinian crowd to violence and called the stoning of Jewish worshipers "a terrible criminal act."

The perceived dilemma for the United States on this matter—to support action against its longtime ally, Israel, or to block such action and risk endangering the coalition—sharpened when Pérez de Cuéllar proposed in a report issued November 1 that the Security Council involve itself directly in a search for a way to protect Palestinians in the territories. Among the report's recommendations was a meeting of all the countries that had signed the Fourth Geneva Convention of 1949 to discuss possible measures for preventing human-rights violations in the territories. Israel's UN mission issued a statement in response indicating that Israel had "sole responsibility" for administering the territories, adding that "this responsibility is not subject to review or intervention by other authorities."

On November 4, Israel's Foreign Ministry issued a statement criticizing the UN report for being one-sided and for "not calling for a stop to Palestinian violence." Concerning the call to convene the nations that had signed the Fourth Geneva Convention, the statement said: "For the 40 years since the Geneva Convention was signed there have been dozens of wars with millions killed and wounded. The international community has not found reason to convene the signatories even once." And the statement suggested that the continuing preoccupation with this matter would "only serve those forces who are interested in creating a link between the Arab-Israeli conflict and the Gulf crisis."

On November 11, Yosef Ben Aharon, Shamir's chief of staff, told the *New York*

Times that, while the government "cannot entertain any kind of investigation mission from the Security Council resolutions," it would be willing to see a single UN envoy, Jean-Claude Aimé, to hold talks on "the situation in general, the peace process, the entire gamut of human rights in the territories," instead of specifically raising the killings at the Temple Mount or protection for Palestinians in the territories. Ben Aharon also said that the envoy would have to agree not to discuss the proposed convening of the Geneva Convention signatories. Later that day Israel formally invited Aimé through the secretary-general.

FURTHER PEACE EFFORTS

On the broader front, November was a critical month because of President Bush's decision to increase dramatically the number of American forces and the Security Council decision to authorize the use of force. On November 8, Bush announced that U.S. land, sea, and air forces might reach 400,000 by early 1991. The president said it was being done to provide an "adequate offensive military option," which was the first public declaration that U.S. forces might take an offensive role. When asked how long he would wait for sanctions to work, the president said: "I hope that the sanction will work within a two-month period."

Meanwhile, congressional skepticism of the Bush approach appeared to be growing. On November 27, the Senate Armed Forces Committee heard a host of witnesses asking the administration to give sanctions a chance. But Secretary Cheney told the committee, on December 3, that there was no guarantee that sanctions would work even over five years, and that military action might be the only sure way to end the occupation.

Earlier, on November 11, King Hassan of Morocco called for an emergency Arab summit meeting, which he described as a "last chance" for peace. The next day the Iraqi regime indicated that it would not reject the proposal flatly, but reiterated its insistence that any solution of the Gulf crisis should be tied to a settlement of the Palestinian issue.

Tensions between Washington and Jerusalem mounted when it was announced that President Bush would meet Hafez al-Assad of Syria. On November 23, Prime Minister Shamir told reporters that he hoped the Bush-Assad meeting would "not encourage the oppressive policies of Syria against Israel." Defense Minister Arens went further in criticism of the U.S. decision, saying that if Bush met with King Fahd, Mubarak, and then Assad, but pointedly did not meet with Shamir, "there is a danger of the wrong message being sent." At the same time, Shamir struck a conciliatory note, pointing out that "the paramount goal, over and above all else, at this time in the region, is the existence and strengthening of the international coalition" against Iraq. However, other Israeli officials reportedly were asserting that the U.S. administration was misjudging Assad and Syria, the same as it had Saddam and Iraq.

Not surprisingly, Yasir Arafat, a frequent visitor to Baghdad during the crisis, expressed strong support for Saddam's assertion that any Iraqi withdrawal would have to be tied to other conflicts in the region, including the Palestinian-Israeli one. On November 22, in Tunisia, Arafat said: "One thing has to be understood clearly. We, the Palestinians, are not just a number in the equation. We are the difficult number. There can be no solution in the Gulf crisis without a solution to the Palestinian problem."

On November 29, in a historic decision, the Security Council voted 12 to 2, with one abstention, to authorize the United States and its allies to expel Iraq from Kuwait by force if Saddam did not withdraw his forces by January 15, 1991. This was only the second time the UN provided authority for individual member states to wage war against another country. Three council members—Yemen, Cuba, and Malaysia—sought to put another resolution critical of Israel's treatment of Palestinians living in the territories on the agenda ahead of the Iraq vote. Although the anti-Israel resolution was put off, attention returned to it soon after the resolution on Iraq was passed. Secretary Baker, at a news conference following the Iraq vote, denied that the United States had only avoided a fight over an Israel resolution before the Iraq vote by promising to withhold its veto when the Palestinian resolution did come up for a vote. Baker said there was no commitment except to "discuss with them next week in good faith the resolution which is now pending—and which is unacceptable to the United States in its present form—to see if we can come up with something we can support." It was noted that the PLO-backed resolution endorsed convening a Geneva conference, while a proposed substitute resolution introduced by Finland merely "welcome[d] the idea" of such a conference and called for further discussion and study, with no decision to be made until the end of the year.

Meanwhile, the day after the UN vote, Bush announced that he would "go the extra mile for peace" and offered to meet in Washington with the Iraqi foreign minister and send Baker to Baghdad to meet with Saddam. On December 1, the first hope for a breakthrough in the months-long Gulf crisis emerged when Iraq accepted the Bush offer for talks. In its statement of acceptance, however, the regime not only castigated the president as being the "enemy of God" and "arrogant," but said that it would continue to link the Kuwait issue to Israeli occupation of Arab lands. A White House spokesperson immediately rejected this avenue: "Our approach all along is that there is no linkage of the Gulf crisis to other issues, including the Middle East." And Vice-President Dan Quayle reiterated on CNN, "Palestine is not an issue on the table. There is no linkage."

The U.S. diplomatic initiative generated anxiety among Israelis and led several Israeli leaders to say openly what they had been reported to be saying privately for some time. Moshe Arens, Benjamin Netanyahu, and Ariel Sharon, as well as other members of the Knesset, all offered sharp public warnings that Saddam should not be left with his army and weapons intact, reflecting new concern in Israel that a diplomatic solution might be reached that would leave Iraq's military power in place.

In Montevideo, on December 4, Bush said he would not be "in a negotiating mood" if he met with Iraqi foreign minister Tariq Aziz, and indicated that there "will be no linkage whatsoever" between the Palestinian issue and the Gulf crisis. Despite these comments, Israeli concern mounted in the next few days, leading Foreign Minister Levy to warn, on December 5, against "a situation in which all the Western armies will leave the Gulf and Saddam Hussein will emerge with certain advantages." The ministry indicated that Levy told U.S. ambassador William Brown that the original U.S. position vis-à-vis Saddam "was one of the factors which Israel considered in adopting its low profile policy." And Levy later told Israeli television that whoever "thinks that if Israel alone has to stand up against this danger, that Israel will continue with a low profile, is making a mistake. In order to defend herself, like in the past, Israel will not call on anyone to fight its war or anyone else's soldiers, but will reply with all its might."

Five days later, while in the United States on a visit, Shamir said in a speech in New York, "We trust the American Government's determined stand not to permit Saddam Hussein to link the Gulf crisis with the Arab-Israeli conflict and the Palestinian issue." At the same time, he said that Israel would not acquiesce in any "move to appease Saddam Hussein at the expense of Israel."

On December 11, Bush and Shamir met in the White House for two hours. The Israeli prime minister emerged from the meeting with a positive statement: "We have been delighted to express our full support for the leadership of the President, for the policy of the United States in this recent crisis of the Gulf, and the President also expressed his support for our behavior, for our policy, and for our problems." Shamir adviser Avi Pazner told the *New York Times* that the Israeli leader assured Bush that Israel would not abandon its low-profile response to the crisis. He said, too, that Shamir came away from the meeting "more assured about American intentions and determination to bring the crisis in the Gulf to a solution" based on UN resolutions.

On the U.S. side, Assistant Secretary of State for Near East and South Asian Affairs John Kelly said that the two leaders "talked about the peace process in the Middle East and the fact that after the Gulf crisis has been solved, that it'll be advisable to try to reinvigorate the peace process." The meeting was widely seen as a U.S. effort to soothe Israeli fears about the growing military and diplomatic ties between Washington and Israel's Arab neighbors, reflected in the fact that Baker had been to the region three times and Bush once during the crisis without even paying a visit to Jerusalem.

While the UN vote authorizing the use of force against Saddam heated up the Gulf crisis and led the president to initiate his diplomatic initiative, efforts also increased at the UN to pass a new resolution against Israel. Throughout December, negotiations were taking place between the United States and nonaligned countries on wording critical of Israel, with the former seen as trying to avoid excessively harsh language and proposals but apparently ready to support a resolution in order to sustain the coalition against Saddam.

Finally, on December 20, the United States joined other members of the Security

Council in adopting a resolution that referred to lands held by Israel since 1967 as "Palestinian territories," criticized an Israeli deportation order against four Palestinians, called for the UN to monitor the Palestinians' safety in the territories "on an urgent basis," and carried with it a nonbinding statement by the council's president, Yemen, backing a Middle East peace conference. U.S. representative to the UN Thomas Pickering insisted that his vote "in no way indicates a change in United States policy on any issue related to the Arab-Israeli conflict." The resolution was the third one critical of Israel since the start of the Gulf crisis to be backed by the United States. Israeli representative Yoram Aridor called it a "biased, unbalanced resolution in which Arab violent provocations are being condoned, and Israeli defense against these violations is being condemned."

The resolution's statement on an international conference was subject to different interpretations. Some saw the fact that it was nonbinding and its language—"at an appropriate time, properly structured"—as being not inconsistent with the longstanding U.S. approach to Israel. Others, however, deemed it a change of tone even to consider the idea of an international conference in a Security Council statement, especially in light of recent U.S. support for three anti-Israel resolutions.

Clearly, the Gulf conflict was a dominant element in U.S. strategy. As noted earlier, a U.S. veto might allow Saddam to portray the Arab allies as siding with Israel's friend and protector. On the other hand, the administration was seen as wary of approving a resolution too favorable to the Palestinian cause for fear that it might be interpreted as part of a concession to Iraq.

Pazner said that Israel was "dismayed" by this resolution because it was one-sided and unjustified, but added that it would "simply be one more anti-Israel UN resolution that will have no effect and will be filed in the vault with all the previous ones." Israel's reaction to the U.S. vote was depicted as low-key because Israel believed that overall its previously strained relations with the administration had rebounded in the wake of Shamir's visit to Washington earlier in December.

As the year came to a close, talk of war was in the air, with reports that the Pentagon was telling the president that offensive military action against Iraq should be deferred at least until February. On December 21, in Saudi Arabia, Secretary of Defense Cheney said that it looked increasingly as if Hussein was "not getting the message and we'll have to use force to get him out." And the Pentagon issued a statement on December 26 to the effect that the threat of an Iraqi attack on Israel was "very realistic." It noted that, as a last resort, if Saddam feared war was inevitable, he could initiate conflict "which may include a provocation with Israel as an attempt to decouple the coalition forces." Meanwhile, Arens told the Knesset on December 25 that Israel did not "rule out the possibility of the Iraqis striking at us first." Arens said that Saddam's missiles had the range to reach Israel but their capability was "very restricted." In the same vein, Army Chief of Staff Dan Shomron said: "We must remember that Iraq's ability to harm us is limited while our ability to seriously harm the Iraqi homefront is proven beyond declarations. Saddam Hussein understands this simple equation."

These comments were seen as a signal that Israel would not launch a preemptive strike against Baghdad, hinted at a while back when Israel expressed frustration over a lack of strategic coordination between Israel and the U.S. military. The comments seemed to reflect the improved situation between the two militaries in response to Israeli complaints.

Absorption of Soviet Jews

Significant as it was, the major event of the year for Israel was not the Gulf crisis but the massive immigration of Soviet Jews. This movement, expected to continue for a number of years, was seen as a historic turning point for Israel, the fulfillment of its raison d'être. The large-scale immigration to Israel was initiated by two events: the opening of Soviet doors to Jewish emigration and new U.S. regulations limiting the number of Soviet Jews coming to the United States to 50,000 per year.

Early in the year, with projections emerging in Israel that as many as a million Soviet Jews could immigrate to Israel over the next few years, Israel turned to the American Jewish community for assistance. In January, Simcha Dinitz, chairman of the Jewish Agency, met with heads of the United Jewish Appeal and other Jewish organizations to ask for a greater sum than had been committed to earlier.

In mid-January, Shamir gave a speech to Likud party members that reverberated throughout the Arab world and elsewhere. In his talk, the prime minister appeared to connect Soviet immigration to the issue of the territories. "A big immigration requires Israel to be big as well," he said, adding that Israel should hold onto the territories because "we need the space to house the people." Criticized for his remark, the prime minister asserted in an interview with the *New York Times* that he had been misunderstood and did not advocate settling any Soviet Jews in the territories unless they chose on their own to go there.

Despite his clarification, the speech, together with the dramatic increase in the number of Soviet Jewish immigrants in January, generated great anxiety in the Arab world. King Hussein said the influx was "not a threat to Jordan only" but "threatens the depth of the Arab world and the Palestinian people's national rights." Egyptian president Mubarak called on the Arab states to protest. A Persian Gulf magazine in Qatar summed up the feelings when it warned that quick action was necessary, "otherwise a great Israel will become a fact."

Under heavy Arab pressure, the Soviet Foreign Ministry issued a condemnation of any settlement plan that would "endanger Soviet émigrés by using them to crowd Palestinians out of their own land," and suggested that such a move could undercut Moscow's efforts to liberalize emigration laws. In response, on January 30, Israel denied having any plan to settle Soviet Jews in the territories, saying that "anyone who comes to Israel can go wherever he chooses." It was pointed out that fewer than 1 percent of the Soviet Jews were, in fact, settling in the territories. On March 3, President Bush held a press conference in Palm Springs, California, at the time of a visit by Japanese prime minister Toshiki Kaifu. He used the occasion to express publicly his objection to Israeli settlements: "We do not believe there should be new settlements in the West Bank or in East Jerusalem." The president's inclusion of Jerusalem set off a furor, since it was clearly aimed at Israel's insistence that less than 1 percent of Soviet Jews were settling in the territories. Reportedly, advisers to the president had pointed out that the Israeli statistics were correct only if East Jerusalem was not considered part of the West Bank. If East Jerusalem was included, they noted, the actual figure was closer to 10 percent.

The magnitude of the influx of Soviet Jews led Israeli leaders to conclude that the absorption process could not be dealt with by Israel itself. As a result, Israel requested that the United States provide a $400-million loan guarantee to enable Israel to borrow the money from commercial banks at reasonable interest rates. On March 1, Secretary of State Baker, testifying before Congress, indicated administration support for the $400-million loan guarantee provided Israel stopped expanding settlements. Administration logic was that even if the money was not spent in the territories, the guarantee would free other Israeli funds to be spent on settlements. Two days later, the president added his remarks at Palm Springs, making clear that the administration still viewed Jerusalem as occupied territory. Israeli leaders reacted with bitterness. Shamir said, on March 5, that "there are no settlements in Jerusalem. It is part of Israel and it will never be divided again." And he insisted that new Jewish neighborhoods in Jerusalem would be expanded with "as many Soviet Jewish immigrants as possible." Meanwhile, on March 5, according to White House spokesman Marlin Fitzwater, the president told Seymour Reich, chairman of the Conference of Presidents of Major American Jewish Organizations, that he would support the loan guarantees "provided the United States and Israel can work out assurances that satisfy the United States on settlement activity."

Efforts to soften the impact of the president's comments soon began to emerge. In a letter dated March 16, Baker wrote to Mel Levine, Democratic congressman from California, that he was "very aware of the great significance which Jerusalem has for the Jewish people as well as for people of other religions" and said that Jews and others can live where they want, East or West, and the city must remain undivided."

In late April, Congress approved the FY 90 supplemental appropriations bill, which included the $400-million loan guarantee.

By May, Arab efforts to generate international opposition to Soviet Jewish immigration to Israel had taken a new turn. Negotiations were being conducted between the United States and Arab countries on a UN Security Council resolution criticizing Israeli settlements as a breach of international law. On May 10, Defense Minister Arens formally protested the negotiations to U.S. ambassador Brown, accusing the United States of supporting Arab efforts to halt the flow of Soviet immigrants into Israel altogether. One week later, the State Department announced that discussions between the United States and the Arabs on this matter had been suspended, reportedly because the Arabs continued to insist on including language which asserted that settlements violated international law, a concept the administration was unwilling to support.

Late in May the Arab states called a three-day Arab summit in Baghdad, primarily to discuss the perceived threat to the Arab world posed by the mass movement of Soviet Jews to Israel. At the summit Saddam Hussein urged economic reprisals against countries supporting the influx. The summit's final communiqué, however, merely appealed to countries to avoid aid to Israel "that would facilitate the implanting of the immigrants in Palestine and other occupied territories." The communiqué summed up Arab attitudes on the subject: "The conference is fully convinced that the transfer of Soviet and other Jews to Palestine and other occupied Arab territories represents a new aggression against the rights of the Palestinian people, and a grave threat to the Arab nation."

Arab pressure seemed to pay some dividends when President Gorbachev, in Washington for meetings with President Bush, intimated at a news conference on June 3 that the emigration flow could be stopped if Israel did not give assurances that Soviet Jews would not be settled in the territories. Responding to a question on the issue, he said that either "our concern will be heeded in Israel and they will make certain conclusions, or else we must give further thought to it in terms of what we can do with issuing permits for exit." Israel continued to insist, in response, that it was "not sending, not encouraging, and not giving incentives to Soviet Jews to settle in the areas of Judea, Samaria and Gaza." On June 5, however, Shamir also made clear that Soviet Jews would not be stopped from moving to the territories if they so desired: "If the Soviet Union or President Gorbachev does not think it can today tell its citizens where to live, it is as clear as the sun that we, as followers of freedom and democracy, cannot limit this category."

With foreign concern on the rise, the Israeli government announced on June 24 that it would not, as a matter of policy, settle Soviet immigrants in the territories. The announcement was made by Housing Minister Sharon to the Jewish Agency and was deemed significant as the clearest government public stand against settlement of immigrants in the territories. Sharon made the distinction between settlements generally and those for Soviet Jews: "The building policy, according to the government, is to be implemented in every part of the land of Israel. But immigrants, due to the problems we have, will not be settled beyond the green line. We will not send any Jew who comes from Russia to Judea, Samaria or to Gaza because we understand the seriousness of the situation. But that doesn't mean that other people cannot settle in any place." Immigration officials explained that Sharon's policy involved a modest change: before, Israel made no attempt to direct immigrants to any particular place, but from then on Israel would actively encourage Soviet immigrants to all points inside Israel; no new immigrant housing would be built in the West Bank or in Gaza.

As the months passed, even though the brouhaha between the United States and Israel over Jerusalem quieted down, the $400- million loan guarantee was still not approved. Finally, early in October, Secretary Baker reported that he and Israeli foreign minister Levy, after meeting in Washington, had reached agreement, with Israel confirming that "it is the policy of Israel that immigrants will not be settled beyond the green line." Baker also said that Israel had agreed to give the United

States periodic information about the financing of settlements, commitments described by Baker that "go beyond the traditional assurances that Israel has provided us with respect to the use of our aid in the territories." Back in Jerusalem, Levy gave a different reading on the agreement, saying that while new immigrants would not be steered to the territories, Israel was not eager to report on its settlement activities: "Our operations aren't subject to any approvals except that of the Cabinet and the Knesset. If our friends want to know from time to time, they can turn to the Foreign Ministry and receive the information."

Several days later Shamir announced that a new neighborhood would be built in East Jerusalem, making clear that the agreement regarding immigrants did not include Jerusalem.

U.S.-PLO Relations

The first year of the Bush administration, 1989, was a year of dialogue between the United States and the PLO. It was as well a year in which Israel continually criticized that dialogue on the grounds that the PLO had not ceased its terrorism and was not a fit party for peace negotiations.

Early in 1990, the Prime Minister's Office stepped up its efforts to persuade the United States to break off the dialogue, issuing a report that documented PLO violations of its commitment to stop terrorism. Referring to the talking points which the United States had conveyed to the PLO in 1988, making the talks contingent both on cessation of terrorism "by the PLO or any of its factions" and PLO condemnation and discipline of the factions responsible for any terrorism, the Israeli report said: "Not only has the PLO failed to fulfill these requirements, but Arafat's own Fatah organization, in particular, has itself engaged in terrorist acts. It has encouraged and lauded these attacks even in the midst of the dialogue." Israel claimed that since the beginning of 1989 there had been at least six attempts to penetrate Israel's northern border by guerrillas associated with the Democratic Front for the Liberation of Palestine, a leftist faction within the PLO.

The report also referred to evidence presented to Washington that Arafat's own Fatah movement had launched a raid from Egypt into the Negev on December 5, 1989. Five heavily armed guerrillas crossed the border that night, but were killed by Israeli troops before they could carry out any attacks. Reports indicated that American officials had raised the Negev raid with the PLO leadership in Tunis and had concluded that the attack had occurred without Arafat's knowledge or authorization. Israeli officials continued to insist that the United States was ignoring its own policy by keeping the incident quiet and by not calling on the PLO to denounce the attacks and expel members responsible for them.

In response to some congressional urging as well as to Israeli persistence on this matter, the State Department initiated a review of PLO conduct since the dialogue began. On March 19, it sent a report to Congress in which it concluded that Arafat had stuck to his word on renouncing terrorism. Concerning some 30 border and rocket attacks by Palestinian groups against Israel, the report attributed them to "disparate elements with different views" and said the PLO was deficient in controlling all of its groups. The report said that this lack of control was not a reason to excuse PLO activities and that "we have made it clear to the PLO that these activities raise serious questions about the PLO's commitment to renounce terrorism." The bottom line, however, was that the United States found that the PLO "has adhered to its commitment undertaken in 1988 to renounce terrorism."

Sen. Connie Mack (R., Fla.), who with Sen. Joseph Lieberman (D., Conn.) had cosponsored the legislation that prompted the State Department review, strongly condemned the report, saying that it "reads more like a defense of the PLO than a balanced account of the PLO's record since its 1988 commitments." Mack added that the report would "further erode confidence in the administration's will to effectively hold the PLO to its commitments." And Lieberman accused the State Department of "bend[ing] over backward to not be too critical of the PLO," for fear of jeopardizing any Middle East peace initiative.

PLO attitudes toward the administration were reflected in an interview that Arafat had with the *New York Times* on March 2. Usually critical of the United States, Arafat went out of his way to offer words of praise: "This Administration is the first American Administration that speaks of the end of Israeli occupation." He praised Secretary Baker for telling Israelis "to forget the dream of Greater Israel."

On the morning of May 30, an attempted terrorist raid on Israel changed the equation. Israeli forces foiled a speedboat attack by Palestinian guerrillas off the coast of Tel Aviv, killing 4 and capturing 12 of the raiders. Only one of the six guerrilla boats reached shore; the rest either broke down or were intercepted at sea. In Lebanon, a spokesperson for the Palestine Liberation Front headed by Abul Abbas, the mastermind of the *Achille Lauro* affair, said the raid was initiated to avenge "the Zionist massacre against our workers," a reference to the shooting on May 20 of seven Palestinian day laborers in Rishon LeZion by an emotionally unstable Israeli. Israeli officials immediately demanded that the United States end its dialogue with the PLO, since Abbas was a member of the PLO executive committee. Moshe Arens said that Israel hoped this last event "will convince the Administration," adding, "You can't fool all the people all the time."

The following day, Arafat denied PLO responsibility for the raid but did not denounce the operation or take any action against the PLO faction involved. Concerning Abul Abbas, Arafat said that since he was elected by the Palestine National Council, the "PNC has to decide on Abul Abbas, not me." An unnamed administration official expressed dissatisfaction with the PLO response: "It is not good enough for him to say, 'We are not part of it. We didn't know about it.' That is good to hear, but it is not enough—not just for us, but, more important, for the Israelis. This was a real opportunity for Arafat to send a signal to the Israelis that he truly is committed to a moderate approach. Once again, it's an opportunity missed." Concerning future U.S.-PLO relations, White House spokesman Fitzwater said the administration wanted "to investigate the information and reach conclusions about what happened and who was responsible and why, before we would try to change our policy in any way."

Meanwhile, Presidents Conference head Seymour Reich called on the administration to "reassess the policy of talking with the PLO," saying that the United States "cannot lead a campaign against worldwide terrorism while holding ongoing discussions with the world's most notorious terrorists."

On May 31, U.S. ambassador in Tunis Robert Pelletreau, the link to the PLO during 1989, asked the PLO to condemn the raid and expel or suspend Abul Abbas. Two days later, Abu Iyad, a top PLO official, rejected the U.S. demand because it "considers any military act a type of terrorism." As the days passed, the State Department indicated that it was putting pressure on the PLO to expel Abul Abbas from its executive committee, but was ready to give Arafat sufficient opportunity to take the necessary steps to prevent a breaking off of the U.S.-PLO dialogue. After meeting for three days in Baghdad, the PLO executive committee issued a statement on June 7 which failed to condemn the raid or to take any action against Abul Abbas, warning that a break in U.S.-PLO contacts would be a "blow to the peace process" in the region.

Secretary Baker, who was attending a NATO foreign ministers' meeting in Scotland, reflected on June 8 on the U.S. dilemma in this matter. He spoke of terrorism as something that had to be taken "very, very seriously," but added that "peace in the Middle East is also a serious matter." He concluded that when all the facts were in, "we will act in a way that reflects our dual commitment to promoting peace and being resolute in countering terrorism." Bush too called on Arafat to "speak up," saying that the U.S.-PLO dialogue is "predicated in part on renunciation of terror," and in his view, "this is sheer terror." Pressure on the administration to act was coming not only from Israel but from members of Congress. Senators Frank Lautenberg (D., N.J.), Charles Grassly (R., Iowa), Connie Mack (R., Fla.), and Joseph Lieberman (D., Conn.) introduced legislation early in June urging the administration to end the dialogue.

On June 11, a statement issued by the PLO press agency said that the PLO was "against any military action that targets civilians, whatever form it may take." The statement was issued after Egyptian president Mubarak warned Arafat that failure to speak out would almost certainly lead to suspension of the dialogue. The administration, however, said it was "disappointed" with the PLO because it had "not explicitly condemned the Tel Aviv raid and refrained from any public comment on Abul Abbas."

Finally, on June 20, President Bush announced that the United States was suspending the 18-month discussions with the PLO. He said that "we have given the PLO ample time" and that the United States can't digest the dialogue as long as this terrorist act is sticking in our throat." Finally, speaking in Huntsville, Alabama, the president said the suspension was "not an easy call" because of the negative effect it was likely to have on the peace process. He indicated as well that if the PLO condemned the attack and began "to take steps" to discipline Abul Abbas, the United States would be prepared to resume the dialogue immediately. Clearly, one factor pushing the administration was the imminence of a Senate resolution calling for suspension. According to one official, the White House "wanted to be seen as driving this process, not being driven by it."

Not surprisingly, the PLO criticized the move as "an unfriendly and provocative act" and called for economic sanctions against Israel. On the other hand, Israel welcomed the suspension as "an important and positive decision" and said it would be sending the administration new proposals on how to advance the peace process without the PLO. Egypt and Jordan offered muted responses, expressing "regret," but, in the words of Egypt, the hope that "this suspension of the U.S.-Palestinian dialogue will be lifted as soon as possible."

Clearly, the administration, which during the previous year had repeatedly articulated the view that the dialogue with the PLO was an important element in moving the peace process forward, took the step because events left it with no other choice. It is questionable whether in the months ahead the parties could have found a formula to renew the dialogue. With the emergence of the Gulf crisis at the beginning of August, attention moved away from the Arab-Israeli conflict, and relations between Washington and the PLO were further hurt by the PLO's decided tilt toward Baghdad from the outset of the crisis.

St. John's Hospice Affair

On April 11, over 100 Orthodox Jews moved into a vacant building, the St. John's Hospice, in the Christian quarter of the Old City of Jerusalem. The action set off a protest by hundreds of Christian clericals and soon became an international affair. The Greek Orthodox Church claimed that it owned the property and that its tenant, an Armenian, had no right to sublease the building to Jews. The Jews said their move was intended to reestablish a Jewish presence in buildings they asserted had been inhabited by Jews in the 1920s, though several days later they dropped this argument. This was the first Jewish move into the Christian quarter since Israel captured the Old City in 1967. One focus of the criticism of the settlers was the fact that the action had taken place during Easter week. Mayor Teddy Kollek urged Jews to consider "how they would feel if singing and dancing Christians or Muslims moved into the Jewish quarter on Passover."

On April 18, Israel's High Court issued an eviction notice for the more than 100 Jewish residents of the buildings, but the law allowed them 21 days to respond. On April 22, what had started out as one more story of ideologically motivated Israeli citizens making claims for a Jewish presence turned into a more serious issue when the government acknowledged that it had secretly provided almost $2 million to help establish the group in the hospice. The following day, the State Department sharply criticized the government of Israel, calling the aid "deeply disturbing," and saying that Ambassador William Brown would be "taking this issue up with the government of Israel." State Department officials called the takeover of the hospice "an insensitive and provocative action" and expressed pleasure "that the Israeli courts have ordered the settlers' eviction."

Israel, however, reacted defiantly to the criticism. The Foreign Ministry stated, "It is the right of Jews to live everywhere, and to purchase or rent property in all parts of the land of Israel, and especially in Jerusalem." And the Prime Minister's Office called the matter an "ordinary commercial real estate transaction," with no affront intended to the Greek Orthodox Church. As for the financial assistance, it was deemed consistent with government aid provided for housing projects across Israel.

On April 26, Israel's Supreme Court upheld the eviction order. The settlers had until May 1 to leave the premises. The controversy began to die out, but not before Pope John Paul, in his Sunday address in St. Peter's Square on April 29, expressed "profound concern" over the "grave incidents that have occurred recently in the Holy City."

KENNETH JACOBSON

Communal

Jewish Communal Affairs

THE YEAR 1990 BROUGHT A NOTICEABLE shift in the mood of the American Jewish community, as old priorities were questioned and new anxieties emerged. Despite their continuing commitment to the security of the State of Israel—strengthened toward the end of the year by the threat of an Iraqi attack on Israel—there was a growing sense that Israeli insistence on holding on to the occupied territories would, sooner or later, result in conflict with the American administration. The issue of saving Soviet Jewry, which for so many years had provided a focus for American Jewish energies, had been transformed by *glasnost* from an idealistic demand to "let my people go" into a less lofty search for the money to resettle the émigrés who were pouring out of the USSR.

Just at the time that the traditional issues that had mobilized American Jewry for a generation began losing their luster, Jewish intellectuals, subjecting the internal workings of their community to intensive scrutiny, questioned its long-term viability. Toward the end of the year, data from an ambitious new survey of American Jews provided hard numbers that seemed to reinforce these forebodings. And the Jewish religious movements, each in its own way, struggled to provide compelling visions of Judaism that might disprove the pessimists and inspire the next generation.

American Jews and Israel

At the beginning of the year, American Jewry confronted the first of a series of disturbances in U.S.-Israeli relations. With the peace process languishing, the administration of President George Bush making no secret of its unhappiness about the settlement of Soviet Jewish refugees in the West Bank, and Senate minority leader Robert Dole (R., Kan.) calling for a cut in American aid to the Jewish state, Israeli prime minister Yitzhak Shamir publicly advocated, on January 14, "a bigger Israel, a strong Israel, Eretz Yisrael" to absorb the immigrants. Since "a greater Israel" was the code expression for permanent Israeli control over the territories, his words were widely taken to mean that immigrants would be channeled there. The American government's official response was that Shamir's remarks were "not helpful."

American Jewry was split over how to respond. The mainstream leadership sought to contain the damage. Reporting on a phone conversation he had with Shamir, Seymour Reich, chairman of the Conference of Presidents of Major American Jewish Organizations, explained that Israel had no deliberate policy of settling Soviet Jews in the West Bank or Gaza; while admittedly the Shamir government intended to hold on to the territories, this had no connection with where the immigrants were sent.

In the eyes of some American Jews who favored Israeli withdrawal from the territories, the American Jewish establishment proved its own bankruptcy by backing the Israeli line. In Los Angeles, *Tikkun* magazine convened a Southern California Conference of Liberal and Progressive Intellectuals that attracted over 1,300 people. *Tikkun* editor Michael Lerner claimed that most American Jews opposed Israeli retention of the territories, but that "people who give big money and who have created organizations that stifle debate" created the illusion that American Jewry backed Shamir. Prof. David Biale of the Graduate Theological Union in Berkeley compared the occupation of the West Bank and Gaza to a cancer eating away, not only at "democracy in Israel," but also at the American Jewish community. The participants resolved to place an ad in Israeli newspapers calling for negotiations that would lead to a demilitarized Palestinian state.

Questions raised about American Jewish leaders' support for Israeli policies attracted the attention of public-opinion professionals. Two surveys were completed—one done for Tel Aviv University's Israel-Diaspora Institute by Steven M. Cohen, the other for the American Jewish Committee by Jacob B. Ukeles. Both demonstrated that, far from espousing a more hawkish view than their constituents, as alleged by the "liberal and progressive intellectuals," American Jewish leaders were actually more conciliatory toward the Arabs than rank-and-file Jews. As Earl Raab noted in the pages of *Commentary* (June 1990), "Despite debate in the American Jewish community over some Israeli strategies, any politician who thinks that a large number of Jewish voters would now look favorably upon cuts in aid to Israel, or other forms of diminished support, will soon discover that he has been misled by a false and tendentious reading of American Jewish opinion." Yet the Cohen study also contained findings that could only disturb supporters of the official Israeli line: many of the American Jewish leaders expressing public solidarity with the Shamir government privately agreed with the more flexible stand of the Labor opposition.

DIFFERENCES AT NJCRAC CONFERENCE

When the annual plenary of the National Jewish Community Relations Advisory Council (NJCRAC) convened in Phoenix on February 20, the vexed issue of the settlement of Soviet Jews in the territories split the assembled delegates down the middle. NJCRAC—an umbrella organization that coordinates the activities of Jewish national and local community relations bodies—debated a resolution critical of

Israeli policies. It expressed concern that "the construction of new housing in the administered territories will have the direct effect of encouraging settlement there," a result that allegedly would "detract from the *aliyah* potential and our fund raising" and "increase tensions between Israelis and Palestinians living there, possibly disrupting delicate negotiations."

Theodore Mann, a former president of the American Jewish Congress, defended this language on the ground that the prospect of Soviet *olim* settling in the West Bank might dampen the enthusiasm of philanthropists and discourage the Soviet Union from initiating direct flights to Israel. But Seymour Reich expressed opposition to what he saw as an "inappropriate and mischievous" resolution. Since, he said, Israel had no plans for large-scale construction projects in the West Bank, it made no sense to allude to such a possibility.

A motion to remove the controversial clauses resulted in a tie vote, 199–199, so the language stayed in. The resolution then passed 216–207—though NJCRAC officials pointed out that it was not yet official policy, but only a recommendation to the organization's Israel Task Force. (Two months later, that body rejected the resolution.)

The next day, February 21, found NJCRAC divided again over Israeli policy. When a statement on the Middle East was proposed, representatives of the American Jewish Congress circulated two amendments affirming that "many within the Jewish community" favored a "two-state solution" to the Israeli-Palestinian conflict, and that American Jewry "expressed concern" that Prime Minister Shamir, by rejecting "the concept of land for peace," seemed to "rule out sovereignty of any kind" for the Palestinians, in alleged violation of Security Council Resolution 242.

When AJCongress withdrew the amendments to avoid an acrimonious debate, Maynard Wishner, who chaired the NJCRAC Israel Task Force, praised the decision. "There is not argument," he said, "that there is diversity of opinion. But umbrella organizations which are tempted to separate on bare majorities can stop being umbrellas very soon." Those who favored the amendments felt that the publicity attending their efforts could not fail to have an impact. David Saperstein of the Union of American Hebrew Congregations expressed his confidence "that the concerns of the American Jewish public are being heard in Israel."

PRESIDENTS CONFERENCE

During the annual Israel seminar in Jerusalem in late February of the Presidents Conference, chairman Seymour Reich—always careful not to criticize Israeli policy in public—did suggest to reporters that Israel might move faster to implement the peace initiative that it had proposed in 1989. And for the first time, the seminar program included a session with Peace Now activists.

In private meetings with Yitzhak Shamir, the 75 delegates explained how important it was in terms of American public opinion for the prime minister to dispel the notion that there was a concerted effort to settle Soviet Jews in the territories. Shamir acquiesced, stating at the closing dinner of the seminar that "it is not the policy of the government of Israel to direct the *olim* to the areas of Judea, Samaria, and Gaza. Nor are there special incentives for those that do go there." The Americans responded with loud applause. In striking contrast was their hostile reaction to a presentation by Housing Minister Ariel Sharon, who had threatened to quit the cabinet in protest over Shamir's alleged willingness to negotiate with the Palestinians. Howard Squadron, a former chairman of the Presidents Conference, found Sharon's hard-line ideas "extraordinarily unrealistic." "They will happen when the Messiah comes," he said.

Organized American Jewry barely had time to savor Yitzhak Shamir's disavowal of any plan to direct immigrants to the territories when, on March 3, President Bush implied during a news conference that Jews should not settle in East Jerusalem. Even dovish Jewish leaders who could envisage an Israeli withdrawal from the West Bank were appalled at the idea that any part of the Holy City could be off limits to Jews. One such dove, Rabbi Alexander Schindler of the Union of American Hebrew Congregations (UAHC), wrote to Bush requesting that he "articulate our government's policy regarding Jerusalem clearly and consistently, so that there is no room for doubt or fear that this administration considers East Jerusalem a part of the West Bank."

Attempts to clarify the administration's position were not successful, and Seymour Reich declared on March 11 that "mixed signals" on Jerusalem undermined Israeli confidence in the peace process. Indeed, fallout from the president's statement was a contributing factor in the fall, two days later, of Israel's Likud-Labor coalition.

When Labor party leader Shimon Peres, with his positive position on peace talks, was given the first opportunity to form a new coalition, mainstream Jewish leaders in the United States made no secret of their preference for him over the Likud's Shamir. And they reacted with fury when Peres failed to garner a majority because two Orthodox Knesset members followed the guidelines of the Brooklyn-based Rabbi Menachem Schneerson, the Rebbe of Lubavitch, who opposed giving up any of the occupied territories. Seymour Reich declared that it was "reprehensible for anyone in the Diaspora to interfere with the Israeli political system." Alexander Schindler attacked Schneerson directly: "How can a religious leader in good conscience reject the idea of moving toward peace when the young men in his own movement are exempted from military service so they can pursue their yeshiva studies?" There were calls for federations to retaliate by cutting off funding to Lubavitch institutions, until it was learned that no federation money went to Lubavitch headquarters.

CONFLICT OVER JERUSALEM

Meanwhile, to counter the impression left by President Bush that Jewish sovereignty over East Jerusalem was uncertain, the Senate passed a nonbinding resolution affirming that united Jerusalem was the capital of Israel. American Jewish gratification quickly turned to apprehension, however, when Senator Dole, on April 15, announced his intention to get the Senate to rescind its vote—adding, for good measure, that American Jewish leaders were so greedy in their quest for American aid to Israel that "they wouldn't give a penny to anyone else." Seymour Reich characterized Dole's remarks as "ill-advised, without foundation, and not becoming a leader of the U.S. Senate," and he cited the Jewish community's consistent support for aid to other countries in need. After several leading Republicans dissociated themselves from his views, Dole backed down.

But a much more serious crisis in American-Israeli relations loomed. On April 11—during the Christian holy day season leading up to Easter—150 Jews occupied a building in the Christian Quarter of East Jerusalem, claiming that they had purchased the lease. The local Greek Orthodox Church, however, said it was the rightful owner and the transaction was illegal. And on April 23, Israel's Housing Ministry admitted that it had financed the purchase.

Fearing that the incident would further damage Israel's image in the United States and endanger the passage of $400 million in loan guarantees to Israel then pending in Congress, American Jewish organizations—the same ones that had recently insisted that Jews had every right to move into East Jerusalem—denounced the move. The American Jewish Congress said it was "appalled" that the Israeli regime involved itself in "a clandestine effort to settle Jews in the Christian Quarter of Jerusalem." Alexander Schindler called the government's role "unconscionable and self-destructive." Even the Anti-Defamation League, which usually backed Israeli policies to the hilt, expressed "deep concern" that the settlers had received government help. Both Seymour Reich and officials of the American Israel Public Affairs Committee (AIPAC) warned Prime Minister Shamir over the telephone of adverse political consequences in the United States.

Time magazine, in its May 7 issue, carried a report—"The Agony Over Israel: American Jews face a dilemma: how to criticize the Jewish state without seeming disloyal"—written by the star investigative journalist Carl Bernstein. In his assessment, based on extensive interviews, the Jewish takeover of the East Jerusalem building had been the last straw. It was not only AIPAC, but "leaders of the Reform and Conservative branches of Judaism and scores of men and women who have held leadership positions in organizations ranging from B'nai B'rith to Hadassah" who were disenchanted with a whole series of Israeli policies. Israel's dealings with South Africa, its alleged role in the Iran-Contra affair, the Pollard spy case, and the disproportionate power of the ultra-Orthodox—added to "Israel's provocative settlement policies and intransigence toward the Palestinians," wrote Bernstein, provided the recipe for American Jewish "agony."

Yet even so, when Prime Minister Shamir succeeded, on June 11, in forming a right-wing government explicitly committed to "strengthen, expand, and develop" West Bank and Gaza settlements, the organized American Jewish community closed ranks. Alexander Schindler, longtime critic of Likud's approach, expressed the consensus, saying that "whatever differences some of us may have with specific policies, American Jews stand as one with Israel." Of the major organizations, only AJCongress dissented; Robert Lifton, its president, predicted that the new government coalition would "split American Jews as well as Israelis" and announced that his organization felt free now, as in the past, to criticize the policies of Israel's government. Nine days later American Jewish leaders expressed considerable satisfaction when the Bush administration announced a suspension of its dialogue with the PLO, after the latter refused to renounce a May 30 terrorist attack on Israel.

In light of the common perception of growing strain between Israel and the United States, American Jews were understandably sensitive to the results of public-opinion surveys that gauged American attitudes about the Middle East. On July 9, the release of a new *New York Times*/CBS News poll showing a decline in support for Israel and a rise in support for the Palestinians provided cause for concern. Jewish spokespersons sought to control the damage by attributing the changes to short-term problems rather than a permanent erosion. Abraham Foxman of the Anti-Defamation League felt that "if relations between the U.S. and Israeli officials were to improve and Israel were to get its act together, including some progress in the peace process, then the fundamentals that have led the American people to support Israel overwhelmingly will reassert themselves." That polling is far from an exact science was demonstrated two weeks later when the American Jewish Committee released a Roper poll it had commissioned which showed a rise in American sympathy for Israel. "We find most heartening that most Americans remain steadfast in their regard for Israel," said AJCommittee executive vice-president Ira Silverman.

GULF CRISIS; TEMPLE MOUNT

In August, however, such matters were relegated to the back burner by Iraq's invasion of Kuwait. American Jewry solidly backed American economic sanctions against Iraq, as Seymour Reich put it, to restrain Saddam Hussein "from striking at some other Arab oil-producing state and to prevent him from carrying out his threats against Israel." Jewish organizations also noted that this crisis showed how important it was for the United States to have a strong and trustworthy ally— Israel—in the region. As the administration pushed legislation through Congress providing Saudi Arabia with advanced weaponry to repel a potential Iraqi invasion, Jewish leaders sought new American aid for Israel to preserve the Jewish state's military superiority in the region. On September 28, the day after administration officials met with a 50-member delegation of the Conference of Presidents, the State

Department issued a public pledge to respond swiftly to any Iraqi attack on Israel.

Just as organized American Jewry began getting used to the welcome notion of Israel and the United States as allied against the common Iraqi threat, new violence in Jerusalem threatened the newfound harmony. On October 8, during the Sukkot holiday, Arabs on the Temple Mount hurled rocks on Jews praying at the Western Wall. In dispersing the Arabs, Israeli police killed 17 of them. The United States then helped draft a UN Security Council resolution condemning Israel for responding with excessive force. The Presidents Conference called the resolution "harsh and hypocritical" for failing even to mention the attack on the Jewish worshipers. NJCRAC charged the United States with "joining with those forces at the UN which routinely use that forum to isolate Israel diplomatically." Several Orthodox organizations declared Saturday, October 20, a "Sabbath of Protest." And the next day there were several well-attended rallies in New York City protesting the UN action.

A crack in the wall of American Jewish unanimity did develop over whether Israel should cooperate with a UN team sent to investigate the incident. A broad spectrum of Jewish organizations supported Israel's decision not to cooperate, citing the UN's historic hostility to the Jewish state and the threat to Jewish sovereignty over Jerusalem that a UN investigation would represent. Alexander Schindler, however, advised the Israelis that from a public-relations point of view there was much to gain from working with the UN group.

On November 8, five Jewish leaders—Seymour Reich, Abraham Foxman, Presidents Conference executive director Malcolm Hoenlein, AIPAC president Mayer Mitchell, and AIPAC executive director Thomas Dine—met for an hour with President Bush in the White House. The five expressed concern that administration interest in piecing together an anti-Iraq coalition had led to a neglect of Israel's interests, and they cited as an example American support for the UN condemnation of Israel over the Temple Mount violence. Bush assured them that there had been no change in American policy toward the Jewish state—a position he repeated publicly at a news conference minutes later—and that the United States was coordinating its strategy regarding Iraq together with Israel. The president also suggested that Israel cooperate with the UN team investigating the Temple Mount deaths, a message that the Jewish leaders quickly conveyed to Israel.

On November 28, another anti-Israel resolution was proposed in the Security Council, this one calling for a UN observer to be stationed in the West Bank, urging Israel to accept the application of the Fourth Geneva Convention to the territories, and supporting the idea of an international peace conference on the Middle East. The Presidents Conference, arguing that this amounted to interference in Israel's internal affairs, urged the United States to exercise its veto. It did not; the final version of the resolution, which also condemned Israel for deporting Palestinians from the West Bank, passed the Security Council unanimously on December 20. The Presidents Conference expressed the American Jewish consensus: "By failing to exercise its right of veto, the Bush Administration has seriously wounded our one staunch and democratic ally in the region."

Ironically, a week later it was Seymour Reich himself, the outgoing chairman of the Presidents Conference, who publicly criticized Israeli policy. After Israeli housing minister Ariel Sharon announced plans to construct 2,500 new homes for Jews in the West Bank—possibly endangering $400 million in loan guarantees from the United States—Reich said there was "no good reason to place Israel in the position to be a target of additional criticism from the United States and others." Thus, the year ended on a sour note for American Jewish–Israeli relations.

American Jews and Soviet Jewry

On January 2, the National Conference on Soviet Jewry (NCSJ) announced that over 71,000 Jews had left the USSR in 1989, four times as many as the previous year. Proclaiming 1989 "the record year to date for Jewish emigration from the Soviet Union," NCSJ chairwoman Shoshana Cardin expressed the hope "that 1990 will also prove to be a milestone year." It was. Over 181,000 Soviet Jews emigrated, more than had left the country in the previous 21 years combined. At year's end Cardin announced: "The Soviet Union continues to live up to its international commitment to provide for free emigration for its citizens, including its still sizable Jewish population."

After years of exerting pressure on the Soviets to let the Jews leave, the American Jewish community now faced the challenge of raising the money to help Israel absorb the immigrants. On January 20, the United Jewish Appeal announced Operation Exodus, a special $420-million campaign for the resettlement of Soviet Jews. UJA expected to solicit pledges for this huge amount over one year, while the money could be paid out over three years. By earmarking the entire sum for Israel, the organizers hoped to avoid the frictions that marred the 1989 Passage to Freedom campaign, which set aside some of the money for resettlement costs in the United States. Reports of rising anti-Semitism in the Soviet Union made accelerated emigration to Israel more likely, inducing leaders of local federations not to insist on receiving any of the proceeds of Operation Exodus.

To help finance the absorption of Soviet Jews in American communities, Jewish social-service agencies sought $70 million from the State Department's refugee budget. Yet even this amount, if forthcoming, would be a mere drop in the bucket for the 40,000 Jews expected to arrive in the United States during 1990.

The Council of Jewish Federations convened a special general assembly in Miami on February 6 to deal with the problem. There was widespread agreement that the federations would share the resettlement costs, and not simply leave individual Jewish communities to cope with the refugees who ended up coming to them. Underlying this consensus was the sense that saving Soviet Jewry was a one-time historic opportunity that must not be missed.

Controversy developed over just how to apportion resettlement costs among the communities. Smaller communities objected to a formula based on money raised in the 1988 campaign, arguing that it penalized the most sucessful fund-raisers. These federations suggested, instead, that only half the assessment be based on the 1988 campaign, with the other half allocated according to the size of the Jewish community. The larger communities with weaker fund-raising records, however, doubted they could reach such ambitious goals. A compromise was reached: 85 percent of each community's "fair share" would be based on the 1988 campaign, 15 percent on size. Ultimately, 121 of the 141 eligible communities participated in this arrangement.

Meanwhile, congressional legislation providing Israel with $400 million in loan guarantees to pay for housing Soviet emigrants ran into an unexpected snag. On March 1, Secretary of State Baker said that the administration would only approve the bill if none of the funds from these loans were used for settlements in the territories. After discussions with Vice-President Dan Quayle, Jewish leaders expressed confidence that this did not mean that the loan guarantees depended on an end to Jewish settlement in Gaza and the West Bank. Such settlement could continue, so long as the loan money did not finance it.

OPERATION EXODUS

Operation Exodus opened strongly. A "millionaires' meeting" hosted on February 28 by businessman Leslie Wexner raised $58 million from 16 individuals. On April 4, a congressional seder to promote Operation Exodus took place in Washington. It attracted 500 people and featured an address by Vice-President Quayle. Marvin Lender, chairman of Operation Exodus, announced that $109 million had already been raised. By early May, several of the federations—those with very wealthy givers—were well on their way toward their assigned goals; indeed, Baltimore had already topped it, and San Francisco had decided to raise double the original projection. Leaders in such communities reported tremendous enthusiasm. Yet two-thirds of the federations, still busy with their regular campaigns, had not even started on Operation Exodus.

On June 3, American Jews were taken aback by Soviet threats to restore limits on the emigration of Jews. Responding to complaints by Arabs—echoed in more subdued tones by the U.S. administration—that Israel was settling Soviet Jews in the territories, President Mikhail Gorbachev, who was in the United States for a summit meeting with President Bush, raised the possibility of cutting off the emigration unless Israel guaranteed that no Soviet Jews would be steered to the West Bank or Gaza. (Ironically, this was two days after Rabbi Arthur Schneier of the Appeal for Conscience Foundation presented Gorbachev with an award for "changing the course of world events in our time.") American Jewish organizations denounced any linkage between the humanitarian question of emigration and the territorial issue, and denied, in any case, that Israel was settling immigrants in the disputed territories. Efforts by the NCSJ to reach the Soviet president before his return to Moscow were unsuccessful. But the crisis blew over quickly. On June 6, the Associated Press reported that Gorbachev had "retracted" his threat.

In late June, the annual Jewish Agency Assembly in Jerusalem discussed the progress of Operation Exodus. "In less than four months," announced chairman Marvin Lender, "we have raised $311 million," three-quarters of the projected target figure. Forty-two individuals had donated over a million dollars apiece. But more than twice as many Soviet Jews were entering Israel than had been projected when Operation Exodus began, creating what the chairman of the United Israel Appeal termed a "substantial emergency." To help meet the unanticipated costs, UJA officials resolved to urge their Operation Exodus donors to pay off their pledges in two years rather than three, and began talking of a new special drive for 1991.

In September, however, they decided to hold off on a new campaign. With pledges for Operation Exodus just $20 million shy of the $420 million goal, the UJA and the federations decided to concentrate on collection of pledges so that the money could be put to use quickly in Israel, rather than on any immediate "Exodus II" drive. And with other causes seriously underfunded—Ethiopian Jewish relief as well as American Jewish social-service and educational institutions—the fund-raisers were eager to devote more attention to their regular campaigns, which they hoped would benefit from the sense of excitement generated by Operation Exodus. In November, when the Jewish Agency Board of Governors called on world Jewry to raise another $1.3 billion for resettlement of Soviet Jews in Israel, board chairman Mendel Kaplan acknowledged that only a portion would come from philanthropy of the traditional kind. "We are now looking for other financial instruments to be provided by Diaspora Jews," he said, probably referring to loans and investments.

On November 30, President Bush told a news conference that he was considering waiving the provisions of the 1974 Jackson-Vanik Amendment restricting trade with the Soviet Union. Jackson-Vanik, which predicated the granting of trade benefits upon Soviet adherence to a policy of free emigration, had long been a symbol to Jews of American determination to fight for human rights in the USSR. American Jewish organizations had till now insisted that no waiver be issued without firm guarantees, written into law, that the Soviets would maintain an open-door policy. The Union of Councils for Soviet Jews immediately announced opposition to a waiver, but the National Conference on Soviet Jewry, in a shift of position, supported a one-year waiver. In the light of high levels of emigration, it reasoned, Soviet adherence to the conditions previously demanded could be left to private conversations between the administration and the USSR. Shoshana Cardin, chairwoman of the NCSJ, explained that Jackson-Vanik had previously been "used as a stick"; now it could be "used as a carrot."

On December 11, President Bush announced that he was waiving certain restrictions of Jackson-Vanik through the following July, so that the Soviet Union could receive up to $1 billion in credits to buy American food products. This was acceptable even to the Union of Councils for Soviet Jews, since the waiver did not cover the provision barring the Soviets from most-favored-nation trade benefits. The president's decision drew a chorus of praise from American Jewish organizations. While the future of the Soviet Union and its Jews was unpredictable, the American

Soviet Jewry movement, in the form in which it had captured the imagination of a generation of American Jews, was essentially over.

The Kahane Assassination

The successful culmination of the Soviet Jewry movement coincided almost exactly with the violent death of Meir Kahane, the man most associated in the public mind with the campaign to save Soviet Jews. Kahane was a highly controversial figure. Born in Brooklyn in 1932, he worked as an Orthodox rabbi, journalist, and FBI informant until 1968, when, outraged by a rise in anti-Semitic incidents in New York City, he founded the Jewish Defense League. Kahane's JDL did not shrink from the use of force to defend Jews against attacks and sought to instill a greater sense of Jewish pride in the Jewish community. Kahane regularly raised the charge that American Jewry had failed to rescue European Jews from the Nazi Holocaust and that only his form of militance could prevent a recurrence. He was contemptuous of the mainstream Jewish leadership which, he charged, failed to stand up for Jewish rights. Kahane's slogan "Never Again!" voiced the sentiments of many Jews who, stirred by the Six Day War and the early writings of Elie Wiesel, were starting to come to grips with the annihilation of six million of their brothers and sisters a generation earlier.

American Jews had organized to call attention to the plight of Soviet Jews several years before Kahane seized upon the issue. Yet he was the first to sanction violence to further the cause. After several shootings and bomb attacks directed at Soviets and Soviet institutions that were traced to the JDL, Kahane was convicted in federal court in 1971, but fled the country while out on bail. He was imprisoned for a year when he returned to the United States in 1974. Kahane shifted his base of operations to Israel after his release. He founded the Kach party, advocating the removal of Arabs from Israel, and sat in the Knesset from 1984 to 1988 as the party's sole representative. Kach was barred from participation in the 1988 election on the grounds that it was racist and undemocratic.

On November 5, Kahane was shot to death after making a speech in a Manhattan hotel. Egyptian-born El Sayyid A Nosair, who was seen holding the murder weapon immediately before the shots rang out, and who then fled the scene, was arrested and charged with the crime.

Kahane's death and the funeral that was held in a Brooklyn synagogue evoked mixed emotions from American Jews. Many of his hard-core supporters—stunned, distraught, outraged—called for vengeance against Arabs. A few anti-Kahane Jews, generally secular intellectuals, wasted no tears: Leon Wieseltier, for example, the literary editor of the *New Republic*, dismissed Kahane as "a great fear artist." Orthodox Jews were ambivalent. On the one hand, the late rabbi had been a proud Orthodox Jew—eulogist Rabbi Moses Tendler went so far as to say that the deceased had "talked with God"—and had expressed contempt for any other form of Judaism. Furthermore, his bitter attacks on the secular leadership of American

Jewry resonated well in the Orthodox world. Yet Kahane's advocacy of violence was quite foreign to the politically quietistic tradition of Orthodoxy. A common Orthodox response, then, was to praise him as an exemplary Jew while at the same time disagreeing with his tactics.

Most intriguing was the reaction of the mainstream leaders of American Jewry. Seymour Reich, chairman of the Presidents Conference, and Abraham Foxman, executive director of the Anti-Defamation League, attended the funeral, though both told reporters that they did not agree with Kahane's approach to Jewish issues. The American Jewish Committee, which was not represented at the funeral, nevertheless stated in a press release: "Despite our considerable differences, Meir Kahane must always be remembered for the slogan 'Never Again,' which for so many became the battle-cry of post-Holocaust Jewry." The markedly polite tone of these organizations that had considered Kahane, when alive, beneath contempt, could be interpreted in either of two ways. Kahane loyalists suggested that the new note of respect marked a belated recognition of Kahane's influence on the American Jewish masses. Others denied that the Jewish establishment had changed its stance. Rather, it was responding sympathetically to the tragic fact that a Jew—it could have been any Jew—was gunned down by an Arab. Had Kahane died of a heart attack, the argument ran, there would have been no such outpouring of sympathy.

Shifting Organizational Patterns

Just as Israel and Soviet Jewry showed signs of losing their priority status on the American Jewish agenda, the ramified organizational structure of American Jews that traditionally dealt with these issues faced new problems. The tribulations experienced by Jewish organizations in 1990 stemmed at least in part from problems in the American economy that cut deeply into the level of charitable giving. The lack of money— in itself probably a short-term problem—forced the community to confront certain long-term questions it had previously managed to avoid.

One of these was the changing role of women. The largest Jewish women's organization—indeed, the largest American Jewish organization of any kind—was Hadassah, the women's Zionist organization. As the other American Zionist groups declined in the years of Israel's statehood, Hadassah thrived by avoiding ideological debates and focusing on concrete, high-quality health-care projects in Israel. But in 1990, for the first time, Hadassah leadership noted that membership had leveled off at around 385,000, and that income from dues was down.

The reason was simple. In the words of national vice-president Deborah Kaplan, "Women are working. They don't have time to volunteer." Furthermore, young career women, even if they were interested in giving of their spare time to a Jewish cause, tended not to be attracted to Hadassah, which was popularly viewed as an organization for older women. And in keeping with the interests of an older generation of women, Hadassah programming stressed Israel, not the "women's issues" like child care and abortion rights that were important to younger Jewish women.

While several of the sessions at Hadassah's July convention were geared to the interests of younger career women, it remained unclear whether the organization would succeed in capturing their loyalty.

The shifting role of women in organized Jewry caused problems of a different sort for B'nai B'rith International. For years, B'nai B'rith Women had functioned as an auxiliary of the main body, participating in service projects and meeting for social purposes. But by the late 1980s the women's group began, independently from the men, to take positions on policy matters that concerned them, and in 1988 it declared itself an independent organization. In January 1990, B'nai B'rith International sent out a mailing to the members of the women's organization offering them membership in a reorganized B'nai B'rith, and threatening to cut off the insurance policies they had purchased through B'nai B'rith if they did not pay dues. B'nai B'rith Women, in turn, charged that the men's organization, suffering from a sharp decline in membership, was desperate for money.

Months of tense negotiations followed. A resolution was finally reached in late August. B'nai B'rith International amended its constitution to make women full and equal members. It also reached agreement with the women's organization, each group recognizing the other as an independent and self-governing body.

One dramatic illustration of the changing role of women in Jewish life was the election of Shoshana Cardin, on December 18, as the first woman to chair the Conference of Presidents of Major American Jewish Organizations. The unanimous choice of the 46 member organizations, Cardin had won extraordinary respect as head of several Jewish organizations—most recently, the National Conference on Soviet Jewry.

A second long-term trend in Jewish organizational life was less obvious but clearly discernible: a growing intolerance of ambiguity in organizational program focus on the part of potential members and donors. Many Jews preferred to target their energies and money to specific causes that excited their commitment rather than support more general programs.

The first national organization to try to come to grips with the new situation was the American Jewish Committee, which worried that its broad spectrum of programs gave it an unclear identity in the public mind. Faced with a growing deficit, the AJC board of governors decided, on February 7, to take drastic action. It voted a 25-percent budget cut for 1991 and eliminated entire program areas—such as urban affairs, education, and women's issues—that were deemed no longer central to the AJC's mission. "We took a look at what we were doing and what other organizations are doing," explained Mimi Alperin, chairwoman of the AJC's national executive council. "We kept what we felt we did better than other organizations and the things that no other organizations are doing." Some months later, AJC's new executive vice-president, David A. Harris, expressed the same realization that the agency had to narrow its focus to survive. Under his stewardship, he said, the agency would pursue "issues of core concern to American Jewry."

The tendency of donors to target gifts to concrete causes brought increased attention in 1990 to relatively new, grass-roots organizations that raised money for needs of Jews and non-Jews not addressed by larger, multipurpose agencies. Examples were the New Israel Fund, which supported civil-rights, Arab-Jewish, and other "socially conscious" programs in Israel; Mazon, which sought to counter hunger and homelessness in the United States; American Jewish World Service, whose grants helped grass-roots organizations around the world; and the Jewish Fund for Justice, which funded community-action projects in the United States. A volunteer for one of these groups explained their appeal: unlike the established organizations, the new charities enabled donors to "see a direct impact in terms of peoples' lives" (*Baltimore Jewish Times*, May 11, 1990).

Prof. Jacob Neusner of the University of South Florida—a prolific scholar and longtime critic of American Jewish life—suggested that changes in organizational patterns marked the beginning of a new era for American Jewry. The mainstream agencies, he argued, "all of them suited three generations that wanted to be Jewish (and had to be Jewish)—but didn't want to be too Jewish." Jews of the new generation, in contrast, "celebrate the now-porous boundaries that separate group from group . . . walking in off the streets for a moment of Jewish experience when they want, walking out of organized Jewry altogether when they want. . . . The middle has not held, the vital center has lost its vitality, and the extremes—assimilated Jews . . . or segregated Jews . . . these outline the road into the future" (*Forward*, November 16, 1990).

Pessimism About the Future

Although Neusner pointedly refused to declare the newly emerging form of Jewish identity any better or worse than the old, the great majority of Jewish intellectuals in 1990 were less than sanguine about American Jewish life. Their mood contrasted sharply with the optimism about the possibilities of Jewish renewal popularized just five years before in Charles Silberman's best-selling *A Certain People*. The pessimists differed among themselves over what was wrong, but agreed that the celebratory rhetoric of the mid-1980s had been inappropriate.

The shrillest critique of American Jewry came from the historian and rabbi Arthur Hertzberg, who had served the community for decades both in the pulpit and as a communal spokesperson. In *The Jews in America: Four Centuries of an Uneasy Encounter*, Hertzberg characterized the history of 20th-century American Jewry as a long, desperate series of attempts to come up with substitute Jewish identities to replace a lost religious faith. There had been Jewish ethnicity, the political liberalism of the 1960s, the focus on Israel, and the preoccupation with the Nazi Holocaust. All these ersatz Judaisms had petered out, argued Hertzberg, and "the momentum of Jewish experience in America is essentially spent." Without a "spiritual revival . . . American Jewish history will soon end, and become a part of American history as a whole."

Reform theologian Eugene Borowitz took a similar approach, though he avoided

Hertzberg's apocalyptic tone. Borowitz recalled the "spontaneous re-Judaization" that swept American Jewry when Israel's survival was endangered in 1967. Now, though, he wrote, "I think I am only reporting the Emperor's nakedness when I say that Israelocentrism no longer can be the engine driving American Jewish life." He felt that the reality of Israel had disillusioned American Jews, and that, as the importance of ethnicity declined in American society, Jews would be increasingly affected by "the pluralism and democracy and equality which let them be like everyone else" (*Sh'ma*, September 21, 1990).

The same skepticism about American Judaism came across in *On Being a Jew: What Does It Mean to Be a Jew? A Conversation About Judaism and Its Practice in Today's World*, by Harvard professor James Kugel. This book, an argument for traditional Judaism written as a dialogue, was modeled on the medieval work *Kuzari* by the Spanish Jewish poet Yehuda Halevi. Yet significantly, whereas Halevi's dialogue was between a Jewish sage and the king of the Khazars, who was searching for the true religion, Kugel's starts as a dialogue between a religiously observant Jew and the son of a business associate who needs help finding a rabbi—to perform the "breaking the glass" ceremony at his upcoming wedding to a Christian.

In the dialogue, Kugel's traditional Jew disapproves of American Jewish concentration on "Israel and the Holocaust." "They are both," he notes, "conveniently perhaps, elsewhere. And so American Judaism in general has an 'elsewhere' quality to it: it is 'there,' in Israel or back in the Old Country, that Jews could be said to be really Jews, and it is 'there' that the significant Jewish events of our age have happened or are happening." American Jewish institutions, "concerned only with what is called 'Jewish survival,' " were, for Professor Kugel's protagonist, "sterile and unappealing."

If Hertzberg, Borowitz, and Kugel, each in his own way, considered American Jewish reliance on Israel for Jewish identity a weakness, there were others offering an opposite diagnosis: American Jewry's fatal flaw was its detachment from the Jewish state. Jerrold S. Auerbach, a history professor at Wellesley, wrote *Rabbis and Lawyers: The Journey from Torah to Constitution* from an unabashedly Zionist, indeed, religiously Zionist, point of view. For him, Jewish law and the Promised Land were basic to Judaism, and therefore "the synthesis of Judaism and Americanism"—which he saw as a mere code phrase for "the Jewish legitimacy of individual preferences"—was "a historical fiction." Thus American Jews supported the State of Israel only so long as it was liberal and secular. But with the rise of the Likud, Israel grew more authentically Jewish and less liberal, and American Jews "found reason to distance themselves from it." From Auerbach's perspective, an American Judaism that "had come to mean little but personal taste" and "excluded anything that differentiated them from other Americans" was doomed.

Another variant of the Zionist critique of American Jewry, this time without the religious ingredient—was that of David Vital of Tel Aviv University, perhaps the most eminent historian of the Zionist movement. In *The Future of the Jews: A People at the Crossroads?* Vital stressed the fundamental distinction between a Jewish community that has the political authority to take responsibility for its fate—Israel—and voluntary Jewish communities without political authority, such as the Jews in the United States. Acknowledging the relative success of American Jews in sustaining a collective identity, he nevertheless wondered, "Can there really be developed by them and among them a secular, indigenous (i.e., English-language) variety or version of Jewish life . . . which is not . . . a mere (necessarily pale) imitation of life, cultural life at all events, in Hebrew-speaking Israel?" He pointed out the irony that those American Jews most conscious of their Jewishness were inevitably drawn toward Israeli themes and concerns and away from American Jewish life, a process that could only weaken the American Jewish community.

Social scientists Charles Liebman of Bar-Ilan University and Steven Cohen of Queens College offered yet another permutation of the pessimistic scenario in their book *Two Worlds of Judaism: The Israeli and American Experiences*. Liebman and Cohen, as critical as any Zionists of the diluted Jewishness of American Jews, did not see an increasingly inward-looking and intolerant Israel as much of an alternative. "Most Jews in America," they claimed, "have reinterpreted the tradition in overly universalistic and cosmopolitan terms, leaving too little of what is especially Jewish. . . . On the other hand, the Israeli conception is too particularistic and parochial for our tastes." The approach of Liebman and Cohen raised the possibility, not only of American Jewish assimilation, but, perhaps just as tragic, the gradual emergence of two very different understandings of Judaism, one American, the other Israeli, sharing little common ground.

STATISTICAL SURVEYS

For those Jews familiar with the mood among the community's intellectuals, there was little that was surprising in the results of several statistical studies of the American Jewish community that appeared in 1990. On September 17, the Jewish Outreach Institute—a new, privately funded think tank dealing with intermarriage—announced the findings of a study of Jewish attitudes toward intermarriage. Fully 74 percent of the over 2,000 American Jewish leaders surveyed said they would not oppose the marriage of their 35-year-old daughter to a non-Jew, and only 21 percent would insist that he convert to Judaism. Clearly, the fear of not having grandchildren overrode the taboo against intermarriage. Over half of these leaders had at least one child who was married to someone not born Jewish. Prof. Egon Mayer of the City University of New York, who conducted the study, argued that hopeless resignation was not the only possible response to these figures. "I don't see despair and fatigue," he said. "We fought this battle one way and we haven't achieved our goal, so let's take a different approach, by reaching out to these families and bringing them into the community."

In October, the Maurice and Marilyn Cohen Center for Modern Jewish Studies at Brandeis University issued a study of intermarriage in eight American Jewish communities. While intermarriage rates varied widely among the communities, there was a common pattern of sharply rising rates among the younger age cohorts. According to the Brandeis survey, mixed-married families—where the non-Jewish partner did not convert—were far less likely to identify Jewishly than families where the non-Jew converted. The latter, in fact, behaved in many respects like inmarried Jewish families. Unfortunately, conversion rates had dropped just as intermarriage rates were rising. Like Egon Mayer, the Brandeis researchers called for greater stress on outreach. Gary Tobin, who directed the study, called on the community "to make conversion more accessible."[1]

On November 15, the Council of Jewish Federations (CJF) issued a summary of the findings of a far more extensive study, its new national Jewish population survey.[2] The immediate response of the community was confusion, largely because the research team that conducted the study utilized several different categories to identify Jews and estimate the size of the Jewish population: Jews by birth or by choice, whether religious or secular; people raised as Jews or having Jewish parents but who now follow a different religion; and a category for non-Jews living in households that contain at least one Jew. CJF research director Barry Kosmin acknowledged that interpreting the survey would not be easy: "You can take out of this net whatever fish you're after," he noted. Thus, the CJF press-release headline optimistically announced "Increase in U.S. Jewish Population"; the headline in the Jewish Telegraphic Agency Daily News Bulletin (November 16) read, more soberly, "Slight Growth, But Downward Trend"; and a full-page ad in the New York *Jewish Week*, sponsored by an Orthodox outreach organization (December 21), warned ominously of "600,000 American Jews Lost to Other Religions."

Since many American Jews considered Jewish education an important element of a strong Jewish identity, considerable interest surrounded the release, in November, of the report of the Commission on Jewish Education in North America that had been organized in 1988 and funded by Cleveland businessman Morton Mandel. The picture emerging from the report was bleak, showing that almost 60 percent of Jewish children received no Jewish education, and that the educational programs that did exist suffered from "deficiencies in educational content; an underdeveloped profession of Jewish education; inadequate community support; and the absence of a research function to monitor results, allocate resources, and plan improvements." None of this came as any surprise. "I don't think it required two years and this much money to get to this point," commented one educational specialist.

Amid this mood of pessimism—and just before the release of the 1990 CJF Jewish population survey—the eminent Harvard sociologist Nathan Glazer noted that all branches of Judaism, even the Orthodox, hardly spoke of faith or theology. He wrote that "the Jewish religion, Judaism, has become the religion of survival," little more

---

[1]See "Jewish Identity in Conversionary and Mixed Marriages," elsewhere in this volume.
[2]See "Profile of American Jewry: Insights from the 1990 Jewish Population Survey," elsewhere in this volume.

than a mechanism to guarantee the continuity of the Jewish people. And he warned that "religion has to be believed, for its own sake, to serve instrumentally" (*Society*, November-December 1990). If Glazer was right, the efforts of the Jewish religious denominations to build and sustain a believable Jewish spirituality held the key to the American Jewish future.

Denominational Developments

REFORM

Reform Judaism in the United States continued to develop on two separate tracks. In the sphere of ritual and liturgy, the movement back to tradition accelerated. Yet on family and personal life-style issues, the movement contined to depart ever further from tradition.

Adherents of classical Reform, which had downgraded the importance of ritual practice in Judaism and emphasized ethical monotheism and prophetic teachings instead, were, by 1990, an embattled minority within American Reform. While Reform Jews were far from accepting Orthodox strictures about the binding nature of Jewish law, they were becoming more and more interested in the experiential dimension of Judaism.

In an attempt to supplement anecdotal evidence of this trend with hard data, the UAHC-CCAR Commission on Religious Living commissioned a study of worship and ritual patterns in Reform congregations. The findings, released in December, confirmed popular impressions. While 77 percent of the congregations reported that Friday night services were their primary form of worship, over half of the synagogues held Saturday morning services. Almost all recited the traditional blessing over bread before communal meals, almost 70 percent said the grace after meals at least sometimes on these occasions, and 59 percent provided worshipers with *kippot* (28 congregations required them to be worn).

Rabbi Sanford Seltzer, director of the commission, suggested that these statistics were "expressions of a post-Holocaust generation of Reform Jews in search of spirituality." "These have not been easy times for Reform congregants whose orientation has been that of Classical Reform," he noted, predicting that the survey "will merely add to their discomfort."

The report of a 17-member CCAR Committee on Homosexuality and the Rabbinate, made public in May, expressed the innovative spirit of American Reform Judaism. The culmination of four years of discussion and debate, this report recommended that otherwise qualified gay and lesbian rabbis be recognized as bona fide members of the Reform rabbinate. Noting that congregations would remain free to use their own criteria in hiring rabbis, the report stated that, regardless of their sexual orientation, as "role models and exemplars," rabbis should conduct their private lives "with discretion and with full regard to the mores and sensibilities of their communities." Although the "centrality of monogamous, heterosexual, procreative marriage in the Jewish tradition" made the committee stop short of endorsing gay and lesbian marriage ceremonies, it did declare that "all Jews are religiously equal, regardless of their sexual orientation."

The CCAR membership adopted the committee report at its convention in June, as Reform became only the third American denomination—after Unitarian Universalists and Reconstructionist Jews—to officially accept gay clergy. Orthodox leaders denounced the move as a further sign of Reform estrangement from tradition, while officials of the Conservative movement, which had just given its approval to equality in synagogue life for gays and lesbians, neither condemned nor approved the Reform innovation. Within Reform there were rabbis with deep misgivings. Prof. Leonard Kravitz of the Hebrew Union College noted that, unlike previous Reform departures from tradition, where sources existed to support change, the biblical and talmudic abhorrence of homosexuality was unequivocal. And Rabbi Philmore Berger of Oceanside, New York, commented: "For the life of me, I cannot see how homosexual rabbis can be the role models our people need and want."

RECONSTRUCTIONISM

Reconstructionist Judaism, building upon the new prayerbook it issued in 1989, continued working toward a distinctive set of principles at the same time that it championed the unity of the Jewish people and welcomed signs of rapprochement between it and the other liberal branch of Judaism, Reform.

In Reconstructionism, more so than in the other versions of American Judaism, the president of the rabbinical college set the theological agenda. Rabbi Arthur Green, who held that position, published two articles in 1990 that charted the movement's direction. In one, entitled "Where We Stand: Theory and Practice of Contemporary Reconstructionism" (*Reconstructionist*, Autumn 1990), Green delineated the unique aspects of Reconstructionism. It considers itself a religious movement, even though its God is the power "who makes us more generous, sensitive, and caring people," rather than a supernatural force that intervenes in history. Unlike the Orthodox, Reconstructionists believe that Judaism evolved historically, and that free choice rather than legal obligation is the basis for observance of *mitzvah*. Green wrote that his movement differs from Conservatism as well, since, rather than seeking to change specific halakhic norms, it frankly acknowledges that the Jewish people is now living in a post-halakhic age. Yet unlike Reform, Green's interpretation of Reconstructionism stressed the value of traditional religious practices, even those that have no obvious rational basis.

In "Twin Centers: Sacred Time and Sacred Space" (*Reconstructionist*, May-June 1990), Green demonstrated how a Reconstructionist might reappropriate the traditional Sabbath in a non-halakhic but rigorous way. This is done by spending time at home with friends and family, reading "something that will edify, challenge, or make you grow," and avoiding business, handling money, "commercial or canned video entertainment," and "encounters in which people are likely to tell you to 'Have a nice day!' "

Elaborating on a central theme of its new prayerbook, the Reconstructionist movement singled out environmentalism as an especially important religious ideal. "Replenish the Earth: Ecology and Jewish Tradition" was the theme of the Federation of Reconstructionist Congregations and Havurot when it met in the Rocky Mountains in June. Shomrei Adama (Guardians of the Earth), founded by Reconstructionists in 1988, was the only identifiably Jewish group to take part in Earth Day, 1990. And in December, the Reconstructionists sponsored a family camp in Michigan with the theme "In God's Image and Nature's Embrace."

Reconstructionists applauded developments in American Reform which, they felt, drew the two movements closer. They saw both the evidence of growing Reform interest in religious ritual and the Reform decision to accept gays and lesbians as rabbis—something Reconstructionists had done for years—as positive signs. And in 1990 Reconstructionism became the first non-Reform movement to be granted observer status in the World Union for Progressive Judaism, the international umbrella organization of Reform groups.

CONSERVATISM

Conservative Judaism continued to feel the impact of the disaffection of its most traditionalist element. While the Union for Traditional Conservative Judaism had emerged in 1983 specifically in opposition to the movement's decision to ordain women, its founding also reflected a more general dissatisfaction with what was seen as Conservatism's insufficient emphasis on Halakhah. Considered an insignificant force by the Conservative leadership, the union struck root nevertheless, and by this year claimed the allegiance of about 5,000 families and over 400 rabbis. In February it announced the establishment of its own rabbinical seminary, which opened in Mt. Vernon, New York, in September. With one million dollars in private funding, the new school attracted prominent personalities (including Elie Wiesel) to its advisory board and named the eminent talmudist David Weiss Halivni as its academic head.

Establishment of the seminary evoked considerable speculation over where it and its backers would ultimately locate themselves on the Jewish denominational spectrum. The proposed curriculum for rabbinical ordination included the critical study of religious texts that characterized the Conservative approach, but also stressed traditional rabbinic methods associated with Orthodox modes of study. Significantly, a number of prominent rabbis and scholars previously associated with the modernist wing of Orthodoxy agreed to serve on the seminary board. And in May, the group officially voted to drop the word "Conservative" from its name, becoming the Union for Traditional Judaism (UTJ). The organization clearly hoped to expand its base beyond traditionalist Conservatives to encompass also those Orthodox Jews uneasy over the increasing influence of extremists within Orthodoxy.

Mainstream Conservatism still hoped to hold its traditionalist wing. Even after the UTJ dropped the denominational identification from its name, Rabbi Jerome Epstein, executive vice-president of the United Synagogue of America, wrote to Conservative rabbis: "I do not believe it is inevitable that the Union for Traditional Judaism members will leave our movement. I hope rather that they will learn to express their disagreement with what they find objectionable without demanding a monolithic approach as the price for their future involvement."

Two official decisions by the Conservative movement in 1990—one on the issue of gay rights, the other on women's rights—reduced the likelihood of such a scenario. While unwilling to go as far as their Reform counterparts in endorsing homosexual rabbis, the Conservatives rabbis voted overwhelmingly, at their national convention in May, to welcome homosexuals into their congregations and to "increase awareness, understanding and concern for our fellow Jews who are gay and lesbian." And although the movement's Cantors Assembly turned down, for the third consecutive year, a motion to admit women to its ranks, the group's executive council subsequently voted to approve the proposal and admit the female cantors. Several of the traditionalist cantors immediately announced plans to leave the Cantors Assembly and form their own association.

Just as in Reform the impulse for change in matters of gender and sexual life-style was accompanied by a felt need to return to tradition in the area of ritual, so in Conservatism there was a strong attraction to more traditional forms of spirituality. At the same Rabbinical Assembly convention that approved a Conservative welcome to gays and lesbians, rabbis complained that Conservative services were too cold and formal, a situation that alienated Jews seeking emotional warmth and spiritual depth. The rabbis took a concrete step to remedy the problem, voting to "reexamine" the late Friday night service—a pre-World War II innovation that, for many, cut short or even eliminated the Sabbath eve family meal at home—and revive "worship services closer to the traditional time of sunset," allowing families once again to enjoy in their homes the festive ritual Sabbath meal. The Jewish Theological Seminary also saw the need for rabbis to leaven their scholarly training with a greater sensitivity to spirituality. It announced that rabbinical students would now be required to write position papers and diary entries on their personal religious quests, to be shared with and commented upon by their classmates.

But the question of what role Halakhah had within the Conservative movement, highlighted by the creation of a rival seminary, remained. JTS professor Joel Roth, who chaired the movement's Committee on Jewish Law and Standards, complained to the biennial convention of the United Synagogue that "in too many synagogues, observant Conservative Jews are told in no uncertain terms that they are not really Conservative, but Orthodox." And Rabbi Irwin Groner, the newly elected president of the Rabbinical Assembly, told his colleagues with remarkable candor: "We are challenged by an assertive and triumphalist Orthodoxy on our right and by a vigorous, growing Reform movement on our left. We are dissatisfied with the state of our movement, we fall short in our own eyes, we are pessimistic about our future."

ORTHODOXY

On the evening of April 26, 20,000 Orthodox Jews packed Madison Square Garden in New York City for the ninth *Siyum Hashas* (completion of the study of the Talmud), sponsored by Agudath Israel. This event grew out of a practice that the Agudah initiated in Poland in 1923 of encouraging Jews to study one page of the Talmud each day, so that the entire Talmud would be completed every seven-and-a-half years. Synchronizing the study cycle would, it was hoped, underline the importance of Talmud study in the life of the Jew and also serve as a unifying force for observant Jews around the world.

The well-publicized and extremely moving ceremonies at Madison Square Garden made many non-Orthodox Jews—and non-Jews—aware, for the first time, of the growing influence of the sectarian Orthodox, for whom proficiency in Talmud was more important than integration in American society. Agudah publicists relished the irony that the growth of their form of Judaism came against a background of pessimism over the future of the rest of American Jewry. "It is true," asserted the *Jewish Observer* (September 1990), "secular-based Judaism and compromise-aimed Judaism are going down the tubes. . . . The American Jewish Committee . . . would be hard pressed to fill the main arena of Madison Square Garden with its entire membership. Yet that very arena overflowed with Orthodox Jews last April—not gathered in protest of any terrible wrong, but convened by Agudath Israel to celebrate the completion of the Talmud. . . ."

But even the rigorous Orthodox were—appearances notwithstanding—hardly monolithic. In 1990, the messianic speculations—some would say, pretensions—of the Lubavitch Hassidic sect, based in Brooklyn, New York, were received coolly by Orthodox Jews of a more rationalist bent. Rabbi Menachem Schneerson, the Lubavitcher Rebbe, stated on numerous occasions that the crisis in the Persian Gulf fulfilled ancient prophecies of a worldwide military conflict that would lead the way to the coming of the messiah. And he made no attempt to contradict the statements of his disciples that the Rebbe himself was the man most qualified to fulfill the role.

The modern or centrist wing of Orthodoxy, which believed in working together with non-Orthodox groups and accommodating, to some extent, to the realities of contemporary society, maintained a defensive posture in the face of the resurgence of the uncompromising Orthodox. The clearest expression of this defensiveness was Rabbi Norman Lamm's book *Torah Umadda: The Encounter of Religious Learning and Worldly Knowledge in the Jewish Tradition*. Lamm was the president of Yeshiva University, the modern Orthodox educational institution that stood for a combined Jewish and secular education. His book assumed that the ideology of the university's Orthodox opponents—that Jewish males should spend all their time in traditional Jewish learning—was undoubtedly legitimate, and that YU's approach was *also* acceptable, but only if secular subjects were studied for the greater glory of God.

Another measure of the decline in moderate Orthodoxy was that critiques of its positions previously made by the sectarian Orthodox were now being voiced within what had been modern Orthodox institutions and by individuals of modern Orthodox background. The Rabbinical Council of America (RCA), at both its midwinter conference in January and its annual convention in June, was seriously divided over both the question of official discussions with other religions and cooperative action with non-Orthodox branches of Judaism, both of which had been accepted for years by the overwhelming majority of modern Orthodox rabbis.

Extremists within the RCA even went so far as to seek the expulsion of some rabbis who were deemed too liberal, either because of their statemements and actions or because they had also taken out membership in the Fellowship of Traditional Orthodox Rabbis, an organization initiated in 1988 by Orthodox rabbis, most of whose synagogues did not have a separation between men and women, who felt that the RCA had moved too far to the right. Largely as a result of unfavorable publicity, the attempt to exclude the Orthodox liberal rabbis failed. One of the threatened rabbis, Irving Greenberg, felt that this episode contained a lesson: "Modern Orthodoxy . . . must renew its own soul and vision. Only thus can it make a major contribution to linking the whole Jewish people and the Torah. . . . In yielding its unique voice and 'going along,' it has weakened itself and its role as one of the key bridges of unity in Judaism."

LAWRENCE GROSSMAN

Jewish Population in the United States, 1991

THE "CORE" JEWISH POPULATION OF the United States was estimated to be 5.5 million in 1990. This figure is based on the findings of the Council of Jewish Federations' 1990 National Jewish Population Survey[1] and represents a modest growth from the 5.4 million reported in the 1970/71 National Jewish Population Study, the last previous effort of such magnitude.

The NJPS-1990 total is about 5 percent less than the 5.8 million total figure for 1991 derived by the alternate method used to estimate the size of the American Jewish community, i.e., adding together all local community counts. The difference, small though it is, between the national and aggregated-local figures is probably explained by the lag in data gathering and reporting on the local level, as well as definitional problems. As more local communities conduct studies over the next few years, declines and increases that have already occurred will be documented. The updated statistics will show national and regional patterns more in line with NJPS findings. Based upon trends revealed in NJPS data, declines can be expected to be reported in Connecticut, New York, New Jersey, Pennsylvania, and most of the Midwestern states. Higher community totals are anticipated for Colorado, Arizona, and the Pacific Northwest.

The NJPS used a scientifically selected sample to project a total number for the United States, but could not provide accurate information on the state and local levels. Therefore, as in past years, in this article we have based local, state, and regional population figures on the usual estimating procedures.

While the Jewish federations are the chief reporting bodies, their service areas vary in size and may represent several towns, one county, or an aggregate of several counties. In some cases we have subdivided federation areas to reflect the more natural geographic boundaries. Some estimates, from areas without federations, have been provided by local rabbis and other informed Jewish community leaders. In still other cases, the figures that have been updated are from past estimates provided by United Jewish Appeal field representatives. Finally, for smaller communities where no recent estimates are available, figures are based on extrapolation from older data. The estimates are for the resident Jewish population, including those in private households and in institutional settings. Non-Jewish family members have been excluded from the total.

The state and regional totals shown in Appendix tables 1 and 2 are derived by

---

[1]See "Profile of American Jewry: Insights from the 1990 National Jewish Population Survey," by Sidney Goldstein, elsewhere in this volume, and Barry A. Kosmin et al., *Highlights of the CJF 1990 National Jewish Population Survey* (New York, Council of Jewish Federations, 1991).

summing the individual estimates shown in table 3 and then making three adjustments. First, communities of less than 100 are added. Second, duplicated counts within states are eliminated. Third, communities whose population resides in two or more states (e.g., Kansas City and Washington, D.C.) are distributed accordingly.

Because population estimating is not an exact science, the reader should be aware that in cases where a figure differs from last year's, the increase or decrease did not come about suddenly but occurred over a period of time and has just now been substantiated. Similarly, the results of a completed local demographic study often change the previously reported Jewish population figure. This should be understood as either an updated calculation of gradual demographic change or a correction of a faulty older estimate.

In determining Jewish population, communities count both affiliated and nonaffiliated residents who are "core" Jews as defined in NJPS.[2] In most cases, counts are made by households, with that number multiplied by the average number of self-defined Jewish persons per household. Similarly to NJPS, most communities also include those born and raised as Jews but who at present consider themselves as having no religion. As stated above, non-Jews living in Jewish households, primarily the non-Jewish spouses and non-Jewish children, are not included in the 1991 estimates presented in the appendix below.

Local Population Changes

The community reporting the largest numeric decline was that of the New York City area[3]—in absolute numbers a drop of about 220,000 since the last estimate was provided. The percentage losses in Jewish population were greatest in the middle-aged suburban regions of Nassau County, Westchester County, and the borough of Queens. It is believed that an aging population in these areas that frequently relocates to Florida is not being replaced in large enough numbers by young persons. Conversely, a Jewish population increase of nearly 15 percent over the past decade took place in Manhattan. These changes were revealed in a recently completed demographic study, further details of which will be provided in next year's article.

Just outside of the immediate New York City area lies Rockland County, the community reporting the largest numerical increase in Jewish population. This suburban county, which was included in the 1991 New York population study, increased its total number by more than 23,000 since the last estimate was provided.

Rapid Jewish population growth also occurred in southeast Florida, where the areas of Hollywood and Boca Raton-Delray Beach grew by at least 5,000. While increases in the former were substantiated in a recently completed population study,

---

[2]Born Jews who report adherence to Judaism, Jews by choice, and born Jews without a current religion ("secular" Jews).

[3]The five boroughs of New York City plus Nassau, Suffolk, and Westchester counties.

the latter is a projected estimate indicative of continued growth. The increase in the Ft. Lauderdale figure is largely based on a reevaluation of its federation list and the methodology used to determine the full-year as against part-year residents. Finally, Miami-Dade County's losses continue to reflect ongoing demographic change, the primary features of which are an aging population, an increase in the numbers of non-Jewish immigrants settling in Jewish areas, and a preference by Jewish newcomers to Florida to locate further up the coast in Broward and Palm Beach counties.

Other declines in excess of 2,000 were reported in Bridgeport and Hartford, Connecticut. As the latter now includes the Meriden area in its total, the actual number for the Hartford area remains the same. Other more moderate declines occurred primarily in Northeastern and Midwestern communities: Champaign-Urbana, Illinois; Gary, Terre-Haute, and Marion, Indiana; Leominister, Massachusetts; Flint, Michigan; Vineland, New Jersey; Kingston and Auburn, New York; and Altoona, Hazelton, and Wilkes-Barre, Pennsylvania. Communities outside these regions that declined included Louisville, Kentucky; Albuquerque, New Mexico; Charleston, South Carolina; Greenville, Mississippi; Chattanooga and Memphis, Tennessee; and Montgomery, Alabama. The Memphis losses were due to the elimination of non-Jews in Jewish households from the community count.

As indicated by the southeast Florida Jewish population increases, growth communities were mainly in the South and West: Portland, Oregon; Atlanta, Georgia; Santa Barbara and Ventura County, California; Denver, Colorado; Dallas, Texas; Brevard County and Sarasota, Florida; Durham-Chapel Hill and Raleigh, North Carolina; and Oklahoma City, Oklahoma. Other parts of the country showing increases included Wichita, Kansas; South Bend, Indiana; Cape Cod, Massachusetts; Ann Arbor, Michigan; and Columbus, Ohio. The new figures for both Dallas and Columbus are reported in their newly completed Jewish population studies. Some of the declines in New Jersey, Massachusetts, and Connecticut reflect the elimination of duplicated counts between communities. In California, the reduction in the Orange County figure is based upon a reevaluation of its federation lists, while the increases in the San Francisco Bay Area reflect the addition of persons born Jewish with no current religion. Inclusion of this group is in keeping with the NJPS definition of the core Jewish population.

BARRY A. KOSMIN
JEFFREY SCHECKNER

APPENDIX

TABLE 1. JEWISH POPULATION IN THE UNITED STATES, 1991

State	Estimated Jewish Population	Total Population*	Estimated Jewish Percent of Total
Alabama...................	9,000	4,041,000	0.2
Alaska	2,400	550,000	0.4
Arizona	72,000	3,665,000	2.0
Arkansas	1,800	2,351,000	0.1
California.................	923,000	29,760,000	3.1
Colorado	51,000	3,294,000	1.5
Connecticut	106,000	3,287,000	3.2
Delaware	9,500	666,000	1.4
District of Columbia.........	25,500	607,000	4.2
Florida...................	593,000	12,938,000	4.6
Georgia	74,000	6,478,000	1.1
Hawaii	7,000	1,108,000	0.6
Idaho	500	1,007,000	(z)
Illinois	257,000	11,431,000	2.2
Indiana...................	18,000	5,544,000	0.3
Iowa.....................	6,000	2,777,000	0.2
Kansas	14,000	2,478,000	0.6
Kentucky.................	11,500	3,685,000	0.3
Louisiana.................	15,500	4,220,000	0.4
Maine....................	8,500	1,228,000	0.7
Maryland.................	211,000	4,781,000	4.4
Massachusetts	275,000	6,016,000	4.6
Michigan	107,000	9,295,000	1.2
Minnesota	30,500	4,375,000	0.7
Mississippi................	1,700	2,573,000	0.1
Missouri..................	61,500	5,117,000	1.2
Montana..................	500	799,000	0.1
Nebraska	7,500	1,578,000	0.5
Nevada...................	20,500	1,202,000	1.7
New Hampshire	7,000	1,109,000	0.6
New Jersey	426,000	7,730,000	5.5
New Mexico	6,000	1,515,000	0.4
New York	1,644,000	17,990,000	9.1

State	Estimated Jewish Population	Total Population*	Estimated Jewish Percent of Total
North Carolina	16,500	6,629,000	0.2
North Dakota	700	639,000	0.1
Ohio	131,000	10,847,000	1.2
Oklahoma.	5,500	3,146,000	0.2
Oregon	15,500	2,842,000	0.5
Pennsylvania	330,000	11,882,000	2.8
Rhode Island	16,000	1,003,000	1.6
South Carolina.	8,000	3,487,000	0.2
South Dakota.	350	696,000	0.1
Tennessee	17,500	4,877,000	0.4
Texas	109,000	16,987,000	0.6
Utah	3,000	1,723,000	0.2
Vermont	4,500	563,000	0.8
Virginia.	67,500	6,187,000	1.1
Washington	33,000	4,867,000	0.7
West Virginia.	2,500	1,793,000	0.1
Wisconsin.	34,500	4,892,000	0.7
Wyoming	500	454,000	(z)
U.S. TOTAL	**5,798,000	248,710,000	2.3

N.B. Details may not add to totals because of rounding.
*Resident population, April 1, 1990. (*Source:* U.S. Bureau of the Census, *Current Population Reports,* series P-25, no. 1044.)
**Exclusive of Puerto Rico and the Virgin Islands which previously reported Jewish populations of 1,500 and 350, respectively.
(z) Figure is less than 0.1 and rounds to 0.

TABLE 2.   DISTRIBUTION OF U.S. JEWISH POPULATION BY REGIONS, 1991

Region	Total Population	Percent Distribution	Jewish Population	Percent Distribution
Northeast	50,809,000	20.4	2,817,000	48.6
New England	13,207,000	5.3	417,000	7.2
Middle Atlantic	37,602,000	15.1	2,400,000	41.4
Midwest	59,669,000	24.0	669,000	11.5
East North Central . .	42,009,000	16.9	548,000	9.5
West North Central . .	17,660,000	7.1	121,000	2.1
South	85,446,000	34.4	1,180,000	20.3
South Atlantic	43,567,000	17.5	1,008,000	17.4
East South Central . . .	15,176,000	6.1	40,000	0.7
West South Central . .	26,703,000	10.7	132,000	2.3
West	52,786,000	21.2	1,133,000	19.5
Mountain.	13,659,000	5.5	153,000	2.6
Pacific	39,127,000	15.7	980,000	16.9
TOTALS.	248,710,000	100.0	5,798,000	100.0

N.B. Details may not add to totals because of rounding.

TABLE 3. COMMUNITIES WITH JEWISH POPULATIONS OF 100 OR MORE, 1991 (ESTIMATED)

State and City	Jewish Population	State and City	Jewish Population	State and City	Jewish Population
ALABAMA		**CALIFORNIA**		Orange County .	80,000
*Birmingham	5,100	Antelope Valley	700	Palmdale (incl. in	
Decatur (incl. in		Bakersfield-Kern		Antelope Valley)	
Florence total)		County	1,400	Palm Springs[N]	9,850
*Dothan	150	Berkeley-Contra		Palo Alto-South	
Florence	150	Costa County (listed		Peninsula (listed	
Huntsville	750	under S.F. Bay Area)		under S.F. Bay Area)	
**Mobile	1,100	*Chico	500	Pasadena (also incl.	
**Montgomery	1,100	Corona (incl. in		in L.A. Metro Area	
Selma	100	Riverside total)		total)	2,000
Sheffield (incl. in		***El Centro	125	Petaluma (listed	
Florence total)		*Eureka	500	under Sonoma	
Tuscaloosa	300	Fairfield	800	County-S.F. Bay Area)	
Tuscumbia (incl. in		Fontana (incl. in		Pomona Valley[N]	6,750
Florence total)		San Bernardino total)		*Redding	145
		*Fresno	2,000	Riverside	1,620
ALASKA		Lancaster		Sacramento[N]	12,500
**Anchorage	2,000	(incl. in Antelope		Salinas	500
***Fairbanks	210	Valley)		San Bernardino area	
Juneau	100	Long Beach (also			2,800
Ketchikan (incl. in		incl. in Los Angeles		*San Diego	70,000
Juneau total)		total)[N]	13,500	San Francisco Bay	
		Los Angeles Metro		Area[N]	210,000
ARIZONA		Area	501,000	San Francisco .	49,500
Cochise County	250	Merced	170	N. Peninsula	24,500
*Flagstaff	250	*Modesto	450	S. Peninsula	21,000
Lake Havesu City	100	Monterey Peninsula		San Jose	33,000
*Phoenix	50,000		1,500	Alameda County	
Prescott	150	Murietta Hot Springs			32,500
*Tucson	20,000		400	Contra Costa County	
Yuma	100	*Napa	450		22,000
		Oakland-Alameda		Marin County .	18,500
ARKANSAS		County (listed		Sonoma County	
Fayetteville	120	under S.F. Bay Area)			9,000
Hot Springs	200	Ontario (incl. in		*San Jose (listed under	
**Little Rock	1,300	Pomona Valley)		S.F. Bay Area)	

[N]See Notes below. *Includes entire county. **Includes all of 2 counties. ***Figure not updated.

State and City	Jewish Population
*San Luis Obispo .	1,500
*Santa Barbara . . .	5,000
*Santa Cruz	1,200
Santa Maria.	300
Santa Monica (also incl. in Los Angeles total)	8,000
Santa Rosa (listed under Sonoma County-S.F. Bay Area)	
Sonoma County (listed under S.F. Bay Area)	
*Stockton.	1,600
Sun City	200
Tulare & Kings counties.	500
***Vallejo	400
*Ventura County	9,000

COLORADO
Aspen.	250
Boulder (incl. in Denver total)	
Colorado Springs	1,500
Denver[N].	46,000
Evergreen.	100
*Ft. Collins	1,000
*Grand Junction. . . .	250
Greely (incl. in Ft. Collins total)	
Loveland (incl. in Ft. Collins total)	
Pueblo	250
Telluride	100
Vail	100

CONNECTICUT
Bridgeport[N]. . . .	13,500
Bristol (incl. in Hartford total)	
Cheshire (incl. in Meriden total)	

State and City	Jewish Population
Colchester	575
Danbury[N]	3,500
Danielson.	100
Darien (incl. in Stamford total)	
Greenwich	3,900
Hartford[N]	26,000
Hebron (incl. in Colchester total)	
Lebanon (incl. in Colchester total)	
Lower Middlesex County[N]	1,475
Manchester (incl. in Hartford total)	
Meriden[N].	3,000
Middletown.	1,300
New Britain (incl. in Hartford total)	
New Haven[N]. . .	28,000
New London[N]. . .	4,000
New Milford	400
Newtown (incl. in Danbury total)	
Norwalk[N]	9,500
Norwich (also incl. in New London total)	1,800
Putnam	100
Rockville (incl. in Hartford total)	
Shelton (incl. in Valley area)	
Southington (incl. in Meriden total)	
Stamford/New Canaan	11,100
Storrs (incl. in Willimantic total)	
Torrington.	560
Valley area[N]	550
Wallingford (also incl. in Meriden total) .	500
Waterbury[N]	2,700

State and City	Jewish Population
Westport (incl. in Norwalk total)	
Willimantic area . . .	700

DELAWARE
Dover[N]	650
Wilmington (incl. rest of state) . . .	9,500

DISTRICT OF COLUMBIA
Greater Washington	165,000

FLORIDA
Boca Raton-Delray Beach (listed under Southeast Fla.)	
Brevard County .	3,750
*Crystal River.	100
**Daytona Beach .	2,500
Fort Lauderdale (listed under Southeast Fla.)	
Fort Myers (incl. in Lee County)	
Fort Pierce	500
Gainesville.	1,200
Hollywood (listed under Southeast Fla.)	
**Jacksonville	7,300
Key West.	170
*Lakeland	800
Lee County	4,000
*Miami-Dade County (listed under Southeast Fla.)	
Naples	750
***Ocala	100
Orlando[N]	18,000
Palm Beach County (listed under Southeast Fla.)	
**Pasco County . .	1,000
**Pensacola.	775
*Port Charlotte-Punta Gorda	400

State and City	Jewish Population
*St. Petersburg- Clearwater	9,500
**Sarasota	10,000
Southeast Florida	515,000
Dade County	189,000
Hollywood[N]	66,000
Ft. Lauderdale[N]	140,000
Boca Raton-Delray Beach	60,000
Palm Beach County (excl. Boca Raton- Delray Beach)	60,000
Stuart-Port St. Lucie	3,000
Tallahassee	1,500
*Tampa	12,500
Venice (incl. in Sarasota total)	
*Vero Beach	300
Winter Haven (incl. in Lakeland total)	

GEORGIA

State and City	Jewish Population
Albany	350
Athens	300
Atlanta Metro Area	67,000
Augusta[N]	1,400
Brunswick	100
**Columbus	1,000
**Dalton	230
Fitzgerald-Cordele	125
Macon	900
*Savannah	2,750
**Valdosta	110

HAWAII

State and City	Jewish Population
Hilo	280
Honolulu (includes all of Oahu)	6,400
Kuaii	100
Maui	210

IDAHO

State and City	Jewish Population
**Boise	220
Lewiston	100
Moscow (incl. in Lewiston total)	

ILLINOIS

State and City	Jewish Population
Aurora area	500
Bloomington-Normal	170
Carbondale (also incl. in S. Ill. total)	100
*Champaign-Urbana	1,300
Chicago Metro Area[N]	248,000
**Danville	100
*Decatur	200
*DeKalb	200
East St. Louis (incl. in S. Ill.)	
Elgin[N]	600
Freeport (incl. in Rockford total)	
*Joliet	850
Kankakee	200
*Peoria	950
Quad Cities[N]	1,250
**Quincy	125
Rock Island (incl. in Quad Cities)	
Rockford[N]	1,000
Southern Illinois[N]	815
*Springfield	1,000
Waukegan	500

INDIANA

State and City	Jewish Population
Bloomington	1,000
Elkart (incl. in South Bend total)	
Evansville	520
**Ft. Wayne	1,085
**Gary-Northwest Indiana	2,200
**Indianapolis	10,000
**Lafayette	500
*Michigan City	280
Muncie	160
South Bend[N]	1,900
*Terre Haute	250

IOWA

State and City	Jewish Population
Ames (also incl. in Des Moines total)	200
Cedar Rapids	430
Council Bluffs (also incl. in Omaha, Neb. total)	150
Davenport (incl. in Quad Cities, Ill.)	
*Des Moines	2,800
*Iowa City	1,200
**Sioux City	600
*Waterloo	170

KANSAS

State and City	Jewish Population
Kansas City (incl. in Kansas City, Mo.)	
Lawrence	175
Manhattan	100
*Topeka	500
Wichita[N]	1,300

KENTUCKY

State and City	Jewish Population
Covington/Newport (incl. in Cincinnati, Ohio total)	
Lexington[N]	2,000
*Louisville	8,700
Paducah (incl. in S. Ill.)	

LOUISIANA

State and City	Jewish Population
Alexandria	250
Baton Rouge[N]	1,200

State and City	Jewish Population

Lafayette (incl. in
  S. Central La.)
Lake Charles...... 300
Monroe.......... 525
**New Orleans.. 12,000
*Shreveport........ 960
South Central La.^{N}
  250

MAINE
Augusta.......... 500
Bangor......... 1,250
Biddeford-Saco (incl.
  in S. Maine)
Brunswick-Bath (incl.
  in S. Maine)
Lewiston-Auburn .. 500
Portland........ 3,900
Rockland......... 110
Southern Maine (incl.
  Portland)^N 5,500
Waterville 300

MARYLAND
*Annapolis 2,000
**Baltimore..... 94,500
Cumberland....... 265
***Easton Park area^N
  100
*Frederick......... 600
*Hagerstown....... 300
*Harford County . 1,000
Howard County . 7,200
Montgomery and Prince
  Georges counties
  104,500
Ocean City 100
**Salisbury 400
Silver Spring (incl. in
  Montgomery County)

MASSACHUSETTS
Amherst.......... 750
Andover^N 3,000

Athol area (also incl.
  in Worcester County
  total) 300
Attleboro......... 200
Beverly (incl. in
  Lynn total)
Boston Metro Region^N
  228,000
Brockton^N...... 8,000
Brookline (also incl.
  in Boston
  total) 26,000
Cape Cod-Barnstable
  County........ 3,000
Clinton (incl. in
  Worcester County)
Fall River 1,780
Falmouth (incl. in
  Cape Cod)
Fitchburg (also incl.
  in Worcester County
  total) 300
Framingham (incl. in
  Boston total)
Gardner (incl. in
  Athol total)
Gloucester (also incl.
  in Lynn total).... 450
Great Barrington (incl.
  in Pittsfield total)
*Greenfield 900
Haverhill 1,500
Holyoke.......... 550
*Hyannis (incl. in
  Cape Cod)
Lawrence (incl. in
  Andover total)
Leominster (also
  incl. in Worcester
  County total) 400
Lowell area 2,000
Lynn-North Shore
  area^N 25,000
*Martha's Vineyard . 260

New Bedford^N .. 3,000
Newburyport...... 280
Newton (also incl. in
  Boston total)
  34,000
North Adams (incl. in
  N. Berkshire County)
North Berkshire
  County.......... 750
Northampton 700
Peabody (incl. in
  Lynn total)
Pittsfield-Berkshire
  County........ 3,100
Plymouth......... 500
Provincetown (incl. in
  Cape Cod)
Salem (incl. in
  Lynn total)
Southbridge (also
  incl. in Worcester
  County total) 105
Springfield^N.... 11,000
Taunton area.... 1,200
Webster (also
  incl. in Worcester
  County total) 125
Worcester area^N
  10,100
*Worcester County
  13,700

MICHIGAN
*Ann Arbor 5,000
Battle Creek 140
Bay City 280
Benton Harbor 450
**Detroit Metro Area
  94,000
*Flint........... 1,725
*Grand Rapids... 1,500
**Jackson 300
*Kalamazoo 1,000
*Lansing 2,100

State and City	Jewish Population	State and City	Jewish Population	State and City	Jewish Population
*Marquette County 150		NEVADA		Camden (incl. in Cherry Hill total)	
Midland.......... 150		Carson City (incl. in Reno total)		Cherry Hill^N ... 28,000	
Mt. Clemens (incl. in Detroit total)		*Las Vegas 19,000		Edison (incl. in Middlesex County)	
Mt. Pleasant^N 150		**Reno 1,400		Elizabeth (incl. in Union County)	
*Muskegon 220		NEW HAMPSHIRE		Englewood (incl. in Bergen County)	
*Saginaw 200		Bethlehem 100		Essex County^N (also incl. in Northeastern N.J. total).... 76,200	
MINNESOTA		Claremont 150		North Essex .. 15,600	
**Duluth.......... 500		Concord.......... 450		East Essex.... 10,800	
*Minneapolis.... 22,000		Dover area....... 600		South Essex... 20,300	
Rochester......... 400		Exeter (incl. in Portsmouth total)		Livingston.... 12,600	
**St. Paul 7,500		Franconia (incl. in Bethlehem total)		West Orange-Orange 16,900	
Winona (incl. in LaCrosse, Wis. total)		Hanover-Lebanon .. 360		Flemington 900	
MISSISSIPPI		*Keene............ 150		Freehold (incl. in Monmouth County)	
Biloxi-Gulfport 150		**Laconia 270		Gloucester (incl. in Cherry Hill total)	
**Greenville 270		Littleton (incl. in Bethlehem total)		Hoboken (listed under Hudson County)	
**Hattiesburg 120		Manchester area 2,500		Hudson County (also incl. in Northeastern N.J. total).... 13,950	
**Jackson 700		Nashua area 1,000		Bayonne 2,500	
MISSOURI		Portsmouth area... 950		Jersey City ... 5,700	
Columbia......... 350		Rochester (incl. in Dover total)		Hoboken 750	
Hannibal (incl. in Quincy, Ill. total)		Salem (also incl. in Andover, Mass. total) 150		North Hudson County^N 5,000	
Kansas City Metro Area 19,100		NEW JERSEY		Jersey City (listed under Hudson County)	
*St. Joseph 265		Asbury Park (incl. in Monmouth County)		Lakewood (incl. in Ocean County)	
**St. Louis 53,500		*Atlantic City (incl. in Atlantic County) 15,800		Livingston (incl. in Essex County)	
Springfield 285		Bayonne (listed under Hudson County)		Middlesex County^N (also incl. in Northeastern N.J. total) 58,000	
MONTANA		Bergen County (also incl. in Northeastern N.J. total).... 85,000			
*Billings.......... 200		***Bridgeton....... 325			
Butte 110		Bridgewater (incl. in Somerset County)		Millville.......... 135	
Helena (incl. in Butte total)					
NEBRASKA					
Grand Island-Hastings (incl. in Lincoln total)					
Lincoln 1,000					
Omaha^N........ 6,500					

State and City	Jewish Population	State and City	Jewish Population	State and City	Jewish Population
Monmouth County (also incl. in Northeastern N.J. total)	33,600	Toms River (incl. in Ocean County) Trenton^N	6,000	Fleischmanns	115
Morris County (also incl. in Northeastern N.J. total)	33,500	Union County (also incl. in Northeastern N.J. total)	30,000	Fredonia (incl. in Dunkirk total) Geneva	300
Morristown (incl. in Morris County)		Vineland^N	2,200	Glens Falls^N	800
Mt. Holly (incl. in Cherry Hill total)		Warren County	400	*Gloversville	380
Newark (incl. in Essex County)		Wayne (incl. in Passaic County)		*Herkimer	180
New Brunswick (incl. in Middlesex County)		Wildwood	425	Highland Falls (incl. in Orange County)	
Northeastern N.J.^{N}	367,000	Willingboro (incl. in Cherry Hill total)		Hudson	470
Ocean County (also incl. in Northeastern N.J. total)	9,500	**NEW MEXICO**		*Ithaca	1,250
Passaic-Clifton (also incl. in Passaic County total)	8,000	*Albuquerque	4,000	Kingston^N	4,300
Passaic County (also incl. in Northeastern N.J. total)	18,700	Las Cruces	525	Lake George (incl. in Glens Falls total)	
Paterson (incl. in Passaic County)		Los Alamos	250	Liberty (also incl. in Sullivan County total)	2,100
Perth Amboy (incl. in Middlesex County)		Santa Fe	900	Middletown (incl. in Orange County)	
Phillipsburg (incl. in Easton, Pa. total)		**NEW YORK**		Monroe (incl. in Orange County)	
Plainfield (incl. in Union County)		*Albany	12,000	Monticello (also incl. in Sullivan County total)	2,400
Princeton	3,000	Amenia (incl. in Poughkeepsie)		Newark (incl. in Geneva total)	
Salem	100	Amsterdam	450	Newburgh (incl. in Orange County)	
Somerset County (also incl. in Northeastern N.J. total)	7,900	*Auburn	115	New Paltz (incl. in Kingston total)	
Somerville (incl. in Somerset County)		Beacon (incl. in Poughkeepsie)		New York Metro Area^N	1,450,000
Sussex County (also incl. in Northeastern N.J. total)	4,100	*Binghamton (incl. all Broome County)	3,000	Bronx	83,700
		Brewster (incl. in Putnam County)		Brooklyn	379,000
		*Buffalo	18,125	Manhattan	314,500
		Canandaigua (incl. in Geneva total)		Queens	238,000
		Catskill	200	Staten Island	33,700
		Corning (incl. in Elmira total)		Nassau County	207,000
		*Cortland	200	Suffolk County	100,000
		Dunkirk	100	Westchester County	94,000
		Ellenville	1,600		
		Elmira^N	1,100		

State and City	Jewish Population	State and City	Jewish Population	State and City	Jewish Population
Niagara Falls	400	Greenville	300	New Philadelphia	
Olean	120	Hendersonville	135	(incl. in	
**Oneonta	250	**Hickory	100	Canton total)	
Orange County	10,000	High Point (incl. in		Norwalk (incl. in	
Pawling	105	Greensboro total)		Sandusky total)	
Plattsburg	260	Jacksonville (incl. in		Oberlin (incl. in	
Port Jervis (also		Wilmington total)		Elyria total)	
incl. in Orange		Raleigh	3,000	Oxford (incl. in	
County total)	560	Whiteville (incl. in		Butler County)	
Potsdam	200	Wilmington total)		**Sandusky	130
*Poughkeepsie	6,500	Wilmington area	500	Springfield	200
Putnam County		Winston-Salem	440	*Steubenville	175
	1,000			Toledo[N]	6,300
**Rochester	22,500	NORTH DAKOTA		Warren (also incl. in	
Rockland County		Fargo	500	Youngstown total)	
	83,100	Grand Forks	150		400
Rome	205			Wooster	135
Saratoga Springs	500	OHIO		Youngstown[N]	4,000
**Schenectady	5,200	**Akron	6,000	*Zanesville	100
South Fallsburg (also		Athens	100		
incl. in Sullivan County		Bowling Green (also		OKLAHOMA	
total)	1,100	incl. in Toledo total)		Norman (also incl.	
Sullivan County			120	in Oklahoma City	
	7,425	Butler County	900	total)	350
Syracuse[N]	9,000	**Canton	2,400	**Oklahoma City	
Troy area	800	Cincinnati[N]	23,000		2,500
Utica[N]	1,900	**Cleveland[N]	65,000	*Tulsa	2,750
Walden (incl. in		*Columbus	15,600		
Orange County)		**Dayton	6,000	OREGON	
Watertown	120	East Liverpool	200	*Corvallis	150
Woodstock (incl. in		Elyria	200	Eugene	2,300
Kingston total)		Fremont (incl. in		**Medford	500
		Sandusky total)		Portland	12,000
NORTH CAROLINA		Hamilton (incl. in		**Salem	250
Asheville[N]	1,350	Butler County)			
**Chapel Hill-Durham		*Lima	365	PENNSYLVANIA	
	3,000	Lorain	600	Allentown	6,000
Charlotte[N]	4,000	Mansfield	180	*Altoona	350
Elizabethtown (incl. in		Marietta (incl. in		Ambridge[N]	350
Wilmington total)		Parkersburg, W.Va.		Beaver Falls (incl.	
*Fayetteville area	300	total)		in Upper Beaver	
Gastonia	240	Marion	110	County)	
Goldsboro	120	Middletown (incl. in		Bethlehem	810
*Greensboro	2,700	Butler County)		**Bradford	100

State and City	Jewish Population
Bucks County (lower portion)[N]	14,500
*Butler	250
**Chambersburg	400
Chester (incl. in Phila. total)	
Chester County (also incl. in Phila. total)	4,000
Coatesville (incl. in Chester County)	
Easton area	1,200
*Erie	800
Farrell (incl. in Sharon total)	
Greensburg (also incl. in Pittsburgh total)	425
**Harrisburg	6,500
Hazleton area	300
Honesdale (incl. in Wayne County)	
Jeanette (incl. in Greensburg total)	
**Johnstown	415
Lancaster	2,100
*Lebanon	350
Lewisburg (incl. in Sunbury total)	
Lock Haven (incl. in Williamsport total)	
McKeesport (incl. in Pittsburgh total)	
New Castle	200
Norristown (incl. in Philadelphia total)	
**Oil City	100
Oxford-Kennett Square (incl. in Chester County)	
Philadelphia area[N]	250,000

State and City	Jewish Population
Phoenixville (incl. in Chester County)	
Pike County	300
Pittsburgh[N]	45,000
Pottstown	700
Pottsville	250
*Reading	2,800
*Scranton	3,100
Shamokin (incl. in Sunbury total)	
Sharon (also incl. in Youngstown, Ohio total)	260
State College	550
*Stroudsburg	400
Sunbury[N]	200
Tamaqua (incl. in Hazleton total)	
Uniontown area	250
Upper Beaver County	200
**Washington (also incl. in Pittsburgh total)	250
Wayne County	500
Waynesburg (incl. in Washington total)	
West Chester (also incl. in Chester County)	300
Wilkes-Barre[N]	3,200
**Williamsport	350
York	1,500
RHODE ISLAND	
Cranston (incl. in Providence total)	
Kingston (incl. in Washington County)	
Newport-Middletown	700
Providence area	14,200

State and City	Jewish Population
Washington County	1,200
Westerly (incl. in Washington County)	
SOUTH CAROLINA	
*Charleston	3,500
**Columbia	2,000
Florence area	210
Georgetown (incl. in Myrtle Beach total)	
Greenville	800
Kingstree (incl. in Sumter total)	
**Myrtle Beach	425
***Orangeburg County	105
Rock Hill (incl. in Charlotte total)	
*Spartanburg	320
Sumter[N]	175
SOUTH DAKOTA	
Sioux Falls	135
TENNESSEE	
Bristol (incl. in Johnson City total)	
Chattanooga	1,350
Johnson City	210
Kingsport (incl. in Johnson City total)	
Knoxville	1,350
Memphis	8,800
Nashville	5,600
Oak Ridge	200
TEXAS	
Amarillo[N]	140
*Austin	5,000
Bay City (incl. in Wharton total)	
Baytown	300

State and City	Jewish Population	State and City	Jewish Population	State and City	Jewish Population
Beaumont	800	Montpelier-Barre	500	WASHINGTON	
*Brownsville	325	Newport (incl. in		Bellingham	300
College Station-Bryan		St. Johnsbury total)		Ellensburg (incl. in	
	400	Rutland	550	Yakima total)	
*Corpus Christi	1,400	**St. Johnsbury	100	Longview-Kelso (incl. in	
**Dallas	35,000			Portland, Oreg. total)	
El Paso	4,900	VIRGINIA		Olympia	300
*Ft. Worth	5,000	Alexandria (incl.		Port Angeles	100
Galveston	800	Falls Church,		Pullman (incl. in	
Harlingen (incl. in		Arlington, and Fairfax		Moscow, Idaho total)	
Brownsville total)		counties)	35,100	*Seattle[N]	29,300
**Houston[N]	42,000	Arlington (incl. in		Spokane	800
Kilgore (incl. in		Alexandria total)		*Tacoma	1,100
Longview total)		Blacksburg	300	Tri Cities[N]	180
Laredo	160	Charlottesville	950	Vancouver (incl. in	
Longview	150	Chesapeake (incl. in		Portland, Oreg. total)	
*Lubbock	225	Portsmouth total)		**Yakima	100
Lufkin (incl. in		Colonial Heights (incl.			
Longview total)		in Petersburg total)		WEST VIRGINIA	
Marshall (incl. in		Danville	100	Bluefield-Princeton	
Longview total)		Fredericksburg	140		225
*McAllen	475	Hampton (incl. in		*Charleston	1,000
Midland-Odessa	150	Newport News)		Clarksburg	115
Paris (incl. in		Harrisonburg (incl. in		Fairmont (incl. in	
Sherman-Denison		Staunton total)		Clarksburg total)	
total)		Lynchburg area	275	Huntington[N]	275
Port Arthur	100	**Martinsville	130	Morgantown	150
San Angelo	100	Newport News-		**Wheeling	300
*San Antonio	10,000	Hampton[N]	2,000		
Sherman-Denison	100	Norfolk-Virginia Beach		WISCONSIN	
Tyler	450		18,000	Appleton	250
Waco[N]	450	Petersburg area	550	Beloit	120
**Wharton	100	Portsmouth-Suffolk		Green Bay	240
Wichita Falls	260	(also incl. in Norfolk		*Kenosha	200
		total)	1,900	LaCrosse	120
UTAH		Radford (incl. in		*Madison	4,500
Ogden	150	Blacksburg total)		Milwaukee[N]	28,000
*Salt Lake City	2,800	Richmond[N]	8,000	Oshkosh	150
		Roanoke	1,050	*Racine	375
VERMONT		Staunton[N]	375	Sheboygan	150
Bennington	100	Williamsburg (incl. in		Superior (also incl.	
Brattleboro	150	Newport News total)		in Duluth, Minn.	
**Burlington	3,000	Winchester[N]	145	total)	100

State and City	Jewish Population	State and City	Jewish Population	State and City	Jewish Population
Waukesha (incl. in Milwaukee total) Wausau[N]	240	WYOMING Casper Cheyenne	100 230	Laramie (incl. in Cheyenne total)	

Notes

CALIFORNIA

Long Beach—includes in L.A. County: Long Beach, Signal Hill, Cerritos, Lakewood, Rosmoor and Hawaiian Gardens. Also includes in Orange County: Los Alamitas, Cypress, Seal Beach, and Huntington Harbor.

Palm Springs—includes Palm Springs, Desert Hot Springs, Cathedral City, Palm Desert, and Rancho Mirage.

Pomona Valley—includes Alta Loma, Chino, Claremont, Cucamonga, La Verne, Montclair, Ontario, Pomona, San Dimas, and Upland. Portion also included in Los Angeles total.

Sacramento—includes Yolo, Placer, El Dorado, and Sacramento counties.

San Francisco Bay Area—North Peninsula includes northern San Mateo County. South Peninsula includes southern San Mateo County and towns of Palo Alto and Los Altos in Santa Clara County. San Jose includes remainder of Santa Clara County.

COLORADO

Denver—includes Adams, Arapahoe, Boulder, Denver, and Jefferson counties.

CONNECTICUT

Bridgeport—includes Monroe, Easton, Trumbull, Fairfield, Bridgeport, Shelton, Stratford and part of Milford.

Danbury—includes Danbury, Bethel, New Fairfield, Brookfield, Sherman, Newtown, Redding, Ridgefield, and part of Wilton; also includes some towns in neighboring Putnam County, New York.

Hartford—includes most of Hartford County and Vernon, Rockville, Ellington, and Tolland in Tolland County, and Meriden area of New Haven County.

Lower Middlesex County—includes Branford, Guilford, Madison, Clinton, Westbrook, Old Saybrook. Portion of this area also included in New London and New Haven totals.

Meriden—includes Meriden, Southington, Cheshire and Wallingford. Most included in Hartford total and a portion also included in New Haven total.

New Haven—includes New Haven, East Haven, Guilford, Branford, Madison, North Haven, Hamden, West Haven, Milford, Orange, Woodbridge, Bethany, Derby, Ansonia and Cheshire.

New London—includes central and southern New London County. Also includes part of Lower Middlesex County and part of Windham County.

Norwalk—includes Norwalk, Weston, Westport, East Norwalk, Darien, Wilton, part of Georgetown and part of New Canaan.

Valley Area—includes Ansonia, Derby, Shelton, Oxford, Seymour, and Beacon Falls. Portion also included in Bridgeport and New Haven totals.

Waterbury—includes Middlebury, Southbury, Naugatuck, Watertown, Waterbury, Oakville and Woodbury.

DELAWARE

Dover—includes most of central and southern Delaware.

DISTRICT OF COLUMBIA

Greater Washington—includes Montgomery and Prince Georges counties in Maryland, Arlington County, Fairfax County, Falls Church, and Alexandria in Virginia.

FLORIDA

Ft. Lauderdale—includes Ft. Lauderdale, Pompano Beach, Deerfield Beach, Tamarac, Margate, and other towns in northern Broward County.

Hollywood—includes Hollywood, Hallandale, Dania, Davie, Pembroke, and other towns in southern Broward County.

Orlando—includes all of Orange and Seminole counties, and part of Lake County.

GEORGIA

Augusta—includes Burke, Columbia, and Richmond counties and part of Aiken County, South Carolina.

ILLINOIS

Chicago—includes all of Cook and DuPage counties and Southern Lake County. For a total of Jewish population of the Chicago Metropolitan Region, please include Northwest Indiana, Joliet, Aurora, Elgin, and Waukegan totals.

Elgin—includes northern Kane County, southern McHenry County, and western edge of Cook County.

Quad Cities—includes Rock Island, Moline (Ill.), Davenport, and Bettendorf (Iowa).

Rockford—includes Winnebago, Boone, and Stephenson counties.

Southern Illinois—includes lower portion of Illinois below Carlinville, adjacent western portion of Kentucky, and adjacent portion of southeastern Missouri.

INDIANA

South Bend—includes St. Joseph and Elkhart counties and part of Berrien County, Mich.

KANSAS

Wichita—includes Sedgwick County and towns of Salina, Dodge City, Great Bend, Liberal, Russel, and Hays.

KENTUCKY

Lexington—includes Fayette, Bourbon, Scott, Clark, Woodford, Madison, Pulaski, and Jessamin counties.

LOUISIANA

Baton Rouge—includes E. Baton Rouge, Ascencion, Livingston, St. Landry, Iberville, Pt. Coupee, and W. Baton Rouge parishes.

South Central—includes Abbeville, Lafayette, New Iberia, Crowley, Opelousus, Houma, Morgan City, Thibadoux, and Franklin.

MAINE

Southern Maine—includes York, Cumberland, and Sagadahoc counties.

MARYLAND

Easton Park Area—includes towns in Caroline, Kent, Queen Annes, and Talbot counties.

MASSACHUSETTS

Andover—includes Andover, N. Andover, Boxford, Lawrence, Methuen, Tewksbury, Dracut, and town of Salem, New Hampshire.

Boston Metropolitan Region—includes all towns south and west of Boston within approximately 30 miles, and all towns north of Boston within approximately 20 miles. All towns formerly part of Framingham area are now included in Boston total.

Brockton—includes Avon, Brockton, Easton, Bridgewater, Whitman, and West Bridgewater. Also included in Boston total.

Lynn—includes Lynn, Saugus, Nahant, Swampscott, Lynnfield, Peabody, Salem, Marblehead, Beverly, Danvers, Middleton, Wenham, Topsfield, Hamilton, Manchester, Ipswich, Essex, Gloucester, and Rockport. Also included in Boston total.

New Bedford—includes New Bedford, Dartmouth, Fairhaven, and Mattapoisett.

Springfield—includes Springfield, Longmeadow, E. Longmeadow, Hampden, Wilbraham, Agwam, and West Springfield.

Worcester—includes Worcester, Northborough, Westborough, Shrewsbury, Boylston, West Boylston, Holden, Paxton, Leicester, Auburn, Millbury, and Grafton. Also included in the Worcester County total.

MICHIGAN

Mt. Pleasant—includes towns in Isabella, Mecosta, Gladwin, and Gratiot counties.

NEBRASKA

Omaha—includes Douglas and Sarpy counties. Also includes Pottawatomie County, Iowa.

NEW HAMPSHIRE

Laconia—includes Laconia, Plymouth, Meredith, Conway, and Franklin.

NEW JERSEY

Cherry Hill—includes Camden, Burlington, and Gloucester counties.

Essex County—East Essex includes Belleville, Bloomfield, East Orange, Irvington, Newark, and Nutley in Essex County, and Kearney in Hudson County. North Essex includes Caldwell, Cedar Grove, Essex Fells, Fairfield, Glen Ridge, Montclair, North Caldwell, Roseland, Verona, and West Caldwell. South Essex includes Maplewood, Millburn, Short Hills, and South Orange in Essex County, and Springfield in Union County.

Middlesex County—includes in Somerset County: Kendall Park, Somerset, and Franklin; in Mercer County: Hightstown; and all of Middlesex County.

Northeastern N.J.—includes Bergen, Essex, Hudson, Middlesex, Morris, Passaic, Somerset, Union, Hunterdon, Sussex, Monmouth, and Ocean counties.

North Hudson County—includes Guttenberg, Hudson Heights, North Bergen, North Hudson, Secaucus, Union City, Weehawken, West New York, and Woodcliff.

Somerset County—includes most of Somerset County and a portion of Hunterdon County.

Trenton—includes most of Mercer County.

Union County—includes all of Union County except Springfield. Also includes a few towns in adjacent areas of Somerset and Middlesex counties.

Vineland—includes most of Cumberland County and towns in neighboring counties adjacent to Vineland.

NEW YORK

Elmira—includes Chemung, Tioga, and Schuyler counties. Also includes Tioga and Bradford counties in Pennsylvania.

Glens Falls—includes Warren and Washington counties, lower Essex County, and upper Saratoga County.

Kingston—includes eastern half of Ulster County.

New York Metropolitan Area—includes the five boroughs of New York City, Westchester, Nassau, and Suffolk counties. For a total Jewish population of the New York metropolitan region, please include Fairfield County, Connecticut; Rockland, Putnam, and Orange counties, New York; and Northeastern New Jersey.

Syracuse—includes Onondaga County, Western Madison County, and most of Oswego County.

Utica—includes southeastern third of Oneida County.

NORTH CAROLINA

Asheville—includes Buncombe, Haywood, and Madison counties.

Charlotte—includes Mecklenberg County. Also includes Lancaster and York counties in South Carolina.

Cincinnati—includes Hamilton and Butler counties. Also includes Boone, Campbell, and Kenton counties in Kentucky.

Cleveland—for a total Jewish population of the Cleveland metropolitan region, please include Elyria, Lorain, and Akron totals.

Toledo—includes Fulton, Lucas, and Wood counties. Also includes Monroe and Lenawee counties, Michigan.

Youngstown—includes Mahoning and Trumbull counties. Also includes Mercer County, Pennsylvania.

PENNSYLVANIA

Ambridge—includes lower Beaver County and adjacent areas of Allegheny County. Also included in Pittsburgh total.

Bucks County (lower portion)—includes Bensalem Township, Bristol, Langhorne, Levittown, New Hope, Newtown, Penndel, Warrington, Yardley, Richboro, Feasterville, Middletown, Southampton, and Holland. Also included in Philadelphia total.

Philadelphia—includes Philadelphia City, Montgomery County, Delaware County, Chester County, and Bucks County. For a total Jewish population of the Philadelphia metropolitan region, please include the Cherry Hill, Salem, and Trenton areas of New Jersey, and the Wilmington area of Delaware.

Pittsburgh—includes all of Allegheny County and adjacent portions of Washington, Westmoreland, and Beaver counties.

Sunbury—includes Shamokin, Lewisburg, Milton, Selinsgrove, and Sunbury.

Wilkes-Barre—includes all of Lucerne County except southern portion, which is included in Hazleton totals.

SOUTH CAROLINA

Sumter—includes towns in Sumter, Lee, Clarendon, and Williamsburg counties.

TEXAS

Amarillo—includes Canyon, Childress, Borger, Dumas, Memphis, Pampa, Vega, and Hereford in Texas, and Portales, New Mexico.

Houston—includes Harris, Montgomery, and Ft. Bend counties, and parts of Brazoria and Galveston counties.

Waco—includes Mclellan, Coryell, Bell, Falls, Hamilton, and Hill counties.

VIRGINIA

Newport News—includes Newport News, Hampton, Williamsburg, James City, York County, and Poquosson County.

Richmond—includes Richmond City, Henrico County, and Chesterfield County.

Staunton—includes towns in Augusta, Page, Shenendoah, Rockingham, Bath, and Highland counties.

Winchester—includes towns in Winchester, Frederick, Clark, and Warren counties, Virginia; and Hardy and Jefferson counties, West Virginia.

WASHINGTON

Seattle—includes King County and adjacent portions of Snohomish and Kitsap counties.
Tri Cities—includes Pasco, Richland, and Kennewick.

WEST VIRGINIA

Huntington—includes nearby towns in Ohio and Kentucky.

WISCONSIN

Milwaukee—includes Milwaukee County, eastern Waukesha County, and southern Ozaukee County.
Wausau—includes Stevens Point, Marshfield, Antigo, and Rhinelander.

Review
of
the
Year

OTHER COUNTRIES

Canada

National Affairs

THE MEECH LAKE ACCORD, A PACKAGE of constitutional amendments designed to induce Quebec to accede to the 1982 constitution, dominated Canadian public life during 1990. The controversial amendments, which recognized Quebec as a distinct society and enabled the provinces to increase their power relative to the federal government, were agreed to in 1987, with a three-year time limit for unanimous ratification by Parliament and the ten provinces. In order to increase the pressure on the doubtful provinces, Prime Minister Brian Mulroney and Premier Robert Bourassa of Quebec encouraged the view that failure to adopt the accord would have dire consequences for the country.

After a dramatic final month leading up to the June 30 deadline, the accord failed to achieve the required unanimity, despite frantic last-minute efforts by many of the key political actors. The process of trying to obtain ratification stirred up nationalist sentiments in Quebec that had been dormant for some years. During the months following the failure, support within Quebec for the independence of that predominantly French-speaking province reached unprecedented heights, nearly 70 percent by some counts. The nominally federalist provincial government felt compelled to act in response to the massive public pressure, ultimately promising a referendum on some aspect of the independence issue by 1992.

The national unity crisis, probably the most severe in Canada's nearly 125-year history, had serious implications for the country's Jewish community, nearly 30 percent of whom live in Montreal, Quebec's largest metropolitan area. Montreal's Jews, who are generally federalist and do not welcome the prospect of living in an independent Quebec, were very unsettled by the developments. There was renewed talk of significant population shifts and fear that the departure of a substantial portion of the productive sector of the population would leave the community shrunken and unable to raise the funds necessary to sustain itself at the accustomed level. Furthermore, as the second-largest Jewish community in the country, Montreal plays a major role in all aspects of countrywide community life. Any weakening of it would have deleterious effects on the entire community. And independence, if it should happen, would create new problems as the Canadian Jewish community tried to maintain its processes and programs.

The intensity of the political debate and the anxiety that it generated led to some divisive developments within the Montreal community. Rabbi Moise Ohana, a francophone of Moroccan origin, took a public stance that was perceived as an endorsement of nationalist goals and generated considerable controversy among Jews from both language groups. In an article in the daily newspaper *La Presse* in March, he tried to distance the francophone Jews from anglophone Jews by expressing support for restrictive language policies. He was motivated by the perception that the relatively new Equality party, the most vehement of anglophone groups in opposition to language policies, which received surprising support from anglophone voters in the 1989 election, was led by a Jew, Robert Libman, and was largely a Jewish party. Stressing that the Jews are not monolithic, Ohana claimed that the Sephardic Jews, who are mainly French-speaking, share the logic of the language laws "and the tangible and real affirmation of the French fact in Quebec, which is the goal sought by these laws." In response, Libman asserted that when he acted politically he was not doing so in a Jewish capacity. Moreover, the quarrel with the language laws was not over the cultural goal per se, but rather the denial of individual rights that such laws entailed. Later in the year, Libman suggested that leaders of the francophone Jews were dividing the community by demonstrating support for Quebec nationalism. In a related development, the Montreal periodical *Tribune Juive* came out in support of sovereignty for Quebec.

In Toronto, Patricia Starr successfully challenged the constitutionality of a provincial inquiry into her activities as a leader of the Toronto section of the National Council of Jewish Women. She was accused of funneling money from NCJW's charitable foundation to Ontario political candidates. Starr, who denied any wrongdoing, still faced criminal-fraud and election-law charges. The Starr scandal was one of the factors that contributed to the disenchantment of the voters with the government of Ontario premier David Peterson. In a September election, Peterson's Liberals fell from power and were replaced by the New Democratic party (NDP). Twelve Jews ran for seats in the legislature. Some prominent Liberals, such as Chaviva Hosek and Ron Kanter, went down to defeat. However, Monte Kwinter and Elinor Caplan, both Liberals, managed to win reelection, as did Progressive Conservative Charles Harnick. Veteran NDP politician Stephen Lewis was appointed to head the transition team of Premier Bob Rae.

In British Columbia, the ruling Social Credit party, meeting in Vancouver in October, finally dropped its contentious constitutional clause that called for adherence to Christian principles. It was replaced with a clause that recognized "the supremacy of God and the rule of law."

The crisis in the Persian Gulf focused attention on the personnel policies of the Canadian Forces. The League for Human Rights of B'nai Brith Canada (BBC) charged in February that Jews and Muslims had been barred from serving in the Middle East since Canada first became involved in peacekeeping operations in 1956. The league pointed to documentary evidence from the 1980s, but military officials denied the existence of such a policy.

Relations with Israel

Canada's foreign policy continued to shift gradually away from Israel and toward the Arabs during the year. Supporters of Israel expressed increasing discontent with the direction and tone of the positions articulated by government spokespersons. In March, for example, after Canada's UN ambassador, Yves Fortier, told the Security Council that Canada did not accept the permanence of Israeli control over any territory occupied since 1967, Mark Entwistle of the Department of External Affairs (DEA) elaborated that that included East Jerusalem. He added that Canada "opposes unilateral actions which are intended to predetermine the outcome of negotiations," which essentially meant settlements. The Canada-Israel Committee (CIC) characterized the notion that East Jerusalem was occupied territory and should not be available for the settlement of Soviet immigrants as "destructive and unacceptable."

In the Security Council, in May, Canada voted for a resolution that would have sent an investigating team to the territories to look into the violence. The United States cast the only negative vote, thereby vetoing the resolution. The pattern of Canada joining with the other members of the council was common during the first year of its two-year term, despite repeated criticism from the CIC and other Jewish groups. DEA spokesman Entwistle stated that the "international community has a responsibility to the Palestinians living in the territories," but reiterated Canada's long-term support for Israel's right to live in peace behind secure borders. Palestinian terrorist attacks, such as the one on May 30 on Israeli beaches, seemed to have no effect on Canadian policy. Even the death of a Canadian teenager, Marnie Kimelman, 17, of Toronto, who was killed by a terrorist bomb on a Tel Aviv beach in July, appeared to leave the policymakers unmoved. Kimelman was the third Canadian woman to die in Israel as the result of terrorist attacks in little over a year.

Prof. David Goldberg, national director of Canadian Professors for Peace in the Middle East, termed Canadian foreign policy insensitive to Israel, in a February speech. He was highly critical of Canada's UN voting record and its upgrading of relations with the PLO in 1989. He bemoaned as well the media's unwarranted and unbalanced fixation on Israel. These sentiments were echoed in a November speech by Moshe Ronen, national executive chairman of the Canadian Jewish Congress (CJC). He charged that "Canada is increasingly being seduced by the UN process" and thus can no longer play the role of honest broker, as it did during the days of the late Lester B. Pearson (1950s and 1960s).

Secretary of State for External Affairs Joe Clark paid a brief visit to Israel in November and met with David Levy, his Israeli counterpart, Prime Minister Yitzhak Shamir, and Palestinian leader Faisal Husseini. In remarks in Israel and later at the UN, Clark emphasized that there was no linkage between the Kuwait crisis and the Arab-Israeli situation. However, he expressed the view that the successful termination of the Gulf crisis would create a window of opportunity for dealing with problems between Israel and the Arabs. Two members of Parliament, Bob Corbett and Svend Robinson, encountered heavy criticism upon their return home from a Baghdad meeting with Yasir Arafat in November. They sought his help in obtaining the release of Western hostages held in Iraq.

The incident at the Temple Mount in Jerusalem during Sukkot (October 8), in which 21 Palestinians were killed, further soured Canada-Israel relations. Ambassador Fortier indicated Canada's willingness to vote for a hard-line Arab resolution in the Security Council, though the one that ultimately passed was softened in order to avoid an American veto. Major Canadian Jewish organizations came to Israel's defense, blaming Palestinians for provoking the attack.

When a June visit to Canada by Israeli cabinet minister Ariel Sharon was announced, the Canadian Arab Foundation (CAF) went to court to try to bar him from Canada on the grounds that he was a war criminal, that he had allegedly plotted aggressive war in Lebanon in 1982. The suit was of dubious legal merit because it was not clear that the CAF had legal standing to file such a suit. In the event, the petition was denied by the Federal Court.

A major public storm emerged over news of the Ontario Science Center's cooperation with the Arab boycott, as a result of which the center's director-general, Mark Abbott, was forced to resign. At issue was a clause in a contract for a children's science exhibit in Oman that called for a boycott of Israeli firms and goods, despite the fact that Ontario law prohibits such provisions. Although Abbott apologized to the Canadian Jewish community for his error of judgment, the controversy was compounded by the revelation that after officials had been made aware that the clause in question violated public policy, they wrote a new clause that was worded less offensively but appeared to have the same objective.

Several Christian religious organizations sponsored a conference on "Israel and the Occupied Territories" in April. In the keynote address, Archbishop and Primate of the Anglican Church of Canada Michael Peers expressed his opposition to the settlement of Soviet immigrants in the West Bank. He called upon Western churches to promote the Palestinian cause in order to "counterbalance the United States and Israel-dominated analysis of the region's needs." In a response to Peers subsequent to the conference, CJC president Les Scheininger asserted that "it is evident that you have fully thrown in your lot with the Palestinians and, indeed, become their advocate." Shirley Carr, president of the largest labor federation, the Canadian Labor Congress (CLC), speaking in May at the group's convention, called upon Israel "to accept a Palestinian state next to its borders," provided that Israeli security would be guaranteed by the PLO and Arab nations. A number of CLC affiliates proposed radically pro-Palestinian resolutions that did not pass. The consensus resolution called for an immediate negotiated resolution of the conflict through a conference in which the PLO would participate.

The Israeli government went to court in September to attempt to suppress the publication of *By Way of Deception: A Devastating Insider's Portrait*, by Victor Ostrovsky and Claire Hoy. Ostrovsky, a Canadian and Israeli dual national, purported to reveal the inside workings of the Israeli intelligence agency Mossad, based on his personal experiences as an agent. Israel claimed that Ostrovsky had violated signed undertakings not to divulge information gained while working for the Mossad and that his revelations could have "dire consequences." A judge issued a temporary order restraining publication for ten days. After it expired, the Israelis dropped their request because the book had already appeared in the United States. Ostrovsky claimed that Israeli agents had tried to intimidate him into withdrawing the book.

In other Israel-related matters, two new Israeli diplomats arrived in Canada. Itzhak Shelef became the ambassador and Itzhak Levanon the consul-general in Montreal. Charles Bronfman and three Diaspora partners launched a new English-language magazine in Israel, *Jerusalem Report*, in October. Its backers expected it to provide what they believed would be more balanced coverage than the rival *Jerusalem Post*, which, under its new owners, also Canadians, had moved from a position highly critical of the Likud-led government to a position much more supportive of it. F. David Radler, president of Canada's Hollinger Inc., owners of the *Post,* indicated that he was pleased with that newspaper's performance during its first year under new management.

Anti-Semitism

There was an alarming number of anti-Semitic incidents during the year in all parts of the country. Most of these involved vandalism of Jewish institutions, such as synagogues, cemeteries, and community buildings. No single thread linked the various incidents, though it appeared that most were of right-wing origin. Others were related to Middle East issues. The annual report of B'nai Brith's League for Human Rights listed 210 incidents in 1990 (up from 176 in 1989), of which 150 were characterized as harassment and 60 as vandalism. The figures were the highest since the organization began to keep such statistics in 1982. Particularly alarming was the recruitment of young people into skinhead groups. According to the report, many of them "have now adopted white supremacist and neo-Nazi beliefs." There was some evidence that several of the desecrations were coordinated, especially those at five synagogues in different cities.

Vancouver experienced three fires set at synagogues in March and vandalism of a cemetery in September. There were two desecrations of Montreal cemeteries, one in April and the other in November, making a total of three such incidents there in little over a year. There were indications of skinhead responsibility in the April incident. Three juveniles were charged in the November action. A similar desecration took place at a cemetery in a Quebec City suburb in May. There was also an attack on a Montreal yeshivah and adjoining synagogue in July, with white supremacists as the suspects. Synagogues were hit in Hamilton in July and Moncton in August. A sign of the seriousness with which the Jewish community viewed the increase in such activity was the offer of rewards by community organizations for information leading to the apprehension of the perpetrators.

290 / AMERICAN JEWISH YEAR BOOK, 1992

In a case from 1989, skinhead Zvonimir Lelas pleaded guilty to three counts of mischief for his vandalism of a synagogue and yeshivah in Toronto. He was sentenced to six months' incarceration, but the Crown appealed the sentence and the Ontario Court of Appeal doubled it to one year. The judges believed that the original sentence was an insufficient deterrent.

In a more direct confrontation, six youths were charged with assault and robbery against Hassidim in the Montreal suburb of Outremont in October. They were accused of attacking at least nine Hassidim in four separate incidents on one night. The intensity of the physical violence against the Hassidim was characterized by one B'nai Brith official as "a pogrom" that "stirs grim memories." The aftermath of the incident was also unsettling to the Jewish community of Montreal. Radio commentator Claude Jasmin, in discussing the incident on his program, charged that the Jews were "the most racist" people in the world. He blamed the Hassidim for creating a negative image for themselves by refusing to integrate. Jasmin had been the center of another controversy in Outremont in 1987 when he also accused the Hassidim of racism in the midst of a fight over a rezoning request by a Hassidic synagogue. Jasmin was later rebuked by the owner of the radio station and ordered to desist from such statements.

In an important legal precedent, the Supreme Court upheld the constitutionality of the antihate laws incorporated in Canada's criminal code. By so doing, the Court reversed a lower appeal court's vacating of James Keegstra's conviction for promoting hatred against Jews. (See AJYB 1990, p. 306.) A fine of $5,000 was also reinstated, thus terminating a case that had dragged on through the courts for years. The Court held by a narrow majority that compelling state interests justified the infringement of free expression that is inherent in the antihate legislation.

In a related matter, convicted Holocaust-denier Ernst Zundel was permitted to appeal to the Supreme Court only on the grounds that the statute under which he was convicted was unconstitutional. That appeal was pending at year's end. An earlier conviction in 1985 for publishing lies about the Holocaust was overturned because of legal errors. He was convicted again in 1988 and sentenced to nine months in jail.

After years of legal jockeying, a human-rights inquiry into the matter of Moncton teacher Malcolm Ross finally got under way. Ross had written several books that depict an international Jewish conspiracy and question the historicity of the Holocaust. A parent, David Attis, requested the hearing into the question of whether the school board fostered a climate of anti-Semitism by employing Ross. In testimony, students described the anti-Semitic taunts and harassment to which they were subjected in the school. Ross was represented by attorney Douglas Christie, who had also defended Keegstra and Zundel. The hearing continued into 1991.

Nazi War Criminals and Holocaust Denial

The government continued its prosecution of accused war criminals who had been allowed to settle in Canada, using a new law passed in 1987. Generally the defendants were non-Germans who had allegedly assisted the Nazis in their destruction of European Jewry. The first case tried was that of Imre Finta, a former Hungarian gendarmerie officer. Eyewitnesses testified at his trial during the first half of the year to such acts as supervising the loading of over 8,000 Jews from Szeged into trains headed for extermination camps, scheduling the deportation trains, and in general, in the view of the Crown attorney, playing a key role in the confinement, robbery, and deportation of the Jews. In a vigorous defense of Finta, lawyer Douglas Christie questioned the veracity of the witnesses and denounced the prosecution of his client as "absurd." He claimed that Finta was only doing his duty and following orders.

In a surprising development, the jury, after hearing six months of testimony, took only 13 hours of deliberation to deliver a not-guilty verdict on all eight counts of war crimes and crimes against humanity, including forcible confinement, kidnapping, robbery, and manslaughter. Critics of the verdict contended that the judge's lengthy charge to the jury made it difficult to convict on the manslaughter charge and raised questions as to whether eyewitness identifications could still be credible after 45 years. Several weeks after the May verdict, the prosecution asked the Ontario Court of Appeal to allow a new trial on the ground that the judge had erred in his charge to the jury. Finta also appealed in an attempt to head off the Crown appeal. He charged that the legislation under which he was prosecuted was unconstitutional. The appeal issue was unresolved at year's end.

Two other war-crimes prosecutions were also in progress. Stephen Reistetter, an official of the fascist governing party in Slovakia during the war, was charged with multiple counts of kidnapping in 1942 in the town of Bardejov, from which some 3,000 Jews were deported. After some legal maneuvering, a commission was sent to Czechoslovakia to gather evidence. The trial was slated to begin in 1991. The merits of gathering evidence abroad were also an issue in the case of Michael Pawlawski, who was accused of complicity in the murder of hundreds of Jews and Poles in parts of the Soviet Union occupied by Germany in 1942. Expectations were that the pretrial phase would be a lengthy one, especially because evidentiary issues were more complex than in the Reistetter case.

The Holocaust-denying historian David Irving visited Canada in the fall and attempted to speak in nine cities, mainly in the West. Several Jewish organizations applied pressure to try to induce those in charge to cancel his appearances. Canada's multiculturalism minister, Gerry Weiner, denounced Irving, stating that his "sympathies and intentions have no place in our society. They are abhorrent to Canadian values and ideals and are an incitement to racism. . . ." Subsequently, lawyer Christie filed a suit against Weiner on behalf of Irving, claiming that the minister's statement was malicious and defamatory and damaging to his reputation.

In comparative perspective, Canada's war-crimes legislation was highly regarded, according to Winnipeg lawyer David Matas, who addressed a human-rights conference in Boston in April. It was the broadest legislation of its kind in the world and resembled postwar proposals for an international legal regime. The visit of Arthur Rudolph to Canada in July set off a major dispute. Rudolph, a German who worked as a rocket scientist during the war, agreed to give up his U.S. residence in 1983, when confronted with evidence of his role in the abuse of slave laborers on the V-2 rocket project, of which he was operations director. In an immigration hearing after his arrival in Canada, a government attorney charged that Rudolph had participated in war crimes, specifically the forcible confinement of slave laborers.

Finally, attorney Douglas Christie, who represented Keegstra, Zundel, and Finta among others, was charged by fellow lawyers Don Weitz and Bert Raphael with unprofessional conduct in two separate complaints, referring to the Finta and Zundel trials, respectively. Both asked that the Law Society of Upper Canada (the Ontario bar) take disciplinary action against Christie. A commissioner, acting on Weitz's complaint, recommended that the discipline committee look into the case. Weitz said that he wanted "to teach Christie and other lawyers like him a lesson." In particular, he objected to the badgering of Jewish witnesses, especially Holocaust survivors.

JEWISH COMMUNITY

Demography

One demographer predicted a major decline for the Canadian Jewish population over the next 70 years. According to Leo Davids, a York University sociologist, the current population of over 300,000 would drop to about 250,000 by the end of the century and perhaps to 150,000 by 2060. The population numbers were affected adversely by declining birthrates. By 2000, the proportion of the Jewish population under age 14 would be about half (15 percent) of what it was in 1961 (28 percent). In addition, the proportion of people over 65 was increasing from 8 percent in 1961 to an estimated 28 percent in 2000. This meant that the community would face increasing pressure to provide services to senior citizens but would have a shrinking base of younger people to support and run the community institutions.

Whereas Davids's data indicated a long-term problem that was largely the result of assimilation and a low birthrate, the Montreal community was extremely sensitive to short-term population changes due to the peculiar political and economic circumstances in Quebec. A study of the 1986 mid-decade census by Charles Shahar of Allied Jewish Community Services (AJCS) in Montreal showed a Jewish population of about 93,000, substantially below the high of over 110,000 reached during the 1970s, before the election of the separatist Parti Québécois. The renewal of sovereignist sentiment in the wake of the Meech Lake failure suggested that there would be significant erosion of the community during the next decade, though the differential effect of various scenarios made it difficult to estimate the changes. What was clear, however, was that the problems of the Canadian Jewish community in general, specifically the growing imbalance toward the older age cohorts, were accentuated in Montreal because of the outmigration of people in their 20s and 30s.

Joseph Levy, a sociologist at the Université de Montréal, did a study comparing French-speaking Sephardim in Montreal with French Canadians. He found that the Sephardim had integrated well into Quebec society but still retained a strong sense of Jewishness and an affinity for Ashkenazi Jews. Religious observance was important to only about half of the Sephardim whom he interviewed. Moreover, Levy claimed that up to half of the young Sephardim were intermarrying. A study of Ontario Jews by York University sociology professor Stuart Schoenfeld found that about 25 percent of Jews marrying between 1984 and 1986 wed a spouse who was not born Jewish. Over half of these outmarrying Jews either converted to another religion or maintained a home where elements of both spouses' religions were present.

The issue of poverty among Canadian Jews continued to be a matter of concern. James Torczyner, a McGill University social-work professor, conducted an extensive analysis of 1981 census data and found that as many as 50,000 Jews lived in poverty, nearly one-sixth of the Jewish population. The highest incidence of Jewish poverty was found in the Maritime provinces and the lowest in Ottawa. Montreal's 20 percent was above the average. Those sectors of the population most likely to be impoverished were the elderly, women, recent immigrants, or people living alone or in small families. The proportion of elderly poor or poor people living alone was substantially higher among Jews than among the general population.

There was modest growth in the number of Israelis settling in Canada. In 1989 there were 1,722 immigrants from Israel, added to some 8,000 who arrived between 1981 and 1988. Since 1948, over 40,000 Israelis had come to Canada. Most gravitated to the two major population centers, Toronto and Montreal.

Communal Affairs

The Canadian Jewish Congress (CJC) took first steps toward implementing the recommendations of the Lithwick report for the restructuring of that organization. The 1989 report represented a joint effort of CJC and the National Budgeting Conference (NBC) to come to grips with CJC's financial and management problems. One of the major proposals of the Lithwick task force was that the federations assume a greater role in giving direction to Congress. Specifically, the various regions of Congress and the local federations in those regions would have to consult on policy matters. The prospect that CJC would be less independent in developing its positions on issues was troubling to many of its leaders, who believed that its role as a spokesman for the community was being compromised.

Despite the reservations, the national CJC executive did decide to adopt the recommendations in February, with some minor changes. The vote was 28–15. Supporters of the report saw it as a way to make CJC "truly representative" of the Canadian Jewish community. Harvey Lithwick, who chaired the task force, believed that the changes were essential in order to create a unified community and reduce competition between organizations. Among the opponents, Zave Ettinger termed the changes an "absolute insult . . . to the history of Congress." In any event, the new reality was that a consensus among the federations that provide the funding would now be required for new CJC initiatives.

CJC was not the only Jewish organization that faced major restructuring. The Canada-Israel Committee (CIC) suffered from competition between its constituent organizations, which reduced its effectiveness as the Jewish community's voice on Israel matters. A committee headed by Donald Carr of Toronto, which began looking into CIC's operation in 1989, singled out the Canadian Jewish Congress and B'nai Brith Canada (BBC) for pursuing their own agendas to the detriment of CIC as a whole. "Neither of these organizations seems content to permit the CIC to exercise its exclusive mandate with respect to Canada-Israel matters in relation to government or media." The report recommended a revised structure to represent CJC, BBC, the Canadian Zionist Federation (CZF), the United Israel Appeal (UIA), and several local federations, with the constituent members being bound by community discipline. CIC would be the sole voice of the community on Israel-related matters, and the member organizations would have to support the agreed-upon policy at all times. Early reactions to the report from CJC and the other groups were critical.

The Canadian Zionist Federation was beset by serious problems, primarily financial. The organization, which encompassed 17 Zionist bodies, had suffered serious cuts in its budget from Israel during the period after 1987. As a result, staff and programming had to be cut, but not before a substantial deficit had accumulated. At his last meeting as president, David Azrieli announced that a plan to pay off the deficit had been worked out. Kurt Rothschild was appointed interim president until the next national convention.

Several other organizations suffered from inadequate funding. BBC eliminated its support for youth programming and for Hillel on campuses because of a budget crunch that necessitated a $1-million reduction in spending at the end of the year. Several staff members were laid off, though the possibility of reinstating some jobs if a fund-raising campaign proved successful was held out. Despite the cuts, BBC president Marilyn Wainberg claimed that the B'nai Brith Youth Organization and Hillel would survive. "We've just had to retrench, like everyone else," she said. CJC, too, faced budget cuts. NBC reduced CJC's Soviet Jewry budget by two-thirds, much to the chagrin of Soviet Jewry activists, some of whom blamed Congress for not resisting more strenuously. In order to meet the rest of a cut imposed by NBC, CJC also reduced its education and young-adult programming and left certain staff posts vacant.

A major cause of the tight financial situation was the intensive fund raising for

Project Exodus for the settlement of Soviet Jews. Canadian Jewry sought pledges of $100 million—and appeared ready to exceed that sum—which effectively meant that increases in regular annual fund raising had to be foregone. This put pressure on agency budgets throughout the community.

In Montreal, plans for a $20-million capital campaign for improving the physical facilities of Jewish educational and health institutions had to be modified, due to the pressure to divert money to Israel for the settlement of the unanticipated numbers of Soviet immigrants. As a result, it was decided to mount a $10-million drive to meet the pressing needs of three schools only, United Talmud Torahs, Hebrew Academy, and Hebrew Foundation School, with parents of students at the three schools expected to raise about one-third of the total amount.

Even the scaled-down plan encountered resistance. Little more than half of the targeted $10 million had been raised when activity was suspended to leave the field clear for the annual Combined Jewish Appeal. The situation was finally resolved when Allied Jewish Community Services, the local federation, borrowed $6.5 million on behalf of the schools. Ecole Maimonide was added to the original group of three schools that would benefit from the plan.

Canada's Sephardi Jews established a new national organization in May, the Congrès Sépharade du Canada (CSC), with Salomon Oziel of Montreal as provisional president. According to Oziel, one of the new body's objectives was to achieve recognition of Sephardi Jews as a "different cultural identity within the Jewish community," analogous to the status attained by Sephardim in Quebec. Another goal was the preservation of the Sephardi heritage.

The Midwest Regional Conference of the World Congress of Gay and Lesbian Jewish Organizations met in Toronto at the end of June. Participants came from the United States and several European countries as well as Canada. One of the themes of the conference was how gays could participate more actively and constructively in Jewish communal affairs.

New Jewish community centers opened in Vancouver and Hamilton. York University in Toronto established a Center for Jewish Studies, headed by Prof. Sydney Eisen, which planned to bring together Jewish studies, Jewish teacher training, and exchange programs with Israeli universities within one framework. It also expected to get involved in work on Canadian Jewish public policy.

In the area of Jewish journalism, Alberta's *Jewish Star* was closed. The founders, Gila and Douglas Wertheimer, decided to sell the independent biweekly publication, which was based in Calgary and had an Edmonton edition, but could not find a suitable buyer. A new paper, the *Jewish Free Press*, was established to replace it, with Judy Shapiro as editor. Vancouver's *Jewish Western Bulletin* celebrated its 60th birthday.

Community Relations

After many years of effort, a Jewish coalition led by BBC and CJC succeeded in getting Parliament to pass an amendment to the Divorce Act that would ease Jewish religious divorce proceedings. Under the new law, each spouse would have to remove all obstacles to the other spouse's religious remarriage before the civil divorce decree could be granted by a civil court. In practice this meant that it would be exceedingly difficult for one spouse to use the issue of granting a *get* as a means to extort concessions from the other spouse.

Quebec's observant Jews were extremely upset over a proposal for a new provincial Animal Protection Act that was drafted and submitted by the Canadian Society for the Prevention of Cruelty to Animals. The proposal contained a clause requiring that animals being prepared for slaughter be rendered unconscious before being killed. In effect this would have banned *shehitah*, Jewish ritual slaughter. A CSPCA background document suggested—inaccurately—that the absence of stunning in Jewish religious practice was "the result of custom rather than a religious requirement. . . ." It also pointed with approval to laws in Sweden and Switzerland that banned *shehitah*. The CSPCA ultimately withdrew its proposal insofar as it would have applied to kosher slaughtering. Subsequently there was a dispute as to whether the government had ever intended to pass the bill.

Ontario was beset with disputes over the role of religion in the public schools. In January the Ontario Court of Appeal ruled that mandatory religious instruction was unconstitutional, a violation of the Charter of Rights and Freedoms, because in effect it amounted to Christian indoctrination. In the particular case before it, the court invalidated religious instruction in Elgin County, prompting the CJC's David Satok to observe that "the Court's decision has finally recognized Ontario's multi-religious nature." Yet, in defiance of the ruling, the board of education in Lanark County maintained the Christian content of opening exercises, prompting a coalition of parents and the CJC to fight the practice. Later in the year, the Ontario government decided to replace devotional religious exercises with the academic study of several religious traditions, a move that was welcomed by Jewish representatives.

The issue of Sunday shopping remained delicate and controversial. Three Toronto rabbis, Moses Burak, Irwin Witty, and Joseph Kelman, testified in affidavits filed with the Ontario Supreme Court that Sunday-closing laws reduced Jews to "second-class citizens." A 1989 law allowed a store to open if the owner closed on another day and registered his or her religion with the government. The CJC called the registration requirement discriminatory and unpalatable. The Quebec Sunday-closing law was amended to make it easier for those closing for another Sabbath to be open on Sunday.

Montreal publisher and business leader Pierre Peladeau set off a storm with approving remarks about Hitler that were quoted in a magazine story and with later comments about Jews in the fashion industry. Among his observations was: "I have a great respect for the Jews, but they take up too much space." A number of organizations, both Jewish and non-Jewish, protested vigorously, demanding a retraction and an apology. The furor led the Université de Montréal to cancel plans to award Peladeau an honorary degree. Eventually Peladeau did issue a statement of regret to the Jewish community and claimed that he had been misquoted about Hitler.

The Peladeau affair illustrated some of the problems that existed between Jews and French Canadians in Montreal. McGill University professor Pierre Anctil urged Jews to engage in dialogue with their French neighbors in order to reduce tensions and eliminate misunderstandings. That advice was followed by a group of Jewish and French Canadian academics, intellectuals, and professionals who met on several occasions. Eventually they issued a manifesto stressing their belief in "the possibility of a shared future which we wish to build together out of a sense of mutual respect."

CJC president Les Scheininger was active in making Jewish views known to leaders of other faiths. When Anglican archbishop Peers circulated an Easter message that focused entirely on the Arab-Israeli conflict and contained a Palm Sunday prayer that many considered an insult to the Jewish people, Scheininger was quick to condemn his action. In June he met with Archbishop James Hayes, the immediate past president of the Canadian Conference of Catholic Bishops, which had issued a statement that was extreme in its condemnation of Israel with regard to the *intifada*. As reported in the *Canadian Jewish News* (June 14, 1990), Scheininger found Hayes and the CCCB to be firmly committed to their position and thus came to the conclusion that the Catholic Church was becoming an advocate of the Arab cause, rather than a mere observer.

Soviet Jewry

A new group composed primarily of immigrants from the Soviet Union and Eastern Europe, the Action Committee for Soviet Jewry, asked the Canadian government to allow large numbers of Soviet Jews to immigrate on the grounds that they were in danger and that Israel could not absorb all those wanting to leave. The committee was critical of decisions taken by Diaspora communities such as Canada to focus efforts on settling Jews in Israel under the circumstances. In contrast, a CJC delegation that met with Joe Clark in June urged him to pressure the Soviet government into allowing direct flights to Israel.

Montreal Yiddish writer Yehuda Elberg visited the Soviet Union and on his return expressed serious doubts regarding the prospects for the Jewish community there. "I just don't see a future," he said. Elberg was particularly disturbed by the evidence of anti-Semitism and the palpable fear of many Jews. Soviet diplomats in Canada tried to play down some of the problems that Elberg reported. For example, the consul in Montreal, Konstantin Grichtchenko, addressing a synagogue audience, claimed that there had been no actual violent incidents against Jews in recent years and that the government was firmly against anti-Semitism. In an April meeting with CJC representatives, the Soviet ambassador, Alexey Rodionov, denounced the right-wing Soviet group Pamyat as "bigots on the fringe of society. . . ." The First Canada-USSR Academic Dialogue on Jewish Themes was held in Toronto in December. Some 20 professors from the two countries presented papers on various aspects of Jewish life in the Soviet Union and elsewhere.

Religion

In January, in response to questions posed by the *Canadian Jewish News*, two Orthodox rabbis commented on the issues of interfaith dialogue and dialogue on theological matters with other movements within Judaism. Rabbi Amram Assayag, president of the Vaad Harabonim of Southern Ontario, saw little use for either type of dialogue. He stated, "Orthodoxy has not moved from its stand in 5,000 years. We are not willing to compromise on halacha." In a similar vein, Rabbi Benjamin Hauer, chairman of the Quebec Region of the Rabbinical Council of America, asserted, "We believe in the ultimate veracity of the Torah, both written and oral, as the immutable word of G-d. All other denominations try to accommodate—they can't accept the implications of Divine revelation." A somewhat different view was expressed by Rabbi Harvey Meirovitch, who had moved to Israel from Toronto and returned there for a lecture, in February, on the subject of tolerance and pluralism in Jewish history. The traditional approach of tolerance recognized alternative formulations of Judaism, but without legitimizing them. Pluralism, by contrast, implies acceptance of differences as legitimate. Meirovitch voiced regret that the idea of pluralism was unacceptable to the Orthodox.

In a lecture in Toronto in March, Rabbi Reuven Bulka of Ottawa tried to steer the Jewish debate away from an emphasis on denominational differences. He asserted that the real struggle was between Judaism and secular values. He also decried increasing polarization within Orthodoxy, calling for moderation rather than extremism.

One Montreal rabbi became engaged in a dispute with supporters of the Lubavitcher Rebbe. Rabbi Allan Nadler, of Congregation Shaar Hashomayim, had strongly criticized the Rebbe in an April op-ed article in the *New York Times* for his involvement in Israeli coalition politics. He was upbraided in a letter from Rabbi Hauer, on behalf of the Montreal Orthodox rabbinate. He suggested a retraction, which Rabbi Nadler declined to offer.

Cantor Eliezer Kirshblum of Toronto resigned from the Conservative Cantors Assembly executive to protest the handling of the decision to admit women members. He claimed that the resolution was "railroaded" through the executive. Nine other Conservative cantors in Toronto stated their total rejection of the decision and indicated that they were considering various unspecified options. In Cantor Kirshblum's view, "What's at stake is the future of the professional cantorate in North America and whether it will be grounded in legitimate halachic tradition."

Rabbi Deborah Brin resigned her post with Congregation Darchei Noam in Toronto because of problems within the Reconstructionist synagogue community. In her resignation statement she said, "I had hoped that the congregation would become willing to deal directly and openly with the challenges of having a woman and a lesbian as their rabbi." Things that she wanted to discuss became "forbidden topics," she said. Speaking in April at a Montreal conference, Rabbi Brin called for new rituals that would recognize the equality of women in the fullest sense. She also advocated the creation of a ceremony for gays and lesbians who want to live as couples.

Education

In Toronto, there were 9,258 students in day schools and 6,081 in supplementary schools. These numbers represented about a 50-percent increase over ten years. About half of the Jewish children in Toronto were receiving some form of Jewish education. In contrast, in Vancouver only 1,300 of some 5,000 Jewish children were receiving a Jewish education.

The Alberta Jewish community received indirect and direct government support for its day schools. The Edmonton Hebrew School and Talmud Torah Society (232 students) were part of the public-school system. The government paid for secular studies while the local federation contributed part of the cost of Jewish studies. The Calgary Akiva Academy (110 students) was funded through the Alberta government as a private school. It also received a grant from the local UJA. The Calgary Jewish Academy (380 students) was funded through the separate (Catholic) school board.

Culture

The highlight of the year was the exhibition "A Coat of Many Colors: Two Centuries of Jewish Life in Canada," which was open from April through September at the Canadian Museum of Civilization in Hull, Quebec, just across the river from the nation's capital. About half a million people visited the exhibition, which was presented in cooperation with the Canadian Friends of Beth Hatefutsoth. It was initiated by Andrea Bronfman and sponsored by Seagram's and the federal government. Prime Minister and Mrs. Brian Mulroney attended the gala opening on March 31. In his remarks, the prime minister observed that "there is hardly a dimension of national life that has not been improved by the dynamic presence of a large and impressive Jewish community in Canada."

The curator of the exhibition was Sandra Morton Weizman, who said that its purpose was to show how Jews had been shaped by Canada and what they had contributed to Canada. There were about 300 items on exhibit, selected to tell the story of Jewish involvement in the history, society, and culture of the country. The major areas touched on were law, education, business, charitable and welfare organizations, medicine, the arts, organized labor, and politics. After the Museum of Civilization showing, the exhibition went on tour across Canada for two years. It was scheduled to be shown in 1993 in New York and then at the Beth Hatefutsoth museum in Tel Aviv. A television program based on the themes of the exhibition was broadcast in October.

Another major exhibition on a Jewish theme was "Planets, Potions, and Parchments: Scientific Hebraica from the Dead Sea Scrolls to the 18th Century," which appeared at the David M. Stewart Museum in Montreal from May through September. The curator, Prof. B. Barry Levy of McGill University, gathered some 200 items illustrating the close connection for Jews between the religious and scientific worlds. The Royal Ontario Museum in Toronto opened a new Judaica Gallery featuring Judaica objects from Europe, 1500–1980.

The most significant drama event of the year was the visit of Montreal's Yiddish Theater, directed by Dora Wasserman, to the Soviet Union. The Saidye Bronfman Center's acting group spent three weeks in the USSR in June, giving a total of 15 performances in Moscow, Kiev, and Odessa. At the University of Toronto, the Disenhouse family established a memorial lecture fund for the advancement of Yiddish.

A concert of the Jewish Music Society of Toronto in January included a dance choreographed by Terrill Maguire to a new musical work by Brian Charney, "River of Fire," which was inspired by a kabbalistic legend dealing with souls who ascend to heaven to be purified.

Publications

In a companion book to the exhibition on Canadian Jewry, also entitled *A Coat of Many Colors: Two Centuries of Jewish Life in Canada*, Irving Abella demonstrates the significant role played by the Jews in Canadian life. The author also documents the effect of the Eastern European immigration late in the 19th century on a previously Anglicized community. The newcomers represented "an alien culture and tradition," thereby encountering hostility that became anti-Semitism.

In *Trauma and Rebirth: Intergenerational Effects of the Holocaust*, John Sigal and Morton Weinfeld present the first empirical study of the long-term consequences of the Holocaust across three generations. Their main finding is that the extent of psychological impairment has been exaggerated.

Frank Chalk and Kurt Jonassohn's *The History and Sociology of Genocide: Analyses and Case Studies* is a comparison of a number of examples of mass murder in different historical periods. Although the authors include the Nazi Holocaust in their comparisons, they recognize its uniqueness as "the most carefully conceived, the most efficiently implemented and the most fully realized case of ideologically motivated genocide in the history of the human race. . . ."

Maintaining Consensus: The Canadian Jewish Polity in the Postwar World by Daniel J. Elazar and Harold M. Waller is a study of how Jewish community organizations govern the community. It examines institutional structures, the political process, policy formation, leadership, and decision making in the countrywide community and in 11 local communities. The authors stress how community governance is changing as the federations become the dominant political actors, largely because of their role in raising and allocating funds.

Lewis Levendel's *A Century of the Canadian Jewish Press* is an exhaustive study of the period 1880–1980. His analysis of the current state of the Canadian Jewish press as "more lap-dog than watch-dog" reflects the problems encountered when community organizations finance the newspapers.

Victor Ostrovsky and Claire Hoy's *By Way of Deception: A Devastating Insider's Portrait* received invaluable publicity from the Israeli government's attempt to suppress it. Although this exposé of the Mossad contains a number of contested revelations, it raises serious questions for Israeli citizens regarding the role of the security services in the political system.

Other new nonfiction books this year included *No Balm in Gilead: A Personal Retrospective of Mandate Days in Palestine* by Sylvia Gelber; *Undiplomatic Notes: Tales from the Canadian Foreign Service* by Sidney Freifeld; *Closing the Doors: The Failure of Refugee Protection* by David Matas and Ilana Simon; *An Everyday Miracle: Yiddish Culture in Montreal*, edited by Ira Robinson, Pierre Anctil, and Mervin Butovsky; *Unfinished Journey*, a biography of David Lewis's family, by Cameron Smith; *Canadian Jewry Today: Who's Who in Canadian Jewry*, edited by Edmond Lipsitz; *The Transliterated English-Yiddish Dictionary* by David Mendel Harduf; *Shylock Reconsidered: Jews, Moneylending and Medieval Society* by Joseph Shatzmiller; *Sefer Ma'amar Mordechai* by Rabbi Mordechai Kalifon; and *A Street Called the Main* by Aline Gubbay.

New works of fiction included *Scorpions for Sale* by Larry Zolf; *Canadian Jewish Short Stories*, edited by Miriam Waddington; *Broadsides* by Mordecai Richler; *Here Comes Hymie: A Novel of Montreal Immigrant Life* by Howard Roiter; *St. Farb's Day* by Morley Torgov; and *The Last Enemy* by Rhoda Kaellis. New works of poetry included *Blendiker Herbst* and *Selected Poems* by Simcha (Sam) Simchovitch.

The following received literary awards this year from the Jewish Book Committee of Toronto Jewish Congress: J. J. Steinfeld for *Forms of Activity and Escape*; Simcha Simchovitch for *Tzaar un Treist* (Sorrow and Consolation); Michael Greenstein for *Third Solitudes*; and Harold Troper and Morton Weinfeld for *Old Wounds*.

Personalia

Charles Dubin was named chief justice of Ontario; Eddie Goldenberg was appointed principal secretary to the new Leader of the Opposition in the House, Jean Chrétien; Sandra Kolber was appointed to the board of the Canadian Broadcasting Corporation; Sen. David Croll was made a member of the Privy Council; Chaviva Hosek became a special adviser on Eastern European affairs to Ontario premier

David Peterson; Judge Sidney Linden was selected chief judge of the criminal division of the Ontario Provincial Court; Judy Rebick was elected president of the National Action Committee on the Status of Women; Harvey Webber was reelected president of the Council for Canadian Unity; and Karen Mock was appointed chairwoman of the Canadian Multicultural Advisory Board.

McGill University chemist Leo Yaffe was awarded the Prix du Québec; Reuben Cohen was appointed chancellor of Dalhousie University; Heather Munroe-Blum became the first female dean of the Faculty of Social Work at the University of Toronto; University of Manitoba professor Nathan Mendelsohn received his province's highest honor, the Order of the Buffalo Hunt, in recognition of his lifelong work in mathematics; and Prof. Irvine Glass of the University of Toronto was named an Einstein Fellow by the Israel Academy of Sciences.

Within the Jewish community, Julia Koschitzky was elected president of United Israel Appeal; Marilyn Wainberg became the first woman president of B'nai Brith Canada; Koschitzky and Sol Lederman were elected to the board of governors of the Jewish Agency; Rhona Blanshay became president of Na'amat Canada and Esther Matlow of Hadassah-WIZO; and Rabbi Baruch Taub received the National Rabbinic Leadership Award from the Union of Orthodox Jewish Congregations of America.

Among leading Jews who died in 1990 were the following: Ray Wolfe, a businessman and major community leader, in January, aged 72; Solomon Birnbaum, a scholar who dated the Dead Sea Scrolls, in January, aged 98; Rabbi Israel Hausman, Montreal Hillel chaplain, in January, aged 58; Ida Baum, the oldest Jew in Montreal, in February, aged 110; Renee Reichmann, matriarch of the Reichmann family, in February, aged 92; Rabbi Stuart Rosenberg, well-known author and Toronto spiritual leader, in March, aged 67; Bernard Wind, Yiddish journalist, in March, aged 79; Rabbi Lipa Wechter, a leading Talmud scholar, in April, aged 79; Harvey Golden, former Montreal Y executive director, in April, aged 86; Rabbi Wolfe Kelman, Toronto native and major figure in the Conservative movement, in June, in New York, aged 66; Johnny Wayne, noted comedian and television personality, in July, aged 72; Max Enkin, community activist, in August, aged 90; Sophie Lewis, wife and mother of noted politicians, in August, aged 78; Sholem Shtern, Yiddish writer, in August, aged 83; Alex Levinsky, former Toronto Maple Leafs player, in September, aged 80; Dr. Daniel Lowe, founder of London's Yizkor Project, in September, aged 45; Marvin Gelber, former public and community official, in October, aged 77; Ben Hatskin, former Winnipeg Blue Bombers player and founder of the Winnipeg Jets hockey franchise, in October, aged 73; G. Sydney Halter, first commissioner of the Canadian Football League, in October, aged 85; Jacob Lowy, businessman and bibliophile, in December, aged 82; and Ben Milner, longtime leader of the Zionist Revisionist-Herut movement in Canada, in December, aged 73.

HAROLD M. WALLER

Western Europe

Great Britain

National Affairs

THE DOMINANT EVENT IN THE COUNTRY'S political life in 1990 was the forced resignation of Prime Minister Margaret Thatcher at the end of November, after 11 years in office. This development climaxed mounting dissatisfaction among Conservatives with their own government's steady decline in popularity. Dramatic evidence of public sentiment was provided in a series of Conservative losses in by-elections during the year.

The principal reason for the government's unpopularity was the community charge (or poll tax), designed to cover the expenses of local government. Despite provisions for rebates and relief, the tax—which had gone into effect in April 1990—was widely felt to be inequitable, to the extent that even many Conservative local councillors resigned rather than implement it. Moreover, it turned out to be far higher than Conservative spokespersons had predicted: an annual average of £363 rather than the anticipated £278. Bitterly opposed by the Labor party and Liberal Democrats, the tax provoked many demonstrations, which culminated in London on March 31 in widespread violence, fights with the police, and looting; 340 arrests were made. In July the government introduced a £3.3-million package intended to hold down the level of the tax by increasing rebates and transitional relief.

The disarray in Conservative ranks was compounded by internal differences over the extent of British participation in the European Community, with Mrs. Thatcher isolated in the strength of her determination to hold out against the possible introduction of a single European currency. The final stage of the crisis was triggered by the resignation in November of Deputy Premier Sir Geoffrey Howe, the only remaining member of Mrs. Thatcher's original cabinet of 1979. In his resignation letter, Sir Geoffrey pointed explicitly to his differences with the prime minister over the issues of European and monetary policy.

On November 3, Michael Heseltine, a former defense secretary who had resigned from the government in 1986 over inter-European industrial cooperation, attacked

Mrs. Thatcher's policies and style of government; on November 13, Heseltine announced that he would stand against Mrs. Thatcher in a contest for the leadership of the Conservative party. At the first round of voting on November 20, Heseltine won enough votes to deny Mrs. Thatcher a decisive majority. Rather than face further humiliation, she withdrew from a second ballot, leaving three candidates in the field: Heseltine, Chancellor of the Exchequer John Major, and Foreign Secretary Douglas Hurd. When Mrs. Thatcher made clear her preference for Major, the other candidates withdrew. John Major was named prime minister on November 28.

Relations with Israel

The Gulf crisis changed Britain's attitude toward the PLO's role in the Middle East peace process, but that took place late in the year. In February, Prime Minister Thatcher was still urging Israel to talk to Palestinians inside and outside the occupied territories and to be prepared to exchange land for a secure peace. PLO leader Yasir Arafat's political adviser, Bassam Abu Sharif, met with Foreign Secretary Douglas Hurd in March, when the PLO's London office was accorded the title "delegation," though the Foreign Office denied that this upgraded the group's status. In May Hurd said that it was only a question of timing, not of principle, before he met with Arafat. Until August, William Waldegrave, minister of state at the Foreign Office, met regularly at the Foreign Office with Abu Sharif. The Board of Deputies of British Jews and Israeli officials continually protested these meetings as not conducive to furthering the peace process.

Following an attack by Palestinian terrorists on Israeli beaches in May, Israel's ambassador told the Foreign Office in June that Israel expected Britain to end the dialogue with the PLO, and Hurd demanded renunciation of terrorism in practice as well as in rhetoric. However, despite Arafat's refusal to condemn the attack, Thatcher claimed, in July, that the U.S. administration had urged Britain to maintain links with the PLO; the U.S. embassy denied the allegation. Hurd told a Board of Deputies delegation voicing concern at Britain's continued relations with the PLO that the government still thought Arafat was trying to follow a policy of nonviolence, though he was under pressure from other Palestinian groups to return to terrorism. A four-point plan drawn up by Hurd for American and European involvement in the peace process called for the PLO to adhere strictly to the renunciation of terrorism and for Israel to begin talks with representative Palestinians.

Hurd continued to favor a meeting between Israelis and Palestinian Arabs, even after Saddam Hussein's August invasion of Kuwait, but when he visited the Gulf states in September, he no longer specifically mentioned the PLO. Further ministerial meetings with the PLO would not be authorized, he said, unless it stopped supporting Baghdad, though meetings below ministerial level would continue. Arafat had made a "serious mistake," he continued, which had dealt a tremendous blow to the Arab cause and weakened the PLO's case for inclusion in any talks with Israel.

Throughout the year, Britain consistently supported an American role in the peace process and favored an international conference as the best forum for settling the dispute. In June, Hurd, visiting Jordan and Saudi Arabia, called for greater international involvement in the Middle East peace process, including a visit by a representative of the United Nations secretary-general. In October Prime Minister Yitzhak Shamir of Israel rejected Hurd's suggestion for permanent members of the UN Security Council to take part in a peace conference on the Middle East.

Although Britain remained critical of Israel's handling of the *intifada,* in February, Waldegrave told Israeli deputy foreign minister Benjamin Netanyahu, in London, that Britain opposed the economic or scientific sanctions against Israel recommended by the European Parliament. In May Hurd described the killings in Israel as "tragic" and warned of future dangers. In June Britain joined other European Community leaders at their Dublin summit in reprimanding Israel for its "lamentable position concerning the observance of human rights in the deteriorating situation in the occupied territories." Visiting Israel in October, Hurd angered Israelis by stating that Israel's security could not rest on closed schools, illegal settlements, and collective punishment. Once Saddam was out of Kuwait, he said, Israel would have to do some fresh thinking. In return, Britain would be prepared to ask Syria and Saudi Arabia to recognize Israel, but only after the dispute was settled.

Although she believed that Jerusalem should remain undivided in any solution, Prime Minister Thatcher criticized Israeli settlement of Soviet immigrants on the West Bank. "We have all worked very hard to secure their right to emigrate," she told the Board of Deputies in February. "It would be a very ironic and unjust reward . . .if their freedom were to be at the expense of the rights, the homes and the land of the peoples of the occupied territories." In April, she told the Kuwaiti newspaper *Al Qabas* that the settlement of Soviet Jewish immigrants in the occupied territories, including East Jerusalem, was illegal and "likely to make the search for peace in the region even harder." In December, British citizens were advised not to visit East Jerusalem and "other occupied territories."

In November Britain resumed the diplomatic ties with Syria it had broken off in 1986, based on evidence of Syrian involvement in a plot to blow up an El Al plane at London's Heathrow airport. Britain had now received "confirmation that Syria rejects acts of international terrorism and will take action against their perpetration," Hurd told the House of Commons.

In March the PLO's British representative, Faisal Oweida, was invited to address the Scottish Labor party conference in Dunoon, against the wishes of Labor's national executive. Tory MPs tabled a motion in Parliament registering "total disapproval" of his presence and condemning Scottish Labor's refusal to allow a reply by a representative of Israel or the Jewish community. George Galloway, MP, former chairman of the Labor party in Scotland, said, "We have had a policy in Scotland of supporting the Palestinian struggle for self-determination for ten years." In October, two leading Jewish benefactors, Sir Trevor Chinn and Cyril Stein, withdrew financial backing from Labor Friends of Israel (LFI), following its joint meeting with the pro-Arab Middle East Council during the Labor party Blackpool conference. The same month, Labor foreign-affairs spokesman Gerald Kaufman presented his view of desired diplomatic developments once Saddam Hussein had withdrawn from Kuwait: an international conference that would achieve justice and self-determination for the Palestinian peoples; an end to the ordeal of the Palestinian refugees; security for the states in the region, including Israel and her neighbors; an end to intervention in Lebanon with the withdrawal of Syrian and Israeli forces; removal of chemical, biological, and nuclear weapons from the entire Middle East; and an end to the "disgusting" arms trade. In December Kaufman committed the Labor party to continuing efforts to convene an international Middle East peace conference under UN auspices.

For seven weeks in October-November, a large-scale festival of Israeli music, theater, and visual arts was held at London's Barbican Center.

Anti-Semitism and Anti-Zionism

Concern over anti-Semitism in Britain rose during the last eight months of the year. Attacks on Orthodox Jews in North London's Stamford Hill district were reported in April; synagogues were daubed (Staines in June; Dollis Hill, North-West London, in August; Watford in November); and cemeteries were desecrated in London (Edmonton and Bushey in May; Willesden in May and August; Enfield in November) and the provinces (Leeds and Blackley, Manchester, in December). In August the Prisoners' Memorial, Dollis Hill, dedicated to those who died in concentration and prisoner-of-war camps, was desecrated. In November, Chief Superintendent Sally Hubbard, head of London's Metropolitan Police community-involvement branch, told a meeting on security convened by the Board of Deputies that since figures of anti-Semitic incidents were first collated in January, the branch had received details of 46 cases: 7 of physical assault, 29 acts of vandalism, 4 cases of anti-Semitic literature, and 6 reports of verbal abuse.

Many of the anti-Semitic incidents were followed by public demonstrations, mainly organized by local antifascist associations and supported by the Jewish Socialist Group and left-wing organizations. Members of the government and the police also gave evidence of taking the anti-Semitic threat seriously. In May Prime Minister Thatcher pledged support for efforts to ensure that Jewish cemeteries were safe from attacks by anti-Semites. In July Metropolitan Police commander Sir Peter Imbert said that Scotland Yard had declared the hunt for the anti-Semitic vandals who desecrated Edmonton top priority. Extra patrols and resources had been made available and there were good links between Scotland Yard and the Board of Deputies. Curbing racial attacks generally would be a prime target of London's police this year, Imbert stated. In August Home Secretary David Waddington, meeting with Jewish leaders, expressed the government's vigorous commitment to tackling racial violence in all its forms.

Still, Scotland Yard's Imbert stated that he was increasingly frustrated by the lack of progress in prosecuting race-hate cases: 19 cases had been forwarded by his office to the Attorney General, who decided whether or not they should be followed up by the Director of Public Prosecutions (DPP). In each case it was decided not to prosecute. In October Dr. Lionel Kopelowitz, president of the Board of Deputies of British Jews, wrote to the DPP expressing "public concern and puzzlement" at its continued failure to take action.

The volume of anti-Semitic literature increased markedly this year. In June, for example, blood-libel leaflets were distributed in Kensington and Chelsea, London, and a broadsheet, "Holocaust News," was circulated in Stanmore, Middlesex; hate leaflets were delivered in Canterbury in July and in Manchester in August. In July the government's law officers ruled that the police should launch an investigation into the publication of two leaflets about ritual murder, "Jewish Tributes to Our Child Martyrs" and "The Ultimate Blasphemy," both distributed by the Dowager Lady Birdwood's Choice Organization.

In November, in an effort to persuade the government to prosecute producers and distributors of anti-Semitic literature, more than 100 MPs signed an early-day motion tabled by Labor's Greville Janner and sponsored by representatives of all the main parties. It called for "swift and effective action" to curb neo-Nazi activities, expressed deep concern at the increase in the dissemination of anti-Semitic materials in the United Kingdom, and pointed out that none of the briefs against 20 racist publications provided since 1986 to the Attorney General by the Jewish Board of Deputies had resulted in prosecution. Also in November, the DPP refused Dr. Kopelowitz's request to meet to discuss the lack of prosecutions because he did not wish "to expose the service to pressures which might threaten its independence." However, a spokesman for Attorney General Sir Patrick Mayhew told the *Jewish Chronicle,* "We are very hopeful that within three months the various strands we are following up will come together."

In December Mayhew told the House of Commons that there had been a considerable increase in racist and anti-Semitic literature in the past year. "The law officers and the Director of Public Prosecutions take extremely seriously the writing, publication and distribution of such odious material." Of the 20 cases highlighted by the Board of Deputies in the past three years, he said, only 7 had not been investigated by the DPP. He maintained that the reason there had been no prosecutions for anti-Jewish literature since 1986 was lack of evidence.

The Board of Deputies of British Jews aroused some criticism because of its measured, low-profile response to anti-Semitic episodes. After the Edmonton cemetery desecration in May, a board spokesman accused the media of "attempting to whip up an atmosphere of anti-Semitism in Britain." The board, he claimed, neither suppressed nor sensationalized news of anti-Semitic incidents. In June board president Kopelowitz said there was no concerted anti-Semitic campaign in Britain. Incidents had increased, he conceded, but the overwhelming majority were minor. This assessment was supported by police officials. According to Scotland Yard's liaison officer to the board, "anti-Semitic incidents constitute a tiny proportion" of all racial crimes, which had risen 22 percent in the past year, and Sally Hubbard said that investigations had uncovered no evidence of any organized campaign against Jews.

One of the Board of Deputies' critics, Gerry Gable, editor of the antifascist magazine *Searchlight,* told the European Parliament's Commission of Enquiry into Racism and Xenophobia, meeting in London in May, that the board had ignored warnings of anti-Semitic attacks. In July, Prof. Geoffrey Alderman of London University accused the Board of Deputies of trying to delude itself and the community that anti-Semitism did not exist. "They like to project an image of a community integrated into society," he said. In August, Chief Rabbi Lord Jakobovits said in an interview with *Sky News:* "I do not think anti-Semitism is in danger of upsetting the stability of the Jewish community in this country." In September, a board representative refused to share a platform with Gable at a meeting on fighting anti-Semitism arranged by the Friends of the Union of Jewish Students, a new body created to maintain post-college links for young Jews.

Despite its reticence, the Board of Deputies was clearly concerned about the broader problem of racism and anti-Semitism in particular. In November it sponsored a series of information meetings about hate attacks. The same month, the board's defense department met with leaders of Afro-Caribbean and Hindu communities eager to develop their own defense structures. In December the board initiated a meeting between North London Orthodox Jews and black leaders of the New Assembly of Churches, in an effort to improve relations.

RIGHT-WING GROUPS

When violence erupted at a British National party (BNP) election meeting in Tower Hamlets, East London, in April, the Board of Deputies expressed "extreme concern" about the growth of right-wing activity in the East End. An unsuccessful attempt by the BNP to hold a rally in Dundee, Scotland, in May, was followed by actions directed against the synagogue and prominent members of that city's Jewish community. In June BNP head John Tyndall was expelled from the United States, and in October Greville Janner successfully lobbied to persuade Home Secretary Waddington to bar German neo-Nazi Manfred Roeder from entering Britain as the BNP's guest. In August the National Front (NF) marched in Enfield; in October, clashes between the BNP and antifascists in the East End led to violence and arrests; and in November the BNP marched through Bethnal Green, East London. Despite these occurrences, Scotland Yard's Sally Hubbard denied that anti-Semitic and racist parties were gaining strength in Britain. "The British National Party and the National Front are in evidence," she said, "but their numbers are pathetic."

CAMPUS ACTIVITY

Although the National Organization of Labor Students (NOLS) became less overtly anti-Zionist after leader Paul Richards espoused political Zionism, following a trip to Israel sponsored by the Union of Jewish Students (UJS), anti-Zionist and anti-Semitic activity on university campuses continued. There were complaints of organized hostility against Jewish students at the London School of Economics (LSE) in April, though these were partially offset by the formation of an Israel-Palestine dialogue group in May and a formal statement by LSE's students'-union executive, issued in July, condemning the equation of Zionism with racism. In October, at Southampton University, the students'-union executive distributed notices advocating a boycott of Israeli produce; Swansea University students'-union members ordered the removal of a booklet on Zionism; at the University of Manchester's Institute of Science and Technology, Islamic Society members complained about the Israeli flag at a Jewish Society booth; Leeds University's Palestinian Solidarity Society mustered heavy support to defeat a Jewish students' motion. In December the students' union at Polytechnic of Central London banned Jewish Society posters on the ground that they were sympathetic to Zionism.

On the positive side, a motion condemning anti-Semitism was passed at Essex Polytechnic in October; Jewish students at Birmingham Polytechnic won a motion calling for mutual recognition between Israel and the Palestinians; and an anti-Israel motion was thrown out at Central London Polytechnic. In November the Leeds Polytechnic Jewish Society persuaded the students' union to pass a resolution against anti-Semitism; and at Manchester University, the students' union defeated an Islamic Society resolution branding Israel as racist and passed a Jewish Society resolution advocating mutual recognition between Israel and the Palestinians.

The Union of Jewish Students took an active part in the campaign against anti-Zionism and anti-Semitism. In March it organized a conference on racism at York University, in conjunction with the commemoration of the 800th anniversary of the massacre of the Jews of York at Clifford's Tower. In October the UJS set up a hot line for reporting anti-Semitic incidents; and in November it held a conference on European anti-Semitism. The UJS joined with the National Union of Students (NUS) and the Student and Academic Campaign for Soviet Jewry (SACSJ) to lobby Parliament, with several items on their agenda: prosecution of publishers of race-hate literature; pressure to be put on Soviet premier Mikhail Gorbachev to condemn Soviet anti-Semitism; and the adoption by Britain of the package of 77 antiracist measures approved by the European Parliament. The UJS walked out of NUS's conference in Newcastle in November after the defeat of its motion protesting attempts to redefine "anti-Semitism" as both anti-Jewish and anti-Arab. The Leeds University students' union subsequently condemned this redefinition. After a sustained and successful effort by Leeds and Manchester Jewish students to obtain seats on their universities' and polytechnics' delegations to NUS's December conference at Blackpool, that body amended the disputed motion, declaring that anti-Zionism was "often a cloak" for anti-Semitism. The group also adopted a major educational campaign against racism, anti-Semitism, and fascist activity. In November the Board of Deputies announced a joint program with the UJS for the board's community security organization to train Jewish students in self-defense. In December the UJS conference reaffirmed its support for mutual Israeli-Palestinian recognition.

Nazi War Criminals

Despite an impassioned plea by Chief Rabbi Lord Jakobovits for its passage, in June the House of Lords rejected the War Crimes Bill on a free vote, by 207 votes to 74. The bill, which would have enabled the prosecution of alleged Nazi war criminals currently living in Britain, had been approved at its second reading in the House of Commons in March, by 273 votes to 60, and had completed its committee stage in April unamended.

Among the peers objecting to the bill were Lord Campbell, who charged that it was "no more than a cruel vendetta against frail old men" whose crimes were committed over 40 years ago; Lord Chancellor Hailsham, who said that fair trials would be impossible because of the difficulties of getting reliable witnesses after so many years, and that the bill referred only to crimes committed in Germany and German-occupied territory; and Lord Shawcross, who maintained that retribution did not cease to be retribution by posting the label "justice" on it.

Following the defeat in the Lords, it was announced in the Commons that the bill would be reintroduced the following year. This was confirmed when Queen Elizabeth, in her speech opening Parliament in October, said, "My government will introduce a Bill to bring to justice suspected war criminals living in this country." Prime Minister John Major affirmed his commitment to the bill in November. It was understood that if the measure failed in the Lords a second time, the government could invoke the Parliament Act and send the bill directly to the queen for Royal Assent.

Despite the bill's defeat, it was reported in June that a Scotland Yard unit would begin to track the movements of alleged war criminals. In July, following an intimation by Sir Geoffrey Howe, deputy leader of the Conservative party, that "suggested amendments" might be attached, 30 peers from all political parties, including the chief rabbi, called on Prime Minister Thatcher not to allow the bill to be watered down when reintroduced. Nevertheless, in November, Home Secretary David Waddington agreed to consider amendments.

In June the Simon Wiesenthal Center handed the Home Office nine new cases of Lithuanian citizens who had found refuge in Britain. Two alleged Nazi war criminals died in Britain during the year: Andrei Pestrak, accused of involvement in the persecution and murder of Jews while serving in the Ukrainian police battalion, died in April, aged 76; Paul Reinhards, alleged to have deported thousands of fellow Latvians to slave labor in Germany, died in Gravesend, Kent, aged 86. His name figured among the original 17 alleged Nazi war criminals living in Britain whose files the Simon Wiesenthal Center presented to the Home Office in 1986.

A £600,000-defamation action brought by Antonas Gecas against Times Newspapers, following the publication of articles alleging his involvement in wartime atrocities, was settled out of court in June. *The Times* apologized and withdrew allegations that Gecas had been an SS officer, had an SS tattoo, and had belonged to an SS death squad during World War II.

JEWISH COMMUNITY

Demography

The Jewish population of Great Britain was estimated at 330,000. The total number of synagogue marriages fell to 1,057 in 1989 from 1,104 in 1988, according to the Board of Deputies Community Research Unit. This was the second lowest level of the century. The number of burials and cremations rose to 4,635 in 1989 from 4,428 in 1988. Total births in 1988, calculated from figures for circumcision, were estimated at 3,681, 4.2 percent more than in 1987.

Increased attention was paid to intermarriage this year. The 120 Jewish partners who attended a seminar for intermarried couples at the Reform Steinberg Center were divided equally between men and women, according to the seminar organizer, Reform rabbi Jonathan Romain. Two-thirds had attended part-time religion classes from ages 5 to 13; 20 percent had been to Jewish day school; three-quarters had attended Jewish youth clubs; nearly half had siblings married out of the faith; 70 percent were synagogue members.

In a *Jewish Chronicle* survey based on a representative sample of 500 of its London readers, 34 percent said they would accept the marriage of one of their children to a non-Jewish partner; 44 percent would not approve but would stay in touch with the couple; only 6 percent would break off contact with their child.

Communal Activities

Twelve percent more children were referred to Norwood Child Care in 1989, according to its annual report published in August. Of the 1,800 children on Norwood's books, 10 percent were "at risk of physical, sexual or emotional abuse." Until recently, the agency had dealt with few child-abuse cases. "Child abuse has always been around," said executive director Sam Brier, "but now the public, as well as the professionals, are much more aware of it as an issue. The Jewish community is no longer immune from almost all of the problems affecting children in the wider community."

Financial hardship among Jews was also increasing. Three-quarters of the London families Norwood helped were receiving government benefits to supplement their incomes. In Manchester, the Jewish poor were worse off now than ten years ago, said Mike Anderson, director of Manchester's Jewish social services, which helped 200–300 individuals yearly. There were, he said in March, "significant pockets of very poor people" in the 35,000-member community. In 1980 they struggled to make ends meet; now they could not afford the basic necessities of life. In August, directors of Jewish social-service agencies in Manchester, Leeds, Liverpool, and Birmingham collaborated to pool ideas and discuss problems, notably their insufficient resources for implementing government policy to resettle mental patients within the community.

Jewish Care, the new welfare agency formed through a merger of the Jewish Welfare Board and the Jewish Blind Society and headed by Lord Young of Graffham, in May took over Waverley Manor, an independent Jewish old-age home in Hendon, North-West London, with 58 residents, which was experiencing financial problems. In June Jewish Care opened the Shalvata Center, also in Hendon, where social workers, psychotherapists, and a consultant psychiatrist assisted individuals with emotional and stress problems. In September the first Jewish Care center offering both permanent and respite care for physically disabled young people opened in North-West London. In November Lord Young issued a four-page document calling for a unified Anglo-Jewish fund-raising structure combining both Israeli and domestic causes. British Jewry, he said, neglected domestic causes by putting support for Israel above all else.

Religion

In April Rabbi Jonathan Sacks was appointed the new chief rabbi. The 200-member Chief Rabbinate Conference approved the recommendation made in February by the selection committee set up by the United Synagogue (US) and headed by its president, Sidney Frosh. The committee's unanimous decision followed the withdrawal from the chief rabbinate contest of Chief Rabbis Cyril Harris of South Africa and Yisrael Lau of Tel Aviv. Current chief rabbi Lord Immanuel Jakobovits agreed to defer his retirement, due to take effect in September 1990, so that Rabbi Sacks could spend a year studying in Israel. "I want to come to the position having immersed myself in an atmosphere of Torah learning and Eretz Yisrael," said 42-year-old Sacks, who would be the first chief rabbi born and reared in a London United Synagogue family. He intended to run a "very open Chief Rabbinate" and would "encourage communal debate," he said. "I am determined as far as possible to emphasize what unites Jews and encourage an atmosphere of mutual respect, but there can be no compromise on matters of halakha (Jewish law)."

In January Rabbi Dr. Louis Jacobs, leading rabbi of the Masorti (Conservative) movement, told a lecture audience that the chief rabbi's authority was not accepted by his movement. Its position was the same as that of the Union of Liberal and Progressive Synagogues (ULPS): "The Chief Rabbi represents only those communities which elect him."

Rabbi Sacks, whose successor as principal of Jews' College was Rabbi Dr. Irving

Jacobs, gave the keynote address at a well-attended seminar in March on "Women and the Jewish Future," hosted by the college, the second in the series "Traditional Alternatives." In November he gave the prestigious BBC Reith lectures on "Religion and Ethics in a Secular Society."

Lord Jakobovits continued to arouse discussion over his views and activities. In July, in Jerusalem, the chief rabbi singled out the Lubavitch movement when criticizing the "streak of messianic fervor" in Jewish life today, in his presidential address to the 25th-anniversary meeting of the Memorial Foundation for Jewish Culture. In the ensuing debate in Britain, an official of the United Synagogue (US) challenged the chief rabbi's implication of a Lubavitch takeover of Jewish schools. The influence of the 45 Lubavitch part-time teachers, out of a total staff of 450, at US religion classes was negligible, according to Michael Cohen, executive director of the US Board of Education. People who worked for the US were US employees, instructed not to use the US as a vehicle for propaganda or to promote ideologies, he said. Nonetheless, Lubavitch director Shraga Vogel claimed that six Lubavitch rabbis served US communities in London and four in the provinces; and there were nine Lubavitch teachers in Jewish day schools in Britain. In addition, there were five Lubavitch centers in London and six in the provinces; two Lubavitch yeshivahs with 79 students; 900 children were educated in Lubavitch day schools; and there was a Lubavitch college for higher rabbinical studies in Leeds.

In September Lord Jakobovits visited Gerald Ronson, who together with Anthony Parnes and Ernest Saunders, all Jewish businessmen, were in Ford open prison, Sussex, convicted of theft, conspiracy, and false accounting during a take-over battle by Guinness for the Distillers' Group four years earlier. Members of the Board of Deputies of British Jews called on fellow board member Prof. Geoffrey Alderman to resign, following his claim in *The Times* in October that certain sections of the British Jewish community accepted "financial wrong-doing," and his appeal for a firm stand by Jewish religious leaders. "I have not heard of one rabbi," wrote Alderman, "who has publicly condemned the Guinness three."

The United Synagogue faced a serious financial crisis, with a deficit in June of £722,000 and with 17 of its synagogues registering losses, as high interest rates made it hard for many members to pay their dues. Two of its major synagogues, Hendon, and Boreham Wood and Elstree, Herts., contemplated changing their relationship with the US from constituent to affiliated status, which would enable them to pay less toward US central services. The US itself announced plans to sell off its valuable silver collection, which came from the now-defunct Great Synagogue. In December, the US council, in an unprecedented move, refused to approve a budget showing a shortfall of £1.1 million until threatened with mass resignations by its president and officers. The Kol Nidre appeal raised only half its goal; *shehitah* (ritual slaughtering) services showed a larger deficit than anticipated; membership fees were seriously in arrears; and receipts from functions catered under London Beth Din auspices had fallen 10 percent. As a result, budget cuts were proposed for the coming year in education expenditure, staffing, and the Jews' College grant.

In December, Sidney Frosh, who had been reelected president in a contested June election, announced a major review of the use of US buildings in the next six to nine months, including three London synagogues—Golders Green and Hampstead in the North-West and the Central in the West End—which might be merged or redeveloped as part of a program to turn assets into cash. The merger between the independent Western and US Marble Arch Synagogues took place in December, forming the Western Marble Arch, the only "associated" synagogue of the United Synagogue, i.e., with its own constitution and allowed to appoint its own ministers, after consulting the chief rabbi. It agreed to make contributions to the US for common religious and charitable purposes.

In February the right-of-center Federation of Synagogues appointed a four-member team to investigate what president Arnold Cohen called the legacy of "financial chaos" he had inherited when he took office the previous year. Team chairman Harold Ragol-Levy said in July that £500,000 recovered in February from previously undocumented accounts in Jersey and London banks "substantially represented the proceeds of the sale of five affiliated synagogues." In June, the federation put up for sale its Whitechapel, East London, headquarters, housing its Beth Din, administrative offices, Great Garden Street Synagogue, and the Kosher Luncheon Club, because of the shift of Jewish population to North-West London suburbs. A new £1.3-million building in Hendon would house the federation offices and the Beth Din. The federation also planned to create a new synagogue in Arkley, Hertfordshire, to cater to that area's growing Jewish population.

Rabbi Tony Bayfield, director of the Sternberg Center, published an essay in the Center's journal, *Manna*, in April—written after consultation with Reform rabbis and lay leaders—emphasizing *kashrut* and Shabbat observance through prayer and study and proclaiming Israel as "central to Jewish life and a focal point for all Jews." In July, Ruth Cohen, new Reform Synagogues of Great Britain chairwoman, indicated in an interview that the movement had become "more traditional in the last ten to twenty years."

In September the Union of Liberal and Progressive Synagogues decided to postpone redevelopment of its London headquarters, described as "the symbol of going into a new era," because of the economic climate.

Conflict between the US and Federation of Synagogues *kashrut* organizations continued throughout the year. In March, El Al, the Israeli airline, transferred responsibility for its *kashrut* to the federation, after the US-sponsored London Beth Din insisted that airline meals be served to passengers in sealed containers. Chief Rabbi Jakobovits, London Beth Din president, expressed "profound regret" that the federation had granted the airline a *kashrut* license which, he claimed, meant a lowering of *kashrut* standards. The London Beth Din announced plans to set up its own airline meals service.

Controversy over new government regulations restricting *shehitah* (ritual slaughter) continued until they became law in July, when Orthodox rabbis agreed to abide by them, "provided strict rabbinical control was maintained." The focus of conflict was the new upright animal pen mandated by the legislation, which the Rabbinical Council of Independent Orthodox Jewish Communities claimed would deprive "thousands of Jewish families of meat," but which the chief rabbi said had been approved by a meeting of British rabbis four years earlier. In June the Federation of Synagogues asked the Board of Deputies of British Jews to inform the government that the Jewish community was deeply divided over the legislation. The board's executive committee replied by castigating the federation's religious authorities for refusing to support the chief rabbi and accept the regulations, claiming that the federation had caused discord in the community and "provided ammunition to our enemies." There were calls to quit the board at the federation's executive meeting.

Education

The new Jewish secondary school in Bushey, Hertfordshire, opened in September, after the Jewish Education Development Trust, which bought the site, pledged £9 million toward the school's £12-million cost, and the local North London community agreed to raise the remaining £3 million. Called "Charles Kalms, Henry Ronson, Immanuel College," after the fathers of businessmen-philanthropists Stanley Kalms and Gerald Ronson, as well as the chief rabbi, the school opened with 23 boys and 17 girls. Girls and boys were taught in separate classes but came together for informal activities.

In April the US council approved plans for a major reorganization of its part-time religion classes. The plans, contained in a hundred-page report, "Jewish Education for US Communities," called for changes in syllabi, examinations, and scheduling, as well as teacher-training and supervision. Changes over the next two years would raise annual US expenditure on the 4,400 children in its 45 centers from the current £850,000 to over £1 million (or one-third of the total US education budget).

Over one-third of British university departments teaching Judaism and subjects of Jewish interest had suffered cuts in faculty and resources, according to a 1989 survey by Dr. Sharman Kadish, research fellow at Royal Holloway and New Bedford College, London University, and published by the Oxford Center for Postgraduate Hebrew Studies and the International Center for the University Teaching of Jewish Civilization, Jerusalem. Out of 37 of these departments, 15 experienced cuts, 9 were expanding, and 4 terminated their Jewish studies courses. The author noted that departments were only able to expand through private donations. "It is likely that Jewish civilization studies will become increasingly dependent on outside funding in future," the survey concluded.

In March the private Spiro Institute agreed to fund courses in Jewish history scheduled to close at Warwick University. In June the *Jewish Chronicle* announced that it was endowing in perpetuity a chair of Jewish studies in the Department of Hebrew and Jewish Studies, University College, London, to commemorate its 150th anniversary in 1991. In August it was reported that the chair in Jewish studies projected for Manchester University would become a visiting professorship for two years, after which its future would be reassessed. In September the Oxford Center for Post-graduate Hebrew Studies inaugurated a visiting lectureship in contemporary Judaism in the name of comedian Jackie Mason.

Publications

This year saw the debuts of the first British Hebrew-language publication, *Hayisraeli shel London* ("The Israeli of London"), and the first scholarly Yiddish journal in 60 years, *Oksforder yiddish,* a yearbook of Yiddish studies, edited by Dovid Katz, who also edited the book *Dialects of the Yiddish Language.* An American, Ned Temko, was appointed the new editor of the weekly *Jewish Chronicle.*

New fiction published during the year included *Exquisite Cadaver* by Wolf Mankowitz; *Kingdom Come* by Bernice Rubens, based on the life of the false messiah Shabbetai Zvi; and *Brief Lives* by Anita Brookner.

Among new studies of British Jewry were *The Making of Modern Anglo-Jewry,* a collection of historical essays, edited by David Cesarani; *The Jews of Britain* by Pamela Fletcher Jones; *Anglia Judaica or a History of the Jews in England,* retold by Elizabeth Pearl, an edited version of the 1738 literary work by D'Blossiers Tovey; and *Second City Jewry* by Kenneth Collins, a history of the Jews of Glasgow. *The Preservation of Jewish Records,* a pamphlet by Bill Williams, aimed to facilitate such activity.

Works on other Jewish communities included *The Ghetto of Venice* by Roberta Curiel and Bernard Dov Cooperman; *The Jews of the Soviet Union: The History of a National Minority* by Benjamin Pinkus; *The Jews of Modern Egypt, 1914–1952* by Gudrun Kramer; *Jews in Contemporary East Germany* by Robin Ostow; and *The Double Eagle: Vienna-Budapest-Prague* by Stephen Brook, who also wrote *Winner Takes All: A Season in Israel. Survey of Jewish Affairs 1989,* edited by William Frankel, should also be noted in this category.

New works of religious significance were the *New Authorized Daily Prayer Book of the United Hebrew Congregations of the Commonwealth,* edited by Chief Rabbi Jakobovits; *Fountain of Blessings, the Code of Jewish Law* by Dayan Pinchas Toledano; *Tradition in an Untraditional Age: Essays on Modern Jewish Thought* by Jonathan Sacks; *A Thread of Gold: Journeys Towards Reconciliation* by Albert H. Friedlander, a description of the interfaith work that earned him the Sternberg medal; *Moments of Insight: Biblical and Contemporary Jewish Themes* by Jeffrey M. Cohen; and *Jews, Idols and Messiahs* by Lionel Kochan.

New works of biography and autobiography included *Lord Jakobovits,* the authorized biography of the chief rabbi by Chaim Bermant; *Arnold Schoenberg: The Composer as Jew* by Alexander L. Ringer; *Ibn Gabirol* by Raphael Loewe; *The False Prophet: Rabbi Meir Kahane—From FBI Informant to Knesset Member* by Robert I. Friedman; *Dangers, Tests and Miracles* by Chief Rabbi Moses Rosen of Romania, as told to Joseph Finklestone; *On Parade, Memoirs of a Jewish Sergeant-Major in World War II,* by Leonard Sanitt; *Marina Tsvetayeva* by Elaine Feinstein; *Recollec-*

tions and Reflections by Bruno Bettelheim; *Gorbals Voices, Siren Song,* the third volume of Ralph Glasser's autobiography; *Dr. Phillips: A Maida Vale Idyll* by Frank Danby; *Montague Burton: The Tailor of Taste* by Eric Sigsworth; and *Marcus Sieff on Management* by Marcus Sieff.

The long list of general scholarly works on the Holocaust included *The Nazi Holocaust: Historical Articles on the Destruction of European Jews,* edited by Michael Marrus: Part 6, *The Victims of the Holocaust,* and Part 9, *The End of the Holocaust;* the *Encyclopaedia of the Holocaust,* edited by Israel Gutman; *Healing Their Wounds: Psycho-Therapy with Holocaust Survivors and Their Families,* edited by P. Marcus and A. Rosenberg; *A Directory of Holocaust Education and Related Activity in the UK,* published by the Holocaust Educational Trust; *In the Shadow of the Holocaust: The Second Generation* by Aaron Hass; *Modernity and the Holocaust* by Zygmunt Bauman; *Unbroken: Resistance and Survival in the Concentration Camps* by Len Crome; *Why Did the Heavens Not Darken? The "Final Solution" in History* by Arno J. Mayer; *All or Nothing: The Axis and the Holocaust, 1941–1943* by Jonathan Steinberg; and *The Blue and the Yellow Stars of David: The Zionist Leadership in Palestine and the Holocaust, 1939–1945* by Dina Porat.

Works relating specifically to Poland and the Holocaust were *The Convent at Auschwitz* by Wladyslaw T. Bartoszewski, who also edited *Polin, A Journal of Polish-Jewish Studies,* volumes 3 and 4; *My Brother's Keeper: Recent Polish Debates on the Holocaust,* edited by Antony Polonsky; *I Remember Nothing More: The Warsaw Children's Hospital and the Jewish Resistance* by Adina Blady Szwajger; and *The Warsaw Ghetto* by Joe J. Heydecker.

Books concerned with the wartime experiences of French Jewry were *Swastika over Paris: The Fate of the French Jews* by Jeremy Josephs; and *Petain's Crime: The Full Story of French Collaboration in the Holocaust* by Paul Webster.

Personal accounts of wartime experiences were contained in *In the Sewers of Lvov* by Robert Marshall; *A Refugee's Flight from Germany in the Thirties* by Frederick G. Cohn; *A Child's War—World War II Through the Eyes of Children* by Kati David; *A Cup of Tears,* a diary of wartime Warsaw, by Abraham Lewin; *Survivors Speak Out,* a collection of poems and accounts; and *Lodz Ghetto: Inside a Community Under Siege,* compiled and edited by Alan Adelson and Robert Lapides. *I Came Alone: The Stories of the Kindertransports,* edited by Bertha Leverton and Shmuel Lowensohn, and *And the Policeman Smiled* by Barry Turner are on the same theme. *We Will Remember Them,* compiled by Henry Morris and edited by Gerald Smith, is a record of the Jews who died in the armed forces of the Crown, 1939–1945.

New works on Israeli-Arab relations included *Judaean Journal* by Jacques Pinto, the diary of an Israeli officer serving in the West Bank at the height of the *intifada;* *Behind the Star* by former BBC correspondent Gerald Butt; *Four Arab-Israeli Wars and the Peace Process* by Sydney D. Bailey; *1948 and After: Israel and the Palestinians,* essays by Benny Morris; *Israel, Palestinians and the Intifada* by Geoffrey Aronson; *Palestine and Israel: The Uprising and Beyond* by David McDowall; *Facts and Fables: The Arab-Israel Conflict* by Clifford A. Wright; *G-Suit: Combat Reports from Israel's Air War* by Merav Halperin and Aharon Lapidot; and *Economic Cooperation and Middle East Peace* by Haim Ben-Shahar. *Mine Enemy* by Amalia and Aharon Barnea tells of the moving friendship of an Arab and an Israeli couple.

Other new works on Israel were *The Elections in Israel-1988,* edited by Asher Arian and Michael Shamir; *Legal Dualism* by Eyal Benvenisti; *Management in the Land of Israel* by Peter Lawrence; *Between East and West: Israel's Foreign Policy Orientations, 1948–1956* by Uri Bialer; *The Suez-Sinai Crisis 1956: Retrospective and Reappraisal,* edited by S.I. Troen and M. Shemesh; ; *The Peace Movement in Israel 1967–87* by David Hall-Cathala; *Journey to the Promised Land,* edited by Nachman Ran; *The Slopes of Lebanon,* a collection of essays, reviews, and addresses by Amos Oz; *Studies in Contemporary Jewry,* vol. 5: *Israel: State and Society, 1948–1988,* edited by Peter Y. Medding; *The Imperfect Spies* by Yossi Melman and Dan Raviv; and *Chariots of the Desert* by David Eshel. Specifically devoted to Jerusalem were *Jerusalem: City of Mirrors* by Amos Elon; and *My Jerusalem: Twelve Walks in the World's Holiest City* by Teddy Kollek and Shulamith Eisner.

Poetry published during the year included *Different Enclosures,* the poetry and prose of Irena Klepfisz; *Sleeping with the Professor's Daughter* by Dan Hershon; *The Hutchinson Book of Post-War British Poets,* edited by Dannie Abse; and *Collected Poems* by Karen Gershon.

Two new works on anti-Semitism were *Anti-Zionism and Anti-Semitism in the Contemporary World,* edited by Robert S. Wistrich; and *The Politics of Marginality: Race, the Radical Right and Minorities in Twentieth-Century Britain,* edited by Tony Kushner and Kenneth Lunn.

Personalia

Sir Jeffrey Sterling, chairman of the P & O shipping, real estate, and hotels group, and Sir David Wolfson, one of Prime Minister Thatcher's advisers, were made barons in her resignation honors. Lady Porter, Westminster Council's Tory leader, became Dame Shirley Porter. Stanley Clinton Davis, former Labor MP and European Commission member, was made a life peer, taking the title of Lord Clinton-Davis of Hackney. Knighthoods went to Sir Brian Wolfson, chairman of Wembley Stadium, the government's National Training Task Force, and the National Economic Development Council's leisure and tourism committee; Sir Ronald Grierson, director of the South Bank Arts Center and Arts Council member; Geoffrey Leigh, chairman of Allied London Properties; Sir Anthony Epstein, professor of pathology at Bristol University; Sir Paul Fox, BBC Network Television managing director; Sir Sydney Lipman, Monopolies and Mergers Commission chairman; and Sir Allan Green, Director of Public Prosecutions.

Among British Jews who died in 1990 were Stuart Albert Samuel Montagu, Lord Swaythling, communal figure, in January, aged 91; Leon Blumenson, Yiddish actor, in January, aged 84; Siegfried Hirsch, former Hendon Adath Yisroel Congregation president, in February, aged 85; Harry Levine, teacher, journalist, and minister of Norwich congregation, in February; Bennie Abrahams, communal worker and Lord Mayor of Newcastle 1981–82, in February, aged 83; Rabbi Icchak Feld, Jewish scholar, in February, aged 79; Vivian Lipman, civil servant and Anglo-Jewish historian, in March, aged 69; Maurice Gaguine, for almost 50 years rabbi of the Withington Spanish and Portuguese Jews' Congregation, in March, aged 71; Nathaniel Mayer Victor, third Baron Rothschild, oil executive and head of Prime Minister Edward Heath's "think tank" 1971–74, in March, aged 79; Harry Mizler, boxer, in March, aged 77; Sir Alan Marre, distinguished civil servant and Britain's first Jewish Ombudsman, in March, aged 76; Beatrice Jeannette Barwell, Zionist champion of Jewish education, in March, aged 75; Rabbi Lipa Baum, minister, Yiddish scholar, and talmudist, in April, aged 70; George Lyttleton, Leeds education worker, in April, aged 86; Alan Silverman, Jewish welfare-work activist, in May, aged 68; Bezalel Stern, vice-president of British Agudas Yisroel and Agudas Yisroel World Organization executive council member, in May, aged 90; Yehuda Lisky, Yiddish writer, in May, aged 90; Asa Benveniste, poet, in May, aged 64; Geoffrey Salmon, former president of J. Lyons and Company, and philanthropist, in May, aged 82; Joe Loss, dance-band leader, in June, aged 80; Samuel Sacks, doctor, Hebrew scholar, talmudist, and Zionist, in June, aged 95; Leonard Sachs, television personality, in June, aged 82; Arthur Sunderland, Jewish journalist, in July, aged 75; Bruno Marmorstein, lawyer, scholar and communal worker, in July, aged 79; Rachel Beth-Zion Abrahams, Zionist historical writer, in August, aged 88; Aryeh Chontow, Torah scholar and philanthropist, in September, aged 74; Harold Altman, communal worker, in October, aged 78; Sir Ben Lockspeiser, aeronautics expert and government administrator, in October, aged 99; Rita Blond, noted Zionist, in October, aged 84; Sidney Bloch, leading welfare worker, in November, aged 66; Sir Alan Mocatta, High Court judge, in November, aged 83; Hyam Morrison, philanthropist, in November, aged 85; Ernst Saly Frankel, leading British Zionist, in November, aged 88; Phyllis Gerson, welfare worker, in December, aged 87; Michael Marchant, for 20 years World Sephardi Federation secretary, in December, aged 98.

LIONEL & MIRIAM KOCHAN

France

THE YEAR 1990 SAW FRANCE facing difficult challenges emanating from both outside and inside the country: outside, the end of the post-Yalta power balance in Europe and the achievement of German unification; inside, growing public impatience in the face of ongoing economic restructuring, expressed through distrust of "classical" political parties and hostility toward immigration. Two events that captured public attention this year were the crisis in the Persian Gulf and the desecration of the Jewish cemetery at Carpentras, the latter taking place against a background of the growing influence of the National Front (FN).

National Affairs

By the end of the 1980s, three clear trends had emerged in French politics: (1) the phenomenon of voter abstention, confirmed in 1990 in all by-elections, which was new in France and thus could be considered a symptom of a social-political crisis; (2) the success of movements which seemed to represent an alternative to the classical parties: the National Front and the Greens; and (3) the focus on themes that had been introduced into the debate and were promoted by the FN, such as immigration, a widespread sense of general insecurity, and national identity. Various scandals linked to the financing of the major political parties contributed to their deteriorating status.

Although virtually absent on the national level—with only one representative in the National Assembly—the FN continued its rise on the local level. According to data released by the end of the year by the Ministry of Interior, 35 mayors, 1,667 town councillors, 4 general councillors (district level), and 116 regional councillors belonged to the FN. The FN claimed some 80,000 members, although the figure of 50,000 seemed closer to reality. At its congress in Nice (March 30–April 1) the party defined the "conquest of power" as its aim.

Although that power seemed far out of the reach of a party considered a threat to democracy by a large majority (around two-thirds) of the French in opinion polls, the polls also showed that a significant minority (20 to 30 percent) shared the FN's ideas and could be considered potential voters. The results of the by-elections that took place in 1990 were particularly revealing. Up to Carpentras, in May, the FN showed a gain of two to nine points over previous elections in the same constituencies. Immediately after Carpentras, one by-election seemed to show that the FN had been harmed, but this proved temporary. The overall trend remained upward. In June, the FN came in second, with 27 percent of the votes, in the first round of the municipal by-election in Villeurbanne (a big, traditionally socialist, working-class suburb close to Lyons) and gained in the second round (36 percent). In December, it came in second in the first round of the municipal by-election in Nice (25 percent of the votes) and was fairly close to taking over the municipality in the second round with 48 percent of the votes.

Political analyst Jean Bothorel (*Le Figaro*, January 7, 1991) claimed that the image of the leader of the National Front, Jean-Marie Le Pen, was "almost normalized," and that the party's growth was no longer linked solely to the issue of North African immigrants. He noted that while Le Pen had found very few allies in intellectual, academic, or cultural circles, or in the world of communication, he was experiencing less and less rejection by business leaders, high public officials, and the military.

Like the FN, the Greens also benefited from the general distrust of the traditional parties, in 1990 gaining 13 to 15 percent in by-elections. Although the Greens definitely opposed the FN's ideology, they refused either to call on their voters to oppose the front or to enter a "republican front" with other parties against the FN (doing so, they argued, would indicate that what distinguished them from the other parties was less meaningful than their differences with the FN, which was not the case).

Middle East Policy

France's involvement in Middle Eastern affairs in the first half of 1990 was fairly limited. The French will to normalize relations with Iran led to a presidential pardon of terrorist Anis Naccache and his expulsion to Iran, in July, along with four other members of the commando unit that had attempted to murder former Iranian prime minister Chappur Bakhtiar in July 1980. France expressed the hope that this gesture would "facilitate the liberation of all Western hostages still detained" in the Middle East. In Lebanon, in October, when Christian general Michel Aoun was defeated in his rearguard battle against the Syrians, he found refuge in the French embassy in Beirut.

Beginning in August, it was the invasion of Kuwait by Iraq and the ensuing crisis in the Persian Gulf area that captured public attention. After attempts to find a diplomatic solution failed, the debate in France centered on two questions: French participation in a possible war that might be declared by the United Nations and France's position vis-à-vis the leader of the coalition against Iraq, the United States. Despite the opposition of Minister of Defense Jean-Pierre Chevènement, who advocated a more lenient position limited to a strict implementation of the first boycott decisions taken by the United Nations, France adopted a policy of firmness, making Iraq responsible for the "logic of war" in the Gulf (the expression came from the mouth of President François Mitterrand in August). Espoused by the president of the Republic, the policy met with consensus among all major parties, whose leaders were regularly consulted, and a broad majority of the public.

Yet, by the end of the year, a line was drawn between the major political parties, on the Right and the Left, which supported the presidential policy in the Gulf, and the protest movements (Communists, FN, the Greens, and the remnants of the far Left), which tried, but with limited success, to mobilize public opinion against a possible war. FN leader Le Pen went to Iraq to negotiate freedom for French hostages and put forth a fairly complex rationale for his position: Iraq was entitled to question its borders; Kuwait, as a state, had no historical roots; French involvement could create a tremendous wave of anti-French feeling in the Arab and Islamic worlds; and, above all, French attention should be entirely devoted to the "real threats": the Soviet Union in Europe and the immigrants at home. Other pacifist movements expressed a more classical anti-American type of argument against what they saw as a war "for oil." It was only natural that, in such a context, the autumn meeting in France of Minister of Foreign Affairs David Levy of Israel with President Mitterrand, Prime Minister Michel Rocard, Minister of Foreign Affairs Roland Dumas, and the chairman of the National Assembly, Laurent Fabius, did not draw any particular attention.

Relations with Israel

As far as the Arab-Israeli conflict was concerned, there were no new French initiatives, and the only noteworthy event was a meeting between President Mitterrand and PLO leader Yasir Arafat, in Paris, on April 4. Arafat's presence on French soil for the third time in 18 months had come to seem almost routine and, unlike the two previous occasions, did not even give rise to a mass protest by the Jewish community. The Representative Council of Jewish Institutions in France (Conseil Représentatif des Institutions Juives de France, CRIF) expressed its "anxiety and failure to understand" such a meeting and its hope that President Mitterrand would tell Arafat that his opposition to Jewish immigration to Israel was unacceptable. The CRIF statement also emphasized that the PLO's "message of peace was a mere pretense," that it remained a "supporter of armed conflict."

Anti-Semitism

According to year-end statistics of the Ministry of Interior on racist and anti-Semitic incidents, anti-Semitic incidents involving violence remained stable in 1990, but there was a sharp rise in the number of incidents that did not directly involve physical violence. For anti-Semitic incidents, the figures were: 20 violent actions (3 injured) and 372 threats and insulting actions (among them 172 in May after the Carpentras desecration, which was more in one month than in any entire previous year). Figures for racist-xenophobic violence were: 52 violent actions (1 dead, 36 injured; 37 of the violent actions directed against North Africans) and 278 threats and insulting actions (among them 198 against North Africans). The figures showed that racist violence was more widespread and more harmful than anti-Semitic violence. At the same time, they highlighted the tremendous snowball effect of

Carpentras, which inspired a wave of incidents, minor in themselves but concentrated in time and numerous enough to create, at least for a while, a real climate of insecurity among Jews.

As in previous years, some of the incidents were linked to supporters of the FN or to what could be called contamination spread by the FN's approach to the "Jewish question." Although Le Pen created no new scandals in 1990, on two occasions he reiterated his view that the Nazi gas chambers were "a detail in the history of World War II," which he had first expressed in 1987: in an interview with the daily *Le Quotidien* (February 9) and two weeks later in an election meeting in Sarcelles (quoted in *Jour J*, February 28). In 1990, Le Pen and the circles close to the FN focused on the theme of "Jewish power," denouncing both the "institutional tools" of Jewish power (B'nai B'rith; CRIF and its president, Jean Kahn) and the "hidden tools" of Jewish power, particularly the press. Le Pen stated as an objective truth the substantial representation of Jews among journalists: "There are many Jews in the press, like there are many Britons in the fleet and Corsicans in the customs."

The FN and its close circles also denounced the alleged privileges of Jews (and of foreigners) who were allowed to be "anti-Catholic" and/or "anti-French," whereas the law prohibited any attack against the Jews. The fundamentalist pro-FN Catholic daily *Présent* (December 28), under the headline "The privilege. One may attack the Church, but not Judaism," wrote: "Any criticism of the Jewish religion or of the policy of the representative institutions of the Jewish community is seen as an act of anti-Semitism; and 'anti-Semitism is not an opinion, it is an offense'—whereas anti-Christianism is not an offense, but an opinion; . . ."

Apart from these themes, which were dominant on the far Right during the entire year, the crisis in the Persian Gulf provided new ground for attacks against Jews, who were accused of supporting a war against Iraq in order to help Israel, in conflict with French interests.

Finally, the mayor of Nice, Jacques Médecin, who had declared that he "shared the theses of the FN up to 99 percent," provoked an incident in April, when he did not protest the presence in his city, to attend the FN congress, of former Waffen SS member and leader of the German Republikaner party Franz Schönhuber. Further, he gave clear hints that he meant to enlarge his municipal majority with the addition of FN town councillors. Three Jewish town councillors immediately resigned. Médecin reacted on the local TV (April 3): "I do not know any Israelite who would refuse a present when offered one. And, as far as I am concerned, I do not know any mayor who could say: 'I refuse votes which are brought to me.' " He added: "I am not the one who has made room [for the FN town councillors]. It is the Jews who have left." (Médecin ran away from France in October in order to escape charges of misappropriation of funds.)

Several initiatives were taken throughout the year against manifestations of racism, anti-Semitism, and intolerance. Among them was an ecumenical statement published on January 24 at the initiative of the Council of Christian Churches and signed by representatives of the Orthodox Interepiscopal Committee, the Catholic Church, the Protestant Federation, the Paris Mosque, and, on behalf of the Jewish community, the chief rabbi of Paris and the president of CRIF. In the summer, the UEJF, the Union of Jewish Students in France, arranged a "protest tour," which took UEJF speakers into 23 main cities in France, where they met with local opinion-makers and press to raise awareness of racism and anti-Semitism. On November 14, 12 mayors of big cities belonging to the major parties of the Right and Left gathered to discuss the problem of racism.

CARPENTRAS

The desecration that was discovered on the morning of May 10 in the Jewish cemetery of Carpentras in the south of France—belonging to one of the oldest Jewish communities in the country—was immediately granted the status of an exceptional and symbolic event. First, the desecration was directed not only against the graves but against the dead themselves. Not only were over 30 graves damaged, but the corpse of an 80-year-old man buried two weeks earlier was dug out of the earth and defiled (an attempt was made to impale it, and a Star of David was placed on the body). Whereas other desecrations in the past had hardly caught the attention of the press, Carpentras, because it trespassed the borders of the "usual" pattern, produced broad coverage in the media and a strong emotional reaction among non-Jews and Jews alike. President François Mitterrand's immediate visit to Chief Rabbi of France Joseph Sitruk, at his home, highlighted the public reaction.

The general climate of opinion supported an unequivocal interpretation of the event as motivated by anti-Semitism. All opinion polls showed the growing popularity of the FN and Jean-Marie Le Pen. The desecration followed the anniversary of the 1945 victory over Nazism, which had featured—on one of the major TV channels—a documentary film on Nazi Germany and anti-Semitism. Thus, just as the bombing of the Rue Copernic Synagogue in October 1980 was presumed to be an attack by French anti-Semites (in fact the police investigation showed later that the bomb had been set by Middle Eastern terrorists), there now seemed every reason to fear an anti-Jewish outbreak in France. Hence the emotion which led some 200,000 French to attend a mass demonstration in Paris on May 14 against anti-Semitism, racism, and intolerance, with the participation of all political leaders (except the FN) and of President Mitterrand himself.

The Carpentras desecration had further repercussions in 1990. In the days and weeks after Carpentras, France was the scene of a wave of cemetery desecrations, both Jewish and non-Jewish, that apparently inspired other desecrations in East Berlin, Canada, Great Britain, Sweden, Israel, Poland, and elsewhere. The attention devoted in France to the most morbid aspect of Carpentras, the outrage to the dead, also had unforeseen consequences. The mere fact that the investigation questioned the reality or the "completeness" of the impalement served to devalue the desecration act itself, as if a "simple" desecration would have been acceptable.

Finally, in the absence of any clear-cut finding by the police inquiry (which was first directed at far Right and skinhead circles but later theorized that drunk youngsters or satanic sects were involved—a thesis that would deny the specifically anti-Semitic nature of the event), some backlash was inevitable. The hasty declaration by French Minister of Interior Pierre Joxe after the desecration ("There is no need for a police investigation in order to know who the criminals are. . . . The criminals have a name. They are called racism, anti-Semitism, intolerance.") was interpreted as a denunciation of the National Front and subsequently opened the door to questions about possible political manipulation of the event.

The backlash was illustrated by a widely discussed article in the bimonthly *Le Débat* (September-October 1990), in which sociologist Paul Yonnet analyzed the main outcome of Carpentras (what he called the "Carpentras machine") as a "purge syndrome." He also denounced the attention devoted to "false or recreational anti-Semitism" and accused French Jews of the very intolerance commonly attributed to French society in general: "It is the Jews who close themselves in a communitarianism that is racist toward non-Jews; they do not accept exogamous marriage, they restrict their schools to their own children, and they denounce the 'non-Jewish Jews.' " According to Yonnet—who fiercely denied being anti-Semitic—the Jews of France want to build "an ethnic-religious, or even an ethnobiological-religious, thus racial, community." In an interview with the weekly *Le Point* (November 5), Yonnet elaborated on these views: "It [the Carpentras machine] is composed of four elements. First, the feeling that the rise of the National Front is inexorable, that the whole society is going to fall into Le Pen-ism. The second element is all the publicity given to anti-Semitism under the pretext of denouncing the real, but soft, anti-Semitism of Le Pen and of the people who surround him. Then comes a kind of back-and-forth movement between Vichy and the present time. . . . Once it is completed, the machine can start isolating Le Pen; the only thing that is needed is the opportunity."

Beyond the problem of the "use" that he felt had been made of the Carpentras desecration, another disturbing point emerged from Yonnet's analysis: his tolerance of even a limited degree of anti-Semitism, what he called "soft" anti-Semitism. Coming from a man who was in no way identified with the far Right, and in the absence of any answer to the basic question of who committed the desecration, Yonnet's line of thought received attention and was taken over by other people, contributing to a perception that Carpentras had been, if not a manipulated event, at least one whose importance had been highly exaggerated.

OPINION POLLS

Polls conducted after Carpentras showed a number of ambiguities. According to one published in the daily *Le Parisien* (May 17), a huge majority (96 percent) were shocked by the event: 41 percent, deeply; 36 percent, very much; 19 percent, somewhat. Yet 35 percent agreed with the statement: "It is acceptable for people to express hostile remarks about Jews, since everyone in a democracy should be able to express themselves." A small majority (56 percent) agreed with this statement: "Taking into account what happened to the Jews during World War II, it is not acceptable for people to express hostile remarks about the Jews." Although a majority (55 percent) felt that the National Front was "an anti-Semitic party," 57 percent felt that "it is acceptable to invite Mr. Le Pen to take part in [TV] programs, since he is the leader of an important political party." Only 33 percent shared the opposite opinion, that "it is acceptable not to invite Mr. Le Pen for he helps to propagate racism and anti-Semitism in the country." A similar question asked in a poll published in the weekly *Le Nouvel Observateur* (May 17) had similar results: 54 percent felt that Jean-Marie Le Pen should be invited to appear on "popular TV programs . . . for he represents part of the voters." The poll in *Le Parisien* also showed that even in the aftermath of Carpentras, the view that "Jews have too much power in France" was shared by a not negligible part of the public: 17 percent totally or somewhat agreed with the statement: "Some people feel that Jews in France today have too much power" (14 percent did not answer).

Holocaust Denial

In the area of "classical" French revisionism, one development in 1990 was the discontinuation of the *Annales d'Histoire Révisionniste*, edited by "leftist" Pierre Guillaume, and its replacement by the *Revue d'Histoire Révisionniste*, edited by Henri Roques, the retired engineer and author of the doctoral thesis on the Kurt Gerstein papers whose doctoral degree was revoked in 1986 by administrative decision. (See AJYB 1988, pp. 276–77.) Together with the production of the new quarterly, the efforts of classical revisionists focused on intensive distribution of revisionist literature—mainly in letter boxes—whose main purpose was to bring to a large audience the results of the "Leuchter report" (by an American revisionist, "proving" that mass murder by Zyklon B was impossible) and videocassettes of Robert Faurisson.

A new phenomenon that started in the autumn of 1989 and grew in 1990 was "post-revisionism," spread through the medium of the monthly *Revision*, edited by Olivier Mathieu and Alain Guionnet. To the post-revisionists, the "scientific" demonstration of the nonexistence of gas chambers was no longer the main purpose. In their openly anti-Semitic publication, the two editors of *Revision* focused on the denunciation of what they called "the Shoah-business," i.e., the moral, political, and financial exploitation of the Holocaust by Jews, and on anti-Zionist and anti-Semitic themes, the latter illustrated by numerous comments on circumcision and the publication in installments of the *Protocols of the Elders of Zion*. On May 14, Guionnet was given three concurrent three-month jail sentences (i.e., a total of three months) for provocation of racial hatred and racial defamation in the September, October, and November 1989 issues of *Revision*.

Yet another demonstration of revisionism received attention in broader circles when the daily *Le Monde* (January 28–29) quoted sections of a recent article in a special issue of a high-level academic journal, *Economies et Sociétés*, devoted to the theme of "vassalized France." The author, a professor of economics at the University of Lyons III, Bernard Notin, expressed clearly racist and revisionist opinions when he denounced "Nobel's band holidaying in Paris at the initiative of the Jewish entourage of the President" (of the Republic)[1] and used the gas chambers to exemplify what he called a "venomous sophism": "The proofs that are proposed in order to demonstrate their existence evolve according to the circumstances and the moment, but they come from a box of tricks with three drawers. In the lowest: a tour of the premises (not very credible). In the middle: the assertion by the victors (they have existed). In the top: hearsay (the story of the man who has seen the man who has seen the man who . . .). On the whole, one postulates their existence, and no matter what the reality of that reality is. One can identify here the basis of all tyrannies."

The novelty in this episode was both the academic position of the author and the high caliber of the publication in which he expressed his views. Reactions to it were, not surprisingly, very strong. The director of CNRS, the National Center for Scientific Research, called Notin's paper "scandalously anti-Semitic and with very little scientific content" and decided to discontinue the CNRS subvention to the journal. In February, the university council of Lyons III suspended Notin until steps could be taken by the minister of education to move him to another university. In May, six well-known academics published an appeal calling for an end to academic cooperation with colleagues who, "acting in the framework of their professional activities or using their [academic] titles . . . call themselves revisionists and are nothing but falsifiers of history or those who publicly support the enterprise of xenophobic and racist hatred which, under the banner of nationalism, is nothing but the negation of the authentic values of Republican France." In July, Notin was tried and fined, after a complaint was filed by the antiracist organization MRAP. The disciplinary section of the administrative council of the Lyons III university decided to suspend him from any teaching and research activity for one year and to fine him half his salary during that period. Notin appealed that decision.

The Notin case highlighted important characteristics of French revisionism generally: the continuous effort of the revisionists to obtain academic recognition, particularly after the Roques-thesis affair; the sensitivity of a large segment of public opinion to the problem, as a result of media denunciation; and, finally, the difficulty of preventing the expression of revisionist views.

---

[1]"Nobel's band" refers to various Nobel prizewinners, such as Elie Wiesel, who were brought to Paris in the early '80s by President Mitterrand in order to promote a humanistic climate of thought. It is also a pun on the title of a book by Louis-Ferdinand Céline, *Guignol's Band*.

LEGAL MEASURES

New regulations aimed at curbing racial and religious discrimination, as well as public denial of the Holocaust, were promulgated on July 13. While antiracist organizations and personalities such as Serge Klarsfeld welcomed the measures—particularly the one that made it an offense to publicly deny the Holocaust—others raised questions about their legitimacy. Nor did opposition come only from the Right. Journalists, for example, objected to more limitations on freedom of the press. There was also a feeling that the measures were directed against Le Pen *ad hominem*, in order to obtain by legal means what political confrontation had been unable to achieve, i.e., stopping the rise of the FN.

Among academics (including militant antirevisionists) it was felt that historical questions should be left to academics. Said historian François Bédarida in an interview with *Le Monde* (May 15): "It is not by law that one establishes the validity of a historical work. As much as it is legitimate to prosecute incitement to racial hatred, it seems to me stupid and counterproductive to forbid a historical lie. The condemnation of revisionism as a gigantic intellectual swindle by the international scientific community is sufficient . . . on condition that the media refrain from providing too big a platform for the holders of counter-truths." Bédarida was the author of a booklet on World War II and the gas chambers that was distributed free of charge by the Nathan publishing house to all schoolteachers in an effort to counter revisionism.

Other Holocaust-Related Matters

The problematic relation of the French to their own past during the Second World War—the attempt to find a balance between the two equally false images of a totally "resistant" or a totally "collaborationist" France—was reflected in the ongoing difficulties involved in bringing René Bousquet to trial. Bousquet had served as secretary general of the Vichy police and was accused of responsibility in the arrests of Jews, particularly the mass arrests in July 1942. In May, 19 new complaints were lodged against him. That the issue was not only a legal one was crudely expressed by Ministerial Delegate to Justice Georges Kiejman, who declared, "Beyond the necessary fight against oblivion, it might seem important to preserve the civil peace," adding: "There are other ways than a trial to denounce the cowardice of the Vichy regime" (*Libération*, October 22). Serge Klarsfeld fiercely denounced Kiejman, "this son of a Jewish deportee, appointed ministerial delegate to justice in order to ensure the impunity of the chief of the Vichy police" (*Le Nouvel Observateur*, October 25). He also deplored "the political refusal to pass judgment on the anti-Jewish actions of the Vichy government, its police and its administration" (quoted in *L'Evénement du Jeudi*, December 27).

These events had to be understood in the context of the widespread ignorance of World War II that prevailed among a good part of the French postwar generation.

A survey published in *Le Monde* (June 13) covered two samples: one of 400 students in secondary schools and universities; the other of 200 persons representing the 18–44-year-old population at large. Fifty percent of the 18–44-year-olds (26 percent of the students) believed that "during the years of the Occupation, the main preoccupation of the majority of the French" was to "resist the occupier"; 33 percent (21 percent of the students) believed that it was "SS" who conducted the arrests of Jews in July 1942, 19 percent (14 percent of the students) that it was "German soldiers"; 44 percent (63 percent of the students) knew that the arrests had actually been carried out by the French police. Even more disturbing was the fact that while 65 percent of the 18–44-year-olds (80 percent of the students) felt that "the use in several concentration camps of toxic gas to kill the deportees" was "clearly proved," 23 percent (15 percent of the students) felt that it was "a fact that happened but which has not been clearly proved"; and 10 percent (2 percent of the students) that it was "a fact that has not been clearly proved."

Apart from highlighting the crucial importance of education, the poll showed the vulnerability of the postwar generation to revisionist or revisionist-type theories, despite intense efforts by both Jewish and non-Jewish bodies to maintain the memory of past events. In 1990, for instance, the city of Lyons hosted an exhibition on Anne Frank which was visited by some 50,000 school pupils. Among other initiatives, an association formed by the Jewish community of Lyons carried out a national fund-raising campaign, with the help of several non-Jewish celebrities, and in March acquired the house in Izieu where 44 Jewish children had been arrested by order of Klaus Barbie in 1944. The purpose of the association was to turn the site into a museum chiefly for children, with a permanent exhibition on the theme "How dictatorships are born." In April the weekly *L'Express* published a heavily documented article on the camps in Beaune-la-Rolande and Pithiviers where Jewish children whose parents had been deported were held and kept in frightful conditions by the French police until their turn came to be deported, without the local population reacting in any way. An exhibition on "Vichy Propaganda," prepared by the Museum of Contemporary History of the Library of Contemporary Documentation, opened in June in the Hôtel des Invalides in Paris. One of the exhibition organizers, historian Denis Peschansky, stated: "In order to fight racism and anti-Semitism effectively, the Vichy period has to be better known."

JEWISH COMMUNITY

Demography

There were no major changes in the estimated Jewish population of France, which remained, according to most sources, 550,000–600,000. Still, new figures made public at the beginning of 1990—from a survey carried out in 1988 under the auspices of the Fonds Social Juif Unifié (FSJU)—showed a number of interesting developments over the previous 15 years. According to Erik H. Cohen, the main author of the 1988 study (writing in the Jewish monthly *L'Arche*, January 1990), one change was in the area of geographical distribution. Whereas in 1976 Jews were distributed roughly 50–50 between the provinces and Paris and surroundings, in 1988, 43.8 percent of Jewish families lived in the provinces, 26.2 percent in Paris suburbs, and 29.9 percent in the city of Paris. In terms of individuals, 41.4 percent resided in the provinces, 31.1 percent in Paris suburbs, and 27.5 percent in the city of Paris. Cohen also noted a movement toward the outer suburbs of Paris, to the detriment of the closer suburbs.

Regarding occupational distribution, he noted a strong movement toward higher executive and managerial positions and the professions (38 percent of the adult Jewish population were in this category), which he interpreted as a sign of a growing integration of the Jews in French society. A rise in intermarriage figures was also notable: 31 percent of 18–29-year-old married Jews were intermarried, with the rate declining by age: 26 percent among 30–49-year-old married Jews, and 14 percent among the 50-and-over married Jews. The birthrate, which had risen steadily from 1951–1955 through 1971–1976, thereafter took a downturn. In religious practice, 45 percent of Cohen's sample said they ate kosher food at home and 24 percent both at home and outside; 15 percent declared themselves to be observant.

According to sources in the Jewish Agency (*Jour J*, January 5), 1,100 Jews from France made *aliyah* in 1989 (up 1 percent). The same sources stressed that France was the only Western country whose immigration to Israel had not dropped.

Communal Affairs

The mass immigration of Soviet Jews to Israel was a matter of top priority for community institutions. Besides the traditional fund raising carried out by the United Jewish Appeal of France (AUJF), CRIF was active in the political sphere, working to counteract the propaganda that depicted Soviet immigration to Israel as a new obstacle to peace in the Middle East, accused Israel of settling the immigrants in the territories, and called on France to use its influence with the Soviet Union to stop emigration. CRIF raised the problem several times in meetings with French authorities (particularly in the meeting of April 26 between President Mitterrand and the president of CRIF, Jean Kahn, who was accompanied by the president of the commission on Soviet Jewry of CRIF). Stressing the fact that only a tiny minority of the immigrants were indeed settling in the territories, CRIF called for France to consider providing economic aid for integration of the new immigrants. Soviet immigration was also discussed in a meeting on February 1 between Chief Rabbi Joseph Sitruk and Prime Minister Michel Rocard. An appeal signed by several dozen intellectuals, published in the general press, called for solidarity with Soviet Jews and Israel and appealed for humanitarian relief. News of the anti-Jewish activities of Pamyat in the USSR and rumors of a possible wave of anti-Semitism created much concern. The French Union of Jewish Students (UEJF) demonstrated against what was perceived as an immediate danger to Soviet Jews. The question of the "Jewishness" of Soviet Jews immigrating to Israel became a subject for internal communal debate, with more traditional circles suggesting that attention should be given not only to material integration but to spiritual integration as well. The broader implication of the debate was a question about the use made in Israel of funds raised in the Diaspora. When asked by the daily *Jour J* (June 15) to comment on the request by some French religious leaders that the United Jewish Appeal set aside 15 percent of the raised funds for "the spiritual integration of Soviet Jews," Chief Rabbi Sitruk replied carefully: "I think this is an interesting approach. . . . One has to negotiate. Today, those who give the money do not want to be only cows waiting to be milked. They also want to give their views on the way their funds are used. This seems to me very healthy and very responsible."

The fate of Syrian Jewry remained of concern, although nothing seemed to change in that situation. March 4 was a day devoted by the community to a national conference on Syrian Jewry.

Other opportunities for communal involvement came in the wake of developments in Eastern Europe. At the beginning of the year, the FSJU put its organization at the disposal of a national movement for solidarity with the Rumanian people and launched an "SOS-Rumania" campaign, together with ten other Jewish organizations, including CRIF and the European Jewish Congress.

Humanitarian efforts were also directed close to home. Despite the high degree of social integration and prosperity in the French Jewish community revealed by the sociological surveys, many Jews in France were caught in the wave of unemployment and poverty affecting the nation as a whole. In December 1989, the FSJU national council decided to include in its 1990 budget the sum of 15 million francs (almost $3 million) for social welfare. In February, the CASIP (Comité d'Action Sociale Israélite de Paris), a philanthropic organization created in 1809, together with the Paris Consistory, organized "Tsedakah Sabbath." This gave the director of CASIP, Gabriel Vadnaï, an opportunity to publicize the fact that his association was providing full support for some 6,500 families and helping the hundred or so families who still came to France every year from North Africa, most of the time in difficult circumstances. CASIP's activity included a clothing service, an employment office, a students' residence, a residence for old people, and a day nursery. "What is important," said Vadnaï, "is that people know that there are in France Jews who are poor, Jews who are unemployed, Jews who are in a social situation of great precariousness. One should know that all Jews are not rich, that the poorest have not all gone to Israel, in contrast with what some would like to believe."

France acquired its first female rabbi in 1990. Rabbi Pauline Bebe, 26, who was ordained in London after three years' study at the Leo Baeck Institute, started her duties as a rabbi on September 1 in the synagogue of the Mouvement Juif Libéral de France (MJLF), created in 1977 by Rabbi Daniel Farhi. The MJLF community included some 1,200 families in Paris and belonged to the World Union of Liberal Judaism.

ISRAEL-RELATED ACTIVITY

The traditional solidarity of French Jewish institutions with Israel was reiterated on different occasions, such as the terrorist attack on a bus transporting Israeli tourists on the road between Cairo and Ismalia in Egypt, in which 10 people were killed and 16 wounded (February 5), an incident that produced intense emotion. In line with its official neutrality in Israeli affairs, the CRIF welcomed the new Israeli government constituted in June by expressing the wish that "in the traces of the peace process initiated by the former [Israeli] government, all efforts will be made to quickly conclude negotiations that will restore peace and put an end to all violence."

The consensus on Israel was disturbed, however, when former CRIF president Théo Klein allowed a letter to be published (*Jour J*, June 18) that he had sent to Israeli president Chaim Herzog on June 1. In the letter, Klein asked what he called an "anguished question," wondering whether, in the event that "the government of Israel was to refuse any meeting with a Palestinian delegation even close to PLO, we Jews in the Diaspora—fraternal allies of Israel directly concerned with its future— would not be led, if not morally forced, to explore the reality of a political opening newly proclaimed in the name of that organization." Klein insisted on the word "explore," which did not mean "negotiate," but his letter evoked strong reactions. CRIF president Jean Kahn repeated the terms of his June message, which he said expressed "the feeling of the whole Jewish community" and to which he was not willing to add anything, for the sake "of the unity of our community." Kahn stressed that Klein had expressed his own personal views (*Jour J*, June 19).

The reaction of the consistory was far more bitter. On June 20, *Jour J* published a message to President Herzog signed by Chief Rabbi Sitruk, Paris chief rabbi Alain Goldmann, the president of the Central Consistory, Jean-Paul Elkann, and the president of the Paris Consistory, Benny Cohen, expressing their "total confidence in the actions taken by Israeli leaders." They maintained that the "democratically appointed" Israeli government "should not be the object of any pressure from the Diaspora," and that "any person who would do so . . . should do it personally and not through the press." The summer vacation period and the tension in the Persian Gulf area more or less put an end to the polemics.

The incident in October on the Temple Mount in Jerusalem was met with a fairly embarrassed statement by CRIF (October 17), which declared that the organization "grieved for the dead of all religions in Beirut, Jerusalem, Kuwait, and the sufferings of the hostages of all countries detained in Iraq." CRIF added that "linking the oil problems, the physical destruction of the independent state of Kuwait, and the future of the Palestinians, went against both common sense and morals."

The Gulf crisis, above all the isolation of Israel—totally deprived of tourism in the last months of 1990—was a matter of deep concern to the Jewish community in this period. CRIF organized a "mission of solidarity" to Israel, with 400 participants, November 25–28. So did several other organizations, among them FSJU, which marked its 40th anniversary by sending a mass mission to Israel by way of Budapest, where the participants met Soviet immigrants and shared the same plane to Israel.

GERMAN UNIFICATION

The process of German unification was carefully followed in Jewish circles, with the full knowledge that whatever one's opinion, the process was ineluctable. Attention focused mainly on the acceptance by a unified Germany of its historical responsibilities. Apart from steps taken together with the head of the German Jewish community, CRIF president Kahn met with Lutz Stavenhagen, the German minister for European Affairs, on September 24, and expressed concern about the absence from the preamble of the unification treaty of any explicit allusion to the years 1933–1945. In an interview with *Le Figaro* (October 5), Kahn repeated his view that "the unification of Germany should not be made at the price of a partial, or, even worse, total, amnesia." But the next day, Kahn expressed his satisfaction with the statements of President Richard von Weizsäcker and Chancellor Helmut Kohl on German responsibility for "Jewish martyrdom" (*Le Monde*, October 6).

Internal Debates

Debate continued this year on the nature of the Jewish community and Jewish pluralism. *Les Nouveaux Cahiers*, the quarterly of the Alliance Israélite Universelle, devoted a large part of its 100th issue, published in the spring, to this question. It included a paper by historian Pierre Birnbaum on "Citizenship and Particularism," one by sociologist Martine Cohen under the title "From Integration . . . to Social Separatism?" in which the author wondered about "the weight of active minorities," and a debate chaired by David Kessler in which Rabbi Gilles Bernheim, philosopher Alain Finkielkraut, and philosopher Sylvie Jessua shared their thoughts on the confrontation between secular and religious Jews.

The nature of the relationship of Jews to the State of Israel became an issue when the French press reported a statement made by Chief Rabbi Sitruk in Israel: "Every Jew from France is a representative of Israel" (*Jour J,* July 10). Philosopher Alain Finkielkraut reacted angrily on a major radio station, saying that he "would have expected to find [those words] in the mouth of an anti-Semite rather than in the mouth of a chief rabbi" (*France-Inter*, July 10, quoted in *Jour J*, July 12). Rabbi Sitruk clarified his point in a statement the same day, in which he said: "I just wanted to express the idea that the Jewish people stand together all around the world and in Israel. . . . I did not have in mind the faintest idea of dual loyalty." He added: "The community does not talk with one voice. It is heterogeneous and pluralistic. I am tired of those maneuvers which try to oppose one part of the community to the other."

The question of Jewish communal representation was also at stake. The gentlemen's agreement that had been in force for several decades, dividing areas of responsibility between the major organizations (political representation to the CRIF, religious and moral authority to the consistories and the chief rabbi, culture and welfare to the FSJU), came under heavy questioning. In an interview with *Jour J* (June 26), the newly elected president of the Paris Consistory, Benny Cohen, was asked: "Are you entitled to speak in the name of the community?" He answered: "We are the only real representatives of the community. The Paris Consistory controls around a hundred synagogues. If one takes into account that two hundred people regularly attend [the services in] each synagogue, we represent 20,000 people. We are the first Jewish organization in France, probably in Europe, maybe in the world." Cohen also presented the chief rabbi of France as the leader of the Jewish community: "The recent events in Carpentras have shown that the leader of the Jewish community in France at the highest level is indeed the chief rabbi of France. I take as proof the presence of President Mitterrand at his home." Benny Cohen then questioned the authority of CRIF: "It is true that the CRIF represents many organizations, but those organizations do not represent very much. I do not see in whose name they speak." He concluded: "The Consistory is recognized and accepted by the entire population. We are very close to the community and the community is very close to us. . . ."

Cohen's statements highlighted a number of existing problems that went beyond institutional or personal ambitions. First, the gap between the size of the Jewish community (around 600,000) and the low rate of participation in Jewish communal life (including the consistories, even with the unavoidable links created through synagogues, weddings, divorces, burials, and consumption of kosher food). Second, the problem of the political representation of a body, the "Jewish community," which was more an aggregation of individuals than an officially constituted entity. Third, the growing conflict between advocates of unconditional support of Israel and a more critical stance, a conflict that CRIF perpetually sought to transcend by adopting "consensual" positions which neither satisfied nor dissatisfied anybody fully. Fourth was the question of the definition of the Jewish community as a religious or as a secular entity. And fifth was the ambiguous role played, consciously or not, by the French authorities. When President Mitterrand chose, after Carpentras, to pay a visit to the chief rabbi of France and not the president of CRIF, he might have (although there was no evidence) been demonstrating his discontent over the fierceness of CRIF's reactions in 1988–89 to the presence of Yasir Arafat in Strasbourg and then in Paris.

CRIF's answer to Benny Cohen took the form of an interview with its president, Jean Kahn, in *Jour J* (June 28). Kahn refered to his agreement with the chief rabbi of France "on a precise definition" of the role of each. If we acknowledged him, said Kahn, as the highest moral authority of the Jewish community in France, he himself wanted CRIF to maintain the political reponsibility for the community, as it had done for the last 40 years. Kahn offered his own experience as president of the Jewish community in Strasbourg as an example of what should be achieved on the national level: "I believe that I have been successful in protecting the unity of that community, since one finds there observant Jews, Jews who are less observant, and Jews who feel linked to Judaism only by cultural and historical ties."

The president of FSJU, David de Rothschild, tried to defuse the debate. "I might be wrong or I might be right, but I tend to think that there is neither a crisis nor a mini-crisis. There is a community leader who recently came into office [Cohen], . . . who made a sharp, a little hasty, a little inopportune statement. It happens. I am convinced that he is aware of that situation." Finally, on June 28, Chief Rabbi Sitruk, president of CRIF Jean Kahn, president of FSJU David de Rothschild, and president of the Paris Consistory Benny Cohen held a meeting and issued a communiqué in which they "jointly assessed the primacy of CRIF in the political representation of the Jewish institutions in France and reiterated their confidence in CRIF's leaders. They acknowledged the absolute necessity of a strengthened cooperation in order to make possible the harmonious coexistence of all trends of thought inside the community." The communiqué put an end to the quarrel and CRIF called on its members to behave as if nothing had happened.

Culture

A number of symposiums and study days took place this year, on more diverse subjects than usual. The 950th anniversary of Rashi's birth was marked by events throughout the year in Rashi's home city of Troyes, where the erection of a Rashi memorial was announced. In February the Rashi European Academic Institute (Institut universitaire européen Rachi, inaugurated in 1989, chaired by René-Samuel Sirat) organized a symposium on Rashi and Bernard de Clairvaux, the founder of the Benedictine monastic order. In April a study day was devoted by WIZO to the theme of "The Jewish Woman and Study." In July the European Association for Jewish Studies gathered several dozen academics from all over the world for a symposium, organized by Gabrielle Sed-Rajna and René-Samuel Sirat. In December, Gallia Judaica, a team of researchers directed by historian Gérard Nahon, held a symposium on the theme "Jewish Culture in Medieval Northern France: From Rashi to the Tosafists, the French Talmud."

Israeli culture was represented in Paris, from January to April, through dance, poetry (the poet Haim Gouri appeared at the Centre Georges Pompidou on February 12), art, and film (starting April 24, the Paris film library showed a series of Israeli films, 30 of them presented in France for the first time). Cinema was also the theme of the "Jewish Culture Days on the Screen" (February 3–8) in the Rachi Cultural Center in Paris, with a program prepared by the Institute for Audiovisual Jewish Memory (Institut de la Mémoire Audiovisuelle Juive).

A European convention of Sephardi youth took place in March—preparatory to the world Sephardi convention planned for the end of the year in Jerusalem—with delegations from Spain, Italy, Greece, Turkey, and Great Britain. The meetings focused on the theme of "Jews and Sephardim, an Identity, a Future." In May the World Jewish Congress, the Center for Hebrew Law (Centre de Droit Hébraïque) of Paris II University, and Paris I University offered a symposium on "Jews and Judaism in Europe After 1492," with the participation of several academics from Eastern Europe. Among the speakers were Michael Chlenov, member of the Moscow Academy of Science; Valeri Engel, president of the Moscow Jewish Historical Association; and, on the French side, Robert Badinter, René-Samuel Sirat, André Kaspi, Doris Bensimon, Mireille Hadas-Lebel, and Haim Vidal Sephiha. Also in May, European B'nai B'rith, WIZO, and the Union of French Jewish Students had a "day of reflection" in which, among others, Annie Kriegel, Joseph Rovan, and Alexandre Adler shared their feelings on "religion and politics in Eastern Europe," "the Jewish condition and the crisis of the nation-state," and "rebirth of anti-Semitism?" In October the Center for Contemporary Jewish Documentation (Centre de Documentation Juive Contemporaine, an archives and research center on the Holocaust) held a symposium organized by Renouveau Juif, the association of sons and daughters of Jewish deportees in France, and the commission for memory of CRIF. The subject was the status of the Jews under Vichy; the chairman was Robert Badinter.

The 1990 Buchman Prize for a work on the history of the Holocaust was awarded to journalist and writer André Frossard, member of the French Academy, a former Resistance member and victim of Klaus Barbie, who published *Le Crime contre l'humanité*, his testimony at the Barbie trial. The 31st colloquium of French-speaking intellectuals was to have taken place in mid-December, but various last-minute difficulties forced the organizers to cancel it.

From November 20 until January 31, 1991, the Museum of Jewish Art in Paris displayed a major exhibition of work by Devi Tuszynski ("the prince of miniature"), on the occasion of his 75th birthday.

In the Jewish press, the major event was the discontinuation of the daily *Jour J* after 15 months of existence. *Jour J* had announced a temporary stoppage in July for the summer vacation, but was unable to restart in September. Despite the widespread feeling in community circles that a daily was an indispensable source of information, *Jour J* had not been able to gather more than 1,400 subscribers, which was not sufficient to ensure its survival.

Publications

Among many books published in 1990, a number were devoted to World War II. *Robert et Jeanne. A Lyon sous l'Occupation* ("Robert and Jeanne: In Lyons during the occupation") by Annette Kahn evoked the memory of the author's parents, Jews and resisters, and their tragic story (the mother was deported to Auschwitz on August 11, 1944, and the father was executed in Lyons on August 24, 1944). *L'oeuvre de secours aux enfants (OSE) sous l'Occupation en France* ("The rescue of children under French occupation") by Sabine Zeitoun is an adaptation of the author's doctoral dissertation, a detailed study of the work of an organization devoted to saving children, which provides insights into the question of UGIF (the Jewish organization created by Vichy). In *Ces enfants qui nous manquent* ("Those children we miss"), Antoine Spire tries to reconstruct the route and life of the children of Izieu, chiefly through use of the letters they sent to their parents. Alain Michel's *L'étoile et la francisque—Des institutions juives sous Vichy* is based on the archives of the consistory during World War II, which were saved and kept after the war by the late Maurice Moch.

Several new publications were devoted to Jewish thought. These included *L'Ecclésiaste et son double araméen* (on Kohelet and its Targum) by Charles Mopsik; *Ouvertures hassidiques* ("Hassidic overtures") by Marc-Alain Ouaknin, an introduction to the world and thought of Hassidism; *Prophètes, talmudistes, philosophes* by Charles Touati, a collection of papers on the debates between Jewish thinkers from antiquity to modern times; and *La littérature rabbinique* by Maurice-Ruben Hayoun.

The attitudes of Christian intellectuals toward Jews and Judaism in medieval Europe is the subject of Gilbert Dahan's carefully documented work *Les intellectuels chrétiens et les juifs au Moyen-Age*. In *Amsterdam au temps de Spinoza, argent et liberté*, Henry Mechoulan analyzes the relationship between the spiritual debates and the economic and social conditions of Amsterdam in that period. Another historical work is a biography of the chief rabbi of the Ottoman Empire, Haim Nahoum, *Un grand rabbin sépharade en politique 1892–1923* by Esther Benbassa. In *Le Bosphore à la Roquette: la communauté judéo-espagnole à Paris: 1914–1940*, Annie Benveniste provides a sociological profile of a Judeo-Spanish community in Paris. Jean Baumgarten is the author of an introduction to the history of the Yiddish language, *Le yiddish*. The relationship of Marx and the Marxists to Judaism is treated in two books: Enzo Traverso's *Les marxistes et la question juive, histoire d'un débat (1843–1943)*, and Francis Kaplan's *Marx antisémite?* André Chouraqui's autobiography, *L'amour fort comme la mort* ("Love as strong as death"), could be considered both a historical document and an account of a fascinating life. The author was born in Algeria, fought in the Resistance in France in 1941, immigrated to Israel in 1956 and became deputy mayor of Jerusalem, where he constantly promoted dialogue and peace between peoples and translated into French both the Bible and the Koran.

Several new books were devoted to French or French-speaking Jewry. In the literary sphere, the *Anthologie des poètes juifs de langue française de la Renaissance à nos jours* by Jacques Eladan contains texts from four centuries. In a philosophical work, *La joie austère*, former chief rabbi René-Samuel Sirat engages in dialogue with interviewer Emmanuel Hirsch. In the area of sociology, in *Les enfants du juif errant* ("The children of the wandering Jew"), Fernande Schulmann presents the results of some 30 interviews with French-speaking Jews living in Israel. The development of the Jewish community in France since the Emancipation is the subject of a collective work published under the editorship of Pierre Birnbaum, *Histoire politique des juifs de France*, with contributions by, among several others, Phyllis Cohen Albert, Alain Dieckhoff, Dominique Schnapper, Aron Rodrigue, and Pierre-André Taguieff. In *Les juifs dans la politique française, de 1945 à nos jours*, Maurice Szafran discusses Jews and politics in France and the relations of Jewish politicians with their community. In *Mitterrand, Israël et les juifs*, Yves Azeroual and Yves Derai provide a journalistic account which contains—together with a few mistakes—some original documents, such as an account of the difficult meeting between the CRIF and President Mitterrand after Arafat's first visit to Paris. *Juif-en-France* is a collection of essays and articles by the former president of the Paris Consistory, Emile Touati, containing his reflections which, he explains in the introduction, are "not academic" but "rooted in the factual experience of a militant and a community leader."

Personalia

The following were made knights in the Order of the Legion of Honor: Albert Mallet, president of the local Jewish radio station Radio-Shalom; lawyer Yves Jouffa, president of the League for Human Rights; Raphael Hadas-Lebel, councillor of state; Gilberte Djian, former president of French WIZO and president of the French section of the World Jewish Congress; Jacques Lévy, general director of the Alliance Israélite Universelle; Dr. Jean Marx, honorary president of the Jewish community of Avignon; lawyer Joseph Roubache, founder of the France-Israel Association of Lawyers and president of the French committee of the International Association of Jewish Lawyers. The following were made officers of the Legion of Honor: Henry Bulawko, honorary president of CRIF; François Bernard, councillor of state and former principal private secretary of Minister of Defense Charles Hernu; Rabbi Charles Liché of the Place des Vosges Synagogue in Paris and president of an association providing financial aid to schools.

William Goldnadel, attorney and leader of Renouveau Juif, was elected president of the Center for Information and Documentation on Israel and the Middle East (CIDIP). Aude Weill-Raynal, lawyer, was elected vice-president. Marc Rocheman was elected the new president of the Union of Jewish Students in France (UEJF) in December 1989. David Kessler, philosopher and official at the Council of State, was chosen as the new president of the Jewish Liberal Movement in France (MJLF). Odette Kurz, president of the French section of WIZO, had to resign for personal reasons and was replaced by Nora Gaillaud-Hofman.

Among prominent Jews who died in 1990 were Rabbi Abraham Edery, director of Ozar Ha-Torah France, a network of Orthodox Jewish schools; Polish-born David Szmulenski, a pioneer in Palestine, fighter in Spain in 1936, Resistance fighter in France, arrested in 1941 and deported to Auschwitz after having been in several jails and camps, who stayed in Poland in 1945 and came back to France in 1968, aged 78; Henri Fiszbin, son of Jewish immigrants from Poland, former member of the Communist party, and leader of a breakaway group that joined the Socialist party in 1988, aged 59; Frédéric Rossif, born in Montenegro, lived in Paris since 1945, cinema and TV film producer (*Mourir à Madrid, Le Temps du Ghetto, Un Mur à Jérusalem, De Nuremberg à Nuremberg*), aged 68; Rabbi Israel Salzer, chief rabbi of Marseilles from 1929 to 1974, a translator of the Gemara into French, wartime chaplain in the underground, aged 85; Dr. Sigismond Hirsch, Resistance member arrested in 1943, later a member of both consistories, aged 84; André Amar, Salonikan-born, studied philosophy at the Ecole Normale Supérieure, member of the Jewish Resistance, arrested in July 1944, escaped from the last convoy to Auschwitz, helped organize postwar services for Jewish deportees, president of the executive of the United Jewish Appeal of France, member of the central committees of the Alliance and of the French section of the World Jewish Congress, member of the planning committee for the colloquiums of French-speaking intellectuals, banker, teacher of the history of ideas, and author, aged 82; Rabbi Haim Yaakov Rottenberg, head of the ultra-Orthodox community in France, founder of a yeshivah and a kollel (150 students) and the Yad Mordekhai network of schools (350 students); Emeric Kohn, born in Hungary, living in France since 1931, honorary director of the Paris Consistory, former secretary general of the Eclaireurs Israélites de France (the Jewish scouts), former head of the section for reception and rehabilitation in the Social Service for Youth, head of the section for fund raising in the FSJU, secretary general of CASIP, secretary general and later director of the Paris Consistory, aged 77; Jean Zacklad, teacher of philosophy in the Yavne Jewish secondary school and author, aged 61; Pierre Auer, president of the Association of Jewish Pharmacists in France, member of the commission for political studies of CRIF, organizer of interfaith meetings on ethics and recent medical research.

NELLY HANSSON

The Netherlands

National Affairs

THE YEAR 1990 WAS ONE OF relative political stability and economic prosperity in the Netherlands. Inflation was negligible—2¼ percent—half that of any other European Community country. However, because the government deficit necessitated cuts in the expenditures of most government departments and the institution of wage controls, the governing coalition (Christian Democrats—CDA, and Labor—PvdA)—which had taken office in 1989 with the slogan of "social renewal"—was unable to implement many of its campaign promises. Inevitable resentment among many of those usually voting Labor resulted in serious losses for that party during the municipal elections of March 21, particularly in Amsterdam, traditionally a Labor bulwark. The extreme right-wing Centrum Democrats (CD) and Centrum parties (CP) increased their representation from 0.9 percent to only 1.1 percent, thus—despite the mass presence of immigrants in the country—remaining a negligible factor.

Unemployment continued to drop, owing to increased job vacancies (though unemployment among recent immigrants remained high). Still, some very large firms announced layoffs, among them Philips Electronics, Fokker Aircraft, KLM Aviation, AKZO, and Shell. They blamed a variety of causes, such as the low exchange rate of the dollar and foreign competition, as well as high wages. It was expected that as a result of the newly relaxed relations between East and West, Dutch defense industries and the armed forces would have to be cut back. In fact, beginning October 29, compulsory service for young men of military age was reduced from 14 to 12 months.

At the end of November, the country registered its 15-millionth inhabitant. The number of Muslims, and, to a lesser extent, of Hindus and Buddhists—the latter two categories mainly so-called Hindustanis from Suriname—had risen dramatically. In 1960 there were only some 1,400 Muslims in Holland and 175 Hindus and Buddhists. In 1990 these figures had risen to 460,000 Muslims and 80,000 Hindus and Buddhists. Whereas in 1960 there had been only one mosque in the country, that of the Ahmadiyyah movement in The Hague, there were now at least 200 mosques, often in premises originally constructed for some other purpose. Nationally, the percentage of so-called *allochthones,* or immigrants, most of them from Asia and Africa, was about 6 percent, but higher in the big cities.

The number of those applying for political asylum amounted to some 22,000 in 1990. Among the applicants were several hundred Palestinians from Lebanon, Syria, and Jordan and some 200 Russian Jews. These 22,000 were in addition to

340

many thousands who were still awaiting a final decision on their applications. This process could take up to three years since applicants who were rejected could appeal twice to a higher court, with the help of specialized lawyers paid by the Ministry of Justice. Some 85 percent of the applications were rejected; however, of those who appealed, close to 62 percent were eventually recognized as political refugees. Many of those whose applications had been finally rejected were still allowed to remain in Holland for the time being, as "tolerated" refugees, because conditions in their countries of origin were too unstable. Throughout their stay in Holland, applicants for political asylum were housed at government expense in absorption centers. There were, in addition, 50,000 to 100,000 illegal residents in Holland.

The fight against environmental pollution was a matter of major concern. On June 14, the government announced a National Milieu Plan, with over $5 billion to be made available for clean-up in 1990, rising to $8 billion in 1994.

Gulf War

Following the Iraqi invasion of Kuwait on August 2 and the subsequent UN decision to place an embargo on Iraqi oil shipments, on August 13 the Dutch government agreed to send two navy frigates to the Persian Gulf, with a crew of 360, including 21 women, to help in enforcing the embargo. They left in September and were later joined by a navy supply ship. The entire Parliament had approved sending the vessels, with the exception of the Green Left—a merger of three extreme left-wing parties, including the Communists.

Between August and December, attention was focused on the fate of the 232 Dutch nationals stranded in Iraq and Kuwait—150 in Iraq and 82 in Kuwait—who were held as hostages there. Those in Iraq included 104 employees of two Dutch dredging companies who were engaged, under contract to Iraq, in dredging the Shatt-al-Arab near Umm al-Qasr. They were not actually considered hostages and for various reasons received little attention from the news media. After a few weeks, all the women, except one, and the children were allowed to leave for Holland. At the insistence of the Dutch government, the Dutch nationals in Kuwait were moved to Baghdad. These Dutch "hostages" included, in addition to a few stranded tourists, employees of Dutch firms and also private businessmen, many of whom had lived in Kuwait or Iraq for many years. A few managed to escape on their own.

Those remaining in Baghdad, as well as their relatives in Holland, who had formed a Committee of Relatives, became increasingly restive when some other countries, such as Belgium and West Germany, sent semi-official missions to Iraq to try and win the release of their own nationals, regardless of the material or political costs involved. Dutch foreign minister Hans van den Broek, however, refused to do the same, for reasons of principle, and his decision received Parliament's approval. Various attempts to send a delegation of the Committee of Relatives or an internationally known Dutch former politician as an emissary to Iraq came to nought. The hostages in Iraq sent a group open letter to the Dutch government demanding that it do everything possible to obtain their release, political principles notwithstanding. In the end, in December, Saddam Hussein suddenly allowed all of them to go. The 104 employees of the two dredging companies, who had actually completed their work in October, were allowed to leave Iraq a little later, along with their very valuable equipment, after protracted inspection by the Iraqi authorities of their work and after—so it was reported—the two firms had made important financial concessions.

Relations with Israel

The Dutch government continued to withhold diplomatic status from Afif Safieh, the PLO representative in The Hague and to consider him only as the director of the PLO Information Office. At his request, an informal meeting took place on April 24 between Foreign Minister van den Broek, himself, and Nabil Sha'ath, of PLO headquarters in Tunisia. The Arabs asked the foreign minister to use his good contacts with Israel and the United States to promote the peace process in the Middle East. Van den Broek in turn insisted that the PLO maintain its unconditional recognition of the State of Israel's right of existence and its renunciation of all terrorism and that it be unequivocal in its statements.

The Dutch Labor party, the PvdA, sent a delegation headed by its party chairwoman, Marianne Sint, to PLO headquarters in the spring, where it met with Yasir Arafat. The PLO leader urged the European Community to play a larger role in promoting an international peace conference on the Middle East.

In January the delegation of the Netherlands Council of Churches that had visited Israel and the occupied areas in September 1989, at the request of the Middle East Council of Churches (see AJYB 1991, p. 281), published its report, which was severely critical of Israel. Relations between the OJEC (the Consultative Council of Jews and Christians) and the Netherlands Council of Churches remained suspended throughout the year. The break occurred after the chairman of the Council of Churches, Prof. Dirk C. Mulder, spoke at a solidarity meeting with Palestinians in The Hague on November 23, 1989.

A delegation of the Middle East Council of Churches paid a visit to the Netherlands in the spring and addressed several meetings. On the advice of their hosts, the Netherlands Council of Churches, the group avoided contact with the OJEC and also with the Dutch branch of the International Council for Peace in the Middle East.

The Women in Black, a small, largely Jewish group, continued to hold their one-hour demonstrations in Amsterdam the second Friday afternoon of each month as a protest against Israel's rule over the occupied areas.

Zeev Suffoth, who had been Israel's ambassador to The Hague for five years, returned to Israel in September. He was succeeded by Michael N. Bavly. Afif Safieh was promoted to PLO representative in London in September. He was succeeded in The Hague by Leila Shahid, a granddaughter of Jamal al-Husseini.

Holocaust-Related Matters

The 50th anniversary of the German invasion of the Netherlands on May 10, 1940, and the 45th anniversary of the country's liberation on May 15, 1945, were observed on a grand scale with official ceremonies, national and local, and with a host of newspaper articles and features, radio and TV programs, and new books. In addition, a number of local monuments were unveiled, dedicated to those who fell during those years as members of the resistance and to Dutch Jews who perished.

On May 3, Dutch television presented the last, the 21st, segment of the documentary series "The Occupation," by Dr. Louis de Jong, former director of the Netherlands State Institute for War Documentation (and, incidentally, a Jew). The first of the weekly installments had been shown in December 1989. The series was a revision, based on new material, of a program first presented between 1960 and 1965. The series was also made available in book form.

A TV program of special Jewish interest was a documentary on the Westerbork transit camp for Jews, made by the Dutch-Jewish documentary filmmaker Willy Lindwer. In *Westerbork, Camp of Hope and Despair,* 17 survivors, some of them now living in Israel, were interviewed. The text of the documentary also appeared in book form and was slated to be published in English translation.

A number of older commercial films based on episodes during the German occupation of the Netherlands were shown again in this period. Films of Jewish interest included *The Ice Cream Parlor,* about the attack on the ice cream parlor owned by two German Jews in Amsterdam in February 1941 that led to the deportation of the first group of over 400 young Jews from that city.

A symposium on the impact of World War II on literature and art was held at the Protestant Free University in Amsterdam. The papers also appeared in book form, with the title *Overal Sporen* ("Traces Everywhere"), edited by D. H. Schram and C. Geljon.

The Netherlands State Institute for War Documentation (RIO), together with the Netherlands Historical Society and the Institute for Dutch History, organized a symposium in May: "Fifty Years After the Invasion," which dealt with World War II and the German occupation of the Netherlands. The younger generation of Dutch historians who took part tended to be critical of historians like Louis de Jong who, in their view, judged events too much in terms of "good" and "bad" and were too subjective, overly influenced by their personal experiences or those of their relatives. They also regarded the term "accommodation" as more suitable than "collaboration."

Among the exhibitions that opened for the anniversaries were "In Hiding" at the Resistance Museum in Amsterdam; "Posters 1940–45" at the Royal Library in The Hague; and "Liberation" at the Jewish Museum in Amsterdam. The Anne Frank Foundation produced nine video portraits in which nine eyewitnesses, including some Jews, told of their experiences during the war. Some of these videotapes—which were available to secondary schools and other institutions—were shown on television.

A historic phonograph record was reissued this year. Titled "Two Kids and a Guitar," it contained the songs of two leading Jewish cabaret artists of the 1930s—"Johnny and Jones" (Arnold van Wesel and Max Kannewasser). The men were imprisoned in Westerbork, where they performed, and from where they were eventually deported.

Compared with ten museums in Holland in 1980 which dealt with World War II and the German occupation of the Netherlands, either as their sole theme or as part of their exhibitions, there were now 20 such museums. Of these, six were devoted exclusively to this theme, two to the fate of the Jews—the one at Westerbork and the Anne Frank House in Amsterdam. The six museums together published a brochure about their programs, which sought not only to show what had happened in the past but also to make connections with the present and future and to warn against racism and discrimination.

The Anne Frank House drew 647,500 visitors in 1990, against some 600,000 in 1989. This placed it third in museum attendance in Amsterdam, after the Rijksmuseum, noted for its Rembrandts, and the Van Gogh Museum.

A group of private individuals proposed to establish a new monument at Westerbork, in addition to the 1971 railway-track monument designed by Ralph Prins. The new work would consist of 102,000 stones—for the 102,000 persons deported from the camp to their deaths—costing 25 Dutch florins ($1.25) each.

A new book about World War II, by Gerard Aalders and Cees Wiebes, published both in Dutch and in Swedish, described the economic collaboration with Nazi Germany of the Swedish Wallenberg Bank, headed by two uncles of Raoul Wallenberg. The authors suggest that this connection may have played a role in the diplomat's arrest by the Soviets in Budapest in January 1945.

The Jewish Social Welfare Foundation (Joods Maatschappelijk Werk, JMW), whose work until recently largely involved processing applications for government payments under the law for payments to war victims (WUV), now devoted much of its attention to the problems of the "second generation," the children of survivors. To that end, in June it organized a weekend for second-generation Jews or "persons with a Jewish background," which attracted 160 participants and was subsidized by the Ministry of Social Welfare and Culture. For many of the participants, this was their first contact with a large group of other Jews. In addition to these 160, some 300 others showed an interest in the counseling offered by the JMW. Among its other activities, the organization decided to arrange regional meetings and discussion groups in which problems of Jewish identity could be dealt with. It also commissioned a playwright to write about the relationships of second-generation Jews with their parents. The resulting play was performed in 20 locations all over the country by a small company consisting entirely of non-Jewish actors.

On the occasion of its tenth anniversary, the Information and Coordination Organization for Service to War Victims, or ICODO, organized the Second European Conference on Post-Traumatic Stress, held September 23–27. The ICODO, which deals with all kinds of traumatic experiences resulting from World War II, and which cooperates closely with the JMW but does not work exclusively with Jews, now gave attention as well to the problems of children of Dutch Nazi parents. A special foundation, KOMBI, financed by the ICODO, which in turn was subsidized by the Ministry of Social Welfare and Culture, organized encounter groups of children of war victims, Jewish and otherwise, with children of Nazi parents.

Anti-Semitism

As in 1989, few cases of overt anti-Semitism were reported in 1990, according to STIBA, the Foundation for Combating Anti-Semitism in the Netherlands. On February 11, STIBA celebrated its tenth anniversary with a symposium, "The Holocaust and the Present," in Amsterdam. Among the participants were Raul Hilberg of the United States and the West German ambassador to The Hague, Otto von der Gablentz (who was appointed ambassador to Israel in October).

One episode this year aroused controversy and charges of anti-Semitism. It concerned a retired professor of sociology and publicist, Johan A. A. van Doorn. Commenting in his regular weekly column of October 18 in the daily *NRC Handelsblad* on the clash on the Temple Mount in Jerusalem in which a number of Palestinians were killed by local police, van Doorn—who on several previous occasions had given indication that he did not like Jews—wrote that not only did Israel apply censorship to journalists there but that "Jewish journalists" elsewhere were expected to practice self-censorship with regard to Israel. This ignited a storm of protests. When asked by the newspaper to apologize, he did so only half-heartedly, at the same time offering "evidence" for his allegation about Jewish journalists. The paper then wrote that van Doorn had "exceeded the limits of propriety," which in turn caused a new storm of protests that the *NRC Handelsblad* had restricted a journalist's freedom of expression. Van Doorn himself then resigned, but immediately found employment as a columnist for the weekly *Haagse Post.*

JEWISH COMMUNITY

Demography

The total number of Jews in the Netherlands was estimated to be about 25,000, the large majority of whom were unaffiliated with the Jewish community.

The Netherlands Ashkenazi community (Nederlands Israelitisch Kerkgenootschap, NIK) this year introduced a different method of counting its members, including as such only those who gave positive evidence of wanting to be considered members. It arrived at a membership of some 6,000, of whom over half were in Amsterdam and the adjoining suburb of Amstelveen. The Hague area and the Rotterdam area each had some 400 members. The remainder were divided among 30 communities, 10 of them medium-sized, with from 220 to 85 members, and 20 smaller.

Communal Affairs

In May the NIK celebrated the 175th anniversary of its founding with a gala concert by eight famous cantors from Israel, the United States, and Canada, held in the large Sephardi synagogue and attended by some 1,300 persons. Interest in the event was so great that many who wanted tickets had to be refused for lack of space. (A cassette of the concert was later made available.)

In connection with the anniversary, the NIK prepared a documentary on its history, which was shown on television, and published a booklet about the organization and its activities. In addition, the NIK contributed the sum of 100,000 Dutch florins ($50,000) for a social-cultural center for the absorption of Jews from the Soviet Union in Kiryat Gat in Israel and funds for two projects in the USSR: a monthlong Jewish education seminar in Moscow in August, which was attended by some 60 future teachers from all over the Soviet Union, and two Jewish day nurseries, in Kharkov in the Ukraine and in Tashkent. The projects were undertaken together with the Mahanayim Jewish Heritage Center in Jerusalem and Moscow.

In Amsterdam the three communal rabbis reached agreement on new procedures for *kashrut* supervision and ritual slaughtering. According to one of the three, Frank Lewis, a newcomer from Great Britain, the system had not been strict enough. The Jewish Communal Center of the Amsterdam Ashkenazi community, located in Van der Boechorst Street, underwent extensive renovations this year. A new, modern, kosher vegetarian restaurant opened in Amsterdam, called Hatikvah.

The first section of the new Beth Shalom Old Age Home, consisting of 66 semidetached apartments, was officially opened in November in the southern suburb of Buitenveldert, now the center of Jewish life in Amsterdam. It replaced the ten-year-old Beth Shalom in the western suburb of Osdorp, which was situated too far from most of Amsterdam's Jews.

The Ashkenazi community of Maastricht, which now included the whole of the province of Limburg, in the extreme south of the country, celebrated the 150th anniversary of its synagogue with a special religious service, an exhibition, and the publication of a book on the history of the community.

A delegation of The Hague Ashkenazi community, led by Rabbi Pinchas Meijers, paid a fortnight's visit to Suriname, former Dutch Guiana, in November, to see what religious and cultural help it could offer to the 120 or so Jews left there, about half of whom were under 18 years of age. The majority of the former Suriname Jews had emigrated to the United States, the Netherlands, or Israel. Those remaining were still divided between two congregations, the Sephardi Tsedek VeShalom and the Ashkenazi Neve Shalom, with Sabbath services alternating between the two synagogues. Among the problems discussed were obtaining kosher meat, supervision of the mikveh, and treatment of persons wanting to belong to the Jewish community who were not Jewish according to Halakhah. The Jews of Paramaribo—the capital, where most of the Jews of Suriname lived—had not had a full-time rabbi for some 20 years.

The Sephardi or Portuguese community in the Netherlands had some 600 members. A major problem facing it was the need to make repairs costing nearly $4 million to its famous Esnoga, a synagogue over 300 years old in Amsterdam. Half of this sum would be covered by government and municipal subsidies, but the remainder had to be raised elsewhere. For this purpose, a committee of Jews and non-Jews was formed, and a fund-raising campaign was started both in the Netherlands and in the United States. Some members of the Amsterdam Sephardi community took the view that since nearly all members now lived beyond walking distance from this famous building, priority should be given to constructing a modest new synagogue in the south of Amsterdam. A related problem was the deterioration of the books and manuscripts in the famous Etz Hayim Library in the annex to the Esnoga, due to the effects of climate.

The Liberal Jewish community had six congregations, of which only those in Amsterdam and The Hague held regular Sabbath services and had rabbis of their own. Together they had some two thousand members. The Leo Baeck Liberal Elementary Day School, which had opened three years earlier, closed its doors in November. Enrollment had fallen to 20 pupils, and the new, non-Jewish, principal, who had started his duties at the beginning of the school year, resigned after only one month.

Following the example of the United States, a modest beginning in interdenominational Jewish dialogue was made in January, with a public meeting attended by members of the Orthodox and Liberal communities. The event was organized by the ad hoc CLAL group. Owing to criticism, the meetings were not continued. However, the three communities—Ashkenazi, Sephardi, and Liberal—cooperated on a number of Jewish issues of common concern, in particular preparations for support to Israel in the event of a Gulf War.

Shalhomo, the Society of Jewish Homosexuals and Lesbians in Holland, organized the Second European Conference of Jewish Homosexuals and Lesbians in Amsterdam in April, with the participation of some 120 persons from 11 European countries. The conference was subsidized jointly by the JMW, the Jewish Social Welfare Foundation in Holland, and the COC, the Netherlands Society of Homosexuals.

Zionism and Israel

As early as the first half of August, when the possibility of a war was envisaged, the executive of the Netherlands Zionist Organization (NZB) took the initiative in establishing an Israel Coordination Bureau. It included representatives of the three nationwide religious communities, the United Israel Appeal (CIA), and the Center for Information and Documentation on Israel (CIDI). In November three non-Jewish pro-Israel organizations joined the bureau: the Israel Committee Netherlands, the Christians for Israel Society, and the Society Netherlands-Israel. The bureau's headquarters were in the offices of the NZB.

Apart from this project, activity within the NZB, in particular in its local branches, was almost nonexistent. At its annual conference in February, at the suggestion of Liberal rabbi David Lilienthal of Amsterdam, the delegates decided, by a small majority, to study the possibility of transforming the NZB into a federation of Zionist parties, in the hope of increasing active participation. A commission was appointed to work out suitable plans.

The United Israel Appeal (called CIA in the Netherlands) this year received a record $5,550,000, of which $4,300,000 was in gifts and $1,250,000 in legacies and wills. While the legacies and wills portion remained more or less stable, cash contributions rose by two million dollars, a response to the campaign for absorption of Soviet Jews in Israel.

Culture

Dr. Rena Mansfeld Fuks delivered her inaugural address as Professor Extraordinary in Jewish History at the University of Amsterdam on February 14. The three-year position was part of a rotating chair established by the Jewish Studies Foundation and was financed by the Jewish Social Welfare Foundation (JMW) with funds received from the government.

The Bibliotheca Rosenthaliana, the Hebraica and Judaica department of the Amsterdam University Library, organized an exhibition of Hebrew incunabula in Dutch libraries, accompanied by a catalogue written by one of the two librarians of the Rosenthaliana, Adrian K. Offenberg.

From April to September, the Jewish Historical Museum exhibited "The Image of the Word: Jewish Tradition in Manuscripts and Books." Most of the works exhibited came from the Rosenthaliana and from other Dutch public and private collections. An important loan came from the Carl Alexander Floersheim Trust for Judaica in Bermuda, established by Michael Floersheim, now of New York but formerly of Amsterdam, in memory of his father. A fine illustrated catalogue in English was published with the financial support of the Yona and Michael Floersheim Charity Foundation in the United States.

There was a surprising growth of interest in Yiddish culture among a group of young people in Amsterdam—some with Jewish backgrounds, others without—who were also extremely critical of Israel. Many of them were members of the group known as "Blanes" (the name of a prewar Jewish street hawker famous for his cry "You must look inside"—not just outside). A Yiddish cabaret group, Galle, began performing this year, and the tiny St. Anthony Theater, with a non-Jewish director, became a venue for Yiddish music. Several of the performers in both were non-Jews.

Publications

The most important new publication this year was *Amsterdam Chazzanuth,* in Dutch and in English, by Hans Bloemendal, the chief cantor of the main Amsterdam Ashkenazi Synagogue for the past 40 years. This two-volume 500-page work, with musical annotation, contained 111 Amsterdam synagogue melodies, 12 of them composed by Bloemendal himself, along with essays by him on Amsterdam synagogue music, and a list of the 25 Ashkenazi hazzanim who had officiated in Amsterdam since 1635.

Also of interest was *The Amsterdam Diamond Exchange*, in Dutch and in English, by Simone Lipschitz. The book was published on the occasion of the transfer of the Amsterdam Diamond Exchange from its 80-year-old building in Weesper Square, in the Jewish quarter, to more modern premises in the southern part of Amsterdam.

Of the many new works published only in Dutch mention may be made of *Anne en Jopie* by Jacqueline van Maarsen. The author claims that she and not Eva Schloss was Anne Frank's closest girlfriend, and that Eva Schloss hardly knew her.

Personalia

Among Jews honored in the Queen's birthday list this year were Dr. Emanuel Wikler, chairman of the Netherlands Ashkenazi community (NIK).

The list of prominent Jews who died this year included Salomon Boas, aged 77, from 1945 on a leader in the Ashkenazi community, the Netherlands Zionist Organization, and many other Jewish organizations, in addition to his work as a lawyer and as a justice on the Amsterdam Higher Court of Justice; Salomon Elzas, aged 68, a former chairman of the Ashkenazi community of The Hague; Leo (Leib) Fuks, aged 81, librarian of the Bibliotheca Rosenthaliana from 1949 till 1973 and an expert on Yiddish; Prof. Juda J. Groen, aged 86, one of the pioneer researchers in psychosomatic illness; Dr. David Hausdorf, aged 85, for many years after the war chairman of the Ashkenazi community of Rotterdam and author of a standard work on its history; Icek Rafalowitz, aged 91, born in Poland, a founder and longtime chairman of the Anski Yiddish Cultural Society, in Amsterdam; Bernard van Tijn, aged 90, for many years a leader of Poale Zion in Holland.

HENRIETTE BOAS

Italy

National Affairs

THERE WAS NO SIGNIFICANT CHANGE in the Italian political framework in 1990. Prime Minister Giulio Andreotti, a Christian Democrat, retained leadership of a delicately balanced coalition government that included Socialists Claudio Martelli as deputy prime minister and Gianni De Michelis as foreign minister.

The Mafia's increasing power and flaunting of authority were high on the list of domestic concerns. Trials continued against the Mafia in Sicily and the Camorra organization in the Naples area, but the war on the criminal faction was severely hampered by public fear and the presumed connections between the Mafia and important political personalities.

Middle East

Two events of international significance also figured prominently on the Italian political scene: PLO leader Yasir Arafat's visit to Europe and the Persian Gulf crisis.

Yasir Arafat, after meeting with French president François Mitterrand, visited Italy April 5–7, where he was welcomed with enthusiasm by leaders of the principal political organizations and trade unions. Arafat was also received by President of the Republic Francesco Cossiga, Prime Minister Andreotti, and President of the Senate Giovanni Spadolini. He asked the Italian government to help stop the immigration of Soviet Jews to Israel and to press for the Palestinians to have their own delegation at the proposed international peace conference.

The reaction of the Italian government to the Iraqi invasion of Kuwait on August 2, which marked the beginning of the Persian Gulf crisis, was ambiguous. Before the actual invasion, the government attempted to draw subtle moral and political distinctions in an effort to downplay any responsibility toward its American ally. After the invasion, Italy sent two frigates, not to the center of the crisis area but to the eastern Mediterranean. During debate on the subject in the Chamber of Deputies, some Catholic and Communist groups tried to link the Gulf crisis to the Arab-Israeli conflict, and Prime Minister Andreotti, in keeping with his pro-Arab sympathies, strongly reiterated his condemnation of the Israeli raid on the Iraqi atomic reactor in 1981. Subsequently, faced with a perplexed and nervous American reaction to its ambivalence, and unhappy with Arafat's unconditional support of Saddam Hussein, the Italian government modified its policy. In September the frigates were moved to the Persian Gulf, and eight Tornado warplanes were sent, with a small contingent of men, to Saudi Arabia.

Relations with Israel

Despite differences of opinion between Israel and Italy on many questions, the two countries worked together to strengthen their political, economic, and cultural ties, looking forward to Israel's prospective integration into the European Community (EC) in 1992.

On March 27, an Italian delegation visited Israel's eighth "Agritech," the most important exhibition of technical innovations in Israeli agriculture. The Italian group, which included members of the Italian Parliament and agriculture officials, met with Israeli politicians and visited farms and kibbutzim.

Italian and Israeli researchers and experts in agricultural genetics attended a three-day conference in Israel, in late March, organized by the Weizmann Institute of Science in Rehovot. A similar meeting was held in Rome in 1978, sponsored by the Accademia dei Lincei. Prof. Francesco D'Amato of Pisa University led the Italian delegation; Prof. Esra Galun, dean of the Biology Faculty at Weizmann, headed the Israeli representation.

The mayor of Naples, Pietro Lezzi, attended an international meeting of mayors in Jerusalem, where he delivered an address on "The Mayor as Ambassador, as First Citizen, and as Administrator," in which he proposed a negotiated solution to the Palestinian problem. Lezzi had last been in Israel in 1974 with a delegation of the Socialist International visiting the Middle East.

Representing the EC Council of Ministers, Italy's minister of foreign affairs, Gianni De Michelis, together with fellow foreign ministers Gerald Collins of Ireland and Jacques Poos of Luxembourg, arrived in Israel July 23. In discussions with Israeli foreign minister David Levy, the "troika" raised a number of issues, including the role of the EC in the Middle East peace process and the tremendous economic potential of relations between the Jewish state and the European Community.

In October, when the Israeli government (in part under pressure from the EC) dropped its protectionist ban on imported pasta products, there began what the Israeli press described as the "pasta war," between Osem, the major domestic producer of pasta, and three other Israeli companies—Elite, Vita, and A.R. Willinger. Those firms imported from Italy the products of, respectively, Barilla, La Molisana, and Federici. The Osem Company lost its battle against free importation of pasta but did persuade the Ministry of Industry and Trade to impose an import duty on the European product.

The general secretary of Italy's Ministry of Foreign Affairs, Bruno Bottai, visited Israel in November, meeting with Prime Minister Yitzhak Shamir, Foreign Minister David Levy, opposition leader Shimon Peres, and the Latin patriarch Michel Sabah. Discussions focused on the Gulf crisis and the Palestinian question. Bottai emphasized the fact that the Jewish state is the only parliamentary democracy in the Middle East.

Political sources in Jerusalem confirmed that, thanks to Italian mediation, the first of 500 Albanian Jewish families arrived in Israel on December 31. According to the

Israeli newspaper *Ma'ariv*, the Israeli ambassador to Italy, Mordechai Drory, was able to bring about the exodus through contacts with the Albanian embassy in Rome, secretly fostered by the Italian government.

Anti-Semitism

A public-opinion poll on prejudice, sponsored by the Center for Contemporary Jewish Documentation (Centro di Documentazione Ebraica Contemporanea, CDEC) of Milan, found that 10 percent of the adult Italian population displayed anti-Semitic feelings. The phenomenon of anti-Semitism, according to Adriana Goldstaub, head of the anti-Semitism section of CDEC, appeared to increase proportionally with the rise in intolerance shown toward blacks.

Some anti-Semitic fallout occurred in connection with the trials this year of Abel and Furlan, two young neo-Nazis from Verona who were convicted of killing several prostitutes, homosexuals, and a priest, in the years 1985–1988. According to Goldstaub, 400 anonymous threatening letters were sent in February and March to families with Jewish surnames in Veneto and Trentino, two regions in the northeast of Italy. The letters were signed by the Gruppo Armato Nazifascista (Armed Nazi Fascist Group). In the same period, in Florence, handbills were distributed praising the "Goebbels Brigades," signed by the Fronte per la liberazione da negri, ebrei e zingari (Front for Liberation from Blacks, Jews, and Gypsies). Later, leaflets were found, signed by the mysterious Ordine Ariano (Aryan Order) and containing a picture of a crematorium and death threats to the non-European "*Untermenschen*," which included Africans and Jews.

On July 12, the Italian branch of the International Association of Jewish Lawyers and Jurists presented a round-table conference on anti-Semitism in Italy and Europe. Tullia Zevi, president of the Union of Italian Jewish Communities (Unione delle Comunità Ebraiche Italiane, UCEI), and the president of the Jewish community of Rome, Sergio Frassineti, opened the conference. Chief Rabbi Elio Toaff of Rome; the rector of the Lateran University, Monsignor Rossano; President of the Republic Cossiga; and President of the Senate Spadolini attended the meeting, which took place in the Parliament building, in the presence of numerous political representatives.

The newly formed Italian committee "Christians Against Anti-Semitism" had its first meeting in Rome on October 10. The group, which is chaired by Annie Cagiati, a leader in Catholic-Jewish dialogue, intends to serve as a forum for those who want to resist anti-Jewish prejudice in Italian society.

On January 17, an article by Dacia Valent, Communist Euro-deputy, appeared in the Italian magazine *Avvenimenti*. She described Israel as the most racist country in the world because, she said, just like their "Nazi jailers," the Jews call themselves the chosen people. She added that, like the Nazis, the Israeli government used criminal propaganda to justify genocide as the only solution to the Palestinian problem. On January 31, following publication of the article, the chairman of the

Italian Communist party (PCI), Achille Occhetto, sent a letter to the Israeli ambassador in Rome, Mordechai Drory, in which he stated that Valent's article did not reflect PCI opinion. He referred to a reply written by Chiara Ingrao, member of the PCI Central Committee and head of the Italian delegation to the international peace demonstration in Jerusalem on December 30, 1989, which appeared in *Avvenimenti*. On February 2, Piero Fassino, of the PCI national secretariat, sent a letter to the president of the Rome Jewish community, Sergio Frassineti, in which he affirmed that the offensive and defamatory article reflected Valent's personal opinion. Dacia Valent was not an official member of the PCI, but had been elected as an independent within the Communist party in the last European election.

On May 14, the Rome Jewish community sponsored a public gathering to express its sorrow and rage over the desecration of Jewish graves in Carpentras, France, five days earlier. The rally was attended by President of the Republic Cossiga, Deputy Prime Minister Martelli, President of the Chamber of Deputies Nilde Jotti, and numerous other political figures. Cossiga's speech was followed by a prayer service, addresses by the president of the community, Frassineti (who said that Italian Jews had full confidence in their country's rule of law, as represented by the president of the Republic), Israeli ambassador Drory, and a doleful rendition of *Ani Maamin* by a chorus. On the same day, the Jewish youth group Federazione Giovanile Ebraica (FGEI) organized a sit-in in front of the French embassy, attended by the youth organizations of the Republican and left-wing parties.

Nazi War Criminals

The Simon Wiesenthal Center of Vienna continued its project, begun in 1989, of collecting information on World War II crimes perpetrated in Italy's northern regions. One objective was to bring to justice Erich Priebke, the Gestapo officer responsible in the area between Bolzano and Brescia, who was accused of committing atrocities against the civilian population.

JEWISH COMMUNITY

Demography

An estimated 32,000 Jews were affiliated with local Jewish communities.

Communal Affairs

The Rome Jewish community, heretofore relatively uninvolved with the situation of Soviet Jewry, this year answered the appeal of the State of Israel for financial aid to help absorb Soviet Jews. On February 19, a big rally supporting Jewish immigration from the Soviet Union took place in Rome at Beth El Synagogue. It was sponsored by the Keren Hayesod and organized by Rafi Luzon.

On February 26, the new academic year of the Italian Rabbinical College-Institute of Advanced Jewish Studies opened in Rome. This inauguration was particularly important because for the first time, according to the 1987 *"Intesa"* (agreement) between the Jewish community and the Italian state, which gives Judaism equal legal standing with other religions, the degree conferred by the college now enjoyed full recognition. Chief Rabbi Toaff presided over the ceremony, while Ariel Toaff, professor of Italian Jewish history at Bar Ilan University, Israel, gave the inaugural lecture.

The 12th conference of the Italian Zionist Federation (FSI) took place in Leghorn on April 29. The president of the local Jewish community, Paola Jarach Bedarida, opened the meetings, attended also by the city's mayor, the Israeli consul in Milan, and the president of the Jewish Lawyers' Association. The FSI continued to play an important role within Italian Jewry, in carrying out public-relations activity directed at political party leaders and the mass media in Israel's behalf.

Tullia Zevi represented Italian Jews at the historic meeting, on May 6, of the World Jewish Congress (WJC), in Berlin, the first such meeting to take place in Germany in 60 years. In the presence of Chancellor Helmut Kohl, WJC president Edgar Bronfman delivered the opening speech, in which he underscored the necessity for both Jews and Germans "not to forget." Referring to the imminent political union of the two Germanys, he maintained that Jews never asked for a recognition of collective blame but an admission of common responsibility. In her remarks, Zevi stressed the importance of retaining historical memory so that younger generations would know what had happened to European Jewry before and during World War II.

On May 26, the second conference of Jewish progressive movements took place in Leghorn. The meeting was organized by the Martin Buber Group of Rome, the Nahum Goldman and Left for Israel organizations of Milan, and by Jewish Studies of Turin. The final resolution passed by the conference expressed deep concern for what was happening in Israel and in the West Bank, "revealing a moral degradation provoked by the prolonged occupation and the refusal to start serious peace negotiations based on mutual recognition between Israelis and Palestinians."

In February, UCEI president Tullia Zevi met with representatives of the Associazione Nazionale ex-Deportati (ANED), a group of Jews and non-Jews who survived the Nazi concentration camps, to discuss the sorry condition of the Italian pavilion at Auschwitz. It was decided to ask the Italian government to intervene in seeking a swift solution of the problem. In June, representatives of the European Jewish communities met in Paris to discuss various concerns relating to the preservation of the Auschwitz-Birkenau concentration camp. The Italian delegation, representing the UCEI, offered Italian Jewry's unconditional support for the restoration project as well as the planned international dialogue center and the removal of the Carmelite nuns from the camp to a new site.

The most important event of the Jewish year was the first congress of the renamed

Unione delle Comunità Ebraiche Italiane (UCEI),[1] which took place in Rome on December 9. It was the first meeting of that body since the signing of the agreement (*Intesa*) with the Italian state, which replaced the 1930 Fascist law, and after the passage of new laws regulating the community's internal life. (See AJYB 1991, p. 294, and AJYB 1989, pp. 328–30.) Twenty-one communities were represented by a total of 92 delegates, half appointed by the communities' councils and the other half selected by the communities' members. Rome had the largest delegation with 36 delegates; Parma and Casale Monferrato were the smallest, with one delegate each. Under the new system, Jewish Italy was divided into three districts: north, center, and south. The rabbinate was represented by five rabbis from Rome and Milan. Tullia Zevi was confirmed by acclamation as president of the UCEI.

Among the problems facing the congress was that of determining the amount of each community's financial contribution to the central body, the Council of the UCEI. Another issue was the Lubavitch presence and activities in Italy. Relations between the Italian rabbinate and the Lubavitch movement appeared to be most tense in Bologna, where a conflict between the local community and the Chabad movement even went to court. The congress approved a resolution urging closer collaboration between the Lubavitch movement and the Rabbinical Assembly. At the same time, it emphasized the need for adherence to community rules and acceptance of the institutions and rabbinical authority developed by Italian Jewry in the course of centuries, in full respect for both Mosaic law and Jewish tradition. The congress urged that greater attention be paid to disseminating Jewish culture and education, to which end a special committee was established. The final resolution reaffirmed the indissoluble bond between Italian Jewry and the State of Israel.

Community Relations

On January 31, a joint statement was issued by the UCEI and UCE (the Union of the Evangelical Churches—all the non-Catholic Christian religious confessions) in response to an order from the Ministry of Education requiring students who did not wish to attend the optional Catholic religion class or an alternative class to remain in school. The two groups charged that this requirement violated the constitutional principle of equality as well as obligations undertaken by the Italian government toward the non-Catholic religions. The Regional Council Administrative Court (TAR) accepted the appeal of the UCEI and UCE in February; however, subsequent action by the minister of education left the matter unresolved.

Two leaders of the Italian Jewish community, Tullia Zevi and Rabbi Elio Toaff, met with Italian political figures on various occasions, on community matters. On February 14, Zevi, together with Seymour Reich, chairman of the Conference of Presidents of Major Jewish Organizations in the United States, met with Prime Minister Giulio Andreotti to discuss Jewish emigration from the USSR to Israel and

---

[1]Formerly UCII. One word was changed in 1987 from "Israelitiche" to "Ebraiche."

the political situation in the Middle East. On April 4, Zevi met with President Francesco Cossiga to voice the general opposition of Italian Jews to Yasir Arafat's visit to Italy. Two days after this meeting, on April 6, Rabbi Toaff was received by President of the Senate Spadolini, who emphasized that the problem of Soviet Jewish emigration to Israel should be treated as a human-rights issue, not a political one.

Jewish-Christian Relations

The 1965 declaration of the Second Vatican Council, *Nostra Aetate*, concerning relations between Jews and Catholics, was read in all Italian churches on January 17, following a decision by the Italian Episcopal Conference (CEI). The bishops also declared a "Day of Judaism" to be observed in January. In Rome, the "day" was highlighted by a meeting between Monsignor Clemente Riva, Tullia Zevi, Chief Rabbi Toaff, and Maria Vingiani, president of the Ecumenical Activities Conference. Also in January, in Parma, a round-table discussion was organized by the CEI and the local Jewish community. The meeting was chaired by the Methodist minister Aquilante, professor of biblical science at Bologna Religious Seminary, Rabbi Kapciowski, and Fausto Levi, president of the local Jewish community.

Culture

In Ferrara, on March 18, the president of the Chamber of Deputies, Nilde Jotti, together with Tullia Zevi, opened the exhibition "*I Tal Ya*" (Isle of the Divine Dew), the Italian version of the American show "Gardens and Ghettos: The Art of Jewish Life in Italy," organized by the Jewish Museum of New York in 1989. The exhibition was divided into four time periods: the Roman Empire (to the 13th century), featuring sarcophagi, bas-reliefs, and precious archaeological finds; the Middle Ages and the Renaissance (13th to 16th centuries), with illuminated manuscripts, the first examples of Jewish book printing, silver, fabrics, and ritual objects; the Age of the Ghettos (16th to 19th centuries), with synagogue furnishings, ritual objects, and artifacts of daily life. Some new objects, not part of the American exhibition, were the Baroque *bimah* of the Carmagnola Synagogue and the precious *aron* (ark) of Livorno. The final section covered the modern period, including a display of works by Jewish artists, among them Ulvi Liegi, Vittorio Corcos, Amadeo Modigliani, Antonietta Rafael Mafai, and Carlo Levi. The exhibition was sponsored by the Ferrara Municipality, the Institute for Artistic and Cultural Properties of the Emilia Romagna Region, the Jewish Museum of New York, and the UCEI.

Official approval was granted in April for the restoration of the Pesaro Synagogue, a fine example of 17th-century Jewish architecture. After restoration, it will be used by the Pesaro municipality, according to the agreement between the UCEI and the municipality, for cultural events, festivals, and exhibitions.

On May 3, the National Jewish Bibliographic Center (Centro Bibliografico dell'-Ebraismo Italiano) in Rome was officially dedicated by Tullia Zevi and Rabbi Toaff.

Created at the initiative of the UCEI, with the financial participation of the Lazio Region, the Rome Province, and the Doron Foundation, the center aims to become the first national library of Italian Jewry, consolidating the archives and books belonging to all the separate Italian Jewish communities. Some 25,000 volumes were already cataloged and stored temporarily in local Jewish schools, awaiting final disposition. The center will eventually have a large audiovisual section on the history, culture, and traditions of the Diaspora's oldest Jewish community, as well as a music section. Rabbi Toaff affixed the ritual mezuzah, an object that inspired the ceramic sculpture by Ariela Bohm in the center's hall. Emanuele Luzzati painted the vault of the main room with themes evoking the wooden synagogues of Central Europe. Akira Kimura made the map of the Jewish settlement that hangs on the wall.

An urban renewal plan for the area of Rome's Jewish ghetto was officially unveiled on April 19, during a meeting organized by the Jewish Cultural Center and the "Centro di studi partecipazione." Local officials approved the project. The ghetto not only is a place of great historic and cultural significance, but is located in one of the most beautiful parts of Rome, surrounded by the Campidoglio, the Roman Forum, the Tiberina Island, and squares with fountains. The restoration of the ghetto was entrusted to a group of leading architects, including Benedetti, Fiorentino, Liistro, Malusardi, Mercurio, and Vittorini. It will be financed by the public works department of the Lazio Region, with contributions from the national government, the EC, and other European Jewish communities.

On February 19, a conference on "The Application of the Anti-Jewish Racial Laws in Turin, 1938–1943" was held in Turin, presided over by Tullia Zevi and sponsored by the Piemonte Region.

The second Israeli film festival took place June 2–7 in Milan. The event was organized by Left for Israel (Sinistra per Israele) in collaboration with the Israel Consulate General; it was financed by the Milan Municipality and the Lombardy Region. The festival opened with *Green Fields*, directed by Itzhaq Yeshurum, a film on the *intifada* that was awarded first prize in the international film festivals of Jerusalem and Rio de Janeiro. The annual conference of the Italian Association for Jewish Studies was held on November 5 in S. Miniato, at the "I Cappuccini" Studies Center. The conference dealt with the subject "Palestinian Judaism from the 1st Century B.C. to the 1st Century A.C.," from archaeological, religious, and historical perspectives.

Also in November, an exhibition of Holocaust-related paintings by Eva Fischer opened at Yad Vashem, in Jerusalem. The exhibition and the catalog were sponsored by the Italian Cultural Institute of Tel Aviv, because it was in Italy that Eva Fischer started her career as a painter.

On November 25, the Jewish Studies Center of Venice held its 15th annual Day of Lectures, in memory of Dante Lattes. The subject was "The First Decade of 20th-Century Italian Jewry—Between Assimilation and Emancipation." The conference was attended by Chief Rabbi Elio Toaff, Prof. Bruno DiPorto, Dr. Mario

Toscano, and Prof. Amos Luzzato, who described his grandfather, Dante Lattes, as a man and as a scholar.

Publications

There is no daily or weekly Jewish press in Italy. A monthly magazine, *Shalom*, is published by the Rome Jewish community, and a *Bollettino* is issued monthly by the Milan Jewish community. The publications of the Italian Zionist Federation and UCEI and the scholarly journal *La Rassegna Mensile di Israel* issued in Rome are quarterlies. The publishers Carucci in Rome and Vogelman in Florence specialize in Jewish works.

Among new studies on the history of Italian Jews was *Memoria della persecuzione degli Ebrei*, issued on the anniversary of the deportation of Tuscany Jews and their spiritual leader, Rabbi Nathan Cassuto of Florence. The pamphlet vividly describes the situation of Tuscany Jewry during the Nazi occupation.

Joseph Baruch Sermoneta, professor of Jewish thought at the Hebrew University of Jerusalem, edited *Ratto della Signora Anna del Monte trattenuta a'Catecumeni tredici giorni dalli 6 fino alli 19 maggio anno 1749* ("The abduction of Anna del Monte, kept in the House of Converts 13 days, from May 6 to 19, 1749") for the Carucci Press. The volume focuses on a tragic episode of forced conversion to Christianity in the period of the ghettos. It includes, in addition to the preface by Sermoneta, the extraordinary diary of Anna del Monte, who was arrested by pontifical soldiers and brought against her will to the House of Converts, and a ballad about her by Sabbato Mois Mieli, a rabbi-poet of the period.

Publication continued of *The Apostolic See and the Jews*, the monumental work of Prof. Shlomo Simonsohn, director of the Diaspora Research Institute at Tel Aviv University. Four volumes of documents were issued this year, covering the years 1464–1521, 1522–1538, 1539–1545, and 1546–1555. The work started in 1988 with the publication of documents covering the period 492–1404, and continued in 1989 with the years 1394–1463. The project was expected to be completed in 1991.

Personalia

The prestigious Yakir Bezalel Prize of Jerusalem's Bezalel Academy of Arts was awarded in April to Bruno Zevi, architect, former professor of architectural history at the universities of Venice and Rome, and author of the influential *Architecture as Space* (1957) and other works. On June 20, an honorary doctorate was conferred on Zevi by the Haifa Technion.

The Italian Jewish pianist Claudio Crismani was appointed artistic director of the first international "Homage to Vladimir Horowitz" festival. Crismani, born in Trieste, studied with Constantinides in Italy and Kazuro in Warsaw, starting his international career in 1979 at the Salle Pleyel in Paris. In 1987, he was chosen to represent Europe at the International Evening of Music of the UNESCO Congress in Paris. That same year, he made his debut in Israel.

On January 11, Rabbi Dr. Aldo Luzzatto died, after a heart attack, in Rishon LeZion, in Israel. Prior to his settling in Israel, he held rabbinical posts in Padua, Genoa, and Milan. For the last 20 years, he worked as a research fellow at the Diaspora Research Institute of Tel Aviv University. He wrote several articles on Italian Jews and compiled a catalog of the Hebrew manuscripts in Milan's Ambrosiana Library, with Luisa Mortara Ottolenghi, published by the Polifilo Press in 1972. Luzzatto edited two important bibliographical volumes on the history of Italian Jewry, the first, *Biblioteca Italo-Ebraica (1964–1973)*, with Moshe Moldavi and Daniel Carpi, and the second, *Biblioteca Italo-Ebraica (1974–1985)*, alone.

Massimo Teglio died at the age of 89 in January. Teglio, better known as the "Red Primrose" of Genoa, played a central role in helping foreign Jewish refugees and Italian Jews during the Nazi occupation. After September 8, 1943, he became the person in charge of Delasem (the Jewish organization that helped Jewish refugees in Italy, 1933–1947) for northern Italy and afterward for the whole country. Teglio remained in Genoa until the end of the war, evading arrest and deportation several times.

Alberto Mortara, the economist, died at age 81 on February 17, in Milan. Born in Venice, he moved to Milan, becoming an active member of the anti-Fascist organization Justice and Liberty. Because of the racial laws, he escaped to Switzerland, joining the Partito d'Azione. In 1956 he founded in Milan the "Ciriec," the Center of Research and Information on the Economy and Public Enterprises.

M. M. CONSONNI

Federal Republic of Germany

National Affairs

 $\mathbf{F}$ ROM THE BEGINNING OF 1990, all signs pointed toward a speedy unification of the two Germanys. The slogan of the East German revolution, "We are the people," had changed into the slogan for unification, "We are one people." The West German political class, especially the governing Christian Democrats and Liberals (CDU-FDP), as well as much of the established media, lent their support to the pro-unification elements inside the German Democratic Republic (GDR). This push for unification among western politicians contrasted sharply with the sentiments of large segments of the West German population who showed little enthusiasm for the influx of East Germans into West Germany and saw their standard of living threatened by the investments necessary to rebuilding the east.

In the political sphere there were divergences as well. The Social Democratic party (SPD) was divided between supporters and opponents of unification, with its leader, Oskar Lafontaine, opposing unification, and later, in light of the overwhelming movement toward unity, favoring a slower process of unification. The Green party was virtually united in its opposition to unification, seeing in it potential for German big-power ambitions and a dangerous new German nationalism. These sentiments on the Left were expressed in a demonstration in Frankfurt-am-Main on May 13, as well as in debates and statements by artists and writers, such as Günter Grass, who took a particularly strong stand against unity.

In the end, it was the will of the East Germans that determined the course of events. In January 1990, the new Social Democratic party of East Germany held its first Party Congress of Delegates, in East Berlin, in which it declared itself almost unanimously in favor of unification. At its founding in October 1989, party leaders had envisioned a separate GDR state, but sentiment shifted quickly toward unification.

In the wake of these largely internal processes, West German leaders moved to gain the agreement of the major powers to unification. On February 12, Chancellor Helmut Kohl and Foreign Minister Hans-Dietrich Genscher flew to Moscow to seek President Mikhail Gorbachev's support. Immediately thereafter, the two, plus the East German foreign minister, met in Ottawa, on the occasion of the "Open Skies" Conference, with the four World War II Allied powers to clarify the issues of Germany's membership in NATO and Germany's borders with its neighbors, especially Czechoslovakia and Poland. In the "two-plus-four talks" that were now being set up, the two Germanys were first to clarify some issues internal to the two states and then negotiate the other issues of relevance to the wartime allies.

360

By July, the Soviet Union had accepted a status of full sovereignty for Germany and its continuing membership in NATO. Germany, in turn, agreed to reduce its armed forces to 370,000 soldiers. In September, Germany and the Soviet Union signed a friendship treaty that involved substantial financial contributions on the part of Germany. A treaty was also signed with Poland, on November 14, which recognized the inviolability of the Oder-Neisse border. The "two-plus-four talks" had already been concluded in Moscow, on September 12, with the signing of a treaty recognizing the unity and sovereignty of Germany. Its European neighbors— Italy, France, and Great Britain—by and large showed little enthusiasm for German unity.

In the spring, especially following April elections in the GDR, the process of unification picked up speed. It took a major step forward with the currency union on July 2, when the Deutsche mark became the official currency in the east. By August, the government of Prime Minister Lothar de Maizière began to weaken, with several coalition partners leaving the cabinet. Later that month, the GDR Volkskammer (parliament), with the exception of the PDS, the renamed former Communist party, voted in favor of unification. This set the stage for the signing of the unity treaty between the two Germanys, on August 31, in East Berlin. On October 3, unification was officially declared and the day proclaimed a new national holiday.

The first all-German national elections took place on December 2, resulting in a resounding victory for the governing conservative-liberal coalition: the Christian Democrats received 43.8 percent of the vote, approximately equally in both East and West Germany; the Free Democrats, previously thought to be moribund, rose to 11 percent, due especially to the popularity in the east of Foreign Minister Genscher, who is of Saxon origin and presented himself as an advocate of the East German population.

Jews and Unification

Although many public pronouncements were made concerning Germany's continuing obligations to the Jews and to Israel, little of this was reflected in the actual unity process. Despite numerous strong appeals by Heinz Galinski, chairman of the Central Council of Jews in Germany (Zentralrat der Juden in Deutschland), the unity treaty contained neither a clear statement of German responsibility for the Nazi past nor a satisfactory formulation of the issue of restitution. The preamble to the *Grundgesetz* (constitution), which had to be revised, contained no more than an oblique reference to the German people's responsibility "before history." Critics of Galinski claimed that his difficult personal relations with major government officials, including the chancellor, were partly to blame for the lack of success of his otherwise admirable attempts at intervention.

In early May, the World Jewish Congress (WJC) met in Berlin—despite the opposition and the boycott of some delegates, especially from Israel. This was the first time since the Holocaust that any major international Jewish body had held a meeting in Germany, and Heinz Galinski proudly announced that with this visit the German Jewish community had once again become a "fully accepted member" of the world Jewish community. In the presence of several government dignitaries, including Chancellor Kohl and Interior Minister Wolfgang Schäuble, a solemn declaration drafted by Elie Wiesel was read at the Wannsee Villa where, in 1942, the Nazi leadership planned the "final solution" and the establishment of the death camps.

Underlying the holding of the meeting was a tacit agreement, a form of "linkage": the WJC would support unification, and the GDR government would accept responsibility for its role in the Holocaust. When the WJC delegation visited East Berlin, Prime Minister de Maizière delivered a strong statement regarding German responsibility for Nazi crimes and his government's firm commitment to the Jewish people; this was a clear departure from the position taken by previous GDR governments. The WJC had originally planned the meeting—held in both East and West Berlin—as a way to press Jewish interests in the GDR and to underscore the importance of the GDR's full recognition of its part in the crimes committed in Hitler's Germany, including acceptance of the framework of restitution agreed to in the 1952 Hague treaty between the Federal Republic and the Conference on Jewish Material Claims Against Germany.

No one, however, had foreseen the speed of developments leading to unification. As a result, the objectives of both sides changed mid-course. Both East and West Germans saw this as a media opportunity, a chance to demonstrate to the world that "nothing really had changed," that the traditional commitments of West Germany would continue to be honored after unification; for this, they sought Jewish blessing. The World Jewish Congress, on the other hand, recognized this as an opportunity to press for continuing commitment from a united Germany to the Jews and to Israel, including a willingness to negotiate claims to Jewish property on the territory of the GDR. The meeting in Berlin was therefore very much in the mutual interest of both Germany and the Jewish/Israeli representatives.

Relations with Israel

Some disharmony was evident this year, particularly because relations between the European Community (EC) and Israel continued to be strained over the *intifada* and continuing West Bank settlement. The deterioration was blamed by the Israeli government on European anti-Semitism, Europe's economic interests in the Middle East, and the failure of Israeli information-propaganda services. Moreover, in this 25th year of diplomatic relations between Israel and West Germany, many Israeli political leaders, including Prime Minister Yitzhak Shamir and other personalities, notably German-born publisher Gershom Schocken, left little doubt about their opposition to unification—an opposition which PDS leader Gregor Gysi attempted to use in his appeal to Jews everywhere to oppose the dissolution of the GDR. (Some Israelis, however, like Moshe Arens, on his visit to Bonn in February, expressed full confidence in a united Germany.) These tensions notwithstanding, the West German government attempted to present itself as the defender of Israel's interests in the EC and continued to cultivate contacts at all levels with the Jewish state.

This attitude reflected the importance the Federal Republic—and similarly the new GDR—attributed to maintaining visibly positive relations with Israel, for internal, symbolic reasons, as well as in foreign policy. The visit of the presidents of the West and East German parliaments, Rita Süssmuth and Sabine Bergmann-Pohl, respectively, to Jerusalem, and especially their much publicized tour of Yad Vashem, was an example of this thinking. Such visits, as well as statements by both East and West German politicians, were intended to demonstrate to the world and to Germans, especially East Germans, that a united Germany would continue to be at least verbally mindful of the Holocaust and to recognize its self-defined political responsibility toward Israel.

Because both countries were occupied with extraordinary problems, political contacts this year were low-key. Berlin mayor Walter Momper visited Israel and toured Yad Vashem; Tel Aviv mayor Shlomo Lahat traveled to Tel Aviv's twin city, Frankfurt. North Rhine–Westphalia's premier, Johannes Rau, used the occasion of a trip to Israel, at the time of the Gulf crisis, to demand a worldwide prohibition of chemical arms, and the German warship *Bayern* anchored in Haifa in order to "strengthen good relations between the marine forces of both countries." Shortly after the Iraqi occupation of Kuwait, Israeli foreign minister David Levy arrived in Bonn to ask Foreign Minister Genscher to put pressure on German firms to stop aiding Iraqi arms development. Other political contacts occurred at the local level: for example, the district of Gilboa and the Hochtaunus region in Hesse established a partnership, and a group of Friends of Ramat-Gan/Weinheim was organized.

CULTURAL RELATIONS

Israel's increasing international political isolation notwithstanding, contacts and exchanges in the cultural sphere continued to grow. German institutions and individuals went out of their way to foster contacts with Israeli artists, musicians, and writers. This was reciprocated on the Israeli side, for example, with the award to German painter Anselm Kiefer of a Wolf Foundation Prize. There was also an invitation to the Berlin Philharmonic to perform in Israel, which became possible only after the death the previous year of conductor Herbert von Karajan, whose Nazi ties had made him unacceptable to the Israelis. Gottfried Wagner, a great-grandson of Richard Wagner, was invited to participate in lectures and discussions. Other visitors were Rector Heinrich Fink of Humboldt University in East Berlin to the Hebrew University of Jerusalem, to draw up an agreement for mutual cooperation; and writer Günter Kunert for his first lecture tour in Israel.

Israeli artists had a considerable presence in West Germany. Public art exhibits included Israeli landscape artists at the Mittelrhein Museum in Koblenz, in late

364 / AMERICAN JEWISH YEAR BOOK, 1992

1989 and early 1990; photographer Moshe Raviv-Vorobeichic at the Bauhaus-Archiv, Berlin; Yaakov Abitbol at the Jewish community building in Heidelberg; and Yigal Ozeri in Wiesbaden. An exhibit of sculptures and drawings by Israelis, previously shown elsewhere in Europe and in the United States, came to the Neukölln district of Berlin; a photographic exhibit, "Encounters Berlin-Jerusalem," was shown in East Berlin.

A meeting of Israeli and German authors took place in late September, in Mainz, with Israelis Aharon Megged, Yoram Kaniuk, Ruth Almog, and David Grossman participating. A gathering of Jewish artists from Tel Aviv, New York, and Berlin took place in Berlin, on the theme "Between Remembrance and the Present." In music, two Israeli musicians who had won the Ariane-Katcz piano competition were invited to perform in the Alte Oper, Frankfurt; and the Kibbutz Chamber Orchestra played in Munich. In theater, Motti Lerner's *Else*, a play about poetess Else Lasker-Schüler's life in Palestine, was staged in Berlin. Omri Nitzan, a visiting director and Brecht specialist, enjoyed success in Munich; and a performance of *Silence*, by the Israeli choreographer Joseph Tmim, was featured in Berlin.

War-Crimes Trials

A number of trials began or continued in 1990, among them that of Ernst-August König, in Siegen, now in its third year. König was accused of the murder of Gypsies. The trial began in Münster of Latvian-born Boleslav Maikovskis, who fled to West Germany in 1987 from the United States, presumably to avoid deportation to the Soviet Union, where he had been convicted of war crimes. In Hildesheim, the trial began of physician Klaus Endruweit, accused of involvement in the Nazi euthanasia program; in Oberhausen, Heinrich Johannes Kühnemann was arrested for war crimes. The trial began in Bonn of Josef Schwammberger, extradited from Argentina after several appeals and accused of responsibility in the killing of some 5,000 Jews in Polish concentration camps. Bruno Karl Blach, a former commandant of labor and concentration camps, who was extradited from the United States in 1989 and arrested for the murder of three concentration-camp inmates, was brought to court in Duisburg, together with Dominik Gleba, another former SS officer.

A center for research into Nazi justice was scheduled to open in Berlin in 1991, to house all available files concerning Nazi trials. On a related matter, the United States refused an early return to German control of the Document Center in Berlin, which housed the archive of the Nazi party. The center's ownership became an issue this year, with the granting of full sovereignty to Germany.

Right-Wing Extremism

A definite, albeit diffuse, increase in right-wing activity took place in West Germany in 1990. It was of two types: that organized by the official ultra-Right parties, on one hand, and the actions of individuals in small and often informal extremist groups, on the other.

As a result of events in East Germany in 1989, the right-wing Republikaner party lost a significant degree of appeal. One of its major platform planks, the call for unification and for a greater Germany, suddenly disappeared when that goal was appropriated by the government in Bonn and showed signs of being realized. Moreover, the party found itself in a dilemma when East Germans began fleeing to the west, arousing the displeasure of precisely those groups in the population that supported the Republicans and similar right-wing parties. Similarly, the "national goal" of helping the East Germans created resentment among the party's erstwhile supporters. These developments, following the party's earlier spectacular rise in popularity, led to deep internal divisions and to the temporary removal of the Republikaner party leader, Franz Schönhuber, in January. At the January meeting, Schönhuber attacked President Richard von Weizsäcker and Jewish community head Heinz Galinski—the latter for slandering German patriots and for "being himself responsible for anti-Semitism" in Germany. Despite some fall-off in support in the Bavarian local elections in March, the party gained over 7 percent nationwide, and Schönhuber was reelected at a party convention in the summer.

This relative decline of the established Right may only have benefited the militant ultra-Right, supporters of the late Michael Kühnen—the major militant neo-Nazi leader—and similar groupings. Many of the most visible actions this year, such as desecration of Jewish cemeteries, could be attributed to these groups. The desecrations of cemeteries in Stuttgart-Bad Cannstadt, in Kusterdingen-Wankheim, Hechingen, and Ihringen—all in the area near Stuttgart—were later identified as the work of a young couple with neo-Nazi beliefs, who were subsequently sentenced to jail; other cemeteries desecrated were in Babenhausen in Southern Hesse and in Paderborn in northwest Germany. In East Berlin the graves of Helene Weigel and Bertolt Brecht were vandalized (possibly engineered by elements close to the old Communist party in order to raise the spectre of a resurgent Nazism that could accompany unification), as were graves in the Weissensee cemetery. Militant ultra-Right groups were buoyed by their new opportunities in East Germany and by the rise in unemployment in the west, which was due largely to the influx of East Germans and the increased visibility of foreigners, mostly people claiming political-refugee status.

The relative political naiveté prevalent in East Germany after the *Wende*, the revolt against Communism, coupled with the passivity of left-wing and democratic elements, offered the Right an open field for its activities. Thus, for example, revisionist historian David Irving gave lectures in Leipzig and elsewhere on the "hoax" of Auschwitz, and Michael Kühnen led marches in the east. Computer games with right-wing and racist themes, which had been available for some time in the Federal Republic, came to East Germany as well; they had titles like "Auschwitz," the "Turkish Test," and "The Nazi."

The mounting rise of neo-Nazism—which looked ever more like equivalent movements in France—met with some public opposition. In February, for example, a conference on "Neofascism and Racism" was held in Frankfurt's Paulskirche. (Although the conference succeeded in assembling an impressive coalition of groups, it failed in the end because of divided views over unification.) In Stuttgart, a march was organized to protest the desecration of the Bad Cannstadt cemetery, and Aktion Sühnezeichen appealed for help to take care of Jewish cemeteries, as a direct response to the desecrations.

Holocaust Commemoration

The Holocaust was commemorated again this year with numerous events throughout West Germany. In Cologne, the opening of an exhibit, *"Im Namen des Deutschen Volkes—Justiz und Nationalsozialismus"* (on justice and law in Nazi Germany), featured a panel discussion, led by the minister of justice for North-Rhine–Westphalia, Rolf Krumsiek. The Jewish Museum in Frankfurt organized an exhibit on the Lodz Ghetto, *"Unser einziger Weg ist Arbeit"* ("Our only road is work"). The city of Münster presented an exhibit on "School and Anti-Semitism in Germany, 1933–1945"; a documentary exhibit on Buchenwald, prepared in the GDR, was shown in Berlin's Martin-Gropius-Bau; and the photodocumentary *"Aus Nachbarn wurden Juden"* ("When neighbors became Jews"), initiated in West Berlin, went to the Nikolai Church in Leipzig, GDR. Berlin also featured an exhibit on women's resistance, *"Lösch nie die Spuren—Frauen leisten Widerstand"* ("Never extinguish the traces—women resist"), organized by Gerda Szepansky.

This year was the 50th anniversary of the deportation of Jews from southern Germany and the Alsace to Gurs concentration camp in southern France. The event was commemorated in Karlsruhe and in a number of other cities in Baden-Württemberg. Mannheim hosted an exhibit, "Gurs, an Internment Camp in Southern France," that later traveled to Konstanz and Hamburg. Other exhibits related to Neuengamme (in Berlin); expulsion of Jews (Düsseldorf), and flight (Darmstadt). The 52nd anniversary of *Kristallnacht* was observed in over 60 German towns and cities.

Two new commemorative sites were opened: in Bergen-Belsen, on the occasion of the 45th anniversary of the liberation of the Jews there; and in Essens (Eastern Frisia), the only Jewish museum and memorial site in this corner of northwest Germany.

Cities inviting their former residents back, usually for a weeklong visit, this year included Frankfurt, Cologne, Düsseldorf, Fürth, Koblenz, Marburg, Bonn, Berlin, Bad Nauheim, and the state of Schleswig-Holstein.

JEWISH COMMUNITY

Demography

As of January 1, 1991, Jewish community membership in West Germany had increased from 27,711 the previous year to 28,468. This substantial rise, the first in about a decade, was almost entirely due to the influx of Eastern European, mostly Soviet, Jews. Most of them chose to settle in those cities where Soviet Jews had settled earlier, i.e., Berlin and, to a lesser degree, Frankfurt and the Ruhr region of North Rhine–Westphalia.

The movement of Soviet Jews to these cities occurred largely because the respective *Länder* (states) were more receptive to Jewish immigration than others, such as Bavaria, which allowed only a tiny number of Jewish immigrants to settle there. (Soviet Jewish immigration to East Germany and especially to East Berlin was much larger, since both the government and individual Jews had made special efforts to welcome Soviet Jews.) Whereas in the seventies and early eighties most Soviet Jews settling in Germany were "dropouts," ostensibly en route to Israel, the vast majority of Soviet Jews arriving in the past four years had Germany as their destination. This direct immigration evoked Israeli protests to the German Jewish leadership and the German government.

Soviet Jewish Immigration

The most important development for German Jewry in many years was undoubtedly the large influx of Soviet Jews into first East and then West Germany. While the small community of Jews in East Germany not only welcomed, but even actively promoted, this flow (see report on the GDR elsewhere in this volume), and while welcoming Soviet refugees was considered a form of restitution by the GDR government, the West German Jewish leadership vacillated between rejection and acceptance. Early in the year, Heinz Galinski, chairman of the Central Council of Jews in Germany, opposed a larger immigration, arguing that Berlin had already absorbed many Soviet Jews and that neither Berlin nor other communities were able to absorb any more.

Due to the pressure of refugees arriving in the East, and critical voices in the Jewish community itself, Galinski subsequently changed his mind and advocated opening the doors to greater numbers of refugees. The West German government, meanwhile, largely opposed the influx; in August it refused to process new visa applications by Jews in its Soviet consulates; moreover, it called on the GDR authorities to act likewise.

In reaction, a special session of the Central Council voted unanimously to demand that the government rescind its decision to refuse visas for Soviet Jews. The International Council of Christians and Jews appealed to Germans to contribute money for plane tickets and, after a special Bundestag debate, that body voted, in November, to grant a special quota and refugee status to Soviet Jews; subsequently, the Zentralrat demanded that the government contribute financially to help absorb the refugees.

Late in the year, however, some German Jewish leaders began to have second thoughts, questioning whether they could morally encourage the settlement of Jews in Germany; others, of course, found this position hypocritical, since they themselves were living in Germany and advocated the right of Jewish refugees to settle wherever they wanted. As the number of refugees grew, and especially as it became apparent that tens of thousands more were planning to go to Germany rather than Israel, the Israeli government stepped up its pressure on the Jewish leadership and the German government to stop the flow of Jews to Germany, on the ground that their "proper place" was in Israel.

Unification of the Jewish Community

While Heinz Galinski warned against swift unification of the two Germanys, he moved very quickly to bring about unification of the two Jewish communities in those states. In February, representatives of the Jewish organizations from West and East Germany, including the respective heads, Heinz Galinski and Siegmund Rotstein, met for the first time and decided to set up a partnership. For the West German Central Council, there were several issues to be resolved: ownership of properties currently held by the East German communities and claims to former Jewish property, including valuable real estate in Berlin; the legitimacy of the community leadership (although East Berlin had democratically elected leaders); and last but not least, the legitimacy of the membership itself, namely, whether the East German Jews were indeed all Jews from the point of view of Halakhah. By December, the two communities, east and west, were officially unified. Some offices of the West German community were moved to the eastern part of the city, and two East Germans, heads of the new regional associations, Siegmund Rotstein of Chemnitz and Hans Levy of Magdeburg, joined the Zentralrat's board of directors. The East Berlin community council dissolved itself, as did the GDR-wide Jewish *Verband*, the Association of Jewish Communities. One member of the former East Berlin leadership, Hans Rotholz, was coopted onto the West Berlin Jewish community council. (Conspicuously bypassed was Peter Kirchner, president of the East Berlin Jewish community, who had hoped to preserve some of that community's distinct identity.)

The haste with which Galinski and the Zentralrat moved to bring about speedy unification on western terms probably had two motives. One was fear that independent new forces among East German Jewry might assert themselves; the other was Galinski's desire to be in a strong negotiating position vis-à-vis Israel and especially the Conference on Jewish Material Claims Against Germany. Indeed, by July, after the currency and economic union came about, Galinski demanded that the Central Council be an equal partner in the restitution negotiations between the GDR, the Claims Conference, and the Israeli representatives, especially over restitution for communal Jewish property.

Jewish-Christian Relations

The major event this year was the presence of a Jewish *Lehrhaus*, or academy—a name with a long, proud tradition in German Jewish history—at the 90th Roman

Catholic Kirchentag (national convention) in Berlin, with several Jewish theologians and lay persons participating. Jewish critics of the event pointed to the church's continuing lack of sensitivity concerning Jewish themes. While acknowledging that the church had taken some initiative in confronting Nazism, they noted that *Kristallnacht* (the November pogrom) was viewed as a "signal from God," and that Carmelite nuns justified their presence in former concentration camps "in order to confront their own faith." Jews were also troubled by aggressive criticism of Israel, such as young Catholics speaking of the "Nazi methods" used by Israelis.

The Buber-Rosenzweig Medal of the Council for Christian-Jewish Cooperation was awarded this year to Charlotte Petersen, the founder of the Wapniarka Aid Society. Otto von Habsburg, of the Austrian imperial family, was awarded an honorary fellowship by the Hebrew University for his help in saving Jews during the war and his involvement in Jewish-Christian cooperation. Johann Waltenberger, the director of a gymnasium in Dachau, was awarded the Federal Cross of Merit, for his involvement in creating a youth meeting center in Dachau.

Communal Affairs

The major developments of the year—unification and the Soviet Jewish influx—had relatively little impact on the ongoing internal affairs of the Jewish communities in the FRG.

The WIZO organization in Germany this year celebrated its 30th anniversary in Germany and the 70th year of its existence worldwide. The group was especially active in Frankfurt, Munich, and Berlin. Helen Israel was elected the new honorary president, and Lala Süsskind, the Berlin chairwoman, became the new president of WIZO in Germany. In recent years, WIZO had emerged as the most dynamic Jewish organization in Germany, sponsoring numerous social events, large and small. With most of the German Jewish community bodies dominated by men, WIZO was the one place in which women could meet, socialize, and develop their own organizational capacities. A large portion of the funds collected by WIZO in Germany went to the Heuss Mother's Convalescence Center in Herzliah, Israel.

Other groups, as well, worked to support medical activity in Israel. A Bavarian committee to support aid to cancer patients in Israel held a benefit on the occasion of its tenth anniversary; a gala dinner was held at Kronberg Castle in support of Israeli children suffering from leukemia; and the Micha Society for Deaf Children in Haifa received support from the Sprecher-Heilbrunn Fund.

The *Allgemeine Jüdische Wochenzeitung*, once an independent weekly but for the past two decades the semi-official organ of the Central Council, dismissed two longtime editors, both non-Jews, without explanation. They were Friedo Sachser, its principal editor, who had been with the paper since 1950, and Boike Jacobs, an associate editor, on staff for about 15 years. The move was seen as an attempt to bring the paper under closer control of the Zentralrat after Galinski's accession to the top position. While the change may have made it harder to attack existing communal structures publicly, criticism persisted. One source was the opposition bimonthly *Semit*, which published at times vitriolic attacks against the Jewish leadership. A Zentralrat-sponsored Jewish youth congress in Berlin criticized the operation of the Jewish communities for excluding the younger generations from the decision-making process.

Culture

Historian Herbert Strauss, longtime faculty member of City College of New York, retired as director of the Berliner Zentrum für Antisemitismusforschung at the Technical University and returned to New York. He was arranging for the transfer to Berlin of an archive of original documents and microfilms, housed in New York, related to the history of German-Jewish immigration.

Among Jewish artists whose work was exhibited in Germany this year were Naftali Bezem, Frank Rödel, Lasar Segal, Fritz Wisten, Emil Orlik, and photographers Sasha and Cami Stone, Herbert Sonnenfeld, and Tim Nachum Gidal. A first German exhibit of Leon Abramowicz was shown in Seebruck in southern Bavaria. El Lissitzky's "Typographical Works" were presented in Darmstadt; the Jewish Museum in Frankfurt arranged an exhibition on the theme "Expressionism and Exile," with works selected from the Fischer family private collection. Hamburg artist and writer Arie Goral presented two exhibits, *"Meine jüdische Bilderwelt"* ("The world of my Jewish pictures") and "Theresienstadt and Other Concentration Camps." He also lectured in his native town of Rheda. Other exhibitions of note included the work of poet and painter Uriel Birnbaum at the University of Hagen; works by Marc Chagall, in Ludwigshafen; photographic portraits of Jewish émigrés by Herlinde Koelbl, in Munich; and a display on Hanukkah, in the Rashi House in Worms.

The 100th birthday of satirist-journalist Kurt Tucholsky was marked by two exhibitions and two new books. Munich's Gasteig featured a comprehensive memorial exhibit, and in Marbach near Stuttgart, at the Schiller Nationalmuseum, an exhibit addressed Tucholsky's role as a writer in the Weimar Republic. The two publications were Fritz J. Raddatz's *Tucholsky—ein Pseudonym*, and *Kurt Tucholsky. Ein Lebensbild*, by Helga Bemmann.

A documentary film of note this year was *Alle Juden raus. Judenverfolgung in einer deutschen Kleinstadt 1933–1945* ("Out with the Jews: Persecution of Jews in a small German town"), by Emanuel Rund. The film portrays the history of Jewish persecution in a small Swabian town, the recollections of former Jewish citizens, and how the town was dealing with its past.

In Cologne's ancient underground city, a mikveh dating from 1170 was restored and reopened.

MUSIC

Klezmer music and Klezmer bands had been enjoying a boom in popularity in West Germany for several years. Advertisements sometimes presented "Klezmer" as an independent musical genre, along with classical music, jazz, and rock. An international Klezmer society was founded that included German (non-Jewish) musicians as well as Jews. Members of at least one American Klezmer band were living and working permanently in Berlin, and others were frequent guests or went on tour throughout Germany. The American Giora Feidman spent much of his time in Germany, giving concerts this year in Munich and Berlin, among other places.

A festival of Jewish music featuring concerts and discussions was organized by the West German Radio Broadcasting Service in Cologne. At the request of President von Weizsäcker, the Berlin Philharmonic Orchestra gave a benefit concert to help restore the Jewish cemeteries in Berlin.

Publications

Among a number of new works of Jewish interest published this year, the following are particularly noteworthy: Arie Goral's *Jüdischer Bestand und Widerstand in der Bundesrepublik Deutschland, Texte 1960–1989* (on Jewish existence in Germany); Dagmar Hartung von Doetinchem and Rudolf Winau, eds., *Zerstörte Fortschritte. Das jüdische Krankenhaus in Berlin 1756–1860–1914–1989* (the history of a Jewish hospital in Berlin); a novel by Karin Lindemann, *Wege heimwärts* (about the effects of Nazism on the second generation, the children of both victims and perpetrators); Jan Lokers's *Die Juden in Emden 1530–1806: eine sozial- und wirtschaftsgeschichtliche Studie zur Geschichte der Juden in Norddeutschland vom ausgehenden Mittelalter bis zur Emanzipationsgesetzgebung* (history of the Jews in Emden); Ilse Losa's *Die Welt in der ich lebte* (memoir of a Jewish woman's childhood and youth in Germany; translated from the Portuguese edition of 1949 by Maralde Meyer-Minnemann and the author); *Briefwechsel Martin Buber–Ludwig Strauss 1913–1953* (the Buber-Strauss correspondence), edited by Tuvia Rübner and Dafna Mach; Helga Schubert's *Judasfrauen* (on women who turned others in to the Gestapo); Günther Schwarberg's *Die Mörderwaschmaschine* (about the German legal establishment's effort after 1945 to block investigations into Nazi crimes); *Der deutsch-israelische Dialog*, 1987–1990, 8 vols., edited by Rolf Vogel (a standard sourcebook on German-Israeli relations); *Solange wie das eingehaltene Licht. Briefe 1966–82* ("As long as the light lasts") by Clara von Bodman and Elazar Benyoetz (correspondence between a German and an Israeli writer).

Lea Rosh and Eberhardt Jäckel received the Geschwister Scholl Prize for their book on the Holocaust, *Der Tod ist ein Meister aus Deutschland* ("Death is a master from Germany").

Personalia

Writer Ralph Giordano—son of a Sicilian father and a Jewish mother—received the award of the Heinz Galinski Foundation, the Federal Cross of Merit, and an honorary doctorate from the University of Kassel. The 66-year-old journalist and TV documentary maker had previously won the prestigious Grimme and Hans-Fallada Prizes. His autobiographical novel *The Bertinis* (1982) was made into a popular TV film. More recent works were *Die zweite Schuld oder von der Last Deutscher zu sein* ("The second guilt, or, about the burden of being a German") and *Wenn Hitler den Krieg gewonnen hätte* ("If Hitler had won the war").

Erich Liebermann, member of the board of the Jewish community organization of Wiesbaden, received the Federal Medal of Merit. Jerusalem mayor Teddy Kollek was invited to the Catholic Church's national meeting in Berlin in May; in the fall he received the 1990 Moses Mendelssohn Prize, from Berlin mayor Walter Momper. Playwright George Tabori was awarded a prize by the Mülheim Theater convention.

Within the Jewish community, Micha Paz was appointed the new director of the Jewish National Fund (KKL) in Germany, and Michel Friedmann, the person responsible for cultural affairs in the Jewish community of Frankfurt, was elected the new chairman of ORT Germany.

Among prominent German-Jewish émigrés who died this year were psychoanalyst Bruno Bettelheim, in Silver Spring, Maryland, aged 86 (he was posthumously awarded the Leopold Lucas Prize); social philosopher Alfred Sohn-Rethel, who had lived in England, aged 91; philanthropist Fred W. Lessing, in New York; and Munich-born Karl Neumeyer, a leader of Shovevei Zion, a settlement of Swabian Jews in Israel, aged 79. Two prominent émigrés who subsequently returned to Germany died this year: banker and philanthropist Eric M. Warburg, long active in Jewish organizations and chairman of the board of the Jewish Hospital in Hamburg, aged 90; and world-renowned sociologist Norbert Elias, who had taught in England, the Netherlands, and later in Bielefeld, aged 93. Hans Seidenberg, a longtime chairman of the Society for Christian-Jewish Cooperation in the Taunus region, died in February, aged 80.

The deaths of several non-Jews who had been important to the Jewish community should be noted. Herbert Wehner, a former leader of the Social Democratic party who was instrumental in setting up numerous German-Israeli contacts, was eulogized at a formal state commemoration in Bonn in the presence of Federal president Richard von Weizsäcker and Zentralrat chairman Heinz Galinski. Charlotte Landgrebe, who died in November 1989, aged 71, fought against Nazism and for the rights of minorities, including those of Gypsies.

Y. MICHAL BODEMANN

German Democratic Republic

National Affairs

THE YEAR 1990 WAS ONE OF POLITICAL, social, and economic chaos in the German Democratic Republic (GDR), climaxing in October in political unification with the Federal Republic of Germany. Over the course of the year, the territory of the GDR was governed by three heads of state in succession, and the formerly dominant Socialist Unity Party (SED) changed its name twice—in December 1989 to Socialist Unity Party-Party for Democratic Socialism (SED-PDS), and in February 1990 to Party for Democratic Socialism (PDS). In reaction to the chaos and uncertainty, 15,000 people, mostly young—of a population of approximately 16 million inhabitants—emigrated each month, in most cases to West Germany.

In January, weekly demonstrations in all major cities (drawing 150,000 in Leipzig alone) protested Communist rule and called for unification with West Germany; former head of state Erich Honecker was arrested but declared unfit to stand trial. On March 18, in the GDR's first free general election by secret ballot, the Alliance for (a united) Germany, led by the Christian Democratic party, scored a sensational victory, winning 40.8 percent of the popular vote. And on April 4, Christian Democratic leader Lothar de Maizière replaced Hans Modrow of the PDS as head of state. July 1 saw the creation of a currency union of the two Germanys, which led to a series of bankruptcies of centralized socialist production units and caused massive layoffs in a country which for 40 years had known no unemployment.

On October 3, the German Democratic Republic formally united with the Federal Republic of Germany, ending its 41 years as an independent state. Five provinces (*Länder*) were created in the territory of the GDR: Brandenburg, Mecklenburg-Pomerania, Saxony, Saxony-Anhalt, and Thuringia. East Berlin maintained a provisional separate existence, with the intention of a future merger with West Berlin. The area that had been the German Democratic Republic was henceforth to be known as the Five New Provinces (FNP).

Jews and the GDR

Jews and the Jewish communities of the GDR experienced and participated in the dissolution of the state and the preparations for German unification in many ways. In March, Gregor Gysi, leader of the PDS (and of partly Jewish descent), called on the Jewish communities of the world to support the continued independence of the GDR. On April 12, the GDR's newly elected Christian Democratic government publicly acknowledged responsibility for the Holocaust and announced its willingness to make restitution payments to survivors. Moreover, it begged forgiveness for the "hypocrisy and hostility of official East German policies toward Israel and for the persecution and degradation of Jewish citizens also after 1945 in our country" and promised that it would grant asylum to persecuted Jews.

The same month, on Easter Sunday, the first East-West Berlin Easter March (for peace) brought 10,000 demonstrators into the streets. Because of heavy participation by the PDS, Konrad Weiss of the citizens' group Democracy Now canceled his scheduled appearance as keynote speaker. His place was taken by Peter Kirchner, president of the East Berlin Jewish community. In his address, Kirchner warned against marginalizing the PDS and praised the party for having learned from its mistakes.

In May the World Jewish Congress held a conference in East and West Berlin, the first time the group had convened any gathering on German soil. The meeting was addressed by the heads of the two German states, Helmut Kohl and Lothar de Maizière, and heard a declaration written for the occasion by Elie Wiesel. As the year progressed, two major issues for Jews assumed high priority: the implementation of GDR restitution payments to Holocaust survivors and the return of property confiscated from individual Jews and Jewish communities in the territory of the GDR. Behind the scenes, negotiations involving the Central Council of Jews in Germany, the Conference on Jewish Material Claims Against Germany, and the governments of Israel and the two Germanys took place regarding the amounts, scheduling, and recipients of GDR restitution payments. In September the Central Council of Jews in Germany hired a lawyer to pursue its claim to 700 former Jewish properties. In the end, the unification contract stipulated that Jews and other victims of the Nazis would be reimbursed only for property in the former GDR that was confiscated between 1933 and 1945.

Anti-Semitism and Extremism

Anti-Semitism became a more serious problem in the GDR/FNP in 1990, often expressed in conjunction with aggression against Russians, foreigners, homosexuals, and Communists. Among many incidents: in January, graves of Soviet soldiers in Pirna and Goerlitz were desecrated with anti-Semitic slogans; in May, the words "Saujud" (Jew Pig) and "Juden Raus" (Jews Out) were sprayed on the graves of Bertolt Brecht and Helene Weigel, and the walls of an East Berlin public swimming pool were painted with swastikas; in September—just before Rosh Hashanah—gravestones were destroyed in the Weissensee cemetery in East Berlin; in October, a fire was set at the construction site of the New Synagogue Berlin-Centrum Judaicum (see below); in November, a plaque on a former synagogue in Potsdam was spray-painted; and in December, the Adass Jisroel cemetery in East Berlin was damaged, and anti-Semitic slogans were painted on the synagogue walls.

For the first time since the establishment of the GDR, the Jewish communities requested and were assigned police protection. By autumn there were almost daily incidents involving right-wing radicals, mostly in Saxony and Thuringia, where economic deterioration was particularly advanced. PDS leader Gregor Gysi was greeted by a right-wing demonstration when he arrived in Dresden for an election rally in November.

The role of external and internal political interests in managing right-wing and anti-Semitic incidents became increasingly clear as the year progressed. In early January the SED-PDS staged a demonstration of 100,000 (the largest demonstration in East Berlin after November 4, 1989) to protest desecration at the Soviet military cemetery in Treptow. However, the fact that the "fascist" slogans ("Occupiers Out," "National Community Instead of Class Struggle," and "Nationalism for a Europe of Free Peoples") were written in party bureaucratese rather than in right-wing youth jargon led to charges that the party had in fact organized the desecration. In the weeks following this demonstration, several thousand members left the SED-PDS, and party president Gregor Gysi called the incident a "mistake."

In February the militant right-wing organization National Alternative, supported by West German and Austrian neo-Nazis, opened shop in East Berlin. Over the summer, the British revisionist historian David Irving lectured in Dresden and Gera with the permission of the local authorities. In autumn two youths who had been convicted of desecrating an East Berlin Jewish cemetery in 1988 had their sentences reduced after appeal proceedings. The youths claimed they had been convicted in a show trial which took place in early autumn 1988 as part of the preparations for the observance of the 50th anniversary of *Kristallnacht* in November of that year. They said they had been drunk the evening of the crime and had caused damage in two non-Jewish cemeteries first, but had been told by the prosecuting attorney that the GDR was interested only in the desecration of the Jewish cemetery.

Relations with Israel

Throughout 1990, state visits, cultural exchanges, and the founding of two Israel-oriented organizations in East Berlin accompanied negotiations toward the establishment of diplomatic relations between the GDR and Israel. However, on October 3, when the GDR united with the FRG, the former had not established diplomatic ties with Israel.

The intense effort expended by a state going out of business to set up a formal relationship with Israel had its own logic. In the early months, the Modrow regime harbored the hope that Israeli fears of German reunification and a positive relation to the GDR might result in Israeli support for the continued existence of the GDR as an independent state. Once the decision was made to unite the two Germanys, the aim of diplomatic initiatives changed to soliciting Israeli acquiescence to the unification. On the Israeli side, the major concern seemed to be East Germany's acceptance of responsibility for the Holocaust and restitution payments to individual survivors and to Israel.

In January GDR head of state Hans Modrow called for the establishment of diplomatic relations with Israel, and in February he assured the Israeli government and the World Jewish Congress that the GDR would acknowledge its role in the Holocaust and would make restitution payments to Jewish survivors. Representatives of Yad Vashem designated six GDR citizens as "Righteous Gentiles" and trees honoring them were planted along the Avenue of the Righteous in Jerusalem. For the first time, guests from the GDR were invited to a seminar held by the Zionist organizations of West Germany and Switzerland. In March the GDR-Israel Society was founded in East Berlin, an initiative of the GDR League for Friendship Among Peoples. However, because it was closely associated with the Foreign Ministry and the Central Committee of the SED, many members and functionaries of the GDR's Jewish communities viewed it as a "laundering" institution for Communists with a compromised past and did not join. In May, Israeli political scientist Shlomo Avineri spoke at East Berlin's Humboldt University at the invitation of the GDR-Israel Society.

In June three Knesset members—Nawaf Massalha, Haggai Meirom, and Shimon Shetreet—visited East Berlin as guests of the Jewish community, and the GDR state travel agency began to offer package tours to Israel. In July Israel's Habimah Theater played for the first time in East Berlin. The presidents of the two German parliaments, Sabine Bergmann-Pohl (East) and Rita Süssmuth (West), visited Jerusalem to solicit Israeli support for German unification.

In August GDR defense minister Rainer Eppelman agreed to discontinue the training of PLO troops and commando units in the GDR. In September the Israeli airline El Al started regular service to Schönefeld airport. The Hebrew University of Jerusalem and the Humboldt University in East Berlin signed an agreement to exchange students and scholars and to develop cooperative research projects. For the first time, an Israeli youth group visited East Berlin; its program included helping with the restoration of the Jewish cemetery in Weissensee.

After unification, in October, the GDR-Israel Society sponsored a lecture and an exhibit and then merged with the (West German) Germany-Israel Society. In November a photographic exhibit, "Berlin-Jerusalem Encounters," was displayed in East Berlin, and in December the Israeli embassy in Bonn announced plans to open a consulate in Berlin to serve the Five New Provinces.

Holocaust-Related Matters

As noted above, on April 12, the GDR formally acknowledged its role in the Holocaust and its willingness to compensate surviving Jewish victims. On April 23, for the first time, Yom Hashoah was observed at the synagogue on the Rykestrasse in East Berlin. On this occasion, announcement was made of the establishment of the GDR branch of Amcha—the international organization that provides counseling and rehabilitation for Holocaust survivors and their descendants in Israel. The GDR government promised to contribute 6.2 million marks to the program, as a humanitarian gesture.

Besides the declaration of April 12, several smaller steps were taken in 1990 by government and public bodies to keep the memory of the Holocaust alive and to honor those who were killed. In turn, the GDR Jewish communities acknowledged these measures by honoring the six GDR citizens designated "Righteous Gentiles" for hiding Jews during the Nazi years.

In May the GDR called for the extradition of Nazi war criminal Alois Brunner, now living in Damascus. Brunner was considered to be one of the most important war criminals still living, and this was the first time the GDR had taken such a step. In August the GDR announced that it would open its archives of the Nazi years to the U.S. Justice Department.

In October, at the request of West German president Richard von Weizsäcker, the (West) Berlin Philharmonic Orchestra gave two benefit concerts, the proceeds going to help restore the extensive and run-down Jewish cemeteries in East Berlin. Daniel Barenboim conducted. And, although fears had been expressed that the opening of the Berlin wall on November 9, 1989, would overshadow the memory of the *Kristallnacht* pogrom of November 9, 1938, several commemorations of the 1938 pogrom did take place in East Berlin in 1990, sponsored by the Jewish community, the churches, citizens' initiatives, and the PDS.

JEWISH COMMUNITY

Demography

On December 31, 1990, 376 Jews belonged to the eight Jewish communities that had constituted the Association of Jewish Communities in the GDR. There were 209 members in East Berlin, 52 in Dresden, 34 in Magdeburg, 32 in Leipzig, 24 in Erfurt, 11 in Chemnitz (formerly Karl-Marx-Stadt), 8 in Halle/Saale, and 6 in Schwerin. An additional 2,000 to 3,000 former GDR citizens of Jewish ancestry did not belong to any organized Jewish community. The Jewish communities reported receiving increasing numbers of membership applications, and again complaints were heard that the processing of membership applications was often prolonged over years, even in cases where the applicant clearly met the halakhic requirements. Reports reached Heinz Galinski, president of the Central Council of Jews in Germany, that in Leipzig and Dresden no new members had been accepted in two years. Especially in the very small communities, new members were often seen primarily as a threat to the internal balance of power.

Adass Jisroel, an independent Orthodox Jewish community in East Berlin, officially recognized by the East German government in December 1989 (see below), reported a membership of 200 families, some from East and some from West Berlin. In December, 13 Jews living in the Province of Brandenburg—of whom 12 had recently arrived from the Soviet Union—announced their intention to establish a new Jewish community in Potsdam. The new body was scheduled to come into being officially in September 1991.

The arrival of Jewish refugees from the Soviet Union, starting in early May (see below), gave a considerable boost to the Jewish population. On December 31, an estimated 2,900 Soviet Jews were living in East Berlin and the Five New Provinces: 1,820 in East Berlin, 450 in Brandenburg, 100 in Pomerania-Mecklenburg, 350 in Saxony, 30 in Saxony-Anhalt, and 150 in Thuringia. Although some Soviet Jews had applied to join the Jewish communities in the New Provinces, as of December 31 the applications were still being processed.

Soviet Jews

One of the most important developments of 1990 was the immigration of almost 3,000 Soviet Jews to the GDR, and then to the united Germany. In February the newly formed Jewish Cultural Association (see below) called upon the GDR to admit Jews fleeing anti-Semitism in the Soviet Union. The GDR government's April 12 declaration of its willingness to grant asylum to persecuted Jews provided the legal basis for the arrival of the first Soviet Jews six days later. On July 11, the GDR Council of Ministers agreed to grant Jews arriving from the USSR residence rights, housing, upkeep, language training, and work permits.

Through the spring and summer, the Soviet Jewish immigrants, arriving at the rate of 40 per week, were looked after largely by the Jewish Cultural Association, the GDR Office for Foreigners, the Lutheran Church, and the new East Berlin Jewish community Adass Jisroel, as well as by individuals and citizens' groups near the barracks where the Soviets were being housed (often ten to a room).

In the fall, the West Berlin Jewish community began to take over. In mid-September, with unification approaching, the West German government ordered its consulates in the USSR to stop processing immigration applications from Jews and advised the GDR to do the same. On October 2, West Germany closed its border to Soviet Jews. From then until the end of the year, Soviet Jews continued to arrive illegally, or semilegally, i.e., with "invitations to visit relatives." They were admitted only in Berlin, however, where they were "tolerated," i.e., allowed to remain, but with no clear legal status and no rights.

In the final months of 1990, Heinz Galinski, president of the Central Council of Jews in Germany and of the Berlin Jewish community, organized a staff of administrators and social workers for the Soviet Jews and publicly insisted that they be admitted to Germany on a nonquota basis and granted residence rights. He maintained this position against pressure from the German government, the Israeli government, and a large part of the membership of his own Jewish community. The Brandenburg Regional Workshop for Foreigners provided support services and counseling for the new arrivals, and the Jewish Cultural Association organized a Russian-German language school.

Although the integration of the Soviets into the chaos of the post GDR threatened to strain the resources of its Jewish communities for years to come, these immigrants represented the only hope for survival of the communities. It was also likely that the newcomers would radically alter the character of Jewish life in the Five New Provinces.

Communal Affairs

The dissolution of the GDR and the reunification of Germany brought about a reorganization of Jewish life in the Five New Provinces. The Association of Jewish Communities in the GDR disbanded in September.

The Jewish communities of Dresden, Leipzig, Erfurt, Halle/Saale, Schwerin, Magdeburg, and Chemnitz (formerly Karl-Marx-Stadt) regrouped into two regional associations based on the division of the Five New Provinces—the Regional Association of Saxony and Thuringia, and the Regional Association of Saxony-Anhalt, Brandenburg, and Mecklenburg-Pomerania—and prepared to carry on with support from their respective provinces. The two regional associations joined the Central Council of Jews in Germany; the presidents of the regional associations, Siegmund Rotstein of Chemnitz and Hans Levy of Magdeburg, became members of the Central Council's board of directors. Some of the former GDR communities were "adopted" by larger Jewish communities in West Germany, which promised them financial and religious support. The East Berlin Jewish community merged with the larger Jewish community of West Berlin, ending a separation of 38 years. Heinz Rothholz of the East Berlin board of directors became a member of the council of representatives of the united Jewish community of Berlin.

In all eight Jewish communities of the former GDR, the intensification of religious and cultural offerings that had characterized the final years of the Honecker regime came to a halt. The members, busy reorganizing their private and family lives, stopped frequenting the lectures and gatherings. The officers and staff members had to redirect their energies toward communal reorganization, the efforts to locate and reclaim formerly Jewish property which had been confiscated by the Nazis and the GDR, and the care and integration of the newly arrived immigrants from the USSR. In Magdeburg, for example, the Jewish community of 34 pensioners found itself responsible for 100 Soviets.

In East Berlin, two new Jewish organizations were founded. These new groups were recognized by the GDR but not by the Central Council of Jews in Germany. The Jewish Cultural Association was started by a group of people around Irene Runge, a sociologist and former member of the board of directors of the East Berlin Jewish community. This group of 300 members considered itself secular but regularly invited ultra-Orthodox rabbis from the United States and Israel to lecture. Its headquarters were located in the building of the former Central Committee of the SED, which supported the group. The Cultural Association took the first initiative toward the admission of Jewish refugees from the Soviet Union to the GDR. It held the first press conference for them when they arrived, and it organized a language school and a cultural program for them, in Russian. It took a leading role in protesting the increasing racism in the GDR, and it organized an extensive cultural program for its German members, many of whom were PDS members of Jewish ancestry, who had little or no relation to traditional Judaism.

In December Irene Runge announced that she had formerly worked for Staatssicherheit (the GDR state security service) and resigned her post as president. To most West Germans, Irene Runge's confession discredited her, and in fact most of her western contacts dropped her immediately. To many East Berliners who had been close to the SED, on the other hand, Runge became something of a martyr. Many others had kept quiet about their pasts and were doing well, and her imaginative and successful initiatives on behalf of the Soviet Jews had brought her a lot of sympathy and admiration. Runge continued to run the Cultural Association, but working mostly behind the scenes.

The second new Jewish group, Adass Jisroel, organized by Mario Offenburg, considered itself Orthodox and claimed to be the surviving remnant of and legal successor to Berlin's prewar Orthodox community of the same name, whose former quarters it now inhabited. This claim was disputed by the Central Council of Jews in Germany. The Central Council's policy was to maintain one unified Jewish community in each city, and the Berlin community already had an Orthodox congregation. Also at stake were the titles to several extremely valuable pieces of real estate owned by the prewar community. In addition, the Central Council did not have the Offenburgs under its control, and Offenburg himself had a dubious past (in the 1960s, he was very close to the PLO and, it was rumored, to Honecker as well).

NEW SYNAGOGUE BERLIN-CENTRUM JUDAICUM

This foundation, now two years old, was the one established Jewish organization in East Berlin that survived the German and German-Jewish unifications. It was integrated intact into the network of Jewish institutions under the auspices of the Central Council of Jews in Germany. It was agreed that its structure and character would be preserved, though changes were made in the membership of the board of directors to accommodate the new political realities.

In June, Dr. Hermann Simon, director of the Centrum Judaicum, reported that the foundation had a balance of 72 million GDR marks and 1.4 million West German marks. In October the Berlin Senate and Magistrate guaranteed the restoration of the New Synagogue's edifice on (East) Berlin's Oranienburgerstrasse, once Berlin's most elegant and important synagogue. The construction, on which 6.8 million marks had already been spent, was expected to be completed in 1995. This year the foundation cosponsored, with (West) Berlin's Pedagogical Center, two exhibits that toured Berlin schools: "From Pogrom to Deportation" and "The World of Anne Frank."

Jewish-Christian Relations

In 1990 the GDR churches as well as the Jewish communities were largely preocccupied with their own restructuring in the wake of German unification. Lutheran churches nevertheless continued to sponsor lectures on Jewish religion and history. Christian youth groups helped restore Jewish cemeteries, and churches collected money, clothing, furniture, and toys for Jewish immigrants from the Soviet Union.

Culture

Despite the social and political chaos of 1990, some cultural events with Jewish content did take place in the GDR/FNP. In East Berlin the once-intensive cultural program of the established Jewish community was poorly attended and ultimately discontinued. However, the independent, secular Jewish Cultural Association offered a full program of lectures, book launchings, observance and explanation of major Jewish holidays, and social gatherings. Many of these events were conducted in Russian or with Russian interpreters present, as an outreach initiative to the newly arrived immigrants from the Soviet Union. East Berlin's Orthodox community, Adass Jisroel, offered a beginner's course in Hebrew and a lecture series on Jewish life in Germany after 1945.

In January Jalda Rebling organized the fourth annual Yiddish Cultural Festival, with guest performers from the USSR, Poland, and Romania. Several events took place in June: an exhibit on Auschwitz was shown in Köpenick; Claude Lanzmann visited East Berlin in connection with the first GDR screening of his film *Shoah* at the French Cultural Center; and the American production *E.G.: A Musical Portrait of Emma Goldman,* by Leonard Lehrman and Karen Kramer, was staged in East Berlin and Dresden.

Cultural events took place in the provinces as well; as in previous years, they were largely under the auspices of the local Jewish communities and Lutheran churches. In February the Warsaw Yiddish Theater played in Weimar and Dresden, and the West German Jewish journalist Günther Ginzel lectured in Leipzig on right-wing radicalism in the FRG and the GDR. In March West Berlin cantor Estrongo Nachamah performed a concert of synagogue music in Magdeburg; in April the Yiddish Theater of Bucharest played in Erfurt; in May the photographic exhibit *"Aus Nachbarn wurden Juden"* ("When Neighbors Became Jews")—originally mounted in West Berlin in 1988—was shown in Leipzig; and in the summer a comprehensive exhibit of Max Beckmann's paintings, 1905–1950, was displayed in Leipzig.

In February Helmut Eschwege, a member of the Dresden Jewish community and the GDR's leading authority on the history of the Jews in the territory of the GDR, was awarded the annual prize of the Technical University of Dresden. The university had nominated him for this award in 1982, but the nomination had been rejected because of Eschwege's criticism of the GDR's anti-Israel policies.

Publications

In 1990, 37 books of Jewish interest were published in the GDR/Five New Provinces. They included ten translations (one each from Spanish, French, Yiddish, Russian, Italian, and Hebrew and two each from English and Polish); five analyses of various aspects of German fascism, one children's book, one Yiddish dictionary, five novels, and three books about Israel and the Middle East. Seven of the books were originally published in West Germany and one had appeared previously in Austria. Of particular interest, this year two of the three published autobiographies of antifascists (Communists) included discussions of Stalinism.

Among this year's most important new publications were: Ilya Ehrenburg, *Menschen, Jahre, Leben. Memoiren* ("People, Years, Life: Memoirs"), the fourth volume of the autobiography of a major socialist writer in the Soviet Union, written between 1964 and 1967 but not published until after the onset of *perestroika,* and including material on Ehrenburg's Jewish identity (translated from Russian); Ralph Giordano, *Die zweite Schuld oder von der Last ein Deutscher zu sein* ("The Second Guilt, or, the Burden of Being a German"), a discussion of guilt and repression in the two postwar Germanys (published in West Germany in 1987); Stefan Heym, *Nachruf* ("Obituary"), the autobiography of a major East German Jewish novelist, describing his struggles against fascism, anti-Semitism, and Stalinism (originally published in West Germany in 1988); A. B. Yehoshua, *Späte Scheidung* ("A Late Divorce"), a work by a major Israeli novelist (translated from Hebrew, published in Israel in 1982 and in West Germany in 1986); Märtin Erwin, *Würde und Bürde. Ein Beitrag zur Geschichte der Leipziger Juden* ("Dignity and Burden: A Contribution to the History of the Jews of Leipzig"), a documentary history of Jewish communal life in Leipzig.

ROBIN OSTOW

Eastern Europe

Soviet Union

National Affairs

IN 1990 POLITICAL CHANGE CONTINUED at an accelerated rate in the once stagnant Soviet system. Mikhail Gorbachev had initiated the policies of *glasnost* and *perestroika*, designed to revive the Soviet economy and political system, but the opening up of the society and system threatened to bring more rapid and far-reaching changes than Gorbachev and his supporters had anticipated. In October Gorbachev was awarded the Nobel Peace Prize for helping to end the cold war, but at the traditional May Day parade, when, for the first time, independent and unofficial organizations were permitted to march, many of the marchers openly jeered him and other leaders as they reviewed the parade from atop Lenin's mausoleum.

In February there were mass demonstrations in support of greater democracy in at least 32 cities. The following month, in elections for local and legislative offices in the three largest Slavic republics—Russia, Belorussia, and Ukraine—opponents of the Communist party won many posts. Opposition candidates won control of the city councils of the three largest cities in the country, Moscow, Leningrad, and Kiev. A bloc calling itself "Democratic Russia," led by Boris Yeltsin, the former head of the Moscow Communist party who had been ousted by Gorbachev, gained a third of the seats in the Supreme Soviet of the Russian Republic. In May, Yeltsin was elected president of the Russian Republic, giving him a power base independent of the Communist party.

When the third Congress of People's Deputies convened in March, it took the historic step of repealing the constitutional monopoly of the Communist party, thus establishing a legal basis for a multiparty system. At the same time, the congress created the new office of executive president, assigning its holder broad powers in foreign policy and military matters. The congress elected Gorbachev to the presidency by a wide margin. Two other fundamental changes were made in June, when the Supreme Soviet passed a law guaranteeing freedom of the press and approving in principle the transition to a market economy.

383

Despite having lost its monopoly of power, the Communist party remained the largest, best organized, and most powerful political grouping in the country. At its 28th congress in July, Gorbachev was reelected first secretary. But Boris Yeltsin resigned from the party, as did the mayors of Moscow and Leningrad, who were leaders of the reform movement.

Persistent ethnic problems and a rapidly deteriorating economy led to widespread pessimism and fears about the future of the country. In December, Foreign Minister Eduard Shevardnadze, one of Gorbachev's closest advisers and supporters, shocked the Congress of People's Deputies by resigning his post and warning that a dictatorship was impending, though he did not identify the future dictator.

Aside from the economy, the major internal problem was interethnic relations. The Baltic states were moving to leave the USSR; Armenians and Azerbaijanis continued their war in the Caucasus; and there were ethnic clashes in several parts of Central Asia.

Latvia and Estonia voted to declare independence after an unspecified transition period, but on March 11, Lithuania declared independence of the Soviet Union, a move Gorbachev declared "illegitimate and invalid." The Soviet Army seized Lithuanian Communist party headquarters in Vilnius, the capital, and an economic embargo was imposed on Lithuania by the other republics. By May, Lithuania agreed to suspend its laws relating to independence, though it would not renounce the declaration itself. The Soviet embargo was lifted in July.

Calls for independence were heard in Ukraine, Georgia, and Moldavia as well. Faced with the possibility of a partial breakup of the union, Gorbachev proposed a new treaty regulating the relations among the union's component parts. Military and foreign policy would remain in central hands; "full autonomy" would be given to the republics in matters relating to their natural resources, territories, and economic systems.

Thus, in both the economic and political spheres there was a great deal of turbulence and proposed change. Having dropped its control of the media and its monopoly of political power, the Communist party was no longer able to control the spontaneous forces released by the attempts at reform.

In foreign relations the Soviet Union continued to move away from confrontation with the West and toward cooperation. In May, Gorbachev met for four days in Washington with President George Bush. They signed more than a dozen bilateral accords and agreed on a framework for reducing strategic nuclear weapons, ending production of chemical weapons, and normalizing trade relations between their countries. On December 12, Bush granted a waiver of the trade restrictions imposed by the 1974 Jackson-Vanik Amendment.

The Soviet Union gave its blessing to the reunification of Germany on October 3, set 1994 as the date for the final withdrawal of Soviet troops from that country, and agreed that reunited Germany could belong to the NATO alliance.

Relations with Israel

A slow warming trend in Soviet-Israeli relations continued. In January, Israel's Habimah Theater, which had originated in Russia, returned to Moscow for the first time since the 1920s and performed in Hebrew in one of Moscow's most prestigious theaters. *Izvestia*, the government newspaper, remarked, "The fact that the Habimah has returned and the two cultures have renewed their acquaintance is very gratifying" (January 10). The next month, the first Soviet-Israeli trade agreement in 23 years was signed, calling for each to set up a chamber of commerce in the other's country. Later in the year, Israel and the USSR signed a three-year agreement to exchange scientific and technological information, engage in joint research, share scientific equipment, and exchange scientists.

On September 30, the USSR and Israel announced that full consular relations had been established and that the general agreement signed in 1989 between El Al and Aeroflot would be implemented "soon."

Anti-Semitism

Several anti-Semitic incidents were reported during the year. The most notorious occurred on January 18, when about 80 people, shouting anti-Semitic slogans and threatening Jews with bodily harm, burst into a Moscow meeting of the liberal "April" group of writers and tried to break up the meeting, while police stood by passively. After some scuffles with the audience, the group left. Later, the minister of the interior, in charge of the police, apologized for their inaction and promised an investigation. The incident was widely reported and discussed in the media. While many writers and others condemned the anti-Semitic group, others claimed publicly that this was a "well-planned provocation" designed by "Zionists and organizations financed by Zionists to incite reprisals against Russian society and instigate a pogrom against its best forces" (letter to *Literaturnaya Rossiya*).

In fact, it was pogroms against Jews that were widely rumored around the country. In February the prosecutor of Moscow stated that there was no credible information about pogroms but that in any case such attempts would be stopped. On February 9, the KGB issued a similar statement and warned the media against blowing rumors out of proportion. One newspaper, *Trud*, reported a pogrom in Kharkov, but this was never confirmed. Rumors about pogroms spread again in May. The Foreign Ministry spokesperson condemned them as the work of those who wished to promote Jewish emigration.

On March 2, nearly 300 writers published a letter in *Literaturnaya Rossiya* in which they complained of the denigration of Russia and its culture. The press and Politburo were accused of "whitewashing the ideological essence of Zionism," which had become a "menacing reality" in the country. Earlier, according to *Izvestia* (February 22), at a meeting in Leningrad, a secretary of the Russian republic writers' union blamed "not only Stalinism but Trotsky, Kamenev, Zinoviev, Uritsky and

Yaroslavsky [all Jews] for undermining the gene pool of the Russian people and their moral and physical strength." In Leningrad, too, some demanded that Russian schools and cultural institutions be staffed only with ethnic Russians.

A *Pravda* writer noted (A. Kalinichenko, March 27) that "anti-Semitism has changed its character. Once diffident and two-faced, it has become aggressive, insolent and defiant." Another example of the emergence of anti-Semitism as a public issue was an article by S. Rogov published in *Pravda* (July 2), which traced the development of anti-Semitism in the Soviet period and argued that it was one of the main spurs to emigration and had led to a widespread fear of pogroms.

Perhaps because of the growing openness of anti-Semitism, the first official legal steps against it in anyone's memory were taken this year. On February 15, the Moscow prosecutor began criminal proceedings against Pamyat, the anti-Semitic organization, because it violated Article 74 of the RSFSR criminal code prohibiting deliberate actions aimed at "stirring up enmity or discord based on nationality or race." In August, Konstantin Smirnov-Ostashvili, a well-known Pamyat leader who had participated in the attempted breakup of the writers' meeting in January, was put on trial for inciting ethnic hatred. In October he was sentenced to two years in jail, the first person to be jailed for anti-Semitic activity. This did not stop his supporters from demonstrating vociferously outside the courtroom. One of Smirnov's colleagues, Alexander Kulakov, gave an interview to the widely read weekly *Argumenty i Fakty* (no. 34, 1990), in which he said that "Russia has no friends. The world is already subjugated to international Jewish capital. . . . We think there should be a trial of the nation which brought the communist evil to the world."

At the same time, citing lack of evidence, the prosecutor in Nikolaev (Ukraine) dropped murder charges against Dmitri Berman, who had been convicted in March 1989. It was widely believed that Berman had been framed, but the Nikolaev authorities pursued the case to conviction, and only considerable international attention brought about a reversal. Berman was given a visa to Israel.

Representatives of the American Anti-Defamation League and the Soviet Jewish Va'ad met in September with more than 40 Moscow city council members and the city's Commission on National Problems. The latter established a joint commission on anti-Semitism with Va'ad. Two council members were to go to New York to study techniques of dealing with bias.

A survey carried out in the Moscow area, funded by the National Science Foundation, the American Jewish Committee, and the University of Houston, involved 508 respondents. Some 15 percent said that "most people" are anti-Semitic, 51 percent said "only some" are anti-Jewish, and 17 percent maintained that "very few" people are anti-Semitic (4 percent said "almost none" are). Respondents were nearly evenly divided on whether anti-Semitism was rising. Equal proportions (19 and 18 percent) said they liked or disliked Jews, and 63 percent were neutral.

JEWISH COMMUNITY

Two strong and contradictory impulses animated the Jewish community during the year. On one hand, there was an unprecedented outburst of communal, cultural, and religious activity. On the other, the emergence of virulent anti-Semitism, publicly expressed by some of the country's leading cultural figures, was a major impetus to the largest emigration of Jews in the entire Soviet period. By year's end, 181,759 Jews had emigrated to Israel, and perhaps several thousand others had gone to the United States and other countries.

Demography

According to the 1989 census, the Jewish population had declined by 20 percent since the 1979 census. A major reason for the decline was intermarriage. Demographer Mark Tolts, writing in *Sovetskaya Kultura* (February 3), pointed out that only Germans in the USSR had a higher rate of intermarriage than Jews. Of all Jewish women marrying in 1988, 47.6 percent married non-Jews, as did 58.3 percent of Jewish men who married that year. A study by Boris Viner, published in *Sovetish Haimland* (No. 2), showed that, whereas in 1923–28, only 3–5 percent of the Jewish marriages in the Ukrainian town of Vinnitsa were mixed, in 1980–84, 20–26 percent were mixed. In Leningrad, in 1955, there were 1,043 marriages where both partners were Jews, but only 362 such marriages in 1985.

The 1989 census data revealed that while the proportion of European Jews giving a Jewish language as their mother tongue had declined between 1979 and 1989 from 12.5 to 11.1 percent, the number of non-Ashkenazic (Georgian, Central Asian, and Mountain) Jews doing so had risen from 52 to 73 percent. It was estimated that 150,000 Jews gave Yiddish as their mother tongue in 1989, with others giving other Jewish languages (Tat, Judaeo-Persian) as their mother tongues.

The census showed that the number of Karaites, a heretical Jewish sect, had declined from 13,000 at the end of the 19th century to 2,500, with only 800 living in the Crimea, once their center. Still, a conference of Karaites drew participants from 23 cities.

There remained a substantial number of Jews in the Communist party: 215,029 party members in 1989, or 1.1 percent of the membership. The figure was perhaps less impressive than might appear, however. Since urban and educated people were highly overrepresented in the party, and Jews were more urbanized and had higher levels of education than other Soviet nationalities, they might actually have been underrepresented. Moreover, no breakdown by age was given, and it might well be that most Jewish party members were middle-aged and older, having joined 40–50 years ago.

Emigration

The 1990 emigration of Soviet Jews was the largest in 70 years. Over 5,000 Jews came to the United States and 181,759 emigrated to Israel, making for the single largest *aliyah* since 1951 and enlarging the Israeli population by 5 percent. The numbers of immigrants to Israel kept increasing as the year went on, with over 35,000 arriving in December, by far the largest number of Soviet immigrants ever to come in one month. Large numbers of Jews were coming even from Birobidzhan, the nominal Jewish autonomous region. Whereas in 1989 only 16 people emigrated from there, in May 1990, 52 people went to Israel and 350 applied to do so. More than a thousand Aeroflot tickets had been ordered by Birobidzhan residents seeking to go to Israel.

These developments set off euphoric expectations among the Israeli public and led some Israeli politicians to predict that "millions" of Soviet Jews would come to Israel. When Prime Minister Yitzhak Shamir told a Likud party meeting in January that a "big immigration requires Israel to be big [*gedolah*] as well," this provoked many Arab and other foreign protests, claiming that the immigration would be used to settle territories occupied by Israel in 1967. At a press conference with President Bush in July, President Gorbachev warned that if Israel did not ensure that Soviet immigrants would not be settled on the West Bank, the USSR would consider "temporarily postponing" the departure of Jews and the issuing of exit permits. Earlier, in reaction to Shamir's remarks, Soviet authorities said they would not permit direct flights of immigrants to Israel, despite a commercial agreement to begin flights to and from Israel in January.

On January 30, the Israeli government said it had no official policy of settling immigrants in the territories, and there were said to be only about 100 Soviet immigrants in the West Bank. Those who considered parts of East Jerusalem part of the West Bank argued that the Israeli statement was misleading, since many Soviet arrivals were housed in those areas of East Jerusalem. Reacting to the criticism, in March, Israeli authorities ordered news organizations to submit all reports on Soviet Jewish immigration to military censors. This, in turn, aroused further protests and the policy was not implemented. While the Hungarian national airline briefly suspended flights of immigrants from Budapest, following Arab protests, the Polish government announced in March that Warsaw could be used as a transit point. Immediately after, two employees of a Polish trade mission in Beirut were murdered.

The large wave of immigration flooded Israeli facilities. According to Israeli president Chaim Herzog and State Comptroller Miriam Ben-Porat, Israel had neither planned nor prepared sufficiently for the *aliyah*. Some Israelis protested that Soviet immigrants were displacing them from housing and were driving up real-estate prices. Absorption Minister Yitzhak Peretz said in July that a quarter of the couples arriving from the USSR were intermarried, and another Israeli official said 30 percent of the arrivals were not Jewish. Later, on a visit to the USSR in November, Peretz said that 35–40 percent of the immigrants were not Jews. These figures were disputed, however, by other sources.

The Ministry of Immigrant Absorption estimated in September that 54 percent of the immigrants had higher education. Over 3,000 physicians and 11,000 engineers were among those who had arrived by September. Many were not employed at all or were working outside their professions. Perhaps because of this, the difficulties in finding housing, and other considerations, about 5,000 Soviet Jews immigrated to Germany in 1990, and 10,000 more were said to have applied for permission to enter.

The New York-based National Conference on Soviet Jewry (NCSJ) said that there were still 300 refusenik families in the USSR, including 106 people who had waited many years for permission to leave.

Culture

The upsurge in Jewish cultural activity continued. An Academy of Jewish Music, designed to train cantors, was founded in Moscow with the help of the American Jewish Joint Distribution Committee. An All-Union Association of Judaica and Jewish Culture was founded at a meeting in Rostov. Its aims were to create an Institute of Judaica in the Academy of Sciences, open libraries, restore monuments, and help produce textbooks.

Jewish cultural associations were founded in Bobruisk, Berdichev, Kherson, Vitebsk, Zhitomir, and other cities. Hebrew and Yiddish classes offered by these groups were especially popular. By September there were 23 Israelis teaching Hebrew in 13 cities, many of them sent by the Jewish Agency from Israel. An Israeli pedagogical center, designed to aid the teaching of Hebrew and Israeli culture, was opened in Moscow. It was equipped with books, tapes, and videos. In Chernovtsy and Berdichev Yiddish courses were introduced in some high schools. In Tallin a Jewish middle school opened. An all-day Jewish school, with ten grades, opened in Riga. Over 800 students applied and some 400 were admitted. The school taught Yiddish from the first grade, Hebrew from the fourth. Part-time schools were opened in several cities, including Minsk and Vilnius. A "Jewish University" opened in Leningrad. It had 200 students in a four-year course of Hebrew and Judaica and was designed to prepare teachers of Jewish studies.

This year saw greater public acknowledgment of the Holocaust in the USSR. A large memorial meeting, attended by high officials, was held at the Ninth Fort in Kaunas, Lithuania, where most of that city's Jews had been murdered. The event was widely covered on radio and in the newspapers. A similar commemoration took place in a Latvian city, Daugavpils. The first public ceremony commemorating the Jewish victims of the Nazis was held in Brest-Litovsk. In Kiev, "Babi Yar Week" was declared in September. Films, concerts, religious ceremonies, and mass meetings marked the observance.

In November the founding congress of the USSR Zionist Federation took place in Moscow, with 100 organizations from 50 cities represented. The federation's aims were to legalize the Zionist movement, propagate Zionist ideology, and influence the USSR's Middle East policy.

Religion

On September 26, the Supreme Soviet passed a law providing freedom to profess any religion and to practice its rites without hindrance. The law declares religious believers equal to nonbelievers in all respects; allows registered congregations to own property, hire labor, and engage in charitable work; and permits religious schooling. These provisions marked a sharp departure from traditional Soviet practice.

Early in the year, "Hineni," the first Reform congregation in the USSR, opened in Moscow. It held services in a private apartment and was led by an engineer. It was being supported by the Reform movement in the United States and elsewhere. The only synagogue in the Ukrainian city of Kharkov opened in September, after having been closed 38 years before. It had been used most recently as a gymnasium. The Ukrainian press reported the reconstruction of the residence of the rabbi of Sadigora. Hassidim planned to turn it into a museum of Hassidism and a prayer house.

Personalia

Iosif Rapaport, a prominent geneticist and chemist, died on December 31, aged 78. Alexander Pechersky, a former Red Army officer who led an uprising in the Sobibor death camp, died in Rostov on January 18, aged 81. Alexander Tverskoi, who wrote in Yiddish and Russian, died on February 10, aged 66. Sociologist Yakov Kopeliush, who studied Soviet Jewry, died on May 3, aged 52.

ZVI GITELMAN

Eastern European Countries

IN 1990, FOLLOWING THE REVOLUTIONARY political changes of late 1989, elections were held in most East European countries. No party emerged with a clear majority in any country. The transition from socialism to a market economy proved painful and controversial; while Poland adopted a radical policy of rapid transition, in the Balkan states there were only tentative moves toward dismantling the socialist economy. Economic crisis and newfound freedoms of expression exacerbated ethnic hostilities, and grass-roots anti-Semitism became visible in several countries, most notably Poland and Hungary.

Against this background, Jewish communities in Eastern Europe set about reorganizing themselves. Three general trends could be observed throughout the region. There were calls for changes in the leadership that had been appointed by, or had cooperated with, Communist authorities; new Jewish groups and organizations were formed; and discussions began on the return of private and Jewish communal properties to their former owners. Nearly all the East European governments reestablished full diplomatic relations with Israel. Contacts between world Jewry and local Jewish communities intensified.

Poland

As part of a plan to move from socialism to capitalism "cold turkey," the government introduced a radical reform program on January 1, including price increases, wage freezes, and currency controls.

On the political scene, the Polish United Workers party (the Communist party, PUWP) voted in January to dissolve itself, and reconstituted itself as a social democratic party. In local elections, held in May, Solidarity-endorsed candidates won more than 40 percent of the vote, the Peasant party 7 percent, and no other party, including the former Communists, got more than 2 percent. In the first round of the presidential election, held in November, Lech Walesa, hero of the Solidarity movement, got only 40 percent of the vote and Prime Minister Tadeusz Mazowiecki only 18 percent. Voters were clearly unhappy with the dislocations and unemployment caused by the rapid transition from socialism. A political unknown who had lived abroad for many years, Stanislaw Tyminski, received 25 percent of the vote. The results of the second round of elections made it clear that the Tyminski vote was a protest vote: this time, Walesa got 74 percent and Tyminski only 25 percent. President Wojciech Jaruzelski resigned, apologizing for any "harm, pain, and injustice" done by his regime. President Walesa nominated Jan Krzysztof Bielecki to be prime minister.

Despite the fact that there were no more than 10,000 Jews in Poland, by the most generous estimate, manifestations of anti-Semitism were amply in evidence. *The Protocols of the Elders of Zion* appeared in two editions, one a reprint from 1937 and the other with a new introduction. Several other anti-Semitic books and pamphlets were available as well. During the campaign for the May 27 elections to local offices, anti-Semitic graffiti were found in several places, including Lodz, Poland's second-largest city. There the Solidarity list was headed by Dr. Marek Edelman, a leader of the 1943 Warsaw Ghetto uprising. Whereas Solidarity got 80 percent of the vote in most large cities, and over 40 percent nationwide, in Lodz it got only 30 percent. Some speculated that this was due to voters' reluctance to vote for a Jew.

In the presidential election, Solidarity split into supporters of Prime Minister Tadeusz Mazowiecki and those favoring Lech Walesa, with several prominent politicians "of Jewish origin" favoring Mazowiecki. The latter, a devout Catholic, was rumored to be a Jew and this was held against him during the presidential election campaign. His rival, Walesa, stated in the course of the campaign, "I can prove my forefathers were all Poles. I am clean. I am a Pole." When he was criticized abroad for these remarks and for saying that when those who are of Jewish origin "hide their nationality, they provoke anti-Semitism," Walesa denied any anti-Semitic intent. Indeed, earlier, in June, he had condemned the 1946 Kielce pogrom, called for a struggle against anti-Semitism, and said that Jews were not a problem for Poland nor had they harmed it.

Full diplomatic relations with Israel were restored in March, after having been broken off unilaterally by Poland in 1967. Israeli foreign minister Moshe Arens discussed economic issues with Finance Minister Leszek Balcerowicz and also met with Prime Minister Mazowiecki and President Jaruzelski.

JEWISH-CATHOLIC RELATIONS

Jewish-Catholic relations continued to engage both world Jewry and the Polish church. In February the World Jewish Congress announced that the groundbreaking had taken place for an interfaith center outside the Auschwitz death camp. Nuns of the Carmelite order, who had established a convent within the camp, thereby eliciting Jewish protests, would move to the new interfaith center on its completion, though no specific date was announced. Within the Auschwitz and Birkenau camps, inscriptions put there by the Communist government, which had ignored or downplayed the role of Jews as victims, were removed. A commission was established to formulate new inscriptions and explanations. At year's end, no new signs had been installed.

In November, Rev. Stanislaw Musial, a Polish priest active in improving Polish-Jewish relations, called on Poles to reexamine their behavior during the Holocaust. He contrasted Germans' "courageous" confrontation with their past with Poles' silence about their attitudes and actions during the mass murder of Jews. A month later, the Polish bishops issued a document, later read at masses throughout the country, condemning anti-Semitism and admitting that some Poles had helped the Nazis kill Jews. The statement called on Catholics to treat Jews as "their elder brethren" in faith and asserted that Jews and Poles had had "special ties" throughout Polish history. While the statement urged that anti-Semitism be confronted and condemned, it maintained that it was wrong "to suggest, as many people do, that so-called Polish anti-Semitism is a particularly virulent form of anti-Semitism." At the same time the statement was being disseminated, the Catholic Theological Seminary in Warsaw published *Jews and Judaism in Church Documents and in the Teachings of John Paul II*, a book designed for Catholic school teachers and seminarians and whose message was similar to that of the bishops' statement.

JEWISH COMMUNITY

The Jewish population of Poland was estimated at less than 10,000.

In April a festival of Jewish culture was celebrated in Krakow. About half the funding for the festival came from the Cultural Affairs Ministry and other state organizations, such as the television network. The Jewish Historical Institute in Warsaw attracted several younger historians to its staff, nearly all of them ethnic Poles. In August a summer camp outside Warsaw, funded by the New York-based Lauder Foundation, was attended by about 100 Jewish youth and adults from Poland, the USSR, Czechoslovakia, and the United States.

Czechoslovakia

Several steps were taken by the new government to reduce the power of the Communist party, which had ruled since February 1948. Prime Minister Marian Calfa resigned from the Communist party in January. That party surrendered more than 100 seats in the Federal Assembly, reducing its representation from 242 to 139 seats out of 350. The Soviet Union agreed to withdraw its forces from Czechoslovakia, with all troops to be out of the country by July 1991. A parallel agreement was reached with Hungary.

After considerable debate centering around Slovak demands for greater autonomy, in April the country was officially renamed the "Czech and Slovak Federative Republic." In national elections, held in June, the Czech Civic Forum and its Slovak counterpart, Public Against Violence, won 170 of 300 contested seats in the Parliament. The Communists won 47, and the Christian Democrats, 40. The Slovak National party got less than ten seats. Alexander Dubcek, who had led the reformist Communist government in 1968 until the Soviet-led invasion had put an end to the reforms, returned from political exile to become chairman of the Parliament. Writer Vaclav Havel, often imprisoned under the Communists, was elected to a two-year term as president.

In January, Israeli vice-premier Shimon Peres became the first Israeli minister to visit Czechoslovakia since 1967. He met with President Havel and Prime Minister Calfa and initialed a trade agreement. A month later full diplomatic relations with Israel were restored when Israeli foreign minister Moshe Arens visited Prague.

JEWISH COMMUNITY

The Jewish population of the country was believed to number about 5,000.

In June, Rabbi Daniel Mayer, the only rabbi in the country, admitted that he had cooperated with the secret police during the Communist era and resigned his post. The lay leaders of the Council of the Jewish Communities of the Czech Lands, Bohumil Heller and Frantisek Kraus, were removed from office on the grounds that they had been tools of the Communist regime. They were replaced by Dr. Desider Galsky, who had headed the Czechoslovak Jewish communities from 1980 to 1985 but who was removed because he was too welcoming of contacts with world Jewry and was "inclined to Zionism." In November Dr. Galsky died in an auto accident. One of the issues his successors would have to deal with was the fate of Jewish properties, including the vast and precious holdings of the State Jewish Museum. Although this had become the property of the state, the new government had pledged to return private property that had been nationalized by the Communists.

In September, representatives of Jewish and Catholic organizations from 16 countries met in Prague and recommended that Catholic-Jewish liaison committees be established in East European countries, as they already had been in Poland and Czechoslovakia. They also suggested that systematic efforts be made to combat anti-Semitism. These would include reviewing textbooks to eliminate anti-Semitic teachings, establishing both seminary courses on Judaism and training programs for priests, and monitoring anti-Semitic outbreaks. These recommendations were later endorsed by Pope John Paul II.

Hungary

Like the other countries, Hungary held elections this year, and these provided some clues to its political character in the post-Communist era. Arpad Goncz, a leader of the Free Democrats, was chosen by the Parliament as acting president. He appointed Jozef Antall of the Democratic Forum, the party that received the most votes in the first post-Communist election, as prime minister. In October, local elections were held; the Democratic Forum captured only 385 electoral districts, whereas the Free Democrats won in 733, and independents, many of them formerly in the Communist party, won in 264. Thus, it was clear that Hungarian politics had not yet settled into stable patterns of partisan affiliation.

There were several anti-Semitic manifestations this year in the political and cultural arenas. Istvan Csurka, a populist writer associated with the Democratic

Forum, the leading party, said in a radio broadcast that Hungarians should wake up to the existence of a "dwarfish minority" that was threatening to take over the country. His talk made it clear that he had the Jews in mind. Writing in a publication appearing in the city of Debrecen, author Imre Kalman charged that Jews were responsible for Hungary's ills. "We cannot afford to be tolerant of Jews who are destroying our country, the country that is giving them their bread." Gustav Zoltai, the new head of the National Representation of Hungarian Israelites, warned that anti-Semitism was on the rise. Indeed, the prewar fascist Arrow Cross organization was revived and issued a manifesto in late 1989 which called for "the immediate deportation of all Jews, Gypsies, and Communists. . . . Public areas that were formerly named for Adolf Hitler, Benito Mussolini, or other National Socialist dignitaries should revert back to their former names."

An Association of Former Slave Laborers was formed to reclaim or be compensated for Jewish property seized in 1944 and then nationalized by the Communists after 1948. It was to have been placed in a trust for the care of Holocaust survivors but Communist governments had not done so. In early 1990 the government conceded that it had misappropriated funds but returned only about $5,000.

JEWISH COMMUNITY

Estimates of the Jewish population varied greatly, ranging from 50,000 to more than four times that number.

Whereas public Jewish life in Hungary had been confined to an officially recognized religious community, with the decline of Communist rule, nonreligious Jewish organizations began to form. In 1988 a Jewish cultural organization began to publish *Mult es Jovo* ("Past and Future"), a 132-page journal that was widely respected in Hungarian intelligentsia circles.

In September two new Jewish day schools opened in Budapest. The Yavneh school, funded by the Lauder Foundation, had a secular orientation. The Masoret Avot school, funded in part by the Reichmann family of Canada, was religious and Zionist in philosophy. Each school enrolled about 400 students. Some Hungarian youth went to Israeli kibbutzim in the summer. A site was purchased for a Jewish youth camp, which would accommodate about 300 children. Hebrew courses for adults became quite popular.

Romania

The governing National Salvation Front scheduled elections for April and said it would itself present candidates. However, the government was challenged by a series of protests and riots throughout the year. In June there were clashes in Bucharest between student anti-Communist demonstrators and coal miners brought in by the government to counter the students. Some 10,000 miners beat civilians, ransacked the headquarters of the National Liberal and National Peasant parties, and were then commended for their actions by President Ion Iliescu. The United States and the European Community suspended aid to Romania in protest against the heavy-handed tactics of the government. In December there were further antigovernment riots in Timisoara, where the original public protests against the Ceausescu regime had been launched in the fall of 1989.

In the May elections, the National Salvation Front got two-thirds of the votes, and President Iliescu won 85 percent of the presidential vote. There were charges of electoral fraud, but foreign observers, while agreeing that there had been violations, could not document that the elections had been fundamentally flawed.

Several anti-Semitic incidents were reported, including the desecration of Jewish graves in Tirgu Mures and Galati.

JEWISH COMMUNITY

The Federation of Jewish Communities reported that of 20,100 Jews in the country, two-thirds were over 50 and only 6 percent under 15 years of age. There were 52 Jewish communities. The Jewish population of Bucharest was 9,114, with 10,986 Jews living in 157 other localities. In 1988, more than 6 percent of the Jewish population (about 1,200 people) emigrated; 4 percent (about 800 people) died; and births amounted to only one-half of 1 percent of the population.

Chief Rabbi Moses Rosen came under fire for his close association with former dictator Nicolae Ceausescu. Rosen replied that he had done what was necessary to protect Jews and improve their lot, including making possible their emigration to Israel.

Bulgaria

Economic, ethnic, and political issues agitated Bulgaria during the year. In a compromise over the status of the Turkish minority, Bulgarian was made the official language, but Turks were given the right to choose Turkish or Bulgarian names. Parliament revoked the constitutional provision guaranteeing the Communist party a dominant role in society and politics, and the Communist party changed its name to the Bulgarian Socialist party. Prime Minister Andrei Lukanov was forced to resign in July, when he admitted that he had called for tanks to crush a prodemocracy protest in December 1989. Lukanov was replaced by opposition leader Zhelyu Zhelev. In the run-off elections for Parliament, the Bulgarian Socialist party won 211 of 400 seats; the United Democratic Front, which encompassed 16 parties, 144 seats; and a Turkish party, 23 seats.

In May, Bulgaria and Israel restored diplomatic relations.

JEWISH COMMUNITY

Within the Jewish community, numbering some 5,000, a new editor of *Evreyski Vesti* (Jewish News) was appointed. In his first editorial, 49-year-old Eliezer Alfandry, who had never joined the Communist party, pledged to put an end to "the old editorial practice of fear and servility, total distortion of news about Israel and all things Jewish, complete lies about life in our Jewish community and communities elsewhere, the falsification of our past, and the complete ignoring of our contribution to society."

Yugoslavia

In republicwide elections in April, an anti-Communist Slovene party won 55 percent of the legislative seats, while the former Communists got only 17 percent. But the candidate of the Democratic Renewal (former Communist) party, Milan Kucan, won the presidency of Slovenia. In the other Catholic republic, Croatia, Franjo Tudjman, representing the Croatian Democratic Union, which was opposed to the Communist party, was elected president of the republic. In Serbian elections, held in December, the socialists (formerly Communists) won 194 seats to the opposition's 48 and independents' 8 seats. Thus, political trends in Serbia were diametrically opposed to those in Croatia and Slovenia. In the latter republic, 95 percent voted for independence in a December plebiscite.

Unlike the other East European countries, Yugoslavia did not restore diplomatic relations with Israel. However, Serbian prime minister Stanko Radmilovic and a group of 300 Serbian citizens came to Israel in June to open the first "Serbian Week" in that country, featuring a commercial and cultural exhibition.

JEWISH COMMUNITY

Yugoslavia's Jewish population was estimated at around 6,000.

The Croatian government agreed to open archives relating to the persecution of Jews in Croatia during World War II to researchers from Yad Vashem. President Franjo Tudjman pledged to allow a Jewish community center and synagogue to be built on the site of the former central synagogue of Zagreb, the republic's capital. The synagogue was constructed in 1867 and destroyed by the Nazis in 1941. The Jewish community had been seeking permission to rebuild it since 1986.

ZVI GITELMAN

Australia

National Affairs

THE AUSTRALIAN LABOR PARTY (ALP) government of Prime Minister Bob Hawke remained in power in 1989–90, although it was returned in the March 1990 federal election with a reduced majority. Hawke, who was on the right of the ALP, was an avowed ally of Jews and Israel, with a proven record of sympathy extending back many years, and was known to have several close friendships with prominent Jews. In 1989–90, however, his government's perceived tilt toward a pro-PLO position—mainly a result of left-wing ALP influences but apparently also because of Hawke's own impatience with the policies of Israeli prime minister Yitzhak Shamir—caused anxiety to Jews and other supporters of Israel.

The bitter and lengthy domestic pilots' dispute of 1989–90, which grounded the airlines, focused public attention on Hawke's close friendship with the Jewish transport magnate Sir Peter Abeles, co-owner of one of the airlines. The alacrity with which the Hawke government moved to compensate the crippled airlines and the unprecedented tactics used against striking pilots raised considerable media and public speculation regarding the extent of Sir Peter's influence in government circles. Although much of the speculation came from antiplutocrats on the Left, it inevitably led to anti-Semitic expressions and allegations of "Jewish" or "Zionist" control by predictable sources, mainly on both the fringe Left and Right.

Relations with Israel

The period 1989–90 witnessed a continued erosion of Australian government support for Israel and an upgrading of contacts with the PLO. These developments did not suggest a drastic or fundamental change in government policy but were nonetheless disturbing.

In 1989 there were two officially sanctioned visits to Australia by official representatives of the PLO. Zebdi Terzi, the PLO's UN representative, arrived in March, and Dr. Nabil Sha'ath, a close associate of Yasir Arafat, in September. Although both men were so-called moderates within the PLO, their publicized meetings with Australian government ministers and officials would have been highly unlikely in previous years. Dr. Clovis Maksoud, a senior envoy from the Arab League, also visited Australia during 1989.

In early March 1989, Minister for Foreign Affairs Sen. Gareth Evans advised the self-styled Australian representative of the PLO, Ali Kazak, that the federal government had no objection to Kazak's Canberra headquarters, the Palestine Information Office, being renamed the "Palestine Liberation Organization Office." Evans stressed, however, that the office could not be accorded diplomatic or consular status and added that certain reported statements of PLO leaders implying a continued dedication to terrorism undermined "the credibility of the PLO position."

In April 1989, the Australian ambassador to the United Nations, Dr. Peter Wilenski (who happened to be Jewish), delivered an extremely one-sided speech condemning Israeli practices in the occupied territories and criticizing what he claimed was the restricted access of Muslim worshipers to the Al Aksa mosque in Jerusalem. He even offered specific apologies for Israel's alleged policy at the mosque to Saudi Arabia's UN ambassador. At the same time, Australia voted with 129 countries to condemn Israeli policy in the West Bank and Gaza.

Following announcement of the Israeli national unity government's peace plan (dubbed the "Shamir Plan" in the press) in March 1989, and after the Solidarity Conference in Jerusalem at which broad consensus among Jewish leaders from around the world was achieved, the Australian Jewish leadership registered appropriate protests at the erosion of government policy toward Israel. In April, Isi Leibler, president of the Executive Council of Australian Jewry (ECAJ), had a lengthy personal meeting with Prime Minister Hawke, to whom he had sent a subsequently published open letter protesting the government's shift. Hawke's response to the letter was acerbic, but he did condemn Wilenski and Foreign Minister Evans over Wilenski's UN speech, the one-sidedness of which had distressed him, he said.

In May 1989, ECAJ president Isi Leibler and Zionist Federation of Australia (ZFA) president Mark Leibler led an unprecedentedly large delegation of 24 Jewish representatives to Canberra, where they met with Hawke and Evans. Although they found Hawke's responses to their concerns disappointing, they believed that they had impressed upon him and Evans the fact that their protests reflected the sentiments of the Jewish community, not merely the opinions of "hard-line" leaders, as had been suggested.

Soon after its reelection in March 1990, the Hawke government issued a Middle East policy statement that called on Israel to halt settlements in the West Bank, on the grounds that the settlements violated international law and significantly hindered peace. The statement also recognized the central importance of the Palestinian issue in the peace process; acknowledged the Palestinians' right of self-determination, including their right to an independent state, if they so chose; and averred that the PLO represented a significant portion of Palestinian opinion and should be party to achieving a comprehensive peace agreement. At the same time, the government—which had never recognized Israel's annexation of East Jerusalem—now explicitly identified East Jerusalem as part of the West Bank.

In June 1990, Leslie Caplan, new president of the ECAJ, and Mark Leibler, president of the ZFA, jointly called on the Australian government to immediately suspend contacts with the PLO in view of recent terrorist attacks on Israeli beaches and Arafat's failure to condemn them. The following month a joint delegation led by Caplan and Leibler met with Hawke and Evans in Canberra. The latter reiterated government policy on East Jerusalem, while the Jewish delegation emphasized that the concept of a united Jerusalem under Israeli sovereignty was nonnegotiable. Subsequently, the government issued the following statement:

> Australia, like the U.S. and international community generally, does not recognize the annexation of East Jerusalem by Israel in 1967. We regard the final status of the territory as remaining to be determined by negotiation.
> Australia would regard an acceptable outcome for these negotiations as being an undivided Jerusalem in which Jews and Arabs were free to live anywhere. . . .
> Australia's approach to future high level dialogue with the PLO representatives is that we will only pursue such contacts where we are satisfied that they will contribute directly and constructively to the achievement of peace in the Middle East.

The Australian government continued to press upon Israel the responsibility to solve the Palestinian problem. In September 1990, the ECAJ and ZFA unavailingly repeated their call to Foreign Minister Evans to halt all dialogue with the PLO in light of the PLO's support for Saddam Hussein.

Throughout this period, Andrew Peacock, leader of the opposition Liberal party until mid-1990, and his successor, Dr. John Hewson, displayed definite pro-Israel sympathies. The Liberal party strongly supported the government's stance on the Gulf crisis. In September 1990, a joint ECAJ-ZFA delegation met with Hewson, who demonstrated a genuine interest in Jewish communal affairs and concerns and displayed a commitment to positive relations with Israel in the spirit of his Liberal predecessors.

Anti-Israel Activity

The number of Muslims in Australia was about 110,000, although the inflated figure of 300,000 was accepted by some politicians, with implications for the Zionist lobby. Most Muslims in Australia came from non-Arab lands, while many Lebanese Arabs were Christians and tended to support Israel. Nevertheless, there was an active pro-Arab lobby in Australia, comprising Arab Muslims and their non-Arab sympathizers. It produced the periodical *Free Palestine*. The followers of Sheik Taj el-Din Hamed al-Hilaly, leader of the Muslim community (see below, "Anti-Semitism and Anti-Zionism"), were involved in anti-Israel propaganda: late in 1989, the Sydney University Islamic Society organized a forum entitled "Zionism—the Other Face of Nazism."

In June 1989, Prime Minister Hawke held a lengthy meeting with a 13-member Arab delegation, which protested Israeli actions during the *intifada* and called on Hawke to pressure Israel to negotiate with the PLO once certain conditions had been met.

In October 1990, at the start of his three-day visit to Australia, Nelson Mandela dubbed Israel a "terrorist state" and made other disparaging remarks that dismayed Australian Jews.

Although in their treatment of foreign affairs the Australian press and media were chiefly preoccupied with other matters such as the turmoil in China, changes in Eastern Europe, and Iraq's invasion of Kuwait, the Arab-Israeli dispute continued to come under close scrutiny. Israel's policies in the occupied territories repeatedly fell victim to blatantly unfair and biased reporting and commentary.

In 1990 the Australian Broadcasting Commission (ABC) presented a "telemovie" depicting Israeli traitor Mordechai Vanunu as a prisoner of conscience. (Rev. John McKnight, the Sydney Anglican cleric who converted Vanunu to Christianity prior to his crime, was at the time in Britain soliciting support for the jailed Israeli.) Terry Lane's almost consistently hostile interviews on ABC radio, Tony Walker's report- age in the Melbourne *Age,* and articles and editorials regularly appearing in the *Adelaide Advertiser* and the *Canberra Times* also gave cause for concern. In general, editorials appearing in the mainstream press were far more responsible and balanced than stories distributed by international press agencies or those written by journal- ists writing primarily for the British press.

In 1989 the Australian Institute of Jewish Affairs organized a major seminar on "Israel and the Media: The Reporters' Viewpoint." The speakers included senior Israeli journalist Hirsh Goodman and a wide cross-section of leading journalists from the Australian print and electronic media. The seminar left little doubt that the Jewish public perceived a definite imbalance in media coverage of Israeli affairs, despite some excellent media presentations which countered the negative picture.

Nazi War Criminals

The prosecution of Nazi war criminals living in Australia remained high on the government's agenda, but it proved a highly divisive issue among the public at large. Andrew Peacock, leader of the opposition Liberal party, foreshadowed his party's intention to scrap the War Crimes Commission if it won power.

In December 1988, following a campaign by the Executive Council of Australian Jewry, the Australian Parliament narrowly passed a controversial War Crimes Act, enabling prosecution of suspected war criminals resident in Australia. The catalyst for this legislation was journalist Mark Aarons's meticulously documented research into the possible entry of Nazi war criminals into Australia in the immediate aftermath of World War II, when thousands of European displaced persons were admitted to the country. Aarons's allegations were broadcast in a series on the Australian Broadcasting Commission (ABC) radio in 1986. (His book based on the series, *Sanctuary,* was published by William Heinemann Australia in 1989.)

Debate leading to the legislation, frequently acrimonious, was often tinged with overt or covert anti-Semitism. The legislation was viewed in many quarters as a specifically Jewish issue, any resultant investigations and prosecutions being depicted as a waste of taxpayers' money. Some opponents of the legislation warned of the difficulties in launching a credible prosecution of alleged offenders after a 50-year time lapse; others deplored what they claimed was a Jewish thirst for vengeance. Vociferous opponents of the legislation included Liberal party senator David Hamer, who declared that the legislation reflected an internationally orchestrated plot by Jews to divert public attention from Israel's troubles; Anglican archbishop Dr. David Penman of Melbourne, who counseled forgiveness; the Melbourne *Age* conservative columnist Michael Barnard; the periodical *News-Weekly,* organ of the right-wing Catholic National Civic Council, headed by B.A. Santamaria; and members of Australia's Baltic and Ukrainian communities.

Among Jews, there was broad if discreetly articulated support for the legislation, the only notable Jewish dissenters being Dr. Frank Knopfelmacher, a seasoned controversialist and retired academic whose family had perished in the Holocaust, and political scientist Robert Manne, columnist for the right-wing periodical *Quadrant.* They argued that the legislation was futile, likely to engender anti-Semitism, and questioned the Soviet evidence that would be involved in any trials. Manne compared Nazi atrocities with the activities of Japanese emperor Hirohito. The subsequent "*Quadrant* affair," which erupted in 1989, focused on a bitter exchange between Manne and another right-wing commentator, Prof. W.D. Rubinstein, a supporter of the legislation who deplored the "obscene false" Hirohito analogy. Manne had complained that the Hawke government was exhibiting double standards in prosecuting "minor European war criminals" while sending mourners to the funeral of Hirohito, whom "many Australians still regard as the most important Japanese war criminal of them all." Rubinstein responded that, for all its undeniable aggression and brutality between 1931 and 1945 (including atrocities against Australian prisoners of war), "imperial Japan at its worst never engaged in genocide . . ." and in fact refused to kill Jews living in its domains, such as Shanghai. The affair threatened to jeopardize what the president of the Executive Council of Australian Jewry, Isi Leibler, called "the long-standing alliance between a significant element of the intellectual right in Australia" and the Jewish community.

The War Crimes Commission, established in 1987 in anticipation of the legislation, reputedly investigated up to 100 alleged offenders, but by the end of 1990 only one had been charged. In January 1990, 74-year-old Adelaide resident Ivan Timofeyevich Polyukovich was accused of the murder of 24 Jewish men, women, and children in the Ukraine and of complicity in the murders of a further 850 people from the Serniki ghetto between August 1941 and May 1943. The trial of Polyukovich, who was free on bail, was scheduled to begin in Adelaide on July 30, 1990, and the court planned to sit in the Ukraine, Israel, and the United States in order to hear testimony. However, on July 29, Polyukovich was admitted to hospital with gunshot wounds, apparently self-inflicted, and he twice attempted to remove his life-support equipment. Doubt as to whether his trial (and any others) would ever proceed increased following a challenge to the constitutionality of the legislation heard in the High Court in September 1990.

Anti-Semitism

Anti-Semitism in Australia remained slight. Yet, possibly as a result of publicity surrounding war-crimes legislation and German reunification, 1989 and 1990 witnessed an escalation of organized anti-Semitic vandalism, graffiti and swastika daubings, hooliganism, verbal abuse on the streets, plus actual or threatened violence against Jews, synagogues, and Jewish property. There were many such incidents in Sydney and Melbourne—including desecration of graves—and Perth and Adelaide also experienced their share. Other minority groups, especially Asians, as well as overseas aid organizations, were the targets of similar attacks. Much of this activity was undoubtedly linked to small neo-Nazi skinhead groups, such as White Power and National Action. Attacks in 1989 seemed to peak around Hitler's 100th birthday in April. Many painted slogans, including one in 1990 warning that a Melbourne park was prohibited to Jews, were written in fluent, sophisticated German. This held disturbing echoes for Melbourne's large population of Holocaust survivors and fueled speculation that some of the perpetrators were of German descent. An anti-Semitic and anti-Asian gang of neo-Nazi skinheads was reported to be operating in Brisbane, too, during 1990.

The most potentially worrisome source of anti-Semitism in Australia remained the League of Rights, an extreme right-wing, avowedly Christian organization associated with several ostensibly respectable front groups that published periodicals and ran bookstores, all promoting anti-Semitism, anti-Zionism, and Holocaust revisionism. At the league's 1990 convention, its elderly leader, Eric Butler, told his mainly rural followers that "Jewish efforts" to outlaw racism had to be vigorously resisted, and he stressed the priority of exposing the Holocaust as "one of the great myths of our time." During recent years, Jewish leaders and others had made concerted efforts to expose the league for the menace it was, especially as some public figures, apparently unaware of the anti-Semitism and racism it peddled along with less sinister views, occasionally lent it credibility by addressing it. As Australia slid deep into economic recession during 1990, Butler found himself in demand as a speaker, particularly in rural Victoria and Queensland. There, his thinly and not-so-thinly veiled references to a world Jewish conspiracy as an explanation for current economic woes appeared to have fallen on some gullible ears and were parroted from time to time in letters to local newspapers.

In 1989, the Executive Council of Australian Jewry presented a detailed report on anti-Semitism to the National Inquiry on Racial Violence. Prepared by Prof. W.D. Rubinstein, the report included information provided by elected Jewish leaders from each state.

In October 1989, a Racial Vilification Amendment to the New South Wales Anti-Discrimination Act provided that individuals who incited hatred, contempt, or severe ridicule toward a person or group because of their race or nationality would face penalties of up to $1,000 (Australian) and six months in jail. Organizations convicted of racial vilification would face fines of up to $A10,000.

Following extensive lobbying by Doron Ur, president of the Council of Western Australian Jewry, the Western Australian Parliament enacted similar legislation in October 1990. The Criminal Code (Incitement to Racial Hatred) Act came in the wake of five years of aggressive racist activity by the white supremacist Australian Nationalist Movement, which vowed to drive Jews, Asians, and coloreds out of Australia. (In September 1990, the movement's leader and five followers were jailed for a series of criminal offenses, mostly against Asians.) The Criminal Code Act imposed tough penalties of up to two years in jail or a $A2,000-fine on persons found guilty of possessing, distributing, or displaying material "intended to cause racial hatred," which had been exemplified by anti-Semitic and anti-Asian posters in Perth.

In Victoria, Jews joined other ethnic minorities in advocating racial vilification legislation at a specially convened hearing of the federal Human Rights Commission in September 1989. Their concern stemmed from recent cases that included neo-Nazi graffiti on synagogues and other Jewish buildings and the slayings of two young Asians in separate attacks in Melbourne in 1989.

The Victorian government, however, rather than following the examples of New South Wales and Western Australia, seemed to place its faith in education as a means of combating racism. Consequently, in 1990 the New South Wales Jewish Board of Deputies, invoking local racial vilification legislation, lodged a complaint with their state's Anti-Discrimination Board about a booklet published in Victoria. The booklet, an annual guide to legal rights by Melbourne lawyer John Bennett, contained gross and disturbing anti-Jewish and anti-Zionist comments. Bennett, a leading proponent of Holocaust revisionism with links to the Institute for Historical Review in California, had been publicizing his allegations of "no gas chambers" and Jewish media control and censorship since 1978, attacking several Australian Jewish leaders by name, and causing deep offense to the Jewish community. Meanwhile, in 1990 the Australian Institute of Jewish Affairs, after consulting other ethnic organizations, produced an innovative and acclaimed television commercial aimed at fighting racial stereotyping.

Arab anti-Semitism, as distinct from anti-Zionism, had not generally surfaced in Australia. But in September 1988, Sheik al-Hilaly, imam of a major Sydney mosque, declared before a public function at Sydney University that Jews constituted "a cancer in European society," considered other humans "animals . . . unworthy of living," were the "underlying cause of all wars," and tried "to control the world through sex, sexual perversion, treason, and economic hoarding." Hilaly, who had arrived in Australia from Egypt on a visitor's permit in 1982, constantly flouted Australian immigration laws and made inflammatory statements against Lebanese Christians and moderate Muslim elements in Australia. His election in 1989 as the first Mufti of Australia, despite vigorous opposition from some Muslims, indicated the level of his support.

Calls to deport Hilaly, in which the Jewish community was joined by public figures and newspaper editorials, brought countercharges of denial of free speech and claims that Islam was under attack. Although Hilaly did not comply with a recommendation made by the chairman of the New South Wales Ethnic Affairs Commission that he apologize to the Jewish community for his 1988 comments, in September 1989 the federal minister for immigration extended Hilaly's visa for a further 12 months, claiming that Hilaly had retracted his anti-Semitic remarks in a letter to Prime Minister Bob Hawke. Hilaly was to be granted permanent residence only on condition that he proved willing to promote "understanding and harmony" between Jews, Muslims, and Christians. Although this proviso went unfulfilled, in September 1990, Hilaly was granted permanent residency, partly on the grounds that he had Australian-born dependent children. The government's decision was widely condemned within and without the Jewish community. Anti-Jewish remarks made by Hilaly during the Gulf War only served to enhanced Jewish wariness of him.

JEWISH COMMUNITY

Australian Jewry in 1990 continued to be a community at ease with itself and with the wider society. Whereas members of the older Jewish community thoroughly identified with Australia's British outlook, a fact that facilitated their acceptance, the development of multiculturalism over the past two decades enabled contemporary Jews to manifest a distinctiveness unknown to their predecessors. Far more *kipot* were worn on the streets than 30 years earlier, and owing to the influx of Holocaust survivors following World War II, far more Yiddish was heard in Australia (predominantly Melbourne) than at the turn of the century, when Eastern European newcomers were actively discouraged from speaking "the jargon" by communal leaders fearful of "conspicuousness." Australian Jewry had become a self-confident ethnic group encompassing all strands of Jewish allegiance and identity, from strict Orthodoxy to secular humanism, from Revisionist Zionism to Bundism. It flourished in its pluralism but was overwhelmingly supportive of Israel. Its numbers and high degree of Jewish commitment were augmented in recent years by immigrants from South Africa, and it boasted an impressive network of Jewish day schools. It had its Cassandras, but overall its prospects seemed bright.

Demography

More evidence became available about Australian Jewry from the 1986 Federal Census and other sources. Australia held a census every five years—most recently in 1981 and 1986—in which there was an optional religion question. The 1986 census revealed 69,089 declared Jews by religion in Australia, distributed by state as follows: Victoria, 32,358; New South Wales, 28,197; Western Australia, 3,919; Queensland, 2,631; South Australia, 1,144; Australian Capital Territory (Canberra), 501; Tasmania, 160; Northern Territory, 98. These figures were known to be substantial underestimates, however. Many Jews failed to respond to the census question for fear of anti-Semitism, for reasons of privacy, or because their identity as Jews was not religious. Most demographers believed that the actual number of Jews in Australia was 90,000–93,000 in 1986 and over 100,000 by the close of 1990. Support for these estimates was provided by the release, for the first time, of a communal list maintained by the Jewish Welfare Society in Melbourne, which showed that there were 41,276 Jews in Victoria (chiefly Melbourne) in 1988—compared with 32,358 found in the census—a figure which was itself believed to be only 90–95 percent complete.

Jews in Melbourne and Sydney—by far the chief centers of Jewish life in Australia—were mainly clustered in a number of recognizably Jewish neighborhoods, chiefly the Caulfield-East St. Kilda districts of Melbourne and, in Sydney, in two distinct areas, Bondi-Randwick in the eastern suburbs and on the near North Shore. In Melbourne, a new area of Jewish settlement, Doncaster, was being developed in the northeast of the city, chiefly by recent South African settlers.

The majority of Australian Jews were still foreign-born. Even though the generation of Holocaust survivors was dying off, they were being replaced by new migrants from South Africa, the Soviet Union, Israel, and North America. In 1986, 3,830 Australian Jews still spoke Yiddish in the home, according to the census, 2,916 of them in Melbourne. Australian Jewry—according to the census figures—was disproportionately elderly, with over 15 percent of Jews identified in the census being 65 or more. However, recent demographic research by Prof. W.D. Rubinstein (Melbourne) and Gary Eckstein (Sydney) indicated that it was also one of the few Diaspora communities with a birthrate above the replacement level, at least in Melbourne and (less certainly) Sydney.

Most Australian Jews were situated in the upper middle class, and Australia's "rich lists" in the 1980s consistently included about 25 percent Jews among the country's 200 wealthiest persons. Most of this group were in Melbourne, chiefly engaged in retailing, property development, finance, light manufacturing, and personal services. Many were immigrant Holocaust survivors who exemplified the traditional "rags-to-riches" story. The majority of Jews were engaged in small and medium-sized businesses and the free professions, such as law and medicine. Australian Jews, especially those in property and finance, suffered heavily in the recession which began in 1990, and there were some spectacular and well-publicized examples of business failures (as there were among Gentiles).

Communal Affairs

At the end of 1989, Isi Leibler of Melbourne ended his term as president of the Executive Council of Australian Jewry (ECAJ), the community's national umbrella organization and principal policy-formulating body. Leslie Caplan of Sydney succeeded Leibler as president, and hence as Australian Jewry's acknowledged spokesperson. During this period, Mark Leibler of Melbourne held the presidency of the

Zionist Federation of Australia (ZFA), the umbrella body of Australian Zionist organizations and the principal communal body concerned with Israel.

Despite financial constraints imposed on many of its wealthy backers as a result of the economic recession, the privately funded Australian Institute of Jewish Affairs (founded 1983), a colloquia-sponsoring and report-issuing body, maintained its invaluable role. It continued to bring international Jewish scholars to Australia and was in the forefront of the fight against anti-Semitism and racism. However, the virtual and often absolute lack of female participation in its forums began to provoke open resentment. In particular, the dearth of official female participants in its major 1990 conference on "The Modern Jew in Crisis" drew sharp public condemnation, not only from feminists.

Indeed, despite some inroads, Australian Jewish women continued to be vastly underrepresented on the communal decision-making level. In 1990 some feminists began to confront publicly the middle-class, volunteer-oriented National Council of Jewish Women, questioning its relevance and appropriateness to the lives and aspirations of modern women and suggesting that its existence impeded the involvement of women in the general Jewish leadership.

Religion

The period 1989–90 saw a number of developments in Jewish religious life. Most Jews in Australia, whether Liberal/Progressive (the terms are used interchangeably and correspond to American Reform) or nominally Orthodox, attended synagogue only on the High Holy Days and special occasions. But in both Melbourne and Sydney there were flourishing Adass Israel (primarily Hungarian ultra-Orthodox) and Lubavitcher congregations, and a Chabad presence had been established in Launceston, Tasmania, which had about 50 Jewish residents.

Liberal congregations existed in all major mainland Jewish population centers; their relations with the Orthodox community were inclined to be tense. Although claims were sometimes made in Melbourne that people visibly connected with Liberal congregations could never hope to be elected to the executive of the representative Jewish Community Council of Victoria, in fact Liberal members did sit on the executive, which in the past included Rabbi John Levi, Australia's senior Liberal rabbi. The traditionally moderate middle ground in Australian Jewish Orthodoxy showed signs of shrinking, owing to incursions made by right-wing Orthodoxy, on the one hand, and the Liberal movement, on the other.

Late in 1989 the Hobart synagogue in Tasmania, dating from 1845, was rededicated. Services were held frequently at the synagogue during 1989–90, with participation by mainland communal leaders, including Lubavitcher figures, but especially Rabbi Daniel Schiff of Melbourne's Temple Beth Israel and members of his congregation.

In February 1990, a third congregation in Perth, which had been informally established during the mid-1980s by South African immigrants and was described as being of "an Orthodox-Conservative character," was formally constituted. In July 1990, Australian governor-general Bill Hayden opened Adelaide's new Nathan and Miriam Solomon Center, a complex housing the Orthodox synagogue, social hall, school, and kindergarten, as well as the offices of the State Zionist Council and the meeting room of the Zionist youth group Habonim.

Most descendants of rural pioneers were either lost to Judaism or had relocated to the main urban centers. However, some Jews did reside in remote localities, for professional or other reasons; they included academics at outlying universities. Adherents of the Lubavitcher movement continued their outreach program to such Jews, especially those in rural New South Wales and Victoria.

In July 1990, plans to found a Liberal temple in Cairns, a coastal city and popular tourist resort in northern Queensland, were announced by Rabbi Brian Fox of Sydney, who estimated that 100 Jews lived there. In September 1990, Jews living in various small and isolated rural localities in northern New South Wales decided to establish ongoing contact through the formation of the Northern Rivers Jewish Community.

Soviet Jewry

In February 1989, the Solomon Mikhoels Cultural Center opened in Moscow, largely as a result of the efforts of veteran Soviet Jewry activist Isi Leibler, then vice-president of the World Jewish Congress, who affixed the *mezuzah* during the opening ceremony. Australian Jews also played major roles in other activities that coincided with the center's opening, including capacity-crowd concerts in Moscow and Leningrad.

In March 1990, the Australian Institute of Jewish Affairs sponsored the visit of Soviet academic Dr. Sergei Rogov, head of the Department of Military and Political Studies at the USSR Academy of Sciences. He lectured on "The New Russian Anti-Semitism and Glasnost" before audiences in Melbourne and Sydney.

During 1990, with the campaign for Soviet Jewry apparently having achieved success, Australian Jewry's almost 30-year involvement in this area diminished. However, the Executive Council of Australian Jewry continued to make representations to the Soviet embassy in Canberra on behalf of the last of the refuseniks; for the implementation of direct flights between the Soviet Union and Israel; and for official condemnation of growing Soviet anti-Semitism. The Australian Senate unanimously adopted a resolution introduced by a Jewish member, Sen. Peter Baume, calling on the USSR to facilitate Jewish migration to Israel by honoring "its agreement permitting direct flights. . . ." This resolution was duly conveyed to the Soviet ambassador.

Toward the end of 1989 the Australian government indicated its intention to curtail its program of humanitarian immigration from the Soviet Union to Australia as a result of the liberalization of Soviet immigration policy. The ECAJ supported this stand and officially resolved to encourage all Soviet Jews to emigrate to Israel, except for intending migrants with relatives already in Australia, to whom the family-reunion principle should be allowed to apply. In official statements, the ECAJ commended the "extraordinary contribution" made by the Lubavitcher movement in the social integration of Soviet Jewish migrants in both Melbourne and Sydney, as well as the role of the Australian Jewish Welfare Society.

The ECAJ also expressed concern for the safety of beleaguered Jews in Syria, Ethiopia, and Iran. Australia's Sephardim, largely of Egyptian and Iraqi origin, successfully raised public awareness of the continuing plight of Syrian Jewry and made representations to the Australian government about bringing this issue to the United Nations and other international forums.

Education

Jewish day-school education continued to expand. In April 1989, the Doncaster Jewish Day School was opened in a Melbourne suburb to serve the children of members of the North Eastern Jewish War Memorial Center. In April 1990, Sinai College, the first Jewish day school in Queensland, was opened in Brisbane. These two new schools brought to 17 the number of Jewish day schools in Australia.

By contrast, Jewish studies at university level were woefully neglected by communal benefactors capable of funding chairs and courses, despite indications of clear interest and an obvious need. Still, the period did see some expansion in Jewish-interest courses at Australian universities as well as adult-education programs arranged by synagogues and other Jewish institutions.

The Australian Association for Jewish Studies, founded in 1988 under the presidency of Adelaide academic Dr. Evan Zuesse, held successful conferences in Melbourne in 1989 and Sydney in 1990. Papers were given on a wide range of topics by academics and others with an interest in Jewish subjects before enthusiastic audiences.

Jewish-Christian Relations

In August 1990, the Australian Institute of Jewish Affairs published a substantial and original report on the attitudes of the Australian church press toward Jews, Israel, and anti-Semitism, co-authored by W.D. Rubinstein and Michael Cohen. The report found that "left-wing" church groups were often very hostile to Israel, while "conservative" church groups either demonstrated some residual anti-Semitism or ignored Jews completely. Overall, the Catholic press was consistently more sympathetic to the Jewish people and much more sensitive to Jewish issues than the Protestant press, but with two glaring exceptions. One was the "almost medieval anti-Semitism" contained in an article by a prominent layman in the Victorian Catholic Church's official weekly, the *Advocate* (since defunct). The other was the "adamant hostility to Nazi war crimes trials" of *News-Weekly,* organ of the Catholic political National Civic Council. (Melbourne's Anglican archbishop, Dr. David

Penman, who died in October 1989, was also the focus of controversy over the war-crimes issue, discussed above.)

In March 1989, a senior Uniting Church (a merger of Methodists and Presbyterians) minister with a background of anti-Israel statements, Rev. Dick Wootton, urged Christian clergy to boycott Israeli-sponsored tours of Israel. He advised clergy to identify with the plight of the Palestinians, who "have risen against their Israeli oppressors." His remarks coincided with a tour by Christian clergy of Israel and Egypt led by Rabbi John Levi of Melbourne's Temple Beth Israel. It was the third such tour Levi had led, and Wootton's remarks were denounced by Levi's colleagues and congregants.

Apart from the Council of Christians and Jews (Victoria), two other notable bodies working to promote Jewish-Christian understanding were the long-established Catholic, Melbourne-based Institute of Social Order and the Catholic Sisters of Sion, who recently celebrated 20 years of work in this field. Indeed, the invaluable Archive of Australian Judaica at Sydney University was administered by a member of that order. Additionally, during 1989–90, a Jewish-Christian dialogue group met regularly in the Sydney suburb of Bondi.

Culture

Among the noteworthy cultural events of 1989–90 were the opening of a second ethnic radio station in Melbourne, with six hours weekly of Jewish programming, and the first Australian Jewish play-writing competition. In general, the extraordinary attendance at public meetings addressed by prominent national and international Jewish religious and cultural personalities suggested that there was a strong desire by Australian Jews to become more involved in their religious and cultural heritage.

The Makor Library, a remarkable resource situated at the Beth Weizmann Community Center in Melbourne, continued to provide a high-level information service for Jews and non-Jews interested in Jews, Judaism, and Israel. By 1990 it had become sorely starved of funds, however, heralding a severe diminution of its staff and services and raising fears that non-Jewish inquirers might be forced to seek their information from less impeccable sources.

Publications

Locally produced Jewish books and periodicals continued to thrive.

The most significant such book of 1989 was undoubtedly Mark Aarons's *Sanctuary,* mentioned above. *The Dunera Affair: A Documentary Source Book,* coedited by Paul Bartrop and Gabrielle Eisen, published by the Melbourne-based Jewish Museum of Australia in 1990, is devoted to an extraordinary episode involving Britain's deportation to Australia of Jewish refugees from Nazism.

In 1990 Dr. Serge Liberman of Melbourne, an award-winning writer, published his fourth collection of short stories, *The Battered and the Redeemed.* Melbourne University Press published two books by the acclaimed poet Lily Brett. *After the War* completes a trilogy of her poetic works, while *Things Could Be Worse* is a collection of short stories with a Jewish theme.

In 1990 the Melbourne-based Asia Pacific Jewish Association published the proceedings of the Second Asian-Jewish Colloquium (held March 1987), entitled *The Jews of Asia: Old Societies and New Images.*

In 1989 a new, high-quality cultural periodical, *Generation,* was launched in Melbourne by a group of young communal activists, and in 1990 the Australian Institute of Jewish Affairs launched *Without Prejudice,* a magazine aimed at combating anti-Semitism and religious and ethnic prejudice generally. In 1990 the Melbourne-based Australian Jewish Democratic Society, a leftist group often critical of the Jewish leadership, began publication of a quarterly, *The Australian Jewish Democrat.* The Australian Jewish Historical Society (Victoria) continued to produce its highly regarded journal, inaugurated in 1988 to augment what were seen as the increasingly inadequate issues produced by its parent body, the society in New South Wales, since 1939. And the Australian Association for Jewish Studies, founded in 1988, continued to produce its scholarly journal *Menorah.*

The weekly Jewish press underwent a transformation in 1990. The Sydney-based *Australian Jewish Times* changed its name to the *Australian Jewish News* (Sydney edition), reflecting the national consolidation of the Jewish press. And Melbourne businessman Richard Pratt sold his interest in both the Sydney and Melbourne editions of the paper to the Klein family of Sydney. The Melbourne edition continued to include the optional Yiddish supplement *Di Yidishe Naies.*

Personalia

Among the Australian Jews who received honors in 1989–90 was Sir David Iser Smith of Canberra, who had served as official secretary to five governors-general of Australia. Sir David received his knighthood upon his retirement in August 1990.

Sir Zelman Cowen, a former governor-general of Australia (1977–82), returned to his native Melbourne in 1990, following his retirement as provost of Oriel College, Oxford. Justice Marcus Einfeld of Sydney resigned in December 1989 after a controversial three-year stint as president of the Human Rights and Equal Opportunity Commission. Prominent Melbourne businessman Isador Magid, a principal benefactor of Progressive Judaism in Australia, retired in 1990 as a long-serving member of the Board of Governors of the Jewish Agency. Major-General Paul Cullen, Australian Jewry's most distinguished living soldier, retired from the Refugee Council of Australia in 1990 after almost a decade of service. Susan Bures, editor of the Sydney edition of the *Australian Jewish News,* was appointed in 1990 to a three-year term as deputy chairperson of the Ethnic Affairs Commission of New South Wales, succeeding Rabbi Uri Themal. Well-known communal leader Isi Leibler in 1990 received an honorary doctorate from Deakin University, Geelong, principally for his services to Soviet Jewry. He became the first person to be honored by an Australian university for devotion to a Jewish cause.

Several prominent personalities, all overseas-born, died during this period: Rabbi Maurice Bernard Benson of Sydney, a founder of the Bankstown and District War Memorial Synagogue in suburban Sydney and a former minister (1949–52) of the Adelaide Hebrew Congregation, May 1989, aged 69; Rabbi Dr. Alfred Fabian of Sydney, minister of the Adelaide Hebrew Congregation (1940–46), chief minister of the Brisbane Hebrew Congregation (1946–62), chief minister of Sydney's North Shore Synagogue (1962–75), and senior Jewish chaplain in Australia (1962–89), October 1989, aged 79; Sydney Alan Field of Sydney, president of the Australian Jewish Welfare Society in New South Wales and founding president of the Australia-Israel Chamber of Commerce, November 1989, aged 70; Paul Fingereth of Brisbane, president of the Queensland Jewish Board of Deputies (1982–86 and again since 1988), April 1990, aged 54; Mina Fink of Melbourne, instrumental in providing humanitarian aid to victims of the Nazis, a former president and a life governor of the National Council of Jewish Women in Australia and an honorary member of the executive of the International Council of Jewish Women, May 1990, aged 76; Abram Landa of Sydney, a former member of the New South Wales Parliament (1930–32, 1941–65) and New South Wales Agent-General in London (1965–70), who played a pivotal role in persuading Australian statesman Dr. H.V. Evatt, then chairman of the ad hoc Committee on Palestine at the United Nations, to commit Australia to support the creation of Israel, July 1989, aged 87; Dr. Wolf Simon Matsdorf, formerly of Sydney, president of the Australian Jewish Welfare Society in New South Wales (1951–59) and a leading analyst of Australian Jewry, who settled in Israel in 1971, in Jerusalem, September 1989, aged 82; Sir Paul Strasser of Sydney, generous benefactor of Jewish educational institutions in Australia, including Shalom College at the University of New South Wales and the Emanuel School, Sydney, March 1989, aged 77; Robert Zablud of Melbourne, a former president of the Victorian Jewish Board of Deputies, of the State Zionist Council of Victoria, and of the Zionist Federation of Australia, and a vice-president of the Executive Council of Australian Jewry, September 1989, aged 76.

HILARY RUBINSTEIN

South Africa

FOR THE PEOPLE OF SOUTH AFRICA, 1990 was one of the most dramatic, exciting, and, at the same time, bewildering periods in recent history. It was a year in which radical government action hastened the dismantling of apartheid and further threatened the traditionally dominant and privileged position of whites. Jews shared the anxieties of other whites about the future and were also mindful of their own potential role as scapegoats during the painful adjustments to come. They were worried, too, about the apparent growth of black anti-Semitism and how this might affect them in the new South Africa.[1]

National Affairs

On February 2, 1990, Pres. F.W. de Klerk stated in his opening speech to Parliament that the government had decided to lift the ban on all prohibited organizations, including the African National Congress (ANC), as well as to release, unconditionally, ANC leader Nelson Mandela and other political prisoners. Furthermore, the three-year-old "state of emergency" would be relaxed in regard to media curbs, conditions imposed on released emergency detainees, and restrictions on some 33 organizations. He also announced the repeal of the Separate Amenities Act of 1953, which comprised the discriminatory laws generally referred to as "petty apartheid."

De Klerk's speech marked the beginning of a new phase in the process of political reform that had been initiated more than a decade earlier by his predecessor, P. W. Botha, in response to growing doubts within the National party about the continued viability of apartheid and to various political and economic developments during the late 1960s and 1970s. By 1986, when his attempts to introduce limited reform had failed to curb growing violence, Botha declared a general state of emergency.

While it appeared that progress toward ending apartheid had halted at the political level, this was not the case in other areas of life in South Africa. "Apartheid is crumbling all about us, and the new society is taking shape," wrote anti-apartheid activist John Kane-Berman. "Post-apartheid SA is not going to be legislated into existence by some future government under a new constitution. It is being forged

---

[1]See Gideon Shimoni, "South African Jews and the Apartheid Crisis," AJYB 1988, vol. 88, pp. 3–58, for an account of developments up to 1987.

in theatres and hotels and restaurants, on trains, on beaches and sports fields, in universities and private schools, in shops and offices, in mines and factories. . . . In our silent revolution the Government has often been more of a spectator than an actor. Change has taken place despite, not because of, its wishes."[2]

What happened in 1990, then, was that the government not only recognized and sanctioned the so-called silent revolution, but also resumed and accelerated legislative and structural reform. De Klerk clearly demonstrated that he and his government were irrevocably committed to the abolition of apartheid and to the establishment of a democratic South Africa with equal rights for all.

Responses to Change

The responses of whites to these events ranged from uncritical optimism about a nonracial, democratic, more egalitarian South Africa, to deep pessimism about the country's viability and the future of whites and, on the extreme Right, to uncompromising rejectionism. For those who accepted that black majority rule was inevitable, hopes for the future depended to an important degree on their assessment of what would happen to the economy. Thus, the immediate concern of lower- and middle-class wage- and salary-earners was the growing competition from blacks, Indians, and coloreds, both in getting jobs and in job advancement, as well as the increasing possibility of having to work under black supervisors and managers. Small white businesses that traded mainly with blacks also faced increased competition. At another level, large employers of labor, both public and private, were constantly under pressure from the powerful black trade unions, legalized only relatively recently. Some factories and commercial firms already had to close down because they could not meet union demands, while many others were involved in a dangerous game of brinkmanship. Looking beyond the present and immediate future, there was great trepidation in the white business community over the implications of ANC rhetoric about nationalization and the redistribution of resources. At the same time, there was hope that black leaders would acknowledge the importance of white capital and know-how in maintaining the economy.

Other, noneconomic, concerns of whites related to the effects of removing discriminatory legislation. Although this had already been happening gradually over the previous 10–15 years, during 1990 the Separate Amenities Act was repealed in its entirety. The Group Areas Act—which designated where members of each racial group could legally own and occupy property—was modified with regard to business premises and was not being enforced against blacks wanting to live in "white areas." Many whites found it difficult to share places of recreation, restaurants, hotels, and amenities such as public lavatories with people whom they still regarded

[2]John Kane-Berman, *South Africa's Silent Revolution* (Southern Book Publishers, Johannesburg, n.d., probably 1990), quoted from *Business Day,* Johannesburg, Aug. 1, 1990, in *Focus on South Africa,* Aug. 1990.

as uncouth, uncivilized, and even "unclean." Many also feared that blacks moving into white neighborhoods would bring noise, litter, overcrowding and, in general, lower their tone—and property values. There was also serious concern about the quality of education as schools, colleges, and universities were opened up to all. There was fear as well that the loosening of control over black political activity would lead to an increase in violence against whites. This fear was reinforced by the ANC's insistence that it was not ready to renounce what it termed "the armed struggle" until it was convinced that there was "real progress" toward majority rule. In the longer term, there was the equally frightening prospect of complete anarchy when expectations by ordinary blacks for a better life could not be fulfilled by a black government.

Black responses to the dismantling of apartheid were also not uniform. At the ideological level, there were groups, like the Pan Africanist Congress, that were reluctant to acknowledge de Klerk's sincerity or to negotiate any compromise with the whites; others would talk to the government, but only on the understanding that such issues as nationalization and majority rule based on one-man one-vote were nonnegotiable preconditions; and still others, like Mandela, who were prepared to lay everything on the negotiating table. There was also an internal struggle for power between the older (and, generally, more moderate) ANC leaders and the younger ones; the unabated violence and bloodshed in the conflict between the ANC and Zulu chief minister Gatsha Buthelezi's Inkatha movement; the ideological gulf between the ANC and the youthful militants of the 1976–1986 uprisings; the probability, at some future date, of a test of strength between leaders of the ANC and those of the powerful black trade unions; and the potential tensions, within the ANC, between the noncommunists and those advocating a socialist state. This lack of unity encouraged some whites, perhaps naively, to believe that there was no great danger of a black government taking over in the near future. For others, probably the majority, the confused situation among blacks simply added to the uncertainty.

Jewish Responses[3]

On February 28, 1990, two-and-a-half weeks after his release from prison, a photograph of Nelson Mandela warmly embracing Yasir Arafat in Lusaka, Zambia, was published on the front pages of several South African dailies. The following day Mandela was quoted as saying, in response to a question, that if his meeting with Arafat and his statements equating the struggle of the Palestinians with that of the blacks were to alienate "South Africa's influential Jewish community," that was "too bad" (*PIJI,* Mar. 2, 1990). These reports, coming on the heels of recent

---

[3]The major sources of information for this section are the news digest *Press Items of Jewish Interest* (*PIJI*), published periodically by the South African Jewish Board of Deputies, Johannesburg, and an early draft of Milton Shain's "What Future for South African Jews?" *Midstream,* Jan. 1992, pp. 17–19.

right-wing anti-Semitic incidents, raised the ire of local Jews—and their anxiety.

To give expression to the community's outrage and, at the same time, to restore calm, mass meetings were organized during March in Johannesburg and Cape Town. These were addressed by leading representatives of the South African Jewish Board of Deputies and the South African Zionist Federation, by Chief Rabbi Cyril Harris, and by Democratic party parliamentarian (now ambassador to Washington) Harry Schwarz. While reaffirming the community's support of Israel, the major thrust of all the speakers was to allay anxiety, cool tempers, and place events in a more realistic perspective. Schwarz assessed the overall situation as follows: The Jewish fate is ultimately tied up with that of the white population as a whole and there can "be no separate deal between blacks and Jews." Clearly it would be in the interest of Jews for South Africa to have a liberal constitution underpinned by a bill of rights. As Schwarz correctly explained: "Only a society which gives everyone rights will give Jews rights." He also suggested, as did other speakers, that insofar as Jews felt that they did have special interests, they should be vigilant while maintaining a low profile.

Since almost all Jews were part of the English-speaking sector, and since a large proportion belonged to the middle and upper classes, it was primarily with these groups that they shared their hopes and fears. Thus, it is probable that the majority supported the government's initiative, though not unlikely that at least some had considerable sympathy with the right-wing rejectionists.

At an official level, the Board of Deputies, as the representative of local Jewish interests, was eager to identify the Jewish community with current political developments. In a press statement following de Klerk's opening speech to Parliament, the board expressed its confidence that the president's proposals would "create an atmosphere for the establishment of genuine democracy for the benefit of the country and all its peoples" (*PIJI,* Feb. 16, 1990).

Attitudes Toward Jews

Over the past several years a number of extreme militant, right-wing groups had come into being. Afrikaner in origin, but welcoming English-speakers who shared their views, their main objective was to counter the unification of South African society. These groups based their appeal on the concept of a white, Christian, Afrikaner national state, in which not only would apartheid continue to be vigorously enforced but the rights of non-Christians would be severely curtailed. The most important and durable of these groups, the Afrikaner Weerstandsbeweging, or Afrikaner Resistance Movement (AWB), had a quasi-military structure, sported brown-shirt-style uniforms, and adopted a swastika-like symbol as its emblem. The leader of the AWB, ex-policeman Eugene Terre'Blanche, was quite explicit about the sinister role of the "five, six, seven hundred thousand (*sic*)" Jews in South Africa who controlled the economy and who were playing a major role in breaking down racial barriers ("They never marry with a non-Jew but they want me to mix with the blacks and with other races"). He also accused them of having "no loyalty for the country and for the Afrikaners . . . [but] are here to make money and to send it to Israel."[4] There seems little doubt that the strident anti-Jewish sentiments so frequently expressed by the AWB encouraged a rash of anti-Semitic incidents over the last two to three years—despite Terre'Blanche's vigorous denial that his movement was in any way involved. These incidents included placing pigs' heads in synagogues, private homes, and other places; desecration of a cemetery; burning the Israeli flag and displaying Nazi flags; and anti-Jewish graffiti. Throughout 1990, a variety of such incidents were widely reported in the general press and in the Board of Deputies' news digest (*PIJI*). The latter included references to numerous statements, letters, and articles—some (by both Jews and non-Jews) condemning the incidents, and others criticizing the Jews.

Anti-Semitic actions were condemned not only by the Jewish community but also by the state president and other members of the government, by Afrikaner academics, and by two right-wing political groups, the Herstigte (Reconstituted) National party and the Conservative party. Dr. Andries Treurnicht, leader of the last-mentioned group, which was also the official parliamentary opposition, was quite unequivocal in his denial that either he or his party (at whose rally some people waved Nazi flags) were anti-Semitic, had any Nazi sympathies or leanings, or that they had ever sanctioned any anti-Jewish behavior by their members. Both the government and police emphasized that these incidents were perpetrated by "insignificant minorities," the "lunatic fringe," and that while they would do all they could to apprehend those responsible, there was no cause for undue alarm.

Officially, the Jewish community took a similar position, warning against overreaction or the creation of vigilante groups. Anti-Semitism had always existed in South Africa, it was felt, and was probably no more prevalent now than it ever had been: it had simply been brought into the open by present conditions. Nevertheless, the board kept a close watch on these activities and maintained contact with the authorities in order to protect the community and its institutions. Knowledgeable South Africans did not discount the possibility that Jews could become primary scapegoats of the Right in the event of economic and political turmoil.

The question of black attitudes to Jews is more complex and requires distinguishing between anti-Zionist and anti-Jewish perspectives. During the 1980s, opponents of apartheid—black and white, South Africans and foreigners—saw Israel as a staunch and active ally of the racist regime. Not only had the Israelis flaunted the UN decision to impose trade sanctions on South Africa but, even worse, there appeared to be strong evidence that they were supplying the South African army with equipment, materials, and expertise. Even after September 1987, when the Israeli government—under pressure from the United States—decided to impose sanctions, the South African press continued to report actual or presumed military

[4]Summarized and quoted from an interview with Eugene Terre'Blanche in Tzippi Hoffman and Alan Fischer, *The Jews of South Africa: What Future?* (Johannesburg, 1988), pp. 185–99.

cooperation between the two countries. The frequency and consistency with which reports, articles, editorials, and correspondence on this topic were published throughout the 1980s and even during 1990 undoubtedly contributed to Israel's negative image in the minds of blacks and liberal whites.

It appears, however, that for blacks, the more salient issue was Israel's occupation of the West Bank and Gaza and the Palestinian struggle for freedom. Parallels between Israel's treatment of Arabs and South Africa's treatment of blacks had long been drawn by supporters and opponents of apartheid, friends and enemies of Israel. For blacks, whose most voluble spokesman in recent years was Anglican archbishop and Nobel Peace Prize winner Desmond Tutu, the *intifada* was seen as analogous to their own desperate fight against the oppressor. Nelson Mandela, too, identified with the Palestinians and frequently expressed his gratitude to, and friendship with, "brothers-in-arms" Yasir Arafat and Muammar Qaddafi.

In addition, local Muslims engaged in a massive ongoing campaign—through meetings, protests, posters, advertisements, and publications—to demonstrate Israel's inhumanity and the illegitimacy of her claim to statehood. The Islamic Propagation Center International in Durban, a well-funded organization, disseminated expensive anti-Zionist and anti-Semitic leaflets to thousands of householders. Animosity between Muslim and Jewish students continued to be a feature of university campus life, particularly at the University of Cape Town and the University of the Witwatersrand. Physical confrontations took place periodically between the two groups.

Jews took the two black leaders far more seriously than they did either right-wing white or Muslim anti-Semites. Each attack on Israel elicited a vigorous counterattack, accusations of anti-Semitism, and a reaffirmation of the community's commitment to the Jewish state. Both Mandela and Tutu denied that their condemnation of Israel's policies meant that they were anti-Jewish. Mandela went further: If Zionism meant the Jewish aspiration for a national home, then he supported it just as he supported Israel's demands for secure borders and Palestinian claims for an independent state. He would like, he said, to visit Israel and even to offer his good offices in bringing about a peaceful settlement (*PIJI,* June 15, 1990). These assurances were offered by Mandela and Tutu on public platforms, in the media, and at meetings with representative Jewish community organizations. Officially, at any rate, some Jewish leaders maintained that, despite their position on the Palestinians, neither Mandela nor Tutu could be accused of being anti-Jewish (*PIJI,* Feb. 13, 1987; June 1 and 29, 1990). However, in the "Jewish street," the tendency was still to equate opposition to Israel's policies with anti-Zionism and anti-Semitism.

An entirely different issue was whether blacks had negative attitudes toward Jews and, if so, whether these attitudes constituted anti-Semitism. Until about 18 years ago, the possible existence of such feelings occasioned no serious concern. In general terms, the relationship between Jews and blacks, like that with other English-speaking urban whites, was based primarily on their respective roles as master and servant, tempered, at best, by a degree of paternalism expressed in terms of more compassionate and humane treatment. Jews were not much concerned what blacks thought of them, assuming that they were, like other whites, resented, but cherishing the belief that they treated "their" blacks better and were, therefore, less disliked than other whites. This belief was shared by many other whites who often accused Jews of "spoiling" their black employees. Many blacks also believed that Jews were more compassionate employers and that, politically, Jews had identified more than other whites with left-wing and liberal groups.

Serious interest in black attitudes to Jews grew out of recent events and increasing black power. In August 1990, the South African Zionist Federation commissioned a survey in which a sample of 1,031 "black elites" and 1,014 whites were asked to say what they felt about Jews. The main findings among blacks were: 17.5 percent said that the Jewish community "irritated" them because, in descending order of frequency, they were parasites, snobs, racists, anti-Christ, and unpatriotic; 16 percent approved of right-wing anti-Semitic actions, and one-third were uncertain whether or not they approved; and, finally, 30 percent considered the Jewish community to be "mostly a liability" to South Africa. Percentages of whites giving the same responses were: 5.7 percent, 0.7 percent, and 3.2 percent, respectively.[5] Unfortunately, the crudeness of the research design—nothing, for example, was asked about black attitudes to other white groups or to whites in general—makes it impossible to draw any conclusion beyond the indication that some anti-Jewish, as distinct from anti-Israel, feeling does exist among blacks.

Whatever other factors might contribute to black attitudes to Jews, it seemed likely that the economic sphere would continue to be the most important determinant of future relations between the two groups. In the first place, for large numbers of black industrial and commercial workers, the boss—and therefore, the exploiter of his labor—was typically a Jew. (Although mining magnate Harry Oppenheimer had not considered himself a Jew since early adulthood, he and his family were still regarded as such by many blacks and whites alike. Anti-Semitic references to Jewish economic power invariably included the Oppenheimer financial and mining empire.) Furthermore, a significant proportion of small businesses catering primarily to a black clientele had been and were owned by Jews—many of whom were perceived to have become rich by taking advantage of blacks' lack of education and their subordinate position.

Whether blacks were anti-Semitic in the classic Western sense was at least debatable. While it could be assumed that there were black anti-Semites, there was evidence that for many blacks these attitudes were situation-related, and that negative attitudes toward Jews were balanced by similar attitudes toward other whites.

Anti-Israel feelings were more serious, however. If no solution were found that

[5]"The Attitudes of Whites and Black-Elites Towards Anti-Semitism," conducted by the Human Sciences Research Council in the series "Opinion Surveys: Research for a New South Africa," Pretoria, Aug. 8–14, 1990. Mimeographed report made available by Jeremy Hayman, Information Officer, South African Zionist Federation, Johannesburg.

completely satisfied the Palestinians, black attitudes could remain negative. On the other hand, once blacks achieved their own goals in South Africa, attitudes to and relations with Israel might—as in many other countries in Africa and elsewhere—be modified by self-interest. Nevertheless, the relationship of South African Jews to Israel was problematic for black leaders and could continue to be so in the future. As black columnist Jon Qwelana wrote in the Johannesburg *Sunday Star* (Apr. 1, 1990): "Personally, I think South Africans of Jewish extraction should expend the great quantities of vigor and energy they pour out in defense of Israel at every drop of a hat on greater concern about what happens right inside their own backyard. Charity begins at home, after all, unless 'home' means somewhere else for them, which I earnestly refuse to believe." A related issue for Jews concerned money raised for Israel: if, under a black government, restrictions on transfer of money abroad remained in force, would current special arrangements be continued?

The Jewish community was also concerned about the effect on Jewish institutions of an inevitably more even-handed, nonracial policy of allocating state funds. Thus, Jewish day schools could expect to receive considerably diminished grants-in-aid, as could Jewish welfare and other government-subsidized services. Furthermore, a black government might insist that all schools (and possibly other institutions) must be open to anyone who wished to attend them, irrespective of race or religion.

In summary: in the negotiations between the government and black nationalists, it seemed unlikely that the Jews would become an issue. Anti-Semitism as such was unlikely to become a problem. On the other hand, the limitations discussed would affect the community and the way it functioned. If imposed, however, these limitations would reflect general policy; they would not be specifically directed against Jews. The notable exception was the connection with Israel, and in this regard the South African Jewish community might find itself facing a serious dilemma.

JEWISH COMMUNITY

Demography[6]

In 1970 the Jews of South Africa numbered 118,200, constituting 3.1 percent of the 3.7 million whites and 0.6 percent of the total population of 21.4 million. The

---

[6]For a detailed analysis, see Sergio DellaPergola and Allie A. Dubb, "South African Jewry: A Sociodemographic Profile," in AJYB 1988, vol. 88, pp. 59–140. The sources of statistical data that have not been specifically referenced are, ultimately, publications of the Central Statistical Service, Pretoria, together with additional, unpublished material made available by the CSS to the South African Jewish Board of Deputies from time to time. It should be noted that a countrywide sociodemographic survey by Allie A. Dubb, sponsored by the Kaplan Centre for Jewish Studies and Research at the University of Cape Town, is now under way. In addition, an official population census was conducted in March 1991. The results of both survey and census were expected to be available early in 1992.

widespread political unrest during the late 1970s led to a dramatic increase in emigration of whites, among them, Jews. While there are no statistics on Jews who left South Africa, it has been estimated that some 14,000 (or almost 12 percent of the 1970 total) had emigrated by the end of 1979. The 1980 census count of 117,963 Jews—down a mere 200 since 1970—was, therefore, unexpected. Detailed analysis of census results and other information led to the conclusion that the loss due to emigration had been offset by an estimated natural increase of 4,200 and an influx of some 9,600 immigrants and returning emigrants. Nevertheless, although the size of the community remained relatively stable, in 1980 it constituted only 2.6 percent of all whites, and 0.5 percent of the total population. By 1990, if a zero migration balance is assumed for the preceding ten years, the Jewish population might be expected to have declined to about 114,000—representing 2.3 percent and 0.4 percent, respectively, of the estimated white and total populations.

The decade 1970–1980 brought a small but significant Jewish immigration from Zimbabwe and other neighboring African states, the United Kingdom, and Western Europe. Although it was generally believed within the Jewish community that there had been a large influx of Israelis after the 1973 Yom Kippur War, in fact, during the whole period, the net Israeli immigration amounted to about 1,300.[7] Only 2,261 Israeli-born and 1,927 Israeli citizens were enumerated in 1980—approximately the same numbers as in 1970. Although popular perceptions of 20,000–30,000 were grossly exaggerated, it is nevertheless probable that there were more Israelis, but that they had escaped enumeration for various reasons. Between 1980 and 1989, 4,030 former Israeli residents immigrated to South Africa and about 685 emigrated, while during the first half of 1990, an additional 539 immigrants arrived. Although it is still impossible to determine the total number of Israelis in the country, at least 7,500 could be accounted for by mid-1990.

Of the estimated 14,000 Jews who emigrated from South Africa during the 1970s, the largest proportion left in the aftermath of the 1976 Soweto uprising. Jews continued to speak of considerable emigration during the 1980s—particularly during the turbulent years of 1986–87—but there is not enough information to make any reasonable estimate. What is known is that only about 3,700 emigrated to Israel and that this number represents an unknown, but undoubtedly much smaller, proportion of the total emigration than it did in the 1970s. Clearly, continued Jewish emigration would depend on actual developments in South Africa and also on whether Jews felt they had a place in the new South Africa—both as whites and as Jews.

The long-term movement of Jews to large urban centers continued, particularly to the two major metropolitan areas of Johannesburg and Cape Town. Whereas in 1970 these two cities accounted for 75 percent of the South African Jewish popula-

---

[7]Figures for Israeli immigrants based on Central Statistical Services, Tourism and Migration, Pretoria, annual reports 1970 to 1988, and monthly Statistical News Release—Tourism and Migration, from Jan. 1989 to June 1990.

tion, this had risen, in 1980, to 80 percent of the total. Conversely, the proportion of Jews in all the smaller cities dropped from 11.7 percent to 10.6 percent. These trends gained momentum during 1980–1989 and, by the end of the decade, several of the smaller city communities were having difficulty maintaining the amenities of Jewish life.

Communal Affairs

Although funds, skilled professional personnel, and committed lay leadership were becoming scarce—related to the emigration of young people and the aging of the community—South African Jewry continued to manifest a cohesive communal life. This was exemplified in its two major organizations, the South African Jewish Board of Deputies (SAJBD) and the South African Zionist Federation (SAZF). Seymour Kopelowitz, who was appointed national director of the SAJBD in 1990, described the SAJBD's role in a changing South Africa in broad terms: acting as a "think tank" for the community, developing and disseminating ideas, and planning for the future needs of the community within the context of the wider society. According to Kopelowitz, the SAJBD would embark on a program to identify the strengths and weaknesses, opportunities and threats facing the Jewish community over the next ten years.

The SAJBD made intensive efforts to establish dialogue with the wider community in general and black leaders in particular. These meetings took place at national and regional levels. Nelson Mandela, "Terror" Lekota, Ahmed Kathrada of the ANC, and Alec Irwin of the Congress of South African Trade Unions (COSATU) were among those who held meetings with the SAJBD. The Transvaal Council of the SAJBD ran Club 44, a group focusing on current affairs that invited speakers such as Aggrey Klaaste, editor of the *Sowetan,* a daily newspaper catering mainly to blacks, and Prof. W. de Klerk, brother of the state president. A range of other cultural activities was coordinated by the SAJBD.

Increasingly, Holocaust memorial services were a feature of the Jewish communal calendar. These ceremonies included poetry readings, songs, and a keynote address, often delivered by a prominent visitor. In addition, Holocaust memorials were erected in major Jewish centers. Since the late 1980s, South African Jews had joined the worldwide pilgrimages to Auschwitz, and in 1988 South African Jews joined world Jewry in commemorating the 50th anniversary of *Kristallnacht.* To mark the event, synagogues kept their lights burning throughout the night. For the occasion, a panel of Holocaust survivors in Johannesburg recounted their experiences to an audience of over 400. Adult education Holocaust study programs were conducted in Cape Town and Johannesburg. In 1990, Dr. Ze'ev Mankowitz of the Hebrew University of Jerusalem held the attention of 350 Jews and Gentiles over a period of six weekly sessions in a course organized by the Isaac and Jessie Kaplan Centre for Jewish Studies and Research at the University of Cape Town. The penultimate lecture was clouded by ugly questions from a "denial" member of the audience. On the whole, however, South Africa did not experience the sort of neo-Nazism currently rife in Europe.

The Jewish community was well served by a vigorous Jewish press consisting of the *Zionist Record,* an organ of the SAZF, the *South African Jewish Chronicle,* and the *Herald Times.* In addition, each region published a monthly newspaper containing mainly local news. The *Johannesburg Jewish Voice* began publication in 1990; although funded by the Jewish community, it gave voice to a wider range of political opinion than the other publications and was somewhat controversial.

Fund Raising

The South African Jewish community had a proud tradition of fund raising for Jewish and Israeli causes. The year under review was a remarkable one for the United Communal Fund (UCF) and the Israel United Appeal (IUA), which had merged in 1987. The single entity, known as the United Communal Fund (UCF), had the effect of unifying the community and ensuring that the two funds did not compete with each other for contributions. The beginning of 1990 saw the start of the highly successful Operation Exodus campaign for Russian Jewry. Shlomo Hillel, a former speaker of Israel's Knesset, was a guest speaker at a number of IUA gatherings. For the first time the organization enlisted the help of the rabbinate and the lay leaders of synagogues, with outstanding results. There appeared to be a newfound spirit of cooperation between the synagogue leadership, both lay and religious, and the fund-raisers.

The major beneficiary of the UCF was Israel; other recipients included the SAJBD, the Jewish day-school movement, the Union of Orthodox Synagogues, the Union of Progressive Judaism, and the Union of Jewish Women. Congregations and other bodies raised their own funds among their members and with fund-raising drives. Although current trends in Jewish demography could eventually force the community to consider rationalizing the range of essential services, at present institutions for the handicapped, aged, and orphaned operated in all major centers. The Union of Jewish Women ran a thriving adult-education program. Their latest project was the Home Instruction Program for Pre-School Youngsters (HIPPY), which was directed at underprivileged black children.

Israel-Related Activity

The *intifada* had little impact on South African Jewry, and the community continued to demonstrate unquestioning support for Israel.

The SAZF was the representative body coordinating Zionist activity, and the various Zionist groupings, organizations, and societies were affiliated with it. Its departments dealt with organization and information, fund raising, youth activities, women's work, and immigration to Israel. The latter dwindled substantially during 1990. Affiliated with the Zionist Federation were a number of Zionist youth movements: Habonim, Bnei Akiva, Betar, and Maginim, which conducted cultural programs, organized youth activities, and ran highly successful summer camps. In addition, university youth had their representative organization, the South African Union of Jewish Students (SAUJS), which was affiliated with the Zionist Federation as well as the SAJBD.

Mendel Kaplan, a South African lawyer and business executive, continued in the post of chairman of the international Jewish Agency board of governors, to which he had been appointed in 1987. He had served previously as world chairman of the board of trustees of the United Israel Appeal.

Education

The South African Board of Jewish Education claimed to control the largest Jewish day-school system in the Diaspora (the King David Schools), though most of its 94 affiliates around the country were afternoon and nursery schools. The system maintained its cohesion and strength, even though apart from Johannesburg and Cape Town, the number of Jewish pupils in day schools had been decreasing over the past few years—a result of demographic shifts within the Jewish population. The system was less threatened by financial considerations than in the past, in part due to a government financial subsidy of 5.5 million rands per annum and increased receipts from the United Communal Fund. (Future scenarios, however, could well exclude a government subsidy.) Jewish day schools provided education from preschool to the completion of high school for approximately 8,000 pupils— more than 60 percent of all Jewish children in South Africa. They received a full education following a state syllabus and a Jewish studies program including Jewish religion, history, literature, and Hebrew language. Although all schools had an Orthodox orientation—often described as "national-traditional"—some provided a more intensive Orthodox religious education than others. The mainstream Jewish day schools accepted children of mixed marriages and Reform converts.

The South African Board of Jewish Education also involved itself with Jewish children who attended state schools, whose main access to Jewish education was through the Cheder program and by means of Religious Instruction Booklets sent into the schools. It also administered a network of Hebrew nursery schools according to the standards laid down by the Nursery School Association of South Africa. The Cape Council of the SAJBD had its own religious-instruction program for Jewish pupils who attended state schools in the Western Cape.

A more intensive Jewish education was provided for approximately 1,700 pupils by the Yeshivah College, the Torah Academy of the Lubavitch Foundation, the Beis Yakov Girls' High School, the Sha'arei Torah Primary School, and the Yeshivat Torat Emet, all in Johannesburg, as well as the Hebrew Academy in Cape Town. The Progressive movement also maintained a network of supplementary Hebrew and religious classes at temples affiliated with it. These schools were affiliated with the Union for Progressive Jewish Education.

At the tertiary level, Hebrew teachers were trained at the Rabbi Zlotnick Hebrew Teachers Training College in Johannesburg. University students were able to take Jewish studies through the Semitics Department of the University of South Africa, the Department of Hebrew and Jewish Studies at the University of Cape Town, the Department of Hebrew and Jewish Studies at Natal University, and the Department of Hebrew at the University of the Witwatersrand. A Jewish Studies University Program (JSUP) combined traditional Jewish studies with university studies through the University of South Africa. Many of these programs reported increased enrollment. In September 1990, an international conference on "Judaism in the Context of World Civilizations" was held at the University of the Witwatersrand.

Religion

According to a study conducted in 1974, 80 percent of South African Jews were affiliated with a religious body, though there was evidence that this number had declined in the interim. About four-fifths belonged to Orthodox congregations and one-fifth to Progressive congregations.[8] These were autonomous bodies, each controlling its own affairs, with religious authority vested in its spiritual leaders. Most of the congregations, however, were affiliated with representative organizations which endeavored to strengthen Jewish religious life. The Union of Orthodox Synagogues of South Africa was the umbrella body for Orthodox congregations throughout South Africa. It consisted of 95 synagogues and claimed a membership enrollment of approximately 18,500 families. Of the 95 synagogues, not more than a handful enjoyed the services of a full-time rabbi. A noteworthy feature of the South African Jewish scene was the inadequate financial compensation of rabbis; the overwhelming majority had to hold down more than one job in order to earn an adequate living.

The activity of the Jews for Jesus—which had attracted a few hundred Jews to its programs—and other evangelical movements was viewed as a serious problem. A special department was established by the Union of Orthodox Synagogues (UOS) to actively counter this process.

The UOS appointed and maintained the office of the chief rabbi, the Johannesburg Beth Din, and the Cape Beth Din. Since 1987 the office of chief rabbi had been held by Cyril Harris. He had been minister of the St. John's Wood Synagogue in London and a fellow of Jews' College, London, before coming to South Africa.

Recently there was tremendous growth in the *ba'al teshuvah* movement (returnees to Judaism), and 34 small *shtieblach* (synagogues) were established mainly in and around Johannesburg. The Lubavitch movement had also made inroads into the community, especially in Johannesburg, where it was established in 1972, and Cape Town, in 1976. Although a relatively small proportion of the community was

---

[8]The countrywide sociodemographic study referred to in note 6, in progress at the time of writing, will provide updated figures.

involved in Lubavitch activities, programs expanded substantially in the past few years. Adult education, youth clubs, and Shabbatons were particularly popular. Outlying communities were visited periodically by a Mobile Jewish Center—"Mitzvah Tank." This specially designed motor vehicle housed exhibits, a library, literature, mezuzahs, tefillin, and so forth. The "tank" periodically visited schools, youth seminars, and predominantly Jewish neighborhoods. In addition, a weekly national radio program, "The Jewish Sound," was initiated and produced by the Lubavitch Foundation.

For the Reform sector, the South African Union for Progressive Judaism (affiliated with the World Union of Progressive Judaism) was the coordinating body. Estimates of the movement's membership ranged from 2,500 to 6,500 families, with a total of 12 congregations in the major centers, though only a few were served by rabbis. Each temple operated a religious school, and there was a separate, independent primary school in Johannesburg under Progressive auspices.

Personalia

Seymour Kopelowitz was appointed national director of the South African Jewish Board of Deputies in 1990. Kopelowitz came to the board with a range of qualifications and awards: he had an MBA degree and was a former Jewish day-school principal and a Jerusalem Fellow.

Harry Schwarz was appointed South African ambassador to Washington in 1990. Mr. Schwarz immigrated to South Africa from Germany as a young boy and spent his entire political career fighting apartheid and social injustice.

Helen Suzman, an internationally renowned anti-apartheid liberal parliamentarian, retired from Parliament in 1990.

ALLIE A. DUBB
MILTON SHAIN

Israel

FOR THE FIRST SEVEN MONTHS OF 1990, Israelis gazed inward: an unprecedented political crisis paralyzed the government; new immigrants poured in from the Soviet Union; the *intifada*, in its third year, moved from the territories into Jerusalem and pre-1967 Israel. The stalled peace process brought down the two-year-old national unity government in March, and the protracted efforts to set up a new government produced a sense of deep revulsion; Israelis were never more disdainful of their leaders. The Soviet immigration, one of the lone surviving matters of national consensus, was embroiled in the divisiveness of settlements in the territories, attitudes toward the Palestinians, and relations with the United States. The latter, in any case, were at an all-time low.

On August 2, Iraq invaded Kuwait, and for the rest of the year, policymakers and public opinion focused outward, on the American campaign against President Saddam Hussein and the specter of war. When the Palestinians, who had succeeded in carving out a unique identity in the *intifada*, threw their support to Saddam, they were once again seen as but a component of the great Arab nation seeking Israel's destruction. This and the perceived external danger at least temporarily erased internal differences and pushed the battle over the territories into the background. The United States emerged as a potential savior, but serious tensions remained between the two governments.

As the year ended, Israelis prepared for the possibility of war; it was clear that their country would be involved. What was not clear, for the first time in its history, was whether Israel would fight back.

NATIONAL SECURITY

The Intifada—Year Three

Judging by the dry statistics alone, it appeared that in 1990 the tensions between Israel and the 1.5 million Palestinians living under military occupation in Judea, Samaria, and Gaza were somewhat relieved. The statistics, however, were misleading. By the end of the year, the emotional gap between Israelis and Palestinians was greater than at any time since the Six Day War, and the *intifada* was not only turning increasingly violent but was slowly crossing the pre-1967 Green Line,

427

threatening Israelis at their hitherto-tranquil homes and offices.

The third year of the Palestinian uprising in the territories, the *intifada*, which ended on December 9, 1990, saw a marked reduction in the number of Arabs killed by the Israeli security forces: according to official statistics, 89 Palestinians were killed by the army in 1990, compared to 270 in 1989. The change was mainly the result of two factors: a decrease in wild street demonstrations by the Palestinians, and far more stringent open-fire instructions for the soldiers. At the same time, internal terror among the Palestinians was on the increase: 192 Palestinians were killed during the year by their own people, by self-appointed masked vigilantes. All of the murders were excused on the basis of the collaboration of the victims with the Israeli authorities; in some cases, however, this was simply a convenient cover for settling old scores in blood.

The policing practices of the army in the territories underwent some changes with the replacement of Yitzhak Rabin by Moshe Arens as defense minister, with the formation of a new government in June. Upon taking office, Arens decided to place greater emphasis on maintaining the security of the roads on which Jewish settlers in the territories travel; one of the results of this policy was that the army now more often than not refrained from entering villages and towns that were not strategically located in the vicinity of major roads. Thus, the potential for deadly confrontations between the army and the local population was significantly reduced. Even critics of Israel's very presence in the territories and of the harsh stifling of the *intifada* praised Arens for reducing the number of casualties. At the same time, the army announced that it was now employing sharpshooters and snipers against masked stone-throwers; this action was criticized both in Israel and abroad.

Between April and July, the mood and attitudes of the population in the territories underwent a dramatic change, influenced by three unrelated developments. By this time, after two and a half years of *intifada*, the Palestinians were described by Israeli authorities as fatigued by the uprising and suffering from its debilitating economic consequences. The first development was President Saddam Hussein of Iraq's threat, in April, to "burn half of Israel" with his "binary chemical weapons." The Palestinian population in the territories, as well as the Arabs in Israel, rallied behind him, applauding the self-proclaimed "liberator" of Palestine, hailing him as the latter-day Saladin. (See "Gulf Crisis," below.) The moderates among them explained the Palestinian reaction as resulting from the despondence created by 23 years of Israeli occupation.

The second episode took place the next month, on May 20, near Rishon LeZion not far from Tel Aviv. An emotionally unbalanced discharged Israeli soldier, armed with an army-issue M-16 automatic rifle, massacred seven Palestinian laborers who were seeking work in Israel. The government claimed that the assailant, Ami Popper, was deranged and roundly condemned the killings. The Prime Minister's Office labeled the massacre "a fearful act of insanity." Arabs, however, saw things differently: they blamed the government for the outrage. The next few days saw a fierce outburst of bloody riots in the territories: 20 Palestinians were killed in confrontations with the army. For several days, the Palestinians refrained from crossing over into Israel, but after a while, economic imperatives sent them back.

The incident near Rishon LeZion further enhanced the identification of Israeli Arabs with their brothers and sisters in the territories, and, for the first time, masked rioters could be seen wielding rocks inside established Arab towns in Israel, such as Nazareth and Shefaram. Prime Minister Yitzhak Shamir told the Likud Knesset caucus that the Israeli Arabs "must be warned that they are crossing a red line."

Some 50,000 Jewish demonstrators, organized by Peace Now, protested the murders; President George Bush sent condolences to the victims—including those who had been killed in the riots in the territories. The United Nations convened a special session in Geneva, with Yasir Arafat in attendance. The Security Council wished to send a delegation to examine the "safety" of the Palestinians under Israeli rule. Israel refused, but subsequently accepted the mission of a top UN official, Jean Claude Aimé.

The third development that embittered Palestinians was the termination of the U.S. dialogue with the PLO. This grew out of an aborted terrorist attack on an Israeli beach, on May 30, during the Shavuot vacation. Two rubber boats carrying 16 heavily armed terrorists were conveyed by a Libyan ship to a point several kilometers from the Israeli coastline. The leader of the terrorist squad, which belonged to the PLO-affiliated Palestine Liberation Front, subsequently stated that the mission of the squad had been to land on the crowded Tel Aviv beach, after the major hotels had been shelled by Katyusha fire from the sea. The boats, however, were detected by the Israel Navy; one was sunk at sea; the other landed on the beach at Nitzanim, some 35 kilometers south of Tel Aviv. Thousands of sunbathing vacationers were in the vicinity as the army and police closed in on the occupants of the second boat, which had succeeded in landing on the beach despite the Israeli patrol boat chasing after it. There were no civilian casualties in the incident, but many questions were raised in its wake about the navy's effectiveness in preventing such incursions, about the fact that, despite being tracked and followed, one of the boats nonetheless succeeded in landing, and about the controversial decision reached jointly by the army and police commanders not to evacuate the crowded beaches.

In July, following the aborted raid, the United States cut off its dialogue with the PLO (see "Diplomatic Developments," below). This move was seen by the Palestinians as a potentially fatal blow to any prospects for progress in the peace process, and they themselves proceeded to boycott American representatives in Israel.

Throughout the summer and fall, acts of violence in Jerusalem and elsewhere heightened apprehension on both sides. On May 28, an explosive device rocked Jerusalem's Mahaneh Yehudah market; one 72-year-old man was killed, nine persons were injured. The Islamic Jihad organization claimed responsibility. In June, riots broke out in the Silwan neighborhood of Jerusalem; these were described as the worst since the start of the *intifada*. Over 30,000 people were placed under curfew inside the capital of Israel. On July 27, a 17-year-old Canadian tourist was killed when a bomb exploded on the beach in Tel Aviv. Again, the Islamic Jihad claimed responsibility. Several days later, on August 6, an act occurred that shocked even the hardened Israeli public: two Jerusalem youths, 17 and 18 years old, were found dead, bound and gagged, near the Jerusalem suburb of Ramot. They had been repeatedly and viciously stabbed.

Jewish Jerusalem exploded with outrage. Unprecedented riots broke out. Arab cars with blue West Bank licenses were stoned; one such car was overturned and its driver killed. Altogether, 12 Palestinians were injured by stone-throwing Jewish youths, some emulating their Palestinian counterparts by covering their faces with masks. Justice Minister Dan Meridor summed up in the Knesset the sentiments of most of the Jewish population: "This murder has reminded us of something about our enemies which we all wished to forget." For the first time, politicians on the Left and on the Right called for a "separation" of the territories from Israel. Those on the Left saw the move as preliminary to a "separation" between Israel and the territories themselves; those on the far Right as a first step toward the "transfer" of the Palestinians out of the territories altogether.

In September a curious calm descended on the territories. For over a month, not one Palestinian was killed by the army in the West Bank; in Gaza, the army had not killed a demonstrator for three months. The change was attributed to Arens's "policy of restraint" and to the general preoccupation with developments in the Gulf.

On Thursday, September 20, during the Jewish New Year holiday, the Israeli public was stunned once again by a particularly gruesome murder. Amnon Pomerantz, a 46-year-old reserve soldier, lost his way in Gaza; instead of reaching his unit, he found himself alone in his car inside the El-Bureij refugee camp in Gaza. The car was stoned, he was beaten, and the car was torched, with his body still inside. In swift retaliation, 34 houses in the camp were demolished. Still, Prime Minister Shamir told a Knesset committee that the *intifada* was "in retreat." Were it not for the murder of Pomerantz, he said, the issue would not even be raised for discussion.

THE TEMPLE MOUNT INCIDENT

Two weeks later, on October 8, Israeli policemen opened fire on Palestinian rioters on the holy Temple Mount, overlooking the Western ("Wailing") Wall in Jerusalem's Old City. It was the most serious incident since the start of the *intifada*, indeed, since the start of the occupation. It injected, as never before, the volatile religious element into the already inflamed nationalistic struggle between Jews and Arabs. It earned Israel worldwide condemnation, and, for the first time, threatened to give credence to Saddam Hussein's attempts to create a "linkage" between his invasion of Kuwait and Israel's presence in the occupied territories.

Since 1968, groups of extremist Jews had railed against "Muslim control" of the Temple Mount. During the festival of Sukkot, they once again announced plans to lay the cornerstone for the "Third Temple" on the Temple Mount. The police, fearing riots, forbade a group of zealots known as the Temple Mount Faithful from approaching the enclosed area where the Mosque of Omar and Al-Aksa mosque are located. They did allow them to demonstrate in the vicinity of the Western Wall, below. On the Temple Mount, thousands of Muslims gathered to "protect" their holy shrines.

Following the incident, it was unclear who had started it. The police and a subsequent government commission of inquiry determined that the rioting had started when the Arabs began to pelt the policemen on the mount, as well as Jewish worshipers down below in the plaza near the Wailing Wall, with thousands of stones, metal rods, and other construction materials. The Arabs and a Jewish human-rights group maintained that it was the other way around: first the police had opened fire on the Muslims; then the stoning began. One thing was clear: only a few policemen and border guards—fewer than 50—had been assigned to stand guard over close to 3,000 agitated Muslims. Outnumbered and driven back by the storm of stones and blocks, the policemen retreated, firing their weapons, including automatic bursts, directly at the rioters. When reinforcements were sent in to disperse the crowds, this was also accompanied by direct fire at the demonstrators. In all, 17 Arabs were killed, including an Israeli Arab, and over 200 people were wounded, including 15 Jews. In the aftermath, riots erupted all over the territories and inside Israel.

The government claimed at first that the incident was a "provocation" organized by the PLO at the behest of Iraq. Facing vociferous worldwide condemnation and a U.S.-sponsored resolution of censure in the UN, on October 10 the government appointed a commission of inquiry, headed by former Mossad head Zvi Zamir. In presenting its report, released on October 26, the Zamir Commission found that the Arabs had started the incident. The commission did, however, sharply criticize the police for not preparing adequately for the volatile Sukkot holiday, for disregarding prior warnings about potential rioting, and for exhibiting a lack of sensitivity to the Temple Mount complex. Despite the censure, Police Minister Ronnie Milo took no action against the police. Toward the end of the year, an independent inquiry was launched by a Jerusalem magistrate at the request of the Arab family of one of the victims. Unlike the Zamir Commission proceedings, these deliberations were held with witnesses testifying under oath.

On October 12, the UN Security Council condemned Israel in a unanimous vote. The Israeli government, in turn, criticized the Security Council's "complete disregard" for the fact that Jewish worshipers had been attacked as well. Once again, the council wished to send a delegation to inquire about the "safety" of Palestinians under Israeli occupation. Once again, the government refused to accept the delegation, claiming that Jerusalem, just like Rishon LeZion, was sovereign Israeli territory. Once again, as in the Rishon massacre, the government finally accepted a personal envoy of the UN Secretary-General, Aimé. This time, the American desire to direct attention away from the Temple Mount incident in order to focus on the

Gulf crisis helped Israel to avert a serious confrontation with the international community.

ESCALATION OF VIOLENCE

Three weeks later, the *intifada* moved further west, into the calm, upper-middle-class Jerusalem neighborhood of Bakaa. In the early morning of October 21, a 19-year-old Arab youth from Obadiya, a village near Bethlehem, ran amok with a carving knife, killing three people and wounding a small child. The murders shocked Israelis as perhaps no others had before. For one thing, many of the residents of Bakaa were activists of the Peace Now movement; for another, Bakaa itself was the epitome of pre-1967 "safe" Israel. Alongside the well-to-do leftists lived poorer, older residents of the neighborhood who supported the Right. The "leftists" faced not only the shock of the murder but the anger of their neighbors, who demonstrated outside their homes with placards reading "death to the traitors."

The next day two women soldiers were stabbed in the north; another Israeli was attacked by a hammer-wielding Arab in Ashkelon.

In the wake of the murders, both Left and Right increased their calls for a "separation" of the two peoples. Peace Now spokesman Amiram Goldblum, whose house had been attacked by irate right-wing residents of the Bakaa neighborhood, said, "Our aim is not to fall in love with the Palestinians; it is to be separated from them." Two days later, Defense Minister Arens appeared to be responding to the call when he ordered all the territories sealed off and the return of all Palestinians from Green Line Israel back to their homes. One of the uglier consequences of this action was the appearance on the scene of Jewish "informers," who summoned the police to evict Palestinians who were trying to evade the orders in order to maintain their jobs.

The government did not plan to make the sealing-off a permanent condition. Opposition to the move was growing from inside the Likud, where several politicians pointed out that by sealing off the territories, the Likud, with its own hands, was resurrecting the Green Line. Nonetheless, the government exerted stricter control over the entry of Palestinians from the territories; over 20,000 Palestinians with police records relating either to security or regular criminal offenses were henceforth to be barred permanently from entering Israel. The Palestinian work force declined from 150,000 to about 70,000. The police announced a campaign against employment of Palestinians without official permits.

The stabbings abated but did not stop. On December 2, bus riders near Tel Aviv were attacked by three knife-bearing terrorists; one bus rider and one assailant were killed. On December 14, three Jewish employees in an aluminum factory in Jaffa were murdered; the Hamas Islamic movement claimed responsibility. The government announced plans to deport four Hamas activists from the Gaza strip; the action was "deplored" by the Security Council, with the United States in support.

In 1990 the character of the *intifada* had changed from mass street demonstrations and rock throwing to deadly stabbings by individuals inside the old Green Line Israel. In December an ominous further escalation appeared to be in the offing: Jewish settlers on the Ramallah-Nablus road were attacked by gunfire from a well-laid ambush; there were several more gunfire incidents; a few days later, an Israeli soldier was killed in Bethlehem by an explosive, detonated by remote control. The security forces expressed concern that the army would henceforth have to contend with an increasing number of terrorist cells in the territories employing "hot weapons," including hand grenades and explosive devices. According to official statistics of the army spokesman, there were 85 incidents of gunfire during 1990; eight hand grenades were thrown; 102 explosive devices of varying sizes were detonated; 648 Molotov cocktails were hurled; 1,196 Israeli soldiers were wounded. The total number of Arabs killed since the start of the *intifada* passed 700.

Other Terrorist Attacks and Border Incidents

On February 4, a bus carrying Israeli tourists from Tel Aviv to Cairo was attacked by three gunmen near the Egyptian town of Ismailia on the Suez Canal. Nine Israelis were killed, 18 others wounded. Two Egyptians were also killed. The incident shocked Israel and put a significant strain on relations between Israel and Egypt.

Deputy Foreign Minister Benjamin Netanyahu accused the PLO of responsibility for the murderous attack; credit was claimed, however, by the Islamic Jihad organization. Israeli intelligence experts told the inner cabinet on February 7 that the PLO was not responsible. The attack had been carried out by three Jordan-based Palestinians, and indeed the Islamic Jihad was the perpetrator. Minister Ariel Sharon revealed a few days later that the perpetrators were Palestinians with links to the Teheran-based Islamic Jihad, who had been deported by Israel to Jordan.

On November 25, the border of peace between the two countries was once again violated by an Egyptian soldier who crossed over into Israeli territory just north of Eilat. The soldier, armed with a submachine gun and hand grenades, succeeded in stopping three vehicles, including a bus; he killed 4 Israelis and wounded 26. The soldier was wounded by return fire but nonetheless succeeded in escaping back to the Egyptian side of the border. He was subsequently apprehended by the Egyptian authorities. Both attacks put strains on Israel's relations with Egypt. Israel stated that it held Cairo responsible for maintaining security on its side of the border. The Egyptians expressed sorrow at the incident but rejected Israeli suggestions that their security measures had not been stringent enough.

Throughout the year, the hitherto tranquil border with Jordan was turning into a source of concern for the Israel Defense Forces. During the first half of the year, these concerns focused on the sporadic but nonetheless consistent infiltrations by terrorists and "crazed" Jordanian soldiers across the border in the eastern Negev, by repeated incidents of gunfire from Jordanian positions across the border, and even (March 24) by Katyusha fire from across the border. In November a terrorist squad that included four Jordanian policemen infiltrated; one Israeli officer was killed before the army disposed of the squad. A few days later, another terrorist infiltrated, killing the Israeli commander of a border position. Hussein had lost control of his army, security sources said.

Israel warned Jordan that it would be held responsible for these incidents, although the military did not believe that Amman had condoned or had any interest in exacerbating relations with Israel. Analysts said that the incidents were a symptom of the growing radical Islamic influence in Jordan in general and in the Jordanian army in particular, as well as of the generally deteriorating economic situation in the Hashemite Kingdom and its consequences for the country's armed forces.

A more benevolent side of Israel's relations with Jordan was exhibited at the beginning of September when the Jordanians returned, unharmed, two boys who had crossed the border several days earlier in an attempt to visit the ruins at Petra. Israel thanked Jordan for its "humanitarian" attitude.

Terrorists continued their attempts to infiltrate into Israel from Lebanon, through the Israeli-controlled security zone and by sea. None of these attempts was successful, although there were several casualties in encounters between army patrols and terrorist squads inside the security zone. On January 21, an Israeli colonel, Yitzhak Rahimov, who was serving as trainer for the Israeli-backed Southern Lebanese Army, was killed in an ambush laid by a squad belonging to the Abu Nidal organization. On November 27, the Israeli army suffered one of its most stinging setbacks in south Lebanon when five soldiers of the crack Givati Brigade were killed in an ambush by terrorists from George Habash's Popular Front for the Liberation of Palestine. The air force continued regular bombing raids of terrorist bases north of the security zone, and there were several land incursions as well, including a relatively large one, with armored forces, which took place on November 10 against Hezballah bases just north of the security zone.

In October, Syria completed its takeover of Lebanon, ejecting by force Christian general Michel Aoun's 5,000-strong militia. The Israeli military was caught by surprise by the general's surrender, and military sources expressed concern about the overall security situation in Lebanon under complete Syrian hegemony. Especially disconcerting were the reports that armed Muslim militias had agreed to leave Beirut and were heading south to fight against Israel. Offering reassurance, Defense Minister Moshe Arens told the Knesset on October 17 that Israeli interests had not been harmed by Aoun's removal and that there was no reason for any Israeli intervention.

Other National Security Matters

Ofek 2, an Israeli-made satellite, was launched on April 3. The 250-lb. satellite, boosted on an Israeli Shavit rocket, was capable of communicating with a land base and receiving instructions from the ground. Science Minister Yuval Ne'eman claimed that the satellite was not military in nature and was aimed mainly at furthering Israel's space exploration. Foreign reports said that the satellite was intended for spying on Arab countries; the London *Guardian* said the rocket that carried Ofek into space was also capable of carrying nuclear warheads over a distance of 900 miles. The United States congratulated Israel on its scientific achievement; Israel denied any link between the timing of the rocket launch and the threats made a day earlier by Iraqi president Saddam Hussein to "burn half of Israel."

Five Israeli soldiers were killed in an artillery accident on July 17 at the southern training base of Ze'elim. The mishap was at first attributed to an individual artillery commander who mistakenly called for the shelling of a position that was still manned. A subsequent internal commission of inquiry found, however, that the accident had been caused by "negligence throughout the command structure." Six officers were dismissed from their posts and three others reprimanded. The incident resulted in a revamping of safety regulations throughout the army. Former chief of staff Rafael Eitan called for the resignation of his successor, Gen. Dan Shomron.

Col. Yehuda Meir went on trial on March 29 for ordering his soldiers, in February 1988, to beat Palestinian residents of the West Bank villages of Beita and Hawara. The trial, which was still in progress at the end of the year, raised questions concerning the responsibility of Defense Minister Yitzhak Rabin and senior army commanders for the "orders" to "break the bones" of Palestinians. In a separate trial, four soldiers of the Givati Brigade were sentenced to various terms of short imprisonment for beating three Arabs in Gaza, also in February 1988; one of the Arabs subsequently died. The four soldiers also claimed that they had been acting on orders; the court reconfirmed the soldier's duty to refuse to carry out illegal orders, but nonetheless sentenced the men to relatively light prison terms.

Air Force Brig. Gen. Rami Dotan, a former head of the Air Force Equipment Squadron, was arrested in October on charges of massive bribe-taking and fraudulent purchase agreements with American arms firms. The arrest, which shocked the country, led to further investigations and arrests of lower-ranking officers and civilian arms dealers. Toward the end of the year, a plea bargain was reportedly being worked out, with Dotan undertaking to return over $11 million in stolen funds and receiving a 12-year prison sentence. The revelation of Dotan's grand larceny tarnished the image of the air force and of its commander, Gen. Avihu Bin Nun, who for a lengthy period before the arrest stood up for Dotan. Dotan was labeled a traitor by several former air force commanders, with one of them, Gen. (res.) Benny Peled saying this about the affair: "In a normal country, they would have left him in a room with a loaded gun on the table."

Mordechai Vanunu's appeal to the Supreme Court to overturn his conviction for espionage and treason was rejected and his 18-year prison sentence confirmed. In a verdict partially released on September 30, the court found that in his 1986 disclosure of top-secret information about Israel's nuclear facility at Dimona to the London *Sunday Times*, Vanunu had "implemented direct and extreme measures in order to expose information which could be exploited by all those who wish to do harm to Israel." On June 13, the European Parliament called on President Chaim Herzog to pardon Vanunu. In the wake of the eruption of the Gulf crisis and the reports of Iraq's nuclear potential, there were those in Israel who maintained that Vanunu's revelations had actually strengthened Israel's power of deterrence.

Victor Ostrovsky, a former low-level Mossad operative, gained worldwide publicity as a result of the Israeli government's ill-advised and unsuccessful attempts to stifle his book *By Way of Deception*. In the book, published in September, Ostrovsky revealed the names of many Mossad operatives and reported on various clandestine activities of the organization, including the damaging allegation that Israel knew in advance of the attempt against the American Marine barracks in Beirut in April 1983, in which 241 American soldiers died. Following publication of the book, Israel claimed that Ostrovsky was a low-level agent who did not have access to the events he claimed knowledge of; the contents themselves were described as fabrications.

DIPLOMATIC DEVELOPMENTS

The Peace Process

The basic situation at the beginning of the year was this: Israel had accepted U.S. secretary of state James Baker's October 1989 "five-point plan," which foresaw an Israeli-Palestinian dialogue in Cairo. From an Israeli perspective, the sole purpose of this dialogue was to discuss the modalities of elections in the territories, proposed in the national unity government's peace initiative of May 1989. The third point of Baker's five stated that "Israel will attend the dialogue only after a satisfactory list of Palestinians has been worked out."

In January, the U.S. administration announced plans for a tripartite meeting of the American, Egyptian, and Israeli foreign ministers, aimed at resolving the final details of the proposed dialogue in Cairo. A date for this meeting was not set; the Americans first wished to overcome the obstacles obstructing the appointment of a Palestinian delegation.

The PLO, in direct contact with the U.S. administration through the American ambassador in Tunis, Robert Pelletreau, and through Egypt, which served as the main Arab interlocutor of the Americans, insisted that the Palestinian delegation to Cairo include representatives from East Jerusalem as well as representatives of the Palestinian "diaspora." The PLO also claimed exclusive jurisdiction in picking and publicly announcing the makeup of the Palestinian delegation.

Prime Minister Shamir and most of his Likud party were adamantly opposed to the participation of East Jerusalemites in the delegation, claiming that this would weaken Israel's claim to exclusive sovereignty over the capital; they were equally opposed to representation of the "diaspora," claiming that this would imply recognition of the Palestinian demand for the "right of return." They did not agree to any role for the PLO in the process and made clear that they would not sit with a delegation chosen by the PLO. Shamir and his colleagues viewed the American support for the inclusion of East Jerusalemites and "outside" Palestinians as a clear warning signal of the degree of collaboration between the administration and the PLO; *Ha'aretz* reported on January 8 that Cabinet Secretary Elyakim Rubinstein, returning in January from a round of talks in Washington, told Prime Minister Shamir and Foreign Minister Arens that the Americans were involving the PLO in the preparations for the Cairo meeting. He added that the United States had already promised the PLO that East Jerusalemites and "outside" Palestinians would indeed be part of the Palestinian delegation.

Even as the diplomatic wheels continued to turn, the administration signaled its rapidly dwindling reserves of patience for the Middle East peace process. On January 9, administration sources leaked the contents of a meeting between Baker and the Norwegian foreign minister. Baker reportedly said that he had given up hope for a breakthrough in the peace process and was thinking of devoting his time to other matters. The next day, State Department spokeswoman Margaret Tutwiler confirmed the essence of Baker's message, saying that Baker would remain "engaged" in the peace process "as long as the parties are determined to make progress." She reminded the attending journalists, however, that other problems in the world were "clamoring for attention."

The Labor contingent in the national unity government played a sort of mediating role between the contradictory demands of the Likud and the PLO; often, this task was carried out in close coordination with both Egypt and the United States. In mid-January, Defense Minister Yitzhak Rabin, coauthor of the May 1989 initiative, held talks in Washington with Baker, while Egyptian foreign minister Esmat Abdel-Meguid was also in town; the following week Finance Minister Shimon Peres met with Egyptian president Hosni Mubarak in Egypt. In these talks, the two Labor leaders, Secretary of State Baker, and the Egyptian president agreed on a formula to solve the problem of the Palestinian representation, which would ultimately find expression in the "Baker question": East Jerusalemites would be represented by Palestinians with a "double address," i.e., Palestinians who lived in the West Bank but maintained offices or another business address in East Jerusalem; the "diaspora" would be represented by Palestinians who had been deported from the territories since 1967, to whom Israel would agree. Egypt undertook to persuade the PLO to accept the compromise formula; Labor would press the national unity government to approve it; and Baker would submit the question to Israel in the most innocuous way possible. Egypt, it was agreed, would publicly announce the makeup of the delegation.

On January 27, in a cabinet meeting, Shamir reacted to the reports of the "agreements" reached by Peres and Rabin in their talks: "If such agreements have been reached," he said, "they are not binding on anyone." The same week, Peres reported explicitly on the agreement to include two East Jerusalemites with "double addresses" and two deported Palestinians in the Palestinian delegation. This time, Shamir did not react at all.

The next week, Baker conveyed his question. It was indeed innocuous enough: would Israel agree to the participation of Palestinians, residents of the territories, on a name-by-name basis? To the harmless question, however, a lethal "assumption" was attached: that these "residents of the territories" would include both East Jerusalemites with a double address and deported Palestinians.

The PLO, in the meantime, was keeping a low profile concerning the Baker-Peres-Mubarak proposals. According to press reports, the organization had agreed to accept the formula, at least as far as the makeup of the delegation was concerned. PLO spokesmen continued to claim, however, that only the PLO would choose the Palestinian delegates, and only it would publicly announce the makeup of the delegation.

On February 23, Baker and Arens met. The Israeli attitude toward the Baker question appeared to be positive. Several days later, unnamed American sources were quoted as saying that Shamir had accepted the Baker formula "in principle." "Things are looking very good," the sources opined. The next day, however, the Prime Minister's Office in Jerusalem formally denied the reports of Shamir's acceptance of the Baker question. The positive "impression" created by Arens in his talks with Baker was apparently based on his own positive attitude toward the Baker proposal, rather than on the sentiments of the prime minister himself. On February 28, in a meeting with his Likud ministers, Shamir himself branded these reports "lies." At the same time, President Bush was still hopeful. He told a press conference in California that he hoped the report of the Likud's agreement to the Baker formula was true so that the peace process could at last move forward.

In the Knesset, Deputy Foreign Minister Netanyahu, who maintained close links with Shamir's office, also sounded as if agreement was the farthest thing from Israel's mind. "Instead of the United States asking stark questions of Israel and demanding clear answers," he said, "I propose that Israel ask the United States some stark questions, and the Administration will give clear responses. If the intention is to create a smoke screen which would allow the PLO to take control of the territory, under conditions of terror, then there is no understanding between us and each one of us has different things in mind." Sources in Foreign Minister Arens's office expressed reservations about Netanyahu's strident tone; it appears, however, that the deputy was more in touch with the mood of the prime minister than his immediate superior, Arens.

On March 5, Shamir's mood became even clearer. In a meeting with the National Religious party, he assailed the United States for "trying to inject the PLO into the process." This, indeed, was the underlying source of Shamir's opposition to the Baker proposal, as Likud ministers confided subsequently: the "Baker question" was but the tip of an iceberg, with the concealed elements including close U.S.-PLO collaboration and an ultimate aim of establishing a Palestinian "entity" in the West Bank and Gaza. As if to corroborate Shamir's accusations, Palestinian sources reported the same day that Baker had agreed that PLO chairman Yasir Arafat would "brief" the Palestinian delegation before the start of the Cairo meeting.

Foreign Minister Arens, who reportedly had let Baker understand in Washington that Jerusalem was amenable to his proposals, now told the Knesset's Foreign Affairs and Defense Committee that Israel should oppose the participation of East Jerusalemites and deported Palestinians. "Their inclusion," he said, "paves the way to negotiations over the status of Jerusalem and the right of return."

On March 6, Baker expressed his growing impatience with Shamir's procrastination by stating that he was no longer willing to deal in "assurances" or "clarifications." The next day, he spoke to Shamir by phone, hoping to spur Israel to finally reach a decision. Shamir reported on the content of his conversation to the Knesset committee. He had told Baker, he said, that Jerusalem was a "crucial question." He asked what the American position would be. "We'll see," Baker replied.

Shamir's continuing refusal to reply to Baker one way or another was now affecting the cohesion of the national unity government. In a March 11 meeting of the inner cabinet, he made no secret of his estimation of American intentions. The dialogue between Washington and the PLO, he said, had now become the cornerstone of Israel's own dialogue with the territories. Four days later, the national unity government fell in a motion of no-confidence in the Knesset (see "Political Developments," below). Spokeswoman Tutwiler commented that "it is clear that the progress in the peace process has now stopped, temporarily."

THE NEW GOVERNMENT

For the next three months, until June 11, Shamir's government functioned as a "transitional government"; there was no substantive discussion in Israel of the proper way to reply to Baker's question. Nonetheless, the issue continued to dog relations between the two countries. In an interview on Israel Radio, in honor of Independence Day, Shamir seemed to be indicating publicly for the first time what he had often said in private: "We cannot be expected to accept every proposal or idea offered by the American Secretary of State." The administration reacted with anger, and the Prime Minister's Office promptly offered a typically "Shamir-esque" interpretation of the prime minister's words: he hadn't said yes to Baker, but he hadn't said no, either. On May 7, American ambassador to Israel William Brown, speaking to high-school students in Arad, made the American attitude clear: We won't take no for an answer, he said. On June 11, the new narrow government was constituted. The government guidelines expressed continued support for the May 1989 initiative, although they explicitly ruled out any participation by East Jerusalemites in the proposed elections in the territories. It was clear, however, that if the old national unity government, of which Labor comprised half, could not bring itself to say yes to Baker, then the new one, composed of parties that were opposed to the May 1989 initiative, would definitely refuse to satisfy the American secretary of state.

Although the U.S. administration refrained from any direct public criticism of the new government, it was clearly not happy with its makeup and with its proposed policies, especially its strong support for expanding the settlement drive in the territories. Indeed, Secretary Baker greeted the new government with one of the most disparaging statements ever made by an American leader about an Israeli government: "The phone number is 1–202–456–1414," he said in testimony in Congress; "when you're serious about peace, call us." Baker said that it was very hard for the United States to understand why Israel had refrained from responding positively to the question identified with his name; the position of the new Israeli government, he said, is that "there will be no dialogue unless the Palestinians accept our positions in advance."

The new government, concerned about the deteriorating state of relations between the two countries, tried to contain the acrimony. The new foreign minister, David Levy, who in previous governments had been one of the three so-called constraints ministers who had railed against Shamir's "concessions," called for a resumption of the dialogue between the two countries. In his new role, Levy suddenly discovered the positive aspects of the American position on the peace process: the United States, he said, agreed with Israel that the PLO should not have a role in the peace process and with Israel's opposition to a Palestinian state. On June 26, he tried to portray Israel's rejection of the "Baker question" in a positive light: "We say yes to the Baker initiative, but no to his questions." Since the Baker question had first come up for discussion in January, this was the first uncategorical statement of Israel's reply: no.

Prime Minister Shamir, for his part, sent President Bush an eight-page letter in reply to Bush's request for clarifications about the new government's attitude toward the peace process. Shamir's letter dealt at length with the need for a peace process with Arab states and for a resolution of the Palestinian refugee problem, both major elements of the May 1989 initiative that had been placed on the back burner while the focus was on the issue of elections in the territories. As far as the Baker question was concerned, and despite Levy's explicit rejection of it, Shamir continued to avoid an explicit no. Israel, he wrote Bush, was interested in having the Cairo dialogue with a Palestinian delegation that would be chosen on a name-by-name basis. Thus, Shamir had replied positively to the open part of the Baker question; he expressed "reservations," however, about its hidden "assumption" regarding the participation of East Jerusalemites and "outside" Palestinians.

On July 14, in an interview with *Ha'aretz*, Shamir went a step further in an effort to convince the administration that his new government was not necessarily an inferior partner, compared to the previous national unity government. He said that he was not concerned whether the Palestinian negotiators "consulted" with the PLO; he was worried that the PLO wished to "run the whole show."

Shamir's continued equivocation concerning the Baker question led the administration to conclude that the peace process should be given another chance (*New York Times*, July 8, 1990). The renewed effort was not to be launched, however. On August 2, Iraq invaded Kuwait. Shamir did not conceal his reading of the significance of this event for the peace process. The Gulf crisis, he said, on August 8, "pushed aside" other problems in the Middle East. In a September meeting, Levy persuaded Baker to forego Israel's reply to his question, asking him whether he wished to bring about the fall of yet another government in Israel. In December, Shamir and Bush agreed not to deal with the peace process at all until the Gulf crisis was resolved.

SYRIA IS HEARD FROM

While the Palestinian question was caught in the representation quagmire, and while Israel was engaged in the protracted process of setting up a new government, the elusive peace process suddenly had a new participant: Syria. This, in any case, was the impression left by Syrian president Hafez al-Assad on several visitors to Damascus; the most prominent of these was former American president Jimmy Carter. Arriving in Israel after talks with Assad, Carter stated on March 18 that Syria was now willing to engage in direct negotiations with Israel, within the framework of an international conference. The purpose of these talks, as far as Assad was concerned, was one: the return of the Golan Heights to Syria.

Accompanying Syria's willingness to change the tone of its attitude toward Israel, at least publicly, were the rapidly warming relations between Damascus and Cairo. Just before the close of 1989, the two countries had restored full diplomatic relations, which had been broken a decade earlier when Egypt agreed to make peace with Israel. On March 24, Assad met with Mubarak in Tobruk. Libyan president Muammar Qaddafi was also present. Israel reacted with marked skepticism to Assad's newfound moderation: Lt. Gen. Dan Shomron, chief of staff of the Israel Defense Forces, said there was "no significance" to Carter's reading of Assad's intentions. The strategic objectives of Syria had not changed, he said.

Deputy Foreign Minister Netanyahu was even more blunt, in an appearance in the Knesset on March 21. "We've heard these songs before," he said. Israel had rejected such signals in the past, Netanyahu said, and will continue to reject them in the future. Assad, according to Netanyahu, was still unwilling to aim for the appropriate final objective: an end to the state of war with Israel. Shamir himself reacted along the same lines a few days later, when he told the Knesset drily that the only new element in Assad's position was his agreement to the convention of an international peace conference. This might be progress from the point of view of Syria, which had refused to attend the 1973 Geneva peace conference, but it was meaningless as far as Israel was concerned.

Mubarak nonetheless continued his efforts to engage Syria in the peace process. He sought a public statement by Assad to this effect. In mid-July, his wish was granted; Assad, visiting Cairo, announced publicly that he was willing to enter into negotiations with Israel, within the framework of an international conference, based on a return of the Golan and appropriate arrangements in Lebanon. The reaction in Israel was more guarded this time, but still skeptical; by this time, however, the

Gulf crisis was brewing. In November, there were reports of the administration's intention to involve Syria in the post-Gulf crisis peace process. But the test of Syria's intentions would have to wait.

U.S.-PLO Dialogue

The American dialogue with the PLO, launched in December 1988, was the main source of friction between the Shamir government and the Bush administration, at least from Israel's vantage point. In principle, the Shamir government viewed the dialogue as American recognition of Israel's sworn enemy and, implicitly, as partial recognition of at least a part of the organization's aims: the establishment of an independent Palestinian state. Israel was suspicious that, while the United States, in theory, accepted Israel's adamant opposition to any PLO role in the peace process, in practice, behind a "smoke screen," the administration was actively negotiating with the organization, directly and through Egypt. A constant accusation hurled at Shamir, from both the Left and the Right, was that while Israel forbade, in law, any contacts with the PLO, in reality it was conducting indirect negotiations with the organization through the United States.

In March, in testimony given by Secretary Baker to Congress, and in an official report submitted to Congress by the State Department, the administration maintained that the PLO was living up to its commitments to desist from terrorism. Shamir called the report "tendentious" and said that the Israeli government disagreed with its findings. The Israeli military also disagreed with the report's findings. General Shomron said that Arafat may indeed have promised to stop terrorism but that his Fatah organization continued to engage in terror. The prime minister told the cabinet that an unnamed senior American official admitted that the administration was being "lenient" with the PLO in order to promote the peace process.

The prestigious *Defense and Foreign Affairs* weekly reported on April 2 that, in light of U.S. satisfaction with the PLO's moderation, the State Department was considering upgrading the level of the dialogue with the PLO: Deputy Secretary of State Lawrence Eagleburger would replace Ambassador Pelletreau as the PLO's interlocutor. The State Department report on world terrorism, released in May, stated bluntly that the U.S.-PLO dialogue was one of the main contributing factors to the diminishing incidence of terrorism in the world in 1989.

Less than a month later, on May 30, this aspect of the American strategy collapsed, when two rubber boats carrying 16 heavily armed terrorists were intercepted near a southern Israeli beach. The aborted attack was carried out by the Palestine Liberation Front, an organization headed by one Muhammad Abul Abbas; he was no less than a full member of the PLO's executive committee.

Israel, which had been claiming all along that even those organizations subservient to Arafat had never desisted from terror, pounced on the opportunity and immediately demanded that the United States stop its dialogue with the PLO. The evidently embarrassed administration procrastinated: it sharply condemned the attack, but said it was seeking "proof" that the PLO was involved. Israel launched a massive public campaign in the American media and in Congress in order to create political pressure that would induce the administration to end the dialogue. In the meantime, Arab states, led by Egypt, and the Soviet Union, including President Mikhail Gorbachev personally, appealed to the United States not to break off its dialogue; this, the PLO lobbyists claimed, would deal a harsh blow to the peace process.

The United States called on Arafat to denounce clearly the beach attack and to take disciplinary action against Abul Abbas. Arafat did his best, but his best wasn't good enough. On June 9, President Bush himself pleaded with the PLO chairman to "raise his voice" about the attack. After some further prodding by Sweden, Arafat tried again: on June 11, the PLO's executive bodies stated that the PLO was "against any military action which targets civilians, regardless of the nature of such actions." There was no mention of any action against Abul Abbas. On June 20, the reluctant United States officially suspended its dialogue with the PLO, until such time as Arafat would fulfill its demands. Against the backdrop of the strained American-Israeli relations, the suspension of the dialogue was greeted in Israel like a breath of fresh air.

A few weeks later, the PLO openly sided with Saddam Hussein in the Gulf conflict. Palestinians in the territories, who had decided on an official boycott of American diplomatic representatives in the wake of the suspension of the dialogue, reacted likewise. Henceforth, and until the end of the year, the gap between the administration and the Palestinian leadership expanded rapidly.

Soviet Jewish Immigration

Another area of friction between the United States and Israel related to Soviet Jewish immigration. On January 14, in a speech before a Likud forum, Prime Minister Shamir told a gathering of Likud activists that "a big *aliyah* requires a big Israel." The statement played directly into the hands of the Arab countries, who were on the verge of launching a concerted international effort against the massive waves of immigration that had started to arrive in Israel toward the end of 1989. Now Israel had to contend with the allegation that the freedom of movement granted to Soviet Jews was being exploited by Israel to strengthen its hold on the occupied territories and greatly expand the settlements there. While the United States had strongly supported the former, it—President Bush in particular—was adamantly opposed to the latter. For a few days, Shamir tried to deny that he had used the word "big"; he had meant "strong"; but in subsequent speeches he repeated the equation—a big Israel for a big *aliyah*.

A few days later, an American "senior official" told the Reuters news agency that the United States would not lend financial assistance to Israel to help absorb the tens of thousands of new Soviet immigrants—if there was no breakthrough in the peace process. The following month, White House chief of staff John Sununu told Congress that Israel's request for $400 million in loan guarantees should be linked to political flexibility by the Shamir government. Sununu indicated that even if Israel committed itself not to spend U.S.-brokered funds to build settlements in the territories, these funds allowed Israel to spend money from other sources on the settlements.

The most vocal of Arab opponents to the *aliyah* was the usually moderate King Hussein of Jordan. The Hashemite monarch, always suspicious of Israeli plans to turn his kingdom into a Palestinian state and thus solve the issue of Palestinian self-determination once and for all, was concerned that hundreds of thousands of new settlers in the West Bank and Gaza would in turn mean hundreds of thousands of new Palestinian refugees in Jordan and, subsequently, further destabilization of the kingdom. On January 18, a few days after Shamir's statement, Hussein told the *Jordan Times* that the wave of immigration to Israel constituted a threat to Jordan and to the Arab world as a whole. President Mubarak then joined the campaign, expressing "discomfort" with the Soviet immigration. Soon the entire Arab world was engaged, and Palestinians as well as Israeli Arabs also joined the fray. (The Palestinians' position on this matter soured their relations with the Israeli Left; most Israelis saw the Arab campaign against the *aliyah* as an indication of the Arab refusal to accept the very idea of Zionism and Israel, and not as a specific objection to the settling of immigrants in the territories.)

The Soviet Union, now under increasing Arab pressure to curtail the immigration, summoned the Israeli consul in Moscow, Arye Levin, and lodged a strong protest against Shamir's statement.

On February 22, Prime Minister Shamir assured President Bush, in a phone conversation, that immigrants were not being directed to the territories. Bush, however, appeared to be viewing East Jerusalem as part of the territories: on March 3, he said that Israel's claims that only 1 percent of the immigrants had settled in the territories were only "partly true," and that a further 10 percent had settled in East Jerusalem. In late February, a senior government official was quoted as projecting an annual immigration rate of 230,000; Immigration Minister Yitzhak Peretz, returning from talks in the United States, reported that the publication of this figure had created a "psychosis" in the United States and among Arab states. (On March 2, the government imposed censorship on the number of arriving immigrants, on projections for the future, and on routes of arrival.)

The Arabs did enjoy partial success in mounting obstacles on the immigrants' path to Israel. In February the Soviet Union promised the PLO that it would not allow direct flights between Israel and the Soviet Union. But that is as far as the Soviets were willing to go; Deputy Foreign Minister Yuli Vorontsov stated flatly, in a press conference on February 12, that there would be no limitations on the exit of Jews. The Soviet Union did make an effort to agree with the United States on a joint statement condemning the settling of immigrants in the territories. Secretary Baker said on February 12 that he had refused the proposal.

Nonetheless, the Arab campaign, which had quickly become a concerted cause of the entire Arab world, was raising concern in Jerusalem. A Baghdad summit meeting of the Arab Cooperation Council (Iraq, Egypt, Jordan, and Yemen) called on the Soviet Union to stop the immigration altogether. Four other Arab foreign ministers (Algeria, Iraq, Syria, and Tunisia) traveled together to Moscow to press their case personally. Defense Minister Rabin told the Knesset, on February 21, that the Arab effort posed a danger to the continuation of the immigration. In March, Hussein spelled out his objections explicitly, in an interview with the French paper *Le Figaro*. The immigrants, he said, would push out the Palestinians. Hussein accused the United States of hypocrisy; on the one hand it had lobbied in favor of their right to emigrate; on the other hand, Washington itself was refusing to accept the emigrating Jews.

In March the Islamic Conference convened in Jedda, labeling the immigration "a threat to peace." It said that the Soviet decision to open the gates was nothing more than "the implementation of a Zionist plot aimed at settling Jews in Palestine and other occupied lands." Also in March, Muhammad Abul Abbas of the PLO Executive Committee swore that the PLO would attack immigrants in their way stations in Europe. Similar threats by the Islamic Jihad organization achieved temporary results in what was then the most important way station, Budapest. Toward the end of the month, Malev, the Hungarian carrier, announced that it would stop bringing immigrants on charter flights because of the security risk. But that was a short-lived refusal; combined American and Israeli pressures brought the Hungarian government, after a week, to express regret at its airline's "surrender to international terrorism." The director general of Malev was sacked, and the flights continued as before. At the same time, Poland, following its resumption of ties with Israel, announced that Warsaw would henceforth serve as a point of transfer for exiting Jews.

Also in March, Secretary Baker spelled out American intentions; the loan guarantees would be linked to an Israeli commitment not to initiate new settlements. This position was rejected categorically by Israel; Shamir described the linkage created by Baker as "completely superfluous." The administration reaction angered Israel even further when the State Department made clear that the restriction on settlements required by Washington also applied to East Jerusalem.

By this time, the Israeli national unity government had fallen. The administration refused to discuss the issue of guarantees before a new government was constituted, although both houses of Congress approved the Israeli request. Throughout the interim period before the establishment of a new government in June, the administration issued several statements criticizing the erection of two new settlements in the West Bank and Gaza.

Tensions reached a peak in May, when the United States appeared to be considering support for an Arab-sponsored resolution in the UN Security Council opposing Soviet Jewish immigration. Foreign Minister Arens accused Washington of coordinating its moves with the Arabs; he spoke of a definite "low point" in relations between the two countries. State Department spokeswoman Margaret Tutwiler reacted by reiterating American support for immigration but opposition to the settling of immigrants in the occupied territories. That same month, a senior official in the Prime Minister's Office described the state of relations between Jerusalem and Washington as "a catastrophe." Shamir himself disagreed; "the situation isn't that bad," he said.

Meanwhile, the immigration issue was raised in each and every meeting held between Arab leaders and Western statesmen and among themselves as well. In May, Soviet president Gorbachev promised visiting Egyptian president Mubarak to press Bush to increase American immigration quotas for Soviet Jews. On June 3, following the summit meeting between Bush and Gorbachev, the Soviet leader announced that his country would review its liberal policy toward the emigration of Jews if Israel did not desist from its policy of settling them in the territories. Gorbachev seemed to imply that Bush agreed with his position; the American side denied this. In any case, Foreign Minister Arens told a Knesset forum, on June 4, that Israel had received assurances from Washington that there would be no change in the Soviet immigration policies.

By now, Israel was intent on repudiating the allegation that it was sending new immigrants to the territories. The Prime Minister's Office announced, in reaction to the Gorbachev statement, that there was no policy of sending immigrants anywhere; Absorption Minister Peretz said that only a few scores of new immigrants had settled in Judea, Samaria, and Gaza; and even Housing Minister Ariel Sharon, now in charge of Israel's massive construction effort for the new immigrants, pledged that Israel would not send new immigrants to the territories. But the United States was not mollified; in testimony to Congress, on July 31, Assistant Secretary of State John Kelly explained that it wasn't enough that the Israeli government was not directly encouraging new immigrants to settle in the territories; veteran young Israelis, he explained, had nowhere to live because of the Russian Jews coming to Israel. Therefore, there was a danger that they would choose to move to the territories, and for them there were ample government incentives.

On September 5, the new foreign minister, David Levy, met with Secretary of State Baker and discussed the loan-guarantees issue. As a result of these talks and other lower-level contacts, an agreement was reached. On October 4, Levy sent a letter to Baker pledging that the loans secured on the basis of the guarantees would be used only in "geographic areas which were subject to the Government of Israel's administration prior to June 5, 1967." Levy also reiterated the government's policy of not "directing" new immigrants to the territories and pledged to submit periodic reports on Israel's building plans in the territories. For the next 30 days, it was unclear whether the government in Israel backed the language of Levy's letter; the right-wing opposition was opposed to it. Prime Minister Shamir himself claimed that the language of the letter excluded East Jerusalem. Responding to the internal criticism, Levy sent yet another letter to Baker, making clear that his letter in no way entailed a commitment not to build in East Jerusalem. On October 21, the government in Israel ratified Levy's letter. In November, Baker authorized a fact-finding delegation of the Agency for International Development to go to Israel to prepare a report that would enable the administration to give the guarantees. At the end of the year, the administration notified Israel officially that the guarantees would be handed over by March 1991.

Jerusalem

On March 3, President Bush threw a bombshell into the already strained atmosphere between Israel and the United States. "We do not believe there should be new settlements in the West Bank or in East Jerusalem," he told a press conference in California. The next day, Margaret Tutwiler reemphasized this American position, saying that the "occupied territories include East Jerusalem." The fact that U.S. policy did not recognize the annexation of East Jerusalem was already well known. But Bush's explicit statement of American opposition to "settlements" in Jerusalem seemed to imply that the United States now opposed Jewish residence in the formerly Jordanian part of Jerusalem. The Prime Minister's Office reacted angrily, saying that "it appears that in the United States there is a lack of understanding of the significance of Jerusalem for every Israeli and Jew in the world. It is inconceivable to restrict the residency of Jews in any part of the city."

In the days following, both President Bush and Secretary Baker tried to mollify the angry Israelis and the American Jewish community: "No peace that I can envision would deny Jews the right to live anywhere in this special city of Jerusalem," Bush wrote to Sen. Rudy Boschwitz, while Baker wrote to Cong. Mel Levine, "Clearly, Jews and others can live where they want, East or West, and the city must remain undivided." The Senate and House of Representatives also passed resolutions stating that "Jerusalem is and should remain the capital of the state of Israel."

The truce lasted less than a month. On April 11, scores of Jewish settlers entered St. John's Hospice in the Christian quarter of the Old City of Jerusalem, which had formerly belonged to the Greek Orthodox Church. It was subsequently revealed that $1.8 million had been transferred from the coffers of the Housing Ministry to a mysterious company in Panama in order to fund the purchase of the building. The goodwill that had been built up in the wake of Bush's controversial statement on Jerusalem in March now dissipated completely: not only was the administration incensed by the action, but traditional allies in Congress as well as American Jewish leaders blasted this "settlement." The status of the hospice itself was being adjudicated in the Israeli courts through the rest of the year, with the settlers maintaining a nominal presence in the building. On May 14, Congress cut $1.8 million from the Israeli aid package, and there was concern that this act would serve as a precedent for the future in expressing American displeasure with Israel's overall settlement policy.

Conflict over Jerusalem erupted once again in the wake of the October 8 massacre of 17 Palestinians on the Temple Mount in Jerualem and ensuing Security Council resolutions 672 and 673 (see above), which called for a fact-finding delegation to visit

Israel and report on the conditions of Palestinians and their "safety." Not only did Israel refuse to accept the mission, it promptly announced plans to build 15,000 additional housing units in East Jerusalem. The United States immediately condemned the Israeli position, Secretary Baker warning that by its refusal to abide by a Security Council resolution, Israel was opening itself up to comparisons with Saddam Hussein. The State Department issued a travel advisory, warning against travel to Jerusalem and the territories, which angered Jerusalem greatly. A few weeks later, Shamir rebuffed a personal appeal by President Bush to accept the UN delegation. Ultimately Israel agreed to accept a personal representative of the UN secretary-general.

THE GULF CRISIS

Israel and Iraq

Throughout 1989 and during the first few months of 1990, some observers suggested that, by virtue of its close ties to Egypt and to relatively moderate Jordan, Baghdad was ready for a historic reconciliation with Israel. In meetings with Israeli leaders, Egyptian president Mubarak claimed that Israel "misunderstood" Iraqi president Saddam Hussein. Some Israeli officials, including top Foreign Ministry experts, were even drawing up theoretical blueprints of potential cooperation between Iraq and Israel. In light of past history, however, this assessment was hard to credit. Iraq had participated in three wars against Israel—in 1948, 1967, and 1973—but unlike the other combatant Arab states, it had never agreed to sign a cease-fire agreement. Moreover, for over a decade Israel had been anxiously following Iraqi attempts to secure sophisticated and unconventional weaponry. It also worried about the considerable battle experience gained by the Iraqi army in its eight-year war against Iran.

Months before the invasion of Kuwait, Iraq was emerging as a serious threat to Israel's security. Clues to this development were contained in reports of close Iraqi-Jordanian cooperation to strengthen the so-called eastern front, which could ultimately plunge Jordan's King Hussein into an open confrontation with Israel.

In February, Iraq formally announced plans to set up a joint jet-fighter squadron with Jordan; Israeli military sources later revealed that the squadron would consist of French Mirage F-1 fighters. Jordan claimed that it felt threatened by the repeated assertions of Israeli leaders, most notably Minister Ariel Sharon, that "Jordan was Palestine" and by the massive waves of Soviet immigration, which King Hussein believed would ultimately "flood" Jordan with hundreds of thousands of additional Palestinian refugees from the West Bank. Israeli sources also revealed that throughout January, Jordan had allowed Iraqi planes to carry out aerial photography and reconnaissance missions near the Israeli border over Jordanian territory. The two armies were also engaged in setting up joint air command and control headquarters, and officers from the two armies regularly trained with each other's units. There were unconfirmed reports that Jordan and Iraq were planning to set up joint land units.

On February 17, Israeli chief of staff Gen. Dan Shomron tried to allay Hussein's fears by stating that Jordan had no reason to feel threatened by Israel. The newspaper *Ma'ariv* reported on February 26 that Prime Minister Yitzhak Shamir also told the cabinet, "Israel does not support the identification of Jordan as Palestine." Similar assurances were conveyed to Jordan directly and through the United States. (Hussein was not appeased; in May, the king's paranoia reached a peak of sorts, when he claimed that an Israeli naval vessel had opened fire on his royal yacht near the Jordanian port of Aqaba. The navy replied that the shots had been fired in another direction altogether, but nonetheless issued instructions to naval commanders in the Gulf of Eilat to steer clear of the king's boats and his nerves.)

Defense Minister Yitzhak Rabin told the Knesset on February 20 that Israel could not treat the expanding military collaboration between Jordan and Iraq with equanimity. On March 22, the prestigious *Jane's Defense Weekly* quoted unnamed senior Israeli defense sources as claiming that Israel was now facing the ominous possibility of a united "eastern front" made up of Syria, Iraq, and Jordan. The Iraqi military potential, the sources said, which included 50 battle-trained divisions, 700 modern aircraft, ballistic capabilities, and chemical warfare experience, posed a real danger to Israel. March and April brought numerous reports of Iraq's attempts to achieve a nuclear potential, of its construction of a super long-range cannon, of its chemical and biological capabilities, and of its surface-to-surface missiles. At the end of March, the *New York Times* reported that Iraq was positioning improved Soviet-made Scud-B surface-to-surface missiles in the southwestern part of the country from where they could reach Israel. The missiles, the newspaper noted, were capable of carrying chemical warheads. Saddam himself made clear in April that Iraqi ballistic missiles were being aimed at Israel, not at Iran, which was confirmed in testimony to Congress by Assistant Secretary of State John Kelly. He added that the United States did not believe Iraq was close to achieving a nuclear potential.

Throughout the first three months of the year, Iraqi president Saddam Hussein reacted to repeated Israeli statements about Iraq's menacing profile by making belligerent statements about the need for a military solution to the question of Palestine, the necessity of a unified Arab military effort, and American and Israeli aggressive designs on Iraq. He warned against an Israeli attempt to repeat the 1981 bombing raid on the Iraqi nuclear reactor at Osirak.

In April, any remaining illusions about Saddam Hussein's intentions were dispelled. In a speech to decorated Iraqi army commanders, on April 2, Saddam said that "if Israel, with the backing of the West, will try to carry out any aggressive act against Iraq, Iraq will make the fire eat up half of Israel," using what he described as "binary chemical weapons." Israel reacted angrily to this statement, and Rabin made the first of numerous counterthreats that would be repeated throughout the year. If Iraq attacked Israel, he warned, the response would hurt Iraq many times over. The Prime Minister's Office issued an official statement, saying, "Israel will not be blackmailed."

On April 18, Saddam expanded his threat to "burn half of Israel" to include any attack by Israel on any Arab state. The next day, he warned that Iraq would attack Israel even without provocation, in order to achieve the "liberation of Palestine." The Iraqi press agency reported that Saddam had ordered the Iraqi Air Force to attack Israel with chemical weapons if Israel launched a nuclear attack against Iraq.

Throughout this period, Egyptian president Mubarak maintained close ties with Saddam; he excused the Iraqi president's belligerent tone by claiming that Iraq was only reacting to the pressures being exerted on it by the West; he called on President Bush and Western leaders to alleviate the tensions with Baghdad. In May, Labor leader Shimon Peres, now in the opposition, quoted Mubarak as describing Saddam as a "realistic leader with both feet on the ground." The world, Mubarak said, should not be overly impressed by Saddam's bellicose statements. The Arab world as a whole expressed public support for Saddam and would continue to do so for as long as the target of his belligerence remained Israel.

Mubarak was also seeking to bring about a rapprochement between Saddam and Syrian president Assad and raised the matter in each of three meetings with the Syrian president. Assad, while impressing Western visitors with a supposedly moderate attitude toward peace, joined in the escalating rhetoric: in a speech before his Ba'ath party in Damascus, on March 7, he called for a *jihad*, or holy war, against Israel; on May 16, he announced that the war against Israel must continue because Arab victory was assured; the next week, he went so far as to pledge Syrian assistance to Iraq if attacked by Israel.

There were other pleaders on behalf of Saddam. U.S. senator Robert Dole, on a Middle East tour with four other senators, said in a press conference in Jerusalem, following a meeting with the Iraqi president, that "Saddam has constructive suggestions which could bring calm to the area." Dole said he had conveyed to Saddam the American wish for improved Iraqi-U.S. relations. Sen. Howard Metzenbaum, who also met with Saddam, came away with rather different impressions: the Iraqi leader, he said, was suffering from a "psychosis of war."

On May 28, an Arab summit convened in Baghdad. Both Saddam and Mubarak spoke at the meeting but presented completely divergent messages. Mubarak said the Arab world must convey a "logical and humanitarian message"; Saddam said the Arab world must unite in order to "liberate Palestine." King Hussein, meanwhile, tried to distance himself from the Israel-Iraq confrontation. In reaction to repeated Israeli warnings that it would not tolerate an Iraqi military presence in Jordan, Hussein announced on June 17 that he would not allow any foreign army to enter Jordan. In mid-June, Saddam once again stepped up his public threats against Israel. He called on the Arab world to stop looking for compromises with Israel. In a rare interview that appeared in the *Wall Street Journal* (June 28 and July 2, 1990), Saddam stated that, if Israel persisted in its absorption of immigrants and continued to adhere to the right of the Jewish people to Palestine, there would be no escaping war. Moshe Arens, now defense minister, said that Israel was extremely concerned about Iraq's ability to wage chemical warfare. He said that there was a danger that Saddam would act against Israel even without an Israeli provocation.

In mid-July, the head of the American Joint Chiefs of Staff, Gen. Colin Powell, visited Israel. Much of his meetings with Arens and with the top echelons of the Israeli army dealt with the Iraqi threat in general and the danger of an Iraqi missile attack on Israel in particular. General Powell pledged American assistance to Israel in the effort to find a response to the missile threat; Arens said that Israel might already have found such a response. (He was referring to the Arrow antimissile missile, an Israeli development heavily funded by the United States, which several weeks later, on August 9, underwent its first test launch. At the same time, the Israeli defense establishment decided against purchase of the American-made Patriot anti-aircraft missile, claiming that it did not provide adequate protection against missile warfare; that decision was reversed within a few weeks of Iraq's invasion of Kuwait.)

On July 17, Saddam launched his campaign, as yet only verbal, against Kuwait and the other Gulf countries, accusing them of "economic sabotage" against Iraq. Three days later, Arens traveled unexpectedly to the United States for meetings with his American counterpart, Secretary of Defense Richard Cheney. It was subsequently revealed that in this meeting Arens warned Cheney of Iraq's aggressive intentions and provided detailed Israeli information about the advanced state of Iraq's nuclear industry. Returning from his visit, Arens declared, on July 24, that "the chances of a war breaking out between Iraq and Israel are now higher than they've been in recent years." Arens was roundly criticized for this statement, which, according to some reports, contradicted the assessment of Israel's own intelligence services. (Some critics accused Arens of making the statement as part of his battle against the government decision to cut the defense budget by $37 million.)

While Arens was in Washington, Science Minister Yuval Ne'eman surprised many in Israel and abroad by declaring that "Israel has a chemical response to Saddam's threats." The U.S. administration did not take kindly to Ne'eman's statement, noting that Israel was admitting for the first time that it had a chemical-warfare potential, something it had denied in the past.

The Crisis Erupts

On August 2, Iraq invaded Kuwait, sending in 26 army divisions which took control of the oil sheikhdom within 48 hours. The immediate and universal assessment in Israel was now in tune with Arens's statement of July 24, that there was indeed a heightened danger of war. Following the U.S. decision to send troops to protect Saudi Arabia, Saddam once again injected Israel into the Gulf equation: Iraq would attack Israel, he said, if the United States attacked Iraq. An Iraqi military spokesman claimed that the American campaign against Iraq was just a cover for Israel's aggressive intentions. Israeli pilots, he said, were flying American aircraft, dressed in American uniforms. A few days later, Saddam created the "linkage" that would haunt Israeli policymakers throughout the Gulf crisis: Iraq, he said, would withdraw from Kuwait only in conjunction with an Israeli withdrawal from the occupied territories.

Despite the threats, there was an understandable sense of relief in Israel in the wake of the Iraqi invasion of Kuwait. Arab solidarity, usually aimed at Israel, collapsed in the face of intra-Arab conflict. The strong response of President George Bush and the international community, including the sanctions imposed by the UN, created hope that Israel would not have to deal with the Iraqi menace on its own.

There were other perceived advantages to be gained from the invasion of Kuwait: most Israeli cabinet ministers felt that the American-Iraqi conflict would alleviate the tensions between Washington and Jerusalem, which had reached a dangerous low just before the invasion. They hoped that the events in the Gulf would also help to reconstruct Israel's image as a vital "strategic asset" for the United States. Israel clearly saw armed conflict in the Gulf as being in its interest, so much so that efforts for a peaceful compromise by diplomatic means, though unchallenged in public, aroused great discomfort.

Israel lent its full support to President Bush's effort to organize an international coalition against Iraq, Prime Minister Shamir repeatedly praising Bush for his determination and tenacity. The support did not erode even though, as the *New York Times* reported on August 14, the United States had asked Israel to maintain a "low profile" concerning the Gulf crisis. The United States was concerned that accentuating the Israeli aspect of the conflict with Iraq would weaken its effort to drum up Arab support for the campaign to eject Iraq from Kuwait. There was also concern that stressing Israel's security could give credence to allegations voiced in some quarters in the United States that American soldiers would be going to war at Israel's behest and in its behalf.

Throughout this period, therefore, relations between the two allies turned more delicate than ever, and careful maneuvering was required by both sides. Israel wished to see the Iraqi menace removed; therefore it was interested in assisting the United States in its efforts to build an international coalition against Iraq. On the other hand, Israel could not maintain too low a profile, lest Saddam interpret this stance as a sign of weakness, misinterpret it as an invitation to attack, and damage Israel's deterrent capabilities in the whole area. The same applied to the United States: it did not want to appear to be cooperating with Israel in any way; at the same time, it could not afford to allow Saddam to believe that it had abandoned Israel altogether. Nor did it wish for Israel to feel abandoned and thus anxious for action. The same balance was required in the strategic relations between the two countries: Israel tried to cooperate with the United States in concealing the strong military links between the two countries; on the other hand, the Gulf crisis had created unforeseen military expenditures, for which Israel sought compensation.

Israel also wanted closer intelligence links with Washington; the United States refused to share information from satellites in "real time."

Another troubling element was Saddam's creation of a "linkage" between Iraq's withdrawal from Kuwait and Israeli withdrawal from the occupied territories. Israel rejected this position, and was closely watching American statements to make sure that Washington would do the same. The administration, for its part, had to show some sympathy for the Arab call to solve the Palestinian issue once the Gulf crisis was over, in order to placate its potential Arab allies; at the same time it could not accept the linkage openly lest it be perceived as bowing to Saddam's demands and risk continued Israeli goodwill.

On September 1, Foreign Minister David Levy received a letter from Secretary Baker reiterating the administration's determination to fight Saddam's aggression but reminding Israel that the Palestinian issue had to be addressed. This letter was already seen in Jerusalem as a sign of the changing times: for the first time, Baker emphasized the need for the peace process to advance on what was termed the "dual track" system, that is, with the Palestinians and with the Arab states concurrently. Israel believed that this acceptance of its own long-held view was one of the first political fruits of the changed international atmosphere following the eruption of the Gulf crisis.

Three Israeli ministers descended on Washington in September: Foreign Minister Levy, Defense Minister Arens, and Finance Minister Modai. Reacting to the American intention to write off $7 billion of the outstanding Egyptian debt, each came up with his own version of what Israel thought was an appropriate parallel measure. Modai and Levy proposed a write-off of $4.6 billion of the Israeli debt; Arens, on the other hand, asked for increased military aid to the tune of an additional $1 billion. Following his own twice-delayed meeting with Secretary Baker, an ebullient Levy declared on September 8 that "the ice between the two countries was now broken; the two countries are once again allies." But Washington was not interested in accentuating the alliance; Baker undertook two trips to the Middle East and in both pointedly refrained from calling on Jerusalem.

Meanwhile, the Israeli military was expressing a healthy respect for the Iraqi military machine. Air force commander Gen. Avihu Bin Nun in September called the Iraqi air force the biggest and qualitatively best in the Middle East, more powerful than the British or German air forces. It was reported that Israel's intelligence and air force had been placed in a state of readiness, though not in a formal state of alert; a limited call-up of reserves was carried out quietly. On September 16, Chief of Staff Shomron said that the close relationship between Iraq and Jordan necessitated a state of preparedness in the army; Prime Minister Shamir said that Israel was prepared to repel an Iraqi air strike through Jordanian airspace. Israel sent several warnings to King Hussein, both publicly and privately, not to entertain the thought of allowing Iraq to use Jordanian airspace against Israel. The same month, the *New York Times* revealed that the United States had undertaken to defend Israel in case of an Iraqi attack.

Publicly, however, Israel continued to threaten retaliation. Foreign Minister David Levy put it starkly in an October 1 speech to the UN General Assembly. Israel, he said, would react immediately and with force if attacked by Iraq; it would not pay with its own security for the economies and freedoms of other nations. In November, Arens said that if attacked, Israel would not respond with a "low profile." The crisis in the Gulf, he said, had already cost Israel $1 billion in unexpected defense expenditures. On five separate occasions, Prime Minister Shamir warned of the "terrible" price that would be exacted from Iraq. His characterization of the possible Israeli retaliation was widely interpreted as a thinly veiled reference to Israel's hitherto denied nuclear capability.

Defense Ministry director general David Ivri went to Washington to submit a preliminary supplemental Israeli request for arms; most of his requests were denied. Defense Minister Moshe Arens followed in his footsteps in mid-September; he asked for a supplemental $1 billion dollars in military assistance. Unnamed American sources said that Arens's request was received with "coolness." Nonetheless, by late October the U.S. Senate approved a "drawdown" of $700-million worth of surplus American military supplies to be transferred to Israel; the Pentagon approved a supplemental plan to "preposition" $200-million worth of supplies that would nominally remain American but in practice would be at Israel's disposal; and President Bush approved the transfer to Israel of two Patriot missile batteries that had originally been earmarked for stationing in Italy.

Arms Sales to Saudi Arabia

Israel was also concerned by the close strategic links being forged between Washington and Saudi Arabia in the wake of the invasion of Kuwait. In addition to the massive troop buildup meant to protect the oil kingdom from Iraqi aggression, Washington announced its intention of selling great quantities of arms and weaponry to Saudi Arabia. This policy put Israel in a quandary; clearly, Israel's long-held argument that weapons in Saudi Arabia's possession would only be turned against Israel was not as credible as before, given the Iraqi threat; on the other hand, Israel was concerned about the aftermath of the Gulf crisis and the ramifications of the Saudi buildup on the postcrisis strategic and military balance. Riyadh had an outstanding order of weapons for $2.2 billion, which had already been approved by the administration. Now suddenly there were reports that the administration planned to supply Saudi Arabia with ten times as much weaponry. The United States assured Israel, at the beginning of September, that the new arms deal would not include the supermodern F-15E combat aircraft, but only the older F-15D and F-15C. However, the *New York Times* reported, on September 2, that the Saudis would be getting 385 M-1A-2 tanks, the most modern in the American arsenal. By the end of September, the administration announced that the total sum of its arms package to Saudi Arabia was $6.7 billion; Israel claimed that this was a ruse and that the second half of the original $20-billion arms deal would be presented at a later date.

U.S.-Israeli relations took a turn for the worse following the Temple Mount incident in October; Jerusalem was also concerned about what was then seen as some equivocation by Bush vis-à-vis Iraq. The American position in the Security Council and its unprecedented condemnation of Israel (Resolution 672 of October 12) reignited suspicion of the administration's intention of "appeasing" the Arabs. On October 23, the Israeli newspaper *Ma'ariv* printed a disparaging assessment of the American situation by Shamir, in what he thought were private remarks: "I am under the impression," he said, "that the Americans don't know what to do about Iraq; they are confused, and that's why they are devoting their attention to us." Foreign Minister Levy suggested that the United States was being "held captive by the very coalition it had formed against Saddam Hussein."

The American inaction and Israel's willingness to continue its "low-profile policy" were greeted with some criticism inside Israel itself. Levy said on November 20 that Israel was taking an "irresponsible risk" by not acting against Saddam. Israel's apprehension increased following President Bush's offer to launch a high-level dialogue with Iraq and Saddam's statement of December 1 accepting the Soviet proposal for an international conference on the Middle East, stipulating only that the Palestinian question be the main item on the agenda. Israel was concerned that the American wish to see an Iraqi withdrawal from Kuwait might induce it to "amend" some of its more pro-Israeli positions; the reservoirs of trust between the two governments were clearly at a low.

At this point, another delicate diplomatic balancing act was necessary: the Arab states had joined the coalition with the sole objective of bringing about the ejection of Saddam's forces; Israel had struck its low profile solely in the belief that the United States would remove the Iraqi military threat. This was made clear to U.S. ambassador to Israel William Brown in a December 4 meeting with Foreign Minister Levy. It was as close as Israel could come to openly warning the administration not to make any deals with Saddam.

In an apparent attempt to placate Israel, whose goodwill was, after all, deemed essential to the American war effort, Bush announced at the end of November that he would meet with Shamir during the next month. After more than a year of virtually no personal contact between the two, the announcement was greeted with much satisfaction by the Prime Minister's Office in Jerusalem. Arriving in the United States, Shamir made Israel's position clearer: we will resist, he said, any appeasement of Iraq at our expense. On December 11, Bush met Shamir; the atmosphere was warmer than expected. The two agreed to put off any further dealings with the peace process. Shamir returned from the United States satisfied and expressing renewed support for the administration's policies toward the Gulf. The reason for Shamir's satisfaction was ultimately revealed: Bush had persuaded him that the United States would not cave in to Saddam.

In the first week of December, Iraq successfully carried out a launch of three El-Hussein modified Scud-B missiles, which military analysts said proved Baghdad's capability of reaching Israel. On December 22, reports surfaced in the foreign press about an Israeli test-launching of a surface-to-surface missile, presumably the Jericho 2, which reportedly had a far longer range than the Iraqi missiles and could carry sophisticated warheads. The reported Israeli launch was widely interpreted as a warning to Saddam.

On December 20, the massive American military presence in the area exacted a steep price. In the bay of Haifa, 20 American soldiers were drowned when their Israeli ferry, the *Altuvia*, capsized and overturned. American officials later expressed warm appreciation for Israeli rescue efforts.

On December 24, a senior army official said that war appeared to be in the offing; the Israel Defense Forces, he added, were in a state of preparedness appropriate for the eve of a war. The focus, once again, was on Jordan, and what was seen as the probability that King Hussein would be compelled to allow Iraqi forces to enter Jordanian territory or to allow the Iraqi Air Force access to Jordanian air space. On December 25, the newspaper *Ha'aretz* quoted Prime Minister Shamir as saying that the danger of war in the Gulf was "very imminent." Shamir expressed grave concern about the possible necessity of Israeli action against Jordan.

CIVIL DEFENSE

Beginning with Saddam's first bellicose statements in April, the Israeli press had started to look into the state of the country's civil defense, particularly the question of whether or not the population should be universally supplied with gas masks. The defense establishment, including the defense minister and the army chief of staff, were opposed to mass distribution; the army had already made plans for a gradual distribution of the masks over a period of several years. In light of the intelligence assessment that the chances for a chemical attack on Israel were very low, the army saw no reason to change its assessment. The cabinet went along with the army's position.

In August, however, Foreign Minister Levy seemed more in tune with the public's apprehension and called for a cabinet review of the army's position. He was criticized for injecting his personal rivalry with Defense Minister Arens into a national security matter. Nonetheless, the inner cabinet then set up a special ministerial committee to review the question. For two months, the committee stuck to its previous position; then, in October, it abruptly reversed its position and opted for mass distribution. The decision emphasized as no other the government's calculated decision to risk an Iraqi missile strike against urban population centers, based on its reported promise to Washington not to launch a preemptive strike. At the same time, the government was forced to dispel speculation abroad about the significance of the distribution: Shamir made clear on October 7 that the decision on the gas masks was not indicative of any Israeli decision to attack.

The decision to distribute masks was also tinged with bitter irony: the decision was made public on the day of Germany's reunification. Memories of the Jewish people's previous experience with gas warfare, as well as modern Germany's assistance in Iraq's chemical warfare effort, led caricaturist Ze'ev of *Ha'aretz* to portray a gas-mask-donning Israeli gazing in wonderment at a newspaper headline heralding the return of a united Germany. Military sources repeated their assessment that Iraq would not attack Israel with chemical weapons; nonetheless, the country's hospitals were preparing themselves to deal with hundreds of possible casualties from a chemical gas attack. Tourism, already down, dropped even further in the wake of the decision to distribute gas masks.

At the end of the year, it appeared that there would be no averting war. Last-minute efforts to arrange compromise talks between Secretary of State James Baker and his Iraqi counterpart, Tariq Aziz, caused some nervousness among policymakers in Jerusalem. Most Israelis seemed to share their government's sense of priorities; they wanted the United States to "take care" of the Iraqi menace. At the same time, most responded to the government's call to pick up their gas masks. Most kept them handy, just in case.

FOREIGN RELATIONS

Europe

Ever since the 1967 Six Day War, Israel's relations with Europe had been completely lopsided. Alongside cordial, if sometimes strained, diplomatic ties and expanding commercial links with Western Europe, Israel's relations with Eastern Europe were virtually nonexistent, with the notable exception of Romania. As part of the aftermath of the liberation of Eastern Europe in the wake of Mikhail Gorbachev's *glasnost*, and in light of increased Western European criticism of Israel's policies in the territories, 1990 saw the return of equilibrium. Relations with Eastern European countries began rapidly thawing; ties with Western Europe were noticeably cooling.

Hungarian foreign minister Gyula Horn visited Israel in the first week of January; diplomatic relations between Israel and Hungary had been renewed in September 1989, and in January the first Hungarian ambassador after the 23-year break submitted his credentials to President Herzog. A few days later, a diplomatic delegation from Czechoslovakia came to Israel to discuss the resumption of ties with Prague. An agreement was signed setting up direct air links between the two countries. On January 20, Finance Minister Shimon Peres visited Czechoslovakia and was informed that diplomatic ties would be renewed in February. This took place on February 9, during a visit by Foreign Minister Arens. In February as well, Israel and Poland resumed full diplomatic ties. In May, Bulgaria followed suit.

There were now full relations with all the former Eastern bloc countries, except the Soviet Union, East Germany, and Yugoslavia. The latter, concerned about the effect that a full resumption of ties with Israel would have on its good ties with the Arabs and its standing as a leader of the Third World, proposed that the links with

Israel be upgraded gradually, starting with consular ties. Israel rejected the offer, saying it would not agree to anything less than an immediate renewal of full ties at the ambassadorial level.

In January, Science Minister Ezer Weizman visited Moscow, after having been "sacked" by Prime Minister Shamir from the prestigious inner cabinet for alleged contacts with the PLO (see "Political Developments," below). Weizman's warm reception by the Soviet authorities was undoubtedly related to his dovish positions and his advocacy of an Israeli dialogue with the PLO. Soviet foreign minister Eduard Shevardnadze told Weizman of the Soviet intention to partially upgrade their relations with Israel and, in a quid pro quo, to allow the PLO to open a full-fledged embassy in Moscow; but only the second part of the deal was kept. In Moscow, Weizman signed an agreement for scientific cooperation between the two countries. The government in Jerusalem, meanwhile, was none too pleased with Weizman's trip to Moscow. Perhaps as a result of this displeasure, Foreign Minister Arens told a Knesset forum that "there is no reason to rush to meetings in the Soviet Union; its influence in the area is on the wane, anyway."

Relations between the two countries deteriorated in the wake of the Arab campaign against immigration to Israel and Prime Minister Shamir's statement of the need for a "large Israel for the large *aliyah*." The Soviet Union could not succumb to Arab pressure to curtail the immigration without risking a serious rupture of its ties with the West, which might imperil its much-needed financial assistance. What the Kremlin did is make much diplomatic and media noise, calling in the senior Israeli representative in Moscow, Arye Levin, for repeated protests about Israeli practices and policies, in general, and its alleged settlement of Soviet Jews in the territories, in particular. On February 19, Shevardnadze announced that the Soviet Union would not be renewing full links with Israel in the foreseeable future. He said that Israel had "complicated" the situation by settling Jews in the occupied territories. "This is an erroneous and irresponsible policy by Tel Aviv," he added.

Nonetheless, economic, tourist, and cultural ties were rapidly being forged. In March the Israel Philharmonic Orchestra went on a first, widely acclaimed, tour of the Soviet Union. The Kremlin also approved, for the first time, the stationing in Moscow of a permanent reporter of the state-owned Israel Broadcasting Authority.

In September, Housing Minister Ariel Sharon visited Moscow to explore Soviet ability to provide Israel with prefab housing for new immigrants. Several days later, President Gorbachev himself entertained two Israeli ministers in a two-hour discussion. Ministers Yitzhak Modai and Yuval Ne'eman said later that the discussion centered around grand visions for future economic cooperation between the two countries, although these were greeted with some skepticism in Jerusalem.

Relations with the Soviet Union were maintained throughout the year at consular level, first established in 1987. The Soviets allowed only six diplomats to serve in the Israeli "consular mission" in Moscow, creating an unbearable workload for the mission, which had to deal with the issuing of hundreds of thousands of visas to Soviet Jews who wished to emigrate to Israel. By the end of the year, following a meeting at the UN between Foreign Ministers Levy and Shevardnadze, the Soviets did allow Israel for the first time to raise the Israeli flag in Moscow. The Israeli consular mission would no longer be formally attached to the Dutch embassy in Moscow but could henceforth function independently. Following a subsequent meeting in December with Prime Minister Shamir, Shevardnadze announced that the Kremlin was no longer attaching any preconditions to the establishment of full relations with Israel, thus dropping the traditional Soviet position that Israel must first agree to attend the Soviet-proposed international conference. Shevardnadze added, however, that the "time is not right yet" for full relations to be resumed.

East Germany made no secret of its wish to establish ties with Israel (the two countries had never had formal ties). On January 28, officials from both countries met in Copenhagen to discuss the matter. Israel demanded, as a precondition to signing an agreement, that East Germany recognize its historic responsibility for crimes committed against the Jewish people by the Nazis and agree in principle to pay compensation to Nazi victims. Israel claimed about 1.5 billion Deutsche marks in compensation, based on the 1953 reparations agreement with West Germany, which had declined at the time to pay a third "owed" by East Germany.

In February, East German prime minister Hans Modrow wrote World Jewish Congress president Edgar Bronfman that his country recognized its historic responsibility for the Holocaust and was willing to give "material compensation" to Nazi war victims. The Copenhagen talks convened again in March; in April, the first non-Communist East German government officially asked the Jewish people for forgiveness for Holocaust crimes. In May, Foreign Minister Arens told the Knesset that Israel had also demanded of East Germany that it express support for the repeal of the 1975 UN "Zionism is racism" resolution and that it introduce study of the Holocaust into all East German schools.

Talks with East Germany were discontinued after unification. The reunification of Germany presented a special diplomatic dilemma for Israel. Foreign Minister Arens angered many in Israel when he declared that German reunification was "inevitable" and therefore not worth resisting. Two other matters were prominent on the Israeli-German agenda: German assistance to the Iraqi chemical-warfare complex, and Israel's request for financial assistance for the new immigration, which in Israel's view was also tied in with East Germany's outstanding debt on reparations for Nazi war crimes. By year's end, there was as yet no reply from the Germans on this matter.

There were some diplomatic breakthroughs with Western European countries as well. Arens, on a first-ever visit to Portugal, in January, concluded that Portugal would send a resident ambassador to Israel. Following a change of regime in Athens, Greece announced that it would henceforth recognize Israel *de jure* as well as *de facto* and would set up full diplomatic ties with Israel.

However, Israel's overall political links with the European Community (EC) suffered as a result of the stalemate in the peace process and European criticism of Israel's policies toward the Palestinians. In January, the European Parliament temporarily suspended scientific ties between the EC and Israel; the EC also rejected an Israeli request for enhanced cooperation in the sphere of energy. In February it was reported that the EC would refrain from concluding new agreements with Israel or from holding high-level visits to the country, because of the situation in the territories. (By the end of the year, in the wake of Israel's revived standing as a result of the Gulf crisis, these sanctions were dropped.)

In June, following the establishment of a new, Likud-led narrow government, relations with the EC continued to deteriorate. A statement issued following an EC summit meeting in London, in June, roundly condemned Israel's behavior in the territories. In July the "troika" of EC foreign ministers, led by the Italian Gianni De Michelis, visited Jerusalem to meet with new foreign minister David Levy. The three warned that relations between Israel and the EC would deteriorate even further unless progress was achieved in the peace process.

Africa and Asia

In January Israel reopened its embassy in Ethiopia. Relations with the Mengistu regime, which was reviled in Washington, were extremely sensitive. The Ethiopian tyrant demanded military assistance, which the United States opposed vehemently. Mengistu, however, held the keys to the exits from Ethiopia, through which Israel wished to see pass the over 15,000 Jews who remained in the country. Jerusalem refused Mengistu's request for outright weaponry, agreeing to send him essentially nonmilitary supplies and to lobby on his behalf in Washington. Immigration from Ethiopia was renewed, then stopped, then renewed again.

In March, Sri Lanka closed down the Israeli interests office there, following the election of an Islamic candidate to the post of prime minister. Relations with China continued to develop slowly, following the 1989 decision to open an Israeli academic center in Beijing and a Chinese tourist center in Tel Aviv. In June, former defense minister Yitzhak Rabin offered a glimpse into the level of military cooperation between the two countries, which was widely reported in the foreign press but censored in Israel. Rabin confirmed that Israel had transferred to China avionic technology of the Lavie fighter, the Israeli-made jet which was scrapped a few years earlier.

DOMESTIC AFFAIRS

Political Developments

On March 15, Prime Minister Yitzhak Shamir's government fell in a vote of no-confidence in the Knesset; it was the first time in the country's history that the parliament voted a government out of power.

During the subsequent 37 days, Labor leader Shimon Peres tried to put together an alternative government, but failed. Then it was Shamir's turn: he spent another 42 days before establishing a coalition comprising his own Likud, parties to its right, and the religious parties. These 87 days of protracted political horse-trading exposed the Israeli political system at its worst. The reason for the political stalemate: the distribution of forces in the Knesset between the two major blocs, Labor and Likud, was split right down the middle. With 60 members of the Knesset pledging their loyalty to each side, any single member of the Knesset could make a coalition by giving it the redeeming 61st vote. For some MKs, this was an opportunity of a lifetime; never had they been the objects of such ardent courtship by the major political leaders. The stalemate was also a godsend for the religious parties; never before had the big secular parties agreed to such far-reaching concessions in exchange for their support. Hitherto obscure rabbis, who proudly proclaimed their antipathy toward the very existence of a modern and secular Jewish state, emerged as political kingmakers; by their word, coalitions were born, and at their whim, the same coalitions promptly died. The largely secular public woke up to find that their system of government had been hijacked by a small group of aged religious zealots.

The result was an unprecedented crisis of confidence between the public and its leaders. Respect for politicians reached an all-time low; many were subjected to insults and abuse and occasional threats on their lives. The public's disenchantment also gave birth to the first apolitical grass-roots mass protest movement in the country's history: the movement for changing the electoral system.

THE WEIZMAN AFFAIR

On December 31, 1989, Prime Minister Yitzhak Shamir dismissed Science Minister Ezer Weizman from the cabinet. Shamir accused Weizman, the flamboyant former Likudnik and former air force commander, of breaking the law and working against the interests of the state by holding a series of meetings with PLO officials in Europe during the summer of 1989. Weizman at first denied the charges; Shamir claimed that he had intelligence reports to prove them. Weizman later admitted to having had indirect contacts with the PLO, aimed at prodding the organization not to reject the American peace initiatives.

The Labor party rejected the legitimacy of Shamir's move and threatened to bring down the government—this, without condoning Weizman's meetings with the PLO. Ultimately, a few hours before Shamir's letter of dismissal to Weizman was to take effect, a compromise was worked out between Labor's defense minister Rabin and the Likud's justice minister Meridor. Weizman would be allowed to retain his post as a minister, but would be barred from membership in the inner cabinet for a period of 18 months. (A subsequent police investigation recommended that no action be taken against Weizman for allegedly violating the law banning contacts with the PLO.)

The crisis was over, but it signaled the fragile condition of the national unity government. Inside the Labor party, the doves attacked the party leadership, especially Rabin, for having capitulated to Shamir. Shamir, in turn, was attacked by his opponents inside the Likud, for capitulating to Labor. It was widely assumed that Shamir had agreed to take back his dismissal because of reports that Labor had concluded secret agreements with some ultra-Orthodox religious parties, which would have allowed it to set up an alternative Labor-led government had the national unity government fallen.

Shamir's "capitulation" on the Weizman affair gave valuable ammunition to his internal opposition, led by the three so-called constraints ministers—Ariel Sharon, Yitzhak Modai, and David Levy. The three had hounded Shamir for his "concessions" in the government's peace intiative of May 1989; they were on the warpath once again, as the government faced the need to make final decisions concerning the makeup of the Palestinian delegation to peace talks. Throughout January, the two camps traded harsher and harsher accusations: Shamir said that Sharon's only purpose was to "divide, obstruct, destroy"; Sharon replied that under Shamir, the Likud had turned into a "pseudo-Labor party." Modai warned that "if Shamir will enter our line of fire, he will be committing suicide." Levy, commenting on the Weizman affair, said that Shamir's government "is not functioning—on any level."

On February 12, the Likud party gathered for what came to be known as the "convention of two microphones." Sharon dropped a bombshell: without any prior warning, even to his fellow "constraints ministers," he announced his resignation, saying that under Shamir's leadership, "the Palestinian terror is running wild, Jewish lives have been abandoned." Shamir then delivered his speech, and, without warning Sharon in advance, asked the convention to approve his policies. At that moment, Sharon stood up and grabbed a second microphone. "Who is in favor of my proposal?" cried Shamir at the exact same moment that Sharon was asking the delegates, "Who is in favor of the eradication of terror?" Most of the delegates raised their hands; Shamir declared victory and left the podium, followed by most of the Likud ministers. Sharon and his colleagues remained, claiming that the victory was theirs. The Likud was close to an open split.

An ironic postscript: in the wake of the government's fall, in March, there were calls for Shamir's resignation, both from Levy and from within the Shamir camp itself. At a critical moment, Sharon expressed support for Shamir's continued leadership, and the attempted "putsch" collapsed. A month earlier Sharon had resigned over Shamir's alleged lack of leadership; now he was salvaging it. When the new government was constituted, the constraints ministers disbanded: Sharon was rewarded for his unexpected loyalty by being appointed housing minister and czar of the absorption process; Levy, now foreign minister, turned into the most moderate of the Likud ministers; Modai indeed split from the Likud on February 28, setting up his own four-member party "For the Advancement of the Zionist Idea."

THE GOVERNMENT FALLS

Only 48 hours before the eruption of the coalition crisis on March 15, the government enjoyed an overwhelming majority in parliament. No less than 92 members out of 120 belonged to the second national unity government, set up following the November 1988 elections. Only 28 members of the Knesset were in the opposition, 16 to the left of the government, 7 to the right, and 5 from the Orthodox religious bloc. The coalition itself consisted of 36 Likud members, 4 members of the Likud splinter led by Minister Yitzhak Modai, 39 Labor members, and another 13 members of the religious parties.

On February 21, three weeks before the eventual fall of the government, Peres and Labor had presented Shamir and the government with an ultimatum: bring the Baker question to a vote in the cabinet, or face the dissolution of the national unity coalition. To underscore the seriousness of its threat, Labor offered a motion of no-confidence in the government (in which it was still a partner) in the Knesset. As Shamir and his Likud colleagues pondered the proper response to the Labor ultimatum, Peres himself made no secret of the fact that his party's threat packed a wallop. According to Labor's calculations, if the government should fall, it would be the party to set up the next government. Labor's 39 members and the 16 members of the Left totaled 55; the 5-member ultra-Orthodox Agudat Israel party was in the opposition and made no secret of its animosity toward Shamir; another 8 ultra-Orthodox members of the coalition, from the Shas and Degel Hatorah parties, were subservient to rabbis with clearly dovish views. Thus, Labor could presumably muster a strong 68-member coalition with relative ease.

For Shamir, there were no good options. He could either cave in to Labor's demand and the American position and agree to the inclusion of East Jerusalemites and deported Palestinians in the delegation to peace talks; or he could refuse and face almost certain relegation to the opposition. Shamir believed that a yes answer to the Baker question was tantamount to an Israeli agreement to negotiate with the PLO; but he was also aware that a Labor-led government would agree to the Baker question, and more. In the days following the Labor ultimatum, reports in the press suggested that rather than lose his post, Shamir intended to give Baker a positive response. Thus, a February 26 appearance by the prime minister in the Knesset's Defense and Foreign Affairs Committee was marked by some interesting reversals of positions: Shamir's usually staunch ideological opponents on the Left treated him with gentle deference, while MK Geula Cohen—a leader of the far-Right opposition Tehiya party and Shamir's colleague in the prestate underground Lehi movement— told the prime minister that it was "embarrassing" to see him in such a state. The usually taciturn prime minister replied in a most unparliamentary manner, indicative of the pressures taxing him: Cohen, he said, was "a lunatic."

On March 3, as the Labor ultimatum was nearing its deadline, the forum of Likud ministers met to discuss the party's attitude toward the Baker question. On that issue they reached no decision; however, they did come up with new demands for

Labor: before bringing the Baker question to a formal vote in the cabinet, the Likud insisted that Labor undertake to agree to new elections in case of an eventual fall of the government. This was intended to prevent Peres from using the same tactic— the threat to set up an alternative coalition—if and when an Israeli-Palestinian dialogue ever got under way.

The Likud added another preliminary condition to the cabinet vote: any Israeli delegation to peace talks, the Likud ministers declared, had to be able to speak "with one voice." Specifically, Labor had to agree in advance that East Jerusalemites would not be allowed to vote in the proposed elections in the territories and undertake not to allow the PLO any role at any stage of the peace process. Labor's defense minister Yitzhak Rabin, who did not share Peres's enthusiasm for an alternative narrow coalition, nonetheless labeled the Likud demands *"hutzpah."* In practical terms, the Likud had rejected the Baker formula.

On March 6, the Labor ministers rejected the Likud's demands and reiterated their request for an immediate cabinet session to discuss and decide on the Baker question. The next day, the government's highest decision-making forum, the inner cabinet, in which Labor and Likud enjoyed a parity of six ministers each, met to discuss the Baker question. Shamir, however, refused to allow a vote. He did make clear what he thought of Labor's latest demands: the PLO, he said, is constantly getting weaker. Its only source of strength is the attitude of the Israeli Labor party.

Peres understood Shamir's procrastination, as well as the Likud "preconditions," as a clear sign that Shamir had no intention of saying yes to Baker. In a television appearance following the inconclusive inner cabinet meeting, he said that "the Likud has decided to bring an end to the national unity government, and with it to the peace process itself." Likud, for its part, launched a series of clandestine contacts with the religious parties aimed at preventing Peres from setting up an alternative narrow coalition. The next day, March 8, Shamir responded to Peres by confirming his suspicions. In a press conference in the north, the prime minister said, "When I am talked to by ultimatums, I turn deaf." Shamir added that "since the establishment of the national unity government, Peres has been counting the days to its demise."

On Sunday, March 11, the inner cabinet met again; again, Shamir refused to bring the Baker question to a vote. The Labor ministers, realizing Shamir's adamance, left the meeting before it was formally closed. The crisis was clearly coming to a head. Peres convened Labor's Central Committee, which had to approve any effort to bring down the government, and the committee unanimously approved Peres's formulation of the issue: "The Likud's refusal to decide on matters which are crucial to progress in the peace process has effectively eliminated the prospects for its advancement." The committee, therefore, authorized Labor's contingent in the Knesset to take the "appropriate parliamentary measures."

On Tuesday, March 13, Shamir precipitated the crisis by dismissing Peres. He did so in order to avert a situation mandated by Israeli law, which prevents cabinet ministers from entering or leaving a transitional government. If the government falls, it automatically becomes such a transitional government. Thus, Shamir decided to dismiss Peres—knowing full well that his Labor colleagues would have no choice but to resign in the wake of the dismissal—so that Labor would not be "trapped" inside the government. If this government was destined to fall, Shamir reasoned, it should at least not be burdened by the presence of his Labor rivals.

In his official letter dismissing Peres, Shamir charged that the Labor leader had "worked toward the dismantling of the national unity government and had undermined its very existence. He [Peres] accuses the government, unjustly, that it is not working for the advancement of peace, which is its main *raison d'être*, and therefore it does not have the right to exist. I say these things with the deepest pain, since I have invested considerably in the establishment and continued existence of the national unity government. I believed, as I continue to believe today, that our situation in these times mandates the existence and the policy of such a government. But subversion against the essence of the national unity government is damaging to the interests of both the people and the state."

Shamir's move surprised the Labor ministers, who until then were calling the shots in the developing government crisis. Their stinging remarks in this, the last meeting of the national unity government, reflected their chagrin. Minister Rafi Edri described Shamir's move as "antidemocratic"; Communications Minister Gad Yaakobi accused Shamir of "dividing the nation and causing severe harm to the country." Political science professor Yitzhak Galnoor, a supporter of the Left, said that Shamir was simply diverting the public agenda away from the external dilemma of the Baker question to the internal political arena.

Peres's dismissal and the resignations of his colleagues were due to take effect 48 hours after the formal submission of the dismissal and resignation letters. Seeking to counter Shamir's designs, and indeed to "trap" its ministers inside the transitional government, Labor sought to force the Knesset to vote on its motion of no-confidence earlier than planned; the party even appealed to the High Court of Justice for this purpose, but to no avail.

Several attempts were made to seek a compromise with Shamir, but these too failed. On the morning of March 15, it appeared that there was no avoiding the vote on the no-confidence motion, but the results were far from certain. Labor appeared to have 60 definite votes: 55 of its own and the leftist bloc, and an additional five of Agudat Israel. It was not clear where the clinching 61st vote would come from.

Before the Knesset started its debate, a last-ditch mediation effort was made. Rabbi Ovadia Yosef, a former Sephardic chief rabbi and spiritual leader of the ultra-Orthodox, Sephardic Shas party, decided to intervene—the first such action by a supposedly nonpolitical religious leader. Israelis, who were anxiously following the drama on live television, were dismayed to see Labor leader Peres, and then the prime minister himself, leave the Knesset building to go to Rabbi Yosef's residence in another Jerusalem neighborhood.

Yosef proposed a five-point compromise: revocation of Peres's dismissal, postponement of the no-confidence vote, a convening of the cabinet within a week, and a positive answer to Baker, coupled with a reaffirmation of Israel's commitment to the indivisibility of Jerusalem and the nonparticipation of the PLO in the peace process. Peres agreed and signed the compromise agreement. Shamir, however, refused to commit himself to a positive reply to Baker; he agreed only to say that the cabinet would "decide" on the Baker question; and not within a week, but within two weeks. Before giving his final negative reply to Rabbi Yosef, Shamir decided to submit the matter to a vote among the ten Likud ministers. Seven Likud ministers voted in favor of the compromise. Shamir, however, disregarded the clear majority.

In later days it would emerge that Labor and Shas's political leader, Interior Minister Arye Deri, were in complete coordination; for weeks, Deri had expressed support for a positive answer to Baker. It was clear to Peres that Shamir would not agree to the rabbi's compromise. It was also clear to Peres that he himself would have to affix his name to the rabbi's offer, if he indeed wished to bring the government down. It was Shas which ultimately defected from the ranks of the coalition and ended the reign of the national unity government.

On March 15, the Knesset passed a no-confidence motion, 60–55. Rabbi Yosef had instructed the six members of Shas not to participate in the vote, but one of the six, Minister Yitzhak Peretz, refused to comply. (In actuality, Peretz was much more in tune with the sentiments of the voters who had put Shas in the Knesset in the first place than the venerated rabbi.) On the following Sunday, Yosef appeared on national television, in an unprecedented nine-minute interview on the prime-time news show *Mabat*. He explained that he had ordered Shas not to provide the votes which would have saved Shamir's government, because "a narrow right-wing government would have led to war. . . . If we would have had such a government, which relies on the extreme right, who shout morning and night 'not an inch,' this would mean that we do not want peace; this is what the nations of the world would believe."

It was strong stuff, especially in light of the fact that Rabbi Yosef was the spiritual leader of hundreds of thousands of Oriental Israelis who were traditionally considered to be supporters of the Likud and even "Arab-haters."

FORMING A NEW GOVERNMENT

In accordance with Israeli law, on Sunday, March 18, President Chaim Herzog opened a series of consultations with all the parties in the Knesset, to determine which candidate had the best chance of forming a new government. Labor's bloc of 60, including Agudat Israel, recommended that Peres be given the job. Surprisingly, the same number of Knesset members expressed support for Shamir. The five members of Shas, who only three days earlier had brought down the government, told Herzog that "someone from the Likud" should form the next government, since the party could not bring itself to support Peres outright. In a statement issued from the President's House, Herzog said that despite the 60–60 tie, he believed Peres had "the best and most reasonable chance" to set up a new government. Herzog based his decision on two factors. First, Labor was the largest party in the Knesset (by virtue of Modai's split from the Likud); second, Herzog maintained that if a certain government policy is defeated in a no-confidence motion in the Knesset, the opposing point of view should be "given a chance."

The Likud did not take kindly to Herzog's decision; their criticism, however, was muted, in light of the general deference accorded the president's position by the public. The Likud did, however, launch its campaign against Peres's efforts; what Israel is facing, the Likud stated, is a government that will be based on "anti-Zionist and pro-fascist" parties.

Peres, meanwhile, was exuberant with confidence. On March 17, the daily *Davar* reported that, in a conversation with World Jewish Congress president Edgar Bronfman, held weeks before the government fell, Peres boasted that he had 72 Knesset members. Peres himself said in a public appearance that he would set up a coalition that would enjoy the support of at least 70 members of the Knesset. On March 21, Peres launched a series of intensive negotiations with all his potential coalition partners, including Modai's previously Likud-linked party For the Advancement of the Zionist Idea. After the first round of talks, however, it was clear that Peres's path to the prime ministership would be more difficult than envisioned in his public statements.

ENTER THE RABBIS

Apart from the Likud leanings of its supporters, another significant reason for Shas's equivocating position in its consultations with the president was to be found in the person of 95-year-old Rabbi Eliezer Schach, of B'nei B'rak, leader of the so-called "Lithuanian," non-Hassidic branch of the ultra-Orthodox. Though himself an Ashkenazi, Schach exerted crucial influence on Shas. Many of the party's political and religious leaders had been educated in his own Poniwez Yeshivah in B'nei B'rak. It was Schach who originally set up Shas as a Sephardi splinter of Agudat Israel before the 1984 elections and installed Rabbi Yosef as its titular spiritual leader. In 1988 he promoted another Ashkenazi party, Degel Hatorah, which gained two Knesset seats. All in all, Schach had direct and indirect control of eight crucial Knesset members.

The rabbi was none too happy with Rabbi Yosef's newfound independence and, in the wake of Yosef's controversial television appearance, ultra-Orthodox circles were rife with rumors about Schach's displeasure with Yosef. Schach's arch-enemy, whom he frequently depicted as a dangerous "false messiah," was Rabbi M.M. Schneerson, the Lubavitcher Rebbe of Brooklyn. In its essence, the rivalry between Schach and the Lubavitcher dated back to 19th-century Eastern Europe and the fierce rivalry, indeed schism, between Hassidism—represented in modern times by the Lubavitcher—and the "*mitnagdim*," of whom Schach was today's most prominent rabbi. In the 1988 elections, the Lubavitcher, who had always been very influential in Agudat Israel, openly pitched his strong Chabad movement behind that party, a move which earned the Agudah an additional couple of seats in the Knesset, at the very least. As a result, if the arch-rival Agudat Yisrael were in favor of Labor, Schach would be in favor of Likud. This, despite the fact that Schach had frequently expressed extremely dovish views, including a willingness to return all the territories captured in the 1967 Six Day War. Thus, Degel Hatorah opted for Shamir in their deliberations with Herzog, and Shas would never again support Labor in the open.

When President Herzog asked Peres to try and form a government, Rabbi Schach reacted by warning Shas that if it joined a Peres government, he would split the party in two. Shas leader Arye Deri, who as early as January had promised Peres that his party would support a Labor-led government, now refused even to enter into coalition negotiations with him.

On March 26, Schach spelled out the ideological underpinnings for his position, in a landmark speech delivered before 10,000 fervent followers at a Tel Aviv basketball arena. The speech, which was televised nationally, was to prove a watershed event in relations between the secular and religious in Israel. Most of the public had never seen Schach before; the overwhelming majority also could not understand a word he said, since the rabbi chose to speak in Yiddish. All in all, it was a surrealistic spectacle: the entire country glued to their television sets, in prime time, watching an indecipherable rabbi arouse thousands of black-garbed adherents to wild enthusiasm. Though many did not understand the language, the message was clear: Schach had declared war on the Labor movement in general, and on its most precious jewel, the kibbutzim, in particular. "The kibbutzim don't know what Yom Kippur is, what is Shabbes, what is the mikve; they raise forbidden pigs and rabbits. One kibbutz member told me that he did not know what 'Shma Yisrael' was; another that she was afraid to enter a synagogue. Is this a Jew? Labor has severed itself from the Torah, from the Sabbath, from the past; they believe in a new Torah."

Schach's diatribe shocked the nation, and the Labor movement in particular. Throughout the ensuing weeks, fierce counterattacks were launched against Schach and the entire ultra-Orthodox community, centering on the fact that yeshivah students did not serve in the army, while the kibbutzim had suffered enormous casualties in Israel's wars, out of all proportion to their share of the population. A veritable kulturkampf was launched; relations between religious and secular sank to an all-time low. The term "Khomeinism" was used to describe Schach and his message. Even the president was embroiled. Herzog mildly criticized Schach in a weekly radio address, and ultra-Orthodox politicians responded by calling for his resignation.

A poll released in early May revealed where the public's sentiments lay: over 60 percent opted for a revocation of the "Orthodox monopoly" in Israel.

THE FALSE GOVERNMENT

On the immediate political level, Schach's speech took all the wind out of Labor's sails. Many in the party said on the day following the speech that Labor should give up the effort to form a new government and should seek early elections instead. It was now clear that the Ashkenazi Degel Hatorah party would never join a coalition with Labor; indeed, several days earlier the party had already concluded a secret agreement with the Likud. More significant, however, was the fact that Rabbi Yosef, who also spoke at the basketball arena, had backtracked completely from his previous support for Labor. "He is the leader, and we shall always walk hand in hand," Yosef said of Schach. This meant that the five members of Shas were now also out of Peres's reach. Now that it was stuck with its basic 60 supporters, Labor reached out for "defectors" from within the Likud itself, and another shameful chapter in the coalition negotiations was launched. On April 3, Peres told surprised and skeptical journalists that he had a majority of 61 members of the Knesset. For 24 hours, the political community and the press scanned the entire political spectrum for the extra Knesset member to whom Peres was referring. After a day, the search was over: the 61st vote was that of Avraham Sharir, a member of the Liberal branch of the Likud party.

Sharir had held two portfolios in the first national unity government, justice and tourism, and had managed to become one of the most unpopular politicians in the country. When Shamir announced the Likud lineup of ministers for the second unity government, Sharir's name was not on the list. The decision gained Shamir rare accolades from both sides of the political arena, but Sharir swore revenge. Peres's effort to set up a government gave him his chance: he signed a secret deal with Peres that would give him a cabinet portfolio in a Labor-led government and ensure his inclusion in the Labor list for the next Knesset.

The parties to Labor's left were not happy with Peres's contract with Sharir, the "defector," a title that quickly stuck to him. (In a country that sanctifies army service, the word "defector" carries an especially negative connotation.) The leftist parties said that they would refrain from joining the Labor coalition for as long as its majority was based solely on a "defector." They did, however, pledge to support Peres's government "from the outside," explaining that they would not block the establishment of a "coalition of peace."

The same day, Peres shored up his coalition by signing a formal agreement with the five-member Agudat Israel party. Now armed with the support of the necessary 61 Knesset members, Peres informed the president that he had succeeded in setting up a government. A special Knesset meeting to approve his new government was set up for Tuesday, April 10. In an interview with a French weekly, Peres already spoke of his new government's policy: the first thing we will do, he said, will be to convene the Cairo dialogue with the Palestinians.

On Monday, April 9, the Labor Central Committee met to approve Peres's list of 11 Labor ministers for the new government. Peres tried to dispel persistent rumors that all was not well among the five supposed supporters from Agudat Israel by saying that "61 Knesset members are signed, and I am convinced that they will keep their word." The new government's guidelines stated that it would reply positively to Baker's question. The committee approved Peres's plans; the atmosphere was one of foreboding, however, not jubilation.

The next day, at 9:00 A.M., 120 members of the Knesset came to hear Peres present his government. Peres never appeared. Overnight, his majority of 61 had become a minority of 59. Two members of Agudat Israel had "defected." One, Avraham Verdiger, tendered his resignation from the Knesset. The other, Eliezer Mizrahi, left Agudat Israel to set up his own single-member list. Both said that, as supporters of the Greater Land of Israel and opponents of any territorial concessions, they could not support a coalition that was dependent on the votes of pro-PLO Arabs and anti-Zionist elements such as the Israel Communist party. More importantly, both were also adherents of the Lubavitcher Rebbe, who forbade them to support such a coalition. Once again, a rabbi had interceded against Peres, and this one didn't even live in Israel. Several days later, the Lubavitcher gave a rare interview to Israel television: The messiah is coming, he said, but until he gets here, we should continue in Shamir's way.

PERES'S SECOND CHANCE

On the afternoon of this hitherto unheard-of parliamentary fiasco, President Herzog extended Peres's deadline for forming a coalition by another 15 days. Once again, the Likud was furious, but this time some of the party's more radical members did not hold their tongues. Zahi Hanegbi, a young Likud firebrand, said that Herzog had acted like a "minor political functionary" and called on the president to resign immediately. The Likud Knesset caucus asked the president to "reconsider" his mistaken decision. Privately, enraged Likud members charged that Herzog's agreement to give Peres another 15 days was a result of cronyism—the two men's common political past as well as repayment by the president for Peres's help in electing him to his post. Never before had such accusations been leveled at a president, not even posthumously. The President's House reacted by issuing a statement explaining that Herzog's decision was based on a firm commitment given to him by the Agudat Israel party, which pledged to "deliver" five Knesset members to support Peres—even if they had to replace the two "rebels." Herzog, the statement read, had been subjected to "stark pressures and ugly threats."

For the next 15 days, Peres tried every available avenue, but his efforts were directed chiefly at two targets: another attempt to persuade Rabbi Ovadia Yosef to allow Shas to support his government and the Likud splinter group led by Yitzhak Modai. Rabbi Yosef rebuffed Peres's advances but he met frequently with both Peres and Shamir, trying to persuade the two to reconstitute the national unity government. Both refused to commit themselves to such a possibility, but refrained from rejecting the rabbi's plea outright. In any case, Rabbi Yosef made clear that he could not order Shas to support a Labor-led government.

In the meantime, the Agudah's Verdiger retracted his resignation from the Knesset. Under pressure from the Agudah's governing body of rabbis, the Council of Torah Sages, he announced that he was now willing to support Labor, in exchange for a commitment from Peres that before any territorial concessions were made, new elections would be called. Peres moved up once again from 59 to 60 seats.

His last chance lay with Modai and his four-member movement For the Advancement of the Zionist Idea. On April 14, the Likud had signed a controversial agreement with Modai, pledging to guarantee the reelection of its four members in the next elections. On April 19, the Likud Central Committee met to approve the agreement, but its concessions to a "defector" aroused widespread resentment. Binyamin Zeev Begin, the former prime minister's son, made a strong impression with an impassioned appeal against the agreement, but party leader Shamir made clear that rejection of the agreement would ensure Peres's becoming the next prime minister. The Central Committee concurred and ratified the agreement with Modai. Shamir even called on the "defector" Avraham Sharir to return to the Likud ranks. "Abrasha, come home," he cried, using the disgraced politician's nickname. Sharir, by this time, was in hiding. Enraged Likud supporters hounded him around the clock, demanding that he revoke his agreement with Labor.

On April 25, during the last 24 hours before the period given to Peres expired, Labor had two last gasps of hope. A rabbinical court in Jerusalem ordered Eliezer Mizrahi, the last Agudah refusenik, to support Peres's government. Mizrahi, however, was nowhere to be found. He too was in hiding. It was left to Modai to maintain the drama until the very last minute. Modai had been one of the three so-called constraints ministers who had plagued Shamir from the Likud's extreme right flanks. Now he was conducting negotiations with Labor. He made clear that he did not believe that the Likud would adhere to the agreement signed with him, despite its approval by the party's Central Committee. Three hours before Peres's term expired, Modai appeared on the nightly *Mabat* television program. After several minutes of avoiding the interviewers' questions, he finally announced, with the semblance of a smile, that he would not support Peres. Thus, after 39 fruitless days, the mandate to set up a government was transferred by Herzog from Peres to Shamir.

SHAMIR'S 42 DAYS

On April 27, Shamir showed that he could be just as overconfident as Peres. "I will set up a narrow coalition very quickly," he said. Negotiations with his potential coalition partners started off under an auspicious sign: the "defector" Sharir had now changed his mind and was "returning home" to the Likud. Sharir, who was by now the most reviled politician in Israel, said that he had posed no conditions

for his return. "You don't make agreements with your own home," he told supporters in Tel Aviv.

Then Shamir's efforts hit a snag. Both the National Religious party and Rabbi
Ovadia Yosef, expressing apprehension at the establishment of an "extreme right-
wing government," announced that they would make a last-ditch effort to reconstitute a national unity government. For more than ten days, both Shas and the NRP
refused to enter substantive discussions with Shamir. By the time they had changed
their minds, Shamir's first 21 days were over. Throughout this period, Shamir had
conducted few meetings with his potential coalition partners. Unlike Peres, Shamir
proceeded at a snail's pace; his advisers, unlike Peres's, did not swamp the press with
supposedly new information every day. Although Shamir's caretaker government
had already been in power for 60 days, and despite the fact that the political
stalemate continued unresolved, the general atmosphere in the country calmed
down.

Shamir's potential coalition partners, as well as senior members of the Likud,
were starting to get suspicious. Shamir, they now thought, was only putting on a
show of conducting serious negotiations. His real aim, they believed, was to use up
his 21-day extension and then lead the country to new elections. On June 3, Ariel
Sharon called a press conference in Tel Aviv and made his suspicions clear. Shamir,
he said, had the pledged support of 61 Knesset members, and "if Shimon Peres had
61 members in the same situation, he would have established a government a long
time ago." The Prime Minister's Office announced a few days later that indeed,
Shamir now enjoyed the support of 61; but the political community continued to
be skeptical of Shamir's ultimate designs.

Now it was the Likud's turn to produce a rabbit from the hat, its own version
of the defecting Sharir: MK Efraim Gur of the Labor party. Gur, born in Georgia
in the Soviet Union, was the first Soviet immigrant to be elected to the Knesset. Since
the downfall of the government, there were persistent rumors of his contacts with
the Likud. On April 9, he described these rumors as "cheap gossip." Several weeks
later he termed them "an insult." On June 4, he categorically denied any intentions
of crossing the political lines. Two days later, he acknowledged signing an agreement
with the rival party: he would be appointed a deputy minister in a Likud government; his reelection would be assured; he would even be allowed to appoint 30
members to the Likud Central Committee.

Shamir's task now was formidable. He had to appease three parties to the right
of the Likud (Tehiya, Moledet, Tzomet) that opposed the Camp David accords and
the government's initiative of May 1989; he had to negotiate with the politicians of
Shas, who were committed to a coalition with the Likud but secretly yearned for
a Labor-led government or at least a return to the national unity government; he
had to deal with four individual Knesset members who were no longer connected
to any previously existing party; and he had to reconcile the contradictory ambitions
of many of his own Likud members, who saw the narrow coalition, with the
attractive portfolios vacated by Labor, as a golden opportunity for political advancement.

Shamir's main gambits were obfuscation and brinkmanship; unlike Peres, who clearly sought a narrow Labor government, Shamir behaved as if it made no difference to him whether he succeeded in setting up a new government, or whether the country faced new elections less than two years after the previous ones, or whether a new national unity government was set up. He postponed the clinching meetings with his potential partners until the very last minute, when there was no time left for bluff and tactics. On June 8, he signed a coalition agreement with 60 members of the Knesset; when Rehavam Zeevi's Moledet party promised to support the government from the outside, Shamir was assured of the support of 62 members of the Knesset. His government comprised the Likud faction—36 (including reformed defector Sharir); the Modai faction—4; the National Religious party—5; Shas—5; Degel Hatorah—2; Tehiya—3; Tzomet—2; and three individuals (Shas resigner Yitzhak Peretz; Labor defector Efraim Gur; and Agudah rebel Eliezer Mizrahi). Nearly half the members of the new government were either ministers (20) or deputy ministers (9). The coalition undertook to curtail abortions, abolish pork growing, and ban "lewd" advertisements. Judging by its makeup, the Shamir coalition was definitely the most right-wing in Israel's history. The Arab world reacted with horror, Yasir Arafat and Hafez al-Assad describing it as a "cabinet of war."

On June 11, the Knesset convened to approve Shamir's government. At the last minute, it looked as if there would be a replay of Peres's debacle of April 10. Shas suddenly threatened not to vote for the proposed coalition. The reason: police investigators had conducted a search at the offices of Interior Minister Deri, who was under investigation for alleged mismanagement of government funds. After a flurry of contacts with Rabbi Yosef, the crisis was resolved. In the end, 62 Knesset members voted for Shamir's coalition; 57 opposed it, and there was one abstention. Many Israelis had misgivings about a coalition composed of so many parties, splinters, and free-roaming individuals. At the same time, there was a collective sigh of relief. The three-month nightmare, which had seen Israel's political leadership sink to previously unimagined depths, was finally over.

PERES VS. RABIN

Defense Minister Rabin was a reluctant participant in the moves leading to the downfall of the national unity government. He had been outmaneuvered by Peres, the party doves, and sympathetic ultra-Orthodox politicians, mainly Interior Minister Arye Deri. But when the plot failed, Rabin decided to seize his chance and challenge Peres for the leadership of the party. He described Peres's aborted attempt to depose Shamir as a "stinking trick." Most of the party's representatives in the Knesset, some of whom had prodded Peres into bringing down the government, jumped on Rabin's bandwagon. Peres's misfortunes were compounded by the publication of an internal party report which pinned on him the blame for Labor's lackluster performance in the elections of November 1988. Rabin was self-confident.

THE NEW CABINET
(installed on June 11, 1990)

Prime Minister, Minister of Labor &
Social Affairs, & Minister for
Environment[1]   Yitzhak Shamir (Likud)

Deputy Prime Minister & Minister of
Foreign Affairs   David Levy (Likud)
Deputy Prime Minister & Minister of
Industry & Trade   Moshe Nissim (Likud)
Defense   Moshe Arens (Likud)
Finance   Yitzhak Modai (Likud)
Agriculture   Rafael Eitan (Tzomet)
Communications   Rafael Pinhasi (Shas)
Economy & Planning   David Magen (Likud)
Education   Zevulun Hammer (National Religious
                                            party)
Energy & Science   Yuval Ne'eman (Tehiya)
Health   Ehud Olmert (Likud)
Housing & Construction   Ariel Sharon
Immigrant Absorption   Yitzhak Peretz (Independent)
Interior   Arye Deri (Shas)
Justice   Dan Meridor (Likud)
Police   Ronnie Milo (Likud)
Religious Affairs   Avner Shaki (National Religious party)
Tourism   Gideon Patt (Likud)
Transportation   Moshe Katsav (Likud)

[1]Shamir retained the Labor and Social Affairs portfolio until Agudat Israel joined the coalition, and the Environment portfolio was left unfilled for Moledet.

The *New York Post* reported (June 20, 1990) his boast that he would topple Peres before the end of June, and then topple Shamir's government and lead the party to elections.

In order to avert a defeat, Peres clung to procedural objections. There was no justification, he said, for Rabin's challenge such a long time before the next elections. Thus, the question facing the party's Central Committee on July 22 was not who should be the party leader but when this leader should be chosen. Nonetheless, it was clear that defeat for Peres would force his resignation.

Peres, however, confounded all the predictions by emerging victorious. The party rank and file, it was reasoned with hindsight, were not comfortable with the idea of deposing a leader, especially one who had proven his loyalty by remaining active and optimistic through the bad times that the party had undergone in the previous decade. Rabin, on the other hand, had stayed aloof from the party during this time; he had also, so it was alleged, stayed aloof from the Central Committee members whose votes he sought. The conventional wisdom regarding Rabin's surprising defeat was ultimately encapsulated in the complaint of a veteran "tea server" at Labor headquarters in Tel Aviv: Rabin had seen her for 20 years, she said, and not once did he say hello. Peres, on the other hand, was always polite. He always remembered to ask about her children.

MOVEMENT FOR ELECTORAL CHANGE

President Herzog was instrumental in drumming up popular support for a concept that was gaining more and more adherents with each passing day of the coalition crisis: the movement to change the Israeli electoral system. Basically, the movement called for direct elections for the post of prime minister. The prime minister would thus not be dependent on the vagaries of a Knesset coalition, and the "extortion" powers of religious parties and other minority elements would be significantly curtailed. Herzog, a longtime supporter of electoral change, approached the limits of his authority to intervene in day-to-day politics when he stated, upon his first announcement of Peres as the candidate for prime minister, that "the public is fed up with an electoral system which causes untold damage." The Knesset was also feeling the heat and anger of the public. Contrary to the recommendation of the justice minister, the parliament gave preliminary approval to four private bills that offered slightly differing blueprints for a new electoral system.

Rabbi Schach's speech gave new impetus for the reformist movement: municipal leaders and mayors, who were themselves chosen in direct elections, joined up with a fledgling group of nonpoliticians to lead the call for electoral change. In April some of these political novices launched a hunger strike. On its 15th day, they called off their hunger strike, in deference to one of the biggest mass demonstrations ever seen in Israel: over 250,000 people showed up at Tel Aviv's Malchei Israel Square on April 7, to demand that the politicians heed *vox populi*. In a public-opinion poll released soon afterward, 61 percent of the public expressed support for the change. American Jewish leaders, dismayed by the ugliness of the Israeli political process, also came out strongly in support of the reform.

Some establishment politicians now lent support to the movement, among them Labor's Yitzhak Rabin and the Likud's Ariel Sharon and Benjamin Netanyahu. Not surprisingly, all three were thought to be driven, *inter alia*, by personal motives, since all three were thought to be popular with the public and thus had a personal stake in direct elections for the prime ministership.

With the establishment of a new government in June and the onset of the Gulf crisis in July, the public lost some interest in the reform movement. Toward the end of the year, the Labor party decided formally to support the change. The Likud, especially Prime Minister Shamir, had yet to openly state its position. It was clear that the reform, if it ever came, would come slowly. The four bills, approved in March, were being discussed in a Knesset committee at the end of the year.

Immigration

Immigration of Jews from the Soviet Union turned from a trickle to a stream by the end of 1989; in the beginning of 1990, it was a steady flow; by the end of the year, it had turned into a veritable flood. More immigrants arrived on a single night in December than the total number of immigrants arriving in some previous years.

Immigration started to pick up toward the end of 1989, with the relaxation of Soviet emigration procedures. The pace grew from 5,000 a month at the beginning of the year to close to an overwhelming 45,000 at its end. All in all, 199,516 immigrants arrived in 1990, more than in any single year since 1949, the first year following the establishment of the state. The bulk of the new immigrants—all but 15,000—came from the Soviet Union. Immigration from Ethiopia also picked up, and over 4,000 new Ethiopian immigrants came, usually by way of Rome. Two thousand Jews came from Bulgaria and Romania, and by the end of the year the last remnant of the small Albanian Jewish community was being transferred to Israel.

Despite numerous projections, Israel was caught unprepared: there were not enough apartments for the newcomers and no jobs. The government debated which of the two deficiencies should be remedied first: without a formal decision, housing won out. For their first six months in the country, the immigrants' upkeep was at the government's expense. The employment problem, therefore, was deferred to the future.

Although the *aliyah* was welcomed by politicians from both the coalition and the opposition, from the outset the absorption process was marked by fierce turf fights between the Jewish Agency and the government, on the one hand, and factions within the government itself, on the other. The agency and the government bickered over their relative shares in absorbing the cost of the immigration and the "absorption basket" given to every immigrant upon his arrival, for a period of six months. In January there were reports that Prime Minister Shamir intended to set up a special oversight committee in his office; Absorption Minister Peretz railed against what he saw as an attempt to intervene in his exclusive sphere of influence, and Shamir backed down.

A sense of emergency took hold in Israel because of increasing reports of wild outbursts of anti-Semitism in the Soviet Union in the wake of the democratization and liberalization there. The head of the Jewish Agency's immigration department, Uri Gordon, said, on February 19, that the agency planned to accelerate the pace of *aliyah* because of the growing anti-Semitism. There were reports of anti-Semitic incidents in Azerbaijan and Moldavia, Leningrad and Moscow. "The Jews of Kiev don't let their children out of their houses for fear of pogroms," it was reported in March. There were insistent reports of a large-scale pogrom planned by the nationalist Russian Pamyat organization, scheduled to take place on May 5. It never did.

The Jewish Agency rejected proposals to open up new way stations in Western Europe, for fear that the Soviet immigrants would then choose not to come to Israel at all; Peretz, on the other hand, surprised the Knesset by stating that Soviet Jews must be rescued, even if they "go to Uganda." The first rule, he said, is that "a drowning Jew must be saved." Peretz's position, however, was not shared by the government. Prime Minister Shamir said: "Sometimes people say the wrong things. That's democracy."

In February, Finance Minister Peres submitted the state budget, which took into account only 40,000 new immigrants for the year. It was clear that the budget was unrealistic even before it had been approved by the Knesset. One reason cited by Peres was concern that a budget covering 100,000 immigrants—the prevailing projection at the time—would arouse "great anger" in the world. Peres said that the Treasury had prepared ample monetary reserves; he also said that there were "tens of thousands" of vacant apartments awaiting the immigrants. Peres's unrealistic budget earned criticism from the Bank of Israel, which said that the budget should have been geared for the absorption of at least 120,000 immigrants. By April, a supplementary one billion shekels was added to the budget for absorption; even the 100,000 figure, which Peres was afraid would needlessly agitate the world, was no longer considered realistic. The Jewish Agency, meanwhile, concluded an agreement with the United Jewish Appeal on a fund-raising campaign goal of $600 million over a period of three years. That figure was subsequently raised to a billion dollars. In March, Peres asked the heads of the Israel Bonds organization to raise no less than $10 billion. Meanwhile, the leaders of the American Jewish community were increasingly disturbed by what they saw as incessant internal bickering in the Israeli government, which was preventing a coordinated policy and threatening the success of the absorption process. When State Comptroller Miriam Ben Porat, who shared these apprehensions, criticized the fact the government had not set up a central absorption authority, Shamir retorted that the comptroller was exceeding the bounds of her authority.

In the latter part of the year, a major construction effort was undertaken under new Housing Minister Ariel Sharon, who had also been appointed head of a special inner cabinet to deal with absorption. Sharon wanted to import 90,000 prefabricated caravans (mobile homes) by the end of 1992; the Finance Ministry replied that Israel didn't have the resources. In the meantime, the army announced that it was vacating military camps, thus producing 20,000 "beds" for new immigrants, and the Housing Ministry unveiled an emergency plan to use dilapidated hotels and guest houses for temporary housing for immigrants.

The arrival of the immigrants rekindled an old internal argument about the proper "distribution" of the population. The Labor party, including Histadrut secretary-general Israel Kessar, said that at least 50 percent of the new immigrants should be directed toward the thinly populated north and south and the under-developed development towns. Most of the new immigrants, however, preferred to settle in the densely populated coastal zone. Those that preferred the periphery did so because of the lower cost of living there.

Contrary to widespread prediction, the waves of new immigrants did not create an immediate conflict with the poorer, largely North African, segments of society, as was the case during the sizable Soviet immigration in the 1970s. The only manifestation of such tension was related to housing and the reports of the massive building plans for the immigrants. From summer onward, homeless veteran Israelis erected tent cities in most major towns; they demonstrated, sometimes violently, demanding that the government solve their housing problems. They were careful not to attack the Soviet immigration, however, which enjoyed consensual support among the Israeli public.

A public-opinion survey conducted among the immigrants toward the end of the year found that 75 percent were satisfied with their situation. Most of those questioned, however, had yet to leave the safety of their "absorption basket" and were still to face the hardships of the unemployment-ridden job market.

Israel was also unprepared for the concerted Arab campaign against the waves of immigration, which succeeded in dissuading the Soviet Union from allowing direct flights to Israel and played a role in toughening the American position on loan guarantees to Israel. Essentially, however, the campaign failed, and was cut short by the onset of the Gulf crisis. (See above, "Soviet Jewish Immigration.")

The Economy

The main challenge facing the Israeli economy in the year 1990 was the arrival of 200,000 immigrants from the Soviet Union. Projections of continued mass immigration indicated that their absorption would be the main factor in the economy for years to come.

The economy reacted positively to the immigration, following two years of slump. Business output increased by 6 percent due to expanding demand, productivity increased while inflation did not accelerate, and there was an improvement in the balance of payments. But unemployment, a critical factor in the eventual success of the absorption process, rose from 8.9 percent in 1989 to 9.6 percent in 1990. Among males, the unemployment rate was 8.4 percent; among females, 11.3 percent. Among non-Jews, the unemployment rate was double, reaching 21.4 percent in 1990.

The immigrants brought about only a modest increase in private consumption (5 percent) but a dramatic leap in investments in housing construction (18 percent). Investments in fixed assets also went up by 17 percent (compared to a 10-percent decrease during the two sluggish years). Disappointingly, exports did not contribute to the increase in business output, mainly because of the significant drop in tourism in the wake of the Gulf crisis. The crisis also created uncertainty in the entire area, dampening the enthusiasm of private firms for investment.

The rate of inflation was 17.2 percent, compared to a slightly higher five-year average of 18.4 percent. The increase in housing prices and increases in government-controlled prices played a significant role in the inflation rate; without these two elements, inflation actually subsided, reaching an average rate of 11–12 percent a year.

The state budget, geared to accommodate the waves of immigration, was criticized by the Bank of Israel for failing to grasp the true ramifications of the impact of the immigrants on the economy. The budget took into account an increase in direct absorption costs and in indirect expenditures such as education and health. But investment in infrastructure actually continued to decrease, and the budget deficit (2 percent) was relatively low in light of the absorption needs. The Bank of Israel also criticized the government for ignoring the need to create macro-economic conditions which would help business prepare for the change. Only in September did the government submit a plan for this purpose, creating greater flexibility in the labor market, liberalizing foreign-trade regulations, and introducing a certain reform in taxes.

To meet the growing housing needs, the government initiated, on April 1, a sweeping reform in mortgages. Responsibility for the mortgages was transferred from the government to private banks; interest on mortgages for government-eligible borrowers was reduced from 5 to 4.5 percent, and the return would henceforth be linked to the cost-of-living index once every three months, and not every month as before. In May the government approved a Treasury plan to build 45,000 housing units and to allocate land for a further 70,000 housing units. The government undertook to purchase 40 to 50 percent of the apartments built by private contractors in central areas and 70 percent on the periphery; this decision was widely criticized, with the critics claiming that the government might ultimately lose up to $2 billion by buying apartments built in undesirable areas. In August, in order to meet the rapidly expanding housing needs, the government decided to purchase 5,000 prefabricated caravans (mobile homes) from the local market and to import a further 9,000; by November the government added another 30,000 caravans to its shopping list. Also in August, the Knesset Finance Committee approved a special allocation of NIS 1.2 billion for housing needs. To further open up the housing market, the Knesset committee approved tax waivers for income from rentals.

On March 1, Value Added Tax was raised from 15 to 16 percent, to spur government income. At the same time, various modest tax reforms were implemented throughout the year, including a slight reduction in personal income tax and a reform in automobile taxes.

The state budget, approved by the Knesset on March 30, amounted to NIS 62.5 billion; another NIS 1.9 billion was added on July 24 to meet the burgeoning expenditures on immigration; the budget for 1991, submitted on November 25, was in the amount of NIS 75.7 billion, in 1990 prices; it was to be for nine months only, following the 1990 decision to conform the budgetary year with the calendar year, as of December 31, 1991.

Other Noteworthy Events

Rabbi Meir Kahane was assassinated on November 5, in New York; the accused gunman was a 37-year-old Egyptian boiler repairman, El Sayyid A Nosair. The 58-year-old American-born rabbi, founder of the Jewish Defense League and the Israeli Kach movement, had served in the Israeli Knesset for four years, between 1984 and 1988, advocating expulsion of Arabs and a state ruled by religious law. In 1988, the Israel Supreme Court approved a decision by the Central Elections Committee to ban the Kach party from competing in the elections because of its "Nazi-like, undemocratic and racist stance." On the day following his death, two Arabs were murdered in the West Bank town of Luban a-Sharkiya, and although the police connected the incident with Kahane's killing, the perpetrators were not found. Kahane's November 7 funeral in Jerusalem was an unruly affair, with anti-Arab and antipress riots breaking out in various spots in the city. Over 15,000 people attended the funeral, including three cabinet ministers. The police warned Palestinian leaders of possible acts of retribution that might be directed against them and even instructed them on self-defense.

John (Ivan) Demjanjuk's appeal to the Supreme Court to overturn his 1988 conviction for Nazi war crimes and sentence of death opened on April 15. Demjanjuk's attorney, Yoram Sheftel, argued that Demjanjuk had been put on trial as a result of mistaken identity, and that he was not at all "Ivan the Terrible" of Treblinka. As in the district court case, the appeal was marked by acrimonious dialogue between Sheftel and the court and between Sheftel and the prosecuting attorney, Michael Shaked, who repeatedly begged the court to restrain his adversary. After hearing arguments for 34 days, the court postponed continuation of the case until 1991, to give both sides time to gather new evidence they claimed was available in the newly opened archives of the Soviet Union.

State Comptroller Miriam Ben Porat emerged as the one of the most popular and respected figures in the country following publication of a series of scathing reports which lambasted political cronyism in government and the mishandling of government funds. Unlike previous comptrollers, Ben Porat made skillful use of the media by releasing individual reports on specific subjects in the limelight. Her year-end report on financial misdeeds in the ultra-Orthodox Shas party paved the way for an extensive police investigation of the party's leaders and also turned Ben Porat into the sworn enemy of *haredi* (ultra-Orthodox) religious circles, a fact which only enhanced her popularity with the general public.

Vital Statistics

At the end of 1990 the Jewish population in Israel comprised, for the first time, over 30 percent of the total number of Jews in the world: 3,947,600 Jews lived in Israel on December 31, 1990. Jews comprised 81.9 percent of the total population; 14.1 percent were Muslims, 2.4 percent were Christians, and 1.7 percent were Druze or "others." In 1990 the Jewish population in Israel grew by over 6 percent, compared to only 4 percent for the non-Jewish population. The reason for this was chiefly the massive immigration from the Soviet Union. Over 195,000 Jewish immigrants came to Israel during the year; 72,496 Jews were born in the country itself. Of the Jewish population in 1990, 62 percent were born in Israel (compared to only a third in 1948). Close to a third of these were already second-generation "sabras." The number of Jews who came from Asia or were born in Israel to Asian-born parents was 744,000; the largest contingent among these came from Iraq (262,000).

Less than 10 percent of the Israeli population was now rural; 2.6 percent of the population lived in kibbutzim, and another 3.1 percent lived in agricultural moshavim. Thirty years ago, close to 16 percent of the population was rural. Twenty-three percent of the population lived in the three biggest cities: Jerusalem (525,000), Tel Aviv (340,000), and Haifa (246,000); 44 percent of the population resided in the coastal area of Tel Aviv and its surroundings.

The average Israeli household numbered 3.64 persons in 1990, including singles. Among Jews, the average household included 3.38 people; among non-Jews, 5.64. There were 31,359 marriages during the course of the year; this figure, in absolute terms, had held steady for the past 20 years, despite the increase in population. Divorce, on the other hand, was a growth industry: 6,301 couples were divorced in 1990, compared to only 2,442 in 1970. The divorce rate among Jews was 4 per 1,000 population; among Muslims, the rate was 3 per 1,000. The number of babies born was 103,349; of these, close to 30,000 were born to non-Jewish parents; 26 percent were first-born; close to 20 percent were born into families with six or more children.

The number of approved abortions carried out in 1990 was 15,509 (15 approved abortions for every 100 live births). (Abortions in Israel must be approved by a public committee, and are granted on the grounds of the woman's age, out-of-wedlock-pregnancy, malformed fetus, or danger to the woman's life.) Of the abortions performed, 6,715 were approved for out-of-wedlock pregnancies, 3,022 for malformed fetus, 3,994 for danger to the woman's life, and the balance for older women.

Slightly over a million tourists came to Israel in 1990, down by almost 400,000 from 1987; the decline is explained by the security situation inside Israel, the increasing tension in the Gulf toward the end of the year, and high tourist prices in Israel. Fifty-eight percent of the tourists came from Western Europe; 23 percent from the United States. The average tourist stayed 21.5 days in Israel.

Traffic congestion continued to worsen. There were 13,181 kilometers of paved roads at the end of 1990 (compared to 6,572 in 1960); but there were also 1,015,000 motor vehicles on the road—compared to only 70,000 in 1960. There were 17,496 accidents, in which 427 people were killed and another 27,000 injured. The number of people killed in accidents actually declined, from 475 in 1989 and 511 in 1988.

A total of 1,510,382 pupils were enrolled in 1990 in the various educational institutions, an increase of close to 60,000 over the previous year. Universities and other higher-education institutions had a combined enrollment of 105,000; in 1970, the number was 45,000. Tel Aviv University was the country's largest, with 19,440 students; the Hebrew University of Jerusalem was a close second, with 17,700 students (close to a thousand more than in the previous year). Slightly over 50 percent of the university students were women (their proportion has been steadily increasing). The average number of pupils in an elementary-school class was 27, up from 25 a decade ago; 32 pupils studied in the average high-school class. Among Jewish elementary-school pupils, 71 percent attended the secular state-run schools; 21.7 percent attended the religious state-run schools, and 7 percent attended the independent school system run by the ultra-Orthodox. The 895 newspapers and periodicals published in Israel during 1990 included 22 dailies and another 77 that appeared more than once a month. The numbers represent a decline: in 1978 there were 27 daily newspapers and 96 periodicals that appeared more than once a month. Of the current newspapers and periodicals, 483 were published in Hebrew, 204 in English, 63 in Arabic, and 25 in Russian.

In the West Bank and the Gaza Strip, the Arab population numbered 1,597,000; it grew in 1990 at an annual rate of 4.3 percent in the West Bank, 5.2 percent in Gaza. There were 75,465 live births—3,000 more than in the entire Jewish population of Israel. Over 103,000 Palestinians worked inside Green Line Israel. The number of Arab pupils enrolled in various educational institutions was 509,000. Close to 12 percent of those 15 and over had a post-high-school education; in 1970, the rate was 0.9 percent.

Personalia

Prof. John Strugnell of Harvard University was dismissed on December 31 as editor-in-chief of the Dead Sea Scrolls, for making anti-Semitic remarks in a November interview with *Ha'aretz* newspaper. The Israel Antiquities Authority announced that his replacement would be Prof. Emanuel Tov of the Hebrew University in Jerusalem.

Ephraim Katzir, former president of Israel and an internationally renowned biochemist, was made a commander in the French Legion of Honor by President François Mitterrand, in July. It is the highest honor granted by France to foreigners. Nadav Henefeld, an Israeli basketball player at the University of Connecticut, was named Rookie of the Year of the Big East NCAA conference, in March. He was the first foreigner to win the title.

Among leading personalities who died in 1990 were Avraham Ofek, Israel's leading contemporary muralist, in January, aged 54; Prof. Carl Frankenstein, a pioneer in the development of teaching techniques for mentally handicapped children, a founder of the Hebrew University's education department, and Israel Prize recipient, in January, aged 84; Prof. Yitzhak Hans Klinghoffer, a former Member of Knesset for the Liberal party in the Likud and one of Israel's leading theorists of constitutional law, in January, aged 85; Yaakov Tsur, Zionist leader and diplomat, onetime chairman of the Jewish National Fund and Israeli ambassador in Paris, in February, aged 83; Shin Shalom, honorary president of the Hebrew Writers Union and one of the country's leading poets for more than a generation, in March, aged 85; Joshua Prawer, world-renowned scholar of the Crusader period, instrumental in reforming the country's elementary and secondary school systems, and the spirit behind the Museum of the History of Jerusalem in the Citadel, in May, aged 73; Eliahu Elath, Israel's first ambassador to the United States and former president of the Hebrew University of Jerusalem, in June, aged 86; Levin Kipnis, the father of children's literature in modern Hebrew, the most prolific and popular author of children's stories for over a generation, in June, aged 96; Haim Gvati, one of the leaders of the kibbutz movement and agriculture minister in two governments, in October, aged 89; Gideon Hausner, leader of the Independent Liberal party and former cabinet minister, who achieved world fame when, as attorney general, he served as prosecutor in the trial of Adolf Eichmann, in November, aged 75; Gershom Schocken, longtime editor of the *Ha'aretz* daily newspaper, son of the founder of the Schocken publishing house, in December, aged 78.

MENACHEM SHALEV

World Jewish Population, 1990

Updated Estimates

THIS ARTICLE PRESENTS UPDATES, for the end of 1990, of the Jewish population estimates for the various countries of the world.[1] The estimates reflect some of the results of a prolonged and ongoing effort to study scientifically the demography of contemporary world Jewry.[2] Data collection and comparative research have benefited from the collaboration of scholars and institutions in many countries, including replies to direct inquiries regarding current estimates. It should be emphasized, however, that the elaboration of a worldwide set of estimates for the Jewish populations of the various countries is beset with difficulties and uncertainties.

Over 96 percent of world Jewry is concentrated in ten countries. The aggregate of these ten major Jewish population centers virtually determines the assessment of the size of total world Jewry, estimated at 12.8 million persons in 1990. The country figures for 1990 were updated from those for 1989 in accordance with the known or estimated changes in the interval—migrations, vital events (births and deaths), and identificational changes (accessions and secessions). In addition, corrections were introduced in the light of newly accrued information on Jewish populations. Corresponding corrections were also applied retrospectively to the 1989 figures, which appear below in revised summary (see table 1), so as to allow adequate comparison with the 1990 estimates.

During the year 1990 under review here, operations of data collection and analysis relevant to Jewish population estimates were in planning or already under way in

---

[1]The previous estimates, as of 1989, were published in AJYB 1991, vol. 91, pp. 441–65.

[2]Many of these activities have been carried out by, or in coordination with, the Division of Jewish Demography and Statistics at the Institute of Contemporary Jewry, the Hebrew University of Jerusalem. The authors acknowledge with thanks the collaboration of the many institutions and individuals in the different countries who have supplied information for this update. The paper was revised during DellaPergola's stay at the Institute for Advanced Studies of the Hebrew University of Jerusalem.

several countries. Some of this ongoing research is part of a coordinated effort to update the sociodemographic profile of world Jewry at the outset of the 1990s.[3] Two important sources recently yielded results on major Jewish populations: the official population census of the Soviet Union held in 1989, and the National Jewish Population Survey (NJPS) in the United States completed in 1990.[4] The respective results basically confirmed the estimates we had reported in previous AJYB volumes and, perhaps more importantly, our interpretation of the trends now prevailing in the demography of world Jewry. At the same time, these new data highlighted the increasing complexity of the sociodemographic and identificational processes underlying the definition of Jewish populations—hence the estimates of their sizes. While we address below some of these conceptual problems, users of population estimates should be aware of these difficulties and of the consequent limitations of the estimates.

Concepts and Definitions

In many respects Jewish populations share in the general difficulties met when trying to define, identify, and enumerate minority groups. Difficulties are augmented by the uniquely blended character of Jewry, with its religious, ethnic, cultural, historical, and other components, as well as by the wide geographical scatter and distinctive socioeconomic structure of Jewish groups.

In contemporary societies experiencing intense processes of secularization, acculturation, and social interaction, the ideational (and statistical) boundaries between different religious, ethnic, or cultural groups are no longer clearly and rigidly defined, as they may have been in the past. Multiple bases of identification between individual and community can coexist. Since group identity is not regulated by legal provisions, individuals may change their preferences during their lifetimes. Individuals of Jewish origin may feel varying degrees of personal attachment to Judaism or the Jewish community, and may choose to cut the respective links, whether or not formally adopting another group identity. These identificational changes are reversible: persons who disclaim being Jews at some stage of life may change their minds later. Even at the same time, some may admit or deny their Jewishness under different circumstances. Another element of this general picture

---

[3]Following an international conference in 1987 on Jewish population problems, sponsored by the major Jewish organizations worldwide, an International Scientific Advisory Committee (ISAC) was established. Cochaired by Dr. Roberto Bachi of the Hebrew University and Dr. Sidney Goldstein of Brown University, ISAC's function is to coordinate and monitor Jewish population data collection internationally.

[4]The 1989–1990 National Jewish Population Survey was conducted under the auspices of the Council of Jewish Federations with the supervision of a National Technical Advisory Committee chaired by Dr. Sidney Goldstein of Brown University. Dr. Barry Kosmin of the North American Jewish Data Bank and City University of New York Graduate Center directed the study.

is the growing frequency of mixed marriage. Some of the couples in interfaith marriages prefer to unify the home, one of the partners adopting the group identity of the other; other couples do not. Children of these marriages are likely to be exposed to the different religious and cultural backgrounds of their parents, out of which their own eventual identities will be shaped.

These fluid and voluntaristic patterns of group identification imply that the concept of Jewish population is no longer simple and uniform but offers ground for alternative interpretations and even some confusion and misunderstanding—especially when large and heterogeneous amounts of data are handled and compared. In an attempt to clarify these matters, we briefly outline here one conceptual framework—applied throughout this article—that appears useful in the sociodemographic study of contemporary Jewries.

Core Jewish population. In contemporary social-scientific research on Jews, including demography, it is usual to consider as Jews all those who, when asked, identify themselves as such; or, if the respondent is a different person in the same household, are identified by him/her as Jews. We define this aggregate as the "core" Jewish population. It includes all those who converted to Judaism or joined the Jewish group informally. It excludes those of Jewish descent who formally adopted another religion, as well as other individuals who did not convert out but currently disclaim being Jewish. This categorization is intentionally comprehensive, reflecting subjective feelings rather than halakhic (Rabbinic) or other legal definitions.[5] Our definition of a person as a Jew does not depend on any measure of that person's Jewish commitment or behavior—in terms of religiosity, beliefs, knowledge, communal affiliation, or otherwise. The core Jewish population is the conceptual target of our population estimates. In estimating the size of a Jewish population, we include, in principle, all marginal individuals who have not ceased to consider themselves Jewish.

Extended Jewish population. We adopt the term "extended" for the sum of the core Jewish population and all other persons of Jewish parentage who are not Jews currently (or at the time of investigation). These non-Jews with Jewish background, as far as they can be ascertained, include: (a) persons who have themselves adopted another religion, even though they may claim to be still Jews ethnically; (b) other persons of Jewish parentage who disclaim to be Jews currently. In survey-taking it is usual, for both conceptual and practical reasons, to consider in this context parentage only and not any more distant ancestry.

Enlarged Jewish population. We designate by the term "enlarged" the sum of the

---

[5]The definition of "Who is a Jew?" according to Halakhah constituted the cardinal criterion of Jewish identification across history. Normatively, it continues to bind all Orthodox and many other Jewish communities in contemporary times. The constraints typical of empirical research do not allow for ascertaining on a case-by-case basis the halakhic identity of each individual included in surveys. Therefore, it is usual in most social-scientific research to rely on the subjective criteria defined here.

core Jewish population and all other persons of Jewish parentage included in the extended Jewish population, as well as their non-Jewish household members (spouses, children, etc.). For both conceptual and practical reasons, this definition does not include any non-Jewish relatives living elsewhere.

These various definitions point to the importance of the household as the primary—and in social terms truly significant—reference unit for the study of Jewish demography. For demographic research purposes, "eligible Jewish households" are all those including at least one individual who is either currently Jewish or of Jewish parentage.[6] Ideally, information should be collected on all the members of Jewish households, Jews and others, to enable researchers to apply the above—and perhaps additional—definitions and to estimate the respective sizes of the various groups and subgroups involved.

In the past, core, extended, and enlarged Jewish populations tended to overlap; today, however, the respective sizes and characteristics may be quite different. One relevant example is provided by the findings of the U.S. NJPS reported below in the section on American Jewry. The time perspective employed in these definitions mainly relates to the two generations of the surveyed individuals and their parents. Other, more extended generational or time perspectives might be considered in the attempt to estimate the size of populations of Jewish origin, based on prolonged genealogical reconstructions. Such approaches, albeit of some interest for historical research, will not be considered here.

Another definitional framework stems from the special position of Israel as a country of destination for Jewish international migration, recently chiefly from the (former) Soviet Union. Israel's most distinctive legal framework for the acceptance and absorption of new immigrants is provided by the Law of Return (*Hok Hashvut*), first passed in 1950 and amended in 1954 and 1970. That basic law awards Jewish new immigrants immediate citizenship and other civil rights in Israel. According to the current, amended version of the Law of Return, a Jew is any person born to a Jewish mother or converted to Judaism (regardless of denomination—Orthodox, Conservative, or Reform). Conversion from Judaism, as in the case of some "ethnic" Jews who currently identify with another religion, entails loss of eligibility for Law of Return purposes. Significantly, the law extends its provisions to all current Jews, and to their Jewish or non-Jewish spouses, children and grandchildren, as well as to the spouses of such children and grandchildren. It can readily be seen, therefore, that due to its three-generational time perspective and lateral extension, the Law of Return applies to a wide population. This population may be of wider scope not only than the core but even than the enlarged Jewish population, as defined above.

Finally, it should be noted that the actual contents and patterns of Jewish identity and behavior may widely vary within the core Jewish population itself, from strongly committed to very marginal. The respective differentials are associated with

---

[6]This approach was followed in the two U.S. National Jewish Population Studies of 1970–1971 and 1989–1990.

sociodemographic trends that may ultimately affect Jewish population size. These issues are, however, beyond the scope of the present article, which is mostly concerned with the bare attempt to estimate the size of core Jewish populations in the countries of the world.

Jewish Population Trends

The world's Jews are highly dispersed. In most countries their number is now rather small and they constitute no more than a minute fraction of the entire population. Consequently, though Diaspora Jews tend to cluster in large cities, they are greatly exposed to assimilation. While the major thrust of the assimilatory process tends to be associated with secessions from the Jewish population (whether formal or informal), there also are gains through accessions of non-Jewish-born persons. It is the net balance of these identificational changes that matters demographically. Outmarriages may involve demographic losses to the Jewish population if less than half of the children are themselves Jews. Moreover, in the longer run, the overall cohesion of a Jewish community may be affected, with consequences for its size as well. What counts in the demographic balance of Diaspora Jewries is "effectively Jewish" fertility and birthrate, including only those newborns who are Jews.[7]

The Jews in most countries of the Diaspora are characterized by very low fertility, which is the major cause for great population aging. An increased proportion of elderly in the population actually implies not only many deceased and a higher death rate, but also a reduced proportion of persons of reproductive age and therefore a relatively lower birthrate. While there are differences in the levels of these demographic factors between the Jews in various regions and countries, in all major Diaspora populations the joint balance of the natural and identificational changes is now close to nil or outrightly negative, with Jewish deaths frequently outnumbering Jewish births. These negative tendencies have been taken into account in updating the estimates of the Jews in many countries.

A notable paradox of Diaspora Jewish demography is that growth of an enlarged Jewish population—following intense outmarriage and an increasing number of persons in households with both Jewish and non-Jewish members—may go hand in hand with stagnation or even diminution of the respective core Jewish population. A case in point is provided by the recent demographic transformations of the Jewish population in the United States (see below).

With regard to the balance of external migrations, there is no regularity among the various Diaspora populations or even in the same population over time. In 1990, the overall volume of international migrations of Jews was much greater than in

---

[7]A fuller discussion of the subject can be found in U.O. Schmelz, "Jewish Survival: The Demographic Factors," AJYB 1981, vol. 81, pp. 61–117; and, by the same author, *Aging of World Jewry* (Jerusalem, 1984).

earlier years, after many of the previous restrictions on the outflow of Jewish emigration from the Soviet Union were lifted. Where the migratory balance is positive—e.g., in North America—it counteracts or even outweighs any numerically negative influence of internal demographic developments. Where the migratory balance is negative, as in Eastern Europe, it may cause or aggravate the decrease of a Jewish population. Any attempt to understand the current and potential flow of Jewish international migration should make reference not only to the internal transformations of Jewish populations and societies but also to the major political and socioeconomic trends shaping world society in general.[8]

In contrast, in Israel the impact of outmarriage and secessions from Judaism is statistically negligible. The fact that Israeli society has a Jewish majority encourages accessions (formal or informal) of non-Jewish members in mixed immigrant households. A positive net balance of accessions and secessions results. Moreover, until the early 1980s and again since 1990 Israel had a positive migration balance.

Jewish fertility levels in Israel are comparatively high, and the Jewish age structure is significantly younger than among Diaspora Jews and the general populations of the other developed countries. The previously substantial fertility differentials between Jews ingathered in Israel from Asia-Africa and Europe-America are no longer in evidence. Remarkably, European Jews in Israel have not participated in the drastic fertility decline that has characterized the developed nations and particularly the Diaspora Jews during the last few decades, but have actually raised their fertility somewhat. In recent years, both major origin groups among Israel's Jews have displayed a fertility level surpassing not only the vast majority of Diaspora Jewry but also the general populations in other developed countries.

In the overall demographic balance of World Jewry, the natural increase of Israel has, so far, made up for the losses in the Diaspora. But such compensation will not be possible for much longer. As a consequence of the intensifying demographic deficit in the Diaspora, a trend toward some reduction in the total size of world Jewry is probably setting in. The relative share of Israel among that total is on the increase, regardless of *aliyah* and *yeridah* (immigration to, and emigration from, Israel), which obviously constitute only internal transfers within the global Jewish framework.

Sources of Data and Estimation Problems

Available demographic information on Jews is deficient in both quantity and quality. Besides the conceptual problems discussed above, difficulties involved in

---

[8]Sergio DellaPergola, "*Aliyah* and Other Jewish Migrations: Toward an Integrated Perspective," in U.O. Schmelz and G. Nathan, eds., *Studies in the Population of Israel in Honor of Roberto Bachi, Scripta Hierosolymitana*, vol. 30 (Jerusalem, 1986), pp. 172–209; and, by the same author, "Mass *Aliyah*: A Thing of the Past?" *Jerusalem Quarterly*, no. 51, 1989, pp. 96–114.

estimating the size of Jewish populations reflect the substantive complexity of Diaspora demography. Relevant aspects are the great geographical scattering of Jews—a factor that makes multiple data collection mandatory but also hinders its feasibility; and the Jews' unusually strong demographic dynamics in many respects—migrations, social mobility, family formation patterns (including outmarriage), etc. More specific difficulties in estimating the up-to-date size of Jewish populations are due to measurement problems.

Particular difficulties exist with regard to the countries of Eastern Europe, whose Jewish populations were drastically reduced during and after World War II. Prolonged antireligious policies in these countries have had a negative effect on the identity of genealogically Jewish persons, many of whom may have severed, insofar as it depends on themselves, all links with Jewishness. The resulting uncertainties have led to wishful thinking in terms of exaggerated estimates, and account for the widely differing numbers of Jews that have been circulated for these countries.

Figures on Jews from population censuses are unavailable for most Diaspora communities, though they do exist for some important ones. In general, the practice of self-determination is followed in relevant censuses and surveys which inquire into religion or ethnicity, thus providing results close to our definitions of a "core" or an "extended" Jewish population—the latter, if religion and ethnicity can be cross-classified, as in Canada. Even where census statistics on Jews are forthcoming, they are usually scant, because the Jews are a small minority of the total population. There have been instances where detailed tabulations on Jews were undertaken, through Jewish initiative, from official census material; examples are Canada, Argentina, and South Africa. In some countries where Jewishness is associated with actual or feared discrimination, individuals may prefer not to describe themselves as Jews. Elsewhere, as has happened in some Latin American countries, non-Jews may be erroneously included as Jews. These problems require statistical evaluation whose feasibility and conclusiveness depend on the relevant information available. Reliable figures are currently forthcoming for the Jews of Israel from official statistics.

Surveys are the major way of obtaining comprehensive information on Jewish populations in the absence of official censuses. In the Diaspora, Jewish-sponsored surveys have the additional advantage of being able to inquire into matters of specifically Jewish interest, e.g., Jewish education, religious practices, and attitudes. However, since they address themselves to a small and scattered minority with identification problems, surveys are not easy to conduct competently and may encounter difficulties with regard to both coverage and response, especially from marginal Jews. Again, these aspects require evaluation. Over the last decades, countrywide Jewish population surveys were undertaken in the United States, South Africa, France, Italy, and the Netherlands. Local surveys were carried out in many cities of the United States, the United Kingdom, Argentina, Brazil, Australia, and some smaller communities. However, these several initiatives have so far been uncoordinated with regard to content and method.

In certain countries or localities, Jewish community registers include the largest part of the Jewish population. Often the same communities keep records of Jewish vital events—especially marriages performed with a Jewish ceremony and Jewish burials. However, communal registers tend to cover mixed households insufficiently. In addition, although the amount and quality of updating varies from place to place, communal registers generally lag behind the actual situation of the respective Jewish populations.

Finally, many estimates of Jewish Diaspora populations for which no solid data from censuses or surveys exist are regrettably of unspecified or dubious source and methodology. This situation contrasts with the amount and quality of demographic information available for Jews in Israel. Israel took its latest census in 1983, but has constantly updated statistics of its Jewish population size and characteristics.

Besides the conceptual and measurement difficulties affecting baseline figures on Jewish population size, similar problems recur with regard to the updating information which should account for all the various types of changes in the time elapsed since that base date. Age-sex-specific models can be of use for vital events and identificational changes. They may be applied after studying the evolution of the respective or similar Jewish populations. With regard to the migratory balance in any updating interval, concrete information must be gathered, because of the above-mentioned irregularity, over time, in the intensity of many migratory streams.

Not a few Jews have some residential status in more than one country. This may be due to business requirements, professional assignments in foreign countries, climatic differences between countries, periods of prolonged transit for migrants, etc. The danger of double-counting or omissions is inherent in such situations. This is particularly critical regarding some countries in Central and tropical South America, Africa, and South or East Asia, where the relatively few Jews living permanently may be outnumbered by a floating population of temporary Jewish residents or tourists. As far as possible we have tried to account for such persons only once, giving precedence to the usual country of residence.

The problem is even more acute with regard to residential status in more than one locality of the same country. This may adversely affect—through omissions or, more likely, double-counting—the accuracy of national Jewish population estimates obtained by summing up reports for individual localities.

Presentation of Data

The detailed estimates of Jewish population distribution in each continent and country (tables 2–7 below) aim at the concept of "core" Jewish population as defined earlier in this article. The reader will recall that "extended" or "enlarged" Jewish populations, including Jews, non-Jews of Jewish parentage, and respective non-Jewish household members, may result in significantly higher estimates. Separate figures are provided for each country with at least 100 resident Jews. Residual estimates of "other" Jews living in smaller communities supplement some of the continental totals. For each of the reported countries, the four columns in the following tables provide the United Nations estimate of mid-year 1990 total population,[9] the estimated end-1990 Jewish population, the proportion of Jews per 1,000 of total population, and a rating of the accuracy of the Jewish population estimate.

There is wide variation in the quality of the Jewish population estimates for different countries. For many Diaspora countries it would be best to indicate a range (minimum-maximum) rather than a definite figure for the number of Jews. It would be confusing, however, for the reader to be confronted with a long list of ranges; this would also complicate the regional and world totals. Yet, the figures actually indicated for most of the Diaspora communities should be understood as being the central value of the plausible range of the respective core Jewish populations. The relative magnitude of this range varies inversely to the accuracy of the estimate.

ACCURACY RATING

The three main elements which affect the accuracy of each estimate are the nature and quality of the base data, the recency of the base data, and the method of updating. A simple code combining these elements is used to provide a general evaluation of the reliability of the Jewish population figures reported in the detailed tables below. The code indicates different quality levels of the reported estimates: (A) base figure derived from countrywide census or relatively reliable Jewish population survey; updated on the basis of full or partial information on Jewish population movements in the respective country during the intervening period; (B) base figure derived from less accurate but recent countrywide Jewish population investigation; partial information on population movements in the intervening period; (C) base figure derived from less recent sources, and/or unsatisfactory or partial coverage of Jewish population in the particular country; updating according to demographic information illustrative of regional demographic trends; (D) base figure essentially conjectural; no reliable updating procedure. In categories (A), (B), and (C), the years in which the base figures or important partial updates were obtained are also stated. For countries whose Jewish population estimate of 1990 was not only updated but also revised in the light of improved information, the sign "X" is appended to the accuracy rating.

Distribution of World Jewish Population by Major Regions

Table 1 gives an overall picture of Jewish population for the end of 1990 as compared to 1989. For 1989 the originally published estimates are presented along with somewhat revised figures that take into account, retrospectively, the correc-

---

[9]See United Nations, Department of International Economic and Social Affairs, Statistical Office, *World Population Prospects 1990*, Population Studies no. 120 (New York, 1991). The figures reflect the 1990 UN revision of world population estimates.

TABLE 1. ESTIMATED JEWISH POPULATION, BY CONTINENTS AND MAJOR GEO-
GRAPHICAL REGIONS, 1989 AND 1990

Region	1989			1990		% Change 1989–1990
	Original Abs. N.	Revised				
		Abs. N.	Percent	Abs. N.	Percent	
World	12,810,300	12,813,800	100.0	12,806,400	100.0	−0.1
Diaspora	9,093,200	9,096,700	71.0	8,859,700	69.2	−2.6
Israel	3,717,100	3,717,100	29.0	3,946,700	30.8	+6.2
America,						
Total	6,261,700	6,261,700	48.9	6,278,400	49.0	+0.3
North[a]	5,825,000	5,825,000	45.5	5,845,000	45.6	+0.3
Central	46,700	46,700	0.4	46,700	0.4	—
South	390,000	390,000	3.0	386,700	3.0	−0.8
Europe,						
Total[b]	2,558,400	2,558,400	20.0	2,307,300	18.0	−9.8
EC	1,019,200[b]	1,019,200[b]	8.0	999,600	7.8	−1.9
West, other	52,300[b]	52,300[b]	0.4	44,000	0.3	−15.9
East and Balkans[c]	1,486,900	1,486,900	11.6	1,263,700	9.9	−15.0
Asia, Total	3,750,700	3,750,900	29.3	3,979,400	31.1	+6.1
Israel	3,717,100	3,717,100	29.0	3,946,700	30.8	+6.2
Rest[c]	33,600	33,800	0.3	32,700	0.3	−3.3
Africa,						
Total	149,900	153,200	1.2	148,700	1.2	−2.9
North	12,700	11,000	0.1	10,600	0.1	−3.6
Central	22,100	27,100	0.2	23,100	0.2	−14.8
South[d]	115,100	115,100	0.9	115,000	0.9	−0.1
Oceania	89,600	89,600	0.7	92,600	0.7	+3.3

[a]U.S.A. and Canada.
[b]Including Jewish migrants in transit.
[c]The Asian regions of USSR and Turkey are included in "East Europe and Balkans."
[d]South Africa and Zimbabwe.

tions made in 1990 in certain country estimates, in the light of improved information. These corrections resulted in a net increase of the 1989 world Jewry's estimated size by 3,500, primarily due to a better estimate for Ethiopia. Some explanations are given below for the countries whose estimates were revised.

The size of world Jewry at the end of 1990 is assessed at 12,806,400. According to the revised figures, between 1989 and 1990 there was an estimated loss of 7,400 people, or about −0.1 percent. Despite all the imperfections in the estimates, it is clear that world Jewry has reached "zero population growth" or is slightly shrinking, with the natural increase in Israel barely or insufficiently compensating for the demographic decline in the Diaspora.

The number of Jews in Israel rose from a figure of 3,717,100 in 1989 to 3,946,700 at the end of 1990—an increase of 229,600 people, or 6.2 percent. In contrast, the estimated Jewish population in the Diaspora declined from 9,096,700 (according to the revised figures) to 8,859,700—a decrease of 237,000 people, or 2.6 percent. These changes primarily reflect the upsurge of Jewish emigration from the Soviet Union. In 1990, the Israel-Diaspora estimated net migratory balance amounted to a gain of about 181,400 Jews for Israel. Internal demographic evolution produced further growth among the Jewish population in Israel and further declines in the Diaspora.

About half of the world's Jews reside in the Americas, with over 45 percent in North America. Thirty-one percent live in Asia, excluding the Asian territories of the USSR and Turkey—nearly all of them in Israel. Europe, including the Asian territories of the USSR and Turkey, accounts for less than one-fifth of the total. Less than 2 percent of the world's Jews live in Africa and Oceania. Among the major geographical regions listed in table 1, the number of Jews in Israel—and, consequently, in total Asia—increased in 1990. Moderate Jewish population gains were also estimated for North America and Oceania. Latin America, Europe, Africa, and the Asian countries other than Israel sustained decreases in Jewish population size. World Jewry constitutes about 2.4 per 1,000 of the world's total population. One in about 414 people in the world is a Jew.

Individual Countries

THE AMERICAS

In 1990 the total number of Jews in the American continents was somewhat more than six and a quarter million. The overwhelming majority (93 percent) resided in the United States and Canada, less than 1 percent lived in Central America (including Mexico), and about 6 percent lived in South America—with Argentina and Brazil the largest Jewish communities (see table 2).

United States. The 1989–1990 National Jewish Population Survey (NJPS), sponsored by the Council of Jewish Federations and the North American Jewish Data Bank (NAJDB), provided the much awaited benchmark information about size and

TABLE 2. ESTIMATED JEWISH POPULATION DISTRIBUTION IN THE AMERICAS, 1990

Country	Total Population	Jewish Population	Jews per 1,000 Population	Accuracy Rating
Canada	26,521,000	310,000	11.7	B 1981–86
United States	249,224,000	5,535,000	22.2	A 1990
Total North America	275,865,000a	5,845,000	21.2	
Bahamas	253,000	300	1.2	C 1973
Costa Rica	3,015,000	2,000	0.7	C 1986
Cuba	10,608,000	700	0.1	C 1990
Dominican Republic	7,170,000	100	0.0	D
Guatemala	9,197,000	800	0.1	C 1983
Jamaica	2,456,000	300	0.1	B 1988
Mexico	88,598,000	35,000	0.4	C 1990
Netherlands Antilles	188,000	400	2.1	D
Panama	2,418,000	5,000	2.1	C 1990
Puerto Rico	3,480,000	1,500	0.4	C 1990
Virgin Islands	116,000	300	2.6	C 1986
Other	23,862,000	300	0.0	D
Total Central America	151,361,000	46,700	0.3	
Argentina	32,322,000	215,000	6.7	C 1990
Bolivia	7,314,000	700	0.1	B 1990
Brazil	150,368,000	100,000	0.7	C 1980
Chile	13,173,000	15,000	1.1	C 1988
Colombia	32,978,000	6,500	0.2	C 1986
Ecuador	10,587,000	900	0.1	C 1985
Paraguay	4,277,000	900	0.2	B 1990
Peru	21,550,000	3,300	0.2	B 1985
Suriname	422,000	200	0.5	B 1986
Uruguay	3,094,000	24,200	7.8	C 1990
Venezuela	19,735,000	20,000	1.0	C 1989
Total South America	296,716,000a	386,700	1.3	
Total	723,942,000	6,278,400	8.7	

aIncluding countries not listed separately.

characteristics of U.S. Jewry and the basis for subsequent updates. According to the official report of the results of this important national sample study,[10] the "core" Jewish population in the United States comprised 5,515,000 persons in the summer of 1990. Of these, 185,000 were converts to Judaism. An estimated 210,000 persons, not included in the previous figures, were born or raised as Jews but converted to another religion. A further 1,115,000 people, thereof 415,000 adults and 700,000 children below age 18, were of Jewish parentage but were not Jews themselves and followed a religion other than Judaism at the time of survey. All together, these various groups formed an "extended" Jewish population of 6,840,000. NJPS also covered 1,350,000 non-Jewish-born members of eligible (Jewish or mixed) households. The study's "enlarged" Jewish population thus consisted of about 8,200,000 persons.

Comparison with the results of the previous National Jewish Population Study, conducted in 1970–1971, is complicated by the fact that various versions were published of the 1970–71 results; moreover, there are margins of error when two sample studies are compared, especially if they were taken under differing circumstances 20 years apart. The 1990 Jewish population estimates are within the range of a sampling error of plus or minus 3.5 percent.[11] This means a range between 5.3 and 5.7 million for the core Jewish population. The 1970–71 estimates of the core Jewish population varied between 5.4 and 6.0 million persons.[12] Even if the lower 1970–71 estimate is preferred, it is sufficiently clear—and very relevant to the assessment of trends—that the core Jewish population hardly grew over the last 20 years, whereas the extended and especially the enlarged Jewish population in the United States increased significantly. This attests numerically to the strengthening of assimilatory trends and to intensifying sociodemographic integration of American Jews with the general population. The new data also reflect the use of more systematic random surveying methods, and the somewhat wider definition of eligible households in the 1989–1990 NJPS, in comparison to the 1970–1971 study. Referring again to our conceptual and definitional framework, it is worth noting that in

---

[10]Barry A. Kosmin, Sidney Goldstein, Joseph Waksberg, Nava Lerer, Ariella Keysar, and Jeffrey Scheckner, *Highlights of the CJF 1990 National Jewish Population Survey* (New York, Council of Jewish Federations, 1991).

[11]See Kosmin et al., p. 39.

[12]The 1970–1971 NJPS results were reported by the study director, Fred Massarik, in "National Jewish Population Study," AJYB 1974–75, vol. 75, pp. 296–97; and, by the same author, "The Boundary of Jewishness: Some Measures of Jewish Identity in the United States," in U.O. Schmelz, P. Glikson, and S. DellaPergola, eds., *Papers in Jewish Demography 1973* (Jerusalem, 1977), pp. 117–39. According to Massarik, the "core" Jewish population amounted to about 5.4 million, out of an "enlarged" Jewish population of about 5.9 million. A different set of estimates was prepared by the 1970–1971 NJPS chief statistician, Bernard Lazerwitz, in "An Estimate of a Rare Population Group: The U.S. Jewish Population," *Demography*, vol. 15, 1978, pp. 389–94. According to Lazerwitz, the U.S. Jewish population amounted to 5.8 million, plus or minus a sampling error of about 200,000. The matter was summarized in U.O. Schmelz, *World Jewish Population: Regional Estimates and Projections* (Jerusalem, 1981), pp. 32–36. Schmelz suggested a base figure of 5.6 million Jews for 1970.

1990 the core Jewish population comprised about two-thirds of the enlarged Jewish population in the U.S.; conversely, the latter exceeded the former by roughly one-half.

Over the whole 1970–1990 period, several hundred thousand Jews migrated to the United States, especially from the USSR, Israel, Iran, and Latin America. During fiscal years 1989 and 1990 alone, respectively 39,553 and 37,770 refugees from the Soviet Union were admitted to the United States.[13] The international migration balance of U.S. Jewry should have generated an actual increase of Jewish population size. The fact that the expected influence of international migration did not show up in the size of U.S. core Jewish population according to NJPS indicates that the balance of other factors of core population change over that whole 20-year period must have been somewhat negative. First detailed analyses of the new NJPS data actually provide evidence of low levels of Jewish fertility and the "effectively Jewish" birthrates, increasing outmarriage rates, declining rates of conversion to Judaism (or "choosing" Judaism), increasing rates of conversion from Judaism, rather low proportions of children of mixed marriages being identified as Jewish, and increasing aging among the Jewish population.[14] A recent temporary increase in the Jewish birthrate appears to have occurred, because the large cohorts born during the "baby boom" of the 1950s and early 1960s have been in the main procreative ages; however, this echo effect is about to fade away, as the much smaller cohorts born since the late 1960s reach the stage of parenthood.

Taking into account this evidence, our estimate of U.S. Jewish population size at the end of 1990 starts from the NJPS benchmark core Jewish population of 5,515,000; assumes that the current balance of demographic and identificational changes in the core Jewish population is overall close to nil; and attempts to account for Jewish immigration which arrived in the latter part of 1990, after completion of NJPS. Assuming a total net migration gain of about 50–60,000 from the USSR, Israel, and other origins for the whole of 1990, we apportioned 20,000 to the final months of 1990. We thus suggest a tentative estimate of 5,535,000 Jews in the United States at the end of 1990. This estimate is of course conditional on further detailed scrutiny and interpretation of the NJPS findings.

The research team of the NAJDB, which is responsible for the primary handling of NJPS data files, has also continued its yearly compilation of local Jewish population estimates. These are reported elsewhere in this volume.[15] NAJDB estimated the

---

[13]Figures from U.S. Department of Justice, Immigration and Naturalization Service, 1990, presented in unpublished table reported in Barry R. Chiswick, "Soviet Jews in the United States: A Preliminary Analysis of Their Linguistic and Economic Adjustment," paper prepared for the Sapir Forum, Hebrew University of Jerusalem (Chicago, 1991); HIAS, news release, New York, Oct. 11, 1991.

[14]See the article by Sidney Goldstein in the present volume. See also U.O. Schmelz and Sergio DellaPergola, *Basic Trends in U.S. Jewish Demography*, Jewish Sociology Papers (New York, American Jewish Committee, 1988).

[15]The first in a new series of yearly compilations of local U.S. Jewish population estimates appeared in Barry A. Kosmin, Paul Ritterband, and Jeffrey Scheckner, "Jewish Population

U.S. Jewish population in 1986 at 5,814,000, including "under 2 percent" non-Jewish household members. This was very close to our own pre-NJPS estimate of 5,700,000. The NAJDB estimate was updated as follows: 1987—5,943,700; 1988—5,935,000; 1989—5,944,000; 1990—5,981,000. These changes do not reflect actual sudden growths or declines, but rather corrections and adaptations made in the figures for several local communities. It should be realized that compilations of local estimates, even if as painstaking as in the case of the NAJDB, are subject to a great many local biases and tend to fall behind the actual pace of national trends. This is especially true in a context of vigorous internal migration, as in the United States. The new NJPS figure, in spite of sample-survey biases, provides a more reliable national Jewish population baseline.

Canada. In Canada the 1981 census enumerated 296,425 Jews according to religion. By adding 9,950 persons who reported "Jewish" as their single reply to the census question on ethnic origin, while not reporting any non-Jewish religion (such as Catholic, Anglican, etc.), the figure rises to 306,375. There were additional persons who did not report a non-Jewish religion but mentioned "Jewish" as part of a multiple response to the question on ethnic origin. It is likely that some of them were merely thinking in terms of ancestry and did not actually consider themselves as Jews at the time of the census. Yet, after including a reasonable portion of the latter group, a total core Jewish population of 310,000 was suggested for 1981. A further 5,140 Canadians who reported being Jewish by ethnic origin but identified with another religion were not included in our estimate.

The population census held in Canada in 1986 provided data on ethnic origins but not on religious groups. A total of 245,855 persons reported being Jewish as a single reply to the question on ethnic origin, as against 264,020 in the same category in 1981. A further 97,655 mentioned a Jewish origin as part of a multiple response to the 1986 question on ethnic origin, as compared to apparently 30,000–40,000 in 1981. Thus, a substantial increase in the number of Canadians reporting partially Jewish ancestry seemed to offset the decline in the number of those with a solely Jewish identification according to the ethnic criterion. Besides actual demographic and identificational trends, changes in the wording of the relevant questions in the two censuses may have influenced these variations in the size of the "ethnically" (or, in our terminology, "extended") Jewish population of Canada.[16]

The 1986 census data indicated that about 9,000 Jews migrated to Canada between 1981 and 1986; more immigration arrived in the following years. In the light of this admittedly partial evidence, and considering the increasingly aged Jewish population structure, it is suggested that a migratory surplus may have roughly

---

in the United States, 1986," AJYB 1987, vol. 87, pp. 164–91. The 1991 update appears elsewhere in the present volume.

[16]Statistics Canada, *1981 Census of Canada: Population: Ethnic Origin; Religion* (Ottawa, 1983, 1984); Statistics Canada, *Population by Ethnic Origin, 1986 Census: Canada, Provinces and Territories and Census Metropolitan Areas* (Ottawa, 1988).

offset the probably negative balance of internal evolution since the 1981 census. Consequently, the 1981 figure of 310,000 was kept unchanged throughout 1990. The 1991 census again included questions on both religion and ethnic origin, and its results will provide a new baseline for the estimate of Canada's Jewish population.

Central America. The estimate for Mexico was kept unchanged at 35,000. The official Mexican censuses have given widely varying figures—17,574 in 1950; 100,750 in 1960; 49,277 in 1970; 61,790 in 1980. It is generally admitted that the last three censuses mistakenly included among the Jews many thousands of non-Jews living outside the known regions of Jewish residence in that country. In 1990 a new census was undertaken, but the figure of Jews was not reported. A Jewish-sponsored population survey of Mexican Jewry was completed in 1991, and its analysis will contribute to refining the current estimate. Panama's Jewish population—the second largest in Central America—is estimated at about 5,000.

South America.[17] The Jewish population of Argentina, the largest in that geographical region, is marked by a negative balance of internal evolution. Since the 1960s, the balance of external migrations was strongly negative; after the restoration of a democratic regime in the early 1980s, emigration diminished and there was some return migration. In 1989, emigration increased again; in 1990, over 2,000 Jews migrated to Israel alone, while others possibly went to North America and Western Europe. Accordingly, the estimate for Argentinian Jewry was reduced from 218,000 in 1989 to 215,000 in 1990.

The official population census of Brazil in 1980 showed a figure of 91,795 Jews. Since it is possible that some otherwise identifying Jews failed to declare themselves as such in the census, a corrected estimate of 100,000 was adopted for 1980 and has been kept unchanged through 1990, assuming that the overall balance of vital events and external migrations was close to zero. The national figure of approximately 100,000 fits the admittedly rough estimates that are available for the size of local Jewish communities in Brazil.

On the strength of fragmentary information that is accumulating, the estimates for Uruguay and Peru were slightly reduced, while those for Venezuela, Chile, and Colombia were not changed.

EUROPE

Of the estimated over 2,300,000 Jews in Europe in 1990, 45 percent lived in Western Europe and 55 percent in Eastern Europe and the Balkan countries— including the Asian territories of the USSR and Turkey (see table 3). In 1990 Europe

---

[17]For a more detailed discussion of the region's Jewish population trends, see U.O. Schmelz and Sergio DellaPergola, "The Demography of Latin American Jewry," AJYB 1985, vol. 85, pp. 51–102; Sergio DellaPergola, "Demographic Trends of Latin American Jewry," in J. Laikin Elkin and G.W. Merks, eds., *The Jewish Presence in Latin America* (Boston, 1987), pp. 85–133.

TABLE 3. ESTIMATED JEWISH POPULATION DISTRIBUTION IN EUROPE, 1990

Country	Total Population	Jewish Population	Jews per 1,000 Population	Accuracy Rating
Belgium	9,845,000	31,800	3.2	C 1987
Denmark	5,143,000	6,400	1.2	C 1990
France	56,138,000	530,000	9.4	C 1990
Germany	77,573,000	40,000	0.5	C 1990
Great Britain	57,237,000	315,000	5.5	C 1990
Greece	10,047,000	4,800	0.5	B 1990
Ireland	3,720,000	1,800	0.5	B 1990
Italy	57,061,000	31,200	0.5	B 1990
Luxembourg	373,000	600	1.6	B 1990
Netherlands	14,951,000	25,700	1.7	C 1990
Portugal	10,285,000	300	0.0	B 1986
Spain	39,187,000	12,000	0.3	D
Total European Community	341,560,000	999,600	2.9	
Austria	7,583,000	7,000	0.9	C 1990
Finland	4,975,000	1,300	0.3	A 1990
Gibraltar	30,000	600	20.0	C 1981
Norway	4,212,000	1,000	0.2	B 1987
Sweden	8,444,000	15,000	1.8	C 1990
Switzerland	6,609,000	19,000	2.9	C 1980
Other	982,000	100	0.1	D
Total other West Europe	32,835,000	44,000	1.3	
Albania	3,345,000	300	0.1	B 1990
Bulgaria	9,010,000	3,100	0.3	C 1990
Czechoslovakia	15,667,000	7,800	0.5	D
Hungary	10,552,000	57,000	5.4	D
Poland	38,423,000	3,800	0.1	C 1990
Romania	23,272,000	17,500	0.8	B 1988
Turkey[a]	55,868,000	19,700	0.4	C 1990
USSR[a,b]	288,595,000	1,150,000	4.0	B 1990
Yugoslavia	23,807,000	4,500	0.2	C 1986
Total East Europe and Balkans	468,539,000	1,263,700	2.7	
Total	842,934,000	2,307,300	2.7	

[a]Including Asian regions.
[b]See also table 4.

lost about 10 percent of its estimated Jewish population, mainly through the emigration of over 200,000 Jews from the Soviet Union, and the final resettlement of another 28,000 who were staying in temporary accommodations in Italy and Austria at the end of 1989.

European Community. The twelve countries that form the European Community (EC) together had an estimated permanent Jewish population of about one million. Decline against the 1989 estimate of 1,019,200 reflects the final resettlement of about 19,000 Jewish migrants from the Soviet Union who were temporarily staying at Ladispoli and other localities near Rome. The process of economic and political integration of the EC countries is slowly moving ahead. The free movement of goods and manpower expected to become effective after January 1, 1993, and accompanying changes in occupational needs and opportunities within the EC, could affect geographical mobility, possibly altering the distribution of Jews among the respective countries. EC policies toward immigration from other, non-EC, countries may be affected as well.

France has the largest Jewish population in Western Europe, estimated at 530,000. Monitoring the plausible trends of both the internal evolution and external migrations of Jews in France suggests that there has been little net change in Jewish population size since the major survey that was taken in the 1970s.[18] A study conducted in 1988 at the initiative of the Fonds Social Juif Unifié (FSJU) confirmed the basic demographic stability of French Jewry.[19]

Periodic reestimations of the size of British Jewry are carried out by the Community Research Unit (CRU) of the Board of Deputies. Based on an analysis of Jewish deaths during 1975–1979, the population baseline for 1977 was set at 336,000, with a margin of error of plus or minus 34,000.[20] An excess of deaths over births is clearly shown by the vital statistical records annually compiled by the Jewish community. Allowing for emigration and some assimilatory losses, the update for 1984, as elaborated by the CRU, came to 330,000. Continuation of the same trends suggested an estimate of 320,000 for 1989. A new study of Jewish synagogue membership indicates a decline of over 7 percent between 1983 and 1990.[21] While this should not be taken as an automatic proxy for Jewish population decline, our reduced estimate to 315,000 in 1990 aims at characterizing the ongoing trend.

In 1990, the momentous process of German political reunion was formally completed. In the former (West) German Federal Republic, the 1987 population census

---

[18]Doris Bensimon and Sergio DellaPergola, *La population juive de France: socio-démographie et identité* (Jerusalem and Paris, 1984).

[19]Erik H. Cohen, *L'Etude et l'éducation juive en France ou l'avenir d'une communauté* (Paris, 1991).

[20]Steven Haberman, Barry A. Kosmin, and Caren Levy, "Mortality Patterns of British Jews 1975–79: Insights and Applications for the Size and Structure of British Jewry," *Journal of the Royal Statistical Society*, ser. A, 146, pt. 3, 1983, pp. 294–310.

[21]Marlena Schmool and Frances Cohen, *British Synagogue Membership in 1990* (London, 1991).

reported 32,319 Jews. Jewish community records reported about 28,500 affiliated Jews at the end of 1990—an increase over previous years. Immigration continuously compensated for the surplus of deaths over births in this aging Jewish population. From the scarce information that existed about the number of Jews in the former (East) German Democratic Republic, we gave an estimate of 500 for 1988. Our 1989 estimate for unified Germany was 35,000, the increase over the sum of Jewish populations in the previous West and East Germanys reflecting assumed recent immigration. In 1990, an estimated 5,000 Jewish migrants from the Soviet Union were admitted to settle in Germany, thus bringing the total Jewish population estimate to 40,000.

Belgium, Italy, and the Netherlands each have Jewish populations ranging around 30,000. There is a tendency toward internal shrinkage of all these Jewries, but in some instances this is offset by immigration. In Belgium, the size of Jewish population is probably quite stable, owing to the comparatively strong Orthodox element in that community. In Italy, until 1984, Jews were legally bound to affiliate with the local Jewish communities, but then membership in these communities became voluntary. Although most Jews reaffiliated, the new looser legal framework may facilitate the ongoing attrition of the Jewish population.

Other EC member countries have smaller and, overall, slowly declining Jewish populations. An exception may be Spain, whose Jewish population is very tentatively estimated at 12,000.

Other Western Europe. Countries which are not EC members together account for a Jewish population of 44,000. Decline from the 1989 estimate of 52,300 reflects the departure of most of the Jewish migrants that were accommodated in transit in Austria. The estimate of Austria's permanent Jewish populaton was increased to 7,000. Switzerland's Jews are estimated at below 20,000. While there is evidence of a negative balance of births and deaths, connected with great aging and frequent outmarriage, immigration may have offset the internal losses. The Jewish populations in Scandinavian countries are, on the whole, numerically rather stable.

USSR. The demographic situation of East European Jewry is rapidly changing as a consequence of the extensive geopolitical changes in the region. The major event was the economic and political crisis that culminated in the disintegration of the Soviet Union as a state in 1991. Closely related to the same fateful complex of factors was the upsurge in Jewish emigration in 1990, which continued, slightly attenuated, in 1991. While mass emigration is an obvious factor in population decrease, the demography of East European Jewry has been characterized for years by very low levels of "effectively Jewish" fertility, frequent outmarriage, and heavy aging. Therefore the shrinking of the Jewish populations there must be comparatively rapid.

At the end of 1990, the timing of our present update, by far the largest Jewish population in Eastern Europe was still concentrated in the USSR, including its Asian republics. Data on "nationalities" (ethnic groups) from the Soviet Union's official population census, carried out in January 1989, revealed a total of 1,451,000

Jews.[22] The new figure confirmed the declining trend already apparent since the previous three population censuses: 2,267,800 in 1959; 2,150,700 in 1970; and 1,810,900 in 1979. Our own estimate of the number of Jews in the USSR at the end of 1988, projected from the 1979 population census, was 1,435,000; it thus deviated by only 1 percent from the new official baseline figure.

Our reservation about USSR Jewish population figures in previous AJYB volumes bears repeating: some underreporting is not impossible, but it cannot be quantified and should not be exaggerated. One should keep in mind the possible effects on census declarations of the prolonged existence of a totalitarian regime and also of societal preferences for other than Jewish nationalities in the various parts of the Soviet Union. As they are, the figures of successive censuses appear to be remarkably consistent with one another—taking into account also the known volume of emigration, on the one hand, and the probable internal demographic evolution of the Jewish population in recent decades, on the other. The latter was characterized by very low fertility and birthrates; high frequencies of outmarriage, especially in the Slavic republics, which have a large share of the total Jewish population; a preference for non-Jewish nationalities among the children of outmarriage; aging; and a clear surplus of Jewish deaths over Jewish births.[23] Viewed conceptually, the census figures represent the core Jewish population in the USSR. They provide a good example of a large and empirically measured core Jewish population in the Diaspora, consisting of the aggregate of self-identifying Jews.

The respective figures for the enlarged Jewish population—including all current Jews, as well as any other persons of Jewish parentage and their non-Jewish household members—must be substantially higher in a societal context like that of the USSR, which has been characterized by high intermarriage rates for a considerable time. It is not possible to provide an actual estimate of this enlarged Jewish population for lack of appropriate data. Nor can any information be derived about the ratio between Jews and non-Jews in an enlarged Jewish population in the USSR from the

---

[22]First data from the 1989 census results, by "nationalities," appeared in *Goskomstat SSSR, Natsional'nii sostav naseleniia* (Moscow, 1989); "Po dannym goskomstata SSSR," *Gazeta Soyuz*, Mar. 11, 1990; Mark Kupovetzky, "Yidish-dos mame-loschen fun 150 toysent Sovetische yiden," *Sovetisch Heimland*, no. 3, 1990, p. 131.

[23]U.O. Schmelz, "New Evidence on Basic Issues in the Demography of Soviet Jews," *Jewish Journal of Sociology*, 16, no. 2, 1974, pp. 209–23; Mordechai Altshuler, *Soviet Jewry Since the Second World War: Population and Social Structure* (Westport, 1987); Leonid E. Darski, "Fertility in the USSR: Basic Trends," paper presented at European Population Conference, Paris, 1991; Mark Tolts, "Jewish Marriages in the USSR: A Demographic Analysis," Moscow, 1991. Indeed, consistency between the censuses, i.e., the respective declarations of self-identification by Jews, was such that our estimate for 1975 turned out to fit well as a demographic interpolation between the results of the 1970 census and the subsequent one held in 1979. See Schmelz, *World Jewish Population: Regional Estimates and Projections.*

statistics of immigrants to Israel. Due to the highly self-selective character of *aliyah*, non-Jews have constituted a relatively small minority of all new immigrants from the USSR.[24] It is obvious, though, that the wide provisions of Israel's Law of Return (see above) apply to virtually the maximum emigration pool of self-declared Jews and close non-Jewish relatives. Any of the large figures attributed in recent years to the size of Soviet Jewry, insofar as they are based on demographic reasoning, do not relate to the core but to various estimates of an enlarged Jewish population. The evidence also suggests that in the USSR, core Jews constitute a smaller share of the total enlarged Jewish population than in some Western countries, including the United States.

Just as the number of declared Jews remained consistent between censuses, the number of persons of Jewish descent who preferred not to be identified as Jews was rather consistent, too, at least until 1989. However, the recent political developments, and especially the emigration urge impressively illustrated by the exodus of 1990–1991, have probably led to greater readiness to declare Jewish self-identification by persons who did not describe themselves as such in the 1989 census. In terms of demographic accounting, these "returnees" imply an actual net increment to the core Jewish population of the USSR, as well as to world Jewry.

With regard to updating the January 1989 census figure to the end of 1990, Jewish emigration has played the major role among the intervening changes. An estimated 71,000, thereof about 60,000 declared Jews, left in 1989, as against 19,300 in 1988, 8,100 in 1987, and only 7,000 during the whole 1982–1986 period. In 1990, according to Soviet, Israeli, American, and other sources, an estimated 201,000 Jews left the Soviet Union.[25] For the first time since 1976, a substantial majority of the Jewish emigrants who left the Soviet Union in 1990 went to Israel rather than to another Western country, as in the preceding years. Concurrently, a further 28,000 emigrants from the previous year who were in temporary accommodations—19,000 in Italy and 9,000 in Austria—were permanently resettled, and the transit camps closed. In total, an estimated 229,000 Jews originating in the USSR were involved in these international migrations in 1990. Of these, 180,000 emigrated to Israel.

At the same time, the heavy deficit of internal population dynamics continued and even intensified due to the great aging which is known to have prevailed for many decades. Aging cannot but have been exacerbated by the significantly younger age

---

[24]Israel's Ministry of Interior records the religion-nationality of each new immigrant for identification purposes. Such attribution is made on the basis of documentary evidence which is supplied by the immigrants themselves and is checked by competent authorities in Israel. According to data available from the Interior Ministry's Central Population Register, 94.2 percent of all new immigrants from the Soviet Union during the period Oct. 1989–Feb. 1991 were registered as Jewish. See Sergio DellaPergola, "The Demographic Context of the Soviet Aliya," *Jews and Jewish Topics in the Soviet Union and Eastern Europe* 3 (16), Winter 1991, pp. 41–56.

[25]See Sidney Heitman, "Soviet Emigration in 1990," *Berichte des Bundesinstitut fur Ostwissenschaftliche und internationale Studien*, vol. 33, 1991.

composition of the emigrants.[26] On the strength of these considerations, our estimate of the core Jewish population in the USSR was reduced from the census figure of 1,450,000 at the end of 1988/beginning of 1989 to 1,370,000 at the end of 1989, and to 1,150,000 at the end of 1990.

At the end of 1990, the Soviet Union still constituted one country, and it is referred to as such in our statistical presentation. However, in view of its subsequent political disintegration, it is relevant to review the distribution of Jewish population in the 15 former Soviet republics that were to become its independent successor states (see table 4).[27] Of the total estimate of 1,150,000 Jews, 30,500 lived in the three Baltic states of Estonia, Latvia, and Lithuania, which were the first to reach independence and international recognition in 1991; 920,000 in the three Slavic republics of Byelorussia (Belarus), Russia, and Ukraine; 50,000 in Moldavia (Moldova); 44,500 in the three trans-Caucasian republics of Armenia, Azerbaijan, and Georgia; and 105,000 in the five central-Asian republics of Kazakhstan, Kirghizstan, Tajikistan, Turkmenistan, and Uzbekistan.

Other East Europe and Balkans. The Jewish populations in Hungary and Romania and the small remnants in Bulgaria, Czechoslovakia, Poland, and Yugoslavia are all reputed to be very overaged and to experience frequent outmarriage. In each of these countries, the ongoing processes of political liberalization have permitted greater autonomy of the organized Jewish communities and their registered membership. More Jews or persons of Jewish origin are known or believed to exist than previously thought, some having come out in the open after years of hiding their identity. Yet, the inevitable numerical decline of Jewish populations in Eastern Europe is reflected in reduced estimates for 1990. (In 1991, the entire Jewish community of Albania, amounting to some 300, emigrated to Israel.) The size of Hungarian Jewry—the largest in Eastern Europe outside the USSR—is quite insufficiently known. Our estimate of 57,000 only attempts to reflect the declining trend that prevails there, too, according to the available indicators. Comparatively large emigration of Jews continued to take place from Romania and was reflected in the

---

[26]Age structures of the Jewish population in the Russian Federal Republic in 1970 and 1979 were reported in *Goskomstat SSSR, Itogi vsesoiuznoi perepisi naseleniia 1970 goda*, vol. 4, table 33 (Moscow, 1973); *Goskomstat SSSR, Itogi vsesoiuznoi perepisi naseleniia 1979 goda*, vol. 4, part 2, table 2 (Moscow, 1989). Data from the 1989 census are in the course of publication. Age structures of recent Jewish migrants from the USSR to the United States and to Israel are available, respectively, from: HIAS, Statistical Abstract, vol. 30, no. 4 (New York, 1990); Israel Central Bureau of Statistics, Immigration to Israel 1990, Special Series, no. 900 (Jerusalem, 1991).

[27]These estimates are based on the detailed geographical origins of new immigrants to Israel. They repeat, with minor adaptations, those of Yoel Florsheim, "Immigration to Israel from the Soviet Union in 1990," *Jews and Jewish Topics in the Soviet Union and Eastern Europe* 2 (15), 1991, pp. 5–14. Our estimates of the total population of USSR republics in 1990 were adapted from Academy of Sciences of the USSR, Institute of Sociology, Center for Social Demography, *Selected Statistical Data on Demographic Processes in the USSR* (Moscow, 1991).

detailed community records available there. Romania's Jewish population was estimated at 17,500 in 1990.

TABLE 4. ESTIMATED JEWISH POPULATION DISTRIBUTION IN THE USSR, 1990

Republic	Total Population	Jewish Population	Jews per 1,000 Population	Accuracy Rating
Estonia	1,600,000	3,500	2.2	B 1990
Latvia	2,700,000	18,000	6.7	B 1990
Lithuania	3,700,000	9,000	2.4	B 1990
Byelorussia	10,295,000	75,000	7.3	B 1990
Russia	147,945,000	470,000	3.2	B 1990
Ukraine	51,780,000	375,000	7.2	B 1990
Moldavia	4,400,000	50,000	11.4	B 1990
Armenia	3,300,000	500	0.2	B 1990
Azerbaijan	7,095,000	21,000	3.0	B 1990
Georgia	5,495,000	23,000	4.2	B 1990
Kazakhstan	16,695,000	17,000	1.0	B 1990
Kirghizstan	4,400,000	5,000	1.1	B 1990
Tajikistan	5,300,000	11,500	2.2	B 1990
Turkmenistan	3,600,000	1,500	0.4	B 1990
Uzbekistan	20,290,000	70,000	3.4	B 1990
Total	288,595,000	1,150,000	4.0	

The Jewish population of Turkey, where a surplus of deaths over births had been reported for several years, was estimated at about 20,000.

ASIA

Israel accounts for 99 percent of all the nearly four million Jews in Asia, excluding the Asian territories of the USSR and Turkey (see table 5). By the end of 1990, Israeli Jews constituted 31 percent of total world Jewry. Israel's Jewish population grew in 1990 by about 230,000, or 6.2 percent. This was the highest rate of growth since the end of the initial wave of mass *aliyah* in 1951. About 79 percent of this growth was due to the net migration balance; 21 percent to natural increase.[28] The total number of immigrants from all countries was 201,500, of whom 195,600 were Jewish. (This last is the second highest in Israel's history, and the highest since 1949, when 239,950 Jewish immigrants arrived.) Included in the figures are 185,000 immigrants from the USSR, of whom 180,000 were Jewish.

It is difficult to estimate the Jewish population of Iran for any given date, but it continues to dwindle. The estimate for 1990 was reduced to 19,000. In other Asian countries with small veteran communities—such as India—the Jewish population tends to decline slowly. On the basis of research conducted by recent visitors to Yemen, firm statistical evidence was obtained for the first time for the small remnant of the Jewish population in that country. Very small communities, partially of a transient character, exist in several countries of Southeast Asia.

AFRICA

Less than 150,000 Jews are estimated to remain now in Africa. The Republic of South Africa accounts for 77 percent of total Jews in that continent (see table 6). In 1980, according to the official census, there were about 118,000 Jews among South Africa's white population.[29] Substantial Jewish emigration after that was compensated in good part by Jewish immigration. Considering a moderately negative migration balance, and an incipient negative balance of internal changes, the Jewish population estimate for 1988 was reduced to 114,000. In 1989 and 1990, the numbers of emigrants, on the one hand, and immigrants and returning residents, on the other, possibly balanced—suggesting no considerable change in Jewish population size. A Jewish-sponsored survey of South African Jewry was completed in 1991, and results will be forthcoming along with the results of a new official population census.

In recent years, the Jewish community of Ethiopia has been at the center of an international effort of rescue. In 1990, over 4,000 Jews migrated to Israel. (In the course of 1991, the overwhelming majority of Ethiopian Jews—about 20,000 people—were brought to Israel, most of them in a one-day dramatic air-lift operation.) A few of these migrants were non-Jewish members of mixed households. In connection with these events, the size of Ethiopian Jewry could eventually be estimated on a more accurate basis than had been the case previously. Taking into account the numbers of those who subsequently left or yet remained in the country, it can be

---

[28]Israel Central Bureau of Statistics, *Statistical Abstract of Israel 1991* (Jerusalem, 1991). For a comprehensive review of sociodemographic changes in Israel, see U.O. Schmelz, Sergio DellaPergola, and Uri Avner, "Ethnic Differences Among Israeli Jews: A New Look," AJYB 1990, vol. 90, pp. 3–204.

[29]Sergio DellaPergola and Allie A. Dubb, "South African Jewry: A Sociodemographic Profile," AJYB 1988, vol. 88, pp. 59–140.

TABLE 5.   ESTIMATED JEWISH POPULATION DISTRIBUTION IN ASIA, 1990[a]

Country	Total Population	Jewish Population	Jews per 1,000 Population	Accuracy Rating
Hong Kong	5,841,000	1,000	0.2	D
India	853,094,000	4,800	0.0	C 1981
Iran	54,607,000	19,000	0.3	D
Iraq	18,920,000	200	0.0	D
Israel	4,822,000[b]	3,946,700	818.5	A 1990
Japan	123,460,000	1,000	0.0	C 1988
Korea, South	42,793,000	100	0.0	D
Philippines	62,413,000	100	0.0	C 1988
Singapore	2,723,000	300	0.1	B 1990
Syria	12,530,000	4,000	0.3	D
Thailand	55,702,000	200	0.0	C 1988 X
Yemen	9,196,000	1,700	0.2	B 1990 X
Other	1,810,938,000	300	0.0	D
Total	3,057,039,000	3,979,400	1.3	

[a]Not including Asian regions of USSR and Turkey.
[b]End 1990.

TABLE 6.   ESTIMATED JEWISH POPULATION DISTRIBUTION IN AFRICA, 1990

Country	Total Population	Jewish Population	Jews per 1,000 Population	Accuracy Rating
Egypt	52,426,000	200	0.0	C 1988
Ethiopia	49,240,000	21,000	0.4	B 1990 X
Kenya	24,031,000	400	0.0	B 1990
Morocco	25,061,000	8,000	0.3	D X
South Africa	35,282,000	114,000	3.2	C 1980
Tunisia	8,180,000	2,400	0.3	D
Zaire	35,568,000	400	0.0	D
Zambia	8,452,000	300	0.0	D
Zimbabwe	9,709,000	1,000	0.1	B 1990
Other	394,162,000	1,000	0.0	D
Total	642,111,000	148,700	0.2	

estimated that the Jewish population was about 25,000 at the end of 1989, and 21,000 at the end of 1990. This implies an upward revision of 5,000 in comparison with our original estimate for 1989.

The remnants of Moroccan and Tunisian Jewry tend to shrink slowly through emigration. In the light of available information, our 1989 estimate was reduced retrospectively, and a further moderate decline was introduced in the estimates for 1990. It should be pointed out, though, that not a few Jews have a foothold both in Morocco or Tunisia and in France and other Western countries, and their geographical attribution is uncertain.

OCEANIA

The major country of Jewish residence in Oceania (Australasia) is Australia, where 95 percent of the estimated total of nearly 93,000 Jews live (see table 7). The 1986 census of Australia, where the question on religion is optional, enumerated 69,065 declared Jews but also indicated that about 25 percent of the country's whole population either did not specify their religion or stated explicitly that they had none.[30] This large group must be assumed to contain persons who identify in other ways as Jews. In addition, Australian Jewry has received migratory reinforcements during the last decade, especially from South Africa and the Soviet Union. At the same time, there are demographic patterns with negative effects on Jewish population size, such as strong aging, low or negative natural increase, and some assimilation. We raised our estimate for 1990 to a provisional figure of 88,000. The new census of 1991, as well as a Jewish survey now being planned, will hopefully provide firmer data on Jewish population size and trends in Australia. The Jewish community in New Zealand—now estimated at 4,500—attracted some immigrants, but incurred a negative migration balance with Australia.

TABLE 7. ESTIMATED JEWISH POPULATION DISTRIBUTION IN OCEANIA, 1990

Country	Total Population	Jewish Population	Jews per 1,000 Population	Accuracy Rating
Australia	16,873,000	88,000	5.2	C 1986
New Zealand	3,392,000	4,500	1.3	C 1988
Other	6,216,000	100	0.0	D
Total	26,481,000	92,600	3.5	

[30]Walter M. Lippmann, *Australian Jewry 1986* (South Yarra, Victoria, 1987).

TABLE 8. DISTRIBUTION OF THE WORLD'S JEWS, BY NUMBER AND PROPORTION
(PER 1,000 POPULATION) IN VARIOUS COUNTRIES, 1990

Number of Jews in Country	Jews per 1,000 Population					
	Total	Below 1	1–4.9	5–9.9	10–24.9	25+
	Number of Countries					
Total	74a	49	15	6	3	1
100–900	24	19	4	—	1	—
1,000–4,900	18	17	1	—	—	—
5,000–9,900	6	4	2	—	—	—
10,000–49,900	15	8	6	1	—	—
50,000–99,900	2	—	—	2	—	—
100,000–999,900	6	1	1	3	1	—
1,000,000 and over	3	—	1	—	1	1
	Jewish Population Distribution (Absolute Numbers)					
Total	12,806,400b	375,100	1,408,000	1,229,200	5,845,600	3,946,700
100–900	9,600	7,400	1,600	—	600	—
1,000–4,900	47,500	43,000	4,500	—	—	—
5,000–9,900	40,700	29,300	11,400	—	—	—
10,000–49,900	346,100	195,400	126,500	24,200	—	—
50,000–99,900	145,000	—	—	145,000	—	—
100,000–999,900	1,584,000	100,000	114,000	1,060,000	310,000	—
1,000,000 and over	10,631,700	—	1,150,000	—	5,535,000	3,946,700
	Jewish Population Distribution (Percent of World's Jews)					
Total	100.0b	2.9	11.0	9.6	45.6	30.8
100–900	0.1	0.1	0.0	—	0.0	—
1,000–4,900	0.3	0.3	0.0	—	—	—
5,000–9,900	0.3	0.2	0.1	—	—	—
10,000–49,900	2.7	1.5	1.0	0.2	—	—
50,000–99,900	1.1	—	—	1.1	—	—
100,000–999,900	12.4	0.8	0.9	8.3	2.4	—
1,000,000 and over	83.0	—	9.0	—	43.2	30.8

aExcluding countries with fewer than 100 Jews.
bIncluding countries with fewer than 100 Jews.

Dispersion and Concentration

Table 8 demonstrates the magnitude of Jewish dispersion. The individual countries listed above as each having at least 100 Jews are scattered over all the continents. In 1990, more than half (42 out of 74 countries) had fewer than 5,000 Jews each. In relative terms, too, the Jews were thinly scattered nearly everywhere in the Diaspora. There is not a single Diaspora country where they amounted even to 3 percent of the total population. In most countries they constituted a far smaller fraction. Only three Diaspora countries had more than 1 percent Jews in their total population, and only nine countries had more than 5 Jews per 1,000 of population. The respective nine countries were, in descending order of the proportion, but regardless of the absolute number of their Jews: United States (22.2 per 1,000), Gibraltar (20.0), Canada (11.7), France (9.4), Uruguay (7.8), Argentina (6.7), Great Britain (5.5), Hungary (5.4), and Australia (5.2). The other major Diaspora Jewries, having lower proportions of Jews per 1,000 of total population, were the USSR (4.0), South Africa (3.2), and Brazil (0.7 per 1,000). Although by the end of 1990 the constituent republics of the Soviet Union were not independent states, and therefore were not reported as such in table 8, it may be noted that four had more than 5 Jews per 1,000 of population: Moldova (11.4), Belarus (7.3), Ukraine (7.2), and Latvia (6.7).

In the state of Israel, by contrast, the Jewish majority amounted to 818.5 per thousand in 1990, compared to 815.2 per thousand in 1989—not including the Arab population of the administered areas.

While Jews are widely dispersed, they are also concentrated to some extent (see table 9). In 1990 over 96 percent of world Jewry lived in the ten countries with the

TABLE 9. TEN COUNTRIES WITH LARGEST JEWISH POPULATIONS, 1990

| | | | % of Total Jewish Population | | | |
| | | Jewish | In the World | | In the Diaspora | |
Rank	Country	Population	%	Cumulative %	%	Cumulative %
1	United States	5,535,000	43.2	43.2	62.5	62.5
2	Israel	3,946,700	30.8	74.0	—	—
3	Soviet Union	1,150,000	9.0	83.0	13.0	75.5
4	France	530,000	4.1	87.1	6.0	81.5
5	Great Britain	315,000	2.5	89.6	3.5	85.0
6	Canada	310,000	2.4	92.0	3.5	88.5
7	Argentina	215,000	1.7	93.7	2.4	90.9
8	South Africa	114,000	0.9	94.6	1.3	92.2
9	Brazil	100,000	0.8	95.4	1.1	93.3
10	Australia	88,000	0.7	96.1	1.0	94.3

largest Jewish populations; and 83 percent lived in the three countries that had at least a million Jews each (United States, Israel, Soviet Union). Similarly, nine leading Diaspora countries together comprised over 94 percent of the Diaspora Jewish population; two countries (United States and Soviet Union) accounted for 75 percent, and the United States alone for over 62 percent of total Diaspora Jewry.

U.O. SCHMELZ
SERGIO DELLAPERGOLA

Directories
Lists
Obituaries

National Jewish Organizations[1]

UNITED STATES

Organizations are listed according to functions as follows:

COMMUNITY RELATIONS

AMERICAN COUNCIL FOR JUDAISM (1943). PO Box 9009, Alexandria, VA 22304. (703)836–2546. Pres. Alan V. Stone; Exec. Dir. Allan C. Brownfeld. Seeks to advance the universal principles of a Judaism free of nationalism, and the national, civic, cultural, and social integration into American institutions of Americans of Jewish faith. *Issues of the American Council for Judaism; Special Interest Report.*

AMERICAN JEWISH ALTERNATIVES TO ZIONISM, INC. (1968). 347 Fifth Ave., Suite 900, NYC 10016. (212)213–9125. FAX: (2l2)213–9142. Pres. Elmer Berger; V.-Pres. Mrs. Arthur Gutman. Applies Jewish values of justice and humanity to the Arab-Israel conflict in the Middle East; rejects nationality attachment of Jews, particularly American Jews, to the State of Israel as self-segregating, inconsistent with American constitutional concepts of individual citizenship and separation of church and state, and as being a principal obstacle to Middle East peace. *Report.*

AMERICAN JEWISH COMMITTEE (1906). Institute of Human Relations, 165 E. 56 St., NYC 10022. (212)751–4000. FAX: (212)-319–6156. Pres. Alfred H. Moses; Exec. V.-Pres. David A. Harris. Seeks to prevent infraction of civil and religious rights of

---

[1]The information in this directory is based on replies to questionnaires circulated by the editors.

Jews in any part of the world; to advance the cause of human rights for people of all races, creeds, and nationalities; to interpret the position of Israel to the American public; and to help American Jews maintain and enrich their Jewish identity and, at the same time, achieve full integration in American life. Includes Jacob and Hilda Blaustein Center for Human Relations, William E. Wiener Oral History Library, William Petschek National Jewish Family Center, Jacob Blaustein Institute for the Advancement of Human Rights, Institute on American Jewish–Israeli Relations. AMERICAN JEWISH YEAR BOOK (with Jewish Publication Society); *Commentary; AJC Journal; Capital Update. Published in Israel: Alon Yedi'ot, a monthly bulletin of the Institute on American Jewish-Israeli Relations.*

AMERICAN JEWISH CONGRESS (1918). Stephen Wise Congress House, 15 E. 84 St., NYC 10028. (212)879–4500. FAX: (212)-249–3672. Pres. Robert K. Lifton; Exec. Dir. Henry Siegman. Works to foster the creative cultural survival of the Jewish people; to help Israel develop in peace, freedom, and security; to eliminate all forms of racial and religious bigotry; to advance civil rights, protect civil liberties, defend religious freedom, and safeguard the separation of church and state. *Congress Monthly; Judaism; Boycott Report.*

ANTI-DEFAMATION LEAGUE OF B'NAI B'RITH (1913). 823 United Nations Plaza, NYC 10017. (212)490–2525. Chmn. Melvin Salberg; Dir. Abraham H. Foxman. Seeks to combat anti-Semitism and to secure justice and fair treatment for all citizens through law, education, and community relations. *ADL Bulletin; Face to Face; Fact Finding Report; International Reports; Law Notes; Rights; Law; Research and Evaluation Report; Discriminations Report; Litigation Docket; Dimensions; Middle East Notebook; Nuestro Encuentro.*

ASSOCIATION OF JEWISH COMMUNITY RELATIONS WORKERS (1950). 1522 K St., NW, Suite 920, Washington, DC 20005. (202)347–4628. Pres. Marlene Gorin. Aims to stimulate higher standards of professional practice in Jewish community relations; encourages research and training toward that end; conducts educational programs and seminars; aims to encourage cooperation between community relations workers and those working in other areas of Jewish communal service.

CENTER FOR JEWISH COMMUNITY STUDIES (1970). Temple University, Center City Campus, 1616 Walnut St., Suite 513, Philadelphia, PA 19103. (215)787–1459. FAX: (215)787–7784. Jerusalem office: Jerusalem Center for Public Affairs. Pres. Daniel J. Elazar. Worldwide policy-studies institute devoted to the study of Jewish community organization, political thought, and public affairs, past and present, in Israel and throughout the world. Publishes original articles, essays, and monographs; maintains library, archives, and reprint series. *Jerusalem Letter/Viewpoints; Survey of Arab Affairs; Jewish Political Studies Review.*

COMMISSION ON SOCIAL ACTION OF REFORM JUDAISM (1953, joint instrumentality of the Union of American Hebrew Congregations and the Central Conference of American Rabbis). 838 Fifth Ave., NYC 10021. (212)249–0100. 2027 Massachusetts Ave., NW, Washington, DC 20036. Chmn. Evely Laser Shlensky; Dir. Rabbi Eric Yoffie; Emer. Dir. Albert Vorspan; Dir. Religious Action Center, Rabbi David Saperstein. Policy-making body that relates ethical and spiritual principles of Judaism to social-justice issues: implements resolutions through the Religious Action Center in Washington, DC, via advocacy, development of educational materials, and congregational programs. *Briefings (social action newsletter); Chai Impact (legislative update).*

CONFERENCE OF PRESIDENTS OF MAJOR AMERICAN JEWISH ORGANIZATIONS (1955). 110 E. 59 St., NYC 10022.(212)-318–6111. FAX: (212)644–4135. Chmn. Shoshana S. Cardin; Exec. Dir. Malcolm Hoenlein. Seeks to strengthen the U.S.-Israel alliance and to protect and enhance the security and dignity of Jews abroad. Toward this end, the Conference of Presidents speaks and acts on the basis of consensus of its 48 member agencies on issues of national and international Jewish concern. *Annual report.*

CONSULTATIVE COUNCIL OF JEWISH ORGANIZATIONS-CCJO (1946). 420 Lexington Ave., Suite 1733, NYC 10170. (212)808–5437. Pres.'s Adolphe Steg, Clemens Nathan, Joseph Nuss; Sec.-Gen. Warren Green. A nongovernmental organization in consultative status with the UN, UNESCO, ILO, UNICEF, and the Council of Europe; cooperates and consults with, advises and renders assistance to the

Economic and Social Council of the UN on all problems relating to human rights and economic, social, cultural, educational, and related matters pertaining to Jews.

COORDINATING BOARD OF JEWISH ORGANIZATIONS (1947). 1640 Rhode Island Ave., NW, Washington, DC 20036. (202)-857-6545. Pres. Kent E. Schiner; Exec. V.-Pres. Dr. Sidney Clearfield; Dir. Internatl. Affairs Daniel S. Mariaschin; Dir. Internatl. Council Warren Eisenberg; Dir. UN Off. Harris Schoenberg. Coordinates the UN activities of B'nai B'rith and the British and South African Boards of Jewish Deputies.

COUNCIL OF JEWISH ORGANIZATIONS IN CIVIL SERVICE, INC. (1948). 45 E. 33 St., Rm. 604, NYC 10016. (212)689–2015. Pres. Louis Weiser. Supports merit system; encourages recruitment of Jewish youth to government service; member of Coalition to Free Soviet Jews, NY Jewish Community Relations Council, NY Metropolitan Coordinating Council on Jewish Poverty, Jewish Labor Committee, America-Israel Friendship League. *Council Digest.*

INSTITUTE FOR PUBLIC AFFAIRS (*see* Union of Orthodox Jewish Congregations of America)

INTERNATIONAL CONFERENCE OF JEWISH COMMUNAL SERVICE (*see* World Conference of Jewish Communal Service)

INTERNATIONAL LEAGUE FOR THE REPATRIATION OF RUSSIAN JEWS, INC. (1963). 2 Fountain Lane, Suite 2J, Scarsdale, NY 10583. (800)448–1866. Pres. Morris Brafman; Chmn. James H. Rapp. Helped to bring the situation of Soviet Jews to world attention; advocates in world forums for the right of Soviet Jews to repatriation.

JEWISH LABOR COMMITTEE (1934). Atran Center for Jewish Culture, 25 E. 21 St., NYC 10010. (212)477–0707. FAX: (212)-477–1918. Pres. Lenore Miller; Exec. Dir. Martin Lapan. Serves as liaison between the Jewish community and the trade-union movement; works with the AFL-CIO to combat anti-Semitism and engender support for the State of Israel and Soviet Jewry; strengthens support within the Jewish community for the social goals and programs of the labor movement; supports Yiddish cultural institutions. *Jewish Labor Committee Review; Alumni Newsletter.*

———, NATIONAL TRADE UNION COUNCIL FOR HUMAN RIGHTS (1956). Atran Center for Jewish Culture, 25 E. 21 St., NYC

10010. (212)477–0707. FAX: (212)477–1918. Chmn. Sol Hoffman; Exec. Sec. Michael Perry. Works with the American labor movement in advancing the struggle for social justice and equal opportunity and assists unions in every issue affecting human rights. Fights discrimination on all levels and helps to promote labor's broad social and economic goals.

JEWISH PEACE FELLOWSHIP (1941). Box 271, Nyack, NY 10960. (914)358–4601. FAX: (914)358–4924. Pres. Rabbi Philip Bentley; Sec. Naomi Goodman. Unites those who believe that Jewish ideals and experience provide inspiration for a nonviolent philosophy and way of life; offers draft counseling, especially for conscientious objection based on Jewish "religious training and belief"; encourages Jewish community to become more knowledgeable, concerned, and active in regard to the war/peace problem. *Shalom/Jewish Peace Letter.*

JEWISH WAR VETERANS OF THE UNITED STATES OF AMERICA (1896). 1811 R St., NW, Washington, DC 20009. (202)265–6280. FAX: (202)234–5662. Natl. Exec. Dir. Herb Rosenbleeth; Natl. Commander Albert L. Cohen. Seeks to foster true allegiance to the United States; to combat bigotry and prevent defamation of Jews; to encourage the doctrine of universal liberty, equal rights, and full justice for all; to cooperate with and support existing educational institutions and establish new ones; to foster the education of ex-servicemen, ex-servicewomen, and members in the ideals and principles of Americanism. *Jewish Veteran.*

———, NATIONAL MEMORIAL, INC. (1958). 1811 R St., NW, Washington, DC 20009. (202)265–6280. FAX: (202)462–3192. Pres. Florence G. Levine. Operates a museum and library archive dedicated to telling the story of the activities and service of American Jews in the armed forces of the U.S. *Quarterly newsletter, Routes to Roots.*

NATIONAL CONFERENCE ON SOVIET JEWRY (formerly AMERICAN JEWISH CONFERENCE ON SOVIET JEWRY) (1964; reorg. 1971). 10 E. 40 St., Suite 1701, NYC 10016. (212)679–6122. FAX: (212)686–1193. Chmn. Shoshana S. Cardin; Exec. Dir. Martin A. Wenick. Coordinating agency for major national Jewish organizations and local community groups in the U.S., acting on behalf of Soviet Jewry through public education and social action; stimulates all segments of the community to maintain an interest in the problems of Soviet Jews by publishing reports and special pamphlets, sponsoring special programs and projects, organizing public meetings and forums. *Newsbreak; annual report; action and program kits; Wrap-Up Leadership Report.*

————, SOVIET JEWRY RESEARCH BUREAU. Chmn. Charlotte Jacobson. Organized by NCSJ to monitor emigration trends. Primary task is the accumulation, evaluation, and processing of information regarding Soviet Jews, especially those who apply for emigration.

NATIONAL JEWISH COALITION (1980). 415 2nd St., NE, Suite 100, Washington, DC 20002. (202)547-7701. FAX: (202)544-2434. Hon. Chmn. Max M. Fisher; Cochmn. Richard J. Fox, George Klein; Exec. Dir. Matt Brooks. Promotes Jewish involvement in Republican politics; sensitizes Republican leaders to the concerns of the American Jewish community; promotes principles of free enterprise, a strong national defense, and an internationalist foreign policy. *NJC Bulletin.*

NATIONAL JEWISH COMMISSION ON LAW AND PUBLIC AFFAIRS (COLPA) (1965). 787 Seventh Ave., 44th fl., NYC 10019. (212)554-2360. Pres. Allen L. Rothenberg; Exec. Dir. Dennis Rapps. Voluntary association of attorneys whose purpose is to represent the observant Jewish community on legal, legislative, and public-affairs matters.

NATIONAL JEWISH COMMUNITY RELATIONS ADVISORY COUNCIL (1944). 443 Park Ave. S., 11th fl., NYC 10016. (212)-684-6950. FAX: (212)686-1353. Chmn. Maynard I. Wishner; Sec. Joel Reck; Exec. V.-Chmn. Lawrence Rubin. National coordinating body for the field of Jewish community relations, comprising 13 national and 117 local Jewish community relations agencies. Promotes understanding of Israel and the Middle East; freedom for Soviet Jews; equal status for Jews and other groups in American society. Through the NJCRAC's work, its constituent organizations seek agreement on policies, strategies, and programs for effective utilization of their resources for common ends. *Joint Program Plan for Jewish Community Relations.*

NEW JEWISH AGENDA (1980). 64 Fulton St., #1100, NYC 10038. (212)227-5885. FAX: (212)962-6211. Cochmn. Lois Levine, Ira Grupper; Exec. Dir. Irena Klepfisz. Grass-roots, multi-issue organization with over 45 chapters in N. America. Founded as "a progressive voice in the Jewish community and a Jewish voice among progressives." Works for peace in the Middle East and Central America, feminism, gay and lesbian rights, and economic justice, and against anti-Semitism and racism. *Agenda In-Brief.*

SHALOM CENTER (1983). 7318 Germantown Ave., Philadelphia, PA 19119. (215)247-9700. Bd. Chmn. Viki List; Exec. Dir. Arthur Waskow. National resource and organizing center for Jewish perspectives on moving from the cold war toward "One Earth"—in dealing with nuclear and other environmental dangers. Trains community organizers, holds conferences, assists local Jewish committees and coalitions on nuclear weapons and environmental issues. Sponsors Sukkat Shalom and Ira Silverman Memorial. Provides school curricula, sermon materials, legislative reports, adult-education texts, and media for Jewish use. *Shalom Report.*

STUDENT STRUGGLE FOR SOVIET JEWRY, INC. (1964). 50 W. 97 St., Suite 3F, NYC 10025. (212)799-8900. FAX: (212)663-5784. Natl. Dir. Jacob Birnbaum; Natl. Coord. Glenn Richter; Chmn. Rabbi Avraham Weiss. Provides information and action guidance to adult and student organizations, communities, and schools throughout the U.S. and Canada; assists Soviet Jews by publicity campaigns; helps Soviet Jews in the U.S.; maintains speakers bureau and research documents. *Soviet Jewry Action Newsletter.*

UNION OF COUNCILS FOR SOVIET JEWS (1970). 1819 H St., NW, Suite 230, Washington, DC 20006. (202)775-9770. Natl. Pres. Pamela B. Cohen; Natl. Dir. Micah H. Naftalin. Its 50 local councils and 100,000 members throughout the U.S. support and protect Soviet Jews by gathering and disseminating news on the condition and treatment of Soviet Jews; advocacy; publications and educational programs, including briefings and policy analyses. The Moscow Bureau on Human Rights, established 1990, monitors anti-Semitism and ethnic intolerance, advocates for Refuseniks and political prisoners, seeks to advance democracy and rule of law in USSR successor states. *Monitor! (weekly summary of developments affecting the Jewish and human rights movements); Congressional Handbook for Soviet Jewry; Anti-Semitism in the Russian Press; Status Reports on Anti-Semitism; Russia Inside (a publication of Moscow Bureau).*

WORLD CONFERENCE OF JEWISH COMMUNAL SERVICE (1966). 3084 State Highway 27, Suite 9, Kendall Park, NJ 08824-1657. (908)821-0282. FAX: (908)821-5335. Pres. Arthur Rotman; Sec.-Gen. Joel Ollander. Established by worldwide Jewish communal workers to strengthen their understanding of each other's programs and to communicate with colleagues in order to enrich the quality of their work. Conducts quadrennial international conferences in Jerusalem and periodic regional meetings. *Proceedings of international conferences; newsletters.*

WORLD JEWISH CONGRESS (1936; org. in U.S. 1939). 501 Madison Ave., 17th fl., NYC 10022. (212) 755-5770. FAX: (212)-755-5883. Pres. Edgar M. Bronfman; Co-chmn. N. Amer. Branch Prof. Irwin Cotler (Montreal) and Evelyn Sommer; Sec.-Gen. Israel Singer; Exec. Dir. Elan Steinberg. Seeks to intensify bonds of world Jewry with Israel as central force in Jewish life; to strengthen solidarity among Jews everywhere and secure their rights, status, and interests as individuals and communities; to encourage development of Jewish social, religious, and cultural life throughout the world and coordinate efforts by Jewish communities and organizations to cope with any Jewish problem; to work for human rights generally. Represents its affiliated organizations—most representative bodies of Jewish communities in more than 70 countries and 35 national organizations in Amer. section—at UN, OAS, UNESCO, Council of Europe, ILO, UNICEF, and other governmental, intergovernmental, and international authorities. Publications (including those by Institute of Jewish Affairs, London): *Christian Jewish Relations; Coloquio; News and Views; Boletín Informativo OJI; Batfutsot; Gesher; Patterns of Prejudice; Soviet Jewish Affairs.*

CULTURAL

AMERICAN ACADEMY FOR JEWISH RESEARCH (1929). 3080 Broadway, NYC 10027. (212)678-8864. FAX: (212)678-

8947. Pres. Arthur Hyman. Encourages Jewish learning and research; holds annual or semiannual meeting; awards grants for the publication of scholarly works. *Proceedings of the American Academy for Jewish Research; Texts and Studies; Monograph Series.*

AMERICAN BIBLICAL ENCYCLOPEDIA SOCIETY (1930). 24 W. Maple Ave., Monsey, NY 10952. (914)352-4609. Pres. Irving Fredman; Author-Ed. Rabbi M.M. Kasher. Fosters biblical-talmudical research; sponsors and publishes *Torah Shelemah* (Heb., 42 vols.), *Encyclopedia of Biblical Interpretation* (Eng., 9 vols.), *Divrei Menachem* (Heb., 4 vols.), and related publications. *Noam.*

AMERICAN JEWISH HISTORICAL SOCIETY (1892). 2 Thornton Rd., Waltham, MA 02154. (617)891-8110. FAX: (617)899-9208. Pres. Ronald C. Curhan; Exec. Dir. Dr. Michael Feldberg. Collects, catalogues, publishes, and displays material on the history of the Jews in America; serves as an information center for inquiries on American Jewish history; maintains archives of original source material on American Jewish history; sponsors lectures and exhibitions; makes available historic Yiddish films and audiovisual material. *American Jewish History; Heritage.*

AMERICAN JEWISH PRESS ASSOCIATION (1943). c/o Northern California Jewish Bulletin, 88 First St., San Francisco, CA 94105. (415)957-9340. FAX: (415)957-0266. Pres. Marc S. Klein. Natl. Admin. Off.: 11312 Old Club Rd., Rockville, MD 20852-4537. (301)881-4113. Exec. Dir. L. Malcolm Rodman. Seeks the advancement of Jewish journalism and the maintenance of a strong Jewish press in the U.S. and Canada; encourages the attainment of the highest editorial and business standards; sponsors workshops, services for members. *Membership bulletin newsletter; Roster of Members.*

AMERICAN SOCIETY FOR JEWISH MUSIC (1974). 129 W. 67 St., NYC 10023. (212)-362-8060 X307. Pres. Jack Gottlieb; Co-V.-Pres. Michael Leavitt, Phillip Miller. Promotes the knowledge, appreciation, and development of Jewish music, past and present, for professional and lay audiences; seeks to raise the standards of composition and performance in Jewish music, to encourage research, and to sponsor performances of new and rarely heard works. *Musica Judaica Journal.*

ASSOCIATION FOR THE SOCIAL SCIENTIFIC STUDY OF JEWRY (1971). University of Connecticut, Dept. of Sociology, Center for Judaic Studies, Storrs, CT 06269-2068. (203)486-2271. FAX: (203)486-6356. Pres. Arnold Dashefsky; V.-Pres. Sherry Israel; Sec.-Treas. J. Alan Winter. Arranges academic sessions and facilitates communication among social scientists studying Jewry through meetings, newsletter, and related materials. *Contemporary Jewry; ASSSJ Newsletter.*

ASSOCIATION OF JEWISH BOOK PUBLISHERS (1962). 838 Fifth Ave., NYC 10021. (212)-249-0100. Pres. Rabbi Elliot L. Stevens. As a nonprofit group, provides a forum for discussion of mutual problems by publishers, authors, and other individuals and institutions concerned with books of Jewish interest. Provides national and international exhibit opportunities for Jewish books. *Combined Jewish Book Catalog.*

ASSOCIATION OF JEWISH GENEALOGICAL SOCIETIES (1988). 1485 Teaneck Rd., Teaneck, NJ 07666. (201)837-2700. FAX: (201)837-8506. Pres. Gary Mokotoff. Confederation of over 35 Jewish Genealogical Societies (JGS) in the U.S. and Canada. Encourages Jews to research their family history, promotes membership in the various JGSs, acts as representative of organized Jewish genealogy, implements projects of interest to persons researching their Jewish family history. Annual conference where members learn and exchange ideas. Each local JGS publishes its own newsletter.

ASSOCIATION OF JEWISH LIBRARIES (1965). c/o National Foundation for Jewish Culture, 330 Seventh Ave., 21st fl., NYC 10001. (212)629-0500. FAX: (212)678-8998. Pres. Linda P. Lerman; V.-Pres. and Pres.-Elect Ralph R. Simon. Seeks to promote and improve services and professional standards in Jewish libraries; disseminates Jewish library information and guidance; promotes publication of literature in the field; encourages the establishment of Jewish libraries and collections of Judaica and the choice of Judaica librarianship as a profession; cocertifies Jewish libraries (with Jewish Book Council). *AJL Newsletter; Judaica Librarianship.*

B'NAI B'RITH KLUTZNICK MUSEUM (1956). 1640 Rhode Island Ave., NW, Washington, DC 20036. (202)857-6583. FAX: (202)857-0980. Dir. Ori Z. Soltes. A center of Jewish art and history in nation's capital, maintains temporary and permanent exhibition galleries, permanent collection of Jewish ceremonial and folk art, B'nai B'rith International reference archive, outdoor sculpture garden, and museum shop, as well as the American Jewish Sports Hall of Fame. Provides exhibitions, tours, educational programs, research assistance, and tourist information. *Semiannual newsletter; permanent collection catalogue; exhibition brochures.*

CENTER FOR HOLOCAUST STUDIES, DOCUMENTATION & RESEARCH (1974). Merged into A Living Memorial to the Holocaust-Museum of Jewish Heritage, Jan. 1991.

CENTRAL YIDDISH CULTURE ORGANIZATION (CYCO), INC. (1943). 25 E. 21 St., 3rd fl., NYC 10010. (212)505-8305. Mgr. Jacob Schneidman. Promotes, publishes, and distributes Yiddish books; publishes catalogues.

CONFERENCE ON JEWISH SOCIAL STUDIES, INC. (formerly CONFERENCE ON JEWISH RELATIONS, INC.) (1939). 2112 Broadway, Rm. 206, NYC 10023. (212)724-5336. Publishes scientific studies on Jews in the modern world, dealing with such aspects as anti-Semitism, demography, economic stratification, history, philosophy, and political developments. *Jewish Social Studies.*

CONGREGATION BINA (1981). 600 W. End Ave., Suite 1-C, NYC 10024. (212)873-4261. Pres. Joseph Moses; Exec. V.-Pres. Moses Samson; Hon. Pres. Samuel M. Daniel; Secy. Gen. Elijah E. Jhirad. Serves the religious, cultural, charitable, and philanthropic needs of the Children of Israel who originated in India and now reside in the U.S. Works to foster and preserve the ancient traditions, customs, liturgy, music, and folklore of Indian Jewry and to maintain needed institutions. *Kol Bina.*

CONGRESS FOR JEWISH CULTURE (1948). 25 E. 21 St., NYC 10010. (212)505-8040. Co-pres.'s Prof. Yonia Fain, Dr. Barnett Zumoff; Exec. Dir. Michael Skakun. An umbrella group comprising 16 constituent organizations; perpetuates and enhances Jewish creative expression in the U.S. and abroad; fosters all aspects of Yiddish cultural life through the publication of the journal *Zukunft,* the conferring of literary awards, commemoration of the Holocaust and the martyrdom of the Soviet Jewish writers under Stalin, and a series of topical readings, scholarly conferences, symposiums, and concerts. *Zukunft.*

ELAINE KAUFMAN CULTURAL CENTER (1952; formerly HEBREW ARTS CENTER). 129 W. 67 St., NYC 10023. (212)362-8060. FAX: (212)874-7865. Chmn. Lewis Kruger; Pres. Alvin E. Friedman; Exec. Dir. Lydia Kontos. Offers instruction in music, dance, art, and theater to children and adults, combining Western culture with Jewish traditions. Presents frequent performances of Jewish and general music by leading artists and ensembles in its Merkin Concert Hall and Ann Goodman Recital Hall. The Birnbaum Library houses Jewish music scores and reference books. *Kaufman Cultural Center News; bimonthly concert calendars; catalogues and brochures.*

HEBREW ARTS CENTER (*see* Elaine Kaufman Cultural Center)

HEBREW CULTURE FOUNDATION (1955). 110 E. 59 St., NYC 10022. (212)339-6000. Chmn. Milton R. Konvitz; Sec. Herman L. Sainer. Sponsors the introduction and strengthening of Hebrew language and literature courses in institutions of higher learning in the United States.

HISTADRUTH IVRITH OF AMERICA (1916; reorg. 1922). 47 W. 34 St., Rm. 609, NYC 10001. (212)629-9443. Pres. Dr. David Sidorsky; Exec. V.-Pres. Dr. Aviva Barzel. Emphasizes the primacy of Hebrew in Jewish life, culture, and education; aims to disseminate knowledge of written and spoken Hebrew in the Diaspora, thus building a cultural bridge between the State of Israel and Jewish communities throughout the world. *Hadoar; Lamishpaha; Tov Lichtov; Hebrew in America.*

HOLOCAUST CENTER OF THE UNITED JEWISH FEDERATION OF GREATER PITTSBURGH (1980). 242 McKee Pl., Pittsburgh, PA 15213. (412)682-7111. Pres. Holocaust Comm. Jeffrey W. Letwin; Bd. Chmn. David Shapira; Dir. Linda F. Hurwitz. Develops programs and provides resources to further understanding of the Holocaust and its impact on civilization. Maintains a library, archive; provides speakers, educational materials; organizes community programs.

HOLOCAUST MEMORIAL RESOURCE & EDUCATION CENTER OF CENTRAL FLORIDA (1981). 851 N. Maitland Ave., Maitland, FL 32751. (407)628-0555. FAX: (407)-645-1172. Pres. Dr. William Michael Hooks; Exec. V.-Pres. Tess Wise. An interfaith educational center devoted to teaching the lessons of the Holocaust. Houses permanent multimedia educational exhibit; maintains library of books, videotapes, films, and other visuals to serve the entire educational establishment; offers lectures, teacher training, and other activities. *Newsletter.*

INSTITUTE FOR RUSSIAN JEWRY, INC. (1989). PO Box 96, Flushing, NY 11367. (718)969-0911. Exec. Dir. Rosa Irgal. Disseminates knowledge of Judaism in Russian language, from historical and cultural perspectives; promotes knowledge of the religious and cultural heritage of Russian Jews through Russian folk and fine art exhibits, lecture series, music and dance workshops.

INTERNATIONAL JEWISH MEDIA ASSOCIATION (1987). U.S.: c/o St. Louis Jewish Light, 12 Millstone Campus Dr., St. Louis, MO 63146. (314)432-3353. FAX: (314)-432-0515. Israel: PO Box 92, Jerusalem (2-533-296). Pres. Robert A. Cohn; Staff Consultant Malcolm Rodman. A worldwide network of Jewish journalists in the Jewish and general media, which seeks to provide a forum for the exchange of materials and ideas, and to enhance the stature of Jewish media and journalists. *Presidents Bulletin; proceedings of international conferences on Jewish media.*

JCC ASSOCIATION LECTURE BUREAU (1922; formerly JWB). 15 E. 26 St., NYC 10010-1579. (212)532-4949. FAX: (212)481-4174. Dir. Sesil Lissberger. A nonprofit program service of JCC Association of N. America providing lecturers and performers from a broad range of Jewish and public life; also offers photo exhibits to stimulate Jewish programming of communal organizations. *The Jewish Arts—A Listing of Performers; Learning for Jewish Living—A Listing of Lecturers; Available Lecturers from Israel; Lecturers on the Holocaust.*

JEWISH ACADEMY OF ARTS AND SCIENCES, INC. (1926). 888 Seventh Ave., Suite 403, NYC 10106. (212)757-1627. Acting Pres. Milton Handler; Hon. Pres. Abraham I.

Katsh; Dir./Treas. Zvi Levavy. An honor society of Jews who have attained distinction in the arts, sciences, professions, and communal endeavors. Encourages the advancement of knowledge; stimulates scholarship, with particular reference to Jewish life and thought; recognition by election to membership and/or fellowship; publishes papers delivered at annual convocations.

JEWISH BOOK COUNCIL (1943). 15 E. 26 St., NYC 10010. (212)532–4949. Pres. Leonard S. Gold; Dir. Paula Gribetz Gottlieb. Promotes knowledge of Jewish books through dissemination of booklists, program materials; sponsors Jewish Book Awards, Jewish Book Month; presents literary awards and library citations; cooperates with publishers of Jewish books. *Jewish Book Annual; Jewish Books in Review; Jewish Book World.*

JEWISH HERITAGE PROJECT (1981). 150 Franklin St., #1W, NYC 10013. (212) 925–9067. FAX: (212) 925–9067. Exec. Dir. Alan Adelson. Strives to bring to the broadest possible audience authentic works of literary and historical value relating to Jewish history and culture. Distributor of the film *Lodz Ghetto*, which it developed, as well as its companion volume *Lodz Ghetto: Inside a Community Under Siege.*

JEWISH MUSEUM (1904, under auspices of Jewish Theological Seminary of America). Exhibitions, programs, and shop at the New-York Historical Society through 1992: 170 Central Park W., NYC; offices c/o American Bible Society Bldg., 1865 Broadway, NYC 10023. (212)399–3430. Dir. Joan H. Rosenbaum; Bd. Chmn. H. Axel Schupf. "New," expanded museum will open in 1993. Repository of the largest collection of Judaica—paintings, prints, photographs, sculpture, coins, medals, antiquities, textiles, and other decorative arts—in the Western Hemisphere. Includes the National Jewish Archive of Broadcasting. Tours, lectures, film showings, and concerts; special programs for children. *Special exhibition catalogues; annual report.*

JEWISH MUSIC COUNCIL (1944). 15 E. 26 St., NYC 10010. (212)532–4949. Chmn. Joseph Hurwitz; Coord. Paula Gribetz Gottlieb. Promotes Jewish music activities nationally; annually sponsors and promotes the Jewish Music season; encourages par-

ticipation on a community basis. *Jewish Music Notes* and numerous music resource publications for national distribution.

JEWISH PUBLICATION SOCIETY (1888). 1930 Chestnut St., Philadelphia, PA 19103. (215)564–5925. FAX:(215)564–6640. Pres. Martin D. Cohn; Exec. V.-Pres. Rabbi Michael A. Monson. Publishes and disseminates books of Jewish interest for adults and children; titles include contemporary literature, classics, art, religion, biographies, poetry, and history. AMERICAN JEWISH YEAR BOOK (with American Jewish Committee); *The Bookmark; JPS Catalogue.*

JUDAH L. MAGNES MUSEUM—JEWISH MUSEUM OF THE WEST (1962). 2911 Russell St., Berkeley, CA 94705. (415)849–2710. FAX: (415)849–3650. Pres. Gary J. Shapiro; Dir. Seymour Fromer. Collects, preserves, and makes available Jewish art, culture, history, and literature from throughout the world. Permanent collections of fine and ceremonial art, rare Judaica library, Western Jewish History Center (archives), the museum changing exhibits, traveling exhibits, docent tours, lectures, numismatics series, poetry award, a museum shop. *Magnes News; special exhibition catalogues; scholarly books.*

JUDAICA CAPTIONED FILM CENTER, INC. (1983). PO Box 21439, Baltimore, MD 21208–0439. Voice (after 4 PM) (410)-655–4750; TDD (410)655–6767. Pres. Lois Lilienfeld Weiner. Developing a comprehensive library of captioned and subtitled films and tapes on Jewish subjects; distributes them to organizations serving the hearing-impaired, including mainstream classes and senior adult groups, on a free-loan, handling/shipping-charge-only basis. *Quarterly newsletter.*

LEAGUE FOR YIDDISH, INC. (1979). 200 W. 72 St., Suite 40, NYC 10023. (212)787–6675. Pres. Dr. Sadie Turak; Exec. Dir. Dr. Mordkhe Schaechter. Encourages the development and use of Yiddish as a living language; promotes its modernization and standardization; publishes linguistic resource materials. *Afn Shvel (quarterly).*

LEO BAECK INSTITUTE, INC. (1955). 129 E. 73 St., NYC 10021. (212)744–6400. FAX: (212)988–1305. Pres. Ismar Schorsch; Exec. Dir. Robert A. Jacobs. A library, archive, and research center for the history of German-speaking Jewry. Offers lectures, exhibits, faculty seminars; publishes a series of monographs, yearbooks, and journals. *LBI Bulletin; LBI News; LBI Yearbook; LBI Memorial Lecture; LBI Library & Archives News.*

A LIVING MEMORIAL TO THE HOLO-CAUST–MUSEUM OF JEWISH HERITAGE (1984). 342 Madison Ave., Suite 706, NYC 10173. (212)687–9141. FAX: (212)-573–9847. Cochmn. George Klein, Hon. Robert M. Morgenthau, Peter Cohen, Sen. Manfred Ohrenstein; Museum Dir. David Altshuler. The museum will be New York's principal public memorial to the six million Jews murdered during the Holocaust. Scheduled to open in 1994, it will include permanent and temporary exhibition galleries, a computerized interactive learning center, a Memorial Hall, and education facilities. *Brochures; bimonthly newsletter.*

MAALOT (1987). 1719 Wilmart St., Rockville, MD 20852. (301)231–9067. FAX: (301)984–9031. Pres./Exec. Off. David Shneyer. An educational program established to train individuals in Jewish music, the liturgical arts, and the use, design, and application of Jewish customs and ceremonies. Offers classes, seminars, and an independent study program.

MARTYRS MEMORIAL & MUSEUM OF THE HOLOCAUST OF THE JEWISH FEDERATION COUNCIL OF GREATER LOS ANGELES (1963; reorg. 1978). 6505 Wilshire Blvd., 12th fl., Los Angeles, CA 90048. (213)651–3175. FAX: (213)852–1494. Chmn. Jack I. Salzberg; Cochmn. Dr. Sam Goetz; Dir. Dr. Michael Nutkiewicz. A photo-narrative museum and resource center dedicated to Holocaust history, issues of genocide and prejudice, and curriculum development. *Pages (quarterly newsletter).*

MEMORIAL FOUNDATION FOR JEWISH CULTURE, INC. (1964). 15 E. 26 St., NYC 10010. (212)679–4074. Pres. the Right Hon., the Lord Jakobovits; Exec. V.-Pres. Jerry Hochbaum. Through the grants that it awards, encourages Jewish scholarship and Jewish education, supports communities that are struggling to maintain their Jewish identity, makes possible the training of Jewish men and women for professional careers in communal service in Jewishly deprived communities, and stimulates the documentation, commemoration, and teaching of the Holocaust.

NATIONAL FOUNDATION FOR JEWISH CULTURE (1960). 330 Seventh Ave., 21st fl., NYC 10001. (212)629–0500. FAX: (212)-629–0508. Pres. Sandra Weiner; Exec. Dir. Richard A. Siegel. The leading Jewish organization devoted to promoting Jewish culture in the U.S. Administers the Council of American Jewish Museums, the Council of Archives and Research Libraries in Jewish Studies, and the Council of Jewish Theatres; supports Jewish scholarship through Doctoral Dissertation Fellowships; provides funding to major Jewish cultural institutions through the Joint Cultural Appeal; organizes conferences, symposia, and festivals in the arts and humanities. *Jewish Cultural News.*

NATIONAL YIDDISH BOOK CENTER (1980). Old East Street School, Amherst, MA 01002. (413)256–1241. FAX: (413)253–4261. Pres. Aaron Lansky; Exec. Dir. Stephen Hays. Collects and disseminates Yiddish books; conducts activities contributing to the revitalization of Yiddish culture in America. *Der Pakn-treger/The Book Peddler.*

ORTHODOX JEWISH ARCHIVES (1978). 84 WILLIAM ST., NYC 10038. (212) 797-9000. Dir. Rabbi Moshe Kolodny. Founded by Agudath Israel of America; houses historical documents, publications, and photos relating to the growth of Orthodox Jewry in the U.S. and the correlating history of Orthodox communities in Europe, Israel, and elsewhere. Of special note are its holdings relating to rescue activities organized during the Holocaust.

RESEARCH FOUNDATION FOR JEWISH IMMIGRATION, INC. (1971). 570 Seventh Ave., NYC 10018. (212)921–3871. Pres. Curt C. Silberman; Sec. and Coord. of Research Herbert A. Strauss; Archivist Dennis E. Rohrbaugh. Studies and records the history of the migration and acculturation of Central European German-speaking Jewish and non-Jewish Nazi persecutees in various resettlement countries worldwide, with special emphasis on the American experience. *International Biographical Dictionary of Central European Emigrés, 1933–1945; Jewish Immigrants of the Nazi Period in the USA.*

ST. LOUIS CENTER FOR HOLOCAUST STUDIES (1977). 12 Millstone Campus Dr., St. Louis, MO 63146. (314)432–0020. Chmn. Leo Wolf; Dir. Rabbi Robert Sternberg.

Develops programs and provides resources and educational materials to further an understanding of the Holocaust and its impact on civilization. *Audio Visual and Curriculum Resources Guides.*

SEPHARDIC HOUSE (1978). 8 W. 70 St., NYC 10023. (212)873–0300. Bd. Chmn. Rabbi Marc D. Angel; Exec. Dir. Janice E. Ovadiah. A cultural organization dedicated to fostering Sephardic history and culture; sponsors a wide variety of classes and public programs; publication program disseminates materials of Sephardic value; outreach program to communities outside of the New York area; program bureau provides program ideas, speakers, and entertainers. *Sephardic House Newsletter.*

SIMON WIESENTHAL CENTER, Los Angeles, ÇA (*see* Yeshiva University)

SKIRBALL MUSEUM, HEBREW UNION COLLEGE (1913; 1972 in Calif.). 3077 University Ave., Los Angeles, CA 90007. (213)-749–3424. FAX: (213)747-6128. Dir. Nancy Berman; Curator Barbara Gilbert. Collects, preserves, researches, and exhibits art and artifacts made by or for Jews, or otherwise associated with Jews and Judaism. Provides opportunity to faculty and students to do research in the field of Jewish art. *Catalogues of exhibits and collections.*

SOCIETY FOR THE HISTORY OF CZECHOSLOVAK JEWS, INC. (1961). 87–08 Santiago St., Holliswood, NY 11423. (718)468–6844. Pres. and Ed. Lewis Weiner; Sec. Joseph Abeles. Studies the history of Czechoslovak Jews; collects material and disseminates information through the publication of books and pamphlets. *The Jews of Czechoslovakia (3 vols.); Review I; Review II; Review III; Review IV.*

SOCIETY OF FRIENDS OF THE TOURO SYNAGOGUE, NATIONAL HISTORICAL SHRINE, INC. (1948). 85 Touro St., Newport, RI 02840. (401)847–4794. Pres. Jacob Temkin; Coord. Kirsten L. Mann. Helps maintain Touro Synagogue as a national historic site, opening and interpreting it for visitors; promotes public awareness of its preeminent role in the tradition of American religious liberty; annually commemorates George Washington's letter of 1790 to the Hebrew Congregation of Newport. *Society Update.*

SPERTUS MUSEUM, SPERTUS COLLEGE OF JUDAICA (1968). 618 S. Michigan Ave., Chicago, IL 60605. (312)922–9012. FAX: (312)922–6406. Pres. Spertus College, Dr. Howard A. Sulkin; Museum Dir. Dr. Morris A. Fred. The largest, most comprehensive Judaic museum in the Midwest with 12,000 square feet of exhibit space and a permanent collection of some 3,000 works spanning 3,500 years of Jewish history. Also includes the Zell Holocaust Memorial, Field Gallery of Contemporary Art, changing special exhibitions, and the Rosenbaum Children's Artifact Center, plus traveling exhibits for Jewish educators, life-cycle workshops, programs for seniors and the disabled, and community-generated art projects. *Newsletter; exhibition catalogues; educational pamphlets.*

TOURO NATIONAL HERITAGE TRUST (1984). 85 Touro St., Newport, RI 02840. (401)847-0810. Pres. Bernard Bell; Exec. Dir. Kirsten L. Mann. Works to establish national conference center within Touro compound; sponsors Touro Fellow through John Carter Brown Library; presents seminars and other educational programs; promotes knowledge of the early Jewish experience in this country within the climate of religions which brought it about.

UNITED STATES HOLOCAUST MEMORIAL COUNCIL (1980). 2000 L St., NW, Suite 588, Washington, DC 20036. (202)653–9220. Chmn. Harvey M. Meyerhoff; Exec. Dir. Sara J. Bloomfield. Established by Congress as an independent federal establishment, to plan, build and operate the United States Holocaust Memorial Museum in Washington, DC, which will open in April 1993, and to encourage and sponsor observances of an annual, national, civic commemoration of the victims of the Holocaust known as the Days of Remembrance. Also engages in Holocaust education and research programs. Composed of 55 members of all faiths and backgrounds appointed by the president, plus five U.S. senators and five members of the House of Representatives. *Newsletter (monthly); Directory of Holocaust Institutions in the U.S. and Canada.*

YESHIVA UNIVERSITY MUSEUM (1973). 2520 Amsterdam Ave., NYC 10033. (212)-960–5390. Chmn. Bd. of Govs. Erica Jesselson; Dir. Sylvia A. Herskowitz. Collects, preserves, and interprets Jewish life and culture through changing exhibitions of ceremonial objects, paintings, rare books and documents, synagogue architecture, textiles, decorative arts, and photographs. Oral history archive. Special events, holiday workshops, live performances, lectures, etc. for adults and children. Guided tours and workshops are offered. *Seasonal calendars; special exhibition catalogues.*

YIDDISHER KULTUR FARBAND—YKUF (1937). 1133 Broadway, Rm. 1023, NYC 10010. (212)691–0708. Pres. and Ed. Itche Goldberg. Publishes a monthly magazine and books by contemporary and classical Jewish writers; conducts cultural forums; exhibits works by contemporary Jewish artists and materials of Jewish historical value; organizes reading circles. *Yiddishe Kultur.*

YIVO INSTITUTE FOR JEWISH RESEARCH, INC. (1925). 1048 Fifth Ave., NYC 10028. (212)535–6700. FAX: (212)879–9763. Chmn. Bruce Slovin; Exec. Dir. Samuel Norich. Engages in social and cultural research pertaining to East European Jewish life; maintains library and archives which provide a major international, national, and New York resource used by institutions, individual scholars, and the public; trains graduate students in Yiddish, East European, and American Jewish studies; offers exhibits, conferences, public programs; publishes books. *Yidishe Shprakh; YIVO Annual; YIVO Bleter; Yedies fun Yivo; Jewish Folklore and Ethnology Review.*

———, MAX WEINREICH CENTER FOR ADVANCED JEWISH STUDIES (1968). 1048 Fifth Ave., NYC 10028. (212)535–6700. FAX: (212)879–9763. Dean Allan Nadler. Provides advanced-level training in Yiddish language and literature, ethnography, folklore, linguistics, and history; offers guidance on dissertation or independent research. *YIVO Annual; YIVO Bleter; Jewish Folklore & Ethnology Review.*

ISRAEL-RELATED

ALYN—AMERICAN SOCIETY FOR HANDICAPPED CHILDREN IN ISRAEL (1934). 19 W. 44 St., NYC 10036. (212)869–8085. FAX: (212)768-0979. Pres. Caroline W. Halpern; Chmn. Simone P. Blum; Exec. Dir. Joan R. Mendelson. Supports the work of ALYN Hospital, long-term reha-

bilitation center for severely orthopedically handicapped children, located in Jerusalem. It serves as home, school, and hospital for its patients, with a long-term goal for them of independent living.

AMERICA-ISRAEL CULTURAL FOUNDATION, INC. (1939). 41 E. 42 St., Suite 608, NYC 10017. (212)557–1600. FAX: (212)-557-1611. Bd. Chmn. Isaac Stern; Pres. Carl Glick. Supports and encourages the growth of cultural excellence in Israel through grants to cultural institutions; scholarships to gifted young artists and musicians. *Hadashot newsletter.*

AMERICA-ISRAEL FRIENDSHIP LEAGUE, INC. (1971). 134 E. 39 St., NYC 10016. (212)213–8630. FAX: (212)683-3475. Pres. Samuel M. Eisenstat; Exec. V.-Pres. Ilana Artman. A nonsectarian, nonpartisan organization which seeks to broaden the base of support for Israel among Americans of all faiths and backgrounds. Activities include educational exchanges, tours of Israel for American leadership groups, symposia and public education activities, and the dissemination of printed information. *Newsletter.*

AMERICAN ASSOCIATES, BEN-GURION UNIVERSITY OF THE NEGEV (1973). 342 Madison Ave., Suite 1924, NYC 10173. (212)-687–7721. FAX: (212)370-0686. Pres. Harold L. Oshry; Exec. V.-Pres. Dr. Lee Katz. Bd. Chmn. Michael W. Sonnenfeldt. Serves as the university's publicity and fund-raising link to the U.S.; is committed to programs for the absorption of Soviet émigrés in the Negev, publicizing university activities and curricula, securing student scholarships, transferring contributions, and encouraging American interest in the university. *AABGU Reporter; BGU Bulletin; Negev; Overseas Study Program Catalog.*

AMERICAN COMMITTEE FOR SHAARE ZEDEK HOSPITAL IN JERUSALEM, INC. (1949). 49 W. 45 St., Suite 1100, NYC 10036. (212)354–8801. Pres. Charles H. Bendheim; Bd. Chmn. Ludwig Jesselson; Sr. Exec. V.-Pres. Morris Talansky. Raises funds for the various needs of the Shaare Zedek Medical Center, Jerusalem, such as equipment and medical supplies, nurses' training, and research; supports exchange program between Shaare Zedek Medical Center and Albert Einstein College of Medicine, NY. *Heartbeat Magazine.*

AMERICAN COMMITTEE FOR SHENKAR COLLEGE IN ISRAEL, INC. (1971). 855 Ave. of the Americas, NYC 10001. (212) 947–1597. FAX: (212)643–8275. Pres. David Pernick; Exec. Dir. Charlotte Fainblatt. Raises funds for capital improvement, research and development projects, laboratory equipment, scholarships, lectureships, fellowships, and library/archives of fashion and textile design at Shenkar College in Israel, Israel's only fashion and textile technology college. Accredited by the Council of Higher Education, the college is the chief source of personnel for Israel's fashion and apparel industry. *Shenkar News.*

AMERICAN COMMITTEE FOR THE WEIZMANN INSTITUTE OF SCIENCE (1944). 51 Madison Ave., NYC 10010. (212)779–2500. FAX: (212)779–3209. Chmn. Alan A. Fischer; Pres. Saul Waring; Exec. V.-Pres. Bernard N. Samers. Through 14 regional offices in the U.S. raises funds for the Weizmann Institute in Rehovot, Israel, and disseminates information about its 800 ongoing scientific research projects. *Rehovot; Interface; Research.*

AMERICAN FRIENDS OF ASSAF HAROFEH MEDICAL CENTER (1975). 19 W. 44 St., Suite 1118, NYC 10036. (212)764–6130. FAX: (212)575–0408. Pres. Martin Lifland; Chmn. Kenneth Kronen; Exec. V.-Pres. Donald L. Gartner. Raises funds for the various needs of the Assaf Harofeh Medical Center in central Israel near Tel Aviv, such as equipment and medical supplies, medical training for immigrants, nurses' training, physiotherapy training, research, and construction of new facilities. *Newsletter.*

AMERICAN FRIENDS OF BAR-ILAN UNIVERSITY (1955). 91 Fifth Ave., Suite 200, NYC 10003. (212)337–1270. FAX: (212)337–1274. Chancellor Rabbi Emanuel Rackman; Chmn. Global Bd. of Trustees Aharon Meir; Pres. Amer. Bd. of Overseers Belda Lindenbaum; Exec. V.-Pres. Gen. Yehuda Halevy. Supports Bar-Ilan University, a traditionally oriented liberal arts and sciences institution, where all students must take Basic Jewish Studies courses as a requirement of graduation; located in Ramat-Gan, Israel, and chartered by the Board of Regents of the State of NY. *Update; Bar-Ilan News.*

AMERICAN FRIENDS OF BETH HATEFUTSOTH (1976). 110 E. 59 St., NYC 10022. (212)339–6000. FAX: (212)318–6176. Pres. Abraham Spiegel; V.-Pres. Sam E. Bloch; Exec. Dir. Gloria Golan. Supports the maintenance and development of Beth Hatefutsoth, the Nahum Goldmann Museum of the Jewish Diaspora in Tel Aviv, and its cultural and educational programs for youth and adults. Circulates its traveling exhibitions and provides various cultural programs to local Jewish communities. Includes the Douglas E. Goldman Jewish Genealogy Center (DOROT); the Center for Jewish Music, and the Grunstein Shamir Photodocumentation Center. *Beth Hatefutsoth quarterly newsletter.*

AMERICAN FRIENDS OF HAIFA UNIVERSITY (1972). 488 Madison Ave., 10th fl., NYC 10021. (212)838–8069. FAX: (212)838–3464. Pres. David I. Faust. Promotes, encourages, and aids higher and secondary education, research, and training in all branches of knowledge in Israel and elsewhere; aids in the maintenance and development of Haifa University; raises and allocates funds for the above purposes; provides scholarships; promotes exchanges of teachers and students. *Newsletter; Focus.*

AMERICAN FRIENDS OF TEL AVIV UNIVERSITY, INC. (1955). 360 Lexington Ave., NYC 10017. (212)687–5651. FAX: (212)-687–4085. Board Chmn. Stewart M. Colton; Pres. Saul B. Cohen; Exec. V.-Pres. Harriet Kendell Kessler. Promotes higher education at Tel Aviv University, Israel's largest and most comprehensive institution of higher learning. The university has a law school, medical school, and more than 50 research institutes, including the Moshe Dayan Center for Middle East & African Studies and the Jaffe Center for Strategic Studies. *Tel Aviv University News; Tau FAX Flash.*

AMERICAN FRIENDS OF THE HEBREW UNIVERSITY (1925; inc. 1931). 11 E. 69 St., NYC 10021. (212)472–9800. FAX: (212)-744–2324. Pres. Barbara A. Mandel; Bd. Chmn. Harvey M. Krueger; Exec. V.-Pres. Robert A. Pearlman. Fosters the growth, development, and maintenance of the Hebrew University of Jerusalem; collects funds and conducts programs of information throughout the U.S., highlighting the university's achievements and its significance. *News from the Hebrew University of Jerusalem; Scopus magazine.*

AMERICAN FRIENDS OF THE ISRAEL MUSEUM (1972). 10 E. 40 St., Suite 1208, NYC 10016. (212)683-5190. FAX: (212)-683-3187. Pres. Maureen Cogan; Exec. Dir. Michele Cohn Tocci. Raises funds for special projects of the Israel Museum in Jerusalem; solicits works of art for exhibition and educational purposes. *Newsletter.*

AMERICAN FRIENDS OF THE SHALOM HARTMAN INSTITUTE (1976). 280 Grand Ave., Englewood, NJ 07631. (201)894-0566. FAX: (201)894-0377. Pres. Robert P. Kogod; Dir. Rabbi Donniel Hartman; Admin. Dorothy Minchin. Supports the Shalom Hartman Institute, Jerusalem, an institute of higher education and research center, devoted to applying the teachings of classical Judaism to the issues of modern life. Founded in 1976 by David Hartman, the institute includes a Beit Midrash and centers for philosophy, theology, Halakhah, political thought, and medical science, an experimental school, and programs for lay leadership.

AMERICAN FRIENDS OF THE TEL AVIV MUSEUM OF ART (1974). 133 E. 58 St., Suite 704, NYC 10022. (212)593-5771. Cochmn. David Genser, Hanno Mott. Exec. Dir. Ursula Kalish. Raises funds for the Tel Aviv Museum of Art in Tel Aviv, Israel; enables Americans to better understand and become involved in Israeli art and culture.

AMERICAN FRIENDS/SARAH HERZOG MEMORIAL HOSPITAL-JERUSALEM (EZRATH NASHIM) (1895). 40 E. 34 St., Suite 907, NYC 10016. (212)725-8175. FAX: (212)-683-3871. Pres. Irwin S. Meltzer. Supports research, education, and patient care at Ezrath Nashim Association in Jerusalem, which includes a 290-bed hospital, comprehensive outpatient clinic, drug-abuse clinic, geriatric center, and the Jacob Herzog Psychiatric Research Center; Israel's only independent, nonprofit, voluntary geriatric and psychiatric hospital; used as a teaching facility by Israel's major medical schools. *Friend to Friend; To Open the Gates of Healing.*

AMERICAN ISRAEL PUBLIC AFFAIRS COMMITTEE (AIPAC) (1954). 440 First St., NW, Washington, DC 20001. (202)639-5200. FAX: (202)347-4921. Pres. David Steiner; Exec. Dir. Thomas A. Dine. Registered to lobby on behalf of legislation affecting U.S.-Israel relations; represents Americans who believe support for a secure Israel is in U.S. interest. Works for a strong U.S.-Israel relationship. *Near East Report; AIPAC Papers on U.S.-Israel Relations.*

AMERICAN-ISRAELI LIGHTHOUSE, INC. (1928; reorg. 1955). 30 E. 60 St., NYC 10022. (212)838-5322. Pres. Mrs. Leonard F. Dank; Sec. Frances Lentz. Provides education and rehabilitation for the blind and physically handicapped in Israel to effect their social and vocational integration into the seeing community; built and maintains Rehabilitation Center for the Blind (Migdal Or) in Haifa. *Tower.*

AMERICAN JEWISH LEAGUE FOR ISRAEL (1957). 130 E. 59 St., NYC 10022. (212)-371-1583. Pres. Rabbi Reuben M. Katz; Bd. Chmn. Joseph Landow. Seeks to unite all those who, notwithstanding differing philosophies of Jewish life, are committed to the historical ideals of Zionism; works, independently of class, party, or religious affiliation, for the welfare of Israel as a whole. Not identified with any political parties in Israel. Member, World Confederation of United Zionists. *Bulletin of the American Jewish League for Israel.*

AMERICAN PHYSICIANS FELLOWSHIP FOR MEDICINE IN ISRAEL (1950). 2001 Beacon St., Brookline, MA 02146. (617)232-5382. Pres. Leonard F. Gottlieb, MD. Exec. Dir. Daniel C. Goldfarb. Helps Israel become a major world medical center; secures fellowships for selected Israeli physicians and arranges lectureships in Israel by prominent American physicians; runs medical seminars in Israel; coordinates U.S. and Canadian medical and paramedical emergency volunteers to Israel; supports research and health-care projects in Israel. *APF News.*

AMERICAN RED MAGEN DAVID FOR ISRAEL, INC. (1940). 888 Seventh Ave., Suite 403, NYC 10106. (212)757-1627. FAX: (212)757-4662. Pres. Robert L. Sadoff, MD; Natl. Chmn. Louis Cantor; Exec. V.-Pres. Benjamin Saxe. An authorized tax-exempt organization; the sole support arm in the U.S. of Magen David Adom, Israel's Red Cross Service; raises funds for MDA's emergency medical services for Israel's military and civilian population, supplies ambulances, bloodmobiles, and mobile cardiac rescue units serving all hospitals and communities throughout Israel; supports MDA's 73 emergency medical clinics and helps provide training and equipment for volunteer emergency paramedical corps. *Lifeline.*

AMERICAN SOCIETY FOR TECHNION-ISRAEL INSTITUTE OF TECHNOLOGY (1940). 810 Seventh Ave., 24th fl., NYC 10019. (212)-262–6200. FAX: (212)262–6155. Pres. Lewis M. Weston; Natl. Chmn. Leonard Sherman; Exec. V.-Pres. Melvyn H. Bloom. Supports the work of the Technion-Israel Institute of Technology, Haifa, which trains nearly 10,000 students in 20 departments and a medical school, and conducts research across a broad spectrum of science and technology. *Technion USA.*

AMERICAN SOCIETY FOR THE PROTECTION OF NATURE IN ISRAEL (1986). 330 Seventh Ave., NYC 10001. (212)947–2820. FAX: (212)629–0509. Hon. Pres. Samuel W. Lewis. Seeks to increase the American public's awareness of, and support for, the critical conservation efforts conducted in Israel by the Society for the Protection of Nature in Israel (SPNI). Conducts educational programs and outdoor activities in the U.S.

AMERICAN SOCIETY FOR YAD VASHEM (1981). 48 W. 37 St., NYC 10018. (212)-564–9606. FAX: (212)268–0529. Chmn. Eli Zborowski; Exec. Dir. Selma Schiffer. Development arm of Yad Vashem, Jerusalem, the central international authority created by the Knesset in 1953 for the purposes of commemoration and education in connection with the Holocaust. *Martyrdom and Resistance (newsletter).*

AMERICAN ZIONIST FEDERATION (1939; reorg. 1949 and 1970). 110 E. 59 St., NYC 10022. (212)318–6100. FAX: (212)935–3578. Pres. Simon Schwartz; Exec. Dir. Karen Rubinstein. Coordinates the work of the Zionist constituency in the areas of education, *aliyah,* youth and young leadership and public and communal affairs. Seeks to involve the Zionist and broader Jewish community in programs and events focused on Israel and Zionism (e.g., Zionist Shabbat, Scholars-in-Residence, Yom Yerushalayim) and through these programs to develop a greater appreciation for the Zionist idea among American Jewry. Composed of 16 national Zionist organizations, 10 Zionist youth movements, and

affiliated organizations. Offices in Chicago, Los Angeles, New York. Groups in Baltimore, Detroit, Philadelphia, Pittsburgh, Rochester, Washington, DC. *HaMakor.*

AMERICAN ZIONIST YOUTH FOUNDATION, INC. (1963). 110 E. 59 St., NYC 10022. (212)751–6070. Pres. Rabbi Joseph P. Sternstein; Exec. Dir. Ruth Kastner. Heightens Zionist awareness among Jewish youth through programs and services geared to high-school and college-age youngsters. Sponsors educational tours to Israel, study in leading institutions; sponsors field workers on campus and in summer camps; prepares and provides specialists who present and interpret the Israel experience for community centers and federations throughout the country. *Activist Newsletter; Guide to Education and Programming Material; Programs in Israel.*

AMERICANS FOR A SAFE ISRAEL (1971). 147 E. 76 St., NYC 10021. (212)628–9400. FAX: (212)988–4065. Chmn. Herbert Zweibon. Seeks to educate Americans in Congress, the media, and the public in general about Israel's role as a strategic asset for the West; through meetings with legislators and the media, in press releases and publications, promotes the notion of Jewish rights to Judea and Samaria and the concept of "peace for peace" as an alternative to "territory for peace." *Outpost.*

AMERICANS FOR PEACE NOW (1984). 27 W. 20 St., 9th fl., NYC 10011. (212)645–6262. FAX: (212)929–3459. Pres. Jonathan Jacoby. Conducts educational programs and raises funds to support the Israeli peace movement, Shalom Achshav (Peace Now), and coordinates U.S. advocacy efforts through APN's Washington-based Center for Israeli Peace and Security. *National Newsletter.*

AMERICANS FOR PROGRESSIVE ISRAEL (1952). 224 W. 35 St., Suite 403, NYC 10001. (212)868–0386. Pres. Naftali Landesman. A socialist Zionist organization that calls for a just and durable peace between Israel and all its Arab neighbors, including the Palestinian people; works for the liberation of all Jews; seeks the democratization of Jewish communal and organizational life; promotes dignity of labor, social justice, and a deeper understanding of Jewish heritage. Affiliate of American Zionist Federation and World Union of Mapam, with fraternal ties to Hashomer

Hatzair and Kibbutz Artzi Federation of Israel. *Israel Horizons; API Newsletter.*

AMIT WOMEN (formerly AMERICAN MIZ-RACHI WOMEN) (1925). 817 Broadway, NYC 10003. (212)477-4720. Pres. Norma Holzer; Exec. Dir. Marvin Leff. The State of Israel's official *reshet* (network) for religious secondary technological education; conducts innovative children's homes and youth villages in Israel in an environment of traditional Judaism; promotes cultural activities for the purpose of disseminating Zionist ideals and strengthening traditional Judaism in America. *AMIT Woman.*

AMPAL—AMERICAN ISRAEL CORPORATION (1942). 10 Rockefeller Plaza, NYC 10020-1956. (212)586-3232. FAX: (212)649-1745. Pres. Lawrence Lefkowitz; Bd. Chmn. Michael Arnon. Finances and invests in industrial, agricultural, real estate, hotel, and tourist enterprises in Israel. *Annual report; quarterly reports.*

ARZA—ASSOCIATION OF REFORM ZION-ISTS OF AMERICA (1977). 838 Fifth Ave., NYC 10021. (212)249-0100. FAX: (212)-517-7968. Pres. Norman D. Schwartz; Exec. Dir. Rabbi Eric Yoffie. Individual Zionist membership organization devoted to achieving Jewish pluralism in Israel and strengthening the Israeli Reform movement. Chapter activities in the U.S. concentrate on these issues and on strengthening American public support for Israel. *ARZA Newsletter.*

BETAR ZIONIST YOUTH ORGANIZATION (1935). 218 E. 79 St., NYC 10021. (212)-353-8033. Central Shlihim Arie Salman, Tova Vagami; Dir. Glenn Mones. Organizes youth groups across North America to teach Zionism, Jewish pride, and love of Israel; sponsors summer programs in Israel for Jewish youth ages 13-21; sponsors Tagar Zionist Student Activist Movement on college campuses. *Etgar.*

BOYS TOWN JERUSALEM FOUNDATION OF AMERICA INC. (1948). 91 Fifth Ave., Suite 601, NYC 10003. (212)242-1118. FAX: (212)242-2190. Pres. Michael J. Scharf; Chmn. Josh S. Weston; V.-Chmn. Alexander S. Linchner; Exec. V.-Pres. Rabbi Ronald L. Gray. Raises funds for Boys Town Jerusalem, which was established in 1948 to offer a comprehensive academic, religious, and technical education to disadvantaged Israeli and immigrant boys from over 45 different countries, including Ethiopia, Russia, and Iran. Enrollment: over 1,400 students in jr. high school, academic and technical high school, and a college of applied engineering. *BTJ Newsbriefs; Your Town Magazine.*

CAMERA—COMMITTEE FOR ACCURACY IN MIDDLE EAST REPORTING IN AMER-ICA (1982). PO Box 428, Boston, MA 02258. (617) 789-3672. FAX: (617) 787-7853. Natl. Pres. Andrea Levin. Monitors and responds to media distortion in order to promote better understanding of Middle East events; urges members to alert the media to errors, omissions, and distortions; unites all friends of Israel regardless of politics or religion to correct unbalanced or inaccurate coverage of Middle East. *CAMERA Media Report (quarterly); CAMERA on Campus; Action Alerts.*

COUNCIL FOR A BEAUTIFUL ISRAEL ENVI-RONMENTAL EDUCATION FOUNDATION (1973). 350 Fifth Ave., 19th fl., NYC 10118. (212)947-5709. Pres. Alice M. Weiss; Admin. Dir. Donna Lindemann. A support group for the Israeli body, whose activities include education, town planning, lobbying for legislation to protect and enhance the environment, preservation of historical sites, the improvement and beautification of industrial and commercial areas, and renovating bomb shelters into parks and playgrounds. *Yearly newsletter.*

EMUNAH WOMEN OF AMERICA (formerly HAPOEL HAMIZRACHI WOMEN'S ORGA-NIZATION) (1948). 7 Penn Plaza, NYC 10001. (212)564-9045. FAX: (212)643-9731. Pres. Sondra H. Fisch; Exec. Dir. Shirley Singer. Maintains and supports 200 educational and social-welfare institutions in Israel within a religious framework, including day-care centers, kindergartens, children's residential homes, vocational schools for the underprivileged, senior-citizen centers, a college complex, and Holocaust study center. Also involved in absorption of Soviet and Ethiopian immigrants (recognized by Israeli government as an official absorption agency). *The Emunah Woman; Lest We Forget; Emunah Connection.*

FEDERATED COUNCIL OF ISRAEL INSTITU-TIONS—FCII (1940). 4702 15th Ave., Brooklyn, NY 11219. (718)972-5530. Bd. Chmn. Z. Shapiro; Exec. V.-Pres. Rabbi Julius Novack. Central fund-raising organization for over 100 affiliated institutions; handles and executes estates, wills, and bequests for the traditional institutions in Israel; clearinghouse for information on budget, size, functions, etc., of traditional educational, welfare, and philanthropic institutions in Israel, working cooperatively with the Israeli government and the overseas department of the Council of Jewish Federations. *Annual financial reports and statistics on affiliates.*

FRIENDS OF LABOR ISRAEL (1987). 27 W. 20 St., 9th fl., NYC 10011. (212)255–1796. FAX: (212)929–3459. Chmn. Rabbi Daniel Polish; Exec. Dir. Rabbi Stanley A. Ringler. American organization committed to a program of education in America and Israel on behalf of institutions, organizations, and projects in Israel designed to promote democracy, pluralism, social justice, and peace. FLI is an affinity group of the Israel Labor party and represents the concerns of progressive American Jews in Labor party circles. *Labor Political Briefs.*

FRIENDS OF THE ISRAEL DEFENSE FORCES (1981). 21 W. 38 St., 5th fl., NYC 10018. (212)575–5030. FAX: (212)575–7815. Bd. Chmn. Marvin Josephson. Sec. Stephen Rubin. Supports the Agudah Lema'an Hahayal, Israel's Assoc. for the Well-Being of Soldiers, founded in the early 1940s, which provides social, recreational, and educational programs for soldiers, special services for the sick and wounded, and much more.

FUND FOR HIGHER EDUCATION (1970). 1768 S. Wooster St., Los Angeles, CA 90035. (213)202–1879. Chmn. Amnon Barness; Chmn. Exec. Com. Max Candiotty. Raises funds and disseminates information in the interest of institutions of higher education in the U.S. and Israel. Over $18 million distributed to over 100 institutions of higher learning, including over $11 million in Israel and $6 million in the U.S. *In Response.*

GESHER FOUNDATION (1969). 421 Seventh Ave., #905, NYC 10001. (212) 564–0338. FAX: (212)967–2726. Pres. Matthew J. Maryles; Exec. V.-Pres. Hillel Wiener. Seeks to bridge the gap between Jews of various backgrounds in Israel by stressing the interdependence of all Jews. Runs encounter seminars for Israeli youth; distributes curricular materials for public schools; offers Jewish identity classes for Russian youth, and a video series in Russian and English on famous Jewish personalities.

GIVAT HAVIVA EDUCATIONAL FOUNDATION, INC. (1966). 27 W. 20 St., #902, NYC 10011. (212)255–2992. FAX: (212)-627–1287. Chmn. Bruno Aron. Supports programs in Israel to further Jewish-Arab rapprochement, narrow economic and educational gaps within Israeli society, and improve educational opportunities for various disadvantaged youth. Affiliated with the Givat Haviva Center of the Kibbutz Artzi Federation, the Menachem Bader Fund, and other projects. In the U.S., GHEF, Inc., sponsors educational seminars, public lectures and parlor meetings with Israeli speakers, as well as individual and group trips to Israel. *News from Givat Haviva; special reports.*

GOLDA MEIR ASSOCIATION (1984). 33 E. 67 St., NYC 10021. (212)570–1443. FAX: (212)737–4326. Chmn. Alfred H. Moses; Pres. Robert C. Klutznick. Consultant, Robert I. Evans: 2300 Computer Ave., Bldg. G., Willow Grove, PA, 19090. (215) 830–1406. FAX: (215) 657–5161. North American support group for the Israeli association, whose large-scale educational programs address the issues of democracy in Israel, Sephardi-Ashkenazi integration, religious pluralism, the peace process, and relations between Israeli Jews and Arabs. Its "Project Democracy" has been adapted to help new Soviet immigrants integrate into Israeli society by providing them an education in democratic ideals and principles. *Newsletter.*

HABONIM-DROR NORTH AMERICA (1934). 27 W. 20 St., 9th fl., NYC 10011. (212)-255–1796. Sec.-Gen. Melody Robens-Paradise; Exec. Off. Aryeh Valdberg. Fosters identification with pioneering in Israel; stimulates study of Jewish life, history, and culture; sponsors community-action projects, seven summer camps in North America, programs in Israel, and *garinei aliyah*. *Batnua; Progressive Zionist Journal; Bimat Hamaapilim.*

HADASSAH, THE WOMEN'S ZIONIST ORGANIZATION OF AMERICA, INC. (1912). 50 W. 58 St., NYC 10019. (212)355–7900. FAX: (212)303–8282. Pres. Deborah Kaplan; Exec. Dir. Beth Wohlgelernter. In America helps interpret Israel to the American people; provides basic Jewish education as a background for intelligent and creative Jewish living; sponsors Young Judaea/Hashachar, largest Zionist youth movement in U.S., which has four divisions: Young Judaea, Intermediate Judaea, Senior Judaea, and Hamagshimim; operates six Zionist youth camps in this country; supports summer and all-year courses in Israel. Maintains in Israel Hadassah-Hebrew University Medical Center for healing, teaching, and research; Hadassah College of Technology; and Hadassah Career Counseling Institute. *Update; Headlines; Hadassah Magazine; Textures; Bat Kol; The Catalyst; The American Scene.*

———, YOUNG JUDAEA/HASHACHAR (1909; reorg. 1967). 50 W. 58 St., NYC 10019. (212)355–7900. Natl. Dir. Glen Karonsky; Coord. Hamagshimim (college level) Michael Balaban; Pres. of Sr. Judaea (high-school level) Evan Shereck. Seeks to educate Jewish youth aged 9–27 toward Jewish and Zionist values, active commitment to and participation in the American and Israeli Jewish communities; maintains summer camps and year programs in Israel. *Hamagshimim Journal; Kol Hat'nua; The Young Judaean.*

HASHOMER HATZAIR, SOCIALIST ZIONIST YOUTH MOVEMENT (1923). 224 W. 35 St., Suite 403, NYC 10001. (212)929–4955. FAX: (212)627–1287. Sec. David Suskauer; Natl. Dir. Yossi Amir. Seeks to educate Jewish youth to an understanding of Zionism as the national liberation movement of the Jewish people. Promotes *aliyah* to kibbutzim. Affiliated with AZYF and Kibbutz Artzi Federation. Espouses socialist-Zionist ideals of peace, justice, democracy, and brotherhood. *Young Guard.*

INTERNS FOR PEACE (1976). 270 W. 89 St., NYC 10024. (212)580–0540. FAX: (212)-580–0693. Dir. Rabbi Bruce M. Cohen. An independent, nonprofit, nonpolitical organization, dedicated to fostering understanding and respect between Jewish and Arab citizens of Israel.

ISRAEL HISTADRUT FOUNDATION (1960). 276 Fifth Ave., Suite 901, NYC 10001. (212)683–5454. FAX: (212)213–9233. Pres. Herbert Rothman; Exec. V.-Pres. Alvin Smolin. Specializes in planned giving, which includes testamentary bequests, charitable trusts, and endowment funds that benefit over 85% of the people of Israel through Histadrut social-service agen-

cies: 17 major hospitals; over 1,300 medical, dental, and pharmaceutical clinics; several schools of medicine and nursing; 158 vocational trade schools; 6 senior-citizen geriatric centers; 5 children's villages; and 4 colleges.

JEWISH COMMITTEE FOR ISRAELI-PALESTINIAN PEACE (1982). PO Box 4991, Washington, DC 20008. (301)530–1737. Seth Grimes, Ellen Siegel, representatives. Promotes a two-state solution to the Israeli-Palestinian conflict to be achieved through negotiations with the PLO in order to ensure Israeli security and Palestinian rights. Sponsors educational and dialogue programs, writes articles and editorials, assists the Israeli peace movement. *Israeli-Palestinian Digest.*

JEWISH INSTITUTE FOR NATIONAL SECURITY AFFAIRS (JINSA) (1976). 1717 K St., NW, Suite 300, Washington, DC 22202. (202)833–0020. FAX: (202)296–6452. Pres. Sen. Rudy Boschwitz; Exec. Dir. Tom Neumann. A nonprofit, nonpartisan educational organization working within the American Jewish community to explain the link between American defense policy and the security of the State of Israel; and within the national security establishment to explain the key role Israel plays in bolstering American interests. *Security Affairs.*

JEWISH NATIONAL FUND OF AMERICA (1901). 42 E. 69 St., NYC 10021. (212)-879–9300. FAX: (212)517–3293. Pres. Ruth W. Popkin; Exec. V.-Pres. Dr. Samuel I. Cohen. Exclusive fund-raising agency of the world Zionist movement for the afforestation, reclamation, and development of the land of Israel, including construction of roads, parks, and recreational areas, preparation of land for new communities and industrial facilities; helps emphasize the importance of Israel in schools and synagogues throughout the U.S. *JNF Almanac; Land and Life.*

JEWISH PEACE LOBBY (1989). 8401 Colesville Rd., Suite 317, Silver Spring, MD 20910. (301)589–8764. FAX: (301)589–2722. Pres. Jerome M. Segal. A legally registered lobby promoting changes in U.S. policy vis-à-vis the Israeli-Palestinian conflict. Supports Israel's right to peace within secure borders; a political settlement based on mutual recognition of the right of self-determination of both peoples; a two-state solution as the most likely means to a stable peace. *Washington Action Alerts.*

KEREN OR, INC. (1956). 1133 Broadway, NYC 10010. (212)255–1180. Bd. Chmn. Dr. Edward L. Steinberg; Pres. Dr. Albert Hornblass; Exec. V.-Pres. Paul H. Goldenberg. Funds the Keren-Or Center for Multihandicapped Blind Children, at 3 Abba Hillel Silver St., Ramot, Jerusalem, housing and caring for 70 children, 1½ to 16 years of age. Provides long-term basic training, therapy, rehabilitative, and early childhood education to the optimum level of the individual; with major hospitals, is involved in research into causes of multihandicapped blind birth.

LABOR ZIONIST ALLIANCE (formerly FARBAND LABOR ZIONIST ORDER; now uniting membership and branches of POALE ZION—UNITED LABOR ZIONIST ORGANIZATION OF AMERICA and AMERICAN HABONIM ASSOCIATION) (1913). 33 E. 67 St., NYC 10021. (212)628–0042. Pres. Henry L. Feingold. Seeks to enhance Jewish life, culture, and education in U.S. and Canada; aids in building State of Israel as a cooperative commonwealth, and its Labor movement organized in the Histadrut; supports efforts toward a more democratic society throughout the world; furthers the democratization of the Jewish community in America and the welfare of Jews everywhere; works with labor and liberal forces in America. *Jewish Frontier; Yiddisher Kempfer.*

LEAGUE FOR LABOR ISRAEL (1938; reorg. 1961). 33 E. 67 St., NYC 10021. (212)628–0042. Pres. Henry L. Feingold; V.-Pres. Ben Cohen. Conducts Labor Zionist educational and cultural activities for youth and adults in the American Jewish community. Promotes educational travel to Israel.

LIKUD USA (1925). 4 East 34 St., 4th fl., NYC 10016. (212)447–7887. FAX: (212)-447–7492. Exec. Dir. David Borowich; Pres. George S. Meissner. Educates the Jewish community and the American public about the views of Israel's Likud party; encourages support for a strong, secure State of Israel in all of its territory. *The Likud Newsletter.*

MEDICAL DEVELOPMENT FOR ISRAEL (1982). 130 E. 59 St., NYC 10022. (212)-759–3370. FAX: (212)759–0120. Bd. Chmn. Howard M. Squadron; Pres. Dr. Samuel C. Klagsbrun. Raises funds to help improve the quality of health care in Israel, its primary goal the construction of the Children's Medical Center of Israel, a 224-bed tertiary care facility for the entire region. *Brochures and newsletters.*

MERCAZ U.S.A. (1979). 155 Fifth Ave., NYC 10010. (212)533–7800. Pres. Rabbi Matthew H. Simon; Exec. Dir. Renah L. Rabinowitz. The U.S. Zionist organization for Conservative/Masorti Judaism; works for religious pluralism in Israel, defending and promoting Conservative/Masorti institutions and individuals; fosters Zionist education and *aliyah* and develops young leadership. *Mercaz News & Views.*

NA'AMAT USA, THE WOMEN'S LABOR ZIONIST ORGANIZATION OF AMERICA, INC. (formerly PIONEER WOMEN/NA'AMAT) (1925; reorg. 1985). 200 Madison Ave., Suite 1808, NYC 10016. (212)725–8010. FAX: (212)447–5187. Pres. Harriet Green. Part of a world movement of working women and volunteers, NA'AMAT USA helps provide social, educational, and legal services for women, teenagers, and children in Israel. It also advocates legislation for women's rights and child welfare in the U.S., furthers Jewish education, and supports Habonim-Dror, the Labor Zionist youth movement. *NA'AMAT Woman magazine.*

NATIONAL COMMITTEE FOR LABOR ISRAEL—HISTADRUT (1923). 33 E. 67 St., NYC 10021. (212)628–1000. FAX: (212)-517–7478. Pres. Jay Mazur; Exec. V.-Pres. Yehuda Ebstein; Chmn. Trade Union Council Morton Bahr. Raises funds for the educational, health, social and cultural institutions of the Israeli Federation of Labor-Histadrut. Promotes relations between American trade unions and the Histadrut and the American Jewish community. *Backdrop Histadrut; Amal Newsletter.*

NEW ISRAEL FUND (1979). 1101 15 St., NW, Suite 304, Washington, DC 20005. (202)-223–3333. FAX: (202)659–2789. Pres. Mary Ann Stein; Exec. Dir. Norman S. Rosenberg. A partnership of Israelis and North Americans dedicated to strengthening democracy and advancing social justice in Israel. The Fund strengthens Israel's democratic fabric by providing funds and technical assistance to the independent, public-interest sector; cultivating a new generation of public-interest leaders; and educating citizens—both in Israel and abroad—to create a constituency for democracy. *Quarterly newsletter; annual report.*

PEC ISRAEL ECONOMIC CORPORATION (formerly PALESTINE ECONOMIC CORPORATION) (1926). 511 Fifth Ave., NYC 10017. (212)687-2400. Chmn. R. Recanati; Pres. Joseph Ciechanover; Sec.-Asst. Treas. William Gold. Primarily engaged in the business of organizing, financing, and administering business enterprises located in or affiliated with enterprises in the State of Israel, through holdings of equity securities and loans. *Annual report.*

PEF ISRAEL ENDOWMENT FUNDS, INC. (1922). 41 E. 42 St., Suite 607, NYC 10017. (212)599-1260. Chmn. Sidney A. Luria; Pres. Abraham J. Kremer; Sec. Harvey Brecher. Uses funds for educational, research, religious, health, and other philanthropic institutions in Israel. *Annual report.*

PIONEER WOMEN/NA'AMAT (*see* NA'AMAT USA)

POALE AGUDATH ISRAEL OF AMERICA, INC. (1948). 4405 13th Ave., Brooklyn, NY 11219. (718)435-5449. Pres. Rabbi Fabian Schonfeld; Exec. V.-Pres. Rabbi Moshe Malinowitz. Aims to educate American Jews to the values of Orthodoxy and *aliyah;* supports kibbutzim, trade schools, yeshivot, moshavim, kollelim, research centers, and children's homes in Israel. *PAI News; She'arim; Hamayan.*

———, WOMEN'S DIVISION OF (1948). Pres. Aliza Widawsky; Presidium: Sarah Ivanisky, Miriam Lubling, Bertl Rittenberg. Assists Poale Agudath Israel to build and support children's homes, kindergartens, and trade schools in Israel. *Yediot PAI.*

PROGRESSIVE ZIONIST CAUCUS (1982). 27 W. 20 St., 9th fl., NYC 10011. (212)675-1168. FAX: (212)929-3459. Dir. Alexandra Wall; Shaliach Aryeh Valdberg. A campus-based grass-roots organization committed to a progressive Zionist agenda. Students organize local and regional educational, cultural, and political activities, such as speakers, films, *Kabbalot Shabbat,* and Arab-Jewish dialogue groups. The PZC Kvutzat Aliyah is a support framework for individuals interested in *aliyah* to a city or town. *La'Inyan; Makor.*

PROJECT NISHMA (1988). 1225 15 St., NW, Washington, DC 20005. (202)462-4268. FAX: (202)462-3892. Cochmn. Theodore R. Mann, Edward Sanders, Henry Rosovsky; Exec. Dir. Thomas R. Smerling. Conducts educational programs on Israeli security and the peace process; arranges military briefings for Jewish leaders; publishes articles by senior Israeli defense experts; analyzes U.S. Jewish opinion; and articulates pragmatic positions. Sponsored by over 100 nationally active Jewish leaders from across the country.

RELIGIOUS ZIONISTS OF AMERICA. 25 W. 26 St., NYC 10010. (212)689-1414.

———, BNEI AKIVA OF NORTH AMERICA (1934). 25 W. 26 St., NYC 10010. (212)-889-5260. V.-Pres. Admin. Marc Haber; Natl. Dir. Noah Slomowitz. The only religious Zionist youth movement in North America, serving over 10,000 young people from grade school through graduate school in 16 active regions across the United States and Canada, six summer camps, seven established summer, winter, and year programs in Israel. Stresses communal involvement, social activism, leadership training, and substantive programming to educate young people toward a commitment to Judaism and Israel. *Akivon; Hamvaser; Pinkas Lamadrich; Daf Rayonot; Ma'Ohalai Torah; Zraim.*

———, MIZRACHI-HAPOEL HAMIZRACHI (1909; merged 1957). 25 W. 26 St., NYC 10010. (212)689-1414. FAX: (212)779-3043. Pres. Rabbi Sol Roth; Exec. V.-Pres. Israel Friedman. Disseminates ideals of religious Zionism; conducts cultural work, educational program, public relations; raises funds for religious educational institutions in Israel, including *yeshivot hesder* and Bnei Akiva. *Newsletters; Kolenu.*

———, MIZRACHI PALESTINE FUND (1928). 25 W. 26 St., NYC 10010. Chmn. Joseph Wilon; Sec. Israel Friedman. Fundraising arm of Mizrachi movement.

———, NATIONAL COUNCIL FOR TORAH EDUCATION OF MIZRACHI-HAPOEL HAMIZRACHI (1939). 25 W. 26 St., NYC 10010. Pres. Rabbi Israel Schorr; Dir. Rabbi Meyer Golombek. Organizes and supervises yeshivot and Talmud Torahs; prepares and trains teachers; publishes textbooks and educational materials; organizes summer seminars for Hebrew educators in cooperation with Torah Department of Jewish Agency; conducts ulpan. *Hazarkor; Chemed.*

———, NOAM-MIZRACHI NEW LEADERSHIP COUNCIL (formerly NOAM-HAMISHMERET HATZEIRA) (1970). 25 W. 26 St., NYC 10010. (212)684–6091. Chmn. Rabbi Marc Schneier; V.-Chmn. Sheon Karol. Develops new religious Zionist leadership in the U.S. and Canada; presents young religious people with various alternatives for settling in Israel through *garinei aliyah* (core groups); meets the religious, educational, and social needs of Jewish young adults and young couples. *Forum.*

SOCIETY OF ISRAEL PHILATELISTS (1948). 27436 Aberdeen, Southfield, MI 48076. (313)557–0887. Pres. Dr. Emil Dickstein; Exec. Sec. Irvin Girer. Promotes interest in, and knowledge of, all phases of Israel philately through sponsorship of chapters and research groups, maintenance of a philatelic library, and support of public and private exhibitions. *Israel Philatelist; monographs; books.*

STATE OF ISRAEL BONDS (1951). 730 Broadway, NYC 10003. (212)677–9650. Internatl. Chmn. David B. Hermelin; Pres. Ambassador Meir Rosenne. Seeks to provide large-scale investment funds for the economic development of the State of Israel through the sale of State of Israel bonds in the U.S., Canada, Western Europe, and Latin America.

THEODOR HERZL FOUNDATION (1954). 110 E. 59 St., NYC 10022. (212)752–0600. FAX: (212)826–8959. Chmn. Kalman Sultanik; Sec. Zelig Chinitz. Offers cultural activities, lectures, conferences, courses in modern Hebrew and Jewish subjects, Israel, Zionism, and Jewish history. *Midstream.*

———, HERZL PRESS. Chmn. Kalman Sultanik. Serves as "the Zionist Press of record," publishing books that are important for the light they shed on Zionist philosophy, Israeli history, contemporary Israel and the Diaspora, and the relationship between them. They are important as contributions to Zionist letters and history. *Midstream.*

THEODOR HERZL INSTITUTE. 110 E. 59 St., NYC 10022. (212)339-6000. Chmn. Jacques Torczyner; Dir. Ida Reich. Program geared to review of contemporary problems on Jewish scene here and abroad, presentation of Jewish heritage values in light of Zionist experience of the ages, study of modern Israel, and Jewish social research with particular consideration of history and impact of Zionism. Lectures, forums, Encounter with Creativity; musicales, recitals, concerts; holiday celebrations; visual art programs, Nouveau Artist Introductions. *Annual Program Preview; Herzl Institute Bulletin.*

UNITED CHARITY INSTITUTIONS OF JERUSALEM, INC. (1903). 1467 48 St., Brooklyn, NY 11219. (718)633–8469. Chmn. Rabbi Pollak. Raises funds for the maintenance of schools, kitchens, clinics, and dispensaries in Israel; free loan foundations in Israel.

UNITED ISRAEL APPEAL, INC. (1925). 110 E. 59 St., NYC 10022. (212)688–0800. FAX: (212)754–4293. Chmn. Norman H. Lipoff; Exec. V.-Chmn. Herman S. Markowitz. Provides funds raised by UJF/Federation campaigns in the U.S. to aid the people of Israel through the programs of the Jewish Agency for Israel, UIA's operating agent. Serves as link between American Jewish community and Jewish Agency for Israel; assists in resettlement and absorption of refugees in Israel, and supervises flow and expenditure of funds for this purpose. *Annual report; newsletters; brochures.*

UNITED STATES COMMITTEE SPORTS FOR ISRAEL, INC. (1948). 1926 Arch St., Philadelphia, PA 19103. (215)561–6900. Pres. Robert E. Spivak; Exec. Dir. Barbara G. Lissy. Sponsors U.S. participation in, and fields and selects U.S. team for, World Maccabiah Games in Israel every four years; promotes education and sports programs in Israel; provides funds and technical and material assistance to Wingate Institute for Physical Education and Sport in Israel; sponsors coaching programs in Israel. *USCSFI Newsletter; commemorative Maccabiah Games journal; financial report.*

VOLUNTEERS FOR ISRAEL (1982). 330 W. 42 St., NYC 10036-6902. (212)643–4848. FAX: (212)643–4855. Pres. Dr. Meyer Ashpitz; Natl. Coord. Arthur W. Stern. Provides aid to Israel through volunteer work, building lasting relationships between Israelis and Americans. Affords persons aged 18–70 the opportunity to participate in various duties currently performed by overburdened Israelis on IDF bases and in other settings, enabling them to meet and work closely with Israelis and to gain an inside view of Israeli life and culture. *Quarterly newsletter; information documents.*

WOMEN'S LEAGUE FOR ISRAEL, INC. (1928). 160 E. 56 St., NYC 10022. (212)838-1997. FAX: (212)888-5972. Pres. Trudy Miner; Sr. V.-Pres. Annette Kay; Exec. Dir. Dorothy Leffler. Promotes the welfare of young people in Israel; built and maintains Homes in Jerusalem, Haifa, Tel Aviv; Natanya Vocational Training and Rehabilitation Center, and the National Library of Social Work. Also many facilities and programs on the campuses of the Hebrew University. *WLI Bulletin.*

WORLD CONFEDERATION OF UNITED ZIONISTS (1946; reorg. 1958). 130 E. 59 St., NYC 10022. (212)371-1452. Copres. Bernice S. Tannenbaum, Kalman Sultanik, Melech Topiol. Promotes Zionist education, sponsors nonparty youth movements in the Diaspora, and strives for an Israel-oriented creative Jewish survival in the Diaspora. *Zionist Information Views.*

WORLD ZIONIST ORGANIZATION—AMERICAN SECTION (1971). 110 E. 59 St., NYC 10022. (212)339-6000. FAX: (212)826-8959. Chmn. Bernice S. Tannenbaum; Exec. V.-Chmn. Zelig Chinitz. As the American section of the overall Zionist body throughout the world, it operates primarily in the field of *aliyah* from the free countries, education in the Diaspora, youth and Hechalutz, organization and information, cultural institutions, publications; conducts a worldwide Hebrew cultural program including special seminars and pedagogic manuals; disperses information and assists in research projects concerning Israel; promotes, publishes, and distributes books, periodicals, and pamphlets concerning developments in Israel, Zionism, and Jewish history. *Midstream; The Zionist Voice.*

———, DEPARTMENT OF EDUCATION AND CULTURE (1948). 110 E. 59 St., NYC 10022. (212)339-6000. FAX: (212)826-8959. Renders educational services to boards and schools: study programs, books, AV aids, instruction, teacher intraining service. Judaic and Hebrew subjects. Annual National Bible Contest; Israel summer and winter programs for teachers and students.

———, NORTH AMERICAN ALIYAH MOVEMENT (1968). 110 E. 59 St., NYC 10022. (212)339-6060. FAX: (212)826-8959. Exec. Dir. Nellie Neeman. Promotes and facilitates *aliyah* and *klitah* from the U.S. and Canada to Israel; serves as a social framework for North American immigrants to Israel. *Aliyon; NAAM Newsletter; Coming Home.*

ZIONIST ORGANIZATION OF AMERICA (1897). ZOA House, 4 E. 34 St., NYC 10016. (212)481-1500. FAX: (212)481-1515. Pres. Jim Schiller; Exec. V.-Pres. Paul Flacks. Seeks to safeguard the integrity and independence of Israel, assist in its economic development, and foster the unity of the Jewish people and the centrality of Israel in Jewish life in the spirit of General Zionism. In Israel, owns and maintains both the ZOA House in Tel Aviv, a cultural center, and the Kfar Silver Agricultural and Technical High School in Ashkelon, with a full-time student enrollment of 700 students. Kfar Silver, under the supervision of the Israel Ministry of Education, focuses on academic studies, vocational training, and programs for foreign students. *American Zionist Magazine; Zionist Information Service Weekly News Bulletin (ZINS); Public Affairs Action Guidelines; Public Affairs Action Report for ZOA Leaders.*

OVERSEAS AID

AMERICAN ASSOCIATION FOR ETHIOPIAN JEWS (1969). 1836 Jefferson Place, NW, Washington, DC 20036. (202)223-6838. FAX: (202)223-2961. Pres. Nathan Shapiro; Exec. Dir. William Recant. Informs world Jewry about the plight of Ethiopian Jews; advocates reunification with family members in Israel as a major priority; provides aid in refugee areas and Ethiopia; and helps resettlement in Israel. *Release; Newsline.*

AMERICAN FRIENDS OF THE ALLIANCE ISRAÉLITE UNIVERSELLE, INC. (1946). 420 Lexington Ave., Suite 1733, NYC 10170. (212)808-5437. FAX: (212)983-0094. Pres. Henriette Beilis; Exec. Dir. Warren Green. Participates in educational and human-rights activities of the AIU and supports the Alliance System of Jewish schools, teachers' colleges, and remedial programs in Israel, North Africa, the Middle East, Europe, and Canada. *Alliance Review.*

AMERICAN JEWISH JOINT DISTRIBUTION COMMITTEE, INC.—JDC (1914). 711 Third Ave., NYC 10017. (212)687–6200. FAX: (212)370–5467. Pres. Sylvia Hassenfeld; Exec. V.-Pres. Michael Schneider. Provides assistance to Jewish communities in Europe, Asia, Africa, and the Mideast, including welfare programs for Jews in need. Current concerns include Israel's social needs and absorption efforts for Soviet and Ethiopian immigrants; program expansions emphasize Jewish education in Eastern Europe and the former USSR and nonsectarian development and disaster assistance. *Annual report; JDC Challenge (newsletter); Historical Album.*

AMERICAN JEWISH PHILANTHROPIC FUND (1955). 386 Park Ave. S., 10th fl., NYC 10016. (212)OR9–0010. Pres. Charles J. Tanenbaum. Provides resettlement assistance to Jewish refugees primarily through programs administered by the International Rescue Committee at its offices in Western Europe and the U.S.

AMERICAN ORT FEDERATION, INC.—ORGANIZATION FOR REHABILITATION THROUGH TRAINING (1924). 817 Broadway, NYC 10003. (212)677–4400. FAX: (212)979–9545. Pres. Murray Koppelman; Exec. V.-Pres. Marshall M. Jacobson. Provides vocational/technical education to more than 220,000 students in 38 countries throughout the world. The largest ORT operation is in Israel, where 96,000 students attend 140 ORT schools and training centers. Expanded programs meet the needs of emigration of Jews from the Soviet Union: in Israel, special vocational training and job placement programs; in the U.S. special programs in New York, Chicago, and Los Angeles, with courses in English as a second language, bookkeeping, computer operations, and business math. Annual cost of program is approximately $187 million. *American ORT Federation Bulletin; American ORT Federation Yearbook.*

————, AMERICAN AND EUROPEAN FRIENDS OF ORT (1941). 817 Broadway, NYC 10003. (212)677–4400. FAX: (212)-979–9545. Pres. Simon Jaglom; Hon. Chmn. Jacques Zwibak. Promotes the ORT idea among Americans of European extraction; supports the Litton ORT Auto-Mechanics School in Jerusalem and the ORT School of Engineering in Jerusalem.

Promotes the work of the American ORT Federation.

————, AMERICAN LABOR ORT (1937). 817 Broadway, NYC 10003. (212)677–4400. FAX: (212)979–9545. Pres. Sam Fine. Promotes the vocational/technical training of more than 200,000 young people with the marketable skills they need to become productive members of society. Promotes the work of the American ORT Federation in 35 countries around the world.

————, BUSINESS AND PROFESSIONAL ORT (1937). 817 Broadway, NYC 10003. (212)-677–4400. FAX: (212)979–9545. Pres. Rose Seidel Kalich. Promotes work of American ORT Federation.

————, NATIONAL ORT LEAGUE (1914). 817 Broadway, NYC 10003. (212)677–4400. FAX: (212)979–9545. Pres. Judah Wattenberg; First V.-Pres. Tibor Waldman. Promotes ORT idea among Jewish fraternal *landsmanshaften* and individuals. Promotes the work of the American ORT Federation.

————, WOMEN'S AMERICAN ORT (1927). 315 Park Ave. S., NYC 10010. (212)505–7700. FAX: (212)674–3057. Pres. Sandy Isenstein; Exec. Dir. Thila Elpern. Advances the programs and self-help ethos of ORT through membership, fund raising, and educational activities. Supports 120 vocational schools, junior colleges and technical training centers in Israel; helps meet the educational needs of Jewish communities in 30 countries; spearheads growing ORT-U.S. school operations in New York, Los Angeles, and Chicago, and associate programs in Miami and Atlanta. Maintains a wide-ranging domestic agenda which espouses quality public education, combats anti-Semitism, champions women's rights, and promotes a national literacy campaign. *Women's American ORT Reporter; Close-Ups; Direct Line; The Highest Step; Women's American ORT Yearbook.*

CONFERENCE ON JEWISH MATERIAL CLAIMS AGAINST GERMANY, INC. (1951). 15 E. 26 St., Rm. 1355, NYC 10010. (212)-696–4944. FAX: (212)679–2126. Pres. Dr. Israel Miller; Sec. and Exec. Dir. Saul Kagan. Monitors the implementation of restitution and indemnification programs of the German Federal Republic (FRG) arising from its agreements with West Germany and most recently with the united Germany, especially with respect to the new restitution law for property lost by Jewish Nazi victims on the territory of the former German Democratic Republic. Administers Hardship Fund, which distributes funds appropriated by FRG for Jewish Nazi victims unable to file timely claims under original indemnification laws. Also assists needy non-Jews who risked their lives to help Jewish survivors.

HIAS, INC. (HEBREW IMMIGRANT AID SOCIETY) (1880; reorg. 1954). 333 Seventh Ave., NYC 10001-5004. (212)967-4100. FAX: (212)967-4442. Pres. Ben Zion Leuchter; Acting Exec. Dir. Dail Stolow. The international migration agency of the organized American Jewish community, assists in the rescue, protection and movement of Jewish refugees and other Jewish migrants. HIAS also responds to the migration needs of other peoples at risk and represents and advocates on behalf of all these peoples, Jewish and other. *Annual report; HIAS Reporter (quarterly newsletter).*

INTERNATIONAL COALITION FOR THE REVIVAL OF THE JEWS OF YEMEN (ICROJOY) (1989). 150 Nassau St., Suite 1238, NYC 10038. (212)766-5556. Chmn. Dr. Hayim Tawil; V.-Chmn. Shlomo Grafi; Sec. Lester Smerka. Seeks to enrich and assist the Jewish community of the Republic of Yemen.

JEWISH RESTITUTION SUCCESSOR ORGANIZATION (1947). 15 E. 26 St., Rm. 1355, NYC 10010. (212)696-4944. FAX: (212)-679-2126. Sec. and Exec. Dir. Saul Kagan. Acts to discover, claim, receive, and assist in the recovery of Jewish heirless or unclaimed property; to utilize such assets or to provide for their utilization for the relief, rehabilitation, and resettlement of surviving victims of Nazi persecution.

NORTH AMERICAN CONFERENCE ON ETHIOPIAN JEWRY (NACOEJ) (1982). 165 E. 56 St., NYC 10022. (212)752-6340. FAX: (212)980-5294. Pres. Joseph Feit; Exec. Dir. Barbara Ribakove Gordon. Provides assistance to Ethiopian Jews in Ethiopia and in Israel; informs American and other Jewish communities about their situation; works to increase involvement of world Jewish communities in assisting, visiting,

and learning about Ethiopian Jews. *Lifeline (membership newsletter).*

RE'UTH WOMEN'S SOCIAL SERVICE, INC. (1937). 130 E. 59 St., NYC 10022. (212)-836-1570. FAX: (212)836-1114. Pres. Rosa Strygler; Chmn. Ursula Merkin. Maintains in Israel subsidized housing for self-reliant elderly; old-age homes for more dependent elderly; Lichtenstadter Hospital for chronically ill and young accident victims not accepted by other hospitals; subsidized meals; Golden Age clubs. *Annual dinner journal.*

THANKS TO SCANDINAVIA, INC. (1963). 745 Fifth Ave., Rm. 603, NYC 10151. (212)-486-8600. FAX: (212)486-5735. Natl. Chmn. Victor Borge; Pres. Richard Netter; Exec. Dir. Judith S. Goldstein. Provides scholarships and fellowships at American universities and medical centers to students and doctors from Denmark, Finland, Norway, and Sweden in appreciation of the rescue of Jews from the Holocaust. Informs current and future generations of Americans and Scandinavians of these singular examples of humanity and bravery; funds books about this chapter of history. *Annual report.*

UNITED JEWISH APPEAL, INC. (1939). 99 Park Ave., Suite 300, NYC 10016. (212)-818-9100. FAX: (212)818-9509. Natl. Chmn. Marvin Lender; Chmn. Bd. of Trustees Morton A. Kornreich; Exec. V.-Pres. Rabbi Brian L. Lurie. The annual UJA/Federation Campaign is the primary instrument for the support of humanitarian programs and social services for Jews at home and abroad. In Israel, through the Jewish Agency, campaign funds help absorb, educate, and settle new immigrants, build villages and farms in rural areas, support innovative programs for troubled and disadvantaged youth, and promote the revitalization of distressed neighborhoods. The Operation Exodus Campaign provides funds for the settlement of Soviet and Ethiopian Jews in Israel. UJA/Federation funds also provide for the well-being of Jews and Jewish communities in 34 other countries around the world through the American Jewish Joint Distribution Committee. Constituent departments of the UJA include the Rabbinic Cabinet, University Programs Department, Women's Division, Young Leadership Cabinet, the Women's Young Leadership Cabinet, and the Business and Professional Women's Council.

RELIGIOUS AND EDUCATIONAL ORGANIZATIONS

AGUDATH ISRAEL OF AMERICA (1922). 84 William St., NYC 10038. (212)797–9000. Pres. Rabbi Moshe Sherer; Exec. V.-Pres. Rabbi Shmuel Bloom; Exec. Dir. Rabbi Boruch B. Borchardt. Mobilizes Orthodox Jews to cope with Jewish problems in the spirit of the Torah; sponsors a broad range of projects aimed at enhancing religious living, education, children's welfare, protection of Jewish religious rights, outreach to the assimilated and to Soviet Jewish arrivals, and social services. *Jewish Observer; Dos Yiddishe Vort; Coalition.*

———, AGUDAH WOMEN OF AMERICA–N'SHEI AGUDATH ISRAEL (1940). 84 William St., NYC 10038. (212)363–8940. Presidium Esther Bohensky, Aliza Grund; Exec. Dir. Rita Siff. Organizes Jewish women for philanthropic work in the U.S. and Israel and for intensive Torah education.

———, BOYS' DIVISION—PIRCHEI AGUDATH ISRAEL (1925). 84 William St., NYC 10038 (212)797–9000. Natl. Dir. Rabbi Joshua Silbermintz; Natl. Coord. Rabbi Moshe Weinberger. Educates Orthodox Jewish children in Torah; encourages sense of communal responsibility. Branches sponsor weekly youth groups and Jewish welfare projects. National Mishnah contests, rallies, and conventions foster unity on a national level. *Darkeinu; Leaders Guides.*

———, GIRLS' DIVISION—BNOS AGUDATH ISRAEL (1921). 84 William St., NYC 10038. (212)797–9000. Natl. Dirs. Devorah Streicher and Leah Zagelbaum. Sponsors regular weekly programs on the local level and unites girls from throughout the Torah world with extensive regional and national activities. *Newsletters.*

———, YOUNG MEN'S DIVISION—ZEIREI AGUDATH ISRAEL (1921). 84 William St., NYC 10038. (212)797–9000. Dir. Rabbi Labish Becker. Educates youth to see Torah as source of guidance for all issues facing Jews as individuals and as a people. Inculcates a spirit of activism through projects in religious, Torah-educational, and community-welfare fields. *Zeirei Forum; Am Hatorah; Daf Chizuk; Ohr Hakollel.*

AGUDATH ISRAEL WORLD ORGANIZATION (1912). 84 William St., NYC 10038. (212)-797–9000. Chmn. Rabbi Moshe Sherer, Rabbi Yehudah Meir Abramowitz. Represents the interests of Orthodox Jewry on the national and international scenes. Sponsors projects to strengthen Torah life worldwide.

AMERICAN ASSOCIATION OF RABBIS (1978). 350 Fifth Ave., Suite 3304, NYC 10118. (212)244–3350. Pres. Rabbi Harold Lerner; Exec. Dir. Rabbi David L. Dunn. An organization of rabbis serving in pulpits, in areas of education, and in social work. *Quarterly bulletin; monthly newsletter; membership directory.*

ASSOCIATION FOR JEWISH STUDIES (1969). Widener Library M., Harvard University, Cambridge, MA 02138. Pres. Herbert H. Paper; Exec. Sec. Charles Berlin. Seeks to promote, maintain, and improve the teaching of Jewish studies in American colleges and universities by sponsoring meetings and conferences, publishing a newsletter and other scholarly materials, setting standards for programs in Jewish studies, aiding in the placement of teachers, coordinating research, and cooperating with other scholarly organizations. *AJS Review; newsletter.*

ASSOCIATION OF HILLEL/JEWISH CAMPUS PROFESSIONALS (1949). c/o B'nai B'rith Hillel Foundation, Tufts University, Curtis Hall, 474 Boston Ave., Medford, MA 02155. Pres. Rabbi Jeffrey Summit. Seeks to promote professional relationships and exchanges of experience, develop personnel standards and qualifications, safeguard integrity of Hillel profession; represents and advocates before National Hillel Staff, National Hillel Commission, B'nai B'rith International, Council of Jewish Federations. *Handbook for Hillel Professionals; Guide to Hillel Personnel Practices.*

ASSOCIATION OF ORTHODOX JEWISH SCIENTISTS (1948). 1364 Coney Island Ave., Brooklyn, NY 11230. (718)338–8592. Pres. Neil Maron; Bd. Chmn. Reuben Rudman; Exec. Dir. Joel Schwartz. Seeks to contribute to the development of science within the framework of Orthodox Jewish tradition; to obtain and disseminate information relating to the interaction between the Jewish traditional way of life and scientific developments—on both an ideological and practical level; to assist in the solution of problems pertaining to Orthodox Jews engaged in scientific teaching or research. Two main conventions are held each year. *Intercom; Proceedings; Halacha Bulletin; newsletter.*

B'NAI B'RITH HILLEL FOUNDATIONS, INC. (1923). 1640 Rhode Island Ave., NW, Washington, DC 20036. (202)857–6560. FAX: (202)857–6693. Chmn. B'nai B'rith Hillel Comm. David L. Bittker; Internatl. Dir. Richard M. Joel. Provides cultural, social, community-service, educational, and religious activities for Jewish college students of all backgrounds. Maintains a presence on 400 campuses in the U.S., Canada, and overseas. Sponsors National Leaders Assembly, Charlotte and Jack J. Spitzer Forum on Public Policy, Jacob Burns Endowment in Ethics and the Campus, Sarah and Irving Pitt Institute for Student Leadership, National Jewish Law Students Network. *Campus Connection; Mekorot; Igeret; The Hillel Guide to Jewish Life on Campus: A Directory of Resources for Jewish College Students.*

B'NAI B'RITH YOUTH ORGANIZATION (1924). 1640 Rhode Island Ave., NW, Washington, DC 20036. (202)857–6633. FAX: (212)857–1099. Chmn. Youth Comm. Dennis Glick; Dir. Sam Fisher. Helps Jewish teenagers achieve self-fulfillment and make a maximum contribution to the Jewish community and their country's culture; helps members acquire a greater knowledge and appreciation of Jewish religion and culture. *Shofar; Monday Morning; BBYO Parents' Line; Hakol; Kesher; The Connector.*

CANTORS ASSEMBLY (1947). 150 Fifth Ave., NYC 10011. (212)691–8020. FAX: (212)-633–1020. Pres. Nathan Lam; Exec. V.-Pres. Samuel Rosenbaum. Seeks to unite all cantors who adhere to traditional Judaism and who serve as full-time cantors in bona fide congregations to conserve and promote the musical traditions of the Jews and to elevate the status of the cantorial profession. *Annual Proceedings; Journal of Synagogue Music.*

CENTRAL CONFERENCE OF AMERICAN RABBIS (1889). 192 Lexington Ave., NYC 10016. (212)684–4990. FAX: (212)689–6419. Pres. Rabbi Walter Jacob; Exec. V.-Pres. Rabbi Joseph B. Glaser. Seeks to conserve and promote Judaism and to disseminate its teachings in a liberal spirit.

The CCAR Press provides liturgy and prayerbooks to the worldwide Reform Jewish community. *CCAR Journal: A Reform Jewish Quarterly; CCAR Yearbook.*

CLAL—NATIONAL JEWISH CENTER FOR LEARNING AND LEADERSHIP (1974). 47 W. 34 St., 2nd fl., NYC 10001. (212)279–2525. FAX: (212)465–8425. Pres. Rabbi Irving Greenberg; Exec. V.-Pres. Alan Bayer. Dedicated to preparing Jewish leaders to respond to the challenges of a new era in Jewish history; challenges which include the freedom to accept or reject one's Jewish heritage, the liberty to choose from an abundance of Jewish values and lifestyles, and the exercise of Jewish power after the Holocaust and the rebirth of the State of Israel. *News & Perspectives.*

COALITION FOR THE ADVANCEMENT OF JEWISH EDUCATION (CAJE) (1976). 261 W. 35 St., #12A, NYC 10001. (212)268–4210. FAX: (212)268–4214. Chmn. Rabbi Michael A. Weinberg; Exec. Dir. Dr. Eliot G. Spack. Brings together Jews from all ideologies who are involved in every facet of Jewish education and are committed to transmitting the Jewish heritage. Sponsors annual Conference on Alternatives in Jewish Education and Curriculum Bank; publishes a wide variety of publications; organizes shared-interest networks; offers mini grants for special projects. *Bikurim; Mekasher (a human resources directory); CAJE Jewish Education News.*

CONGRESS OF SECULAR JEWISH ORGANIZATIONS (1970). 1130 S. Michigan Ave., #2101, Chicago, IL 60605. (312)922–0386. Pres. Harold Gales; Exec. Dir. Gerry Revzin. An umbrella organization of schools and adult clubs; facilitates exchange curricula and educational programs for children and adults stressing our Jewish historical and cultural heritage and the continuity of the Jewish people. *Newsletter; Holiday Celebration Book.*

COUNCIL FOR JEWISH EDUCATION (1926). 426 W. 58 St., NYC 10019. (212)713–0290. FAX: (212)586–9579. Pres. Solomon Goldman; Consultant Philip Gorodetzer. Fellowship of Jewish education professionals—administrators and supervisors and teachers in Hebrew high schools and Jewish teachers colleges—of all ideological groupings; conducts annual national and regional conferences; represents the Jewish education profession before the Jewish community; cosponsors, with the Jewish Education Service of North America, a personnel committee and other projects; cooperates with Jewish Agency Department of Education and Culture in promoting Hebrew culture and studies; conducts lectureship at Hebrew University. *Jewish Education; Sheviley Hahinnukh.*

FEDERATION OF JEWISH MEN'S CLUBS, INC. (1929). 475 Riverside Dr., Rm. 244, NYC 10115. (212)749–8100. FAX: (212)316–4271. Pres. J. Harold Nissen; Exec. Dir. Rabbi Charles Simon; Dir. Dr. Joel Sperber. Promotes principles of Conservative Judaism; develops family-education and leadership-training programs; offers the Art of Jewish Living series and Yom Hashoah Home Commemoration; sponsors Hebrew literacy adult-education program; presents awards for service to American Jewry. *Torchlight.*

INSTITUTE FOR COMPUTERS IN JEWISH LIFE (1978). 7074 N. Western Ave., Chicago, IL 60645. (312)262–9200. FAX: (312)262–9298. Pres. Thomas Klutznick; Exec. V.-Pres. Irving J. Rosenbaum. Explores, develops, and disseminates applications of computer technology to appropriate areas of Jewish life, with special emphasis on Jewish education; provides access to the Bar-Ilan University Responsa Project; creates educational software for use in Jewish schools; provides consulting service and assistance for national Jewish organizations, seminaries, and synagogues. *Monitor.*

JEWISH CHAUTAUQUA SOCIETY, INC. (sponsored by NATIONAL FEDERATION OF TEMPLE BROTHERHOODS) (1898). 838 Fifth Ave., NYC 10021. (212)570–0707 or (800)-765-6200. FAX: (212)570–0960. Pres. Alvin R. Corwin; 1st V.-Pres./Chancellor Roger B. Jacobs; Exec. Dir. Lewis Eisenberg. Working to promote interfaith understanding, sponsors accredited courses and lectures on Judaic topics, makes book grants, produces interfaith videos and convenes interfaith institutes. JCS also works with Hillel to support extracurricular intergroup programming on college campuses and is a founding sponsor of the National Black/Jewish Relations Center at Dillard University. *Brotherhood.*

JEWISH EDUCATION IN MEDIA (1978). PO Box 180, Riverdale Sta., NYC 10471. (212)362–7633; (203)968-2225. Pres. Bernard Samers; Exec. Dir. Rabbi Mark S.

Golub. Devoted to producing radio, television, film, video-cassette and audio-cassette programming for a popular Jewish audience, in order to inform, entertain, and inspire a greater sense of Jewish identity and Jewish commitment. "L'Chayim," JEM's weekly half-hour program, airs on WOR Radio in New York and in radio and television syndication; it features outstanding figures in the Jewish world addressing issues and events of importance to the Jewish community.

JEWISH EDUCATION SERVICE OF NORTH AMERICA (JESNA) (1981). 730 Broadway, NYC 10003–9540. (212)529–2000. FAX: (212)529–2009. Pres. Neil Greenbaum; Exec. V.-Pres. Dr. Jonathan S. Woocher. The trans-denominational planning, coordinating, and service agency for Jewish education of the organized Jewish community in North America. Works with federations, central agencies for Jewish education, and other local, national, and international institutions, and undertakes activities in the areas of research, program and human-resource development, information and resource dissemination, consultation, conferences and publications. *Agenda: Jewish Education; TRENDS; Media Meida; Information Research Bulletins; JESNA Update.*

JEWISH MINISTERS CANTORS ASSOCIATION OF AMERICA, INC. (1896). 3 W. 16 St., NYC 10011. (212)229–5699. Pres. Cantor Nathan H. Muchnick. Furthers and propagates traditional liturgy; places cantors in synagogues throughout the U.S. and Canada; develops the cantors of the future. *Kol Lakol.*

JEWISH RECONSTRUCTIONIST FOUNDATION (1940). Church Rd. and Greenwood Ave., Wyncote, PA 19095. (215)887–1988. Pres. Rabbi Elliot Skiddell; Exec. Dir. Rabbi Mordechai Liebling. Dedicated to the advancement of Judaism as the evolving religious civilization of the Jewish people. Coordinates the Federation of Reconstructionist Congregations and Havurot, Reconstructionist Rabbinical Association, and Reconstructionist Rabbinical College.

———, FEDERATION OF RECONSTRUCTIONIST CONGREGATIONS AND HAVUROT (1954). Church Rd. and Greenwood Ave., Wyncote, PA 19095. (215)887–1988. FAX: (215)576–6143. Pres. Valerie Kaplan; Exec. Dir. Rabbi Mordechai Liebling. Services affiliated congregations and havurot educationally and administratively; fosters the establishment of new Reconstructionist congregations and fellowship groups. Runs the Reconstructionist Press and provides programmatic materials. Maintains regional offices in New York and Los Angeles. *Reconstructionist; newsletter.*

———, RECONSTRUCTIONIST RABBINICAL ASSOCIATION (1974). Church Rd. and Greenwood Ave., Wyncote, PA 19095. (215)576-5210. FAX: (215)576-6143. Pres. Rabbi Lee Friedlander; Exec. Dir. Rabbi Robert Gluck. Professional organization for graduates of the Reconstructionist Rabbinical College and other rabbis who identify with Reconstructionist Judaism; cooperates with Federation of Reconstructionist Congregations and Havurot in furthering Reconstructionism in N. America. *Raayanot; newsletter.*

———, RECONSTRUCTIONIST RABBINICAL COLLEGE (*see* p. 553)

JEWISH TEACHERS ASSOCIATION—MORIM (1931). 45 E. 33 St., Suite 604, NYC 10016. (212)684-0556. Pres. Joseph M. Varon; V.-Pres. Eli Nieman. Protects teachers from abuse of seniority rights; fights the encroachment of anti-Semitism in education; provides legal counsel to protect teachers from discrimination; offers scholarships to qualified students; encourages teachers to assume active roles in Jewish communal and religious affairs. *Morim JTA Newsletter.*

MACHNE ISRAEL, INC. (1940). 770 Eastern Pkwy., Brooklyn, NY 11213. (718)774-4000. FAX: (718)774-2718. Pres. Menachem M. Schneerson (Lubavitcher Rebbe); Dir., Treas. M.A. Hodakov; Sec. Nissan Mindel. The Lubavitcher movement's organ dedicated to the social, spiritual, and material welfare of Jews throughout the world.

MERKOS L'INYONEI CHINUCH, INC. (THE CENTRAL ORGANIZATION FOR JEWISH EDUCATION) (1940). 770 Eastern Pkwy., Brooklyn, NY 11213. (718)493-9250. Pres. Menachem M. Schneerson (Lubavitcher Rebbe); Dir., Treas. M.A. Hodakov; Sec. Nissan Mindel. The educational arm of the Lubavitcher movement. Seeks to promote Jewish education among Jews, regardless of their background, in the spirit

of Torah-true Judaism; to establish contact with alienated Jewish youth; to stimulate concern and active interest in Jewish education on all levels; and to promote religious observance as a daily experience among all Jews. Maintains worldwide network of regional offices, schools, summer camps, and Chabad-Lubavitch Houses; publishes Jewish educational literature in numerous languages and monthly journal in five languages. *Conversaciones con la juventud; Conversations avec les jeunes; Schmuessen mit Kinder un Yugent; Sihot la-No-ar; Talks and Tales.*

NATIONAL COMMITTEE FOR FURTHERANCE OF JEWISH EDUCATION (1941). 824 Eastern Pkwy., Brooklyn, NY 11213. (718)735-0200. Pres. Joseph Fisch; Chmn. Exec. Com. Rabbi Sholem Ber Hecht. Seeks to disseminate the ideals of Torah-true education among the youth of America; provides education and compassionate care for the poor, sick, and needy in U.S. and Israel; provides aid to Iranian Jewish youth; sponsors camps; Operation Survival, War on Drugs; Hadar HaTorah, Machon Chana, and Ivy League Torah Study Program, seeking to win back college youth and others to Judaism; maintains schools and dormitory facilities, family and vocational counseling services. *Panorama; Passover Handbook; Seder Guide; Cultbusters; Intermarriage; Brimstone & Fire.*

NATIONAL COUNCIL OF YOUNG ISRAEL (1924). 3 W. 16 St., NYC 10011. (212)929-1525. Pres. Chaim Kaminetsky; Exec. V.-Pres. Rabbi Ephraim H. Sturm. Maintains a program of spiritual, cultural, social, and communal activity aimed at the advancement and perpetuation of traditional, Torah-true Judaism; seeks to instill in American youth an understanding and appreciation of the ethical and spiritual values of Judaism. Sponsors kosher dining clubs and fraternity houses and an Israel program. *Viewpoint; Hashkafa series; Masorah newspaper.*

———, AMERICAN FRIENDS OF YOUNG ISRAEL IN ISRAEL—YISRAEL HATZA'IR (1926). 3 W. 16 St., NYC 10011. (212)929-1525. FAX: (212)727-9526. Pres. Alter Goldstein; Treas. Steve Mostofsky. Promotes Young Israel synagogues and youth work in Israel; works to help absorb Russian and Ethiopian immigrants.

———, ARMED FORCES BUREAU (1912). 3 W. 16 St., NYC 10011. (212)929–1525. Advises and guides the inductees into the armed forces with regard to Sabbath observance, *kashrut,* and Orthodox behavior. *Guide for the Orthodox Serviceman.*

———, INSTITUTE FOR JEWISH STUDIES (1947). 3 W. 16 St., NYC 10011. (212)929–1525. Pres. Chaim Kaminetsky; Exec. V.-Pres. Rabbi Ephraim H. Sturm. Introduces students to Jewish learning and knowledge; helps form adult branch schools; aids Young Israel synagogues in their adult education programs. *Bulletin.*

———, YOUNG ISRAEL COLLEGIATES AND YOUNG ADULTS (1951; reorg. 1982). 3 W. 16 St., NYC 10011. (212)929–1525. Chmn. Kenneth Block; Dir. Richard Stareshefsky. Organizes and operates kosher dining clubs on college and university campuses; provides information and counseling on *kashrut* observance at colleges; gives college-age youth understanding and appreciation of Judaism and information on issues important to Jewish community; arranges seminars and meetings, weekends and trips; operates Achva summer mission to Israel for ages 18–21 and 22–27.

———, YOUNG ISRAEL YOUTH (reorg. 1968). 3 W. 16 St., NYC 10011. (212)929–1525. Dir. Richard Stareshefsky. Fosters a program of spiritual, cultural, social, and communal activities for the advancement and perpetuation of traditional Torah-true Judaism; strives to instill an understanding and appreciation of high ethical and spiritual values and to demonstrate compatibility of ancient faith of Israel with good Americanism. Operates Achva Summer Mission study program in Israel. *Monthly newsletter.*

NATIONAL HAVURAH COMMITTEE (1979). PO Box 2621, Bala Cynwyd, PA 19004-6621. (215)843–1470. FAX:(215)843-1470. Chmn. Dr. Herbert Levine; Coord. Rivkah Walton. A center for Jewish renewal devoted to spreading Jewish ideas, ethics, and religious practices through *havurot,* participatory and inclusive religious mini-communities. Maintains a directory of N. American *havurot* and sponsors a weeklong summer institute, regional weekend retreats, and a D'var Torah newspaper column. *Havurah (newsletter).*

NATIONAL JEWISH CENTER FOR LEARNING AND LEADERSHIP (*see* CLAL)

NATIONAL JEWISH COMMITTEE ON SCOUTING (Boy Scouts of America) (1926). 1325 Walnut Hill La., PO Box 152079, Irving, TX 75015–2079. (214)580–2059. FAX: (214)580– 2502. Chmn. Harry R. Rosen; Dir. Andrew Hoffman. Assists Jewish institutions in meeting their needs and concerns through use of the resources of scouting. Works through local Jewish committees on Scouting to establish Tiger Cub groups (1st grade), Cub Scout packs, Boy Scout troops, and coed Explorer posts in synagogues, Jewish community centers, day schools, and other Jewish organizations wishing to draw Jewish youth. Support materials and resources on request. *Hatsofe (quarterly); Expressions (annually).*

NATIONAL JEWISH GIRL SCOUT COMMITTEE (1972). Synagogue Council of America, 327 Lexington Ave., NYC 10016. (212)686–8670. FAX: (212)686–8673. Chmn. Rabbi Herbert W. Bomzer; Field Chmn. Adele Wasko. Under the auspices of the Synagogue Council of America, serves to further Jewish education by promoting Jewish award programs, encouraging religious services, promoting cultural exchanges with the Israel Boy and Girl Scouts Federation, and extending membership in the Jewish community by assisting councils in organizing Girl Scout troops and local Jewish Girl Scout committees. *Newsletter.*

NATIONAL JEWISH HOSPITALITY COMMITTEE (1973). 201 S. 18 St., Rm. 1519, Philadelphia, PA 19103. (215)546–8293. Pres. Rabbi Allen S. Maller; Exec. Dir. Steven S. Jacobs. Assists persons interested in Judaism—for conversion, intermarriage, or to respond to missionaries. *Special reports.*

NATIONAL JEWISH INFORMATION SERVICE FOR THE PROPAGATION OF JUDAISM, INC. (1960). 3761 Decade St., Las Vegas, NV 89121. (702)454–5872. Pres. Rabbi Moshe M. Maggal; V.-Pres. Lawrence J. Epstein; Sec. and P.R. Dir. Rachel D. Maggal. Seeks to convert non-Jews to Judaism and return Jews to Judaism; maintains College for Jewish Ambassadors for the training of Jewish missionaries, and the Correspondence Academy of Judaism for instruction on Judaism through the mail. *Voice of Judaism.*

OZAR HATORAH, INC. (1946). 1 E. 33 St., NYC 10016. (212)689–3508. Pres. Joseph Shalom; Sec. Sam Sutton. An international educational network which provides religious and secular education for Jewish youth worldwide.

P'EYLIM—AMERICAN YESHIVA STUDENT UNION (1951). 805 Kings Highway, Brooklyn, NY 11223. (718)382-0113. Pres. Jacob Y. Weisberg; Exec. V.-Pres. Avraham Hirsch. Aids and sponsors pioneer work by American graduate teachers and rabbis in new villages and towns in Israel; does religious, organizational, and educational work and counseling among new immigrant youth; maintains summer camps for poor immigrant youth in Israel; belongs to worldwide P'eylim movement which has groups in Argentina, Brazil, Canada, England, Belgium, the Netherlands, Switzerland, France, and Israel; engages in relief and educational work among North African immigrants in France and Canada, assisting them to relocate and reestablish a strong Jewish community life. *P'eylim Reporter; News from P'eylim; N'shei P'eylim News.*

RABBINICAL ALLIANCE OF AMERICA (IGUD HARABONIM) (1944). 3 W. 16 St., 4th fl., NYC 10011. (212)242-6420. Pres. Rabbi Abraham B. Hecht; Admin. Judge of Beth Din (Rabbinical Court) Rabbi Herschel Kurzrock. Seeks to promulgate the cause of Torah-true Judaism through an organized rabbinate that is consistently Orthodox; seeks to elevate the position of Orthodox rabbis nationally and to defend the welfare of Jews the world over. Also has Beth Din Rabbinical Court for Jewish divorces, litigation, marriage counseling and family problems. *Perspective; Nahalim; Torah Message of the Week; Registry.*

RABBINICAL ASSEMBLY (1900). 3080 Broadway, NYC 10027. (212)678-8060. Pres. Rabbi Gerald Zelizer; Exec. Dir. Rabbi Joel H. Meyers. Seeks to promote Conservative Judaism and to foster the spirit of fellowship and cooperation among rabbis and other Jewish scholars; cooperates with the Jewish Theological Seminary of America and the United Synagogue of Conservative Judaism. *Conservative Judaism; Proceedings of the Rabbinical Assembly; Rabbinical Assembly Newsletter.*

RABBINICAL COUNCIL OF AMERICA, INC. (1923; reorg. 1935). 275 Seventh Ave., NYC 10001. (212)807-7888. FAX: (212)-727-8452. Pres. Rabbi Marc D. Angel; Exec. V.-Pres. Rabbi Binyamin Walfish. Promotes Orthodox Judaism in the com-

munity; supports institutions for study of Torah; stimulates creation of new traditional agencies. *Hadorom; Record; Sermon Manual; Tradition.*

RESEARCH INSTITUTE OF RELIGIOUS JEWRY, INC. (1941; reorg. 1964). 471 W. End Ave., NYC 10024. (212)874-7979. Chmn. Rabbi Oswald Besser; Sec. Rabbi Marcus Levine. Engages in research and publishes studies concerning the situation of religious Jewry and its history in various countries.

SHOMREI ADAMAH/KEEPERS OF THE EARTH (1988). Church Rd. and Greenwood Ave., Wyncote, PA 19095. (215)-887-3106. Dir. Ellen Bernstein. A research, development, and education institute involved with nature and environmental issues from a Jewish perspective. Provides liturgical, educational, and other materials to members, including ecologically oriented services, sermons, and children's activities for school, camp, and home, as well as guides for study and action. Works with congregations and groups across North America on "greening" their communities. *Kol Hailanot/ Voice of the Trees (newsletter); Judaism and Ecology.*

SOCIETY FOR HUMANISTIC JUDAISM (1969). 28611 W. Twelve Mile Rd., Farmington Hills, MI 48334. (313)478-7610. FAX: (313)477-9014. Pres. Robert Sandler; Exec. Dir. Miriam Jerris; Asst. Dir. M. Bonnie Cousens. Serves as a voice for Jews who value their Jewish identity and who seek an alternative to conventional Judaism, who reject supernatural authority and affirm the right of individuals to be the masters of their own lives. Publishes educational and ceremonial materials; organizes congregations and groups. *Humanistic Judaism* (quarterly journal); *Humanorah* (quarterly newsletter).

SYNAGOGUE COUNCIL OF AMERICA (1926). 327 Lexington Ave., NYC 10016. (212)-686-8670. FAX: (212)686-8673. Pres. Rabbi Jerome K. Davidson; Bd. Chmn. Martin C. Barell; Exec. V.-Pres. Rabbi Henry D. Michelman. Represents congregational and rabbinic organizations of Conservative, Orthodox, and Reform Jewry; acts as "one voice" for religious Jewry. *SCA News; special reports.*

TORAH SCHOOLS FOR ISRAEL—CHINUCH ATZMAI (1953). 40 Exchange Pl., NYC 10005. (212)248-6200. FAX: (212)248-

6202. Pres. Abraham Pam; Exec. Dir. Henach Cohen. Conducts information programs for the American Jewish community on activities of the independent Torah schools educational network in Israel; coordinates role of American members of international board of governors; funds special programs of Mercaz Hachinuch Ha-Atzmai B'Eretz Yisroel. *Israel Education Reporter.*

TORAH UMESORAH—NATIONAL SOCIETY FOR HEBREW DAY SCHOOLS (1944). 160 Broadway, NYC 10038. (212)227–1000. Pres. Sheldon Beren; Bd. Chmn. David Singer; Exec. V.-Pres. Rabbi Joshua Fishman. Establishes Hebrew day schools in U.S. and Canada and provides a full gamut of services, including placement and curriculum guidance, teacher-training on campuses of major yeshivahs, an annual intensive teacher institute in July, and regional seminars and workshops. Publishes textbooks; runs Shabbatonim, extracurricular activities. National PTA groups; national and regional teacher conventions. *Olomeinu–Our World; Visions; Parshah Sheets; Torah Umesorah News.*

——, NATIONAL ASSOCIATION OF HEBREW DAY SCHOOL ADMINISTRATORS (1960). 1114 Ave. J, Brooklyn, NY 11230. (718)258–7767. Pres. David H. Schwartz. Coordinates the work of the fiscal directors of Hebrew day schools throughout the country. *NAHDSA Review.*

——, NATIONAL ASSOCIATION OF HEBREW DAY SCHOOL PARENT-TEACHER ASSOCIATIONS (1948). 160 Broadway, NYC 10038. (212)227–1000. Natl. PTA Coord. Bernice Brand. Acts as a clearinghouse and service agency to PTAs of Hebrew day schools; organizes parent education courses and sets up programs for individual PTAs. *Fundraising with a Flair; Monthly Sidrah Series Program; PTA with a Purpose for the Hebrew Day School.*

——, NATIONAL CONFERENCE OF YESHIVA PRINCIPALS (1956). 160 Broadway, NYC 10038. (212)227–1000. Pres. Rabbi Yitzchok Merkin; Bd. Chmn. Rabbi Baruch Hilsenrath; Exec. V.-Pres. Rabbi A. Moshe Possick. A professional organization of primary and secondary yeshivah/day-school principals providing yeshivah day schools with school visitations, teacher and principal conferences—including a Mid-Winter Conference—and a National Convention. *Directory of High Schools.*

——, NATIONAL LAY LEADERSHIP COMMITTEE (LLC) (1991). Chmn. Barry Ray; Dir. Rabbi Zvi Shachtel. Provides a lay leaders' executive report-professional journal; national lay leadership convention; national policy setting committees.

——, NATIONAL YESHIVA TEACHERS BOARD OF LICENSE (1953). 160 Broadway, NYC 10038. (212)227–1000. Exec. V.-Pres. & Dir. Rabbi Joshua Fishman. Issues licenses to qualified instructors for all grades of the Hebrew day school and the general field of Torah education.

UNION FOR TRADITIONAL JUDAISM (1984). 261 E. Lincoln Ave., Mt. Vernon, NY 10552. (914)667–1007. FAX: (914)667–1023. Pres. Dr. Miriam Klein Shapiro; Exec. V.-Pres. Rabbi Ronald D. Price. Through innovative outreach programs, seeks to bring the greatest possible number of Jews closer to an open-minded observant Jewish life-style. Activities include the Kashrut Initiative, Operation Pesah, the Panel of Halakhic Inquiry, Speaker's Bureau, adult and youth conferences, and congregational services. *Hagahelet (quarterly newsletter); Cornerstone (journal); Tomeikh Kahalakhah (Jewish legal responsa).*

UNION OF AMERICAN HEBREW CONGREGATIONS (1873). 838 Fifth Ave., NYC 10021. (212)249–0100. Pres. Rabbi Alexander M. Schindler; Bd. Chmn. Melvin Merians; Sr. V.-Pres. Rabbi Daniel B. Syme. Serves as the central congregational body of Reform Judaism in the Western Hemisphere; serves its approximately 850 affiliated temples and membership with religious, educational, cultural, and administrative programs. *Reform Judaism.*

——, AMERICAN CONFERENCE OF CANTORS (1956). 1 Kalisa Way, Suite 104, Paramus, NJ 07652. (201)599–0910. FAX: (201)599–1085. Pres. Vicki L. Axe; Exec. V.-Pres. Howard M. Stahl; Admin. Cantor Nancy Hausman. Members receive investiture and commissioning as cantors at recognized seminaries, i.e., Hebrew Union College–Jewish Institute of Religion, Sacred School of Music, or Jewish Theological Seminary, as well as full certification through HUC-JIR-SSM. Through Joint Cantorial Placement Commission, serves Reform congregations seeking cantors and music directors. Dedicated to creative Judaism, preserving the best of the past, and encouraging new and vital approaches to religious ritual, music, and ceremonies. *Koleinu.*

——, COMMISSION ON JEWISH EDUCATION OF THE UNION OF AMERICAN HEBREW CONGREGATIONS, CENTRAL CONFERENCE OF AMERICAN RABBIS, AND NATIONAL ASSOCIATION OF TEMPLE EDUCATORS (1923). 838 Fifth Ave., NYC 10021. (212)249–0100. Chmn. Rabbi Jonathan A. Stein; Cochmn. Robert E. Tornberg; Dir. Rabbi Howard I. Bogot. Long-range planning and policy development for congregational programs of lifelong education; network projects with affiliates and associate groups including: special-needs education, Reform Jewish outreach, and Reform Day Schools; activities administered by the UAHC Department for Religious Education.

——, COMMISSION ON SOCIAL ACTION OF REFORM JUDAISM (*see* p. 516)

——, COMMISSION ON SYNAGOGUE MANAGEMENT (UAHC-CCAR) (1962). 838 Fifth Ave., NYC 10021. (212)249–0100. FAX: (212)734–2857. Chmn. Paul Vanek; Dir. Joseph C. Bernstein. Assists congregations in management, finance, building maintenance, design, construction, and art aspects of synagogues; maintains the Synagogue Architectural Library.

——, NATIONAL ASSOCIATION OF TEMPLE ADMINISTRATORS (NATA) (1941). c/o Stephen S. Wise Temple, 15500 Stephen S. Wise Dr., Los Angeles, CA 90077-1598. (213)476–8561. FAX: (213)476–3587. Pres. Norman Fogel. Prepares and disseminates administrative information and procedures to member synagogues of UAHC; provides training of professional synagogue executives; formulates and establishes professional standards for the synagogue executive; provides placement services. *NATA Journal; Temple Management Manual.*

——, NATIONAL ASSOCIATION OF TEMPLE EDUCATORS (NATE) (1955). 707 Summerly Dr., Nashville, TN 37209-4253. (615)352–6800. FAX: (615)352–7800. Pres. Robin L. Eisenberg; Exec. V.-Pres. Richard M. Morin. Represents the temple educator within the general body of Reform Judaism; fosters the full-time profession of the temple educator; encourages the growth and development of Jewish religious education consistent with

the aims of Reform Judaism; stimulates communal interest in and responsibility for Jewish religious education. *NATE News; Compass.*

——, NATIONAL FEDERATION OF TEMPLE BROTHERHOODS (1923). 838 Fifth Ave., NYC 10021. (212)570–0707. Pres. Alvin R. Corwin; Exec. Dir. Lewis Eisenberg. Dedicated to enhancing the world through the ideal of brotherhood, NFTB and its 300 affiliated clubs are actively involved in education, social action, youth activities, and other programs which contribute to temple and community life. Supports the Jewish Chautauqua Society, an interfaith educational project. *Brotherhood.*

——, NATIONAL FEDERATION OF TEMPLE SISTERHOODS (1913). 838 Fifth Ave., NYC 10021. (212)249–0100. Pres. Judith Hertz; Acting Exec. Dir. Marjorie Epstein. Serves more than 640 sisterhoods of Reform Judaism; promotes interreligious understanding and social justice; awards scholarships and grants to rabbinic students; provides braille and large-type Judaic materials for Jewish blind; supports projects for Israel, Soviet Jewry, and the aging; is an affiliate of UAHC and the women's agency of Reform Judaism; works in behalf of the Hebrew Union College–Jewish Institute of Religion; cooperates with World Union for Progressive Judaism. *Leaders Line; Notes for Now.*

——, YOUTH DIVISION AND NORTH AMERICAN FEDERATION OF TEMPLE YOUTH (1939). 838 Fifth Ave., NYC 10021. (212)249–0100. FAX: (212)517–7863. Dir. Rabbi Allan L. Smith; Pres. Jon Crane. Seeks to train Reform Jewish youth in the values of the synagogue and their application to daily life through service to the community and congregation; runs department of summer camps and national leadership-training institute; arranges overseas academic tours, work-study programs, international student-exchange programs, and college-student programs in the U.S. and Israel, including accredited study programs in Israel. *Ani V'Atah; The Jewish Connection.*

UNION OF ORTHODOX JEWISH CONGREGATIONS OF AMERICA (1898). 333 Seventh Ave., NYC 10001. (212)563–4000. Pres. Sheldon Rudoff; Exec. V.-Pres. Rabbi Pinchas Stolper. Serves as the national central body of Orthodox synagogues; sponsors Institute for Public Affairs; National Conference of Synagogue Youth; LAVE—Learning and Values Experiences; Israel Center in Jerusalem; *aliyah* department; national OU *kashrut* supervision and certification service; Marriage Commission; "Taste of Torah" radio program; provides educational, religious, and organizational programs, events, and guidance to synagogues and groups; represents the Orthodox Jewish community to governmental and civic bodies and the general Jewish community. *Jewish Action magazine; OU Kosher Directory; OU Passover Directory; OU News Reporter; Synagogue Spotlight; Our Way magazine; Yachad magazine; Luach Limud Torah Diary Home Study Program.*

———, INSTITUTE FOR PUBLIC AFFAIRS (1989). 333 Seventh Ave., NYC 10001. (212)563-4000. FAX: (212)564-9058. Pres. Sheldon Rudoff; Chmn. Mandell Ganchrow; Exec. Dir. William E. Rapfogel. Serves as the policy analysis, advocacy, mobilization, and programming department responsible for representing Orthodox/traditional American Jewry. *Orthodox Advocate (quarterly newsletter); Briefing (monthly updates).*

———, NATIONAL CONFERENCE OF SYNAGOGUE YOUTH (1954). 333 Seventh Ave., NYC 10001. (212)563-4000. Dir. Rabbi Raphael Butler. Central body for youth groups of Orthodox congregations; provides educational guidance, Torah study groups, community service, programs consultation, Torah library, Torah fund scholarships, Ben Zakkai Honor Society, Friends of NCSY; weeklong seminars, Travel America with NCSY, Israel Summer Seminar for teens and collegiates, and Camp NCSY East Teen Torah Center. Divisions include Senior NCSY in 18 regions and 465 chapters, Junior NCSY for preteens, Our Way for the Jewish deaf, Yachad for the developmentally disabled, Mesorah for Jewish collegiates, Israel Center in Jerusalem, and NCSY in Israel. *Keeping Posted with NCSY; Face the Nation—President's Newsletter; Oreich Yomeinu—Education Newsletter; Mitsvah of the Month.*

———, WOMEN'S BRANCH (1923). 156 Fifth Ave., NYC 10010. (212)929-8857. Pres. Deborah M.F. Turk. Seeks to spread the understanding and practice of Orthodox Judaism and to unite all Orthodox women and their synagogal organizations; services affiliates with educational and programming materials, leadership, and organizational guidance, and has an NGO representative at the UN. Supplies candelabra for Jewish patients in hospitals and nursing homes; supports Stern and Touro College scholarship funds and Jewish braille publications. *Hachodesh; Hakol.*

UNION OF ORTHODOX RABBIS OF THE UNITED STATES AND CANADA (1902). 235 E. Broadway, NYC 10002. (212)964-6337. Dir. Rabbi Hersh M. Ginsberg. Seeks to foster and promote Torah-true Judaism in the U.S. and Canada; assists in the establishment and maintenance of yeshivot in the U.S.; maintains committee on marriage and divorce and aids individuals with marital difficulties; disseminates knowledge of traditional Jewish rites and practices and publishes regulations on synagogal structure; maintains rabbinical court for resolving individual and communal conflicts. *HaPardes.*

UNION OF SEPHARDIC CONGREGATIONS, INC. (1929). 8 W. 70 St., NYC 10023. (212)873-0300. Pres. Rev. Dr. Salomon Gaon; Bd. Chmn. Victor Tarry. Promotes the religious interests of Sephardic Jews; prints and distributes Sephardic prayer books; provides religious leaders for Sephardic congregations.

UNITED LUBAVITCHER YESHIVOTH (1940). 841-853 Ocean Pkwy., Brooklyn, NY 11230. (718)859-7600. Supports and organizes Jewish day schools and rabbinical seminaries in the U.S. and abroad.

UNITED SYNAGOGUE OF CONSERVATIVE JUDAISM (1913). 155 Fifth Ave., NYC 10010-6802. (212)533-7800. FAX: (212)-353-9439. Pres. Alan J. Tichnor; Exec. V.-Pres./CEO Rabbi Jerome M. Epstein. International organization of 800 Conservative congregations. Maintains 12 departments and 20 regional offices to assist its affiliates with religious, educational, youth, community, and administrative programming and guidance; aims to enhance the cause of Conservative Judaism, further religious observance, encourage establishment of Jewish religious schools, draw youth closer to Jewish tradition. Extensive Israel programs. *United Synagogue Review; Art/Engagement Calendar; Program Suggestions; Directory & Resource Guide; Book Service Catalogue of Publications.*

——, COMMISSION ON JEWISH EDUCATION (1930). 155 Fifth Ave., NYC 10010. (212)533–7800. FAX: (212)353–9439. Cochmn. Joshua Elkin, Dr. Miriam Klein Shapiro; Dir. Rabbi Robert Abramson. Develops educational policy for the United Synagogue of America and sets the educational direction for Conservative congregations, their schools, and the Solomon Schechter Day Schools. Seeks to enhance the educational effectiveness of congregations through the publication of materials and in-service programs. *Tov L'Horot; Your Child; Dapim; Shiboley Schechter; Advisories.*

——, COMMITTEE ON SOCIAL ACTION AND PUBLIC POLICY (1958). 155 Fifth Ave., NYC 10010. (212)533–7800. FAX: (212)353–9439. Chmn. Scott Kaplan . Develops and implements positions and programs on issues of social action and public policy for the United Synagogue of America; represents these positions to other Jewish and civic organizations, the media, and government; and provides guidance, both informational and programmatic, to its affiliated congregations in these areas.

——, JEWISH EDUCATORS ASSEMBLY (1951). 15 E. 26 St., Rm. 1350A, NYC 10010. (212)532–4949. FAX: (212)481–4174. Pres. Dr. Miriam Klein Shapiro; Exec. Dir. Bernard Dov Troy. Advances the development of Jewish education on all levels in consonance with the philosophy of the Conservative movement. Promotes Jewish education as a basis for the creative continuity of the Jewish people; sponsors an annual convention. Serves as a forum for the exchange of ideas, programs, and educational media. *Bulletins; V'aleh Hachadashot Newsletter.*

——, KADIMA (formerly PRE-USY; reorg. 1968). Cong. B'nai Jacob, 75 Rimmon, Woodbridge, CT 06525. (203)389–2111. FAX: (212)353–9439. Acting Exec. Dir. Jules A. Gutin. Involves Jewish preteens in a meaningful religious, educational, and social environment; fosters a sense of identity and commitment to the Jewish community and the Conservative movement; conducts synagogue-based chapter programs and regional Kadima days and weekends. *Mitzvah of the Month; Kadima Kesher; Chagim; Advisors Aid; Games; quarterly Kadima magazine.*

——, NATIONAL ASSOCIATION OF SYNAGOGUE ADMINISTRATORS (1948). Cong. B'nai Jacob, 75 Rimmon, Woodbridge, CT 06525. (203)389–2111. Pres. Rhoda F. Myers. Aids congregations affiliated with the United Synagogue of America to further the aims of Conservative Judaism through more effective administration (Program for Assistance by Liaisons to Synagogues—PALS); advances professional standards and promotes new methods in administration; cooperates in United Synagogue placement services and administrative surveys. *NASA Connections Newsletter; NASA Journal.*

——, UNITED SYNAGOGUE YOUTH OF (1951). 155 Fifth Ave., NYC 10010. (212)-533–7800. FAX: (212)353–9439. Pres. Joel Levenson; Acting Exec. Dir. Jules A. Gutin. Seeks to strengthen identification with Conservative Judaism, based on the personality development, needs, and interests of the adolescent, in a mitzvah framework. *Achshav; Tikun Olam; A.J. Heschel Honor Society Newsletter; SATO Newsletter; USY Alumni Assn. Newsletter; USY Program Bank; Hamad'rich Newsletter for Advisors.*

VAAD MISHMERETH STAM (1976). 4902 16th Ave., Brooklyn, NY 11204. (718)-438–4963. FAX: (212)435–0374. Pres. Rabbi David L. Greenfeld; Exec. Dir. Rabbi Yakov Basch. A nonprofit consumer-protection agency dedicated to preserving and protecting the halakhic integrity of Torah scrolls, phylacteries, and *mezuzot.* Makes presentations and conducts examination campaigns in schools and synagogues; created an optical software system to detect possible textual errors in *stam.* Offices in Israel, Strasbourg, Chicago, London, Manchester, Montreal, and Zurich. Publishes *Guide to Mezuzah* and *Guide to the Letters of the Aleph Beth. The Jewish Quill.*

WOMEN'S LEAGUE FOR CONSERVATIVE JUDAISM (1918). 48 E. 74 St., NYC 10021. (212)628–1600. Pres. Audrey Citak; Exec. Dir. Bernice Balter. Parent body of Conservative (Masorti) women's groups in U.S., Canada, Puerto Rico, Mexico, and Israel; provides programs and resources in Jewish education, social action, Israel affairs, American and Canadian public affairs, leadership training, community service programs for persons with disabilities, conferences on world affairs, study institutes, publicity techniques; publishes books of Jewish interest; contributes to support of Jewish Theological Seminary of America and its residence halls. *Women's League Outlook magazine; Ba'Olam newsletter.*

WORLD COUNCIL OF SYNAGOGUES (1957). 155 Fifth Ave., NYC 10010 (212)533–7693. Pres. Rabbi Zachary Heller; Exec. Dir. Bernard Barsky. International representative of Conservative organizations and congregations; promotes the growth and development of the Conservative movement in Israel and throughout the world; supports educational institutions overseas; holds biennial international conventions; represents the world Conservative movement on the Executive of the World Zionist Organization. *World Spectrum.*

WORLD UNION FOR PROGRESSIVE JUDAISM, LTD. (1926). 838 Fifth Ave., NYC 10021. (212)249–0100. FAX: (212)517–3940. Pres. Donald Day; Exec. Dir. Rabbi Richard G. Hirsch; N. Amer. Dir. Martin Strelzer; Dir. Internatl. Relations & Development Rabbi Clifford Kulwin. International umbrella organization of Liberal Judaism; promotes and coordinates efforts of Liberal congregations throughout the world; starts new congregations, recruits rabbis and rabbinical students for all countries; organizes international conferences of Liberal Jews. *Ammi; Rodnik; Newsupdates.*

SCHOOLS, INSTITUTIONS

ACADEMY FOR JEWISH RELIGION (1955). 15 W. 86 St., NYC 10024. (212)932–3184. Chmn. Presidential Council Rabbi Manuel Gold; Exec. Dean Rabbi Shohama Wiener. The only rabbinic seminary in the U.S. at which students explore the full range of Jewish spiritual learning and practice. Graduates serve in Conservative, Reform, Reconstructionist, and Orthodox congregations, chaplaincies, and educational institutions. Programs include rabbinic and cantorial studies in NYC and on/off-campus nonmatriculated studies.

ANNENBERG INSTITUTE (formerly DROPSIE COLLEGE FOR HEBREW AND COGNATE LEARNING) (1907; reorg. 1986). 420 Walnut St., Philadelphia, PA 19106. (215)238–1290. FAX: (215)238–1540. Dir. Eric M. Meyers; Assoc. Dir. David M. Goldenberg. A center for advanced research in

Judaic and Near Eastern studies at the postdoctoral level. *Jewish Quarterly Review.*

BALTIMORE HEBREW UNIVERSITY (1919). 5800 Park Heights Ave., Baltimore, MD 21215. (301)578–6900. FAX: (301)578–6940. Pres. Leivy Smolar; Bd. Chmn. Dr. Earl Diamond. Offers PhD, MA, and BA programs in Jewish studies, biblical and Near Eastern archaeology, philosophy, literature, history, Hebrew language and literature; School of Continuing Education; Joseph Meyerhoff Library; community lectures, film series, seminars. *The Scribe (annual newsletter).*

———, BALTIMORE INSTITUTE FOR JEWISH COMMUNAL SERVICE. Coord. Judith Yalin; Dean Robert O. Freedman. Trains Jewish communal professionals; offers joint degree program: MA in Jewish studies from BHU; MSW from U. of Maryland.

———, BERNARD MANEKIN SCHOOL OF UNDERGRADUATE STUDIES. Dean Judy Meltzer. BA program; the Isaac C. Rosenthal Center for Jewish Education; on-site courses in Maryland and Jerusalem; interdisciplinary concentrations: contemporary Middle East, American Jewish culture, and the humanities.

———, PEGGY MEYERHOFF PEARLSTONE SCHOOL OF GRADUATE STUDIES. Dean Robert O. Freedman. PhD and MA programs; MA and MSW with University of Maryland School of Social Work and Community Planning in federation, community organization, center, and family services; MA and MEd in Jewish education and double MA in journalism with Towson State University; MA program in the study of Christian-Jewish relations with St. Mary's Seminary and University; MA program in community relations with University of Maryland Graduate School.

BETH MEDROSH ELYON (ACADEMY OF HIGHER LEARNING AND RESEARCH) (1943). 73 Main St., Monsey, NY 10952. (914)356–7065. Bd. Chmn. Emanuel Weldler; Treas. Arnold Jacobs; Sec. Yerachmiel Censor. Provides postgraduate courses and research work in higher Jewish studies; offers scholarships and fellowships. *Annual journal.*

BRAMSON ORT TECHNICAL INSTITUTE (1977). 69-30 Austin St., Forest Hills, NY 11375. (718)261–5800. Dir. Dr. Seymour

B. Forman; Admissions, Lois E. Shallit. A two-year Jewish technical college offering certificates and associate degrees in high technology and business fields, including computer programming, electronics technology, business management, word processing, and ophthalmic technology. Houses the Center for Computers in Jewish Education. Extension sites in Manhattan, Brooklyn, and the Bronx.

BRANDEIS-BARDIN INSTITUTE (1941). 1101 Peppertree Lane, Brandeis, CA 93064. (818)348–7201. FAX: (805)526–1398. Pres. Gary Brennglass; Exec. V.-Pres. Dr. Alvin Mars. A pluralistic, nondenominational Jewish institution providing programs for people of all ages: Brandeis Camp Institute (BCI), a leadership program for college-age adults; Camp Alonim, a positive Jewish experience for children 8–16; House of the Book Shabbat weekends for adults 25+, at which scholars-in-residence discuss historical, cultural, religious, and spiritual aspects of Judaism; Family Weekends and Grandparents Weekends. *Brandeis-Bardin Institute Newsletter; BCI Alumni News.*

BRANDEIS UNIVERSITY (1948). 415 South St., Waltham, MA 02254. (617)736–2000. Bd. Chmn. Louis Perlmutter; Pres. Samuel O. Thier. Founded under Jewish sponsorship as a nonsectarian institution offering to all the highest quality undergraduate and graduate education. The Lown School is the center for all programs of teaching and research in the areas of Judaic Studies, Ancient Near Eastern Studies, and Islamic and Modern Middle Eastern Studies. The school includes the Department of Near Eastern Studies, which offers academic programs in the major areas of its concern; the Hornstein Program for Jewish Communal Service, a professional training program; and the Cohen Center for Modern Jewish Studies, which conducts research and teaching in contemporary Jewish studies, primarily in the field of American Jewish studies. *Various newsletters, scholarly publications.*

CLEVELAND COLLEGE OF JEWISH STUDIES (1964). 26500 Shaker Blvd., Beachwood, OH 44122. (216)464–4050. Pres. David S. Ariel; V.-Pres. Thomas N. Sudow; Dean Lifsa Schachter. Provides courses in all areas of Judaic and Hebrew studies to adults and college-age students; offers continuing education for Jewish educators and administrators; serves as a center for Jewish life and culture; expands the availability of courses in Judaic studies by exchanging faculty, students, and credits with neighboring academic institutions; grants bachelor's and master's degrees.

DROPSIE COLLEGE FOR HEBREW AND COGNATE LEARNING (*see* Annenberg Institute)

GRATZ COLLEGE (1895). Old York Rd. and Melrose Ave., Melrose Park, PA 19126. (215)635–7300. FAX: (215)635–7320. Bd. Chmn. Steven Fisher; Pres. Dr. Gary S. Schiff. Offers a wide variety of undergraduate and graduate degrees and continuing education programs in Judaic, Hebraic, and Middle Eastern studies. High-school level programs are offered by the affiliated Jewish Community High School of Gratz College. Grants BA and MA in Jewish studies, MA in Jewish education, MA in Jewish music, MA in Jewish liberal studies, certificates in Jewish communal service, Jewish education, Israel studies, Jewish librarianship, and other credentials. Joint graduate program in Jewish communal service with the U. of Pennsylvania. *Various newsletters, annual academic bulletin, and scholarly publications.*

HEBREW COLLEGE (1921). 43 Hawes St., Brookline, MA 02146. (617)232–8710. Acting Pres. Barry Mesch; Bd. Chmn. Herbert L. Berman. Provides intensive programs of study in all areas of Jewish culture from high school through college and graduate-school levels, also at branch in Hartford; offers the degrees of MA in Jewish studies, Bachelor and Master of Jewish education, Bachelor of Hebrew letters, and teacher's diploma; degrees fully accredited by New England Assoc. of Schools and Colleges. Operates Hebrew-speaking Camp Yavneh in Northwood, NH; offers extensive Ulpan program and courses for community. *Hebrew College Today.*

HEBREW THEOLOGICAL COLLEGE (1922). 7135 N. Carpenter Rd., Skokie, IL 60077. (312)267–9800. Acting Pres. Rabbi Dr. Jerold Isenberg. An institution of higher Jewish learning which includes a graduate school; school of liberal arts and sciences; division of advanced Hebrew studies; Fasman Yeshiva High School; Anne M. Blitstein Teachers Institute for Women. *Or Shmuel; Torah Journal; Likutei P'shatim; Turrets of Silver.*

HEBREW UNION COLLEGE–JEWISH INSTI-
TUTE OF RELIGION (1875). 3101 Clifton
Ave., Cincinnati, OH 45220. (513)221–
1875. FAX: (513)221–2810. Pres. Al-
fred Gottschalk; Exec. V.-Pres. Uri D.
Herscher; V.-Pres. Academic Affairs
Samuel Greengus; V.-Pres. Paul M.
Steinberg; Chmn. Bd. of Govs. Stanley P.
Gold. Academic centers: 3101 Clifton
Ave., Cincinnati, OH 45220 (1875), Dean
Kenneth Ehrlich; 1 W. 4 St., NYC 10012
(1922), Dean Norman J. Cohen; 3077
University Ave., Los Angeles, CA 90007
(1954), Dean Lee Bycel; 13 King David
St., Jerusalem, Israel 94101 (1963), Dean
Michael Klein. Prepares students for Reform rabbinate, cantorate, religious-
school teaching and administration, community service, academic careers;
promotes Jewish studies; maintains libraries and a museum; offers master's
and doctoral degrees; engages in archaeological excavations; publishes scholarly
works through Hebrew Union College
Press. *American Jewish Archives; Biblio-
graphica Judaica; HUC-JIR Catalogue;
Hebrew Union College Annual; Studies in
Bibliography and Booklore; The Chronicle.*

——, AMERICAN JEWISH ARCHIVES
(1947). 3101 Clifton Ave., Cincinnati, OH
45220. (513)221–1875. FAX: (513)221–
7812. Dir. Jacob R. Marcus; Admin. Dir.
Abraham Peck. Promotes the study and
preservation of the Western Hemisphere
Jewish experience through research, publications, collection of important source
materials, and a vigorous public-outreach
program. *American Jewish Archives; monographs, publications, and pamphlets.*

——, AMERICAN JEWISH PERIODICAL
CENTER (1957). 3101 Clifton Ave., Cincinnati, OH 45220. (513)221–1875. Dir.
Jacob R. Marcus; Codir. Herbert C.
Zafren. Maintains microfilms of all American Jewish periodicals 1823–1925, selected
periodicals since 1925. *Jewish Periodicals
and Newspapers on Microfilm (1957); First
Supplement (1960); Augmented Edition
(1984).*

——, EDGAR F. MAGNIN SCHOOL OF
GRADUATE STUDIES (1956). 3077 University Ave., Los Angeles, CA 90007. (213)-
749–3424. FAX: (213)747–6128. Dir.
Stanley Chyet. Supervises programs leading to PhD (Education), DHS, DHL, and
MA degrees; participates in cooperative

PhD programs with the University of
Southern California.

——, JEROME H. LOUCHHEIM SCHOOL
OF JUDAIC STUDIES (1969). 3077 University Ave. Los Angeles, CA 90007. (213)-
749–3424. FAX: (213)747–6128. Dir.
David Ellenson. Offers programs leading
to MA, BS, BA, and AA degrees; offers
courses as part of the undergraduate program of the University of Southern California.

——, NELSON GLUECK SCHOOL OF BIBLI-
CAL ARCHAEOLOGY (1963). 13 King
David St., Jerusalem, Israel 94101. FAX:
2–251–478. Dir. Avraham Biran. Offers
graduate-level research programs in Bible
and archaeology. Summer excavations are
carried out by scholars and students. University credit may be earned by participants in excavations. Consortium of colleges, universities, and seminaries is
affiliated with the school.

——, RHEA HIRSCH SCHOOL OF EDUCA-
TION (1967). 3077 University Ave., Los
Angeles, CA 90007. (213)749–3424. FAX:
(213)747–6128. Offers PhD and MA programs in Jewish and Hebrew education;
conducts joint degree programs with University of Southern California; offers
courses for Jewish teachers, librarians, and
early educators on a nonmatriculating
basis; conducts summer institutes for professional Jewish educators.

——, SCHOOL OF EDUCATION (1947). 1
W. 4 St., NYC 10012. (212)674–5300.
FAX: (212)533–0129. V.-Pres. and Dean
of Faculty Paul M. Steinberg; Dean Norman J. Cohen; Dir. Kerry M. Olitzky.
Trains teachers and principals for Reform
religious schools; offers MA degree with
specialization in religious education; offers
extension programs in various suburban
centers.

——, SCHOOL OF GRADUATE STUDIES
(1949). 3101 Clifton Ave., Cincinnati, OH
45220 (513)221–1875. FAX: (513)221–
0321. Dir. Alan Cooper. Offers programs
leading to MA and PhD degrees; offers
program leading to DHL degree for rabbinic graduates of the college.

——, SCHOOL OF JEWISH COMMUNAL
SERVICE (1968). 3077 University Ave.,
Los Angeles, CA 90007. (213)749–3424.
FAX: (213)747–6128. Dir. H. Jack Mayer.
Offers certificate and master's degree to
those employed in Jewish communal ser-

vices, or preparing for such work; offers joint MA in Jewish education and communal service with Rhea Hirsch School; offers MA and MSW in conjunction with the University of Southern California School of Social Work, with the George Warren Brown School of Social Work of Washington University, and with the University of Pittsburgh School of Social Work; offers joint master's degrees in conjunction with USC in public administration or gerontology.

————, SCHOOL OF JEWISH STUDIES (1963). 13 King David St., Jerusalem, Israel, 94101. FAX: 2–251–478. Dean Michael Klein; Assoc. Dean Rabbi Shaul R. Feinberg. Offers first year of graduate rabbinic, cantorial, and Jewish education studies (required) for American students; program leading to ordination for Israeli rabbinic students; undergraduate semester in Jerusalem and one-year work/study program on a kibbutz in cooperation with Union of American Hebrew Congregations; public outreach programs (lectures, courses, concerts, exhibits).

————, SCHOOL OF SACRED MUSIC (1947). 1 W. 4 St., NYC 10012. (212)674–5300. FAX: (212)533–0129. Dir. Israel Goldstein. Trains cantors and music personnel for congregations; offers MSM degree. *Sacred Music Press.*

————, SKIRBALL MUSEUM (*see* p. 524)

HERZLIAH-JEWISH TEACHERS SEMINARY (1967). Division of Touro College. 844 Ave. of the Americas, NYC 10001. (212)-447–0700. Pres. Bernard Lander; Dir. Jacob Katzman.

————, GRADUATE SCHOOL OF JEWISH STUDIES (1981). 844 Ave. of the Americas, NYC 10001. (212)447–0700. Pres. Bernard Lander; Dean Michael A. Shmidman. Offers courses leading to an MA in Jewish studies, with concentrations in Jewish history or Jewish education. Students may complete part of their program in Israel, through MA courses offered by Touro faculty at Touro's Jerusalem center.

————, JEWISH PEOPLE'S UNIVERSITY OF THE AIR. (212)447–0700. Dir./Producer Jacob Katzman. The educational outreach arm of Touro College, it produces and disseminates Jewish educational and cultural programming for radio broadcast and on audio-cassettes.

INSTITUTE OF TRADITIONAL JUDAISM (1990). 261 E. Lincoln Ave., Mt. Vernon, NY 10552. (914)667–1007. FAX: (914)-667–1023. Rector (*Reish Metivta*) Rabbi David Weiss Halivni; Dean Rabbi Ronald D. Price. A nondenominational rabbinical school dedicated to genuine faith combined with intellectual honesty and the love of Israel. Graduates receive "*yoreh yoreh*" *smikhah*.

JEWISH THEOLOGICAL SEMINARY OF AMERICA (1886; reorg. 1902). 3080 Broadway, NYC 10027–4649. (212)678–8000. Chancellor Dr. Ismar Schorsch; Bd. Chmn. Gershon Kekst. Operates undergraduate and graduate programs in Judaic studies; professional schools for training Conservative rabbis and cantors; Melton Research Center for Jewish Education; the Jewish Museum; and such youth programs as the Ramah Camps and the Prozdor high-school division. Produces network television programs in cooperation with interfaith broadcasting commission. *Academic Bulletin; Masoret; The Melton Journal.*

————, ALBERT A. LIST COLLEGE OF JEWISH STUDIES (formerly SEMINARY COLLEGE OF JEWISH STUDIES-TEACHERS INSTITUTE) (1909). 3080 Broadway, NYC 10027. (212)678–8826. Dean Dr. Anne Lapidus Lerner. Offers complete undergraduate program in Judaica leading to BA degree; conducts joint programs with Columbia University and Barnard College enabling students to receive two BA degrees.

————, CANTORS INSTITUTE AND SEMINARY COLLEGE OF JEWISH MUSIC (1952). 3080 Broadway, NYC 10027. (212)678–8038. Dean Rabbi Morton M. Leifman. Trains cantors, music teachers, and choral directors for congregations. Offers fulltime programs in sacred music leading to degrees of MSM and DSM, and diploma of *Hazzan.*

————, DEPARTMENT OF RADIO AND TELEVISION (1944). 3080 Broadway, NYC 10027. (212)678–8020. Dir. Marjorie Wyler. Produces radio and TV programs expressing the Jewish tradition in its broadest sense, including hour-long documentaries on NBC and ABC. Distributes cassettes of programs at minimum charge.

————, GRADUATE SCHOOL (formerly INSTITUTE FOR ADVANCED STUDY IN THE HUMANITIES) (1968). 3080 Broadway,

NYC 10027. (212)678–8024. Acting Dean Dr. Stephen P. Garfinkel. Programs leading to MA, MPhil, DHL, and PhD degrees in Jewish studies, Bible, Jewish education, history, literature, ancient Judaism, philosophy, rabbinics, and medieval Jewish studies; dual degree with Columbia University School of Social Work.

———, JEWISH MUSEUM (see p. 522)

———, LIBRARY OF THE JEWISH THEOLOGICAL SEMINARY. 3080 Broadway, NYC 10027. (212)678–8075. FAX: (212)678–8998. Librarian Dr. Mayer E. Rabinowitz. Contains one of the largest collections of Hebraica and Judaica in the world, including manuscripts, incunabula, rare books, and Cairo Geniza material. The 270,000-volume collection is housed in a state-of-the-art building and is open to the public. *New Acquisitions List; Friends of the Library Newsletter.*

———, LOUIS FINKELSTEIN INSTITUTE FOR RELIGIOUS AND SOCIAL STUDIES (1938). 3080 Broadway, NYC 10027. (212)678–8815. Dir. Irving Levine; Assoc. Dir. Carlotta Damanda. A scholarly and scientific fellowship of clergy and other religious teachers who desire authoritative information regarding some of the basic issues now confronting spiritually minded individuals.

———, MELTON RESEARCH CENTER FOR JEWISH EDUCATION (1960). 3080 Broadway, NYC 10027. (212)678–8031. Dirs. Dr. Eduardo Rauch, Dr. Barry W. Holtz. Develops new curricula and materials for Jewish education; prepares educators through seminars and in-service programs; maintains consultant and supervisory relationships with a limited number of pilot schools; develops and implements research initiatives; sponsors "renewal" retreats for teachers and principals. *The Melton Journal.*

———, NATIONAL RAMAH COMMISSION (1951). 3080 Broadway, NYC 10027. (212)678–8881. FAX: (212)749–8251. Pres. Dr. Saul Shapiro; Natl. Dir. Sheldon Dorph. Sponsors 7 overnight Conservative Jewish camps in U.S. and Canada, emphasizing Jewish education, living, and culture; offers opportunities for qualified college students and older to serve as counselors, administrators, specialists, etc. Also programs for children with special needs (Tikvah program); offers special programs in U.S. and Israel, including Weinstein National Ramah Staff Training Institute, Ramah Israel Seminar, Ulpan Ramah Plus, and Tichon Ramah Yerushalayim. Family and synagogue tours to Israel and summer day camp in Israel for Americans.

———, PROZDOR (1951). 3080 Broadway, NYC 10027. (212)678–8824. Principal Dr. Michael Panitz. The high-school department of JTS, it provides a supplementary Jewish education for students who attend a secular (public or private) full-time high school. Classes in classical Jewish studies, with emphasis on Hebrew language, meet twice a week.

———, RABBINICAL SCHOOL (1886). 3080 Broadway, NYC 10027. (212)678–8816. Dean Rabbi Gordon Tucker. Offers a program of graduate and professional studies leading to the degree of Master of Arts and ordination; includes one year of study in Jerusalem and an extensive field-work program.

———, SAUL LIEBERMAN INSTITUTE OF JEWISH RESEARCH (1985). PO Box 196, Jerusalem, Israel 92102. (02)631121. Dir. Shamma Friedman. Engaged in preparing for publication a series of scholarly editions of selected chapters of the Talmud. The following projects support and help disseminate the research: Talmud Text Database; Bibliography of Talmudic Literature; Catalogue of Geniza Fragments; Teachers Training and Curriculum Development in Oral Law for Secondary Schools.

———, SCHOCKEN INSTITUTE FOR JEWISH RESEARCH (1961). 6 Balfour St., Jerusalem, Israel, 92102. (02)631288. Dir. Shmuel Glick; Coord. for Educ. Programs Simcha Goldsmith. Comprises the Schocken collection of rare books and manuscripts and a research institute dedicated to the exploration of Hebrew religious poetry (*piyyut*). *Schocken Institute Yearbook (P'raqim).*

———, UNIVERSITY OF JUDAISM (1947). 15600 Mulholland Dr., Los Angeles, CA 90077. (310)476–9777. FAX: (310)471–1278. Pres. Dr. David L. Lieber; Dean of Academic Affairs Dr. Hanan Alexander; Dean of Student Affairs Rabbi Daniel Gordis. The undergraduate school, Lee College of Arts and Sciences, is an accredited liberal arts college offering a core curriculum of Jewish and Western studies, with majors including psychology, business, literature, political science, and Jewish studies. Accredited graduate programs in nonprofit business management, Jewish education, and Jewish studies, plus a preparatory program for the Conservative rabbinate. Two institutes for research and program development, the Wilstein Institute for Jewish Policy Studies and the Whizin Center for the Jewish Future. A broad range of continuing-education courses, cultural-arts programs, and a variety of outreach services for West Coast Jewish communities. *Direction Magazine; Focus Newsletter; Bulletin of General Information.*

MESIVTA YESHIVA RABBI CHAIM BERLIN RABBINICAL ACADEMY (1905). 1593 Coney Island Ave., Brooklyn, NY 11230. (718)377-0777. Exec. Dir. Y. Mayer Lasker. Maintains fully accredited elementary and high schools; collegiate and postgraduate school for advanced Jewish studies, both in America and Israel; Camp Morris, a summer study retreat; Prof. Nathan Isaacs Memorial Library; Gur Aryeh Publications.

NER ISRAEL RABBINICAL COLLEGE (1933). 400 Mt. Wilson Lane, Baltimore, MD 21208. (301)484-7200. FAX: (301)484-3060. Rabbi Yaakov S. Weinberg, Rosh Hayeshiva; Rabbi Herman N. Neuberger, Menahel. Trains rabbis and educators for Jewish communities in America and worldwide. Offers bachelor's, master's, and doctoral degrees in talmudic law, as well as teacher's diploma. College has four divisions: Mechina High School, Rabbinical College, Teachers Training Institute, Graduate School. Maintains an active community-service division. Operates special program for Iranian Jewish students. *Ner Israel Update; Alumni Bulletin; Ohr Hanair Talmudic Journal; Iranian B'nei Torah Bulletin.*

RABBINICAL COLLEGE OF TELSHE, INC. (1941). 28400 Euclid Ave., Wickliffe, OH 44092. (216)943-5300. Pres. Rabbi Mordecai Gifter; V.-Pres. Rabbi Abba Zalka Gewirtz. College for higher Jewish learning specializing in talmudic studies and rabbinics; maintains a preparatory academy including a secular high school, postgraduate department, teacher-training school, and teachers seminary for women. *Pri Etz Chaim; Peer Mordechai; Alumni Bulletin.*

RECONSTRUCTIONIST RABBINICAL COLLEGE (1968). Church Rd. and Greenwood Ave., Wyncote, PA 19095.(215)576-0800. FAX: (215)576-6143. Pres. Arthur Green; Bd. Chmn. Jacques G. Pomeranz; Genl. Chmn. Aaron Ziegelman. Coeducational. Trains rabbis for all areas of Jewish communal life: synagogues, academic and educational positions, Hillel centers, federation agencies; confers title of rabbi and grants degrees of Master and Doctor of Hebrew Letters. *RRC Report.*

SPERTUS COLLEGE OF JUDAICA (1924). 618 S. Michigan Ave., Chicago, IL 60605. (312)922-9012. FAX:(312)922-6406. Pres. Howard A. Sulkin; Bd. Chmn. Gary Edidin; V.-Pres. for Academic Affairs Byron L. Sherwin; Dir. Spertus Museum Morris A. Fred; Dir. Asher Library Michael Terry. An accredited liberal arts institution of higher learning offering five master's degree programs in Jewish studies, Jewish education, Jewish communal service, and human-services administration, plus an extensive program of continuing education. Offers classes at the main campus, a suburban center, and extension locations. Major resources of the college encompass Spertus Museum, the Asher Library, including the Chicago Jewish Archives, and Spertus College of Judaica Press.

———, SPERTUS MUSEUM (*see* p. 524)

TOURO COLLEGE (1970). Executive Offices: Empire State Bldg., 350 Fifth Ave., Suite 5122, NYC 10018. (212)643-0700. Pres. Bernard Lander. Bd. Chmn. Max Karl. Chartered by NY State Board of Regents as a nonprofit four-year college with business, Judaic studies, health sciences, and liberal arts programs leading to BA, BS, and MA degrees; emphasizes relevance of Jewish heritage to general culture of Western civilization. Also offers JD degree and a biomedical program leading to the MD degree from Technion-Israel Institute of Technology, Haifa.

———, BARRY Z. LEVINE SCHOOL OF HEALTH SCIENCES AND CENTER FOR BIOMEDICAL EDUCATION (1970). 135 Common Rd., Bldg. #10, Dix Hills, NY 11746. (516)673-3200. Dean Dr. Joseph Weisberg. Along with the Manhattan campus, offers 5 programs: 5-year program leading to MA from Touro and MD from Faculty of Medicine of Technion-Israel Institute of

Technology, Haifa; BS/MA—physical therapy and occupational therapy programs; BS—physician assistant and health-information management programs.

———, COLLEGE OF LIBERAL ARTS AND SCIENCES. 844 Sixth Ave., NYC 10001. (212)447–0700. FAX: (212)779–2344. Exec. Dean Stanley Boylan. Offers comprehensive Jewish studies along with studies in the arts, sciences, humanities, and preprofessional studies in health sciences, law, accounting, business, computer science, education, and finance, health sciences, and law.

———, GRADUATE SCHOOL OF JEWISH STUDIES (1981) 844 Sixth Ave., NYC 10001. (212)447–0700 X 514. Pres. Bernard Lander; Dean Michael A. Shmidman. Offers courses leading to an MA in Jewish studies, with concentrations in Jewish history or Jewish education. Students may complete part of their program in Israel, through MA courses offered by Touro faculty at Touro's Jerusalem center.

———, INSTITUTE OF JEWISH LAW. (516)-421–2244. Based at Fuchsberg Law Center, serves as a center and clearinghouse for study and teaching of Jewish law. Coedits *Dinei Israel* (Jewish Law Journal) with Tel Aviv University Law School.

———, JACOB D. FUCHSBERG LAW CENTER (1980). Long Island Campus, 300 Nassau Rd., Huntington, NY 11743. (516)421–2244. Dean Howard A. Glickstein. Offers studies leading to JD degree.

———, JEWISH PEOPLE'S UNIVERSITY OF THE AIR. (1979). 844 Sixth Ave., NYC 10001. (212)447–0700 X 589. Producer/Dir. Jacob Katzman. Produces and disseminates courses in Jewish subject matter for radio broadcasting and on audio-cassettes. Printed course outlines for all courses and discussion; leader's guides for some.

———, MOSCOW BRANCH. 5 Jablockkova St., 127254 Moscow, USSR. 210–86–69; 210–61–73. Offers BS program in business and BA program in Jewish studies.

———, SCHOOL OF GENERAL STUDIES. 240 E. 123 St., NYC 10021. (212)722–1575. Dean Stephen Adolphus. Offers educational opportunities to minority groups and older people; courses in the arts, sciences, humanities, and special programs of career studies.

———, TOURO COLLEGE FLATBUSH CENTER (1929). 1277 E. 14 St., Brooklyn, NY 11230. (718)253–7538. Dean Robert Goldschmidt. A division of the College of Liberal Arts and Sciences; options offered in accounting and business, education, mathematics, political science, psychology, and speech. Classes are given on weeknights and during the day on Sunday.

———, TOURO COLLEGE ISRAEL CENTER. 23 Rechov Shivtei Yisrael, Jerusalem. 2–894–086/088. Assoc. Dean Dr. Carmi Horowitz; Resident Dir. Dr. Chana Sosevsky. Offers undergraduate courses in business, computer science, and education. Houses the MA degreee program in Jewish studies. The Touro Year Abroad Option for American students is coordinated from this center.

WEST COAST TALMUDICAL SEMINARY (Yeshiva Ohr Elchonon Chabad) (1953). 7215 Waring Ave., Los Angeles, CA 90046. (213)937–3763. Dean Rabbi Ezra Schochet. Provides facilities for intensive Torah education as well as Orthodox rabbinical training on the West Coast; conducts an accredited college preparatory high school combined with a full program of Torah-talmudic training and a graduate talmudical division on the college level. *Torah Quiz; Kobetz Migdal Ohr.*

YESHIVA UNIVERSITY (1886). Joel Jablonski Campus, 500 W. 185 St., NYC 10033-3299. (212)960–5400. FAX: (212)960–0055. Pres. Dr. Norman Lamm; Chmn. Bd. of Trustees Ludwig Jesselson. The nation's oldest and largest independent university founded under Jewish auspices, with a broad range of undergraduate, graduate, and professional schools, a network of affiliates, a widespread program of research and community outreach, publications, and a museum. Curricula lead to bachelor's, master's, doctoral, and professional degrees. Undergraduate schools provide general studies curricula supplemented by courses in Jewish learning; graduate schools prepare for careers in medicine, law, social work, Jewish education, psychology, Jewish studies, Semitic languages, literatures, and cultures, and other fields. It has six undergraduate schools, seven graduate and professional schools, and three affiliates. *Alumni Review/Inside.*

Yeshiva has four campuses in Manhattan and the Bronx: Joel Jablonski Campus, 500 W. 185 St., NYC 10033-3299; Jack and Pearl Resnick Campus, Eastchester Rd. & Morris Pk. Ave., Bronx, NY 10461; Midtown Center, 245 Lexington Ave., NYC 10016; Brookdale Center, 55 Fifth Ave., NYC 10003.

Undergraduate schools for men at Joel Jablonski Campus: Yeshiva College (Dean Dr. Norman S. Rosenfeld) provides liberal arts and sciences curricula; grants BA degree. Isaac Breuer College of Hebraic Studies (Assoc. Dean Dr. Michael D. Shmidman) awards Hebrew teacher's diploma, AA, BA, and BS. James Striar School of General Jewish Studies (Assoc. Dean Dr. Michael D. Shmidman) grants AA degree. Yeshiva Program/Mazer School of Talmudic Studies (Dean Rabbi Zevulun Charlop) offers advanced course of study in talmudic texts and commentaries.

Undergraduate school for women at Midtown Center, 245 Lexington Ave., NYC 10016. (212)340–7700: Stern College for Women (Dean Dr. Karen Bacon) offers liberal arts and sciences curricula supplemented by Jewish studies programs offered through the Rebecca Ivry Department of Jewish Studies; awards BA, AA, and Hebrew teacher's diploma.

Sy Syms School of Business at Joel Jablonski Campus (Dean Dr. Michael Schiff) offers undergraduate business curricula in conjunction with study at Yeshiva College or Stern College; grants BS degree.

Sponsors one high school for boys (Manhattan) and one for girls (Queens).

Universitywide programs serving the community and the nation include the Carl C. Icahn Foundation Institutes for Child Protection; Irving and Hanni Rosenbaum Aliyah Incentive Fund; Ivan L. Tillem Program for Special Services for the Jewish Elderly; Holocaust Studies Program; Interdisciplinary Conference on Bereavement and Grief; Yeshiva University Museum; Yeshiva University Press.

——, ALBERT EINSTEIN COLLEGE OF MEDICINE (1955). Eastchester Rd. & Morris Pk. Ave., Bronx, NY 10461. (212)430–2000. Pres. Dr. Norman Lamm; Chmn. Bd. of Overseers Burton P. Resnick; Dean Dr. Dominick P. Purpura. Prepares physicians and conducts research in the health sciences; awards MD degree; includes Sue Golding Graduate Division of Medical Sciences (Dir. Dr. Barbara K. Birshtein), which grants PhD degree. Einstein College's clinical facilities, affiliates, and resources encompass Jack D. Weiler Hospital of Albert Einstein College of Medicine, Montefiore Medical Center, Bronx Municipal Hospital Center, and the Rose F. Kennedy Center for Research in Mental Retardation and Human Development. *Einstein; AECOM Today; Einstein Quarterly Journal of Biology and Medicine.*

——, ALUMNI OFFICE, 500 W. 185 Street, NYC 10033. (212)960–5373. Dir. Toby Hilsenrad Weiss. Seeks to foster a close allegiance of alumni to their alma mater by maintaining ties with all alumni and servicing the following associations: Yeshiva College Alumni (Pres. Emanuel J. Adler); Stern College for Women Alumnae (Pres. Jan Schechter); Albert Einstein College of Medicine Alumni (Pres. Dr. Bernard Zazula); Ferkauf Graduate School of Psychology Alumni (Pres. Dr. Abraham Givner); Wurzweiler School of Social Work Alumni (Pres. Ilene Stein Himber); Rabbinic Alumni (Pres. Rabbi Bernard Rosensweig); Benjamin N. Cardozo School of Law Alumni (Chmn. Noah Gordon, Jay H. Ziffer). *Alumni Review/Inside; AECOM Alumni News; Jewish Social Work Forum.*

——, BELFER INSTITUTE FOR ADVANCED BIOMEDICAL STUDIES (1978). Eastchester Rd. & Morris Pk. Ave., Bronx, NY 10461. (212)430–2801. Dir. Dr. Ernst R. Jaffé. Integrates and coordinates the Medical College's postdoctoral research and training-grant programs in the basic and clinical biomedical sciences. Awards certificate as Research Fellow or Research Associate on completion of training.

——, BENJAMIN N. CARDOZO SCHOOL OF LAW (1976). 55 Fifth Ave., NYC 10003. (212)790–0200. Pres. Dr. Norman Lamm; Chmn. Bd. of Dirs. Jacob Burns; Dean Frank J. Macchiarola. Provides innovative courses of study within a traditional legal framework; program includes judicial internships; grants Doctor of Law (JD) degree. Programs and services include institute for advanced legal studies; center for ethics in the practice of law; Bet Tzedek Legal Services Clinic; institute of Jewish law; center on corporate governance; program in communications law; center for professional development; international law and human-rights program. *Cardozo Studies in Law and Literature; Cardozo*

Law Review; Arts and Entertainment Law Journal; Women's Annotated Legal Bibliography; New Europe Law Review; Cardozo Law Forum.

———, BERNARD REVEL GRADUATE SCHOOL (1937). 500 W. 185 St., NYC 10033. (212)960–5253. Dean Dr. Leo Landman. Offers graduate programs in Judaic studies and Semitic languages, literatures, and cultures; confers MS, MA, and PhD degrees.

———, DAVID J. AZRIELI GRADUATE INSTITUTE OF JEWISH EDUCATION AND ADMINISTRATION (1945). 245 Lexington Ave., NYC 10016. (212)340–7705. Dir. Dr. Yitzchak S. Handel. Offers MS degree in Jewish elementary and secondary education; specialist's certificate and EdD in administration and supervision of Jewish education. Block Education Program, initiated under a grant from the Jewish Agency's L.A. Pincus Fund for the Diaspora, provides summer course work to complement year-round field instruction in local communities; grants MS, specialist's certificate, and EdD degrees.

———, FERKAUF GRADUATE SCHOOL OF PSYCHOLOGY (1957). Eastchester Rd. & Morris Pk. Ave., Bronx, NY 10461. (212)-430–4201. Dean Dr. Barbara G. Melamed. Offers MA in general psychology; PsyD in clinical and school psychology; and PhD in clinical, school, developmental, and health psychology. Programs and services include Center for Psychological and Psychoeducational Services.

———, HARRY FISCHEL SCHOOL FOR HIGHER JEWISH STUDIES (1945). 500 W. 185 St., NYC 10033. (212)960–5253. Dean Dr. Leo Landman. Offers summer graduate programs in Judaic studies and Semitic languages, literatures, and cultures; confers MS, MA, and PhD degrees.

———, (affiliate) RABBI ISAAC ELCHANAN THEOLOGICAL SEMINARY (1896). 2540 Amsterdam Ave., NYC 10033. (212)960–5344. Chmn. Bd. of Trustees Judah Feinerman; V.-Pres. for Administration & Professional Education Rabbi Robert S. Hirt; Dean Rabbi Zevulun Charlop. Grants *semikhah* (ordination) and the degrees of Master of Religious Education, Master of Hebrew Literature, Doctor of Religious Education, and Doctor of Hebrew Literature.

The seminary includes Rabbi Joseph B. Soloveitchik Center of Rabbinic Studies; Morris and Nellie L. Kawaler Rabbinic Training Program; Irving I. Stone Rabbinic Internship Program; Brookdale Chaplaincy Internship Program; Chaver Program (Dir. Rabbi J. David Bleich); Carl and Sylvia Freyer Professional Training Program in Community Outreach; Gindi Program for the Enhancement of Professional Rabbinics; Rudin Continuing Rabbinic Education Program.

Kollelim include Marcos and Adina Katz Kollel (Institute for Advanced Research in Rabbinics—Dir. Rabbi Hershel Schachter); Kollel l'Horaah (Yadin Yadin) and External Yadin Yadin (Dir. Rabbi J. David Bleich); Caroline and Joseph S. Gruss Kollel Elyon (Postgraduate Kollel Program—Dir. Rabbi Aharon Kahn); Caroline and Joseph S. Gruss Institute in Jerusalem (Dir. Rabbi Aharon Lichtenstein).

The service arm of the seminary, Max Stern Division of Communal Services (Dir. Rabbi Robert S. Hirt), provides personal and professional service to the rabbinate and related fields, as well as educational, consultative, organizational, and placement services to congregations, schools, and communal organizations around the world; coordinates a broad spectrum of outreach programs, including Kiruv College Outreach Program, Orthodox Forum, Torah Tours, and off-campus lecture series.

Other seminary programs are Jacob E. Safra Institute of Sephardic Studies and the Institute of Yemenite Studies; Maybaum Sephardic Fellowship Program; Dr. Joseph and Rachel Ades Sephardic Community Outreach Program; Sephardic Community Program; Stone-Sapirstein Center for Jewish Education; National Commission on Torah Education.

PHILIP AND SARAH BELZ SCHOOL OF JEWISH MUSIC (1954). 560 W. 185 St., NYC 10033. (212)960–5353. Dir. Cantor Bernard Beer. Provides professional training of cantors and courses in Jewish liturgical music; maintains a specialized library and conducts outreach; awards associate cantor's certificate and cantorial diploma.

———, WOMEN'S ORGANIZATION (1928). 500 W. 185 St., NYC 10033. (212)960–0855. Natl. Chmn. and Pres. Dinah Pinczower; Exec. Comm: Ann Arbesfeld, Judy Kirshenbaum, Mindy Lamm, Inge Rennert, Judy Schwartz, Alice Turobiner. Supports Yeshiva University's national scholarship program for students training in education, community service, law, medicine, and other professions, and its development program. *YUWO News Briefs.*

——, WURZWEILER SCHOOL OF SOCIAL WORK (1957). 500 W. 185 St., NYC 10033. (212)960–0800. Pres. Norman Lamm; Chmn. Bd. of Govs. Herbert H. Schiff; Dean Dr. Sheldon R. Gelman. Offers graduate programs in social group work, social casework, community social work; grants MSW and DSW degrees and certificate in Jewish communal service. MSW programs are: Concurrent Plan, 2-year, full-time track, combining classroom study and supervised field instruction; Extended Plan, permitting up to five years to complete requirements; Accelerated Plan, granting MSW in 14 months; Plan for Employed Persons (PEP), for people working in social agencies; Block Education Plan (Dir. Dr. Adele Weiner), which combines summer course work with regular-year field placement in local agencies; Clergy Plan, training in counseling for clergy of all denominations; Part-Time Professional Education Plan, enabling human-services professionals to take up to 12 credits as nondegree students. *Jewish Social Work Forum.*

——, (affiliate) YESHIVA OF LOS ANGELES (1977). 9760 W. Pico Blvd., Los Angeles, CA 90035. (213)553–4478. Dean Rabbi Marvin Hier; Bd. Chmn. Samuel Belzberg; Dir. Academic Programs Rabbi Sholom Tendler. Grants BA degree in Jewish studies. Has university program and graduate studies department. Also provides Jewish studies program for beginners. Affiliates are high schools, Jewish Studies Institute for Adult Education, and Simon Wiesenthal Center.

SIMON WIESENTHAL CENTER (1977). 9760 W. Pico Blvd., Los Angeles, CA 90035. (213)553–9036. FAX: (213)553–8007. Dean Rabbi Marvin Hier; Assoc. Dean Rabbi Abraham Cooper; Dir. Dr. Gerald Margolis. Regional offices in New York, Chicago, Miami, Orange County (CA), Jerusalem, Paris, Toronto, Vienna. Dedicated to preserving the memory of the Holocaust through education and awareness. Programs: museum; library; archives; "Testimony for the Truth" oral history; educational outreach; Beit Hashoah—Museum of Tolerance; interactive exploration of social dynamics of bigotry and racism; computerized learning center. In cooperation with Yeshiva of Los Angeles: Jewish Studies Institute; international social action; "Page One" (syndicated weekly radio news magazine presenting contemporary Jewish issues). *Simon Wiesenthal Center Annual; Response Magazine; Commitment; Museum Update.*

YESHIVATH TORAH VODAATH AND MESIVTA RABBINICAL SEMINARY (1918). 425 E. 9 St., Brooklyn, NY 11218. (718)-941–8000. Bd. Chmn. Chaim Leshkowitz. Offers Hebrew and secular education from elementary level through rabbinical ordination and postgraduate work; maintains a teachers institute and community-service bureau; maintains a dormitory and a nonprofit camp program for boys. *Chronicle; Mesivta Vanguard; Thought of the Week; Torah Vodaath News; Ha'Mesifta.*

——, ALUMNI ASSOCIATION (1941). 425 E. 9 St., Brooklyn, NY 11218. (718)941–8000. Pres. Marcus Saffer; Bd. Chmn. Seymour Pluchenik. Promotes social and cultural ties between the alumni and the schools through fund raising; offers vocational guidance to students; operates Camp Torah Vodaath; sponsors research fellowship program for boys. *Annual Journal; Hamesivta Torah periodical.*

SOCIAL, MUTUAL BENEFIT

ALPHA EPSILON PI FRATERNITY (1913). 8815 Wesleyan Rd., Indianapolis, IN 46268–1171. (317)876–1913. Natl. Pres. Richard H. Stein; Exec. V.-Pres. Sidney N. Dunn. International Jewish fraternity active on over 100 campuses in the U.S. and Canada; encourages Jewish students to remain loyal to their heritage and to assume leadership roles in the community; active in behalf of Soviet Jewry, the State of Israel, the United States Holocaust Memorial Museum, and other Jewish causes. *The Lion of Alpha Epsilon Pi (quarterly magazine).*

AMERICAN ASSOCIATION OF RUSSIAN JEWS (1989). 257 Bayview Ave., Amityville, NY 11701. (516)598–3375; (708) 433–0144. FAX:(516)826–7152/(708)433–5530.Pres. Leonid Stolov; V.-Pres. Inna Arolovich. Assists Soviet Jews in emigration from the former USSR and immigration to U.S.; helps Russian Jewish immigrants in resettlement, Jewish acculturation, and adjusting to all aspects of American society, including participation in social and civic activities; informs the American people about the situation of Soviet Jews and the Russian-Jewish community in the U.S. *Chronicle of Anti-Semitic Incidents in the USSR.*

AMERICAN FEDERATION OF JEWS FROM CENTRAL EUROPE, INC. (1938). 570 Seventh Ave., NYC 10018. (212)921-3871. Pres. Robert L. Lehman; Bd. Chmn. Curt C. Silberman; Exec. Asst. Katherine Rosenthal. Seeks to safeguard the rights and interests of American Jews of German-speaking Central European descent, especially in reference to restitution and indemnification; through its affiliate Research Foundation for Jewish Immigration sponsors research and publications on the history, immigration, and acculturation of Central European émigrés in the U.S. and worldwide; through its affiliate Jewish Philanthropic Fund of 1933 supports social programs for needy Nazi victims in the U.S.; undertakes cultural activities, annual conferences, publications; member, Council of Jews from Germany, London.

AMERICAN SEPHARDI FEDERATION (1973). 133 E. 58 St., Suite 404, NYC 10022. (212)-308-3455. FAX: (212)980-9354. Pres. Leon Levy; Exec. Dir. Suri Kasirer. Central umbrella organization for all Sephardic congregations, organizations, and agencies. Seeks to preserve and promote Sephardi culture, education, and traditions. Disseminates resource material on all aspects of Sephardic life. Strives to bring a Sephardic agenda and perspective to American Jewish life. *Sephardic Highlights Newsletter.*

AMERICAN VETERANS OF ISRAEL (1949). 136 E. 39 St., NYC 10016. (516)431-8316. Pres. Paul Kaye; Sec. Sidney Rabinovich. Maintains contact with American and Canadian volunteers who served in Aliyah Bet and/or Israel's War of Independence; promotes Israel's welfare; holds memorial services at grave of Col. David Marcus; is affiliated with World Mahal. *Newsletter.*

ASSOCIATION OF YUGOSLAV JEWS IN THE UNITED STATES, INC. (1941). 130 E. 59 St., Suite 1202, NYC 10022. (212)371-6891. Pres. Mary Levine; Exec. Off. Emanuel Salom; Treas./V.-Pres. Mirko Goldschmidt. Assists all Jews originally from Yugoslavia; raises funds for Israeli agencies and institutions. *Bulletin.*

BNAI ZION—THE AMERICAN FRATERNAL ZIONIST ORGANIZATION (1908). 136 E. 39 St., NYC 10016.(212)725-1211. FAX: (212)684-6327. Pres. Werner Buckold; Exec. V.-Pres. Mel Parness. Fosters principles of Americanism, fraternalism, and Zionism; offers life insurance and other benefits to its members. The Bnai Zion Foundation supports various humanitarian projects in Israel and the USA, chiefly the Bnai Zion Medical Center in Haifa and homes for retarded children—Maon Bnai Zion in Rosh Ha'ayin and the Herman Z. Quittman Center in Jerusalem. In the U.S. sponsors program of awards for excellence in Hebrew for high school and college students. Chapters all over U.S. and a New Leadership division in Greater N.Y. area. *Bnai Zion Voice; Bnai Zion Foundation Newsletter.*

BRITH ABRAHAM (1859; reorg. 1887). 136 E. 39 St., NYC 10016. (212)725-1211. Grand Master Robert Freeman. Protects Jewish rights and combats anti-Semitism; supports Soviet and Ethiopian emigration and the safety and dignity of Jews worldwide; helps to support Bnai Zion Medical Center in Haifa and other Israeli institutions; aids and supports various programs and projects in the U.S.: Hebrew Excellence Program—Gold Medal presentation in high schools and colleges; Camp Loyaltown; Brith Abraham and Bnai Zion Foundations. *Voice.*

BRITH SHOLOM (1905). 3939 Conshohocken Ave., Philadelphia, PA 19131. (215)878-5696. Pres. Jay W. Malis; Exec. Dir. Mervin L. Krimins. Fraternal organization devoted to community welfare, protection of rights of Jewish people, and activities which foster Jewish identity and provide support for Israel; sponsors Brith Sholom House for senior citizens in Philadelphia and Brith Sholom Beit Halochem in Haifa, a rehabilitation center for Israel's permanently war-wounded. *Brith Sholom Presents;* monthly news bulletin.

CENTRAL SEPHARDIC JEWISH COMMUNITY OF AMERICA (1941). 8 W. 70 St., NYC 10023. (212)787-2850. Pres. Emilie Levy; Treas. Victor Tarry. Pres. Women's Div. Irma Cardozo; Treas. Laura Capelluto. Promotes Sephardic culture by awarding scholarships to qualified needy students in New York and Israel; raises funds for hospital and religious institutions in U.S. and Israel. *Annual journal.*

FREE SONS OF ISRAEL (1849). 180 Varick St., 14th fl., NYC 10014. (212)924–6566. Grand Master Herbert Silverstein; Grand Sec. Stanley Siflinger. The oldest Jewish fraternal order in the U.S.; supports the State of Israel; fights anti-Semitism; helps Soviet Jewry. Maintains scholarship fund for members and children of members, insurance fund, and credit union; social functions. *Free Sons Reporter.*

JEWISH LABOR BUND (Directed by WORLD COORDINATING COMMITTEE OF THE BUND) (1897; reorg. 1947). 25 E. 21 St., NYC 10010. (212)475–0059. Exec. Sec. Benjamin Nadel. Coordinates activities of Bund organizations throughout the world and represents them in the Socialist International; spreads the ideas of socialism as formulated by the Jewish Labor Bund; publishes books and periodicals on world problems, Jewish life, socialist theory and policy, and on the history, activities, and ideology of the Jewish Labor Bund. *Unser Tsait* (U.S.); *Lebns-Fragn* (Israel); *Unser Gedank* (Australia); *Unser Shtimme* (France).

SEPHARDIC JEWISH BROTHERHOOD OF AMERICA, INC. (1915). 97–45 Queens Blvd., Rm. 610, Rego Park, NY 11374. (718)459–1600. Pres. Esther Toledo; Sec. Michael Cohen. A benevolent fraternal organization seeking to promote the industrial, social, educational, and religious welfare of its members. *Sephardic Brother.*

WORKMEN'S CIRCLE (1900). 45 E. 33 St., NYC 10016. (212)889–6800. FAX: (212)-532–7518. Pres. Harold Ostroff; Exec. Dir. Robert A. Kaplan. Provides fraternal benefits and activities, Jewish educational programs, secularist Yiddish schools, and summer camps; promotes public-affairs activities in the U.S. on international and national issues. Underwrites "Folksbiene" theater; sponsors Yiddish cultural, music, and theatrical festivals in U.S. and Canada. *Workmen's Circle Call; Kultur un Leben; Horizons.*

SOCIAL WELFARE

AMC CANCER RESEARCH CENTER (formerly JEWISH CONSUMPTIVES' RELIEF SOCIETY, 1904; incorporated as AMERICAN MEDICAL CENTER AT DENVER, 1954). 1600 Pierce St., Denver, CO 80214. (303)233–6501. Acting Dir. Thomas Kean; Pres./CEO Bob R. Baker. A nationally recognized leader in the fight against cancer; employs a three-pronged, interdisciplinary approach that combines laboratory, clinical, and community cancer-control research to advance the prevention, early detection, diagnosis, and treatment of the disease. *Quarterly bulletin; annual report.*

AMERICAN JEWISH CORRECTIONAL CHAPLAINS ASSOCIATION, INC. (formerly NATIONAL COUNCIL OF JEWISH PRISON CHAPLAINS) (1937). 10 E. 73 St., NYC 10021–4194. (212)879–8415. FAX: (212)-772–3977. (Cooperates with the New York Board of Rabbis.) Pres. Rabbi Irving Koslowe; Exec. Off. Rabbi Moses A. Birnbaum. Supports spiritual, moral, and social services for Jewish men and women in corrections; stimulates support of correctional chaplaincy; provides spiritual and professional fellowship for Jewish correctional chaplains; promotes sound standards for correctional chaplaincy; schedules workshops and research to aid chaplains in counseling and with religious services for Jewish inmates. Constituent, American Correctional Chaplains Association. *Chaplains Manual.*

AMERICAN JEWISH SOCIETY FOR SERVICE, INC. (1949). 15 E. 26 St., Rm. 1304, NYC 10010. (212)683–6178. Pres. Arthur Lifson; Exec. Dir. Elly Saltzman. Conducts voluntary work-service camps each summer to enable high-school juniors and seniors to perform humanitarian service.

AMERICAN JEWISH WORLD SERVICE (1985). 15 W. 26 St., 9th fl., NYC 10010. (212)683–1161. FAX: (212)683–5187. Exec. Dir. Andrew Griffel. Provides a Jewish vehicle for responding, on a nonsectarian basis, to hunger and poverty worldwide. Funds international sustainable, environmentally sound development projects and disaster relief; promotes awareness of these issues in the American Jewish community through volunteer groups located in major cities nationwide. *AJWS Report (quarterly newsletter).*

ASSOCIATION OF JEWISH CENTER PROFESSIONALS (1918). c/o JCC, 3505 Mayfield Rd., Cleveland Heights, OH 44118 (216)-382–4000. FAX: (216)382–5401. Pres. Leonard S. Freedman; Exec. Sec. Paulette Buchler. Seeks to enhance the standards, techniques, practices, scope, and public understanding of Jewish Community Center and kindred agency work. *Kesher.*

560 / AMERICAN JEWISH YEAR BOOK, 1992

ASSOCIATION OF JEWISH COMMUNITY OR-
GANIZATION PERSONNEL (AJCOP)
(1969). 1750 Euclid Ave., Cleveland, OH
44115. (216)566–9200. FAX: (216)861–
1230. Pres. Karl Zukerman; Exec. Dir.
Howard R. Berger. An organization of
professionals engaged in areas of fund raising, endowments, budgeting, social planning, financing, administration and coordination of services. Objectives are to
develop and enhance professional practices
in Jewish communal work; to maintain and
improve standards, practices, scope and
public understanding of the field of community organization, as practiced through
local federations, national agencies, other
organizations, settings, and private practi-
tioners.

ASSOCIATION OF JEWISH FAMILY AND
CHILDREN'S AGENCIES (1972). 3084 State
Hwy. 27, Suite 1; PO Box 248, Kendall
Park, NJ 08824–0248. (908)821-0909;
(800)634–7346. FAX:(908)972–8705. Pres.
Marc S. Salisch; Exec. Dir. Bert J. Goldberg. The national service organization for
Jewish family and children's agencies in
Canada and the U.S. Reinforces member
agencies in their efforts to sustain and enhance the quality of Jewish family and
communal life. Operates the Elder Support
Network for the National Jewish Community. *Bulletin (bimonthly); Directory; Professional Opportunities Bulletin; Resettlement Bulletin (monthly).*

ASSOCIATION OF JEWISH FAMILY AND
CHILDREN'S AGENCY PROFESSIONALS
(1965). c/o NYANA, 17 Battery Pl., NYC
10004. (212)425–2900. FAX: (212)344–
1621. Pres. Mark Handelman. Brings together Jewish caseworkers and related professionals in Jewish family, children's, and
health services. Seeks to improve personnel
standards, further Jewish continuity and
identity, and strengthen Jewish family life;
provides forums for professional discussion at national conference of Jewish communal service and regional meetings; takes
action on social-policy issues. *Newsletter.*

BARON DE HIRSCH FUND (1891). 130 E. 59
St., NYC 10022. (212)836–1358. FAX:
(212)888–7538. Pres. Francis F. Rosenbaum, Jr.; Mng. Dir. Lauren Katzowitz.
Aids Jewish immigrants and their children
in the U.S. and Israel by giving grants to
agencies active in educational and vocational fields; has limited program for study
tours in U.S. by Israeli agriculturists.

B'NAI B'RITH (1843). 1640 Rhode Island
Ave., NW, Washington, DC 20036. (202)-
857–6600. FAX: (202)857–1099. Pres.
Kent E. Schiner; Exec. V.-Pres. Dr. Sidney
Clearfield. International Jewish organization, with affiliates in 47 countries. Offers
programs designed to ensure the preservation of Jewry and Judaism: Jewish education, community volunteer service, expansion of human rights, assistance to Israel,
housing for the elderly, leadership training,
rights of Soviet Jews and Jews of other
countries to emigrate and study their heritage. *International Jewish Monthly.*

———, ANTI-DEFAMATION LEAGUE OF
(*see* p. 516)

———, HILLEL FOUNDATIONS, INC. (*see* p.
539)

———, KLUTZNICK MUSEUM (*see* p. 520)

———, YOUTH ORGANIZATION (*see* p. 539)

B'NAI B'RITH WOMEN (1897). 1828 L St.,
NW, Suite 250, Washington, DC 20036.
(202)857–1370.   FAX:(202)857–1380.
Pres. Joan Kort; Exec. Dir. Elaine K.
Binder. Supports Jewish women in their
families, in their communities, and in society. Offers programs that contribute to
preservation of Jewish life and values; supports treatment of emotionally disturbed
children in BBW Residential Treatment
Center in Israel; advocates for Israel and
for family issues. *Women's World.*

CITY OF HOPE NATIONAL MEDICAL CEN-
TER AND BECKMAN RESEARCH INSTI-
TUTE (1913). 1500 E. Duarte Rd., Duarte,
CA 91010. (818)359–8111. Pres. and Chief
Exec. Off. Dr. Sanford M. Shapero; Bd.
Chmn. Richard Ziman. Offers care to
those with cancer and major diseases, med-
ical consultation service for second opin-
ions, and pilot research programs in genet-
ics, immunology, and the basic life process.
*City News; City of Hope Cancer Center Re-
port.*

CONFERENCE OF JEWISH COMMUNAL SER-
VICE (*see* Jewish Communal Service Association of N. America)

COUNCIL OF JEWISH FEDERATIONS, INC.
(1932). 730 Broadway, NYC 10003. (212)-
475–5000. Pres. Charles H. Goodman;
Exec. V.-Pres. Martin Kraar. Provides national and regional services to more than
200 associated federations embracing 800

communities in the U.S. and Canada, aiding in fund raising, community organization, health and welfare planning, personnel recruitment, and public relations. *Directory of Jewish Federations, Welfare Funds and Community Councils; Directory of Jewish Health and Welfare Agencies (biennial); What's New in Federations; Newsbriefs; annual report.*

HOPE CENTER FOR THE DEVELOPMENTALLY DISABLED (1965). 3400 Elizabeth, Denver, CO 80205. (303)388–4801. Bd. Chmn. Albert Cohen; Exec. Dir. George E. Brantley; Sec. Helen Fonda. Provides services to developmentally disabled of community: preschool training, day training and work activities center, speech and language pathology, occupational arts and crafts, recreational therapy, and social services.

INTERNATIONAL ASSOCIATION OF JEWISH VOCATIONAL SERVICES (formerly JEWISH OCCUPATIONAL COUNCIL) (1939). 101 Gary Court, Staten Island, NY 10314. (718)370-0437. FAX: (718)370–1778. Pres. Burton H. Olin; Exec. Dir. Richard M. Africk. Coordinating body of vocational and family-service agencies whose purpose is to support affiliated members, volunteers, and professional leaders in their service to the Jewish and general community.

INTERNATIONAL COUNCIL ON JEWISH SOCIAL AND WELFARE SERVICES (1961). c/o American Jewish Joint Distribution Committee, 711 Third Ave., NYC 10017. (NY liaison office with UN headquarters.) (212)687–6200. Chmn. The Hon. L.H.L. Cohen; Exec. Sec. Cheryl Mariner. Provides for exchange of views and information among member agencies on problems of Jewish social and welfare services, including medical care, old age, welfare, child care, rehabilitation, technical assistance, vocational training, agricultural and other resettlement, economic assistance, refugees, migration, integration and related problems, representation of views to governments and international organizations. Members: six national and international organizations.

JEWISH BRAILLE INSTITUTE OF AMERICA, INC. (1931). 110 E. 30 St., NYC 10016. (212)889–2525. FAX: (212)689–3692. Pres. Dr. Jane Evans; Exec. V.-Pres. Gerald M. Kass. Provides Judaic materials in braille, talking books, and large print for blind, visually impaired, and reading-disabled; offers counseling for full integration into the life of the Jewish community. Comprehensive braille and talking-book library on Judaic topics; many titles in large print. *Jewish Braille Review; JBI Voice.*

JEWISH COMMUNAL SERVICE ASSOCIATION OF N. AMERICA (1899; formerly CONFERENCE OF JEWISH COMMUNAL SERVICE). 3084 State Hwy. 27, Suite 9, Kendall Park, NJ 08824–1657. (908)821–1871. FAX: (908)821–5335. Pres. Ronald I. Coun; Exec. Dir. Joel Ollander. Serves as forum for all professional philosophies in community service, for testing new experiences, proposing new ideas, and questioning or reaffirming old concepts; umbrella organization for seven major Jewish communal service groups. Concerned with advancement of professional personnel practices and standards. *Concurrents; Journal of Jewish Communal Service.*

JEWISH COMMUNITY CENTERS ASSOCIATION OF NORTH AMERICA (1917; formerly JWB). 15 E. 26 St., NYC 10010–1579. (212)532–4949. FAX: (212)481–4174. Pres. Lester Pollack; Exec. V.-Pres. Arthur Rotman. Central leadership agency for 275 Jewish community centers, YM-YWHAs, and camps in the U.S. and Canada, serving over one million Jews. Provides a variety of consulting services and staff training programs to member centers, as well as informal Jewish educational and cultural experiences through Jewish Book and Music Councils and JCC Association Lecture Bureau and many projects related to Israel. U.S. government-accredited agency for the religious, Jewish educational, and recreational needs of Jewish military personnel, their families, and hospitalized VA patients through JWB Jewish Chaplains Council. *Circle; Briefing; Zarkor; Personnel Reporter.*

————, JEWISH BOOK COUNCIL (*see* p. 522)

————, JEWISH MUSIC COUNCIL (*see* p. 522)

————, JWB JEWISH CHAPLAINS COUNCIL (formerly COMMISSION ON JEWISH CHAPLAINCY) (1940). 15 E. 26 St., NYC 10010–1579. Chmn. Rabbi Abraham Avrech; Dir. Rabbi David Lapp. Recruits, endorses, and serves Jewish military and Veterans Administration chaplains on behalf of the American Jewish community and the major rabbinic bodies; trains and assists

Jewish lay leaders where there are no chaplains, for service to Jewish military personnel, their families, and hospitalized veterans. *CHAPLINES* newsletter.

———, LECTURE BUREAU (*see* p. 521)

JEWISH CONCILIATION BOARD OF AMERICA, INC. (A DIVISION OF THE JEWISH BOARD OF FAMILY AND CHILDREN'S SERVICES) (1920). 120 W. 57 St., NYC 10019. (212)582–9100. FAX: (212)245–2096. Pres. Fredric W. Yerman; Exec. V.-Pres. Dr. Alan B. Siskind. Offers dispute-resolution services to families, individuals, and organizations. Social-work, rabbinic, and legal expertise are available for family and divorce mediation and arbitration. Fee—sliding scale.

JEWISH FUND FOR JUSTICE (1984). 920 Broadway, Suite 605, NYC 10010. (212)-677–7080. Bd. Chmn. Lawrence S. Levine; Exec. Dir. Marlene Provizer. A national grant-making foundation supporting efforts to combat the root causes of poverty in the U.S. Provides diverse opportunities for individual, family, and synagogue involvement through memorial, youth endowment, and synagogue challenge funds; works cooperatively with other denominational funders and philanthropies promoting social and economic justice. *Newsletter; Five-Year Report.*

JWB (*see* Jewish Community Centers Association of North America)

LEVI HOSPITAL (sponsored by B'nai B'rith) (1914). 300 Prospect Ave., Hot Springs, AR 71902. (501)624–1281. FAX: (501)-622–3500. Pres. Steven Kirsch; Admin. Patrick G. McCabe. Offers arthritis treatment, stroke rehabilitation, orthopedic rehabilitation, Levi Life Center, a hospice program, and a work capacity center. *Quarterly newsletter.*

MAZON: A JEWISH RESPONSE TO HUNGER (1985). 2940 Westwood Blvd., Suite 7, Los Angeles, CA 90064. (213)470–7769. FAX: (213)470–6736. Bd. Chmn. Lee H. Javitch; Exec. Dir. Irving Cramer. Raises funds by asking American Jews to contribute a suggested amount of 3% of the cost of life-cycle celebrations; funds are granted to nonprofit organizations in the U.S. and abroad that work to alleviate hunger, malnutrition, and poverty. 1991 grants totaled $1.28 million. *Mazon Newsletter.*

NATIONAL ASSOCIATION OF JEWISH FAMILY, CHILDREN'S AND HEALTH PROFESSIONALS (*see* Association of Jewish Family and Children's Agency Professionals)

NATIONAL CONGRESS OF JEWISH DEAF (1956; inc. 1961). c/o Dr. Barbara Boyd, Temple Beth Solomon of the Deaf, 13580 Osborne St., Arleta, CA 91331. Pres. Dr. Barbara Boyd. Congress of Jewish congregations, service organizations, and associations located throughout the U.S. and Canada, advocating religious spirit and cultural ideals and fellowship for the Jewish deaf. Affiliated with World Organization of Jewish Deaf. Publishes *Signs of Judaism*, a guide to sign language of Judaism. *NCJD Quarterly; Jewish Deaf Trivia.*

NATIONAL COUNCIL OF JEWISH PRISON CHAPLAINS, INC. (*see* American Jewish Correctional Chaplains Association, Inc.)

NATIONAL COUNCIL OF JEWISH WOMEN (1893). 53 W. 23 St., NYC 10010. (212)-645–4048. Pres. Joan Bronk; Exec. Dir. Iris Gross. Furthers human welfare through program of community service, education, advocacy for children and youth, aging, women's issues, constitutional rights, Jewish life and Israel. Promotes education for the disadvantaged in Israel through the NCJW Research Institute for Innovation in Education at Hebrew University, Jerusalem. Promotes welfare of children in U.S. through Center for the Child. *NCJW Journal; Washington Newsletter.*

NATIONAL INSTITUTE FOR JEWISH HOSPICE (1985). 8723 Alden Drive, Suite 652, Los Angeles, CA 90048. (213) HOSPICE. Pres. Rabbi Maurice Lamm; Exec. Dir. Levana Lev. Serves as a national Jewish hospice resource center. Through conferences, research, publications, video training courses, referral, and counseling services offers guidance, training, and information to patients, family members, clergy of all faiths, professional caregivers, and volunteers who work with seriously ill Jews. *Jewish Hospice Times.*

NATIONAL JEWISH CENTER FOR IMMUNOLOGY AND RESPIRATORY MEDICINE (formerly NATIONAL JEWISH HOSPITAL/NATIONAL ASTHMA CENTER) (1899). 1400 Jackson St., Denver, CO 80206. (800)222-LUNG. Pres. Leonard M. Perlmutter; Bd. Chmn. Joseph Davis. Seeks to discover and disseminate knowledge that will prevent the occurrence of respiratory, allergic, and immunologic disorders and to develop improved clinical programs for those already afflicted. *New Direction (quarterly); Lung Line Letter (quarterly); Medical Scientific Update.*

NORTH AMERICAN ASSOCIATION OF JEWISH HOMES AND HOUSING FOR THE AGING (1960). 10830 North Central Expressway, Suite 150, Dallas, TX 75231-1022. (214)696–9838. FAX:(214)360–0753. Pres. Bonnie G. Fass; Exec. V.-Pres. Dr. Herbert Shore. Represents a community of not-for-profit charitable homes and housing for the Jewish aging; promotes excellence in performance and quality of service through fostering communication and education and encouraging advocacy for the aging; conducts annual conferences and institutes. *Perspectives (newsletter); Directory; Membership Handbook.*

UNITED ORDER TRUE SISTERS, INC. (UOTS) (1846). 212 Fifth Ave., NYC 10010. (212)679–6790. Pres. Laurette Blumenkrantz; Exec. Admin. Dorothy B. Giuriceo. Charitable, community service, especially home supplies etc. for indigent cancer victims; supports camps for children with cancer. *Echo.*

WORLD CONFEDERATION OF JEWISH COMMUNITY CENTERS (1947; reorg. 1977). 12 Hess St., Jerusalem, Israel 94185. 2–251–265. FAX: 2–247–767. Pres. Leonard Rubin; Exec. Dir. Menachem Revivi. Composed of national center movements in Europe, Israel, Latin America, and North America; seeks to strengthen cooperation among center associations and individual centers; provides programs to enhance Jewish educational opportunities for lay leaders of centers and professional staffs. *Bamerkaz.*

PROFESSIONAL ASSOCIATIONS*

AMERICAN ASSOCIATION OF RABBIS (Religious, Educational)

AMERICAN CONFERENCE OF CANTORS, UNION OF AMERICAN HEBREW CONGREGATIONS (Religious, Educational)

AMERICAN JEWISH CORRECTIONAL CHAPLAINS ASSOCIATION, INC. (Social Welfare)

AMERICAN JEWISH PRESS ASSOCIATION (Cultural)

AMERICAN JEWISH PUBLIC RELATIONS SOCIETY (1957). 234 Fifth Ave., NYC 10001. (212)697–5895. Pres. Henry R. Hecker; Treas. Hyman Brickman. Advances professional status of workers in the public-relations field in Jewish communal service; upholds a professional code of ethics and standards; serves as a clearinghouse for employment opportunities; exchanges professional information and ideas; presents awards for excellence in professional attainments, including the "Maggid Award" for outstanding achievement which enhances Jewish life. *AJPRS Newsletter; AJPRS Directory.*

ASSOCIATION OF HILLEL/JEWISH CAMPUS PROFESSIONALS (Religious, Educational)

ASSOCIATION OF JEWISH CENTER PROFESSIONALS (Social Welfare)

ASSOCIATION OF JEWISH COMMUNITY ORGANIZATION PERSONNEL (Social Welfare)

ASSOCIATION OF JEWISH COMMUNITY RELATIONS WORKERS (Community Relations)

CANTORS ASSEMBLY (Religious, Educational)

CENTRAL CONFERENCE OF AMERICAN RABBIS (Religious, Educational)

COUNCIL OF JEWISH ORGANIZATIONS IN CIVIL SERVICE (Community Relations)

INTERNATIONAL JEWISH MEDIA ASSOCIATION (Cultural)

JEWISH CHAPLAINS COUNCIL, JWB (Social Welfare)

JEWISH COMMUNAL SERVICE ASSOCIATION OF N. AMERICA (Social Welfare)

JEWISH EDUCATORS ASSEMBLY, UNITED SYNAGOGUE OF AMERICA (Religious, Educational)

JEWISH MINISTERS CANTORS ASSOCIATION OF AMERICA, INC. (Religious, Educational)

JEWISH TEACHERS ASSOCIATION—MORIM (Religious, Educational)

*For fuller listing see under categories in parentheses.

NATIONAL ASSOCIATION OF HEBREW DAY SCHOOL ADMINISTRATORS, TORAH UMESORAH (Religious, Educational)

NATIONAL ASSOCIATION OF SYNAGOGUE ADMINISTRATORS, UNITED SYNAGOGUE OF AMERICA (Religious, Educational)

NATIONAL ASSOCIATION OF TEMPLE ADMINISTRATORS, UNION OF AMERICAN HEBREW CONGREGATIONS (Religious, Educational)

NATIONAL ASSOCIATION OF TEMPLE EDUCATORS, UNION OF AMERICAN HEBREW CONGREGATIONS (Religious, Educational)

NATIONAL CONFERENCE OF YESHIVA PRINCIPALS, TORAH UMESORAH (Religious, Educational)

RABBINICAL ASSEMBLY (Religious, Educational)

RABBINICAL COUNCIL OF AMERICA (Religious, Educational)

RECONSTRUCTIONIST RABBINICAL ASSOCIATION, JEWISH RECONSTRUCTIONIST FOUNDATION (Religious, Educational)

UNION OF ORTHODOX RABBIS OF THE U.S. AND CANADA (Religious, Educational)

WORLD CONFERENCE OF JEWISH COMMUNAL SERVICE (Community Relations)

WOMEN'S ORGANIZATIONS*

AMIT WOMEN (Israel-Related)

B'NAI B'RITH WOMEN (Social Welfare)

BRANDEIS UNIVERSITY NATIONAL WOMEN'S COMMITTEE (1948). PO Box 9110, Waltham, MA 02254-9110. (617)-736-4160. FAX: (212)736-4183. Natl. Pres. Marsha Stoller; Exec. Dir. Harriet J. Winer. Provides financial support for the Brandeis Libraries and works to enhance the image of Brandeis, a Jewish-sponsored, nonsectarian university. Offers its members opportunity for intellectual pursuit, continuing education, community service, social interaction, personal enrichment, and leadership development. *Imprint.*

HADASSAH, THE WOMEN'S ZIONIST ORGANIZATION OF AMERICA (Israel-Related)

NA'AMAT USA, the Women's Labor Zionist Organization of America (Israel-Related)

NATIONAL COUNCIL OF JEWISH WOMEN (Social Welfare)

NATIONAL FEDERATION OF TEMPLE SISTERHOODS, UNION OF AMERICAN HEBREW CONGREGATIONS (Religious, Educational)

UOTS (Social Welfare)

WOMEN'S AMERICAN ORT, AMERICAN ORT FEDERATION (Overseas Aid)

WOMEN'S BRANCH OF THE UNION OF ORTHODOX JEWISH CONGREGATIONS OF AMERICA (Religious, Educational)

WOMEN'S DIVISION OF POALE AGUDATH ISRAEL OF AMERICA (Israel-Related)

WOMEN'S DIVISION OF THE JEWISH LABOR COMMITTEE (Community Relations)

WOMEN'S DIVISION OF THE UNITED JEWISH APPEAL (Overseas Aid)

WOMEN'S LEAGUE FOR CONSERVATIVE JUDAISM (Religious, Educational)

WOMEN'S LEAGUE FOR ISRAEL, INC. (Israel-Related)

WOMEN'S ORGANIZATION, YESHIVA UNIVERSITY (Religious, Educational)

YOUTH AND STUDENT ORGANIZATIONS*

AGUDATH ISRAEL OF AMERICA (Religious, Educational)

AMERICAN ZIONIST YOUTH FOUNDATION (Israel-Related)

B'NAI B'RITH HILLEL FOUNDATIONS (Religious, Educational)

B'NAI B'RITH YOUTH ORGANIZATION (Religious, Educational)

BNEI AKIVA OF NORTH AMERICA, RELIGIOUS ZIONISTS OF AMERICA (Israel-Related)

HABONIM-DROR NORTH AMERICA (Israel-Related)

HASHOMER HATZAIR, SOCIALIST ZIONIST YOUTH MOVEMENT (Israel-Related)

KADIMA, UNITED SYNAGOGUE OF AMERICA (Religious, Educational)

---

*For fuller listing see under categories in parentheses.

NATIONAL CONFERENCE OF SYNAGOGUE YOUTH, UNION OF ORTHODOX JEWISH CONGREGATIONS OF AMERICA (Religious, Educational)

NATIONAL JEWISH COMMITTEE ON SCOUTING (Religious, Educational)

NATIONAL JEWISH GIRL SCOUT COMMITTEE (Religious, Educational)

NOAM-MIZRACHI NEW LEADERSHIP COUNCIL, RELIGIOUS ZIONISTS OF AMERICA (Israel-Related)

NORTH AMERICAN FEDERATION OF TEMPLE YOUTH, UNION OF AMERICAN HEBREW CONGREGATIONS (Religious, Educational)

NORTH AMERICAN JEWISH STUDENTS APPEAL (1971). 165 Pidgeon Hill Rd., Huntington Station, NY 11746-9998. (516)385-8771. FAX: (516)385-8772. Pres. Seth Kamil; Chmn. Magda S. Leuchter; Exec. Dir. Brenda Gevertz. Serves as central fund-raising mechanism for six national, independent Jewish student organizations; ensures accountability of public Jewish communal funds used by these agencies; assists Jewish students undertaking projects of concern to Jewish communities; advises and assists Jewish organizations in determining student project feasibility and impact; fosters development of Jewish student leadership in the Jewish community. Beneficiaries include local and regional Jewish student projects; current constituents include Jewish Student Press Service, Student Struggle for Soviet Jewry, Response Magazine, Yugntruf Youth for Yiddish, Progressive Zionist Caucus, and the newest constituent, Project Orchim for outreach on campus.

STUDENT STRUGGLE FOR SOVIET JEWRY (Community Relations)

YOUNG JUDAEA/HASHACHAR, HADASSAH (Israel-Related)

YUGNTRUF YOUTH FOR YIDDISH (1964). 200 W. 72 St., Suite 40, NYC 10023. (212)-787-6675. Cochmn. David Braun, Itzek Gottesman; Editor Gitl Schaechter-Viswanath. A worldwide, nonpolitical organization for high school and college students with a knowledge of, or interest in, Yiddish. Spreads the love and use of the Yiddish language; organizes artistic and social activities, including annual conference for young adults; sponsors Yiddish-speaking preschool for non-Orthodox children; disseminates new Yiddish teaching materials. Yugntruf.

CANADA

B'NAI BRITH CANADA (1875). 15 Hove St., Downsview, ONT M3H 4Y8. (416)633-6224. FAX: (416)630-2159. Pres. Marilyn Weinberg; Exec. V.-Pres. Frank Dimant. Canadian Jewry's senior organization; makes representations to all levels of government on matters of Jewish concern; promotes humanitarian causes and educational programs, community volunteer projects, adult Jewish education, and leadership development; dedicated to human rights. Covenant Newspaper.

———, INSTITUTE FOR INTERNATIONAL AND GOVERNMENTAL AFFAIRS (1987). 15 Hove St., Downsview, ONT M3H 4YB. (416)633-6224. FAX: (416)630-2159. Natl. Chmn. Brian Morris; Natl. Dir. Paul Marcus. Identifies and protests the abuse of human rights throughout the world. Monitors the condition of Jewish communities worldwide and advocates on their behalf when they experience serious violations of their human rights. Comment.

———, LEAGUE FOR HUMAN RIGHTS (1970). 15 Hove St., Downsview, ONT M3H 4Y8. (416)633-6227. FAX: (416)-630-2159. Natl. Chmn. Prof. Stephen Scheinberg; Natl. Dir. Dr. Karen Mock. A national volunteer association dedicated to combatting racism and bigotry. Objectives include human rights for all Canadians, improved inter-community relations, and the elimination of racial discrimination and anti-Semitism. Conducts eduational programs, engages in community action, and provides legal advice and action. Canadian distributor of ADL material. Review of Anti-Semitism; Annual Audit of Anti-Semitic Incidents.

CANADIAN ASSOCIATION FOR LABOR ISRAEL (HISTADRUT) (1944). 7005 Kildare Rd., Suite 14, Cote St. Luc, PQ H4W 1C1. (514)484-9430. FAX: (514)487-6727. Pres. Harry J. F. Bloomfield. Conducts fund-raising and educational activities on behalf of Histadrut, Kupat Holim, and Amal schools in Israel.

CANADIAN FOUNDATION FOR JEWISH CULTURE (1965). 4600 Bathurst St., Willowdale, ONT M2R 3V2. (416)635-2883.

Pres. Mira Koschitzky; Exec. Sec. Edmond Y. Lipsitz. Promotes Jewish studies at university level and encourages original research and scholarship in Jewish subjects; awards annual scholarships and grants-in-aid to scholars in Canada.

CANADIAN FRIENDS OF THE ALLIANCE ISRAÉLITE UNIVERSELLE (1958). PO Box 578, Victoria Station, Montreal, PQ H3Z 2Y6. (514)481-3552. Pres. Joseph Nuss. Supports the educational work of the Alliance.

CANADIAN FRIENDS OF THE HEBREW UNIVERSITY (1944). 3080 Yonge St., Suite 5024, Toronto, ONT M4N 3P4. (416)485-8000. FAX: (416)485-8565. Pres. J. Stephen Lipper; Exec. V.-Pres. Shimon Arbel. Represents the Hebrew University of Jerusalem in Canada; serves as fund-raising arm for the university in Canada; accepts Canadians for study at the university; sponsors educational programs. *Dateline Jerusalem.*

CANADIAN JEWISH CONGRESS (1919; reorg. 1934). 1590 Dr. Penfield Ave., Montreal, PQ H3G 1C5. (514)931-7531. FAX: (514)931-0548. Pres. Les Scheininger; Exec. V.-Pres. Alan Rose. The official voice of Canadian Jewish communities at home and abroad; acts on all matters affecting the status, rights, concerns and welfare of Canadian Jewry; internationally active on behalf of Soviet Jewry, Jews in Arab lands, Holocaust remembrance and restitution; largest Jewish archives in Canada. *National Small Communities Newsletter; Intercom; Ottawa Digest; National Soviet Jewry Newsletter; National Archives Newsletter; regional newsletters.*

CANADIAN ORT ORGANIZATION (Organization of Rehabilitation Through Training) (1942). 5165 Sherbrooke St. W., Suite 208, Montreal, PQ H4A 1T6. (514)481-2787. Pres. Bernard Gross; Exec. Dir. Mac Silver. Carries on fund-raising projects in support of the worldwide vocational-training-school network of ORT. *ORT Reporter.*

———, WOMEN'S CANADIAN ORT (1948). 3101 Bathurst St., Suite 604, Toronto, ONT M6A 2A6. (416)787-0339. Natl. Pres. Lydia London; Natl. Exec. Dir. Diane Uslaner. ·Chapters in 11 Canadian cities raise funds for ORT's nonprofit global network of schools where Jewish

students learn a wide range of marketable skills, including the most advanced high-tech professions. *Focus Magazine.*

CANADIAN YOUNG JUDAEA (1917). 788 Marlee Ave., Suite 205, Toronto, ONT M6B 3K1. (416)781-5156. FAX: (416)-787-3100. Natl. Exec. Dir. Risa Epstein-Gamliel; Natl. Shaliach Shmuel Levkowitz. Strives to attract Jewish youth to Zionism, with goal of *aliyah;* educates youth about Jewish history and Zionism; prepares them to provide leadership in Young Judaea camps in Canada and Israel and to be concerned Jews. *The Judaean.*

CANADIAN ZIONIST FEDERATION (1967). 5250 Decarie Blvd., Suite 550, Montreal, PQ H3X 2H9. (514)486-9526. FAX: (514)483-6392. Pres. Kurt Rothschild. Umbrella organization of all Zionist and Israel-related groups in Canada; carries on major activities in all areas of Jewish life through its departments of education and culture, *aliyah,* youth and students, public affairs, and fund raising, for the purpose of strengthening the State of Israel and the Canadian Jewish community. *Canadian Zionist.*

———, BUREAU OF EDUCATION AND CULTURE (1972). Pres. Kurt Rothschild. Provides counseling by pedagogic experts, in-service teacher-training courses and seminars in Canada and Israel; national pedagogic council and research center; distributes educational material and teaching aids; conducts annual Bible contest and Hebrew-language courses for adults.

FRIENDS OF PIONEERING ISRAEL (1950s). 1111 Finch Ave. W., Suite 154, Downsview, ONT M3J 2E5 (416)736-1339. Pres. Joseph Podemsky. Acts as a voice of Socialist and Zionist points of view within the Jewish community and a focal point for progressive Zionist elements in Canada; Canadian representative of Mapam; affiliated with Hashomer-Hatzair and the Givat Haviva Education Foundation.

HADASSAH—WIZO ORGANIZATION OF CANADA (1917). 1310 Greene Ave., Suite 900, Montreal, PQ H3Z 2B8. (514)937-9431. FAX: (514)933-6483. Natl. Pres. Esther Matlow; Exec. V.-Pres. Lily Frank. Extends material and moral support to the people of Israel requiring such assistance; strengthens and fosters Jewish ideals; encourages Hebrew culture in Canada and promotes Canadian ideals of democracy. *Orah Magazine.*

JEWISH IMMIGRANT AID SERVICES OF CANADA (JIAS) (1919). 5151 Cote Ste. Catherine Rd., Suite 220, Montreal, PQ H3W 1M6. (514)342-9351. FAX: (514)342-8452. Pres. Robert Kleinman; Exec. Dir. Joel Moss. Serves as a national agency for immigration and immigrant welfare. *JIAS Bulletin.*

JEWISH NATIONAL FUND OF CANADA (KEREN KAYEMETH LE'ISRAEL, INC.) (1901). 1980 Sherbrooke St. W., Suite 500, Montreal, PQ H3H 1E8. (514)934-0313. Pres. Allan Posluns; Exec. V.-Pres. Morris Zilka. Fund-raising organization affiliated with the World Zionist Organization; involved in afforestation, soil reclamation, and development of the land of Israel, including the construction of roads and preparation of sites for new settlements; provides educational materials and programs to Jewish schools across Canada.

LABOR ZIONIST ALLIANCE OF CANADA (1909). 7005 Kildare Rd., Suite 10, Cote St. Luc, PQ H3W 1C1. (514)484-1789. FAX: (514)487-6727. Pres. David Kofsky; Chmn. Toronto City Committee Harry Weinstock; Chmn. Montreal City Committee Harry Froimovitch. Associated with the World Labor Zionist movement and allied with the Israel Labor party. Provides recreational and cultural programs, mutual aid, and fraternal care to enhance the social welfare of its membership; actively promotes Zionist education, cultural projects, and forums on aspects of Jewish and Canadian concern.

MIZRACHI-HAPOEL HAMIZRACHI ORGANIZATION OF CANADA (1941). 159 Almore Ave., Downsview, ONT M3H 2H9. (416)-630-7575. Natl. Pres. Kurt Rothschild; Natl. Exec. V.-Pres. Rabbi Menachem Gopin. Promotes religious Zionism, aimed at making Israel a state based on Torah; maintains Bnei Akiva, a summer camp, adult education program, and touring department; supports Mizrachi-Hapoel Hamizrachi and other religious Zionist institutions in Israel which strengthen traditional Judaism. *Mizrachi Newsletter; Or Hamizrach Torah Quarterly.*

NATIONAL COUNCIL OF JEWISH WOMEN OF CANADA (1897). 1110 Finch Ave. W., #518, Downsview, ONT M3J 2T2. (416)-665-8251. Pres. Gloria Strom; Exec. Dir. Eleanor Appleby. Dedicated to furthering human welfare in Jewish and non-Jewish communities, locally, nationally, and internationally; provides essential services and stimulates and educates the individual and the community through an integrated program of education, service, and social action. *New Edition.*

NATIONAL JOINT COMMUNITY RELATIONS COMMITTEE OF CANADIAN JEWISH CONGRESS (1936). 4600 Bathurst St., Willowdale, ONT M2R 3V2. (416)635-2883. FAX: (416)635-1408. Chmn. Joseph J. Wilder; Exec. Dir. Manuel Prutschi. Seeks to safeguard the status, rights, and welfare of Jews in Canada; to combat anti-Semitism and promote understanding and goodwill among all ethnic and religious groups.

STATE OF ISRAEL BONDS (CANADA-ISRAEL SECURITIES, LTD.) (1953). 1255 University St., Suite 200, Montreal, PQ H3B 3B2. (514)878-1871. FAX: (514)874-7693. Pres. Alex Grossman; Bd. Chmn. and CEO Melvyn A. Dobrin. Mobilizes productive investment capital for the economic development of the State of Israel.

Jewish Federations, Welfare Funds, Community Councils

UNITED STATES

ALABAMA

BIRMINGHAM

BIRMINGHAM JEWISH FEDERATION (1936; reorg. 1971); PO Box 130219 (35213); (205)-879–0416. FAX: (205)879–0466. Pres. Steven Brickman; Exec. Dir. Richard Friedman.

MOBILE

MOBILE JEWISH WELFARE FUND, INC. (inc. 1966); One Office Park, Suite 219 (36609); (205)343–7197. Pres. Nancy Silverboard; Admin. Barbara V. Paper.

MONTGOMERY

JEWISH FEDERATION OF MONTGOMERY, INC. (1930); PO Box 20058 (36120); (205)-277–5820. Pres. Jake Mendel; Exec. Dir. Beverly Lipton.

ARIZONA

PHOENIX

JEWISH FEDERATION OF GREATER PHOENIX (1940); 32 W. Coolidge, Suite 200 (85013); (602)274–1800. FAX: (602)266–7875. Pres. Leonard Miller; Exec. Dir. Harold Morgan.

TUCSON

JEWISH FEDERATION OF SOUTHERN ARIZONA (1942); 3822 East River Rd. (85718); (602)577–9393. FAX: (602)577–0734. Pres. Harold Greenberg; Exec. V.-Pres. Richard Fruchter.

ARKANSAS

LITTLE ROCK

JEWISH FEDERATION OF ARKANSAS (1911); 4942 W. Markham, Suite 5 (72205); (501)-663–3571. Pres. Dr. George Wolff; Exec. Dir. Ariel Barak Imber.

CALIFORNIA

LONG BEACH

JEWISH FEDERATION OF GREATER LONG BEACH AND W. ORANGE COUNTY (1937; inc. 1946); 3801 E. Willow St. (90815); (213)-426–7601. FAX: (213)424–3915. Pres. Morton Stuhlbarg; Exec. Dir. Sandi Goldstein.

LOS ANGELES

JEWISH FEDERATION COUNCIL OF GREATER LOS ANGELES (1912; reorg. 1959); 6505 Wilshire Blvd. (90048); (213)852–1234. FAX: (213)655–4458. Pres. David Finegood; Acting Exec. V.-Pres. Merv Lemmerman.

OAKLAND

JEWISH FEDERATION OF THE GREATER EAST BAY (Alameda and Contra Costa Counties) (1918); 401 Grand Ave. (94610); (415)-839–2900. FAX: (415)839–3996. Pres. Dr. Miles Adler; Exec. V.-Pres. Ami Nahshon.

This directory is based on information supplied by the Council of Jewish Federations.

ORANGE COUNTY

JEWISH FEDERATION OF ORANGE COUNTY (1964; inc. 1965); 1385 Warner Ave., Suite. A, Tustin (92680–6442); (714)259–0655. FAX: (714)259–1635. Pres. William Shane; Exec. Dir. Edward Cushman.

PALM SPRINGS

JEWISH FEDERATION OF PALM SPRINGS (1971); 255 El Cielo N., Suite 430 (92262); (619)325–7281. Pres. Jim Horvitz; Exec. Dir. Irving Ginsberg.

SACRAMENTO

JEWISH FEDERATION OF SACRAMENTO (1948); PO Box 254589 (95865); (916)486–0906. FAX: (916)486–0816. Pres. Barbara Ansel; Exec. Dir. Arnold Feder.

SAN DIEGO

UNITED JEWISH FEDERATION OF SAN DIEGO COUNTY (1936); 4797 Mercury St. (92111–2102); (619)571–3444. FAX: (619)-571–0701. Pres. Murray L. Galinson; Exec. V. Pres. Stephen M. Abramson.

SAN FRANCISCO

JEWISH COMMUNITY FEDERATION OF SAN FRANCISCO, THE PENINSULA, MARIN, AND SONOMA COUNTIES (1910; reorg. 1955); 121 Steuart St. (94105); (415)777–0411. FAX: (415)495–6635. Pres. Donald Seiler; Exec. Dir. Wayne Feinstein.

SAN JOSE

JEWISH FEDERATION OF GREATER SAN JOSE (incl. Santa Clara County except Palo Alto and Los Altos) (1930; reorg. 1950); 14855 Oka Rd., Los Gatos (95030); (408)-358–3033. FAX: (408)356–0733. Pres. Bernie Kotansky; Exec. Dir. Paul Ellenbogen.

SANTA BARBARA

SANTA BARBARA JEWISH FEDERATION (1974); 104 W. Anapamu, Suite A. Mailing Address: PO Box 90110, Santa Barbara (93190); (805)963–0244. FAX: (805)569–5052. Pres. Steven A. Amerikaner; Exec. Dir. Barbara Zonen.

COLORADO

DENVER

ALLIED JEWISH FEDERATION OF DENVER (1936); 300 S. Dahlia St. (80222); (303)321–3399. FAX: (303)322–8328. Pres. Stanton D. Rosenbaum; Exec. Dir. Sheldon Steinhauser.

CONNECTICUT

BRIDGEPORT

JEWISH FEDERATION OF GREATER BRIDGEPORT, INC. (1936; reorg. 1981); 4200 Park Ave. (06604); (203)372–6504. FAX: (203)-374–0770. Pres. Selig Danzig; Exec. Dir. Gerald A. Kleinman.

DANBURY

JEWISH FEDERATION OF GREATER DANBURY (1945); 39 Mill Plain Rd., Suite 4 (06811); (203)792–6353. Pres. Jean Wellington; Exec. Dir. Sharon Garelick.

EASTERN CONNECTICUT

JEWISH FEDERATION OF EASTERN CONNECTICUT, INC. (1950; inc. 1970); 28 Channing St., PO Box 1468, New London (06320); (203)442–8062. FAX: (203)444–0759. Pres. Reuben Levin; Exec. Dir. Jerome E. Fischer.

GREENWICH

GREENWICH JEWISH FEDERATION (1956); 600 W. Putnam Ave. (06830); (203)622–1434. FAX: (203)622–1237. Pres. Paula Lustbader; Interim Exec. Dir. Sol Margulies.

HARTFORD

GREATER HARTFORD JEWISH FEDERATION (1945); 333 Bloomfield Ave., W. Hartford (06117); (203)232–4483. FAX: (203)232–5221. Pres. Robert Siskin; Exec. Dir. Don Cooper.

NEW HAVEN

NEW HAVEN JEWISH FEDERATION (1928); 419 Whalley Ave. (06511); (203)562–2137. FAX: (203)787–3241. Pres. Stephen Saltzman; Exec. Dir. Jay Rubin.

NORWALK

(See Westport)

STAMFORD

UNITED JEWISH FEDERATION (inc. 1973); 1035 Newfield Ave., PO Box 3038 (06905); (203)322–6935. FAX: (203)322–3277. Pres. Benson Zinbarg; Exec. Dir. Sheila L. Romanowitz.

WATERBURY

JEWISH FEDERATION OF WATERBURY, INC. (1938); 359 Cooke St. (06710); (203)756–7234. FAX: (203)573–0368. Pres. Dr. Alan Stein; Exec. Dir. Eli J. Skora.

WESTPORT–WESTON–WILTON–NORWALK

UNITED JEWISH APPEAL/FEDERATION OF WESTPORT-WESTON-WILTON-NORWALK (inc. 1980); 49 Richmondville Ave. (06880); (203)266–8197. FAX: (203)226-5051. Pres. Michael Stashower; Exec. Dir. Robert Kessler.

DELAWARE

WILMINGTON

JEWISH FEDERATION OF DELAWARE, INC. (1934); 101 Garden of Eden Rd. (19803); (302)478–6200. FAX: (302)478–5374. Pres. William N. Topkis; Exec. V.-Pres. Robert N. Kerbel.

DISTRICT OF COLUMBIA

WASHINGTON

UNITED JEWISH APPEAL-FEDERATION OF GREATER WASHINGTON, INC. (1935); 6101 Montrose Rd., Rockville, MD 20852. (301)-230–7200. FAX: (301)230–7272. Pres. Edward Kaplan; Exec. V.-Pres. Ted B. Farber.

FLORIDA

DAYTONA BEACH
(See Volusia & Flagler Counties)

FT. LAUDERDALE

JEWISH FEDERATION OF GREATER FT. LAUDERDALE (1968); 8358 W. Oakland Park Blvd. (33351); (305)748–8400. FAX: (305)748–6332. Pres. Barbara Wiener; Exec. Dir. Kenneth B. Bierman.

JACKSONVILLE

JACKSONVILLE JEWISH FEDERATION (1935); 8505 San Jose Blvd. (32217); (904)-448–5000. FAX: (904)448–5715. Pres. Joan Levin; Exec. V.-Pres. Alan Margolies.

LEE COUNTY

JEWISH FEDERATION OF LEE COUNTY (1974); 6315 Presidential Court, Suite A, Ft. Myers (33919-3568); (813)481–4449. FAX: (813)275–9114. Pres. Dr. Harvey Tritel; Exec. Dir. Helene Kramer.

MIAMI

GREATER MIAMI JEWISH FEDERATION, INC. (1938); 4200 Biscayne Blvd. (33137); (305)576–4000. FAX: (305)573–2176. Pres. Howard R. Scharlin; Exec. V.-Pres. Myron J. Brodie.

ORLANDO

JEWISH FEDERATION OF GREATER ORLANDO (1949); 851 N. Maitland Ave., PO Box 941508, Maitland (32794–1508); (407)-645–5933. FAX: (407)645–1172. Pres. Ina Porth; Exec. Dir. Jordan Harburger.

PALM BEACH COUNTY

JEWISH FEDERATION OF PALM BEACH COUNTY, INC. (1962); 501 S. Flagler Dr., Suite 305, W. Palm Beach (33401); (407)832–2120. FAX: (407)832–0562. Pres. Alec Engelstein; Exec. Dir. Jeffrey L. Klein.

PINELLAS COUNTY

JEWISH FEDERATION OF PINELLAS COUNTY, INC. (incl. Clearwater and St. Petersburg) (1950; reincorp. 1974); 301 S. Jupiter Ave., Clearwater (34615); (813) 446–1033. FAX: (813)461–0700. Pres. Stephen Wein; Exec. Dir. Robert F. Tropp.

SARASOTA

SARASOTA-MANATEE JEWISH FEDERATION (1959); 580 S. McIntosh Rd. (34232); (813)-371–4546. FAX: (813)378–2947. Pres. Doris Loevner; Exec. Dir. Norman Olshansky.

SOUTH BROWARD

JEWISH FEDERATION OF SOUTH BROWARD, INC. (1943); 2719 Hollywood Blvd., Hollywood (33020); (305)921–8810. FAX: (305)-921–6491. Pres. Dr. Howard Barron; Exec. Dir. Sumner G. Kaye.

SOUTH COUNTY

SOUTH COUNTY JEWISH FEDERATION (inc. 1979); 336 NW Spanish River Blvd., Boca Raton (33431); (407) 368–2737. FAX: (407)-368–5240. Pres. Marvin Zale; Exec. Dir. Rabbi Bruce S. Warshal.

TAMPA

TAMPA JEWISH FEDERATION (1941); 2808 Horatio (33609); (813)875–1618. FAX: (813)876–7746. Pres. F. Sanford Mahr; Exec. V. Pres. Gary S. Alter.

VOLUSIA & FLAGLER COUNTIES

JEWISH FEDERATION OF VOLUSIA & FLAGLER COUNTIES, INC.; 793 South Nova Rd., Ormond Beach, 32174. (904)672–0294. FAX: (904)673–8372. Pres. Gary Greenfield; Admin. Marilyn Brown.

GEORGIA

ATLANTA

ATLANTA JEWISH FEDERATION, INC. (1905; reorg. 1967); 1753 Peachtree Rd. NE

(30309); (404)873–1661. FAX: (404)874–7043. Pres. Dr. S. Perry Brickman; Exec. Dir. David I. Sarnat.

AUGUSTA

AUGUSTA JEWISH FEDERATION (1937); PO Box 15443 (30909); (404)737–8001. Pres. Matt Marks; Exec. Dir. Michael Pousman.

COLUMBUS

JEWISH WELFARE FEDERATION OF COLUMBUS, INC. (1941); PO Box 6313 (31907); (404)568–6668. Pres. Jack Hirsch; Sec. Irene Rainbow.

SAVANNAH

SAVANNAH JEWISH FEDERATION (1943); PO Box 23527 (31403); (912)355–8111. FAX: (912)355–8116. Pres. Ricky Eichholz; Exec. Dir. Jeff Feld.

HAWAII

HONOLULU

JEWISH FEDERATION OF HAWAII (1956); 677 Ala Moana, Suite 803 (96813); (808)531–4634. FAX: (808)531–4636. Pres. Michael Washofsky; Exec. Dir. Rabbi Melvin Libman.

ILLINOIS

CHAMPAIGN-URBANA

CHAMPAIGN-URBANA JEWISH FEDERATION (1929); 503 E. John St., Champaign (61820); (217)367–9872. Pres. Helen Levin; Exec. Dir. Janie Yairi.

CHICAGO

JEWISH FEDERATION OF METROPOLITAN CHICAGO (1900); 1 S. Franklin St. (60606–4694); (312)346–6700. FAX: (312)855–2474. Pres. Arthur W. Brown, Jr.; Exec. V.-Pres. Steven B. Nasatir.

JEWISH UNITED FUND OF METROPOLITAN CHICAGO (1900); 1 S. Franklin St. (60606–4694); (312)346–6700. FAX: (312)444–2086. Pres. Arthur W. Brown, Jr.; Exec. Dir. Steven B. Nasatir.

ELGIN

ELGIN AREA JEWISH WELFARE CHEST (1938); 330 Division St. (60120); (312)741–5656. Pres. Dr. Albert Simon; Treas. Richard Cutts.

PEORIA

JEWISH FEDERATION OF PEORIA (1933; inc. 1947); 5901 N. Prospect Rd., Suite 203, Town Hall Bldg., Junction City (61614);

(309)689–0063. Pres. Dr. Irving J. Weigensberg; Exec. Dir. Eunice Galsky.

QUAD CITIES

JEWISH FEDERATION OF QUAD CITIES (incl. Rock Island, Moline, Davenport, Bettendorf) (1938; comb. 1973); 224 18 St., Suite 303, Rock Island (61201); (309)793–1300. Pres. Gordon Ney; Exec. Dir. Ida Kramer.

ROCKFORD

JEWISH FEDERATION OF GREATER ROCKFORD (1937); 1500 Parkview Ave. (61107); (815)399–5497. Pres. Jay Kamin; Exec. Dir. Tony Toback.

SOUTHERN ILLINOIS

JEWISH FEDERATION OF SOUTHERN ILLINOIS, SOUTHEASTERN MISSOURI AND WESTERN KENTUCKY (1941); 6464 W. Main, Suite 7A, Belleville (62223); (618)398–6100. Pres. Ronald Rubin; Exec. Dir. Stan Anderman.

SPRINGFIELD

SPRINGFIELD JEWISH FEDERATION (1941); 730 E. Vine St. (62703); (217)528–3446. Pres. Robert Silverman; Exec. Dir. Gloria Schwartz.

INDIANA

EVANSVILLE

EVANSVILLE JEWISH COMMUNITY COUNCIL, INC. (1936; inc. 1964); PO Box 5026 (47715); (812)477–7050. Pres. Jon Goldman; Exec. Sec. Maxine P. Fink.

FORT WAYNE

FORT WAYNE JEWISH FEDERATION (1921); 227 E. Washington Blvd. (46802); (219)422–8566. Pres. Carol Sandler; Exec. Dir. Vivian Lansky.

INDIANAPOLIS

JEWISH FEDERATION OF GREATER INDIANAPOLIS, INC. (1905); 615 N. Alabama St., Suite 412 (46204–1430); (317)637–2473. FAX: (317)637–2477. Pres. Stanley Talesnick; Exec. V.-Pres. Harry Nadler.

LAFAYETTE

FEDERATED JEWISH CHARITIES (1924); PO Box 708 (47902); (317)742–9081. FAX: (317)742–4379. Pres. Arnold Cohen; Finan. Sec. Louis Pearlman, Jr.

MICHIGAN CITY

MICHIGAN CITY UNITED JEWISH WELFARE FUND; 2800 S. Franklin St. (46360); (219)-874–4477. Pres. & Treas. Harold Leinwand.

NORTHWEST INDIANA

THE JEWISH FEDERATION, INC. (1941; reorg. 1959); 2939 Jewett St., Highland (46322); (219)972-2250. FAX: (219)972-4779. Pres. Jerome Gardberg; Exec. Dir. Marty Erann.

SOUTH BEND

JEWISH FEDERATION OF ST. JOSEPH VALLEY (1946); 105 Jefferson Centre, Suite 804 (46601); (219)233-1164. FAX: (219)288-4103. Pres. Dr. William Gitlin; Exec. V.-Pres. Kimball Marsh.

IOWA

DES MOINES

JEWISH FEDERATION OF GREATER DES MOINES (1914); 910 Polk Blvd. (50312); (515)277-6321. FAX: (515)277-4069. Pres. Harry Bookey; Exec. Dir. Elaine Steinger.

SIOUX CITY

JEWISH FEDERATION (1921); 525 14th St. (51105); (712)258-0618. Pres. Michael Potash; Exec. Dir. Doris Rosenthal.

KANSAS

WICHITA

MID-KANSAS JEWISH FEDERATION, INC. (1935); 400 N. Woodlawn, Suite 8 (67208); (316)686-4741. Pres. Ivonne Goldstein; Exec. Dir. Beverly Jacobson.

KENTUCKY

LEXINGTON

CENTRAL KENTUCKY JEWISH FEDERATION (1976); 333 Waller, Suite 5 (40504); (606)-252-7622. Pres. Michael Ades; Exec. Dir. Linda Ravvin.

LOUISVILLE

JEWISH COMMUNITY FEDERATION OF LOUISVILLE, INC. (1934); 3630 Dutchman's Lane (40205); (502)451-8840. FAX: (502)-458-0702. Pres. Ronald W. Abrams; Exec. Dir. Dr. Alan S. Engel.

LOUISIANA

ALEXANDRIA

THE JEWISH WELFARE FEDERATION AND COMMUNITY COUNCIL OF CENTRAL LOUISIANA (1938); 1227 Southhampton (71303); (318)445-4785. Pres. Alvin Mykoff; Sec.-Treas. Roeve Weill.

BATON ROUGE

JEWISH FEDERATION OF GREATER BATON ROUGE (1971); 11744 Haymarket Ave., Suite B; PO Box 80827 (70898); (504) 291-5895. Pres. Dr. Steven Cavalier; Exec. Dir. Louis Goldman.

NEW ORLEANS

JEWISH FEDERATION OF GREATER NEW ORLEANS (1913; reorg. 1977); 1539 Jackson Ave. (70130); (504)525-0673. FAX: (504)-568-9290. Pres. Alan Rosenbloom; Exec. Dir. Jane Buchsbaum.

SHREVEPORT

SHREVEPORT JEWISH FEDERATION (1941; inc. 1967); 2032 Line Ave. (71104); (318)-221-4129. Pres. William Braunig, Jr.; Exec. Dir. Monty Pomm.

MAINE

LEWISTON-AUBURN

LEWISTON-AUBURN JEWISH FEDERATION (1947); 74 Bradman St., Auburn (04210); (207)786-4201. Pres. Scott Nussinow.

PORTLAND

JEWISH FEDERATION COMMUNITY COUNCIL OF SOUTHERN MAINE (1942); 57 Ashmont St. (04103); (207)773-7254. FAX: (207)761-2406. Pres. Lisa Cohen; Exec. Dir. Meyer Bodoff.

MARYLAND

BALTIMORE

THE ASSOCIATED: JEWISH COMMUNITY FEDERATION OF BALTIMORE (1920; reorg. 1969); 101 W. Mt. Royal Ave. (21201); (301) 727-4828. FAX: (301)783-8991. Chmn. Suzanne F. Cohen; Pres. Darrell D. Friedman.

MASSACHUSETTS

BERKSHIRE COUNTY

JEWISH FEDERATION OF THE BERKSHIRES (1940); 235 East St., Pittsfield (01201); (413)-442-4360. FAX: (413)443-6070. Pres. Joel Greenberg; Exec. Dir. Richard Davis.

BOSTON

COMBINED JEWISH PHILANTHROPIES OF GREATER BOSTON, INC. (1895; inc. 1961); One Lincoln Plaza (02111); (617)330-9500. FAX: (617)330-5197. Chmn. Alan R. Goldstein; Exec. V.-Pres. Barry Shrage.

CAPE COD

JEWISH FEDERATION OF CAPE COD 396 Main St., PO Box 2568, Hyannis (02601); (508)778-5588. Pres. Melvin Cohen.

FRAMINGHAM (Merged with Boston)

LEOMINSTER

LEOMINSTER JEWISH COMMUNITY COUN-
CIL, INC. (1939); 268 Washington St. (01453);
(617)534–6121. Pres. Dr. Milton Kline; Sec.-
Treas. Howard J. Rome.

MERRIMACK VALLEY

MERRIMACK VALLEY UNITED JEWISH
COMMUNITIES (Serves Lowell, Lawrence,
Andover, Haverhill, Newburyport, and 22
surrounding communities) (1988); 805 Turn-
pike St., N. Andover (01845); (508)688–
0466. FAX: (508)682-3041. Pres. Larry
Ansin; Exec. Dir. Howard Flagler.

NEW BEDFORD

JEWISH FEDERATION OF GREATER NEW
BEDFORD, INC. (1938; inc. 1954); 467 Haw-
thorn St., N. Dartmouth (02747); (508)997–
7471. FAX: (508)997–7730. Pres. Elliot Ros-
enfield; Exec. Dir. Jerry S. Neimand.

NORTH SHORE

JEWISH FEDERATION OF THE NORTH
SHORE, INC. (1938); 4 Community Rd., Marblehead (01945); (617)598–1810. FAX:
(617)639–1284. Pres. Linda Lerner; Exec.
Dir. Bruce Yudewitz.

SPRINGFIELD

JEWISH FEDERATION OF GREATER SPRING-
FIELD, INC. (1925); 1160 Dickinson St.
(01108); (413)737–4313. FAX: (413)737–
4348. Pres. Diane Troderman; Exec. Dir. Joel
Weiss.

WORCESTER

WORCESTER JEWISH FEDERATION, INC.
(1947; inc. 1957); 633 Salisbury St. (01609);
(508)756–1543. FAX: (508)798- 0962. Pres.
Michael Sleeper.

MICHIGAN

ANN ARBOR

JEWISH COMMUNITY ASSOCIATION/
UNITED JEWISH APPEAL (1986); 2939 Birch
Hollow Dr. (48108). (313)677–0100. Pres.
Dr. Owen Z. Perlman; Interim Dir. Nancy
N. Margolis.

DETROIT

JEWISH WELFARE FEDERATION OF DE-
TROIT (1899); 6735 Telegraph Rd., Suite 30,
PO Box 2030, Bloomfield Hills (48303-2030);
(313)642–4260. FAX: (313)642–4985 (executive offices); (313)642–4941 (all other depart-

ments). Pres. Mark E. Schlussel; Exec.
V.-Pres. Robert P. Aronson.

FLINT

FLINT JEWISH FEDERATION (1936); 619
Wallenberg St. (48502); (313)767–5922.
FAX: (313)767–9024. Pres. Nancy Hanflik;
Exec. Dir. David Nussbaum.

GRAND RAPIDS

JEWISH COMMUNITY FUND OF GRAND
RAPIDS (1930); 2609 Berwyck SE (49506);
(616)956–9365. Pres. Joseph N. Schwartz;
Admin. Dir. Judy Joseph.

MINNESOTA

DULUTH–SUPERIOR

JEWISH FEDERATION & COMMUNITY COUN-
CIL (1937); 1602 E. Second St. (55812); (218)-
724–8857. Pres. David Blustin; Sec. Admin.
Gloria Vitullo.

MINNEAPOLIS

MINNEAPOLIS FEDERATION FOR JEWISH
SERVICE (1929; inc. 1930); 7600 Wayzata
Blvd. (55426); (612)593–2600. FAX: (612)-
593–2544. Pres. Herbert Goldenberg; Exec.
Dir. Max L. Kleinman.

ST. PAUL

UNITED JEWISH FUND AND COUNCIL
(1935); 790 S. Cleveland, Suite 201 (55116);
(612)690–1707. FAX: (612)690–0228. Pres.
Allen Freeman; Exec. Dir. Sam Asher.

MISSISSIPPI

JACKSON

JACKSON JEWISH WELFARE FUND, INC.
(1945); 5315 Old Canton Rd. (39211–4625);
(601)956–6215. Pres. Ruth Friedman; V.-
Pres. Erik Hearon.

MISSOURI

KANSAS CITY

JEWISH FEDERATION OF GREATER KANSAS
CITY (1933); 5801 W. 115th St., Overland
Park, KS (66211–1824); (913)469–1340.
FAX: (913)451–9358. Pres. Ronald Gold-
smith; Exec. Dir. A. Robert Gast.

ST. JOSEPH

UNITED JEWISH FUND OF ST. JOSEPH
(1915); 509 Woodcrest Dr. (64506); (816)-
279–7154. Pres. Dorathea Polsky; Exec. Sec.
Martha Rothstein.

ST. LOUIS

JEWISH FEDERATION OF ST. LOUIS (incl. St.
Louis County) (1901); 12 Millstone Campus

574 / american jewish year book, 1992

Dr. (63146); (314)432–0020. FAX: (314)-
432–1277. Pres. Alyn V. Essman; Exec. V.-
Pres. Ira Steinmetz.

NEBRASKA

LINCOLN

LINCOLN JEWISH WELFARE FEDERATION,
INC. (1931; inc. 1961); PO Box 80014
(68501); (402)423–5695. Co-Pres. Ruth &
Irwin Goldenberg; Exec. Dir. Robert Pitlor.

OMAHA

JEWISH FEDERATION OF OMAHA (1903);
333 S. 132nd St. (68154–2198); (402)334–
8200. FAX: (402)334–1330. Pres. Jay R.
Lerner; Exec. Dir. Howard Bloom.

NEVADA

LAS VEGAS

JEWISH FEDERATION OF LAS VEGAS (1973);
1030 E. Twain Ave. (89109); (702)732–0556.
FAX: (702)732–3228. Pres. Dr. Marvin M.
Perer; Interim Exec. Dir. Jerry Countess.

NEW HAMPSHIRE

MANCHESTER

JEWISH FEDERATION OF GREATER MAN-
CHESTER (1974); 698 Beech St. (03104);
(603)627–7679. Pres. Dr. David Stahl; Exec.
Dir. Mark Silverberg.

NEW JERSEY

ATLANTIC COUNTY

FEDERATION OF JEWISH AGENCIES OF AT-
LANTIC COUNTY (1924); 505–507 Tilton Rd.,
Northfield (08225); (609)646–7077. FAX:
(609)646–8053. Pres. Howard A. Goldberg;
Exec. Dir. Bernard Cohen.

BERGEN COUNTY

UNITED JEWISH COMMUNITY OF BERGEN
COUNTY (inc. 1978); 111 Kinderkamack Rd.,
PO Box 4176, N. Hackensack Station, River
Edge (07661); (201)488–6800. FAX: (201)-
488–1507. Pres. Irwin Marks; Exec. V.-Pres.
James Young.

CENTRAL NEW JERSEY

JEWISH FEDERATION OF CENTRAL NEW
JERSEY (1940; merged 1973); Green Lane,
Union (07083); (201)351–5060. FAX: (201)-
351–7060. Pres. Murray Pantirer; Exec. V.-
Pres. Burton Lazarow.

CLIFTON–PASSAIC

JEWISH FEDERATION OF GREATER CLIF-
TON-PASSAIC (1933); 199 Scoles Ave., Clifton (07012). (201)777–7031. FAX: (201)777–

6701. Pres. Jon Gurkoff; Exec. Dir. Yosef
Muskin.

CUMBERLAND COUNTY

JEWISH FEDERATION OF CUMBERLAND
COUNTY (inc. 1971); 629 Wood St., Suite
204, Vineland (08360); (609)696–4445. Pres.
Stanley Orlinsky; Exec. Dir. Daniel Lepow.

ENGLEWOOD

(Merged with Bergen County)

MERCER COUNTY

JEWISH FEDERATION OF MERCER AND
BUCKS COUNTIES NJ/PA (1929; reorg.
1982); 999 Lower Ferry Rd., Trenton
(08628); (609)883–5000. FAX: (609)883–
2563. Pres. Richard Dickson; Exec. Dir.
Haim Morag. (Also see listing under Pennsylvania.)

METROWEST NEW JERSEY

UNITED JEWISH FEDERATION OF MET-
ROWEST (1923); 60 Glenwood Ave., E. Orange (07017); (201)673–6800; (212)943–
0570. FAX: (201)673–4387. Pres. Jerome
Waldor; Exec. V.-Pres. Howard E. Charish.

MIDDLESEX COUNTY

JEWISH FEDERATION OF GREATER MID-
DLESEX COUNTY (org. 1948; reorg. 1985);
100 Metroplex Dr., Suite 101, Edison
(08817); (201)985–1234. FAX: (201)985–
3295. Pres. James Stahl; Exec. V.-Pres. Michael Shapiro.

MONMOUTH COUNTY

JEWISH FEDERATION OF GREATER MON-
MOUTH COUNTY (1971); 100 Grant Ave., PO
Box 210, Deal (07723–0210); (201)531–
6200-1. FAX: (201)531–9518. Pres. Arnold
Gelfman; Exec. V.-Pres. Marvin Relkin;
Exec. Dir. Bonnie Komito.

MORRIS–SUSSEX COUNTY

(Merged with MetroWest NJ)

NORTH JERSEY

JEWISH FEDERATION OF NORTH JERSEY
(1933); One Pike Dr., Wayne (07470); (201)-
595–0555. FAX: (201)595–1532. Pres.
Joanne Sprechman; Exec. Dir. Barry Rosenberg.

NORTHERN MIDDLESEX COUNTY

(See Middlesex County)

OCEAN COUNTY

OCEAN COUNTY JEWISH FEDERATION
(1977); 301 Madison Ave., Lakewood

(08701); (201)363–0530. FAX: (201)363–2097. Pres. Zev Rosen; Exec. Dir. Michael Ruvel.

PRINCETON

PRINCETON AREA UJA-FEDERATION; 15 Roszel Rd., Princeton (08540); (609)243–9440. Pres. Dr. Eliot Freeman; Exec. Dir. Jerilyn Zimmerman.

RARITAN VALLEY

(See Middlesex County)

SOMERSET COUNTY

JEWISH FEDERATION OF SOMERSET, HUNTERDON & WARREN COUNTIES (1960); PO Box 6455, Bridgewater (08807); (201)725–6994. FAX: (908)725–9753. Pres. George Blank; Exec. Dir. Alan J. Nydick.

SOUTHERN NEW JERSEY

JEWISH FEDERATION OF SOUTHERN NEW JERSEY (incl. Camden, Burlington, and Gloucester counties) (1922); 2393 W. Marlton Pike, Cherry Hill (08002); (609)665–6100. FAX: (609)665–0074. Pres. Dr. Robert Paul; Exec. V.-Pres. Stuart Alperin.

NEW MEXICO

ALBUQUERQUE

JEWISH FEDERATION OF GREATER ALBUQUERQUE, INC. (1938); 8205 Spain, NE (97109); (505)821–3214. FAX: (505)821–3355. Pres. Brian Ivener; Exec. Dir. Joel Brooks.

NEW YORK

ALBANY

(Merged with Schenectady; see Northeastern New York)

BROOME COUNTY

JEWISH FEDERATION OF BROOME COUNTY (1937; inc. 1958); 500 Clubhouse Rd., Vestal (13850); (607)724–2332. FAX: (607)724–2311. Pres. Marcelene H. Yonaty; Exec. Dir. Victoria Rouff.

BUFFALO

JEWISH FEDERATION OF GREATER BUFFALO, INC. (1903); 787 Delaware Ave. (14209); (716)886–7750. FAX: (716)886–1367. Pres. Dr. Richard Ament; Exec. Dir. Harry Kosansky.

DUTCHESS COUNTY

JEWISH FEDERATION OF DUTCHESS COUNTY; 110 S. Grand Ave., Poughkeepsie

(12603); (914)471–9811. Pres. Marc Ritter; Exec. Dir. Allan Greene.

ELMIRA

ELMIRA JEWISH WELFARE FUND, INC. (1942); Grandview Rd. Ext., PO Box 3087 (14905); (607)734–8122. Pres. Arnold Rosenberg; Exec. Dir. Cy Leveen.

KINGSTON

JEWISH FEDERATION OF GREATER KINGSTON, INC. (inc. 1951); 159 Green St. (12401); (914)338–8131. Pres. Dr. Howard Rothstein.

NEW YORK

UJA-FEDERATION OF JEWISH PHILANTHROPIES OF NEW YORK, INC. (incl. Greater NY; Westchester, Nassau, and Suffolk counties) (Fed. org. 1917; UJA 1939; merged 1986); 130 E. 59th St. (10022); (212)980–1000. FAX: (212)867–1074. Pres. Alan S. Jaffe; Chmn. Joseph Gurwin; Exec. V.-Pres. Stephen D. Solender.

NIAGARA FALLS

JEWISH FEDERATION OF NIAGARA FALLS, NY, INC. (1935); Temple Beth Israel, Rm. #5, College & Madison Ave. (14305); (716)-284–4575. Pres. Howard Rushner.

NORTHEASTERN NEW YORK

UNITED JEWISH FEDERATION OF NORTHEASTERN NEW YORK (1986); Latham Circle Mall, 800 New Loudon Rd., Latham (12110); (518)783–7800. FAX: (518)783–1557. Pres. Rabbi Martin Silverman; Exec. Dir. Norman J. Schimelman.

ORANGE COUNTY

JEWISH FEDERATION OF GREATER ORANGE COUNTY (1977); 360 Powell Ave., Newburgh (12550); (914)562–7860. Pres. Richard Levin; Exec. Dir. Nancy Goldman.

ROCHESTER

JEWISH COMMUNITY FEDERATION OF ROCHESTER, NY, INC. (1939); 441 East Ave. (14607); (716)461–0490. FAX: (716)461–0912. Pres. Linda Cornell Weinstein; Exec. Dir. Lawrence W. Fine.

ROCKLAND COUNTY

UNITED JEWISH COMMUNITY OF ROCKLAND COUNTY (1985); 240 W. Nyack Rd., W. Nyack (10994–1711). (914)627–3700. FAX: (914)627–7881. Pres. Mark Karsch; Exec. Dir. Michael A. Bierman.

SCHENECTADY

(Merged with Albany; see Northeastern New York)

SYRACUSE

SYRACUSE JEWISH FEDERATION, INC. (1918); 101 Smith St.; PO Box 510, DeWitt (13214–0510); (315)445–0161. FAX: (315)-445–1559. Pres. Philip Pinsky; Exec. V.-Pres. Barry Silverberg.

TROY

(Merged with Albany-Schenectady; see Northeastern New York)

UTICA

JEWISH FEDERATION OF UTICA, NY, INC. (1933; inc. 1950); 2310 Oneida St. (13501); (315)733–2343. Pres. Marsha Basloe; Exec. Dir. Meyer L. Bodoff.

NORTH CAROLINA

ASHEVILLE

WESTERN NORTH CAROLINA JEWISH FEDERATION (1935); 236 Charlotte St. (28801); (704)253–0701. FAX: (704)251–9144. Pres. Robert J. Deutsch; Exec. Dir. David Seidenberg.

CHARLOTTE

CHARLOTTE JEWISH FEDERATION (1938); PO Box 13369 (28211); (704)366–5007. FAX: (704)365–4507. Pres. Emily Zimmern; Exec. Dir. Daniel Lepow.

DURHAM–CHAPEL HILL

DURHAM–CHAPEL HILL JEWISH FEDERATION & COMMUNITY COUNCIL (1979); 1310 LeClair St., Chapel Hill (27514); (919)967–1945. FAX: (919)962–1277. Pres. Barry Nakell.

GREENSBORO

GREENSBORO JEWISH FEDERATION (1940); 713-A N. Greene St. (27401); (919)272–3189. FAX: (919)272–0214. Pres. Joslin LeBauer; Exec. Dir. Marilyn Chandler.

WAKE COUNTY

WAKE COUNTY JEWISH FEDERATION, INC. (1987); 3900 Merton Dr., Suite 108, Raleigh (27609); (919)781–5459. FAX: (919)787–0666. Pres. Joseph Woodland.

OHIO

AKRON

AKRON JEWISH COMMUNITY FEDERATION (1935); 750 White Pond Dr. (44320); (216)-867–7850. FAX: (216)867–8498. Pres. Dr. Steven Kutnick; Exec. Dir. Michael Wise.

CANTON

CANTON JEWISH COMMUNITY FEDERATION (1935; reorg. 1955); 2631 Harvard Ave., NW (44709); (216)452–6444. FAX: (216)-452–4487. Pres. Robert Narens; Exec. Dir. Jay Rubin.

CINCINNATI

JEWISH FEDERATION OF CINCINNATI (1896; reorg. 1967); 1811 Losantiville, Suite 320 (45237); (513) 351–3800. FAX: (513)351–3863. Pres. Stanley M. Chesley; Exec. V.-Pres. Aubrey Herman.

CLEVELAND

JEWISH COMMUNITY FEDERATION OF CLEVELAND (1903); 1750 Euclid Ave. (44115); (216)566–9200. FAX: (216)861–1230. Pres. Bennett Yanowitz; Exec. Dir. Stephen H. Hoffman.

COLUMBUS

COLUMBUS JEWISH FEDERATION (1926); 1175 College Ave. (43209); (614)237–7686. FAX: (614)237–2221. Pres. Benjamin L. Zox; Exec. Dir. Alan H. Gill.

DAYTON

JEWISH FEDERATION OF GREATER DAYTON (1910); 4501 Denlinger Rd. (45426); (513)854–4150. FAX: (513)854–2850. Pres. Lawrence T. Burick; Exec. V.-Pres. Peter H. Wells.

STEUBENVILLE

JEWISH COMMUNITY COUNCIL (1938); 300 Lovers Lane (43952); (614)264–5514. Pres. Morris Denmark; Exec. Sec. Jennie Bernstein.

TOLEDO

JEWISH FEDERATION OF GREATER TOLEDO (1907; reorg. 1960); 6505 Sylvania Ave., PO Box 587, Sylvania (43560); (419)885–4461. FAX: (419)885–3207. Pres. James J. Akers; Exec. Dir. Steven J. Edelstein.

YOUNGSTOWN

YOUNGSTOWN AREA JEWISH FEDERATION (1935); PO Box 449, 505 Gypsy Lane (44501); (216)746–3251. FAX: (216)746–7926. Pres. Esther L. Marks; Exec. V.-Pres. Sam Kooperman.

OKLAHOMA

OKLAHOMA CITY

JEWISH FEDERATION OF GREATER OKLAHOMA CITY (1941); 2800 Quail Plaza Dr. (73120). (405)752–7307. FAX: (405)752–7309. Pres. Jerry Bendorf.

TULSA

JEWISH FEDERATION OF TULSA (1938); 2021 E. 71st St. (74136); (918)495–1100. FAX: (918)495–1220. Pres. Curtis S. Green; Exec. Dir. David Bernstein.

OREGON

PORTLAND

JEWISH FEDERATION OF PORTLAND (incl. state of Oregon and adjacent Washington communities) (1920; reorg. 1956); 6651 SW Capitol Highway (97219); (503)245–6219. FAX: (503)245–6603. Pres. Stanley D. Geffen; Exec. Dir. Charles Schiffman.

PENNSYLVANIA

ALLENTOWN

JEWISH FEDERATION OF ALLENTOWN (1948); 702 N. 22nd St. (18104); (215)821–5500. FAX: (215)821–8946. Pres. Lory L. Brenner; Exec. Dir. Ivan C. Schonfeld.

ALTOONA

FEDERATION OF JEWISH PHILANTHROPIES (1920; reorg. 1940; inc. 1944); 1308 17th St. (16601); (814)944–4072. Pres. Morley Cohn.

BUCKS COUNTY

JEWISH FEDERATION OF MERCER AND BUCKS COUNTIES NJ/PA (1929; reorg. 1982); 999 Lower Ferry Rd., Trenton, NJ (08628); (609)883–5000. FAX: (609)883–2563. Pres. Richard Dickson; Exec. Dir. Haim Morag. (Also see listing under New Jersey.)

ERIE

JEWISH COMMUNITY COUNCIL OF ERIE (1946); 701 G. Daniel Baldwin Bldg., 1001 State St. (16501); (814)455–4474. Pres. Richard Levick.

HARRISBURG

UNITED JEWISH COMMUNITY OF GREATER HARRISBURG (1941); 100 Vaughn St. (17110); (717)236–9555. FAX: (717)236–8104. Pres. Lory L. Brenner; Exec. Dir. Elliot Gershenson.

JOHNSTOWN

UNITED JEWISH FEDERATION OF JOHNSTOWN (1938); 601 Wayne St. (15905); (814)-539–9891 (home). Pres. Isadore Suchman.

PHILADELPHIA

JEWISH FEDERATION OF GREATER PHILADELPHIA (includes Bucks, Chester, Delaware, Montgomery, and Philadelphia counties) (1901; reorg. 1956); 226 S. 16th St.

(19102); (215)893–5600. FAX: (215)735–7977. Pres. Theodore Seidenberg; Exec. V.-Pres. Robert P. Forman.

PITTSBURGH

UNITED JEWISH FEDERATION OF GREATER PITTSBURGH (1912; reorg. 1955); 234 McKee Pl. (15213); (412)681–8000. FAX: (412)681–3980. Pres. David S. Shapira; Exec. V.-Pres. Howard M. Rieger.

READING

JEWISH FEDERATION OF READING, PA., INC. (1935; reorg. 1972); 1700 City Line St. (19604); (215)921–2766. FAX: (215)929–0886. Pres. Alma Lakin; Exec. Dir. Daniel Tannenbaum.

SCRANTON

SCRANTON-LACKAWANNA JEWISH FEDERATION (incl. Lackawanna County) (1945); 601 Jefferson Ave. (18510); (717)961–2300. FAX: (717)346–6147. Pres. Irwin Schneider; Exec. Dir. Seymour Brotman.

WILKES-BARRE

JEWISH FEDERATION OF GREATER WILKES-BARRE (1935); 60 S. River St. (18702); (717)-822–4146. FAX: (717)824–5966. Pres. Stephen Alinikoff; Exec. Dir. Ted Magram.

RHODE ISLAND

PROVIDENCE

JEWISH FEDERATION OF RHODE ISLAND (1945); 130 Sessions St. (02906); (401)421–4111. FAX: (401)331–7961. Pres. David M. Hirsch; Exec. V.-Pres. Steve Rakitt.

SOUTH CAROLINA

CHARLESTON

CHARLESTON JEWISH FEDERATION (1949); 1645 Raoul Wallenberg Blvd., PO Box 31298 (29407); (803)571–6565. FAX: (803)556–6206. Pres. Judge Hugo Spitz; Exec. Dir. Michael Abidor.

COLUMBIA

COLUMBIA JEWISH FEDERATION (1960); 4540 Trenholm Rd., PO Box 6968 (29260); (803)787–0580. FAX: (803)787–0475. Pres. Hyman Rubin, Jr.; Exec. Dir. Alexander Grossberg.

SOUTH DAKOTA

SIOUX FALLS

JEWISH WELFARE FUND (1938); National Reserve Bldg., 513 S. Main Ave. (57102); (605)336–2880. Pres. Laurence Bierman; Exec. Sec. Louis R. Hurwitz.

TENNESSEE

CHATTANOOGA

CHATTANOOGA JEWISH FEDERATION (1931); 5326 Lynnland Terrace, PO Box 8947 (37411); (615)894–1317. FAX: (615)894–1319. Pres. Charles B. Lebovitz; Exec. Dir. Louis B. Solomon.

KNOXVILLE

KNOXVILLE JEWISH FEDERATION (1939); 6800 Deane Hill Dr., PO Box 10882 (37939–0882); (615)693–5837. Pres. Barbara Bernstein; Exec. Dir. Conrad J. Koller.

MEMPHIS

MEMPHIS JEWISH FEDERATION (incl. Shelby County) (1935); 6560 Poplar Ave. (38138); (901)767–7100. FAX: (901)767–7128. Pres. Jerome Makowsky; Exec. Dir. Gary Siepser.

NASHVILLE

JEWISH FEDERATION OF NASHVILLE & MIDDLE TENNESSEE (1936); 801 Percy Warner Blvd. (37205); (615)356–3242. FAX: (615)352–0056. Pres. Carolyn Levine; Act. Exec. Dir. Ruth Tanner.

TEXAS

AUSTIN

JEWISH FEDERATION OF AUSTIN (1939; reorg. 1956); 11713 Jollyville Rd. (78759); (512)331–1144. FAX: (512)331–7059. Pres. Rafael Pelc; Exec. Dir. Wayne Silverman.

DALLAS

JEWISH FEDERATION OF GREATER DALLAS (1911); 7800 Northaven Rd., Suite A (75230); (214)369–3313. FAX: (214)369–8943. Pres. Andrea Statman; Exec. Dir. Avrum I. Cohen.

EL PASO

JEWISH FEDERATION OF EL PASO, INC. (incl. surrounding communities) (1937); 405 Wallenberg Dr., PO Box 12097 (79913–0097); (915)584–4437. FAX: (915)584–0243. Pres. Joan Johnson; Exec. Dir. David Brown.

FORT WORTH

JEWISH FEDERATION OF FORT WORTH AND TARRANT COUNTY (1936); 6801 Dan Danciger Rd. (76133); (817)292–3081. FAX: (817)292–3214. Pres. Rowena Kimmell; Exec. Dir. Bruce Schlosberg.

GALVESTON

GALVESTON COUNTY JEWISH WELFARE ASSOCIATION (1936); PO Box 146 (77553); (409)763–5241. Pres. Harold Levine; Treas. Joe Nussenblatt.

HOUSTON

JEWISH FEDERATION OF GREATER HOUSTON (1936); 5603 S. Braeswood Blvd. (77096–3999); (713)729–7000. FAX: (713)-721–6232. Pres. Buster Feldman; Exec. Dir. Hans Mayer.

SAN ANTONIO

JEWISH FEDERATION OF SAN ANTONIO (incl. Bexar County) (1922); 8434 Ahern Dr. (78216); (512)341–8234. FAX: (512)341–2842. Pres. Sterling Neuman; Exec. Dir. Stan Ramati.

WACO

JEWISH FEDERATION OF WACO AND CENTRAL TEXAS (1949); PO Box 8031 (76714–8031); (817)776–3740. Pres. Mike Stupak; Exec. Sec. Martha Bauer.

UTAH

SALT LAKE CITY

UNITED JEWISH COUNCIL AND SALT LAKE JEWISH WELFARE FUND (1936); 2416 E. 1700 South (84108); (801)581–0098. Pres. Fred Tannenbaum; Exec. Dir. Roberta Grunauer.

VIRGINIA

NEWPORT NEWS–HAMPTON–WILLIAMSBURG

UNITED JEWISH COMMUNITY OF THE VIRGINIA PENINSULA, INC. (1942); 2700 Spring Rd., Newport News (23606); (804)930–1422. FAX: (804)872–9532. Pres. Joanne Roos; Exec. Dir. Barbara Rostov.

RICHMOND

JEWISH COMMUNITY FEDERATION OF RICHMOND (1935); 5403 Monument Ave., PO Box 17128 (23226); (804)288–0045. FAX: (804)282–7507. Pres. Helen P. Horwitz; Exec. Dir. Robert S. Hyman.

TIDEWATER

UNITED JEWISH FEDERATION OF TIDEWATER (incl. Norfolk, Portsmouth, and Virginia Beach) (1937); 7300 Newport Ave., PO Box 9776, Norfolk (23505); (804)489–8040. FAX: (804)489–8230. Pres. Dr. Charles J. Goldman; Exec. V.-Pres. Gary N. Rubin.

WASHINGTON

SEATTLE

JEWISH FEDERATION OF GREATER SEATTLE (incl. King County, Everett, and Bremerton) (1926); 2031 Third Ave. (98121); (206)443-5400. FAX: (206)443-0303. Pres. Herbert Pruzan; Exec. Dir. Michael Novick.

WEST VIRGINIA

CHARLESTON

FEDERATED JEWISH CHARITIES OF CHARLESTON, INC. (1937); PO Box 1613 (25326); (304)346-7500. Pres. Carl Lehman; Exec. Sec. William H. Thalheimer.

WISCONSIN

KENOSHA

KENOSHA JEWISH WELFARE FUND (1938); 8041 48th Ave. (53142); (414)694-6695.

Pres. Richard Selsberg; Sec.-Treas. Steven Barasch.

MADISON

MADISON JEWISH COMMUNITY COUNCIL, INC. (1940); 310 N. Midvale Blvd., Suite 325 (53705); (608)231-3426. Pres. Judith Schreiber; Exec. Dir. Steven H. Morrison.

MILWAUKEE

MILWAUKEE JEWISH FEDERATION, INC. (1902); 1360 N. Prospect Ave. (53202); (414)-271-8338. Pres. Joseph M. Bernstein; Exec. Dir. Rick Meyer.

CANADA

ALBERTA

CALGARY

CALGARY JEWISH COMMUNITY COUNCIL (1962); 1607 90th Ave. SW (T2V 4V7); (403)-253-8600. FAX: (403)253-7915. Pres. Robert Kalef; Exec. Dir. Drew J. Staffenberg.

EDMONTON

JEWISH FEDERATION OF EDMONTON (1954; reorg. 1982); 7200 156th St. (T5R 1X3); (403)487-5120. FAX: (403)481-3463. Pres. Michael Goldstein; Exec. Dir. Sidney Indig.

BRITISH COLUMBIA

VANCOUVER

JEWISH FEDERATION OF GREATER VAN-COUVER (1932; reorg. 1987); 950 W. 41st Ave. (V5Z 2N7); (604)266-7115. FAX: (604)266-8371. Pres. Ted Zacks; Exec. Dir. Steve Drysdale.

MANITOBA

WINNIPEG

WINNIPEG JEWISH COMMUNITY COUNCIL (1938; reorg. 1973); 370 Hargrave St. (R3B 2K1); (204)943-0406. FAX: (204)956-0609. Pres. Sidney Halpern; Exec. Dir. Robert Freedman.

ONTARIO

HAMILTON

JEWISH FEDERATION OF HAMILTON, WENTWORTH & AREA (1932; merged 1971);

PO Box 7258, 1030 Lower Lion Club Rd., Ancaster (L9G 3N6); (416)648-0605. FAX: (416)648-8388. Pres. Gerald Swaye Q.C.; Exec. Dir. Claire Mandel.

LONDON

LONDON JEWISH FEDERATION (1932); 536 Huron St. (N5Y 4J5); (519)673-3310. FAX: (519)673-1161. Pres. Robert Siskind; Exec. Dir. Gerald Enchin.

OTTAWA

JEWISH COMMUNITY COUNCIL OF OTTAWA (1934); 151 Chapel St. (K1N 7Y2); (613)232-7306. FAX: (613)563-4593. Pres. Dr. Eli Rabin; Exec. Dir. Gerry Koffman.

TORONTO

JEWISH FEDERATION OF GREATER TORONTO (1917); 4600 Bathurst St.; Willowdale (M2R 3V2); (416)635-2883. FAX: (416)635-1408. Pres. Charles S. Diamond; Exec. Dir. Steven Ain.

WINDSOR

JEWISH COMMUNITY COUNCIL (1938); 1641 Ouellette Ave. (N8X 1R9); (519)973-1772. FAX: (519)973-1774. Pres. Alan R. Orman; Exec. Dir. Allen Juris.

QUEBEC

MONTREAL

ALLIED JEWISH COMMUNITY SERVICES (1965); 5151 Cote Ste. Catherine Rd. (H3W 1M6); (514)735-3541. FAX: (514)735-8972. Pres. Harvey Wolfe; Exec. Dir. John Fishel.

Jewish Periodicals[1]

UNITED STATES

ARIZONA

ARIZONA JEWISH POST (1946). 3812 East River Road, Tucson, 85718. (602)529–1500. FAX: (602)577–0734. Sandra R. Heiman. Fortnightly. Jewish Federation of Southern Arizona.

GREATER PHOENIX JEWISH NEWS (1947). PO Box 26590, Phoenix, 85068. (602)870–9470. FAX: (602)870–0426. Flo Eckstein. Weekly.

CALIFORNIA

B'NAI B'RITH MESSENGER (1897). PO Box 35915, Los Angeles, 90035. (213)659–2952. Rabbi Yale Butler. Weekly.

HADSHOT L.A. (1988). 13535 Ventura Blvd., Suite 200, Sherman Oaks, 91423. (818)783–3090. Meir Doron. Weekly. Hebrew.

HERITAGE-SOUTHWEST JEWISH PRESS (1914). 2130 S. Vermont Ave., Los Angeles, 90007. (213) 737–2122. Dan Brin. Weekly. (Also SAN DIEGO JEWISH HERITAGE, weekly; ORANGE COUNTY JEWISH HERITAGE, weekly; CENTRAL CALIFORNIA JEWISH HERITAGE, monthly.) Heritage Group.

JEWISH BULLETIN OF NORTHERN CALIFORNIA (1946). 88 First St., Suite 300, San Francisco, 94105. (415)957–9340. FAX: (415)957–0266. Marc S. Klein. Weekly. San Francisco Jewish Community Publications Inc.

JEWISH JOURNAL (1986). 3660 Wilshire Blvd., Suite 204, Los Angeles, 90010. (213)738–7778. Gene Lichtenstein. Weekly.

JEWISH NEWS & ISRAEL TODAY (1973). 11071 Ventura Blvd., Studio City, 91604. (818)786–4000. Phil Blazer. Monthly.

JEWISH SPECTATOR (1935). 4391 Park Milano, Calabasas, 91302. (818)591–7481. FAX: (818)591–7267. Robert Bleiweiss. Quarterly. American Friends of Center for Jewish Living and Values.

NORTHERN CALIFORNIA JEWISH BULLETIN See JEWISH BULLETIN OF NORTHERN CALIFORNIA.

JEWISH STAR (1956). 109 Minna St., Suite 323, San Francisco, 94105–3728. (415)-243–4323. FAX: (415)243–0826. Nevon Stuckey. Bimonthly.

SAN DIEGO JEWISH TIMES (1979). 2592 Fletcher Pkwy., El Cajon, 92020. (619)-463–5515. Carol Rosenberg. Biweekly.

TIKKUN: A BIMONTHLY JEWISH CRITIQUE OF POLITICS, CULTURE & SOCIETY (1986). 5100 Leona St., Oakland, 94619. (415)-482–0805. FAX: (415)482–3379. Michael Lerner. Bimonthly. Institute for Labor & Mental Health.

WESTERN STATES JEWISH HISTORY (1968). 2429 23rd St., Santa Monica, 90405. (213)-450–2946. Norton B. Stern. Quarterly. Western States Jewish History Association.

COLORADO

INTERMOUNTAIN JEWISH NEWS (1913). 1275 Sherman St., Suite 214, Denver, 80203. (303)861–2234. FAX: (303)832–6942. Rabbi Hillel Goldberg, Miriam Goldberg. Weekly.

---

[1]The information in this directory is based on replies to questionnaires circulated by the editors. For organization bulletins, see the directory of Jewish organizations.

CONNECTICUT

CONNECTICUT JEWISH LEDGER (1929). 2475 Albany Ave., West Hartford, 06117. (203)233–2148. FAX: (203)232–9756. Berthold Gaster. Weekly.

MITZVAH CONNECTION. PO Box 948, Avon, 06001. (203)675–7763. C. Dianne Zweig. Annually.

DISTRICT OF COLUMBIA

B'NAI B'RITH INTERNATIONAL JEWISH MONTHLY (1886 under the name MENORAH). 1640 Rhode Island Ave., NW, Washington, 20036. (202)857–6645. Jeff Rubin. Ten times a year. B'nai B'rith.

JEWISH DEMOCRATIC ADVOCATE (1990). 711 Second St., NE, Suite 100, Washington, 20002. (202)544–7636. FAX: (202)-544–7645. Lewis Roth. Quarterly. National Jewish Democratic Council.

JEWISH VETERAN (1896). 1811 R St., NW, Washington, 20009. (202)265–6280. FAX: (202)234–5662. Albert Schlossberg. Five times a year. Jewish War Veterans of the U.S.A.

MOMENT (1975). 3000 Connecticut Ave., NW, Suite 300, Washington, 20008. (202)-387–8888. FAX: (202)483–3423. Hershel Shanks. Bimonthly. Jewish Educational Ventures, Inc.

MONITOR! (1990). 1819 H Street, NW, Suite 230, Washington, 20006. (202)775–9770. Stacy Burdett. Weekly. Union of Councils for Soviet Jews.

NEAR EAST REPORT (1957). 440 First St., NW, Suite 607, Washington, 20001. (202)-639–5300. Mitchell G. Bard. Weekly. Near East Research, Inc.

SECURITY AFFAIRS (1978). 1717 K St., NW, Suite 300, Washington, 22202. (202)833–0020. FAX: (202)296–6452. Jim Colbert. Monthly. Jewish Institute for National Security Affairs.

UCSJ QUARTERLY REPORT. See MONITOR!

WASHINGTON JEWISH WEEK. See under MARYLAND.

FLORIDA

BROWARD JEWISH WORLD (1986). 2101 Corporate Blvd., Boca Raton, 33431. (407)997–9971. FAX: (407)997–2910.

Gloria Katz. Weekly. Jewish Media Group, Inc.

JEWISH JOURNAL (Palm Beach–Broward–Dade) (1977). 601 Fairway Dr., Deerfield Beach, 33441. (800)477–1997. FAX: (305)-429–1207. Andy Polin. Weekly. South Florida Newspaper Network.

JEWISH PRESS OF PINELLAS COUNTY (Clearwater-St. Petersburg) (1985). 301 Jupiter Ave. S., Clearwater, 34615–6561. (813)441–4500. FAX: (813)461–0700. Karen Wolfson Dawkins. Biweekly. Jewish Press Group of Tampa Bay (FL), Inc.

JEWISH PRESS OF TAMPA (1987). 2808 Horatio St., Tampa, 33609. (813)871–2332. FAX: (813)461–0700. Karen Wolfson Dawkins. Biweekly. Jewish Press Group of Tampa Bay (FL), Inc.

JEWISH WORLD (1982). 2101 Corporate Blvd., Suite 315, Boca Raton, 33431. (407)-833–8331. FAX: (407)659–5428. Stacy Zolotin. Weekly. Jewish Media Group, Inc.

MIAMI JEWISH TRIBUNE (1986). 3550 Biscayne Blvd., 3rd fl., Miami, 33137–3845. (305)576–9500. FAX: (305)573–9551. Bertram Korn, Jr. Weekly. Jewish Media Group, Inc.

SOUTHERN JEWISH WEEKLY, INC. (1924). 1232-3 Blanding Blvd., Orange Park, 32065. (904)272–1479. FAX: (904)272–3347. Phillip B. Lyon. Weekly. Southern Independent Operators, Inc.

GEORGIA

ATLANTA JEWISH TIMES (1925; formerly SOUTHERN ISRAELITE). 1575 Northside Dr., NW, Atlanta, 30318. (404)352–2400. FAX: (404)355–9388. Vida Goldgar. Weekly.

JEWISH CIVIC PRESS (1972). 3330 Peachtree Rd. NE, Suite 500, Atlanta, 30326. (404)-231–2194. Abner L. Tritt. Monthly.

ILLINOIS

CHICAGO JUF NEWS (1972). One S. Franklin St., Rm. 722, Chicago, 60606. (312)-444–2853. FAX: (312)855–2474. Joseph Aaron. Monthly. Jewish United Fund/Jewish Federation of Metropolitan Chicago.

JEWISH COMMUNITY NEWS (1941). 6464 W. Main, Suite 7A, Belleville, 62223. (618)-

398–6100. Steve Low. Irregularly. Jewish Federation of Southern Illinois.

THE SENTINEL (1911). 150 N. Michigan Ave., Suite 3130, Chicago, 60601. (312)-407–0060. FAX: (312)407–0096. J. I. Fishbein. Weekly.

INDIANA

ILLIANA NEWS (1976). 2939 Jewett St., Highland, 46322. (219)972–2250. FAX: (219)972–4778. Sharon Blumberg. Monthly (except July/Aug.). Jewish Federation, Inc./Northwest Indiana.

INDIANA JEWISH POST AND OPINION (1935). PO Box 449097; 2120 N. Meridian St., Indianapolis, 46202. (317)927–7800. FAX: (317)927–7807. Neila Pomerantz. Weekly.

NATIONAL JEWISH POST AND OPINION (1932). 2120 N. Meridian St., Indianapolis, 46202. (317)927–7800. FAX: (317)927–7807. Gabriel Cohen. Weekly.

KANSAS

KANSAS CITY JEWISH CHRONICLE. See under MISSOURI.

KENTUCKY

KENTUCKY JEWISH POST AND OPINION (1931). 1551 Bardstown Rd., Louisville, 40205. (502)459–1914. Julie D. Segal. Weekly.

LOUISIANA

COMMUNITY. See JEWISH VOICE.

JEWISH CIVIC PRESS (1965). PO Box 15500, 924 Valmont St., New Orleans, 70115. (504)895–8785. Abner Tritt. Monthly.

JEWISH VOICE (1989). 924 Valmont St., New Orleans, 70115. (504)895–8784. FAX: (504)895–8785. Michael Blackman. Semiweekly. Jewish Federation of Greater New Orleans.

MARYLAND

BALTIMORE JEWISH TIMES (1919). 2104 N. Charles St., Baltimore, 21218. (301)752–3504. Gary Rosenblatt. Weekly.

MODERN JUDAISM (1980). Johns Hopkins University Press, 701 W. 40 St., Suite 275, Baltimore, 21211-2190. (410)516–6944. FAX: (410)516–6998. (Editorial address: 92 Riverside Dr., Binghamton, NY 13905.) Steven Katz. Three times a year.

PROOFTEXTS: A JOURNAL OF JEWISH LITERARY HISTORY (1980). Johns Hopkins University Press, 701 W. 40 St., Suite 275, Baltimore, 21211-2190. (410)516–6944. FAX: (410)516–6998. Alan Mintz, David G. Roskies. Three times a year.

WASHINGTON JEWISH WEEK (1930, as the NATIONAL JEWISH LEDGER). 12300 Twinbrook Pkwy., Suite 250, Rockville, 20852. (301)230–2222. FAX: (301)881-6362. Andrew Silow Carroll. Weekly.

MASSACHUSETTS

AMERICAN JEWISH HISTORY (1893). Two Thornton Rd., Waltham, 02154. (617)891–8110. FAX: (617)899–9208. Marc Lee Raphael. Quarterly. American Jewish Historical Society.

BOSTON JEWISH TIMES (1945). 169 Norfolk Ave., Boston, 02119. (617)442–9680. Sten Lukin. Fortnightly.

JEWISH ADVOCATE (1902). 15 School St., Boston, 02108. (617)367–9100. FAX: (617)-367-9310. Robert Israel. Weekly.

JEWISH REPORTER (1970). 76 Salem End Rd., Framingham, 01701. (508)879–3300. FAX: (508)879–5856. Marcia T. Rivin. Monthly. Combined Jewish Philanthropies of Greater Boston.

JEWISH WEEKLY NEWS (1945). PO Box 1569, Springfield, 01101. (413)739–4771. Leslie B. Kahn. Weekly.

JOURNAL OF THE NORTH SHORE JEWISH COMMUNITY (1977). 324 B Essex St., Swampscott, 01907. (617)581–7110. FAX: (617)581–7630. Barbara Wolf. Biweekly. Jewish Federation of the North Shore.

MICHIGAN

DETROIT JEWISH NEWS (1942). 27676 Franklin Rd., Southfield, 48034. (313)354–6060. FAX: (313)354–6069. Gary Rosenblatt. Weekly.

HUMANISTIC JUDAISM (1968). 28611 W. Twelve Mile Rd., Farmington Hills, 48334. (313)478–7610. FAX: (313)477–9014. M. Bonnie Cousens, Ruth D. Feldman. Quarterly. Society for Humanistic Judaism.

MINNESOTA

AMERICAN JEWISH WORLD (1912). 4509 Minnetonka Blvd., Minneapolis, 55416.

(612)920–7000. FAX: (612)920–6205. Marshall Hoffman. Weekly.

MISSOURI

KANSAS CITY JEWISH CHRONICLE (1920). 7373 W. 107 St., Suite 250, Overland Park, KS 66212. (913)648–4620. FAX: (913)381–9889. Ruth Baum Bigus. Weekly. Sun Publications.

MISSOURI JEWISH POST (1948). 9531 Lackland, Suite 207, St. Louis, 63114. (314)–423–3088. Kathie Sutin. Weekly.

ST. LOUIS JEWISH LIGHT (1947). 12 Millstone Campus Dr., St. Louis, 63146. (314)–432–3353. FAX: (314)432–0515. Robert A. Cohn. Weekly. St. Louis Jewish Light, Inc.

NEBRASKA

JEWISH PRESS (1920). 333 S. 132 St., Omaha, 68154. (402)334–8200. FAX: (402)333–5497. Morris Maline. Weekly. Jewish Federation of Omaha.

NEVADA

JEWISH REPORTER (1976). 1030 E. Twain Ave., Las Vegas, 89109. (702)732–0556. Marla Gerecht. Monthly (except July and Aug.). Jewish Federation of Las Vegas.

LAS VEGAS ISRAELITE (1965). PO Box 14096, Las Vegas, 89114. (702)876–1255. FAX: (702)364–1009. Michael Tell. Biweekly.

NEW JERSEY

AVOTAYNU (1985). 1485 Teaneck Rd., Teaneck, 07666. (201)837–2701. FAX: (201)–837–8506. Sallyann Amdur Sack. Quarterly.

JEWISH COMMUNITY VOICE (1941). 2393 W. Marlton Pike, Cherry Hill, 08002. (609)–665–6100. FAX: (609)665–0074. Harriet Kessler. Fortnightly. Jewish Federation of Southern NJ.

JEWISH HORIZON (1981). 1391 Martine Ave., Scotch Plains, 07076. (908)889–9200. FAX: (908)889–9205. Fran Gold. Weekly.

JEWISH RECORD (Atlantic City area) (1939). 1525 S. Main St., Pleasantville, 08232. (609)383–0999. Martin Korik. Weekly.

JEWISH STANDARD (1931). 1086 Teaneck Rd., Teaneck, 07666. (201)837–8818. FAX: (201)833–4959. Rebecca Kaplan Boroson. Weekly.

JEWISH STAR (1975). 100 Metroplex Dr., Edison, 08817. (908)985–1234. FAX: (908)–985–3295. Mindy L. Belfer. Bimonthly. Jewish Federation of Greater Middlesex County.

JOURNAL OF JEWISH COMMUNAL SERVICE (1899). 3084 State Hwy. 27, Suite 9, Kendall Pk, NJ 08824-1657. (908)821–1871. FAX: (908)821–5335. Gail Naron Chalew. Quarterly. Conference of Jewish Communal Service.

JUDAICA NEWS (1989). PO Box 1130, Fair Lawn, 07410. (201)796–6151. Terry Cohn. Quarterly.

METROWEST JEWISH NEWS (1947). 901 Route 10 East, Suite 101, Whippany, 07981-1157. (201)887–3900. David Frank. Weekly. United Jewish Federation of MetroWest.

NEW YORK

AFN SHVEL (1941). 200 W. 72 St., Suite 40, NYC, 10023. (212)787–6675. Mordkhe Schaechter. Quarterly. Yiddish. League for Yiddish, Inc.

AGENDA: JEWISH EDUCATION (1949; formerly PEDAGOGIC REPORTER). JESNA, 730 Broadway, NYC, 10003. (212)529–2000. FAX: (212)529–2009. Rabbi Arthur Vernon. Three times a year. Jewish Education Service of North America, Inc.

ALGEMEINER JOURNAL (1972). 211 63 St., Brooklyn, 11220. (718)492-6420. FAX: (718)492-6571. Gershon Jacobson. Weekly. Yiddish-English.

AMERICAN JEWISH YEAR BOOK (1899). 165 E. 56 St., NYC, 10022. (212)751–4000. FAX: (212)751–4017. David Singer, Ruth R. Seldin. Annually. American Jewish Committee and Jewish Publication Society.

AMERICAN ZIONIST (1910). 4 E. 34 St., NYC, 10016. (212)481–1500. FAX: (212)–481-1515. Paul Flacks. Quarterly. Zionist Organization of America.

AMIT WOMAN (1925). 817 Broadway, NYC, 10003. (212)477–4720. FAX: (212)353–2312. Micheline Ratzersdorfer. Five times a year. AMIT Women (formerly American Mizrachi Women).

AUFBAU (1934). 2121 Broadway, NYC, 10023. (212)873–7400. Henry Marx. Fortnightly. German. New World Club, Inc.

BITZARON (1939). PO Box 623, Cooper Station, NYC, 10003. (212)293–5977. Hayim Leaf. Quarterly. Hebrew; English abstracts. Hebrew Literary Foundation and Jewish Culture Foundation of New York University.

BUFFALO JEWISH REVIEW (1918). 15 E. Mohawk St., Buffalo, 14203. (716)854–2192. FAX: (716)854–2198. Harlan C. Abbey. Weekly. Kahaal Nahalot Israel.

THE CALL (formerly WORKMEN'S CIRCLE CALL) (1933). 45 E. 33 St., NYC, 10016. (212)889–6800. FAX: (212)532–7518. Diane H. Merlin. Bimonthly. The Workmen's Circle.

CCAR JOURNAL: A REFORM JEWISH QUARTERLY (formerly JOURNAL OF REFORM JUDAISM) (1953). 192 Lexington Ave., NYC, 10016. (212)684–4990. FAX: (212)689–1649. Lawrence A. Englander. Quarterly. Central Conference of American Rabbis.

CIRCLE (1943). 15 E. 26 St., NYC, 10010–1579. (212)532–4949. FAX: (212)481–4174. Shirley Frank. Quarterly. Jewish Community Centers Association of North America (formerly JWB).

COMMENTARY (1945). 165 E. 56 St., NYC, 10022. (212)751–4000. FAX: (212)751–1174. Norman Podhoretz, Neal Kozodoy. Monthly. American Jewish Committee.

CONGRESS MONTHLY (1933). 15 E. 84 St., NYC, 10028. (212)879–4500. Maier Deshell. Seven times a year. American Jewish Congress.

CONSERVATIVE JUDAISM (1945). 3080 Broadway, NYC, 10027. (212)678–8049. Rabbi Shamai Kanter. Quarterly. Rabbinical Assembly.

CONTEMPORARY JEWRY (1974 under the name JEWISH SOCIOLOGY AND SOCIAL RESEARCH). Center for Jewish Studies, CUNY Graduate School and University Center, 33 W. 42 St., NYC, 10036. (212)-790–4404. Paul Ritterband. Semiannually. Association for the Social Scientific Study of Jewry.

ECONOMIC HORIZONS (1953). 350 Fifth Ave., Suite 1919, NYC, 10118. (212)971–0310. Ronny Bassan. Annually. American-Israel Chamber of Commerce and Industry, Inc.

FORVERTS (YIDDISH FORWARD) (1897). 45 E. 33 St., NYC, 10016. (212)889–8200. FAX: (212)684–3949. Mordechai Strigler. Weekly. Yiddish-English. Forward Association, Inc.

FORWARD (1897). 45 E. 33 St., NYC 10016. (212)889-8200. FAX: (212)447-6406. Seth Lipsky. Weekly. Forward Publishing Company, Inc.

HADAROM (1957). 275 Seventh Ave., NYC, 10001. (212)807–7888. Rabbi Gedalia Dov Schwartz. Annually. Hebrew. Rabbinical Council of America.

HADASSAH MAGAZINE (1914). 50 W. 58 St., NYC, 10019. (212)333–5946. FAX: (212)-333–5967. Alan M. Tigay. Monthly (except for combined issues of June–July and Aug.–Sept.). Hadassah, the Women's Zionist Organization of America.

HADOAR (1921). 47 W. 34 St., Rm. 609, NYC, 10001. (212)629–9443. FAX: (212)-629–9472. Shlomo Shamir, Yael Feldman. Biweekly. Hebrew. Hadoar Association, Inc.

HAMACHNE HACHAREIDI (1980). PO Box 216. Brooklyn, 11218. (718)438–1263. FAX: (718)438–1263. Rabbi Yisroel Eichler. Weekly. Khal Machzikei Hadas.

ISRAEL HORIZONS (1952). 224 W. 35 St., Rm. 403, NYC, 10001. (212)868–0386. Ralph Seliger. Quarterly. Americans for Progressive Israel.

ISRAEL QUALITY (1976). 350 Fifth Ave., Suite 1919, NYC, 10118. (212)971–0310. Beth Belkin. Quarterly. Government of Israel Trade Center and American-Israel Chamber of Commerce and Industry.

JEWISH ACTION MAGAZINE (1950). 333 Seventh Ave., 18th fl., NYC, 10008. (212)563–4000, X 146. Charlotte Friedland. Quarterly. Union of Orthodox Jewish Congregations of America.

JEWISH BOOK ANNUAL (1942). 15 E. 26 St., NYC, 10010. (212)532–4949. Jacob Kabakoff. English-Hebrew-Yiddish. Jewish Book Council.

JEWISH BOOK WORLD (1945). 15 E. 26 St., NYC, 10010. (212)532–4949. William Wollheim. Quarterly. Jewish Book Council.

JEWISH BRAILLE INSTITUTE VOICE (1978). 110 E. 30 St., NYC, 10016. (212)889–2525.

FAX: (212)689–3692. Dr. Jacob Freid. Monthly (except May/June, July/Aug.) (audio cassettes). Jewish Braille Institute of America, Inc.

JEWISH BRAILLE REVIEW (1931). 110 E. 30 St., NYC, 10016. (212)889–2525. Jacob Freid. Monthly, except May/June, July/ Aug. English braille. Jewish Braille Institute of America, Inc.

JEWISH CURRENT EVENTS (1959). 430 Keller Ave., Elmont, 11003. Samuel Deutsch. Biweekly.

JEWISH CURRENTS (1946). 22 E. 17 St., Suite 601, NYC, 10003-3272. (212)924–5740. Morris U. Schappes. Monthly (July/Aug. combined). Association for Promotion of Jewish Secularism, Inc.

JEWISH EDUCATION (1929). 426 W. 58 St., NYC, 10019. (212)713–0290. FAX: (212)-586–9579. Dr. Alvin I. Schiff. Three times a year. Council for Jewish Education.

JEWISH FRONTIER (1934). 33 E. 67 St., NYC, 10021. (212)988–7339. Nahum Guttman. Bimonthly. Labor Zionist Letters, Inc.

JEWISH JOURNAL (1969). 8723 Third Ave., Brooklyn, 11209. (718)238–6600. FAX: (718)238-6657. Harold Singer. Weekly.

JEWISH LEDGER (1924). 2535 Brighton-Henrietta Town Line Rd., Rochester, 14623. (716)427–2434. Barbara Morgenstern. Weekly.

JEWISH MUSIC NOTES (1945). 15 E. 26 St., NYC, 10010. (212)532–4949. Debra Wachsberger, Norman Summers. Bi-annually. Jewish Music Council.

JEWISH OBSERVER (1963). 84 William St., NYC, 10038. (212)797–9000. Rabbi Nisson Wolpin. Monthly (except July and Aug.). Agudath Israel of America.

JEWISH OBSERVER (1978). PO Box 510, DeWitt, 13214. (315)445–0161. FAX: (315)-445–1559. Mollie Leitzes Collins. Biweekly. Syracuse Jewish Federation, Inc.

JEWISH POST AND RENAISSANCE (1977). 57 E. 11 St., NYC, 10003. (212)420–0042. Charles Roth. Bimonthly.

JEWISH PRESS (1950). 338 Third Ave., Brooklyn, 11215. (718)330–1100. FAX: (718)935–1215. Rabbi Sholom Klass. Weekly.

JEWISH SOCIAL STUDIES (1939). 2112 Broadway, Rm. 206, NYC, 10023. (212)-724–5336. Tobey B. Gitelle. Quarterly. Conference on Jewish Social Studies, Inc.

JEWISH TELEGRAPHIC AGENCY COMMUNITY NEWS REPORTER (1962). 330 Seventh Ave., 11th fl., NYC 10001-5010. (212)643–1890. FAX: (212)643–8498. Mark Joffe, Michael Pariser, Mark A. Seal. Weekly.

JEWISH TELEGRAPHIC AGENCY DAILY NEWS BULLETIN (1917). 330 Seventh Ave., 11th fl., NYC 10001-5010. (212)-643–1890. FAX: (212)643–8498. Mark Joffe, Michael Pariser, Mark A. Seal. Daily.

JEWISH TELEGRAPHIC AGENCY WEEKLY NEWS DIGEST (1933). 330 Seventh Ave., 11th fl., NYC 10001-5010. (212)643–1890. FAX: (212)643–8498. Mark Joffe, Michael Pariser, Mark A. Seal. Weekly.

JEWISH WEEK (1876; reorg. 1970). 1501 Broadway, NYC, 10036-5503. (212)921–7822. FAX: (212)921–8420. Phillip Ritzenberg. Weekly.

JEWISH WORLD (1965). 1104 Central Ave., Albany, 12205. (518)459–8455. FAX: (518)459–5289. Laurie J. Clevenson. Weekly.

JOURNAL OF REFORM JUDAISM. See CCAR JOURNAL.

JUDAISM (1952). 15 E. 84 St., NYC, 10028. (212)879–4500. FAX: (212)249-3672. Dr. Ruth B. Waxman. Quarterly. American Jewish Congress.

KOL HAT'NUA (VOICE OF THE MOVEMENT) (1975). 50 W. 58 St., NYC, 10019. (212)-303–8256. David Dashefsky. Four times a year. Young Judaea-Hashachar.

KOSHER DIRECTORY AND CALORIE GUIDE (1925). 333 Seventh Ave., NYC, 10001. (212)563–4000. FAX: (212)564–9058. Tziporah Spear. Every two years. Union of Orthodox Jewish Congregations of America.

KOSHER DIRECTORY, PASSOVER EDITION (1923). 333 Seventh Ave., NYC, 10001. (212)563–4000. FAX: (212)564–9058. Tziporah Spear. Annually. Union of Orthodox Jewish Congregations of America.

KULTUR UN LEBN—CULTURE AND LIFE (1967). 45 E. 33 St., NYC, 10016. (212)-

889–6800. Joseph Mlotek. Three times a year. Yiddish. The Workmen's Circle.

LAMISHPAHA (1963). 47 W. 34 St., Rm. 609, NYC, 10001. (212)629–9443. Hanita Brand. Monthly (except July and Aug.). Hebrew. Histadruth Ivrith of America.

LIKUTIM (1981). 110 E. 30 St., NYC, 10016. (212)889–2525. Joanne Jahr. Two to four times a year (audio cassettes). Hebrew. Jewish Braille Institute of America, Inc.

LILITH—THE JEWISH WOMEN'S MAGAZINE (1976). 250 W. 57 St., #2432, NYC, 10107. (212)757–0818. Susan Weidman Schneider. Quarterly.

LONG ISLAND JEWISH WORLD (1971). 115 Middle Neck Rd., Great Neck, 11021. (516)829–4000. FAX: (516)829-4776. Jerome W. Lippman. Weekly.

MARTYRDOM AND RESISTANCE (1974). 48 W. 37 St., 9th fl., NYC 10018–4708. (212)-564–1865. FAX: (212)268–0529. Eli Zborowski. Bimonthly. International Society for Yad Vashem.

THE MELTON JOURNAL (1982). 3080 Broadway, NYC, 10027. (212)678–8031. Eduardo Rauch, Barry W. Holtz. Biannually. Melton Research Center for Jewish Education.

MIDSTREAM (1954). 110 E. 59 St., NYC, 10022. (212)339–6000. FAX: (212)826–8959. Joel Carmichael. Monthly. Theodor Herzl Foundation, Inc.

MODERN JEWISH STUDIES ANNUAL (1977). Queens College, NSF 350, 65-30 Kissena Blvd., Flushing, 11367. (718)997–3622. Joseph C. Landis. Annually. American Association of Professors of Yiddish.

NA'AMAT WOMAN (1926). 200 Madison Ave., Suite 2120, NYC, 10016. (212)725–8010. Judith A. Sokoloff. Five times a year. English-Yiddish-Hebrew. NA'AMAT USA, the Women's Labor Zionist Organization of America.

OLOMEINU—OUR WORLD (1945). 5723 18th Ave., Brooklyn, NY 11204. (718)259–1223. FAX: (718)259–1795. Rabbi Yaakov Fruchter, Rabbi Nosson Scherman. Monthly. English-Hebrew. Torah Umesorah-National Society for Hebrew Day Schools.

PEDAGOGIC REPORTER. See AGENDA: JEWISH EDUCATION.

PROCEEDINGS OF THE AMERICAN ACADEMY FOR JEWISH RESEARCH (1920). 3080 Broadway, NYC, 10027. (212)678–8864. FAX: (212)678–8947. Dr. Nahum Sarna. Annually. English-Hebrew-French-Arabic-Persian-Greek. American Academy for Jewish Research.

RCA RECORD (1953). 275 Seventh Ave. NYC, 10001. (212)807–7888. FAX: (212)-727–8452. Rabbi Basil Herring. Quarterly. Rabbinical Council of America.

RECONSTRUCTIONIST (1934). PO Box 1336, Roslyn Heights., 11577. (516)621–2067. Rabbi Joy Levitt. Quarterly. Federation of Reconstructionist Congregations and Havurot.

REFORM JUDAISM (formerly DIMENSIONS IN AMERICAN JUDAISM) (1972). 838 Fifth Ave., NYC, 10021. (212)249–0100. Aron Hirt-Manheimer. Quarterly. Union of American Hebrew Congregations.

REPORTER (1972). 500 Clubhouse Rd., Vestal, 13850. (607)724–2360. FAX: (607)724–2311. Marc S. Goldberg. Weekly. Jewish Federation of Broome County.

THE REPORTER (formerly WOMEN'S AMERICAN ORT REPORTER) (1966). 315 Park Ave. S., NYC, 10010. (212)505–7700. FAX: (212)674–3057. Eve M. Jacobson. Quarterly. Women's American ORT, Inc.

RESPONSE (1967). 27 W. 20 St., 9th fl., NYC, 10011. (212)675–1168. FAX: (212)929–3459. Paul Lerner. Quarterly.

SHEVILEY HA-HINNUKH (1939). 426 W. 58 St., NYC, 10019. (212)713–0290. FAX: (212)586–9579. Quarterly. Hebrew. Council for Jewish Education.

SH'MA (1970). Box 567, 23 Murray Ave., Port Washington, 11050. (516)944–9791. FAX: (516)767–9315. Eugene B. Borowitz. Biweekly (except June, July, Aug.).

SHMUESSEN MIT KINDER UN YUGENT (1942). 770 Eastern Pkwy., Brooklyn, 11213. (718)493–9250. Nissan Mindel. Monthly. Yiddish. Merkos L'Inyonei Chinuch, Inc.

SYNAGOGUE LIGHT AND KOSHER LIFE (1933). 47 Beekman St., NYC, 10038. (212)227–7800. Rabbi Meyer Hager. Semiannually. The Kosher Food Institute.

TRADITION (1958). 275 Seventh Ave., NYC, 10001. (212)807–7888. Rabbi Emanuel

Feldman. Quarterly. Rabbinical Council America.

TRENDS (1982). 730 Broadway, NYC, 10003. (212)529-2000. Leora W. Isaacs. Irregularly. Jewish Education Service of North America, Inc.

UNITED SYNAGOGUE REVIEW (1943). 155 Fifth Ave., NYC, 10010. (212)533-7800. FAX: (212)353-9439. Lois Goldrich. Biannually. United Synagogue of America.

UNSER TSAIT (1941). 25 E. 21 St., 3rd fl., NYC, 10010. (212)475-0055. Editorial committee. Monthly. Yiddish. Jewish Labor Bund.

VOICE OF THE DUTCHESS JEWISH COMMUNITY (1990). 110 Grand Ave., Poughkeepsie, 12603. (914)471-9811. Dena Hirsh. Monthly. Jewish Federation of Dutchess County.

WOMEN'S AMERICAN ORT REPORTER. See THE REPORTER.

WOMEN'S LEAGUE OUTLOOK (1930). 48 E. 74 St., NYC, 10021. (212)628-1600. FAX: (212)772-3507. Janis Sherman Popp. Quarterly. Women's League for Conservative Judaism.

WORKMEN'S CIRCLE CALL. See THE CALL.

YEARBOOK OF THE CENTRAL CONFERENCE OF AMERICAN RABBIS (1890). 192 Lexington Ave., NYC, 10016. (212)684-4990. FAX: (212)689-1649. Rabbi Elliot L. Stevens. Annually. Central Conference of American Rabbis.

YIDDISH (1973). Queens College, NSF 350, 65-30 Kissena Blvd., Flushing, 11367. (718)520-7067. Joseph C. Landis. Quarterly. Queens College Press.

DI YIDDISHE HEIM (1958). 770 Eastern Pkwy., Brooklyn, 11213. (718)493-9250. Rachel Altein. Quarterly. English-Yiddish. Neshei Ub'nos Chabad.

YIDDISHE KULTUR (1938). 1133 Broadway, Rm. 1023, NYC, 10010. (212)691-0708. Itche Goldberg. Bimonthly. Yiddish. Yiddisher Kultur Farband, Inc.—YKUF.

YIDDISHE SHPRAKH (1941). 1048 Fifth Ave., NYC, 10028. (212)231-7905. Dr. Mordke Schaechter. Irregularly. Yiddish. YIVO Institute for Jewish Research, Inc.

DOS YIDDISHE VORT (1953). 84 William St., NYC, 10038. (212)797-9000. Joseph Fried-

enson. Monthly. Yiddish. Agudath Israel of America.

YIDDISHER KEMFER (1900). 275 Seventh Ave., NYC, 10001. (212)675-7808. Mordechai Strigler. Biweekly. Yiddish. Labor Zionist Alliance.

DER YIDDISHER VEG (1981). 1274 49th St., Suite 1974, Brooklyn, 11219. (718)435-9474. FAX: (718)438-1263. Meir Dov Grosz. Weekly. Yiddish. Archives of Chasidai Belz.

YIVO ANNUAL OF JEWISH SOCIAL SCIENCE (1946). 1048 Fifth Ave., NYC, 10028. (212)535-6700. FAX: (212)879-9763. Deborah Dash Moore. Annually. YIVO Institute for Jewish Research, Inc.

YIVO BLETER (1931). 1048 Fifth Ave., NYC, 10028. (212)535-6700. David E. Fishman. Biannually. Yiddish. YIVO Institute for Jewish Research, Inc.

YOUNG ISRAEL VIEWPOINT (1952). 3 W. 16 St., NYC, 10011. (212)929-1525. FAX: (212)727-9526. Tovah Holzer. Quarterly. National Council of Young Israel.

YOUNG JUDAEAN (1910). 50 W. 58 St., NYC, 10019. (212)303-8271. Joel Grishaver. Four times a year between Sept. and June. Hadassah Zionist Youth Commission.

YUGNTRUF (1964). 200 W. 72 St., Suite 40, NYC 10023. Gitl Schaechter-Viswanath. Quarterly. Yiddish. Yugntruf Youth for Yiddish.

THE ZIONIST VOICE (1990). 110 E. 59 St., NYC 10022. (212)339-6000. FAX: (212)-826-8959. Yitzhak Rabi. Quarterly. World Zionist Organization-American Section.

ZUKUNFT (THE FUTURE) (1892). 25 E. 21 St., NYC 10010. (212)505-8040. Yonia Fain. Bimonthly. Yiddish. Congress for Jewish Culture.

NORTH CAROLINA

AMERICAN JEWISH TIMES OUTLOOK (1934; reorg. 1950). PO Box 33218, Charlotte, 28233. (704)372-3296. Ruth Goldberg. Monthly. The Blumenthal Foundation.

OHIO

THE AMERICAN ISRAELITE (1854). 906 Main St., Rm. 508, Cincinnati, 45202. (513)621-3145. FAX: (513)621-3744. Phyllis R. Singer. Weekly.

AMERICAN JEWISH ARCHIVES (1948). 3101 Clifton Ave., Cincinnati, 45220. (513)221–1875. Jacob R. Marcus, Abraham J. Peck. Semiannually. American Jewish Archives of Hebrew Union College–Jewish Institute of Religion.

CLEVELAND JEWISH NEWS (1964). 3645 Warrensville Center Rd., Cleveland, 44122. (216)991–8300. FAX: (216)991–9556. Cynthia Dettelbach. Weekly. Cleveland Jewish Publication Co.

DAYTON JEWISH CHRONICLE (1961). 118 Salem Ave., Dayton, 45406. (513)222–0783. Leslie Cohen Zukowsky. Weekly.

INDEX TO JEWISH PERIODICALS (1963). PO Box 18570, Cleveland Hts., 44118. (216)-381–4846. Lenore Pfeffer Koppel. Annually.

OHIO JEWISH CHRONICLE (1922). 2862 Johnstown Rd., Columbus, 43219. (614)-337–2055. FAX: (614)337–2059. Judith Franklin. Weekly.

STARK JEWISH NEWS (1920). 2631 Harvard Ave. NW, Canton, 44709. (216)452–6444. FAX: (216)452–4487. Adele Gelb. Monthly. Canton Jewish Community Federation.

STUDIES IN BIBLIOGRAPHY AND BOOKLORE (1953). 3101 Clifton Ave., Cincinnati, 45220. (513)221–1875. Herbert C. Zafren. Irregularly. English-Hebrew-German. Library of Hebrew Union College–Jewish Institute of Religion.

TOLEDO JEWISH NEWS (1951). 6505 Sylvania Ave., Sylvania, 43560. (419)885–4461. FAX: (419)885-3207. Laurie Cohen. Monthly. Jewish Federation of Greater Toledo.

OKLAHOMA

TULSA JEWISH REVIEW (1930). 2021 E. 71 St., Tulsa, 74136. (918)495–1100. FAX: (918)495–1220. Ed Ulrich. Monthly. Jewish Federation of Tulsa.

PENNSYLVANIA

JEWISH CHRONICLE OF PITTSBURGH (1962). 5600 Baum Blvd., Pittsburgh, 15206. (412)687–1000. FAX: (412)687-5119. Joel Roteman. Weekly. Pittsburgh Jewish Publication and Education Foundation.

JEWISH EXPONENT (1887). 226 S. 16 St., Philadelphia, 19102. (215)893–5740. Albert Erlick. Weekly. Jewish Federation of Greater Philadelphia.

JEWISH QUARTERLY REVIEW (1910). 420 Walnut St., Philadelphia, 19106. (215)-238–1290. FAX: (215)238–1540. Leon Nemoy, David M. Goldenberg. Quarterly. Annenberg Institute.

JEWISH TIMES (1925). 103A Tomlinson Rd., Huntingdon Valley, 19006. (215)938–1177. FAX: (215)938–0692. Matthew Schuman. Weekly. Jewish Federation of Greater Philadelphia.

NEW MENORAH (1978). 7318 Germantown Ave., Philadelphia, 19119–1793. (215)-242–4074. FAX: (215)247–9703. Arthur Waskow, Rabbi Shana Margolin. Quarterly. P'nai Or Religious Fellowship.

RHODE ISLAND

RHODE ISLAND JEWISH HISTORICAL NOTES (1954). 130 Sessions St., Providence, 02906. (401)331–1360. Judith Weiss Cohen. Annually. Rhode Island Jewish Historical Association.

TENNESSEE

THE HEBREW WATCHMAN (1925). 4646 Poplar Ave., Suite 232, Memphis, 38117. (901)763–2215. Herman I. Goldberger. Weekly.

THE OBSERVER (1934). 801 Percy Warner Blvd., Nashville, 37205. (615)356–3242. FAX: (615)352–0056. Judith A. Saks. Biweekly (except July). Jewish Federation of Nashville.

TEXAS

JEWISH HERALD-VOICE (1908). PO Box 153, Houston, 77001–0153. (713)630–0391. FAX: (713)630–0404. Jeanne Samuels. Weekly.

JEWISH JOURNAL OF SAN ANTONIO (1973). 8434 Ahern, San Antonio, 78216. (512)-341–8234. FAX: (512)341–2842. Marion H. Bernstein. Monthly (11 issues). Jewish Federation of San Antonio.

TEXAS JEWISH POST (1947). 3120 S. Expressway, Fort Worth, 76110. (817)927–2831. FAX: (817)429–0840. 11333 N. Central Expressway, Dallas, 75243. (214)-692–7283. FAX: (214)692–7285. Jimmy Wisch. Weekly.

VIRGINIA

RENEWAL MAGAZINE (1984). 7300 Newport Ave., Norfolk, 23505. (804)489–8040. FAX: (804)489–8230. Reba Karp. Quarterly. United Jewish Federation of Tidewater.

UJF VIRGINIA NEWS (1959). 7300 Newport Ave., Norfolk, 23505. (804)489–8040. FAX: (804) 489–8230. Reba Karp. 21 issues yearly. United Jewish Federation of Tidewater.

WASHINGTON

JEWISH TRANSCRIPT (1924). 2031 Third Ave., Suite 200, Seattle, 98121. (206)441–4553. FAX: (206)443–0303. Craig Degginger. Fortnightly. Jewish Federation of Greater Seattle.

WISCONSIN

WISCONSIN JEWISH CHRONICLE (1921). 1360 N. Prospect Ave., Milwaukee, 53202.

(414)271–2992. FAX: (414)271–0487. Andrew Muchin. Weekly. Milwaukee Jewish Federation.

INDEXES

INDEX TO JEWISH PERIODICALS (1963). PO Box 18570, Cleveland Hts., 44118. (216)-381–4846. Lenore Pfeffer Koppel. Annually.

NEWS SYNDICATES

JEWISH TELEGRAPHIC AGENCY, INC. (1917). 330 Seventh Ave., 11th fl., NYC., 10001–5010. (212)643–1890. FAX: (212)-643–8498. Mark Joffe, Michael Pariser, Mark A. Seal. Daily.

CANADA

CANADIAN JEWISH HERALD (1977). 17 Anselme Lavigne Dollard des Ormeaux, PQ H9A 1N3. (514)684–7667. Dan Nimrod. FAX: (514)737–7636. Irregularly. Dawn Publishing Co., Ltd.

CANADIAN JEWISH NEWS (1971). 10 Gateway Blvd., #420, Don Mills, ONT M3C 3A1. (416)422–2331. FAX: (416)422–3790. Patricia Rucker. Weekly.

CANADIAN JEWISH OUTLOOK (1963). 6184 Ash St., #3, Vancouver, BC V5Z 3G9. (604)324–5101.FAX:(604)325–2470.Henry M. Rosenthal. Monthly. Canadian Jewish Outlook Society.

CANADIAN ZIONIST (1934). 5250 Decarie Blvd., Suite 550, Montreal, PQ H3X 2H9. (514)486–9526. FAX: (514)483–6392. Five times a year. English-Hebrew. Canadian Zionist Federation.

DIALOGUE (1988). 1590 Dr. Penfield Ave., Montreal, PQ H3G 1C5. (514)931–7531. FAX: (514)931–3281. Rebecca Rosenberg. Semiannually. French-English. Canadian Jewish Congress, Quebec Region.

JEWISH POST & NEWS (1987). 117 Hutchings St., Winnipeg, MAN R2X 2V4. (204)694–3332. Matt Bellan. Weekly.

THE JEWISH STANDARD (1930). 77 Mowat Ave., Suite 016, Toronto, ONT M6K 3E3. (416)537–2696. Julius Hayman. Fortnightly.

JEWISH WESTERN BULLETIN (1930). 3268 Heather St., Vancouver, BC V5Z 3K5. (604)879–6575. FAX: (604)879–6573. Samuel Kaplan. Weekly.

JOURNAL OF PSYCHOLOGY AND JUDAISM (1976). 1747 Featherston Dr., Ottawa, ONT K1H 6P4. (613)731–9119. Reuven P. Bulka. Quarterly. Center for the Study of Psychology and Judaism.

OTTAWA JEWISH BULLETIN & REVIEW (1954). 151 Chapel St., Ottawa, ONT K1N 7Y2. (613)232–7306. FAX: (613)563–4593. Cynthia Engel. Biweekly. Jewish Community Council of Ottawa.

UNDZER VEG (1932). 272 Codsell Ave., Downsview, ONT M3H 3X2. (416)636–4024. Joseph Kage. Irregularly. Yiddish-English. Achdut HaAvoda-Poale Zion of Canada.

WINDSOR JEWISH COMMUNITY BULLETIN (1942). 1641 Ouellette Ave., Windsor, ONT N9E 1T9. (519)973–1772. FAX: (519)973–1774. Dr. Allen Juris. Quarterly. Windsor Jewish Community Council.

Obituaries: United States[1]

ASHER, JOSEPH, rabbi; b. Heilbronn, Germany, Jan. 7, 1921; d. San Francisco, Calif., June 1, 1990; in U.S. since 1948. Educ.: Aytz Chaim Yeshivah, London; Hebrew Union Coll., Cincinnati. Served Australian Army WWII. Chaplain, DP camps in Germany, 1946–47. Rabbi: Melbourne, Aust.; Sarasota, Fla.; Tuscaloosa, Ala.; Temple Emanu-El, Greensboro, N.C., 1957–67; Temple Emanu-El, San Francisco, Calif., 1967–86. Pres.: Pacific Assn. of Reform Rabbis; N. Calif. Bd. of Rabbis; v.-pres., Amer. Jewish Cong., N. Calif. Region. Mem.: S.F. Conference on Religion, Race, and Social Concern; bd. govs., Hebrew Union Coll.-Jewish Inst. of Religion. Active in the civil rights movement and in the effort to promote German Jewish dialogue. One of original appointees to the U.S. Holocaust Memorial Council. Author: "Isn't It Time We Forgave the Germans?" (*Look* magazine, 1965). Recipient: West German Grand Cross of Merit; *Festschrift* in his memory: *The Jewish Legacy and the German Conscience* (1991).

BERNSTEIN, LEONARD, composer, conductor; b. Lawrence, Mass., Aug. 25, 1918; d. NYC, Oct. 14, 1990. Educ.: Harvard U.; Curtis Inst. Joined N.Y. Philharmonic as asst. conductor, 1943; appointed music director, N.Y. Philharmonic, 1959, the first American-born conductor to head a major orchestra and the youngest musical dir. ever engaged by the NYP—a post he held for 10 years. Gifted and versatile composer: of musicals—*On the Town*, *Wonderful Town*, *West Side Story*, and *Candide*; of ballets—*Fancy Free* and *Dybbuk*; of works on biblical and Jewish themes—*Jeremiah* and *Kaddish* symphonies, *Chichester Psalms*, and Hebrew songs, as well as *Mass*, song cycles, and scores for films. Lectured and taught at Berkshire Music Center in Tanglewood, Mass., and on television. Musical adviser, Israel Philharmonic, 1948–49; named laureate conductor in 1988. Rushed to Israel during Six Day War, conducted IPO in a festive performance in the amphitheater on Mt. Scopus days after its liberation. Noted for expressive podium style, exuberant personality, and left-leaning politics associated with late-'60s "radical chic." Recipient: Fellow, Amer. Acad. and Inst. of Arts and Letters and recip. of its Gold Medal; Gold Medal, City of Milan; Star of People's Friendship Medal, German Democratic Republic; TV Emmy Award for *N.Y. Philharmonic Young People's Concerts*; 2 Grammy Awards.

BERNSTEIN, MARVER H., professor, university administrator; b. Mankato, Minn., Feb. 7, 1919; d. Cairo, Egypt (in a hotel fire, along with his wife, Sheva Rosenthal Bernstein), Mar. 1, 1990. Educ.: U. Wisconsin; Princeton U. (PhD). Budget examiner and analyst, U.S. Bureau of the Budget, 1942–46; joined Princeton U. faculty 1946, rising from research assoc. in politics to instr., asst. prof., 1948; assoc. prof., 1954; prof., 1958–72; chmn. dept. of politics, 1961–64; assoc. dir. Woodrow Wilson

---

[1]Including American Jews who died between January 1 and December 31, 1990.

School of Public and Internatl. Affairs, 1962–64; dean, 1964–69; prof. politics and public affairs, 1969–72. Pres., Brandeis U., 1972–83; univ. prof. of philosophy and politics, Georgetown U., 1983–89. Mem.: presidential task forces on transportation and on manpower for state and local govt.; legislative apportionment comm., State of N.J.; bd. of trustees, Natl. Civil Service League; bd. dir., WGBH Educ. Found.; U.S. Holocaust Memorial Council; WETA, Washington; visiting com., John F. Kennedy School of Govt., Harvard U.; Amer. studies adv. com., Amer. Council of Learned Societies; comm. on internatl. educ. relations, Amer. Council on Educ.; task force on the sr. exec. service, 20th Century Fund; and many other activities. Consultant: Brookings Inst., U.S. Civil Service Comm., Natl. Acad. of Public Admin., the Israeli govt., and others. Pres.: Natl. Found. for Jewish Culture, 1983–86; Amer. Professors for Peace in the Middle East, 1985; mem.: B'nai B'rith Natl. Hillel Comm. 1966 on, its chmn. 1969–75; Inst. for Jewish Policy Planning and Research, Synagogue Council of Amer., 1972–80; exec. council, Amer. Jewish Hist. Soc., 1973–85; internatl. council of Beth Hatefutsoth, 1981 on; internatl. council of B'nai B'rith, 1982–85; bd. of trustees, Reconstructionist Rabbinical Coll., 1983–86; trustee: Combined Jewish Philanthropies, Greater Boston, 1978–83; Amer. Jewish Joint Distribution Com., 1978 on; Found. for Jewish Studies, Washington, D.C., 1984 on. Author: Regulating Business by Independent Commission (1955); The Politics of Israel (1957); The Job of the Federal Executive (1958); co-author, American Democracy (various eds. since 1951); and numerous scholarly articles. Recipient: Mem. Natl. Acad. Public Admin.; fellow, Amer. Acad. Arts and Sciences; hon. doctorates: Jewish Theol. Sem. of Amer., Northeastern U., Duquesne U., Brandeis U., Hebrew Union Coll., Baltimore Hebrew Coll.

BETTELHEIM, BRUNO, psychoanalyst, author; b. Vienna, Austria, Aug. 28, 1903; d. Silver Spring, Md., March 13, 1990; in U.S. since 1939. Educ.: U. Vienna. After internment of more than a year in the concentration camps of Dachau and Buchenwald was released at the intervention of Eleanor Roosevelt and Herbert Lehman. Research assoc., Progressive Educ. Assn., U. Chicago, 1939–41; assoc. prof., psych., Rockford Coll., 1942–44; asst. prof., educ.

psych., U. Chicago, 1944–47; assoc. prof. 1947–52; prof. 1957–73; dir., Sonia Shankman Orthogenic School, 1944–73, a treatment center for emotionally disturbed children, where he pioneered the creation of a "total therapeutic milieu." His The Informed Heart: Autonomy in a Mass Age (1960) and Surviving and Other Essays (1979) aroused controversy with his views on why some people survived concentration camps while others perished. Author (in addition to the above): Love Is Not Enough (1950); Truants from Life (1954); The Empty Fortress: Infantile Autism and the Birth of the Self (1967); The Uses of Enchantment (1976); A Good Enough Parent: A Book on Child-Rearing (1987); and other works.

BLAUSTEIN, MORTON K., business executive, communal leader; b. Baltimore, Md., Oct. 20, 1926; d. Richmond, Va., Dec. 17, 1990. Educ.: Johns Hopkins U., Stanford U. (PhD). A geologist by training, was associated since 1951 (since 1973 as chmn. bd. and CEO) with family-owned American Trading and Production Corp., originally a petroleum-related company that in his tenure expanded into real estate, communications, and other fields. Chmn., bd. of overseers, Stanford U. dept of geology; bd. mem.: Park School, Sinai Hospital, and Johns Hopkins U., Peale Museum, Baltimore Civic Opera Co., Chamber of Commerce, all in Baltimore. Mem.: Natl. Petroleum Council; public policy com., Advertising Council; Governor's Comm. to Study Maryland Hospital Costs. Following in the footsteps of his father, Jacob, served in various positions in the Amer. Jewish Com.: as natl. v.-pres. for 9 years, as chmn. its natl. exec. council, chmn. Baltimore chap., mem. admin. council of Jacob Blaustein Inst. for the Advancement of Human Rights (which he helped found), and endower of the Hilda Katz Blaustein Leadership Development Program. Bd. mem.: Conf. on Jewish Material Claims Against Germany; Memorial Found. for Jewish Culture; Amer. Associates Ben-Gurion U. of the Negev. Benefactor: Ben-Gurion U. of the Negev and bd. mem. its American Associates; Judaic Studies Program, Yale U. Mem. exec. com. and bd. dirs. and treas., the Jewish Fed. of Baltimore, more than 25 years; rep. Amer. Jewish Com., Baltimore Jewish Council, 1956–70.

BLOOM, ALBERT W., journalist; b. Pittsburgh, Pa., Aug. 9, 1918; d. Pittsburgh, Pa., Jan. 27, 1990. Educ.: Duquesne U.; Columbia U. School of Journalism. Served U.S. Air Force, WWII (lt.-col. reserve; retired). Copy ed., Washington *Times Herald*, 1945–47; reporter and ed., Pittsburgh *Post-Gazette*, 1947–62; journalism instr., Duquesne U., 1947–62; founding ed., exec. ed., ed. emer., Pittsburgh *Jewish Chronicle*, 1962–90; instr., U. of Pittsburgh, 1963–78. Pres.: Amer. Jewish Press Assn.; Young Peoples Synagogue; co-chmn., Amer. Zionist Fed.; bd. mem.: Hebrew Inst. of Pittsburgh; Hillel Acad. of Pittsburgh. Recipient: Simon Rockower Award; Joseph Polakoff Award; Duquesne U. Distinguished Alumnus Award; Smolar Award; honored by Hebrew Inst. MEAH Club, B'nai B'rith McKeesport Lodge, and March of Dimes; Chinese Combat Command commendation, 1945.

BOKSER, BARUCH, professor, rabbi; b. Waltham, Mass., July 25, 1945; d. NYC, July 12, 1990. Educ.: U. Pa.; Jewish Theol. Sem. of Amer.; Brown U. (PhD). Asst. prof., rabbinics and Judaic studies, U. Calif., Berkeley, 1974–82; assoc. prof., Dropsie Coll. (Annenberg Inst.), 1982–85; prof., Talmud and rabbinics, JTS, 1986 on. Author: *Samuel's Commentary on the Mishnah* (1975); *Post Mishnaic Judaism in Transition* (1980); *Origins of the Seder* (1984); ed., *The History of Judaism: The Next Ten Years* (1980). Mem. edit. bd., *Jewish Quarterly Review*; bd. mem., Assn. for Jewish Studies; mem.: Soc. of Bibl. Lit.; Amer. Acad. of Religion; World Union of Jewish Studies. Ready for publication at time of his death: a transl. and explanation of Tractate *pesahim* of the Palestinian Talmud. Author of scholarly studies in various volumes, as well as articles and reviews, and contrib. to *The Encyclopedia of Religion*.

BRAVERMAN, LIBBIE L., educator, author; b. Boston, Mass., Dec. 20, 1900; d. Cleveland, Ohio, Dec. ?, 1990. Educ.: Western Reserve U.; Harvard U., U. Pittsburgh. Educ. dir., Euclid Ave. (Fairmount) Temple, Cleveland, Ohio, 1946–52; Temple Sinai, Stamford, Conn., 1966–67. Mem. bd. govs., Cleveland Coll. Jewish Studies; hon. natl. bd. mem., Hadassah; v.-pres., Natl. Council for Jewish Educ.; pres.: Ohio-Mich.-Ind. Religious Teachers Assn.; Central States region of Hadassah;

head counselor, Camp Tabor, Camp Carmelia. Co-author: *Children of the Emek* (1931); *Children of Freedom* (1953); *Six Day Warriors* (1969); and several textbooks.

COPLAND, AARON, composer; b. Brooklyn, N.Y., Nov. 14, 1900; d. N. Tarrytown, N.Y., Dec. 2, 1990. Educ.: Private musical instruction in U.S. and France. Regarded as "the dean of American composers," was also a noted pianist, conductor, teacher, advocate of American music, and an inspiration to generations of younger American composers. His Symphony for Organ and Orchestra premiered in N.Y. in 1925. Seeking to make modern music more accessible, created "a homespun musical idiom" that often included folk tunes. Among his best-known works from this period: *El Salón Mexico* (1936) and the ballets *Billy the Kid* (1938), *Rodeo* (1942), and *Appalachian Spring* (1944), and concert pieces like *Fanfare for the Common Man* and *Lincoln Portrait* (both 1942). Among his works on Jewish themes are the trio *Vitebsk: Study on a Jewish Theme* (1929), and *In the Beginning* (1947). Pres., Amer. Composers' Alliance, 1937–45; mem. exec. bd., League of Composers; faculty mem. for 25 years, Berkshire Music Center at Tanglewood; first Amer. composer to deliver the Norton lectures at Harvard U., 1951. Author: *The New Music* (1968), a two-vol. autobiog., and other works. Recipient: Pulitzer Prize (for *Appalachian Spring*); Academy Award for score for motion picture *The Heiress* (1948); mem., Amer. Acad. of Arts and Letters; Presidential Medal of Freedom (1964); Henry Howland Memorial Prize, Yale U.; Gold Baton, Amer. Symphony Orchestra League; Kennedy Center Award; the Queens Coll. School of Music named for him in 1981.

COUSINS, NORMAN, writer, editor; b. Union Hill, N.J., June 24, 1915; d. Los Angeles, Calif., Nov. 30, 1990. Educ.: Teachers Coll., Columbia U. Educ. writer, *N.Y. Evening Post*, 1934–35; lit. ed. and mng. ed., *Current History* magazine, 1935–40; ed., *Saturday Review*, 1940–71 and 1973–77; chmn. bd. eds., 1978; ed. emer. 1980 on; founding ed., *World* magazine, 1972–73. Adj. prof., dept. psychiatry and behavioral science, UCLA, 1980s. Hon. pres., United World Federalists; bd. chmn., Natl. Educ.

Television; co-chmn., Citizens Com. for a Nuclear Test Ban Treaty; mem., Hiroshima Peace Center Assn.; trustee: Charles F. Kettering Found., Menninger Found., Ruth Mott Found. Organized medical treatment in U.S. for 24 "Hiroshima Maidens"; after recovering from a life-threatening illness, became an advocate of holistic healing. Author: more than two dozen books, incl. *Modern Man Is Obsolete* (1945); *Who Speaks for Man* (1953); *In Place of Folly* (1961); *The Improbable Triumvirate* (1972); *Anatomy of an Illness* (1983); and *Head First: The Biology of Hope* (1989). Recipient: Albert Schweitzer Prize for Humanitarianism; Japan Niwano Peace Prize; Eleanor Roosevelt Peace Award; Peace Medal, UN; Magazine Publisher of the Year; and many other awards and hon. doctorates.

CROWN, HENRY (KRINSKY), business executive, philanthropist; b. Chicago, Ill., June 13, 1896; d. Chicago, Ill., Aug. 14, 1990. Served U.S. Army, WWII (achieving rank of colonel). A rags-to-riches figure, left school in 8th grade and went on to build one of America's largest fortunes—in hotels, real estate, railroads, coal, sugar, the aerospace industry, and other fields. Clerk, Chicago Fire Brick Co., 1910–12; traffic mgr., Union Drop Forge Co., 1912–16; partner, S.R. Crown & Co., 1916–19; treas. Material Service Corp. (building materials), 1919–21, pres. 1921–41, chmn. bd. 1941–59; dir., chmn. exec. com., General Dynamics Corp., 1959–66, 1970–86; hon. chmn., 1986 on; chmn. bd. Henry Crown & Co., 1967; past dir. Hilton Hotels, Waldorf Astoria Corp. Mem. Chicago CD Corps.; trustee, Chicago Boys Clubs; mem.: bd. trustees, DePaul U.; U. Ill. Citizens. Com., Loyola U. Citizens Bd., Northwestern U. Assn. Benefactor: Northwestern U., Stanford U., Brandeis U., Museum of Science and Industry (Washington, D.C.), Hadassah, Jerusalem Foundation, Technion-Israel Inst. of Technology, Tel Aviv U., Hebrew U. of Jerusalem, Weizmann Inst., UJA, Thanks to Scandinavia, and others. Recipient: hon. doctorates from Syracuse U., Brown U., Northwestern U., Jewish Theol. Sem. of Amer., and others; U.S. Legion of Merit, French Legion d'Honneur; Greek Gold Cross; Nicaraguan Order Ruben Dario; Horatio Alger Award, Amer. Schools and Colleges Assn.; Julius Rosenwald Memorial Award, Chicago Jewish Fed., and many other honors.

DAVIS, SAMMY, JR., entertainer; b. NYC, Dec. 8, 1925; d. Beverly Hills, Calif., May 16, 1990. Served US Army, WWII. The son of vaudeville stars, began performing on stage in childhood; became an internationally acclaimed singer, dancer, impressionist. Youngest member of the Will Mastin Trio, 1930–48; star of hotel and nightclub shows, television, Broadway shows (*Mr. Wonderful*, 1956), 20 films: *Benny Goodman Story* (1956); *Porgy and Bess* (1959); *Sergeants Three* (1962); *Salt and Pepper* (1968); *Sweet Charity* (1968); *Tap* (1989), and scores of hit recordings. Converted to Judaism in late 1950s after an automobile accident in which he lost an eye; claimed to have found "an affinity" between Jews and blacks as oppressed peoples. Author (with others) of three autobiog. vols.: *Yes I Can* (1965); *Hollywood in a Suitcase* (1980); *Why Me?* (1989).

DAWIDOWICZ, LUCY S., professor, writer; b. NYC, June 16, 1915; d. NYC, Dec. 5, 1990. Educ.: Hunter Coll.; Columbia U.; postgrad. research fellow, YIVO Inst., Vilna, 1938–39. Asst. to research dir., YIVO Inst., NYC, 1940–46; Joint Distribution Com. educ. officer, DP camps, Germany, 1946–47; research analyst, Amer. Jewish Com., 1948–68, and research dir., 1968–69; assoc. prof. and prof., social hist., Yeshiva U., 1969–78; prof., Holocaust studies, Yeshiva U., 1970–78. Visiting prof.: SUNY Albany, Stanford U.; Spindel lect., Bowdoin Coll.; Rudolph lect., Syracuse U. Founder and pres., Fund for the Translation of Jewish Literature; bd. mem.: Friends of the Library of the Jewish Theol. Sem. of Amer.; Leo Baeck Inst.; Conf. on Jewish Social Studies; mem.: Assn. for Jewish Studies, Amer. Hist. Assn., Amer. Jewish Hist. Soc. A pioneer in the field of Holocaust studies and author of a classic text, *The War Against the Jews 1933–1945* (1975). Her experiences as a researcher in prewar Poland and in postwar Germany, where she helped to reclaim the YIVO library and archives captured by the Nazis, were described in a memoir, *From That Place and Time* (1989). Author (in addition to the works cited above): *The Golden Tradition: Jewish Life and Thought in Eastern Europe* (1967); *A Holocaust Reader* (1976); *The Jewish Presence: Es-*

says on Identity and History (1977); *The Holocaust and the Historians* (1981); *On Equal Terms: Jews in America, 1981–1991* (1982); articles in *Commentary* (39 pieces between 1951 and 1990) and other periodicals. Co-author, *Politics in a Pluralist Democracy* (1963); co-ed., *For Max Weinreich; Studies in Jewish Language, Literature and Society* (1964). Recipient: Guggenheim fellowship, 1976; Anisfield-Wolf Prize (for *The War Against the Jews*); Disting. Achievement Award, Hunter Coll. Alumni Assn.; National Jewish Book Award (for *From That Place and Time*); hon. ·doctorates: Kenyon Coll., HUC-JIR, Monmouth Coll., Yeshiva U., Spertus Coll. of Judaica.

DOBIN, RUBIN R., rabbi, business executive; b. Brooklyn, N.Y., Oct. 12, 1915; d. Miami Beach, Fla., Sept. 11, 1990. Educ.: U. Texas, Rutgers U., Hebrew Theol. Sem. (ord.), Yeshiva U., Touro Coll,, Fla. Internatl. U. (PhD). Chaplain, U.S. Army, WWII. Founder, with his brother, of "Two Guys" chain of discount stores on Long Island after the war. Founding rabbi, Hewlett-E. Rockaway (N.Y.) Jewish Center; trustee: Cong. Shaaray Tefila, Lawrence, N.Y.; Hebrew Inst. of Long Island. Founder and rabbi emer., Young Israel of Sunny Isles (Fla.); sr. v.-pres., Hebrew Acad. of Greater Miami. Active in POW-MIA movement during Vietnam War and in Israel after 1973 Yom Kippur War. Natl. chmn., Operation Recognition, which seeks to have the Internatl. Com. of Red Cross recognize Magen David Adom in Israel and its emblem, the red star of David; natl. coord., Americans for Haganah, during Israel's War of Independence; active in many Jewish organizations, incl. Bar Ilan U., JNF, Synagogue Council of Amer., Union of Orthodox Jewish Congs. Recipient: awards from JNF, Israel Bonds, UJA, N.J. Conf. of Christians and Jews, and many other honors.

ENDE, GEORGE, rabbi, educator; b. Brooklyn, N.Y., Jan. 12, 1912; d. Rehovot, Israel, Jan. 11, 1990. Educ.: Yeshivat Rabbi Chaim Berlin; Long Island U.; CCNY; Yale U.; Jewish Inst. of Religion (ord.). Dir., Hillel Founds., Tuscaloosa, Ala., and Burlington, Vt.; asst. rabbi and educ. dir., Temple on the Heights, Cleveland, Ohio, 1944–47; prin., Marshalliah Hebrew H.S., NYC, 1954–57 and 1960–64; consultant, Jewish Educ. Com. of N.Y., 1947–72. Set-

tled in Israel, 1975. Mem.: Rabbinical Assembly; Educators' Assembly; Natl. Council for Jewish Educ.; N.Y. Bd. of Rabbis; Histadruth Ivrith. Recipient: Hon. doctorate, Jewish Theol. Sem. of Amer.

FINE, PHIL DAVID, attorney; b. Brookline, Mass., Aug. 20, 1925; d. Boston, Mass., July 31, 1990. Educ.: Northeastern U., Norwich U.; Boston U. Founding partner, Fine and Ambrogne, 1959; partner, White, Fine & Verville, Boston, 1967 on. Deputy admin., Small Business Admin. (1961–62); bd. chmn.: Commonwealth Natl. Corp., Stadium Realty Trust, Commonwealth Bank & Trust Co. Prominent in the creation of such Boston developments as Faneuil Hall Market, Foxboro Stadium, and Exchange Place. Mem.: bd. govs. Mass. Genl. Hosp.; trustee: Newton Public Library; Boston U. Pres. and chmn., Amer. Jewish Hist. Soc.; consultant, Mamilla Project, Jerusalem.

FINEBERG, S. ANDHIL, rabbi, communal worker; b. Pittsburgh, Pa., Nov. 29, 1896; d. Mt. Vernon, N.Y., Feb. 24, 1990. Educ. U. Cincinnati; HUC-JIR; Columbia U. (PhD). Served U.S. Marine Corps, WWI. Rabbi: Niagara Falls, N.Y., 1920–24; Pittsburgh, Pa., 1924–26; White Plains, N.Y., 1926–29; Sinai Temple, Mt. Vernon, N.Y., 1929–37; natl. chaplain, Jewish War Veterans, 1932–36. Natl. community relations consultant, Amer. Jewish Com., 1939–64; consultant, Natl. Conf. Christians and Jews, 1965–78; coord., N.Y. Interracial Colloquy, 1966–78. Pres. Natl. Assn. Jewish Comunity Workers; chmn., professional standards com., Natl. Assn. of Intergroup Relations Officials. Author: *Biblical Myth and Legend*, *Overcoming Anti-Semitism*, *The Rosenberg Case*, *Defrauding Minority Groups*, *The Fallacies of Communism*, *Deflating the Professional Bigot*, and numerous magazine articles. Recipient: hon. doctorate, HUC-JIR; Anisfield-Wolf Literary Award.

FREEHOF, SOLOMON B., rabbi, scholar; b. London, England, Aug. 8, 1892; d. Pittsburgh, Pa., June 12, 1990; in U.S. since 1903. Educ.: U. Cincinnati; Hebrew Union Coll. Chaplain, U.S. Army in Europe, WWI. Teacher, HUC, 1915–24; rabbi: Kehillat Anshe Maarav Temple, Chicago, 1924–34; Rodef Shalom Temple, Pittsburgh, 1934–68; emer. thereafter. Pres.: World Union for Progressive Judaism; CCAR; mem.: exec. bd. UAHC comm. on

Teachers Coll., Harvard U. (PhD). Natl. sec., Hechalutz Org., 1936–37; lived in Palestine 1938–39; ed., Inst. of Jewish Affairs, World Jewish Cong., 1941–45; managing ed., *Jewish Frontier*, 1943–49; assoc. dir., educ. and info. depts., and publications, Jewish Agency, 1949–56; research assoc., Harvard Center for Middle East Studies, 1956 on; joined Brandeis U. faculty 1962; prof., Jewish and Zionist hist., 1968–80. Mem.: Jewish Agency Exec., Amer. sect.; bd. of trustees, Hebrew Coll., Boston; bd. govs., Tel Aviv U. Author: *The American Jew: A Zionist Analysis* (1956, 1988); *The Idea of a Jewish State* (1961); *Jews and Blacks* (1971); *Essays in Modern Jewish History* (1982); *A Clash of Heroes: Brandeis, Weizmann and American Zionism* (1987), and numerous essays and articles. Recipient: Guggenheim Fellowship; hon. doctorates from Gratz Coll., Tel Aviv U.

HAMMER, ARMAND, business executive, philanthropist; b. NYC, May 21, 1898; d. Los Angeles, Calif., Dec. 10, 1990. Educ.: Columbia U. (BS, MD). Pres.: Allied Amer. Corp., NYC, 1923–25; A. Hammer Pencil Co., NYC, London, and Moscow, 1925–30; Hammer Galleries, NYC, 1930 on; J.W. Dant Distilling Co., 1943–54; Mutual Broadcasting System, 1957–58; chmn. bd., chief exec. off., Occidental Petroleum Corp., Los Angeles, 1957 on; chmn., M. Knoedler & Co., 1972 on; dir. and investor in many companies. A controversial figure because of his ties to Soviet leaders and advocacy of world peace and nuclear disarmament. Kept his Israeli connections quiet, presumably because of oil dealings with Libya, but became a close friend of Menachem Begin, helped secure the release of two lifetime refuseniks, David Goldfarb and Ida Nudel, and engaged in private diplomacy on behalf of Soviet Jews. A lifelong art collector and dealer, built a museum in his name in L.A. to house his art collection. Benefactor: Columbia U., Metropolitan Museum of Art, Natl. Gallery of Art, and other museums; cancer research centers at the Salk Inst. and Columbia U.; Assaf Harofeh Med. Center, Israel; Pacific Jewish Center; Jerusalem Coll. of Technology. Author: *Hammer* (autobiog., 1987). Recipient: National Medal for the Arts, 1987; Soviet Order of Friendship Among Peoples, 1978; Maimonides Award, Los Angeles Jewish Community; John Jay Award, Columbia Coll.; Golda

Meir Leadership Award; Humanitarian Award, Internatl. Physicians for Prevention of Nuclear War; Emma Lazarus Statue of Liberty Award, Amer. Jewish Hist. Soc.; and numerous other awards and honors.

HECHT, JACOB J., rabbi; b. Brooklyn, N.Y., Nov. 3, 1923; d. Greenfield Park, N.Y., Aug. 5, 1990. Educ.: Rabbinical Coll. Tomchei Tmimim; Mesivta Torah Vodaath; Yeshiva Rabbi Chaim Berlin. Rabbi, Cong. Yeshiva Rabbi Meir Simcha Hacohen of E. Flatbush, for 50 years; exec. v.-pres., Natl. Com. for Furtherance of Jewish Educ. since 1946; dean, Hadar Hatorah Rabbinical Coll. for men and Machon Chana Inst. of Higher Learning for women; exec. v.-pres., Iranian Jewish Children's Fund; pres., various children's camps; official interpreter for Lubavitcher Rebbe's broadcast discourses; host, "Shema Yisrael" radio show, station WEVD; columnist, the *Jewish Press*. Pres., Rabbinic Bd. E. Flatbush; chmn., Rabbinic Court of E. Flatbush; hon. chaplain, Kings County Jewish War Veterans; mem., President's Task Force on Voluntarism; exec. mem., Morality in Media; v.-chmn., Jewish Political Actions Com.; mem., Assn. of Orthodox Jewish Scientists; exec. mem., Rabbinical Alliance of Amer.; mem. bd. dirs., N.Y. Council of Charitable Orgs.; del.: White House Conf. on Educ., White House Conf. on Aging; mem., Governor's Suicide Prevention Com. Author: *Brimstone and Fire*, numerous teachers' guides, and publications on such topics as morality, violence, pornography, blockbusting, and intermarriage. Recipient: Cert. of Merit, Kings County Council of JWV; State of N.Y. Citation; Educator of the Year Award, Assn. of Teachers of N.Y.; and other honors.

HEXTER, MAURICE B., organization executive, communal worker; b. Cincinnati, Ohio, June 30, 1891; d. NYC, Oct. 28, 1990. Educ.: U. Cincinnati; Harvard U. (PhD). Exec. dir., Milwaukee Fed. of Jewish Charities, 1915–17; supt., United Jewish Charities, Cincinnati, 1917–19; exec. dir., Fed. of Jewish Charities, Boston, 1919–29; instr., tutor, social ethics dept., Harvard U., 1921–29; lect., School of Social Work, Simmons Coll., 1921–29; sec., Joint Palestine Survey Comm., 1927–29. Moved to Jerusalem, 1929, to direct Palestine Emergency Fund, 1929–38, to oversee rebuilding of homes destroyed in Arab riots. Non-Zionist mem. exec., Jewish Agency for Palestine, 1929–38, and head of its colonization dept., 1935–38; mem. negotiating comm. with British cabinet, 1930–31; Jewish Agency rep., Palestine Royal Comm., 1936–37. Returned to U.S. and joined staff of Fed. of Jewish Philanthropies of N.Y., 1938, as asst. to exec. v.-pres.; co-exec. v.-pres. (with Joseph Willen), 1941–67; exec. consultant, 1967 on. Pres., Natl. Conf. of Jewish Social Workers (1924); Dominican Republic Settlement Assn. (1941); mem.: advisory bd. to welfare commissioner of N.Y.; NYC Council Against Poverty; grants com., Silberman Found.; v.-pres., treas., Henry Kaufmann Found.; chmn. bd. of overseers, Florence Heller School for Advanced Studies in Social Work; trustee, Brandeis U.; Amer. Friends of Hebrew U. Credited with bringing about many social reforms and innovations in communal services; a key figure in founding schools of social work at Hunter Coll., Brandeis U., and Yeshiva U.; an active sculptor in his later years, whose works won critical acclaim. Benefactor: Mt. Sinai Medical Center; Jersey City State Coll.; Usdan Center for the Creative and Performing Arts; Jewish Home and Hospital for the Aged. Recipient: award in his name at Hunter Coll. School of Social Work; chairs in his name at Hebrew U. of Jerusalem (in internatl. relations and Middle East studies), at Mt. Sinai Medical Center, N.Y. (in pulmonary medicine), and at Brandeis U. (in philanthropy).

HOENIG, MOSES H., attorney, communal worker; b. NYC, Sept. 18, 1898; d. Long Beach, N.Y., Oct. 30, 1990. Educ.: St. Lawrence U.; Brooklyn Law School. In private law practice for 70 years. Founding mem. and pres., Natl. Council of Young Israel, 1926–57; pres., Brooklyn Jewish Community Council; mem. exec.: Mizrachi Org.; Amer. Jewish Cong. (1932–45); ed. *Viewpoint* magazine (Young Israel).

HOFSTADTER, ROBERT, physicist; b. NYC, Feb. 5, 1915; d. Stanford, Calif., Nov. 17, 1990. Educ.: CCNY; Princeton U. (PhD). Served in WWII as physicist at Natl. Bureau of Standards, working on anti-aircraft weapons. Instr., physics: Princeton U., 1940–41; CCNY, 1941–42; physicist, Norden Lab. Corp., 1943–46; asst. prof., Princeton, 1946–50; assoc. prof., Stanford U., 1950–54, prof., 1954–85; dir.: high en-

ergy physics lab, Stanford, 1967–74; John Fluke Mfg. Co., 1979–88. Mem. bd. govs.: Technion-Israel Inst. of Technology; Weizmann Inst. of Science. Recipient: Nobel Prize, 1961, for research in nuclear particles, providing the first "reasonably" consistent picture of the atomic nucleus; Ford and Guggenheim fellowships; U.S. Natl. Medal of Science; Townsend Harris Medal, CCNY; and many other awards. A physics lab at Brandeis U. named in his honor.

KAHANE, MEIR (MARTIN), rabbi, political activist; b. Brooklyn, N.Y., Aug. 1, 1932; d. NYC, Nov. 5, 1990 (assassinated in a Manhattan hotel). Educ.: Mirrer Yeshiva, Brooklyn; Brooklyn Coll.; New York U. Law School. Rabbi, Howard Beach, Queens, mid-1950s; free-lance journalist; co-founder (with Joseph Churba), Consultant Research Assn., 1963, a think tank collecting information for U.S. intelligence and other orgs. Under the name Michael King, wrote occasional sports stories for *Brooklyn Daily* and infiltrated John Birch Soc. for the FBI. In 1965 founded short-lived Fourth of July movement (reportedly with govt. funding), to build support for Vietnam War on college campuses; assoc. ed., Brooklyn *Jewish Press*, 1967–68; co-author (with Churba), *The Jewish Stake in Vietnam*, 1968. In response to increase in anti-Semitic incidents in New York, founded Jewish Defense League, 1968, an org. devoted to self-defense and Jewish pride, whose motto "Never Again!" struck a responsive chord in Jews determined to prevent future Holocausts. Credited with calling attention to the plight of Soviet Jewry, the group was also condemned for bombing attacks and shootings directed at Soviet facilities and officials. Kahane was convicted in federal court in July 1971 on explosives charges; released on probation; settled in Israel in September; returned to U.S. in 1974, when probation was revoked and he spent a year in prison. In Israel founded political party, Kach ("Thus"), which advocated expulsion of Arabs and a Torah state. Member Knesset, 1984–88, when Kach was disqualified on the ground that it was racist and undemocratic. Kahane was arrested more than 20 times on charges ranging from sedition to inciting riots. One of the most controversial figures in modern Jewish life, his potent mixture of ultranationalism, religiosity, hatred of Arabs, and sanctioning of violence won him ardent support as well as condemnation as a racist, both in U.S. and Israel.

KAHN, LOTHAR, professor; b. Rehlingen, Saarland (then France), June 1, 1922; d. W. Palm Beach, Fla., Jan. 23, 1990; in U.S. since 1937. Educ.: CCNY; Columbia U. (PhD). Ed., French military publications, U.S. War Dept., 1943–45; instr., Univ. High School, Coll. of Educ., Ohio State U., 1945–46; asst. prof., assoc. prof., and prof., French, German, world lit., and philosophy, Central Conn. State Coll./U., 1946–87. Visiting prof.: Trinity Coll.; Wesleyan U. Author: *Mirrors of the Jewish Mind: A Gallery of Our Time* (1968); *Insight and Action: The Life and Work of Lion Feuchtwanger* (1975); *God: What Others Have Said About Him* (1980); and numerous articles and chapters in books, chiefly on German-Jewish literature and current events. Coauthor: *Elementary Conversational German* and other language textbooks; *Book of Insults and Irreverent Quotations; Death in the Balance* (on capital punishment). Recipient: hon. doctorate (posth.), Johann Wolfgang Goethe U. of Frankfurt, W. Germany; College Distinguished Service Award, CCSC.

KELMAN, WOLFE, rabbi, communal worker; b. Vienna, Austria, Nov. 27, 1923; d. NYC, June 26, 1990; in U.S. since 1946. Educ.: U. Toronto; Jewish Theol. Sem. of Amer. Served Royal Canadian Air Force, WWII. Exec. v.-pres., Rabbinical Assembly, 1951–1990; dir., Louis Finkelstein Inst. for Religious and Social Studies, 1990. Dir., Joint Placement Comm., the RA, United Syn., and JTS, 1951–66; visiting prof., homiletics, JTS, 1967–73; adj. asst. prof., Jewish hist., JTS, 1973–88; visiting prof., Hebrew U., Jerusalem, 1984–85. Chmn., World Jewish Cong., Amer. Sect., 1986–90, as well as mem. its governing council, co-chmn. interreligious affairs com., chmn. cultural comm.; v.-pres., Labor Zionist Alliance; non-govt. rep., U.S. Mission to UN; mem.: bd. govs., NY Bd. of Rabbis; bd. dirs, HIAS; exec., Melton Research Center and chmn. its acad. bd.; founding mem., Amer. Jewish World Service; mem. adv. com., Jewish Fund for Justice; pres.; Hebrew Arts Found.; Com. of Neighbors Concerned with the Elderly, Their Rights and Needs. Active in Internatl. Com. on Jewish Religious Consultations, Syn. Council of America, Natl. Jewish Community Relations Council, and N.Y. Bd. of

Rabbis. Instrumental in the revival of Cong. Ansche Chesed on Manhattan's West Side; a leader in the movement to allow ordination of women; accompanied A.J. Heschel on civil-rights marches in the South in '60s. Author: numerous articles in various publications, incl. the AJYB. Recipient: hon. doctorates: JTS; HUC-JIR; vol. of essays in his honor, *Perspectives on Jews and Judaism* (Rabbinical Assembly).

KLEBAN, ANNA, administrator; b. Grodno (Russia), Aug. 1, 1899; d. Philadelphia, Pa., Apr. 16, 1990; in U.S. since 1921. A staff mem. of the library of the Jewish Theol. Sem. of Amer. for over 50 years, first as personal sec. to Dr. Alexander Marx, later as dir. of community education and field activities. Known widely as a knowledgeable, charming, and witty lecturer on the library's collections, especially the rare books; had a reading knowledge of seven languages and spoke five fluently.

KRAMER, SAMUEL NOAH, professor; b. Zashkow, Russia, Sept. 28, 1897; d. Philadelphia, Pa., Nov. 26, 1990; in U.S. since 1906. Educ.: Temple U.; Dropsie Coll.; U. Pa. (PhD). Served U.S. Army, WWI. Participated in archaeological expedition to Iraq, excavating Sumerian tablets, 1930; began transcribing tablets as a Guggenheim fellow in Istanbul, 1931; as research asst. and assoc., worked on Assyrian dictionary being prepared at U. Chicago, 1932–39; joined U. Pa. faculty 1942; Clark Research Prof., U. Pa., 1949–68. Prof., Amer. Schools of Oriental Research, Istanbul and Baghdad, 1946–47; Fulbright research prof., Turkey, 1951–52; Pattern Found. Lect., Indiana U., 1968; visiting prof., U. Copenhagen, 1969–70. Mem.: Amer. Oriental Soc., Archeological Inst. of Amer., Soc. Bibl. Lit., Amer. Philosophical Soc., Amer. Anthropological Assn. Author: *Gilgamesh and the Huluppu Tree* (1938); *Sumerian Mythology* (1944); *History Begins at Sumer: Thirty-Nine "Firsts" in Man's Recorded History* (1959, reissued 1987); *Cradle of Civilization* (1967); *In the World of Sumer: An Autobiography* (1986), and other works. Recipient: John Frederick Lewis Prize, Amer. Phil. Soc.; several hon. degrees.

KREEGER, DAVID LLOYD, insurance executive, philanthropist; b. NYC, Jan. 4, 1909; d. Washington, D.C., Nov. 18, 1990. Educ.: Rutgers U.; Harvard Law School. Private law practice, 1932–34; U.S. govt.,

1934–46; private practice, 1946–57; joined Govt. Employees Ins. Co. (GEICO) and Affiliates, 1957: sr. v.-pres., pres. bd., v. chmn.; chmn. and CEO, 1957–74; chmn. exec. com., 1974–79; hon. bd. chmn., 1979–90. An internationally known art collector and accomplished violinist. Pres., Natl. Symphony Orch., 1970–78; founder, pres., and chmn., Washington Opera, 1980–90; pres., chmn., Corcoran Gallery of Art, 1988–90; trustee, American U.; bd. mem: Georgetown U., Peabody Inst. of Music, Arena Stage, Dumbarton Oaks, Natl. Gallery. Pres., David Lloyd Kreeger Charitable Found. Mem.: DC Comm. on Arts & Humanities; Fed. Res. Bd's. art adv. panel. Natl. v.-pres., Amer. Jewish Com.; v.-pres., trustee, Washington Hebrew Cong. Recipient: Natl. Medal of Arts (1990); Amer. U. Cyrus A. Ansary Award; Georgetown U. John Carroll Medal; George Peabody Medal; Rutgers Hall of Distinguished Alumni; Corcoran Gallery of Art Bronze Medal; and other honors.

LASKER, HARRY, rabbi: b. NYC, Aug. 8, 1917; d. Elizabeth, N.J., Aug. 21, 1990. Educ.: Brooklyn Coll., Jewish Inst. of Religion (ord.). Rabbi, Fairmont, W. Va., 1940–43; part-time pulpits in Plainfield, N.J., 1954–58, and Hillside, N.J., 1959–88; natl. dir., Jewish Relationships, Boy Scouts of Amer., 1943–80. Author: *Ner Tamid Religious Award for Boy Scouts*, *Ner Tamid Guide for Boy Scouts and Explorers*, *Scouting and the Jewish Boy*, and *Jewish Religious Services for Boy Scouts and Explorers*. Recipient: hon. doctorates from HUC-JIR, Jewish Theol. Sem. of Amer.; special citation, Natl. Jewish Com. on Scouting.

LASKY, VICTOR, journalist; b. Liberty, N.Y., Jan. 7, 1918; d. Washington, D.C., Feb. 22, 1990. Educ.: Brooklyn Coll. Served U.S. Army, WWII (*Stars and Stripes* corresp. and ed.). Reporter: *Chicago Sun*, 1941–47; *N.Y. World Telegram and Sun*, 1947–50 (where he assisted on a series on Communist infiltration of U.S. that won a Pulitzer Prize); screenwriter for MGM, 1950–56; dir. public relations, Radio Liberty, 1956–60; syndicated columnist, "Say It Straight," for N. Amer. Newspaper Alliance, 1962–80. Founder and 1st v.-pres., Council Against Communist Aggression; lecturer and writer for Accuracy in Media. Author: *JFK: The Man and the Myth* (1963); *The Ugly Russian* (1965); *Robert F.*

Kennedy: The Myth and the Man (1968); *It Didn't Start with Watergate* (1977); *Never Complain, Never Explain: The Story of Henry Ford II* (1981), and other works. Co-author: *Seeds of Treason* (about Alger Hiss; 1950).

LESTER, ELENORE; writer, editor; b. NYC, (?), 1920; d. NYC, Sept. 9, 1990. Educ.: Hunter Coll.; NYU. Reporter, Newark *Star-Ledger*, 1951–64; free-lance writer and critic, largely on theater and the arts; after 1967, turned increasingly to Jewish subjects. Joined N.Y. *Jewish Week* in 1975, rising to sr. ed. Wrote *N.Y. Times Magazine* cover story on Raoul Wallenberg, Mar. 30, 1980, and lectured widely on him. Consultant, Jewish Women's Task Force, late 1970s; mem. founding com., *Lilith* magazine. Author: *Raoul Wallenberg: The Man in the Iron Web*.

LEVI, S. GERSHON, rabbi, translator; b. Toronto, Canada, June 13, 1908; d. Jerusalem, Israel, Apr. 4, 1990; in U.S. since 1929 (?). Educ.: U. Toronto; Columbia U.; Jewish Theol. Sem. of Amer. Sr. Jewish chaplain, Canadian Armed Forces, WWII. Asst. rabbi, Shaar Hashomayim Cong., Montreal, 1936–41; Hillel rabbi, U. Toronto, 1945–46; rabbi, Jamaica Jewish Center, NYC, 1946–74; upon retirement, settled in Israel. V.-pres., treas., and pres., Rabbinical Assembly; ed., *Conservative Judaism*, 1965–70; registrar, Cantors' Inst., JTS, 1962-'70s. Transl.: *Gates of Bronze* by Hayim Hazaz (1975); *The Jews in Their Land in the Talmudic Age* by Gedaliah Alon, 2 vols. (1980, 1984); short Yiddish fiction of Chaim Grade. Recipient: Order of the British Empire.

LEVIN, HERMAN, business executive, communal worker; b. Brooklyn, N.Y., (?), 1901; d. Palm Beach, Fla., Mar. 31, 1990. Educ.: Wharton School of Business, U. Pa. Pres., Acme Dress Form Corp. Pres.: Jewish Reconstructionist Found.; Society for the Advancement of Judaism (Manhattan); East Midwood Jewish Center, Brooklyn; mem., founding bd. govs., Reconstructionist Rabbinical Coll.

LEWITTES, MORDECHAI H., rabbi, educator; b. Brooklyn, N.Y., Apr. 18, 1911; d. NYC, Nov. 17, 1990. Educ.: CCNY; Hebrew U., Jerusalem; Jewish Theol. Sem. of Amer. Rabbi, Hazelton, Pa., 1935–37; instr., Hebrew, Thomas Jefferson H.S., Brooklyn, 1937–53; religious school prin., Brooklyn

Jewish Center, 1937–62; educ. dir., asst., and assoc. rabbi, Brooklyn Jewish Center, 1938–63; chmn., acad. subjects, Sarah Hale H.S., 1953–62; coord., NYC Bureau of Curriculum Development, 1963; first prin., Enrico Fermi H.S., Brooklyn, 1964–65; dir., Ford Found.-NYC Bd. of Educ. Correlated Curriculum Project, 1966–67; prin., H.S. of Graphic Communication Arts, 1967–74; prin., Solomon Schechter H.S. of Brooklyn, 1974–77; rabbi, Ocean Beach Syn., Fire Island, N.Y., 1976–90. A pioneer teacher of Hebrew in public high schools. Pres., Amer. Assn. of Teachers of Hebrew; v.-pres., Natl. Hebrew Culture Council; mem., Hebrew Regents Com., N.Y. State Dept. of Educ.; ed., *Pedagogic Reporter* (JESNA); trustee, Soc. for the Advancement of Judaism. Author: *The Student Bible* (4 vols.); *Heroes and Highlights of Jewish History* (4 vols.); *My Hebrew Primer*; and *Easy Hebrew*. Co-author: *Selected Readings in Hebrew Literature*; *Modern Hebrew (Ivrit Hayah*; 2 vols.); *Readings to Enjoy*. Recipient: Hon. doctorate, JTS.

LONDON, EPHRAIM S., attorney; b. NYC, June 17, 1911; d. NYC, June 12, 1990. Educ.: NYU; NYU Law School. Served U.S. Army, WWII, and postwar as special investigator, War Crimes Comm. in Germany. Partner, Brennan, London & Buttenwieser, NYC. A specialist in constitutional law, successfully argued cases before the U.S. Supreme Court involving censorship of films (notably *Lady Chatterley's Lover*). Among his clients were comedian Lenny Bruce and convicted spy Robert A. Soblen. Chmn., comm. on law and social action, Amer. Jewish Cong. and pres. its lawyers chap.; mem.: bd. dirs., N.Y. Civil Liberties Union; N.Y. County Lawyers Assn. civil rights comm.; Assn. of the Bar of NYC comm. on bill of rights; Workmen's Circle. Ed. *The World of Law*, a widely used text in law schools.

MOSKOWITZ, MOSES, administrator; b. Stryj, Ukraine, (?), 1910; d. NYC, Mar. 19, 1990; in U.S. since 1928. Educ.: CCNY; Columbia U. Served U.S. Army, WWII. Foreign affairs analyst, Amer. Jewish Com., 1930s-early '40s; sec. gen., Consultative Council of Jewish Organizations (a nongovernmental org. accredited to the UN and Council of Europe), 1947–90. Author: *Human Rights and World Order* (1958); *The Politics and Dynamics of Human Rights* (1968); *International Concern with Human Rights* (1974); *The Roots and Reaches of United Nations Actions and Decisions* (1980).

MUSHER, SIDNEY, business executive, communal worker; b. Newark, N.J., Nov. 9, 1905; d. NYC, Nov. 21, 1990. Educ.: Johns Hopkins U. Engaged in private research in food chemistry, 1925–28; supt., Pompeian Olive Oil Corp., Baltimore, 1928–31; asst. to v.-pres., production, Van Camp Packing Co., in charge of Van Camp Oil Co., 1931–33; pres., Musher Found., Inc., and v.-pres., Aveeno Pharmaceuticals, 1935–63; v.-pres. and dir., Cooper Laboratories, 1963–66; genl. partner, Interlaken Associates. Held over 200 patents. Chmn., trustee, and CEO, PEF Israel Endowment Funds, Inc., for 20 years; bd. mem., PEC Israel Econ. Corp. for 45 years. Initiated and chaired Israel Research and Development Corp.; mem., Israeli Prime Minister's Council for Econ. Devel.; mem. bd. dirs. and hon. mem. bd. govs., Hebrew U., Jerusalem, and v.-pres. its Amer. Friends; mem. bd. govs., Ben-Gurion U. of the Negev, and bd. mem., Amer. Associates of Ben-Gurion U.; mem. adv. council, Amer. Com. for the Weizmann Inst. of Science; bd. mem., Natl. Found. for Jewish Culture; hon. mem. exec. council & sec., Amer. J. Hist. Soc.; mem. bd. regents, Internatl. Center for University Teaching of Jewish Civilization. Chmn., trustee, and mem. adv. council, Society for the Advancement of Judaism; bd. mem. and treas., Jewish Reconstructionist Found.; mem. bd. govs., Reconstructionist Rabbinical Coll.; founding mem. West End Syn. (Manhattan). Recipient: Hon. doctorate, Hebrew U., Jerusalem; Ben-Gurion Award, Ben-Gurion U.; City of N.Y. Citation and Proclamation for Exceptional Service; Agnon Gold Medal, Amer. Friends of Hebrew U.; estab. of Sidney Musher Bldg. for Science Teaching, Weizmann Inst. of Science.

MUSKIN, YAAKOV, rabbi; b. Chicago, Ill., Feb. 27, 1918; d. Cleveland, Ohio, Jan. 8, 1990. Educ.: Ner Israel Rabbinical Coll. Assoc. natl. dir., Vaad Hatzalah (rescue and rehabilitation of Torah scholars who survived the Holocaust), 1945–47; rabbi, Warrensville Center Syn., Cleveland (a merger of 8 syns.), 1950–1990. Chmn. Orthodox Rabbinical Council of Cleveland, 1984–90; hon. lfe mem. bd. of trustees, Hebrew Acad. of Cleveland, 1950–1990 and chmn. its educ. com., 1984–90; chmn., educ. com., Yeshivath Adath Bnai Yisrael afternoon school; mem., Cleveland Bureau of Jewish Educ.; bd. mem.: Telshe Yeshiva; Yeshivat Sha'alvim in Israel; chmn. Israel Bonds Religious Council; bd. mem. Cleveland Jewish Fed., its kashruth comm., chaplaincy com., and central fund for traditional institutions. Recipient: Council of Jewish Federations Community Rabbinical Award (1979, 1989); Center Syn. 30-Year Service Award; adoption of Hebrew name "Kehillat Yaakov" by Center Syn., in his memory.

PALEY, WILLIAM S., broadcasting executive, philanthropist; b. Chicago, Ill., Sept. 28, 1901; d. NYC, Oct. 26, 1990. Educ.: U. Pa. Served U.S. Army, WWII, in psychol. warfare and info. control. Vice-pres., sec., Congress Cigar Co. (his father's firm), 1922–28; entered radio through supervising advertising for his co.; bought into small network which became Columbia Broadcasting System; served as pres., 1928–46; chmn. bd. 1946–83; founder chmn., 1983–86, acting chmn., 1986. Trustee, Museum of Modern Art, 1937 on, pres. 1968–72, chmn. 1972–85, chmn. emer., 1985 on; life trustee, Columbia U.; mem. bd. dirs., Harriman Inst. for Advanced Study of Soviet Union, Columbia U.; founder and bd. chmn., Museum of Broadcasting, NYC; founding mem., Bedford Stuyvesant Devel. Corp. and mem. of many govt. and civic comms. Benefactor: Museum of Modern Art; Metropolitan Museum of Art. Life trustee, Fed. of Jewish Philanthropies of N.Y.; estab. Paley Arts Center, Jerusalem. Recipient: Croix de Guerre with Palm, France; Order of Merit, Italy; Medallion of Honor, City of N.Y.; ADL First Amendment Freedoms Award; two Peabody Awards; and many other honors. Author: *As It Happened* (memoirs).

PROSHANSKY, HAROLD M., professor, university administrator; b. NYC, Sept. 16, 1920; d. NYC, Dec. 13, 1990. Educ.: CCNY; Columbia U.; NYU (PhD). Served U.S. Army WWII (research psychologist). Research assoc. U.S. Haskins Laboratories, 1946–47; fellow, experimental psych., NYU, 1947–48; instr., NYU, 1948–51; research assoc., Amer. Jewish Cong., 1951–52; lect., instr., asst. prof., psych., Brooklyn Coll., 1952–59; NIMH research fellow, U. Michigan, 1959–60; visiting assoc.

prof., U. Michigan, 1960–61; assoc. prof., prof., Brooklyn Coll., 1961–66; prof., PhD program in psych., CUNY, 1963–66; exec. off., PhD program in psych., 1966–68; dean, Graduate Div., CUNY, 1968–70; dean and deputy pres., 1970–72; pres., Graduate School and Univ. Center, CUNY, 1972–90. Among numerous affiliations and directorships: mem. bd. dirs., Bryant Park Restoration Corp.; Feminist Press; Natl. Comm. on Resources for Youth; Inst. for Responsive Educ.; Amer. Com. for the Weizmann Inst. of Science; bd. trustees Long Island U.; Phipps Houses; past pres., Soc. for the Psychol. Study of Social Issues; consultant, NYC Planning Com. A pioneer in the field of environmental psych., lectured widely and wrote on the subject. Author: numerous articles, reports, and book chaps. Recipient: Fellow: Amer. Psychol. Assn., Amer. Assn. for the Advancement of Science, N.Y. Acad. of Sciences.

RADER, ISADORE JACK, organization executive; b. NYC, Mar. 5, 1917; d. NYC, Sept. 24, 1990. Educ.: Brooklyn Coll. Asst. exec. dir., Amer. ORT Fed., 31 years. Hon. mem., World ORT Union central bd.; mem. bd. dirs., *Dissent* magazine. Author: *By the Skill of Their Hands—The Story of ORT.*

ROSEN, NATHAN N., rabbi; b. Borisov, Russia, July 4, 1906; d. Long Island, N.Y., Jan. 23, 1990. Educ.: Rabbinical Coll., New Haven (ord.); Rabbi Isaac Elchanan Theol. Sem. (ord.); Teachers Coll., Columbia U. Served U.S. Army, WWII. Rabbi: Valley Stream, N.Y.; Savannah, Georgia; Brooklyn, N.Y.; Rockville Centre, N.Y. Founded Hillel Found. at Brown U. and Pembroke Coll., Providence, R.I., serving as dir. until 1974. Lect., Hebrew and Yiddish, Brown U., and a founder, Hebrew Day School, Providence. Pres. R.I. Zionist Region, R.I. Bd. of Rabbis; mem.: Natl. Assn. Hillel Directors; Providence Human Relations Com.; chaplain: Natl. Jewish War Veterans of Amer.; Shriners of N. Amer.; Masonic Order of R.I.

ROSENBERG, STUART E., rabbi, author, b. NYC, July 5, 1922; d. W. Palm Beach, Fla., Mar. 12, 1990. Educ.: Brooklyn Coll.; Columbia U. (PhD); Jewish Theol. Sem. of Amer. Rabbi: Temple Beth El, Rochester, N.Y., 1946–56; Beth Tzedec Cong., Toronto, Can., 1956–73; Beth Torah

Cong., Toronto, 1980–89; lect., U. Rochester, 1951–56; visiting prof.: Toronto School of Theol., 1975–78; exec. v.-pres., Canadian Friends of Tel Aviv U., 1977–80. Founding natl. pres., Canadian Found. for Jewish Culture; helped found Ontario Region, United Syn. of Amer., Camp Ramah in Canada, and United Syn. day school in Toronto; v.-pres., Natl. Found. for Jewish Culture (U.S.). An early visitor to USSR and spokesman for Soviet Jews, and a pioneer in Christian-Jewish dialogue in Canada. Canadian ed., *Encyclopedia Judaica*. Author: 20 books, incl. *The Road to Confidence* (1959); *The Bible Is for You* (1961); *Judaism* (1966); *What Do We Believe?* (with Martin E. Marty and Andrew Greeley, 1968); *The Jewish Community in Canada* (2 vols., 1971); *The Real Jewish World: A Rabbi's Second Thoughts* (1984); *Christians and Jews: The Eternal Bond* (1985); and *The Christian Problem: A Jewish View* (1986). Recipient: hon. doctorate, JTS; Sabato Morais hon. fellowship, JTS; a chair in Jewish hist. in his name at JTS.

SHAPIRO, HARRY L., physical anthropologist; b. Boston, Mass., Mar. 19, 1902; d. NYC, Jan. 7, 1990. Educ.: Harvard Coll., Harvard U. (PhD). Tutor, Harvard U., 1925–26; asst., assoc. curator, dept of anthropology, Amer. Museum of Natural History (NYC), 1926–42; curator of physical anthropology and chmn. of the dept., 1942–70, where he created the Hall of the Biology of Man, the first of its kind in the world. Lect., Columbia U., 1938–42, prof., 1943–74. Pres., Amer. Anthropological Assn.; founding mem. and v.-pres., Amer. Assn. Physical Anthropologists; pres., Amer. Ethnological Soc.; chmn., anthropology sect., N.Y. Acad. of Sciences; mem. ed. adv. bd., Natl. Acad. of Sciences; chmn., div. of anthropology and psychology, Natl. Research Council.; mem. bd. dirs.: Louise Wise Services; Field Found. Author: *The Heritage of the Bounty: The Story of Pitcairn Island Through Six Generations* (1936); *Migration and Environment*, a study of physical changes in Japanese immigrants to Hawaii and their descendants (1939); *Aspects of Culture* (1956); *The Jewish People: A Biological History* (1960); *Peking Man* (1974); and other works. Recipient: Fellow: Amer. Acad. Arts and Sciences; Natl. Acad. of Sciences; Theodore Roosevelt Disting. Service Medal; hon. fellow, Anthropologische Gesellschaft, Vienna; N.Y. Acad. of

Sciences Award; Amer. Assn. of Forensic Science Award.

SIMON, KATE, writer; b. Warsaw, Poland, Dec. 5, 1912; d. NYC, Feb. 4, 1990; in U.S. since 1916. Educ.: Hunter Coll. Editor, book reviewer for the *New Republic* and *The Nation*. Author: 10 travel works, incl. the best-selling *New York Places and Pleasures: An Uncommon Guidebook* (1959) and guides to Mexico City, Paris, London, and Rome; 3 vols. of autobiography: *Bronx Primitive: Portraits in a Childhood* (1982); *A Wider World: Portraits in an Adolescence* (1986); and *Etchings in an Hourglass* (posth.). Recipient: Awards from Natl. Book Critics Circle, the English-Speaking Union, Hunter Coll.

SULZBERGER, IPHIGENE OCHS, business executive, communal worker; b. Cincinnai, Ohio, Sept. 19, 1892; d. Stamford, Conn., Feb. 26, 1990. Educ.: Barnard Coll. Daughter, wife, mother-in-law, and mother of publishers of the *N.Y. Times* (Adolph S. Ochs, Arthur Hays Sulzberger, Orvil E. Dryfoos, Arthur Ochs Sulzberger), and granddaughter of a founder of American Reform Judaism, Isaac Mayer Wise. Dir., Times Co., 1917–73, and until her death, trustee of the stock trust established by her father that effectively controlled the co. Pres., Park Assn. of N.Y., 1934–50, chmn., 1950–57; hon. chmn., Central Park Conservancy; trustee: Barnard Coll., 1937–68; HUC-JIR; U. Chattanooga; Girl Scout Council of Greater N.Y. Bd. mem., Fed. of Jewish Philanthropies of N.Y. Also active in behalf of NAACP, United Negro College Fund, Internatl. Rescue Com., Jewish Chaplaincy at Columbia U., and many other organizations. Recipient: Disting. Alumna Award, Barnard Coll.; Gold Medal, Natl. Inst. Social Sciences; hon. doctorates: Jewish Theol. Sem. of Amer.; HUC-JIR; Columbia U.

TILLES, GILBERT, developer, philanthropist; b. Braddock, Pa., Dec. 31, 1916; d. Great Neck, N.Y., Nov. 14, 1990. Educ.: U. Michigan. In the early 1950s, co-developed more than a dozen shopping centers on Long Island; pres., All-State Properties, 1959; in 1961 formed Tilles Development Corp., builder of offices and industrial parks in N.Y. metro. area. V.-chmn., Long Island U. (contributed 2,200-seat Tilles Center for the Performing Arts at C.W. Post campus of Long Island U.); mem. bd.

trustees, Long Island Jewish Medical Center; founder, Assn. for a Better Long Island. Natl. v.-chmn., Union of Amer. Hebrew Congs., hon. chmn., and chmn. its endowment and trust com.; founding chmn., Eisner Camp for Living Judaism; pres., trustee, Temple Beth-El of Great Neck; hon. chmn., L.I. Com. for State of Israel Bonds. Recipient: Commercial Builder of the Year Award.

VISHNIAC, ROMAN; biologist, photographer; b. St. Petersburg, Russia, Aug. 19, 1897; d. NYC, Jan. 22, 1990; in U.S. since 1940. Educ.: U. Moscow (PhD, zoology). Asst. prof. biology, Shanyavsky U. Emigrated to Latvia 1918, and from there to Berlin. In 1932–40, traveled 5,000 miles through Poland, Lithuania, Latvia, Hungary, Rumania, Czechoslovakia, and Germany, making a photographic record of Jewish life on the eve of WWII. Fled to France in 1940; interned 3 months before obtaining visa to U.S. Achieved renown as a science photographer, particularly for using polarized light to film living microscopic creatures. Prof. humanities, Pratt Inst.; prof. biology educ., Yeshiva U. and Albert Einstein Coll. of Medicine. First collection of European photos, *Polish Jews: A Pictorial Record*, published 1942. Other works: *A Day of Pleasure* (1969); *Building Blocks of Life* (1971); *Roman Vishniac* (1974); *A Vanished World* (1983).

WALLACE, IRVING, writer; b. Chicago, Ill., Mar. 19, 1916; d. Los Angeles, Calif., June 29, 1990. Educ.: Williams Inst., Berkeley, Calif. Served U.S. Army, WWII (writer of training films). Free-lance writer of articles, short stories: *Saturday Evening Post*, *Cosmopolitan*, *Reader's Digest*, *Esquire*, and others, 1931–53; screenwriter, late 1940s and '50s. Author of 16 novels—most of them best-sellers, many made into movies—and 17 works of nonfiction. First best-seller, *The Chapman Report* (1960). Others incl. *The Prize* (1962); *The Man* (1964); *The Word* (1972); and *The Guest of Honor* (1989). Collaborated with wife, daughter, and son on *The People's Almanac*, *The People's Almanac No. 2*, and *The Book of Lists*.

WEINBERG, HARRY, business executive, philanthropist; b. (?), Galicia, (?), 1908; d. Honolulu, Hawaii, Nov. 4, 1990; in U.S. since 1912. A successful entrepreneur who left school at age 12; began investing in Baltimore real estate in his 20s; branched out into other businesses, such as retreaded automobile tires during WWII, mass transit (bought Fifth Ave. Coach Corp., NYC, and companies in Baltimore, Scranton, Dallas, and Honolulu), and Hawaii real estate. Established the Harry and Jeanette Weinberg Found., one of 12 largest charitable trusts in the U.S., with 25 percent of its disbursements pledged to Jewish needy.

WEISS, SAMSON RAPHAEL; rabbi b. Emden, Germany, May 9, 1910; d. NYC, Feb. 6, 1990; in U.S. since 1938. Educ.: U. Breslau, U. Berlin, U. Zurich, U. Prague; Mir Yeshiva (ord.); U. Dorpat, Estonia (PhD). Dean, Hebrew dept., Jewish Teachers Coll., Wurzburg, Germany, 1934–38; prof., codes, Ner Israel Rabbinical Acad., Baltimore, 1938–40; dean, Yeshivath Beth Yehuda Talmudical Acad., Detroit, 1941–44; dir., Torah Umesorah, 1944–45; founder, dir., Young Israel Inst. for Jewish Studies, 1945–56; natl. dir., Natl. Council of Young Israel, 1947–56; exec. v.-pres., Union of Orthodox Jewish Congs. in Amer., 1956–72; settled in Israel 1972; chmn. Jerusalem Inst. for Talmudic Research; chmn. Judaic Studies dept., Touro Coll., NYC (lecturing in spring term). Bd. chmn.: Amer. Friends of Shaare Zedek Hosp., Amer. Friends of Mirrer Yeshiva; mem.: Rabbinical Council of Amer., contrib., *Viewpoint*, *Jewish Life* magazines, and German-Jewish press.

ZUCKERMAN, ARTHUR J., rabbi; b. Brooklyn, N.Y., Dec. 16, 1907; d. NYC, Jan. 6, 1990. Educ.: CCNY; Hebrew Union Coll.; Columbia U. (PhD). Rabbi: Winston-Salem, N.C., 1936–38; Lansing, Mich., 1938–40; founding dir., Hillel Found., U. Washington, Seattle, 1940–45; dir., B'nai B'rith Hillel Found., CCNY, 1945–1970; dir., dept. of medieval Jewish civilization, Reconstructionist Rabbinical Coll., 1970–77. Adj. assoc. prof. of hist., CCNY; instr., Jewish hist. and religion, Schools of Sacred Music and Educ., HUC-JIR, NYC; visiting prof. Jewish hist.: Inst. International d'Etudes Hebraiques, Paris, France; New School for Social Research, NYC. Pres., Natl. Assn. of Hillel Directors; mem. ed. bd., the *Reconstructionist*; chmn., NY chap., Religious Educ. Assn. Author: *A Jewish Princedom in Feudal France 768–900*; articles and essays on medieval Jewish history and other subjects. Recipient: hon. doctorate, HUC-JIR; Reconstructionist movement's Keter Shem Tov Award.

Calendars

SUMMARY JEWISH CALENDAR, 5752–5756 (Sept. 1991–Aug. 1996)

HOLIDAY	5752 (1991)	5753 (1992)	5754 (1993)	5755 (1994)	5756 (1995)
Rosh Ha-shanah, 1st day	M Sept. 9	M Sept. 28	Th Sept. 16	T Sept. 6	M Sept. 25
Rosh Ha-shanah, 2nd day	T Sept. 10	T Sept. 29	F Sept. 17	W Sept. 7	T Sept. 26
Fast of Gedaliah	W Sept. 11	W Sept. 30	S Sept. 19	Th Sept. 8	W Sept. 27
Yom Kippur	W Sept. 18	W. Oct. 7	Sa Sept. 25	Th Sept. 15	W Oct. 4
Sukkot, 1st day	M Sept. 23	M Oct. 12	Th Sept. 30	T Sept. 20	M Oct. 9
Sukkot, 2nd day	T Sept. 24	T Oct. 13	F Oct. 1	W Sept. 21	T Oct. 10
Hosha'na' Rabbah	S Sept. 29	S Oct. 18	W Oct. 6	M Sept. 26	S Oct. 15
Shemini 'Azeret	M Sept. 30	M Oct. 19	Th Oct. 7	T Sept. 27	M Oct. 16
Simhat Torah	T Oct. 1	T Oct. 20	F Oct. 8	W Sept. 28	T Oct. 17
New Moon, Heshwan, 1st day	T Oct. 8	T Oct. 27	F Oct. 15	W Oct. 5	T Oct. 24
New Moon, Heshwan, 2nd day	W Oct. 9	W Oct. 28	Sa Oct. 16	Th Oct. 6	W Oct. 25
New Moon, Kislew, 1st day	Th Nov. 7	Th. Nov. 26	S Nov. 14	F Nov. 4	Th Nov. 23
New Moon, Kislew, 2nd day	F Nov. 8		M Nov. 15		F Nov. 24
Hanukkah, 1st day	M Dec. 2	S Dec. 20	Th Dec. 9	M Nov. 28	M Dec. 18
New Moon, Tevet, 1st day	Sa Dec. 7	F Dec. 25	T Dec. 14	Sa Dec. 3	Sa Dec. 23
New Moon, Ṭevet, 2nd day	S Dec. 8		W Dec. 15	S Dec. 4	S Dec. 24
Fast of 10th of Ṭevet	T Dec. 17	S Jan. 3 (1993)	F Dec. 24	T Dec. 13	T Jan. 2 (1996)

	1992	1993	1994	1995	1996
New Moon, Shevat	M Jan. 6	Sa Jan. 23	Th Jan. 13	M Jan. 2	M Jan. 22
Hamishshah-'asar bi-Shevat	M Jan. 20	Sa Feb. 6	Th Jan. 27	M Jan. 16	M Feb. 5
New Moon, Adar I, 1st day	T Feb. 4	S Feb. 21	F Feb. 11	T Jan. 31	T Feb. 20
New Moon, Adar I, 2nd day	W Feb. 5	M Feb. 22	Sa Feb. 12	W Feb. 1	W Feb. 21
New Moon, Adar II, 1st day	Th Mar. 5			Th Mar. 2	
New Moon, Adar II, 2nd day	F Mar. 6			F Mar. 3	
Fast of Esther	W Mar. 18	Th Mar. 4	Th Feb. 24	W Mar. 15	M Mar. 4
Purim	Th Mar. 19	S Mar. 7	F Feb. 25	Th Mar. 16	T Mar. 5
Shushan Purim	F Mar. 20	M Mar. 8	Sa Feb. 26	F Mar. 17	W Mar. 6
New Moon, Nisan	Sa Apr. 4	T Mar. 23	S Mar. 13	Sa Apr. 1	Th Mar. 21
Passover, 1st day	Sa Apr. 18	T Apr. 6	S Mar. 27	Sa Apr. 15	Th Apr. 4
Passover, 2nd day	S Apr. 19	W Apr. 7	M Mar. 28	S Apr. 16	F Apr. 5
Passover, 7th day	F Apr. 24	M Apr. 12	Sa Apr. 2	F Apr. 21	W Apr. 10
Passover, 8th day	Sa Apr. 25	T Apr. 13	S Apr. 3	Sa Apr. 22	Th Apr. 11
Holocaust Memorial Day	Th Apr. 30	S Apr. 18	F Apr. 8*	Th Apr. 27	T Apr. 16
New Moon, Iyar, 1st day	S May 3	W Apr. 21	M Apr. 11	S Apr. 30	F Apr. 19
New Moon, Iyar, 2nd day	M May 4	Th Apr. 22	T Apr. 12	M May 1	Sa Apr. 20
Israel Independence Day	F May 8*	M Apr. 26	Sa Apr. 16†	F May 5*	W Apr. 24
Lag Ba-'omer	Th May 21	S May 9	F Apr. 29	Th May 18	T May 7
Jerusalem Day	S May 31	W May 19	M May 9	S May 28	F May 17*
New Moon, Siwan	T Jun 2	F May 21	W May 11	T May 30	S May 19
Shavu'ot, 1st day	S Jun 7	W May 26	M May 16	S June 4	F May 24
Shavu'ot, 2nd day	M Jun 8	Th May 27	T May 17	M June 5	Sa May 25
New Moon, Tammuz, 1st day	W July 1	Sa June 19	Th June 9	W June 28	M June 17
New Moon, Tammuz, 2nd day	Th July 2	S June 20	F June 10	Th June 29	T June 18
Fast of 17th of Tammuz	S July 19	T July 6	S June 26	S July 16	Th July 4
New Moon, Av	F July 31	M July 19	Sa July 9	F July 28	W July 17
Fast of 9th of Av	S Aug. 9	T July 27	S July 17	S Aug. 6	Th July 25
New Moon, Elul, 1st day	Sa Aug. 29	T Aug. 17	S Aug. 7	Sa Aug. 26	Th Aug. 15
New Moon, Elul, 2nd day	S Aug. 30	W Aug. 18	M Aug. 8	S Aug. 27	F Aug. 16

*Observed Thursday, a day earlier, to avoid conflict with the Sabbath.
†Observed Thursday, two days earlier, to avoid conflict with the Sabbath.

CONDENSED MONTHLY CALENDAR
(1991–1994)

1990, Dec. 18–Jan. 15, 1991] ṬEVET (29 DAYS) [5751

Civil Date	Day of the Week	Jewish Date	SABBATHS, FESTIVALS, FASTS	PENTATEUCHAL READING	PROPHETICAL READING
Dec. 18	T	Ṭevet 1	New Moon, second day; Ḥanukkah, seventh day	Num. 28:1–15 Num. 7:48–53	
19	W	2	Ḥanukkah, eighth day	Num. 7:54–8:4	
22	Sa	5	Wa-yiggash	Gen. 44:18–47:27	Ezekiel 37:15–28
27	Th	10	Fast of 10th of Ṭevet	Exod. 32:11–14 43:1–10 (morning and afternoon)	Isaiah 55:6–56:8 (afternoon only)
29	Sa	12	Wa-yeḥi	Gen. 47:28–50:26	I Kings 2:1–12
Jan. 5	Sa	19	Shemot	Exod. 1:1–6:1	Isaiah 27:6–28:13 29:22–23 *Jeremiah 1:1–2:3*
12	Sa	26	Wa-'era'	Exod. 6:2–9:35	Ezekiel 28:25–29:21

*Italics are for
Sephardi Minhag.*

1991, Jan. 16–Feb. 14]   SHEVAṬ (30 DAYS)   [5751

Civil Date	Day of the Week	Jewish Date	SABBATHS, FESTIVALS, FASTS	PENTATEUCHAL READING	PROPHETICAL READING
Jan. 16	W	Shevaṭ 1	New Moon	Num. 28:1–15	
19	Sa	4	Bo'	Exod. 10:1–13:16	Jeremiah 46:13–28
26	Sa	11	Be-shallaḥ (Shabbat Shirah)	Exod. 13:17–17:16	Judges 4:4–5:31 *Judges 5:1–31*
30	W	15	Ḥamishshah-'asar bi-Shevaṭ		
Feb. 2	Sa	18	Yitro	Exod. 18:1–20:23	Isaiah 6:1–7:6 9:5, 6 *Isaiah 6:1–13*
9	Sa	25	Mishpaṭim (Shabbat Sheḳalim)	Exod. 21:1–24:18 Exod. 30:11–16	II Kings 12:1–17 *II Kings 11:17–12:17*
14	Th	30	New Moon, first day	Num. 28:1–15	

Italics are for Sephardi Minhag.

1991, Feb. 15–Mar. 15] ADAR (29 DAYS) [5751

Civil Date	Day of the Week	Jewish Date	SABBATHS, FESTIVALS, FASTS	PENTATEUCHAL READING	PROPHETICAL READING
Feb. 15	F	Adar 1	New Moon, second day	Num. 28:1–15	
16	Sa	2	Terumah	Exod. 25:1–27:19	I Kings 5:26–6:13
23	Sa	9	Teẓawweh (Shabbat Zakhor)	Exod. 27:20–30:10 Deut. 25:17–19	I Samuel 15:2–34 *I Samuel 15:1–34*
27	W	13	Fast of Esther	Exod. 32:11–14 Exod. 34:1–10 (morning and afternoon)	Isaiah 55:6–56:8 (afternoon only)
28	Th	14	Purim	Exod. 17:8–16	Book of Esther (night before and in the morning)
Mar. 1	F	15	Shushan Purim		
2	Sa	16	Ki tissa'	Exod. 30:11–34:35	I Kings 18:1–39 *I Kings 18:20–39*
9	Sa	23	Wa-yakhel, Pekude (Shabbat Parah)	Exod. 35:1–40:38 Num. 19:1–22	Ezekiel 36:16–38 *Ezekiel 36:16–36*

Italics are for Sephardi Minhag.

1991, Mar. 16–Apr. 14]   NISAN (30 DAYS)   [5751

Civil Date	Day of the Week	Jewish Date	SABBATHS, FESTIVALS, FASTS	PENTATEUCHAL READING	PROPHETICAL READING
Mar. 16	Sa	Nisan 1	Wa-yikra' (Shabbat Ha-hodesh); New Moon	Levit. 1:1–5:26 Exod. 12:1–20 Num. 28:9–15	Ezekiel 45:16–46:18 *Ezekiel 45:18–46:15*
23	Sa	8	Zaw (Shabbat Ha-gadol)	Levit. 6:1–8:36	Malachi 3:4–24
29	F	14	Fast of Firstborn		
30	Sa	15	Passover, first day	Exod. 12:21–51 Num. 28:16–25	Joshua 5:2–6:1, 27
31	S	16	Passover, second day	Levit. 22:26–23:44 Num. 28:16–25	II Kings 23:1–19, 21–25
Apr. 1	M	17	Hol Ha-mo'ed, first day	Exod. 13:1–16 Num. 28:19–25	
2	T	18	Hol Ha-mo'ed, second day	Exod. 22:24–23:19 Num. 28:19–25	
3	W	19	Hol Ha-mo'ed, third day	Exod. 34:1–26 Num. 28:19–25	
4	Th	20	Hol Ha-mo'ed, fourth day	Num. 9:1–14 Num. 28:19–25	
5	F	21	Passover, seventh day	Exod. 13:17–15:26 Num. 28:19–25	II Samuel 22:1–51
6	Sa	22	Passover, eighth day	Deut. 15:19–16:17 Num. 28:19–25	Isaiah 10:32–12:6
11	Th	27	Holocaust Memorial Day		
13	Sa	29	Shemini	Levit. 9:1–11:47	I Samuel 20:18–42
14	S	30	New Moon, first day	Num. 28:1–15	

Italics are for
Sephardi Minhag.

1991, Apr. 15–May 13]   IYAR (29 DAYS)   [5751

Civil Date	Day of the Week	Jewish Date	SABBATHS, FESTIVALS, FASTS	PENTATEUCHAL READING	PROPHETICAL READING
Apr. 15	M	Iyar 1	New Moon, second day	Num. 28:1–15	
19	F*	5	Israel Independence Day		
20	Sa	6	Tazria', Mezora'	Levit. 12:1–15:33	II Kings 7:3–20
27	Sa	13	Ahare mot, Kedoshim	Levit. 16:1–20:27	Amos 9:7–15 *Ezekiel 20:2–20*
May 2	Th	18	Lag Ba-'omer		
4	Sa	20	Emor	Levit. 21:1–24:23	Ezekiel 44:15–31
11	Sa	27	Be-har, Be-hukkotai	Levit. 25:1–27:34	Jeremiah 16:19–17:14
12	S	28	Jerusalem Day		

*Observed Thursday, a day earlier, to avoid conflict with the Sabbath.

Italics are for Sephardi Minhag.

1991, May 14–June 12]   SIWAN (30 DAYS)   [5751

Civil Date	Day of the Week	Jewish Date	SABBATHS, FESTIVALS, FASTS	PENTATEUCHAL READING	PROPHETICAL READING
May 14	T	Siwan 1	New Moon	Num. 28:1–15	
18	Sa	5	Be-midbar	Num. 1:1–4:20	Hosea 2:1–22
19	S	6	Shavu'ot, first day	Exod. 19:1–20:23 Num. 28:26–31	Ezekiel 1:1–28 3:12
20	M	7	Shavu'ot, second day	Deut. 15:19–16:17 Num. 28:26–31	Habbakuk 3:1–19 *Habbakuk 2:20–3:19*
25	Sa	12	Naso'	Num. 4:21–7:89	Judges 13:2–25
June 1	Sa	19	Be-ha'alotekha	Num. 8:1–12:16	Zecharia 2:14–4:7
8	Sa	26	Shelah lekha	Num. 13:1–15:41	Joshua 2:1–24
12	W	30	New Moon, first day	Num. 28:1–15	

1991, June 13–July 11]   TAMMUZ (29 DAYS)   [5751

Civil Date	Day of the Week	Jewish Date	SABBATHS, FESTIVALS, FASTS	PENTATEUCHAL READING	PROPHETICAL READING
June 13	Th	Tammuz 1	New Moon, second day	Num. 28:1–15	
15	Sa	3	Korah	Num. 16:1–18:32	I Samuel 11:14–12:22
22	Sa	10	Hukkat	Num. 19:1–22:1	Judges 11:1–33
29	Sa	17	Balak	Num. 22:2–25:9	Micah 5:6–6:8
30	S	18	Fast of 17th of Tammuz	Exod. 32:11–14 Exod. 34:1–10 (morning and afternoon)	Isaiah 55:6–56:8 (afternoon only)
July 6	Sa	24	Pinehas	Num. 25:10–30:1	Jeremiah 1:1–2:3

Italics are for
Sephardi Minhag.

1991, July 12–Aug. 10]   AV (30 DAYS)   [5751

Civil Date	Day of the Week	Jewish Date	SABBATHS, FESTIVALS, FASTS	PENTATEUCHAL READING	PROPHETICAL READING
July 12	F	Av 1	New Moon	Num. 28:1–15	
13	Sa	2	Maṭṭot, Mas'e	Num. 30:2–36:13	Jeremiah 2:4–28 3:4 *Jeremiah 2:4–28 4:1–2*
20	Sa	9	Devarim (Shabbat Ḥazon)	Deut. 1:1–3:22	Isaiah 1:1–27
21	S	10	Fast of 9th of Av	Morning: Deut. 4:25–40 Afternoon: Exod. 32:11–14 Exod. 34:1–10	(Lamentations is read night before.) Jeremiah 8:13–9:23 (morning) Isaiah 55:6–56:8 (afternoon)
27	Sa	16	Wa-ethannan (Shabbat Naḥamu)	Deut. 3:23–7:11	Isaiah 40:1–26
Aug. 3	Sa	23	'Ekev	Deut. 7:12–11:25	Isaiah 49:14–51:3
10	Sa	30	Re'eh; New Moon, first day	Deut. 11:26–16:17 Num. 28:9–15	Isaiah 66:1–24 I Samuel 20:18, 42

1991, Aug. 11–Sept. 8]   ELUL (29 DAYS)   [5751

Civil Date	Day of the Week	Jewish Date	SABBATHS, FESTIVALS, FASTS	PENTATEUCHAL READING	PROPHETICAL READING
Aug. 11	S	Elul 1	New Moon, second day	Num. 28:1–15	
17	Sa	7	Shofeṭim	Deut. 16:18–21:9	Isaiah 51:12–52:12
24	Sa	14	Ki teze'	Deut. 21:10–25:19	Isaiah 54:1–10
31	Sa	21	Ki tavo'	Deut. 26:1–29:8	Isaiah 60:1–22
Sept. 7	Sa	28	Niẓẓavim	Deut. 29:9–30:20	Isaiah 61:10–63:9

*Italics are for
Sephardi Minhag.*

Civil Date	Day of the Week	Jewish Date	SABBATHS, FESTIVALS, FASTS	PENTATEUCHAL READING	PROPHETICAL READING
Sept. 9	M	Tishri 1	Rosh Ha-shanah, first day	Gen. 21:1–34 Num. 29:1–6	I Samuel 1:1–2:10
10	T	2	Rosh Ha-shanah, second day	Gen. 22:1–24 Num. 29:1–6	Jeremiah 31:2–20
11	W	3	Fast of Gedaliah	Exod. 32:11–14 Exod. 34:1–10 (morning and afternoon)	Isaiah 55:6–56:8 (afternoon only)
14	Sa	6	Wa-yelekh (Shabbat Shuvah)	Deut. 31:1–30	Hosea 14:2–10 Micah 7:18–20 Joel 2:15–27 *Hosea 14:2–10* *Micah 7:18–20*
18	W	10	Yom Kippur	Morning: Levit. 16:1–34 Num. 29:7–11 Afternoon: Levit. 18:1–30	Isaiah 57:14–58:14 Jonah 1:1–4:11 Micah 7:18–20
21	Sa	13	Ha'azinu	Deut. 32:1–52	II Samuel 22:1–51
23	M	15	Sukkot, first day	Levit. 22:26–23:44 Num. 29:12–16	Zechariah 14:1–21
24	T	16	Sukkot, second day	Levit. 22:26–23:44 Num. 29:12–16	I Kings 8:2–21
25–27	W-F	17–19	Hol Ha-mo'ed, first to third days	W Num. 29:17–25 Th Num. 29:20–28 F Num. 29:23–31	
28	Sa	20	Hol Ha-mo'ed, fourth day	Exod. 33:12–34:26 Num. 29:26–31	Ezekiel 38:18–39:16
29	S	21	Hosha'na' Rabbah	Num. 29:26–34	
30	M	22	Shemini 'Azeret	Deut. 14:22–16:17 Num. 29:35–30:1	I Kings 8:54–66
Oct. 1	T	23	Simḥat Torah	Deut. 33:1–34:12 Gen. 1:1–2:3 Num. 29:35–30:1	Joshua 1:1–18 *Joshua 1:1–9*
5	Sa	27	Be-re'shit	Gen. 1:1–6:8	Isaiah 42:5–43:10 *Isaiah 42:5–21*
8	T	30	New Moon, first day	Num. 28:1–15	

Italics are for Sephardi Minhag.

Civil Date	Day of the Week	Jewish Date	SABBATHS, FESTIVALS, FASTS	PENTATEUCHAL READING	PROPHETICAL READING
Oct. 9	W	Ḥeshwan 1	New Moon, second day	Num. 28:1–15	
12	Sa	4	Noaḥ	Gen. 6:9–11:32	Isaiah 54:1–55:5 *Isaiah 54:1–10*
19	Sa	11	Lekh lekha	Gen. 12:1–17:27	Isaiah 40:27–41:16
26	Sa	18	Wa-yera'	Gen. 18:1–22:24	II Kings 4:1–37 *II Kings 4:1–23*
Nov. 2	Sa	25	Ḥayye Sarah	Gen. 23:1–25:18	I Kings 1:1–31
7	Th	30	New Moon, first day	Num. 28:1–15	

Civil Date	Day of the Week	Jewish Date	SABBATHS, FESTIVALS, FASTS	PENTATEUCHAL READING	PROPHETICAL READING
Nov. 8	F	Kislew 1	New Moon, second day	Num. 28:1–15	
9	Sa	2	Toledot	Gen. 25:19–28:9	Malachi 1:1–2:7
16	Sa	9	Wa-yeẓe'	Gen. 28:10–32:3	Hosea 12:13–14:10 *Hosea 11:7–12:12*
23	Sa	16	Wa-yishlaḥ	Gen. 32:4–36:43	Hosea 11:7–12:12 *Obadiah 1:1–21*
30	Sa	23	Wa-yeshev	Gen. 37:1–40:23	Amos 2:6–3:8
Dec. 2–6	M–F	25–29	Ḥanukkah, first to fifth days	M Num. 7:1–17 T Num. 7:18–29 W Num. 7:24–35 Th Num. 7:30–41 F Num. 7:36–47	
7	Sa	30	Mi-kez; New Moon, first day; Ḥanukkah, sixth day	Gen. 41:1–44:17 Num. 28:9–15 Num. 7:42–47	Zechariah 2:14–4:7

Italics are for Sephardi Minhag.

1991, Dec. 8–Jan. 5 1992] ṬEVET (29 DAYS) [5752

Civil Date	Day of the Week	Jewish Date	SABBATHS, FESTIVALS, FASTS	PENTATEUCHAL READING	PROPHETICAL READING
Dec. 8	S	Ṭevet 1	New Moon, second day; Ḥanukkah, seventh day	Num. 28:1–15 Num. 7:48–53	
9	M	2	Ḥanukkah, eighth day	Num. 7:54–8:4	
14	Sa	7	Wa-yiggash	Gen. 44:18–47:27	Ezekiel 37:15–28
17	T	10	Fast of 10th of Ṭevet	Exod. 32:11–14 Exod. 34:1–10 (morning and afternoon)	Isaiah 55:6–56:8 (afternoon only)
21	Sa	14	Wa-yeḥi	Gen. 47:28–50:26	I Kings 2:1–12
28	Sa	21	Shemot	Exod. 1:1–6:1	Isaiah 27:6–28:13 29:22–23 *Jeremiah 1:1–2:3*
Jan. 4	Sa	28	Wa-'era'	Exod. 6:2–9:35	Ezekiel 28:25–29:21

Italics are for Sephardi Minhag.

1992, Jan. 6–Feb. 4]   SHEVAṬ (30 DAYS)   [5752

Civil Date	Day of the Week	Jewish Date	SABBATHS, FESTIVALS, FASTS	PENTATEUCHAL READING	PROPHETICAL READING
Jan. 6	M	Shevaṭ 1	New Moon	Num. 28:1–15	
11	Sa	6	Bo'	Exod. 10:1–13:16	Jeremiah 46:13–28
18	Sa	13	Be-Shallah (Shabbat Shirah)	Exod. 13:17–17:16	Judges 4:4–5:31 *Judges 5:1–31*
20	M	15	Hamishshah 'asar bi-Shevaṭ		
25	Sa	20	Yitro	Exod. 18:1–20:23	Isaiah 6:1–7:6 9:5, 6 *Isaiah 6:1–13*
Feb. 1	Sa	27	Mishpaṭim	Exod. 21:1–24:18	Jeremiah 34:8–22 33:25, 26
4	T	30	New Moon, first Day	Num. 28:1–15	

Italics are for Sephardi Minhag.

1992, Feb. 5–Mar. 5]   ADAR I (30 DAYS)   [5752

Civil Date	Day of the Week	Jewish Date	SABBATHS, FESTIVALS, FASTS	PENTATEUCHAL READING	PROPHETICAL READING
Feb. 5	W	Adar I 1	New Moon, 2nd day	Num. 28:1–15	
8	Sa	4	Terumah	Exod. 25:1–27:19	I Kings 5:26–6:13
15	Sa	11	Teẓawweh	Exod. 27:20–30:10	Ezekiel 43:10–27
22	Sa	18	Ki tissa'	Exod. 30:11–34:35	I Kings 18:1–39 *I Kings 18:20–39*
29	Sa	25	Wa-yaḳhel (Shabbat Sheḳalim)	Exod. 35:1–38:20 Exod. 30:11–16	II Kings 12:1–17 *II Kings 11:17–12:17*
Mar. 5	Th	30	New Moon, first day	Num. 28:1–15	

Italics are for Sephardi Minhag.

1992, Mar. 6–Apr. 3]   ADAR II (29 DAYS)   [5752

Civil Date	Day of the Week	Jewish Date	SABBATHS, FESTIVALS, FASTS	PENTATEUCHAL READING	PROPHETICAL READING
Mar. 6	F	Adar II 1	New Moon, second day	Num. 28:1–15	
7	Sa	2	Peḳude	Exod. 38:21–40:38	I Kings 7:51–8:21 *I Kings 7:40–50*
14	Sa	9	Wa-yikra' (Shabbat Zakhor)	Levit. 1:1–5:26 Deut. 25:17–19	I Samuel 15:2–34 *I Samuel 15:1–34*
18	W	13	Fast of Esther	Exod. 32:11–14 Exod. 34:1–10 (morning and afternoon)	Isaiah 55:6–56:8 (afternoon only)
19	Th	14	Purim	Exod. 17:8–16	Book of Esther (night before and in the morning)
20	F	15	Shushan Purim		
21	Sa	16	Ẓaw	Levit. 6:1–8:36	Jeremiah 7:21–8:3 9:22–23
28	Sa	23	Shemini (Shabbat Parah)	Levit. 9:1–11:47 Num. 19:1–22	Ezekiel 36:16–38 *Ezekiel 36:16–36*

Italics are for Sephardi Minhag.

1992, Apr. 4–May 3]   NISAN (30 DAYS)   [5752

Civil Date	Day of the Week	Jewish Date	SABBATHS, FESTIVALS, FASTS	PENTATEUCHAL READING	PROPHETICAL READING
Apr. 4	Sa	Nisan 1	Tazria' (Shabbat Ha-ḥodesh); New Moon	Levit. 12:1–13:59 Exod. 12:1–20 Num. 28:9–15	Ezekiel 45:16–46:18 *Ezekiel 45:18–46:15*
11	Sa	8	Mezora' (Shabbat Ha-gadol)	Levit. 14:1–15:33	Malachi 3:4–24
17	F	14	Fast of Firstborn		
18	Sa	15	Passover, first day	Exod. 12:21–51 Num. 28:16–25	Joshua 5:2–6:1, 27
19	S	16	Passover second day	Levit. 22:26–23:44 Num. 28:16–25	II Kings 23:1–9, 21–25
20	M	17	Ḥol Ha-mo'ed, first day	Exod. 13:1–16 Num. 28:19–25	
21	T	18	Ḥol Ha-mo'ed, second day	Exod. 22:24–23:19 Num. 28:19–25	
22	W	19	Ḥol Ha-mo'ed, third day	Exod. 34:1–26 Num. 28:19–25	
23	Th	20	Ḥol Ha-mo'ed, fourth day	Num. 9:1–14 Num. 28:19–25	
24	F	21	Passover, seventh day	Exod. 13:17–15:26 Num. 28:19–25	II Samuel 22:1–51
25	Sa	22	Passover, eighth day	Deut. 15:19–16:17 Num. 28:19–25	Isaiah 10:32–12:6
30	Th	27	Holocaust Memorial Day		
May 2	Sa	29	Aḥare Mot	Levit. 16:1–18:30	I Samuel 20:18–42
3	S	30	New Moon, first day	Num. 28:1–15	

Italics are for
Sephardi Minhag.

1992, May 4–June 1] IYAR (29 DAYS) [5752

Civil Date	Day of the Week	Jewish Date	SABBATHS, FESTIVALS, FASTS	PENTATEUCHAL READING	PROPHETICAL READING
May 4	M	Iyar 1	New Moon, second day	Num. 28:1–15	
8	F*	5	Israel Independence Day		
9	Sa	6	Kedoshim	Levit. 19:1–20:27	Amos 9:7–15 *Ezekiel 20:2–20*
16	Sa	13	Emor	Levit. 21:1–24:23	Ezekiel 44:15–31
21	Th	18	Lag Ba-'omer		
23	Sa	20	Be-har	Levit. 25:1–26:2	Jeremiah 32:6–27
30	Sa	27	Be-ḥukkotai	Levit. 26:3–27:34	Jeremiah 16:19–17:14
31	S	28	Jerusalem Day		

*Observed Thursday, a day earlier, to avoid conflict with the Sabbath.

Italics are for Sephardi Minhag.

1992, June 2–July 1]   SIWAN (30 DAYS)   [5752

Civil Date	Day of the Week	Jewish Date	SABBATHS, FESTIVALS, FASTS	PENTATEUCHAL READING	PROPHETICAL READING
June 2	T	Siwan 1	New Moon	Num. 28:1–15	
6	Sa	5	Be-midbar	Num. 1:1–4:20	Hosea 2:1–22
7	S	6	Shavu'ot, first day	Exod. 19:1–20:23 Num. 28:26–31	Ezekiel 1:1–28 3:12
8	M	7	Shavu'ot, second day	Deut. 15:19–16:17 Num. 28:26–31	Habbakuk 3:1–19 *Habbakuk 2:20–3:19*
13	Sa	12	Naso'	Num. 4:21–7:89	Judges 13:2–25
20	Sa	19	Be-ha'alotekha	Num. 8:1–12:16	Zechariah 2:14–4:7
27	Sa	26	Shelaḥ lekha	Num. 13:1–15:41	Joshua 2:1–24
July 1	W	30	New Moon, first day	Num. 28:1–15	

Italics are for Sephardi Minhag.

1992, July 2–July 30]   TAMMUZ (29 DAYS)   [5752

Civil Date	Day of the Week	Jewish Date	SABBATHS, FESTIVALS, FASTS	PENTATEUCHAL READING	PROPHETICAL READING
July 2	Th	Tammuz 1	New Moon, second day	Num. 28:1–15	
4	Sa	3	Korah	Num. 16:1–18:32	I Samuel 11:14–12:22
11	Sa	10	Ḥukkat	Num. 19:1–22:1	Judges 11:1–33
18	Sa	17	Balak	Num. 22:2–25:9	Micah 5:6–6:8
19	S	18	Fast of 17th of Tammuz	Exod. 32:11–14 34:1–10 (morning and afternoon)	Isaiah 55:6–56:8 (afternoon only)
25	Sa	24	Pineḥas	Num. 25:10–30:1	Jeremiah 1:1–2:3

1992, July 31–Aug. 29]   AV (30 DAYS)   [5752

Civil Date	Day of the Week	Jewish Date	SABBATHS, FESTIVALS, FASTS	PENTATEUCHAL READING	PROPHETICAL READING
July 31	F	Av 1	New Moon, first day	Num. 28:1–15	
Aug. 1	Sa	2	Maṭṭot, Mas'e	Num. 30:2–36:13	Jeremiah 2:4–28 3:4 *Jeremiah 2:4–28 4:1–2*
8	Sa	9	Devarim (Shabbat Ḥazon)	Deut. 1:1–3:22	Isaiah 1:1–27
9	S	10	Fast of 9th of Av	Morning: Deut. 4:25–40 Afternoon: Exod. 32:11–14 Exod. 34:1–10	(Lamentations is read the night before.) Jeremiah 8:13–9:23 (morning) Isaiah 55:6–56:8 (afternoon)
15	Sa	16	Wa-etḥannan (Shabbat Naḥamu)	Deut. 3:23–7:11	Isaiah 40:1–26
22	Sa	23	'Ekev	Deut. 7:12–11:25	Isaiah 49:14–51:3
29	Sa	30	Re'eh; New Moon, first day	Deut. 11:26–16:17 Num. 28:9–15	Isaiah 66:1–24 *Isaiah 66:1–24 I Samuel 20:18,42*

Italics are for Sephardi Minhag.

1992, Aug. 30–Sept. 27]   ELUL (29 DAYS)   [5752

Civil Date	Day of the Week	Jewish Date	SABBATHS, FESTIVALS, FASTS	PENTATEUCHAL READING	PROPHETICAL READING
Aug. 30	S	Elul 1	New Moon, second day	Num. 28:1–15	
Sept. 5	Sa	7	Shofeṭim	Deut. 16:18–21:9	Isaiah 51:12–52:12
12	Sa	14	Ki teẓe'	Deut. 21:10–25:19	Isaiah 54:1–10
19	Sa	21	Ki tavo'	Deut. 26:1–29:8	Isaiah 60:1–22
26	Sa	28	Niẓẓavim	Deut. 29:9–30:20	Isaiah 61:10–63:9

Civil Date	Day of the Week	Jewish Date	SABBATHS, FESTIVALS, FASTS	PENTATEUCHAL READING	PROPHETICAL READING
Sept. 28	M	Tishri 1	Rosh Ha-shanah, first day	Gen. 21:1–34 Num. 29:1–6	I Samuel 1:1–2:10
29	T	2	Rosh Ha-shanah second day	Gen. 22:1–24 Num. 29:1–6	Jeremiah 31:2–20
30	W	3	Fast of Gedaliah	Exod. 32:11–14 Exod. 34:1–10 (morning and afternoon)	Isaiah 55:6–56:8 (afternoon only)
Oct. 3	Sa	6	Wa-yelekh (Shabbat Shuvah)	Deut. 31:1–30	Hosea 14:2–10 Micah 7:18–20 Joel 2:15–27 *Hosea 14:2–10* *Micah 7:18–20*
7	W	10	Yom Kippur	Morning: Levit. 16:1–34 Num. 29:7–11 Afternoon: Levit. 18:1–30	Isaiah 57:14–58:14 Jonah 1:1–4:11 Micah 7:18–20
10	Sa	13	Ha'azinu	Deut. 32:1–52	II Samuel 22:1–51
12	M	15	Sukkot, first day	Levit. 22:26–23:44 Num. 29:12–16	Zechariah 14:1–21
13	T	16	Sukkot, second day	Levit. 22:26–23:44 Num. 29:12–16	I Kings 8:2–21
14–16	W–F	17–19	Hol Ha-mo'ed, first to third days	W Num. 29:17–25 Th Num. 29:20–28 F Num. 29:23–31	
17	Sa	20	Hol Ha-mo'ed, fourth day	Exod. 33:12–34:26 Num. 29:26–31	Ezekiel 38:18–39:16
18	S	21	Hosha'na' Rabbah	Num. 29:26–34	
19	M	22	Shemini 'Azeret	Deut. 14:22–16:17 Num. 29:35–30:1	I Kings 8:54–66
20	T	23	Simhat Torah	Deut. 33:1–34:12 Gen. 1:1–2:3 Num. 29:35–30:1	Joshua 1:1–18 *Joshua 1:1–9*
24	Sa	27	Be-re'shit	Gen. 1:1–6:8	Isaiah 42:5–43:10 *Isaiah 42:5–21*
27	T	30	New Moon, first day	Num. 28:1–15	

Italics are for Sephardi Minhag.

1992, Oct. 28–Nov. 25]   ḤESHWAN (29 DAYS)   [5753

Civil Date	Day of the Week	Jewish Date	SABBATHS, FESTIVALS, FASTS	PENTATEUCHAL READING	PROPHETICAL READING
Oct. 28	W	Heshwan 1	New Moon, second day	Num. 28:1–15	
31	Sa	4	Noah	Gen. 6:9–11:32	Isaiah 54:1–55:5 *Isaiah 54:1–10*
Nov. 7	Sa	11	Lekh Lekha	Gen. 12:1–17:27	Isaiah 40:27–41:16
14	Sa	18	Wa-Yera'	Gen. 18:1–22:24	II Kings 4:1–37 *II Kings 4:1–23*
21	Sa	25	Ḥayye Sarah	Gen. 23:1–25:18	I Kings 1:1–31

Italics are for
Sephardi Minhag.

1992, Nov. 26–Dec. 24]   KISLEW (29 DAYS)   [5753

Civil Date	Day of the Week	Jewish Date	SABBATHS, FESTIVALS, FASTS	PENTATEUCHAL READING	PROPHETICAL READING
Nov. 26	Th	Kislew 1	New Moon	Num. 28:1–15	
28	Sa	3	Toledot	Gen. 25:19–28:9	Malachi 1:1–2:7
Dec. 5	Sa	10	Wa-yeze'	Gen. 28:10–32:3	Hosea 12:13–14:10 *Hosea 11:7–12:12*
12	Sa	17	Wa-yishlaḥ	Gen. 32:4–36:43	Hosea 11:7–12:12 *Obadiah 1:1–21*
19	Sa	24	Wa-yeshev	Gen. 37:1–40:23	Amos 2:6–3:8
20–24	S–Th	25–29	Hanukkah, first to fifth days	S Num. 7:1–17 M Num. 7:18–29 T Num. 7:24–35 W Num. 7:30–41 Th Num. 7:36–47	

Italics are for Sephardi Minhag.

1992, Dec. 25–Jan. 22, 1993]   ṬEVET (29 DAYS)   [5753

Civil Date	Day of the Week	Jewish Date	SABBATHS, FESTIVALS, FASTS	PENTATEUCHAL READING	PROPHETICAL READING
Dec. 25	F	Ṭevet 1	New Moon; Hanukkah, sixth day	Num. 28:1–15 Num. 7:42–47	
26	Sa	2	Mi-ḳeẓ; Hanukkah, seventh day	Gen. 41:1–44:17 Num. 7:48–53	Zechariah 2:14–4:7
27	S	3	Hanukkah, eighth day	Num. 7:54–8:4	
Jan. 2	Sa	9	Wa-yiggash	Gen. 44:18–47:27	Ezekiel 37:15–28
3	S	10	Fast of 10th of Ṭevet	Exod. 32:11–14 34:1–10 (morning and afternoon)	Isaiah 55:6–56:8 (afternoon only)
9	Sa	16	Wa-yeḥi	Gen. 47:28–50:26	I Kings 2:1–12
16	Sa	23	Shemot	Exod. 1:1–6:1	Isaiah 27:6–28:13 29:22–23 *Jeremiah 1:1–2:3*

Italics are for
Sephardi Minhag.

1993, Jan. 23–Feb. 21]   SHEVAṬ (30 DAYS)   [5753

Civil Date	Day of the Week	Jewish Date	SABBATHS, FESTIVALS, FASTS	PENTATEUCHAL READING	PROPHETICAL READING
Jan. 23	Sa	Shevaṭ 1	Wa-'era'; New Moon	Exod. 6:2–9:35 Num. 28:9–15	Isaiah 66:1–24
30	Sa	8	Bo'	Exod. 10:1–13:16	Jeremiah 46:13–28
Feb. 6	Sa	15	Be-shallaḥ (Shabbat Shirah); Hamishshah-'asar bi-Shevaṭ	Exod. 13:17–17:16	Judges 4:4–5:31 *Judges 5:1–31*
13	Sa	22	Yitro	Exod. 18:1–20:23	Isaiah 6:1–7:6 9:5–6 *Isaiah 6:1–13*
20	Sa	29	Mishpaṭim (Shabbat Sheḳalim)	Exod. 21:1–24:18 Exod. 30:11–16	II Kings 12:1–17 *II Kings 11:17–12:17* *I Sam. 20:18, 42*
21	S	30	New Moon, first day	Num. 28:1–15	

Italics are for Sephardi Minhag.

1993, Feb. 22–Mar. 22]   ADAR (29 DAYS)   [5753

Civil Date	Day of the Week	Jewish Date	SABBATHS, FESTIVALS, FASTS	PENTATEUCHAL READING	PROPHETICAL READING
Feb. 22	M	Adar 1	New Moon, second day	Num. 28:1–15	
27	Sa	6	Terumah	Exod. 25:1–27:19	I Kings 5:26–6:13
Mar. 4	Th	11	Fast of Esther	Exod. 32:11–14 34:1–10 (morning and afternoon)	Isaiah 55:6–56:8 (afternoon only)
6	Sa	13	Tezawweh (Shabbat Zakhor)	Exod. 27:20–30:10 Deut. 25:17–19	I Samuel 15:2–34 *I Samuel 15:1–34*
7	S	14	Purim	Exod. 17:8–16	Book of Esther (night before and in the morning)
8	M	15	Shushan Purim		
13	Sa	20	Ki tissa' (Shabbat Parah)	Exod. 30:11–34:35 Num. 19:1–22	Ezekiel 36:16–38 *Ezekiel 36:16–36*
20	Sa	27	Wa-yakhel, Pekude (Shabbat Ha-hodesh)	Exod. 35:1–40:38 Exod. 12:1–20	Ezekiel 45:16–46:18 *Ezekiel 45:18–46:15*

Italics are for Sephardi Minhag.

1993, Mar. 23–Apr. 21]   NISAN (30 DAYS)   [5753

Civil Date	Day of the Week	Jewish Date	SABBATHS, FESTIVALS, FASTS	PENTATEUCHAL READING	PROPHETICAL READING
Mar. 23	T	Nisan 1	New Moon	Num. 28:1–15	
27	Sa	5	Wa-yikra'	Levit. 1:1–5:26	Isaiah 43:21–44:24
Apr. 3	Sa	12	Zaw (Shabbat Ha-gadol)	Levit. 6:1–8:36	Malachi 3:4–24
5	M	14	Fast of Firstborn		
6	T	15	Passover, first day	Exod. 12:21–51 Num. 28:16–25	Joshua 5:2–6:1, 27
7	W	16	Passover, second day	Levit. 22:26–23:44 Num. 28:16–25	II Kings 23:1–9, 21–25
8	Th	17	Hol Ha-mo'ed, first day	Exod. 13:1–16 Num. 28:19–25	
9	F	18	Hol Ha-mo'ed, second day	Exod. 22:24–23:19 Num. 28:19–25	
10	Sa	19	Hol Ha-mo'ed, third day	Exod. 33:12–34:26 Num. 28:19–25	Ezekiel 37:1–14
11	S	20	Hol Ha-mo'ed, fourth day	Num. 9:1–14 Num. 28:19–25	
12	M	21	Passover, seventh day	Exod. 13:17–15:26 Num. 28:19–25	II Samuel 22:1–51
13	T	22	Passover, eighth day	Deut. 15:19–16:17 Num. 28:19–25	Isaiah 10:32–12:6
17	Sa	26	Shemini	Levit. 9:1–11:47	II Samuel 6:1–7:17 *II Samuel 6:1–19*
18	S	27	Holocaust Memorial Day		
21	W	30	New Moon, first day	Num. 28:1–15	

Italics are for Sephardi Minhag.

1993, Apr. 22–May 20]   IYAR (29 DAYS)   [5753

Civil Date	Day of the Week	Jewish Date	SABBATHS, FESTIVALS, FASTS	PENTATEUCHAL READING	PROPHETICAL READING
Apr. 22	Th	Iyar 1	New Moon, second day	Num. 28:1–15	
24	Sa	3	Tazria', Mezora'	Levit. 12:1–15:33	II Kings 7:3–20
26	M	5	Israel Independence Day		
May 1	Sa	10	Aḥare mot, Kedoshim	Levit. 16:1–20:27	Amos 9:7–15 *Ezekiel 20:2–20*
8	Sa	17	Emor	Levit. 21:1–24:23	Ezekiel 44:15–31
9	S	18	Lag Ba-'omer		
15	Sa	24	Be-har, Be-ḥukkotai	Levit. 25:1–27:34	Jeremiah 16:19–17:14
19	W	28	Jerusalem Day		

Italics are for Sephardi Minhag.

1993, May 21–June 19] SIWAN (30 DAYS) [5753

Civil Date	Day of the Week	Jewish Date	SABBATHS, FESTIVALS, FASTS	PENTATEUCHAL READING	PROPHETICAL READING
May 21	F	Siwan 1	New Moon	Num. 28:1–15	
22	Sa	2	Be-midbar	Num. 1:1–4:20	Hosea 2:1–22
26	W	6	Shavu'ot, first day	Exod. 19:1–20:23 Num. 28:26–31	Ezekiel 1:1–28 3:12
27	Th	7	Shavu'ot, second day	Deut. 15:19–16:17 Num. 28:26–31	Habbakuk 3:1–19 *Habbakuk 2:20–3:19*
29	Sa	9	Naso'	Num. 4:21–7:89	Judges 13:2–25
June 5	Sa	16	Be-ha'alotekha	Num. 8:1–12:16	Zechariah 2:14–4:7
12	Sa	23	Shelaḥ lekha	Num. 13:1–15:41	Joshua 2:1–24
19	Sa	30	Koraḥ; New Moon, first day	Num. 16:1–18:32 Num. 28:9–15	Isaiah 66:1–24 *Isaiah 66:1–24* *I Samuel 20:18, 42*

Italics are for Sephardi Minhag.

1993, June 20–July 18]   TAMMUZ (29 DAYS)   [5753

Civil Date	Day of the Week	Jewish Date	SABBATHS, FESTIVALS, FASTS	PENTATEUCHAL READING	PROPHETICAL READING
June 20	S	Tammuz 1	New Moon, second day	Num. 28:1–15	
26	Sa	7	Ḥukkat	Num. 19:1–22:1	Judges 11:1–33
July 3	Sa	14	Balak	Num. 22:2–25:9	Micah 5:6–6:8
6	T	17	Fast of 17th of Tammuz	Exod. 32:11–14 34:1–10 (morning and afternoon)	Isaiah 55:6–56:8 (afternoon only)
10	Sa	21	Pineḥas	Num. 25:10–30:1	Jeremiah 1:1–23
17	Sa	28	Maṭṭot, Mas'e	Num. 30:2–36:13	Jeremiah 2:4–28 3:4 *Jeremiah 2:4–28 4:1–2*

*Italics are for
Sephardi Minhag.*

1993, July 19–Aug. 17]   AV (30 DAYS)   [5753

Civil Date	Day of the Week	Jewish Date	SABBATHS, FESTIVALS, FASTS	PENTATEUCHAL READING	PROPHETICAL READING
July 19	M	Av 1	New Moon	Num. 28:1–15	
24	Sa	6	Devarim (Shabbat Ḥazon)	Deut. 1:1–3:22	Isaiah 1:1–27
27	T	9	Fast of 9th of Av	Morning: Deut. 4:25–40 Afternoon: Exod. 32:11–14 34:1–10	(Lamentations is read the night before.) Jeremiah 8:13–9:23 (morning) Isaiah 55:6–56:8 (afternoon)
31	Sa	13	Wa-ethannan (Shabbat Naḥamu	Deut. 3:23–7:11	Isaiah 40:1–26
Aug. 7	Sa	20	'Ekev	Deut. 7:12–11:25	Isaiah 49:14–51:3
14	Sa	27	Re'eh	Deut. 11:26–16:17	Isaiah 54:11–55:5
17	T	30	New Moon, first day	Num. 28:1–15	

1993, Aug. 18–Sep. 15]   ELUL *(29 DAYS)*   [5753

Civil Date	Day of the Week	Jewish Date	SABBATHS, FESTIVALS, FASTS	PENTATEUCHAL READING	PROPHETICAL READING
Aug. 18	W	Elul 1	New Moon, second day	Num. 28:1–15	
21	Sa	4	Shofeṭim	Deut. 16:18–21:19	Isaiah 51:12–52:12
28	Sa	11	Ki teze'	Deut. 21:10–25:19	Isaiah 54:1–10
Sept. 4	Sa	18	Ki tavo'	Deut. 26:1–29:8	Isaiah 60:1–22
11	Sa	25	Nizzavim, Wa-yelekh	Deut. 29:9–31:30	Isaiah 61:10–63:9

Civil Date	Day of the Week	Jewish Date	SABBATHS, FESTIVALS, FASTS	PENTATEUCHAL READING	PROPHETICAL READING
Sep. 16	Th	Tishri 1	Rosh Ha-shanah, first day	Gen. 21:1–34 Num. 29:1–6	1 Samuel 1:1–2:10
17	F	2	Rosh Ha-shanah, second day	Gen. 22:1–24 Num. 29:1–6	Jeremiah 31:2–20
18	Sa	3	Ha'azinu (Shabbat Shuvah)	Deut. 32:1–52	Hosea 14:2–10 Micah 7:18–20 Joel 2:15–27 *Hosea 14:2–10* *Micah 7:18–20*
19	S	4	Fast of Gedaliah	Exod. 32:11–14 34:1–10 (morning and afternoon)	Isaiah 55:6–56:8 (afternoon only)
25	Sa	10	Yom Kippur	Morning: Levit. 16:1–34 Num. 29:7–11 Afternoon: Levit. 18:1–30	Isaiah 57:14–58:14 Jonah 1:1–4:11 Micah 7:18–20
30	Th	15	Sukkot, first day	Levit. 22:26–23:44 Num. 29:12–16	Zechariah 14:1–21
Oct. 1	F	16	Sukkot, second day	Levit. 22:26–23:44 Num. 29:12–16	I Kings 8:2–21
2	Sa	17	Hol Ha-mo'ed, first day	Exod. 33:12–34:26 Num. 29:17–22	Ezekiel 38:18–39:16
3–5	S–T	18–20	Hol Ha-mo'ed, second to fourth days	S Num. 29:20–28 M Num. 29:23–31 T Num. 29:26–34	
6	W	21	Hosha'na' Rabbah	Num. 29:26–34	
7	Th	22	Shemini 'Azeret	Deut. 14:22–16:17 Num. 29:35–30:1	I Kings 8:54–66
8	F	23	Simhat Torah	Deut. 33:1–34:12 Gen. 1:1–2:3 Num. 29:35–30:1	Joshua 1:1–18 *Joshua 1:1–9*
9	Sa	24	Be-re'shit	Gen. 1:1–6:8	Isaiah 42:5–43:10 *Isaiah 42:5–21*
15	F	30	New Moon, first day	Num. 28:1–15	

Italics are for
Sephardi Minhag.

1993, Oct. 16–Nov. 14]   HESHWAN (30 DAYS)   [5754

Civil Date	Day of the Week	Jewish Date	SABBATHS, FESTIVALS, FASTS	PENTATEUCHAL READING	PROPHETICAL READING
Oct. 16	Sa	Heshwan 1	Noah; New Moon, second day	Gen. 6:9–11:32 Num. 28:9–15	Isaiah 66:1–24
23	Sa	8	Lekh Lekha	Gen. 12:1–17:27	Isaiah 40:27–41:16
30	Sa	15	Way-yera'	Gen. 18:1–22:24	II Kings 4:1–37 *II Kings 4:1–23*
Nov. 6	Sa	22	Ḥayye Sarah	Gen. 23:1–25:18	I Kings 1:1–31
13	Sa	29	Toledot	Gen. 25:19–28:9	I Samuel 20:18–42
14	S	30	New Moon, first day	Num. 28:1–15	

*Italics are for
Sephardi Minhag.*

1993, Nov. 15–Dec. 14] KISLEW (30 DAYS) [5754

Civil Date	Day of the Week	Jewish Date	SABBATHS, FESTIVALS, FASTS	PENTATEUCHAL READING	PROPHETICAL READING
Nov. 15	M	Kislew 1	New Moon, second day	Num. 28:1–15	
20	Sa	6	Wa-yeze'	Gen. 28:10–32:3	Hosea 12:13–14:10 *Hosea 11:7–12:12*
27	Sa	13	Wa-yishlaḥ	Gen. 32:4–36:43	Hosea 11:7–12:12 *Obadiah 1:1–21*
Dec. 4	Sa	20	Wa-yeshev	Gen. 37:1–40:23	Amos 2:6–3:8
9–10	Th–F	25–26	Hanukkah, first, second days	Th Num. 7:1–17 F Num. 7:18–29	
11	Sa	27	Mi-ḳez; Hanukkah, third day	Gen. 41:1–44:17 Num. 7:24–29	Zechariah 2:14–4:7
12–13	S–M	28–29	Hanukkah, fourth, fifth days	S Num. 7:30–41 M Num. 7:36–47	
14	T	30	New Moon, first day; Hanukkah, sixth day	Num. 7:42–47 Num. 28:1–15	

Italics are for Sephardi Minhag.

1993, Dec. 15–Jan. 12, 1994] ṬEVET (29 DAYS) [5754

Civil Date	Day of the Week	Jewish Date	SABBATHS, FESTIVALS, FASTS	PENTATEUCHAL READING	PROPHETICAL READING
Dec. 15	W	Ṭevet 1	New Moon, second day; Hanukkah, seventh day	Num. 28:1–15 7:48–53	
16	Th	2	Hanukkah, eighth day	Num. 7:54–8:4	
18	Sa	4	Wa-yiggash	Gen. 44:18–47:27	Ezekiel 37:15–28
24	F	10	Fast of 10th of Ṭevet	Exod. 32:11–14 34:1–10 (morning and afternoon)	Isaiah 55:6–56:8 (afternoon only)
25	Sa	11	Wa-yeḥi	Gen. 47:28–50:26	I Kings 2:1–12
Jan. 1	Sa	18	Shemot	Exod. 1:1–6:1	Isaiah 27:6–28:13 29:22–23 *Jeremiah 1:1–2:3*
8	Sa	25	Wa-'era'	Exod. 6:2–9:35	Ezekiel 28:25–29:21

Italics are for Sephardi Minhag.

SELECTED ARTICLES OF INTEREST IN RECENT VOLUMES
OF THE AMERICAN JEWISH YEAR BOOK

OBITUARIES

Leo Baeck	By Max Gruenewald 59:478–82
Salo W. Baron	By Lloyd P. Gartner 91:544–554
Jacob Blaustein	By John Slawson 72:547–57
Martin Buber	By Seymour Siegel 67:37–43
Abraham Cahan	By Mendel Osherowitch 53:527–29
Albert Einstein	By Jacob Bronowski 58:480–85
Felix Frankfurter	By Paul A. Freund 67:31–36
Louis Ginzberg	By Louis Finkelstein 56:573–79
Jacob Glatstein	By Shmuel Lapin 73:611–17
Sidney Goldmann	By Milton R. Konvitz 85:401–03
Hayim Greenberg	By Marie Syrkin 56:589–94
Abraham Joshua Heschel	By Fritz A. Rothschild 74:533–44
Horace Meyer Kallen	By Milton R. Konvitz 75:55–80
Mordecai Kaplan	By Ludwig Nadelmann 85:404–11
Herbert H. Lehman	By Louis Finkelstein 66:3–20
Judah L. Magnes	By James Marshall 51:512–15
Alexander Marx	By Abraham S. Halkin 56:580–88
Reinhold Niebuhr	By Seymour Siegel 73:605–10
Joseph Proskauer	By David Sher 73:618–28
Maurice Samuel	By Milton H. Hindus 74:545–53
John Slawson	By Murray Friedman 91:555–558
Leo Strauss	By Ralph Lerner 76:91–97
Max Weinreich	By Lucy S. Dawidowicz 70:59–68
Chaim Weizmann	By Harry Sacher 55:462–69
Stephen S. Wise	By Philip S. Bernstein 51:515–18
Harry Austryn Wolfson	By Isadore Twersky 76:99–111

Index